THE HANDBOOK OF MORTGAGE-BACKED SECURITIES

THE HANDBOOK OF MORTGAGE-BACKED SECURITIES

Edited by
Frank J. Fabozzi

Walter E. Hanson/Peat, Marwick, Mitchell
Professor of Business and Finance
Lafayette College
and
Managing Editor, *The Journal of
Portfolio Management*

Probus Publishing
Chicago, Illinois

Library of Congress Cataloging in Publication Data

The Handbook of mortgage-backed securities.

Includes index.
1. Mortgage bonds—United States.   2. Portfolio management—United States.   I. Fabozzi, Frank J.
HG4655.H36   1985   332.63'23   85–9315

ISBN 0–917253–04–3

Library of Congress Catalog Card No. 83–9315

Printed in the United States of America

   3 4 5 6 7 8 9 0

To the memory of Mathew Aprile, Sr., Gloria Fabozzi, Jeanine Fabozzi, Pasquale Fabozzi and Sarah Tartaglione

CONTENTS

CONTRIBUTORS   xi
FOREWORD   xiii
PREFACE   xv

CHAPTER 1   Introduction   *Frank J. Fabozzi*   1

SECTION I
Mortgages and the Mortgage Market 5

CHAPTER 2   The Mortgage Market   *Kenneth H. Sullivan*   7
3   Mortgages   *Dexter Senft*   29
4   Adjustable-Rate Mortgages   *Joseph C. Hu* 63
5   Housing Finance in a Deregulated Environment   *Joseph C. Hu*   79

SECTION II
The Securities and Their Historical Performance 99

CHAPTER 6   Mortgage Pass-through Securities *Kenneth H. Sullivan, Bruce M. Collins and David A. Smilow*   101
7   Mortgage-Backed Bonds   *Kenneth H. Sullivan, Llewellyn Miller and Timothy B. Kiggins*   149
8   The Historical Performance of Mortgage Securities: 1972–1984   *Michael Waldman and Steven Guterman*   201

SECTION III
Analytical Tools   239

CHAPTER 9   The Total Return Calculation for
Mortgage Pass-Throughs   *H. Peter
Wallace*   241

10   Determining the Yield of a Mortgage
Security   *Michael Waldman and Mark
Gordon*   257

11   Forecasting Prepayments Rates for
Mortgages Securities   *David J.
Askin*   279

12   A Framework for Evaluating Treasury-
Based Adjustable Rate Mortgages
*Michael Waldman and Stephen
Modzelewski*   307

SECTION IV
Strategies with Mortgage-Backed Securities   347

CHAPTER 13   Mortgage-Backed Securities from the
Portfolio Manager's Perspective
Richard L. Sega   349

14   Financial Futures and Mortgage-Backed
Securities   *Richard L. Sandor and
Norman E. Mains*   373

15   Return Enhancement: GNMA Time Swap
Using Floaters   *Ronald J. Ryan*   403

16   OTC Options on Mortgage Securities
Mark Pitts   413

17   Hedging the Interest Rate Risk of Fixed
Rate Mortgages with Prepayment Rights
Alden L. Toevs   447

18   Interest Rate Anticipation Strategies
*H. Gifford Fong and Frank J.
Fabozzi*   475

SECTION V
Credit Rating and Taxation 495

CHAPTER 19 The Rating of Mortgage-Backed
Securities *David J. Askin* 497
20 Federal Income Tax Treatment of
Mortgage-Backed Securities *James
M. Peaslee* 569
GLOSSARY OF TERMS 617
INDEX 623

CONTRIBUTORS

David J. Askin, Vice President, Mortgage-Backed Securities, Drexel Burnham Lambert

Bruce M. Collins, Analyst Mortgage Research and Product Development, Drexel Burnham Lambert

Frank J. Fabozzi, Ph.D., C.F.A., Walter E. Hanson/Peat, Marwick, Mitchell, Professor of Business and Finance, Lafayette College

H. Gifford Fong, President, Gifford Fong Associates

Mark Gordon, C.F.A., Mortgage Research, Salomon Brothers Inc

Steven Guterman, Mortgage Research, Salomon Brothers Inc

Joseph C. Hu, Ph.D., Vice President, Salomon Brothers Inc

Timothy B. Kiggins, Associate, Mortgage Research and Product Development, Drexel Burnham Lambert

Norman E. Mains, Ph.D., First Vice President and Director of Research, Institutional Financial Futures Division, Drexel Burnham Lambert

Llewellyn Miller, Vice President, Mortgage Research and Product Development, Drexel Burnham Lambert

Stephen Modzelewski, Vice President, Quantitative Research, Salomon Brothers Inc

James M. Peaslee, Partner, Cleary, Gottlieb, Steen & Hamilton

Mark Pitts, Ph.D., Vice President, Shearson Lehman Brothers Inc.

Ronald J. Ryan, C.F.A., Managing Director, Ryan Financial Strategy Group

Richard L. Sandor, Ph.D., Senior Vice President and Manager, Institutional Financial Futures Division, Drexel Burnham Lambert

Richard L. Sega, F.S.A., Assistant Investment Officer, The Travelers Insurance Companies

Dexter Senft, Managing Director, Fixed Income Research, The First Boston Corporation

David A. Smilow, Analyst Mortgage Research and Product Development, Drexel Burnham Lambert

Kenneth H. Sullivan, Managing Director and Manager, Mortgage Research and Product Development, Drexel Burnham Lambert

Alden L. Toevs, Ph.D., Morgan Stanley and Co. Inc.

Michael Waldman, Vice President & Manager of Mortgage Research, Salomon Brothers Inc

H. Peter Wallace, Vice President, Mortgage Portfolio Strategist, Dean Witter Reynolds

FOREWORD

I recently spoke at a mortgage-backed securities conference in New York which was attended by almost 400 people. Many of the faces were unfamiliar, and I asked how many in the audience had worked in the mortgage securities business for as long as five years. Perhaps as many as 15 people raised their hand. I repeated the question, but substituted four years. A similar number of hands went up. Then, just to confirm the findings, I asked to see the hands of those who had been in the mortgage business for three years or less. Nearly every other hand was raised.

So it is with mortgage securities. The market, barely 15 years old, is larger already than the corporate bond market. Few institutional portfolios lack mortgage components. The public has also become a major investor, primarily through pooled trusts and mutual funds. However, it was not very long ago when mortgages had few friends. Freddie Mac 8's were recently priced to yield about 100 basis points more than 10 year governments, assuming a 6 percent annual rate of mortgage prepayments. In August 1981 the same spread was over 700 basis points.

Despite their current popularity I think that mortgages are less well-understood than most other fixed income securities. The essential difference between mortgages and other securities results from the prepayment contingency of mortgages. Sometimes it seems that the only certainty with respect to mortgages is that the number of prepayments will be greater when we investors want them to be fewer, and conversely. Hence the need for clearer insight into the determinants of prepayments and the interrelationship among interest rates, prepayments, mortgage yields and duration.

The mortgage investor must also choose from an ever expanding menu. ARMs, CMOs, GEMs, GPMs, GNMA II and Midgets are but a few of the acronyms. The growing list of alternatives has created a need for new techniques of analysis with which to compare and evaluate the different forms.

Perhaps I am partial, but I think that mortgages are more interesting than other fixed income securities. They have also been more rewarding. The contributors to *The Handbook of Mortgage-Backed Securities* have been pioneers in mortgage research. They have helped reduce the mystery of mortgages for their firms and their clients. This volume offers to the new initiate insights into the lessons learned, often expensively, by leading practitioners in the mortgage securities market. It should be required reading for every fixed income investor.

RICHARD B. WORLEY
Partner
Miller, Anderson & Sherrerd

PREFACE

The Handbook of Mortgage-Backed Securities is designed to provide not only the fundamentals of these securities and the investment characteristics that make them attractive to a broad range of investors, but also extensive coverage on the state-of-the-art strategies for capitalizing on the opportunities in this market. The book is intended for both the individual investor and the professional money manager.

To be effective, a book of this nature should offer a broad perspective. The experiences of a wide range of experts is more informative than that of a single expert, particularly because of the diversity of opinion on some issues. I have chosen some of the best known practitioners to contribute to this book. Most have been actively involved in the evolution of the mortgage-backed securities market.

ACKNOWLEDGMENTS

I would like to express my appreciation to the contributors. I would also like to thank the following firms who allowed the contributors to participate in this project: Cleary, Gottlieb, Steen & Hamilton; Drexel Burnham Lambert Inc.; Gifford Fong Associates; Merrill Lynch; Morgan Stanley; Ryan Financial Strategy Group; Salomon Brothers Inc; Shearson Lehman/ American Express; The First Boston Corporation; and The Travelers Insurance Companies. Hal Hinkle (Goldman Sachs & Co.) provided me with substantive comments on the entire book. Helen Peters (Merrill Lynch), Mel Stein (Stein, Rubine & Stein), Ivan Gruhl (Gifford Fong Associates) and Dessa Garlicki (Rutgers University) gave generously of their time to comment on portions of the manuscript. Kathy Lucas, Larry Stein and Rosalynd Aronheim assisted at various stages of this project. Finally, I am grateful to Michael Jeffers, Vice President of Probus Publishing, for his encouragement and support at each stage of this project.

FRANK J. FABOZZI

CHAPTER 1

Introduction

Frank J. Fabozzi, Ph.D. C.F.A.
Walter E. Hanson/Peat, Marwick, Mitchell Professor of
Business and Finance
Lafayette College

The market for mortgage-backed securities has undergone one of the most dramatic changes of any market in modern investment times. In 1984, the residential mortgage debt outstanding that was "securitized" exceeded $300 billion. Two types of mortgage-backed securities have been issued—mortgage pass-throughs and mortgage-backed bonds. The characteristic that distinguishes these two types of mortgage-backed securities is that the issuer of a mortgage pass-through treats the transaction as a sale of assets while the issuer of a mortgage-backed bond carries the bonds as a debt obligation on its books. Of the more than $300 billion of mortgage-backed securities, all but about $20 billion are mortgage pass-throughs.

In 1984, more than $1.1 trillion of residential mortgage debt had the potential to be "securitized." When other real estate mortgage debt such as commercial mortgages and multi-family mortgages are considered, the amount of real estate mortgage debt that had the potential to be converted to various forms of securities in 1984 exceeded $1.8 trillion. To place the size of the market in perspective, consider that in 1984 corporate bond debt was about $560 billion, Treasury and agency debt was about $980 billion, and tax-exempt issued debt was about $485 billion. Consequently, the amount of real estate mortgage debt outstanding, both securitized and nonsecuritized, was greater than the other three debt markets combined.

Innovation and growth in the mortgage-backed securities market have been dramatic. New issuers, new buyers, and new instruments are appearing with increasing frequency. Mortgage pools are being created to fit the specific needs of a broadening range of institutional investors. Investors, such as insurance companies and pension funds, have become more active and are now the creators of new investment strategies.

Despite the dramatic growth of this market, there are participants in the fixed income market who are uncomfortable about investing in mortgage-backed securities. The reason is that mortgage-backed securities have investment characteristics that differ from the traditional debt obligations held in portfolios that are structured to satisfy a known liability stream. Specifically, a mortgage-backed security is more difficult to value because of the uncertainty of its cash flow. The uncertainty arises because of the prepayment opportunity available to borrowers (homeowners). It should be noted, however, that a similar problem arises with callable bonds. Yet, portfolio managers do not seem to have any compunctions about using low coupon callable bonds in portfolios designed to satisfy a known liability stream. In fact, it is the difficulty of assessing the value of mortgage-backed securities that results in potential mispricing and, as a result, allows investors who are capable of identifying and exploiting any mispricing to enhance portfolio returns.

OBJECTIVES OF THIS BOOK

The objectives of this book are as follows. The first is to describe the types of mortgage-backed securities. The second is to explain the investment characteristics of mortgage-

backed securities with emphasis on the practical attributes
that make these securities attractive for a wide range of institutional and individual investors. The third is to discuss and
illustrate the state-of-the-art techniques that can be employed
to identify opportunities in this market sector that can lead
to enhanced investment returns. The last objective is to describe various portfolio strategies and their application to the
investment needs of a broad range of investors.

ORGANIZATION OF THIS BOOK

The book is divided into five sections. The four chapters in
Section I describe the mortgage market and the types of mortgages. Because originations of adjustable-rate mortgages
(ARMs) have surpassed those of long-term fixed-rate mortgages in 1984, a separate chapter, Chapter 4, is devoted to
ARMs. Section II describes the two types of mortgage-backed
securities and their historical performance. Mortgage pass-
throughs are described in Chapter 6 and mortgage-backed
bonds are described in Chapter 7. Analytical tools are presented in the four chapters of Section III. Strategies with mortgage-backed securities are illustrated in Section IV. Chapter
14 describes how to use futures in managing a portfolio of
mortgage-backed securities. Although there are exchange-
traded debt options, the currently traded contracts are for
Treasury obligations. There is, however, an over-the-counter
market for options on mortgage-backed securities. A description of this market and how it can be used by participants
in the mortgage-backed securities market are covered in Chapter 16. The unique aspects of hedging a portfolio of mortgage-
backed securities are discussed in Chapter 17. The final section, Section V, includes two chapters. Chapter 19 provides
an in-depth discussion of the credit ratings of mortgage-backed
securities. Chapter 20 explains the tax consequences of transactions involving mortgage-backed securities.

SECTION I

Mortgages and the Mortgage Market

CHAPTER 2

The Mortgage Market

Kenneth H. Sullivan
Managing Director and Manager
Mortgage Research and Product Development
Drexel Burnham Lambert

Mortgages have been central to the American way of life; the fact that nearly two-thirds of families in the U.S. own their own homes stands as the most prominent symbol of the American private property system. It would not have been possible if long-term financing in the form of conventional mortgages had not been plentiful. This chapter describes where the money came from. The system and organizations that supplied the capital have changed substantially over the years, and the changes continue.

At first local in nature, the mortgage markets are now national. They were once funded by a single product, price-regulated deposits by individuals, but are now funded by a broad array of devices designed to meet the many investor preferences for market rates, long or short maturities, safety, improved call protection relative to a conventional mortgage, and a number of other considerations. Once a cumbersome mechanical process performed by the originating institution, the making, approving, and funding of mortgages now involve powerful computers, communications advances in credit checking, and comparisons of funding costs from many potential sources. Needless to say, the number of participants in the mortgage industry has increased substantially as new vendors devise means of making the process more efficient.

Continued growth in demand for mortgage credit is depicted in Exhibit 1. Prices of homes in relation to incomes are such that substantial financing is simply necessary to com-

EXHIBIT 1
Residential Mortgage Credit Outstanding

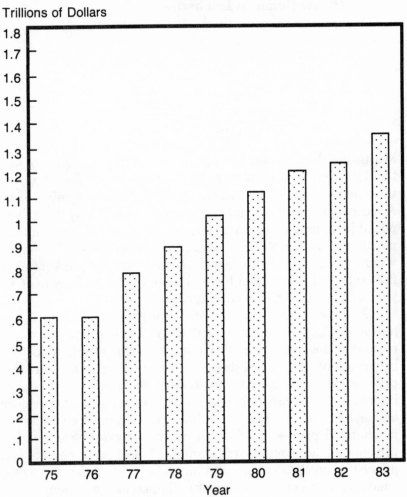

Trillions of Dollars

plete a purchase. In addition, the existing stock of housing units is being driven upward by the growing number of households. The general population has been growing slowly, but the growth is magnified by demographic changes such as a smaller number of people per household and a greater proportion of adults in the population and growth in ownership of second homes. Finally, the deductibility of interest paid on mortgage credit provides a powerful economic incentive to purchase a home, especially since inflation of nominal incomes has pushed larger groups into high marginal tax brackets.

While demand for mortgage credit appears to be stable and relatively predictable, what about the supply of mortgage capital? The greatest changes in the capital markets over the years have been in response to that question. Prior to the 1970s, deposits in financial institutions were the principal source of mortgage credit. When demand exceeded the availability of new deposits as periodically occurred in economic expansions, a "credit crunch" would develop. Since many financial institutions could not raise their rates above the Regulation Q ceiling to attract incremental deposits, they simply stopped lending money. The capital shortage was thus solved in part by causing prospective homebuyers to defer, involuntarily, their purchases to a future period. The changes of the 1970s and early 1980s have been principally directed at making short-term capital available to replace deposits lost to money market funds and at opening up new long-term sources of funds to replace the deposits that in the past were thought to be an ever-increasing source of funds at a maximum rate of 5¼ percent. Thus, the challenge of the 1980s is to complete the unfinished task of opening all sectors of the capital markets to mortgage-related investments by designing instruments with investment characteristics that appeal to the corporate, state, and local pension funds, trust companies, fund managers, insurance companies, and individual investors. The magnitude of the task is indicated in Exhibit 2. Only a little over one quarter of the residential mortgages outstanding have been securitized and new originations have been averaging over $100 billion a year in recent years.

EXHIBIT 2
The Magnitude of the Mortgage Market
in Relation to the Capital Markets

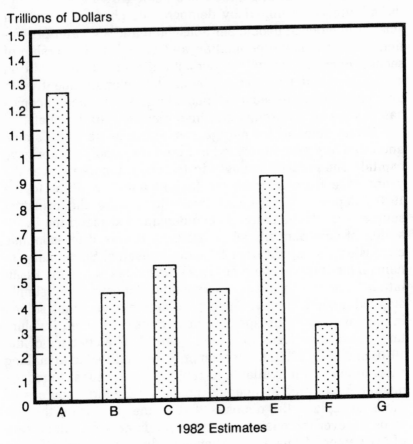

Trillions of Dollars

1982 Estimates

A Residential Mortgages
B Commercial & Farm Mortgages
C Corporate Bonds
D State & Local Governments

E U.S. Treasury, over 1 year
F U.S. Treasury, under 1 year
G Federal Agency

EVOLUTION OF THE PRIMARY
MORTGAGE MARKET

The traditional intermediaries in the U.S. mortgage market
were the thrift institutions—savings and loan associations and
mutual savings banks. Their function was simple. The thrifts

accumulated local household funds kept for liquidity or long-term savings and allocated the money to local mortgage credit. In essence, through the thrifts the local citizens were lending to and borrowing from each other. On occasion local deposits would exceed local mortgage demand, in which case the thrift could purchase loans or participations in loans from outside its area or bonds issued by governments or corporations. Low-

EXHIBIT 3
The Local Primary Mortgage Market

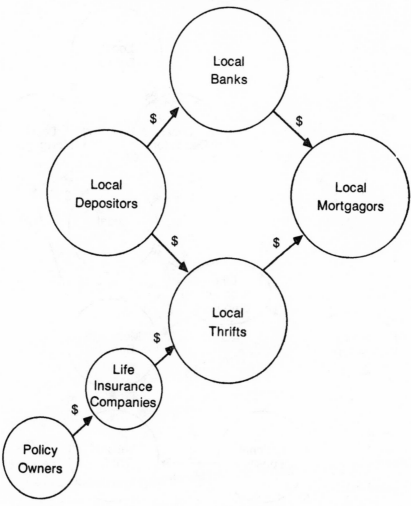

ering the rates offered on deposits to levels below those of
the competition, where possible, would be a less desirable
alternative. If excess demand for credit developed, loans could
be originated and placed with life insurance companies, who
were an early version of "national" deposit-takers with their
whole life insurance policies. This local model of the mortgage
market, depicted in Exhibit 3, survived largely intact for the

EXHIBIT 4
The National Primary Mortgage Market

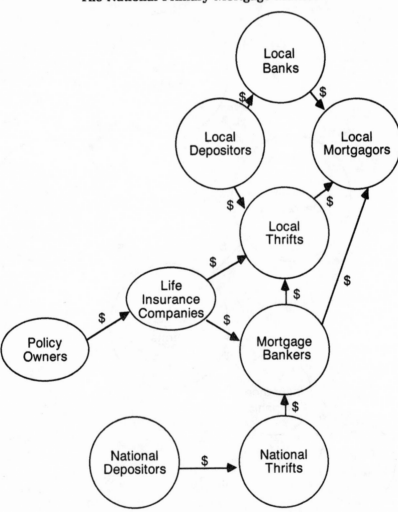

first two post-war decades and is generally referred to as the primary mortgage market. It includes most flows for funding newly originated mortgages.

Increasingly, the local model has required support. Demographic shifts such as increasing affluence, population mobility, regional population life cycles, and others caused local supply and demand to fall out of balance with increasing frequency and severity. To address these imbalances, a new participant in the primary mortgage market evolved. Known as mortgage bankers, these entities can be distinguished from thrifts in two ways. Mortgage bankers neither take deposits nor invest in mortgages for long-term periods. They originate mortgages for resale to investors or lenders in another locale where capital exceeds demand for credit. Some thrifts also developed mortgage banking, that is, resale capabilities along with the mortgage bankers. This model, the national primary mortgage market, successfully intermediated regional supply/demand imbalances throughout the post-war low interest rate environment. Shown below as Exhibit 4, this model's shortcoming, and undoing, was its reliance on regulated deposits, whether local or national.

EVOLUTION OF THE SECONDARY MORTGAGE MARKET

The secondary mortgage market, which exists to facilitate the resale and purchase of existing mortgages, had its roots in the post-depression era but did not contribute significantly to capital market flows until the mid-1970s. The secondary market's function is to alleviate the cyclical funds shortages in the mortgage market. The rise of mortgage bankers and thrifts acting as mortgage bankers demonstrated the need for a more effective means of intermediating the national mortgage market; however, it was the upward trend in interest rates, as well as increasing volatility of rates, that finally forced Federal action to remove impediments to free access to the capital markets.

The mortgage industry became more exposed to credit

crunches as rates rose. High rates (higher than 5¼ percent, the legal maximum on deposits) did two things. First, the high rates diverted new deposits out of direct loan portfolio investments and into other fixed income investments. Not only thrifts but also life insurance companies would take advantage of the less price-sensitive, intermediate-term investments in the

EXHIBIT 5
Disintermediation in the National Primary Market

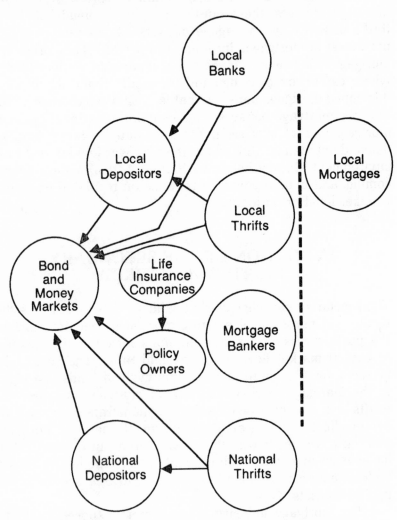

capital markets. There existed no mechanism to attract funds back out of the capital markets in any size. In addition, the high rates caused disintermediation as some existing depositors would withdraw funds, seeking higher returns in alternative investments. Further, life insurance companies experienced disintermediation in the form of increasing policy loans at statutory maximum rates below the market level. Exhibit 5 shows how fund flows could reverse on a short-term basis occasionally causing liquidity problems at some thrifts.

In theory the problem could be solved easily by the thrifts by selling portfolio mortgages to raise the cash necessary to meet both deposit outflows and new credit demand. The disintermediation problem occurred only in high-rate environments, however, when portfolios of fixed-rate mortgage loans could be sold only at a substantial loss, which could leave the thrift with no net worth.

The Role of the Agencies

Several Federal programs have contributed to the establishment and growth of the secondary mortgage market—Government National Mortgage Association (GNMA), Federal Home Loan Mortgage Corporation (FHLMC), and Federal National Mortgage Association (FNMA) (all described in detail later in this chapter), which are known as the "Agencies" because of their varying degrees of Federal support. These three Agencies have important roles in the following secondary market functions:

- The purchase of mortgages from originators. These purchases are financed by Agency borrowings or mortgage pass-through sales.
- The exchange of pass-through securities for mortgages supplied by originators.
- The sale of securities to portfolio investors by originators providing permanent financing for mortgage loans.
- The use of Agency securities as collateral for long-term borrowing by the originator, which provides permanent financing for mortgage loans

- The use of securities to facilitate short-term borrowing by an originator under a reverse repurchase agreement, which provides interim financing or replenishes funds lost to disintermediation.

The evolution of the Agencies and their roles began in the Depression when the Federal government formed the Federal Home Loan Bank System in 1932. Savings and loans that accepted Federal charters gained access to funding support in exchange for assuming the responsibility of maintaining certain uniform regulations and standards as determined by the Federal Home Loan Bank Board. The creation of the Federal Housing Administration (FHA) followed in 1934. The FHA sought to broaden the reach of mortgage credit by offering insurance against mortgage defaults for loans underwritten according to the standards of the FHA. The original FHA standards commenced the long process of homogenizing mortgage contracts so necessary for the efficient operation of a secondary market.

The first Agency purchaser in the secondary market was the FNMA. FNMA (or "Fannie Mae") bought and sold FHA mortgages as early as the late 1930s and Veterans' Administration loans in the late 1940s, but the secondary market did not really develop in a material way until the 1970s. As confidence in the economy was restored after the war, the local and national primary market performed the necessary intermediation. In a credit crunch, the secondary market would play a small role. In response to the rising rate environment and periodic housing crises, two new entities were formed. The Government National Mortgage Association and the Federal Home Loan Mortgage Corporation were created in 1968 and 1970, respectively. GNMA (or "Ginnie Mae") assumed responsibility for supporting the FHA and VA loan markets and was free to use its "full faith and credit of the U.S." backing to do so. FHLMC (or "Freddie Mac") was incorporated to provide needed support for conventional mortgages that met certain standards and were not either insured by the FHA or guaranteed by the VA. While FHLMC is not U.S. Government guaranteed, it has borrowing rights with the Federal Reserve. By

interposing the direct or implied credit of the U.S. Government
between the mortgagors and the investors, the efficiency of
secondary market operations was greatly enhanced. The effec-
tiveness of the secondary market was increased again when
FNMA, which had been converted to a private corporation

EXHIBIT 6
Securities Issuance by the Agencies
Outstanding Pass-Through Securities

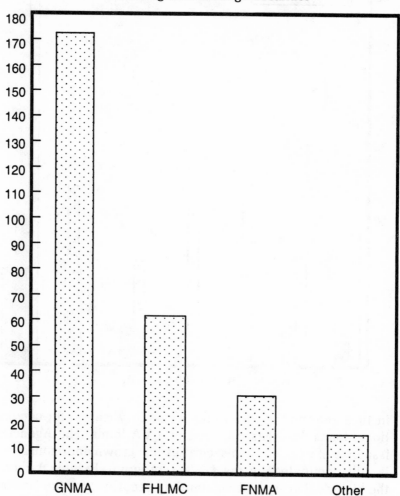

EXHIBIT 6 (concluded)
Issuance of Pass-Through Securities

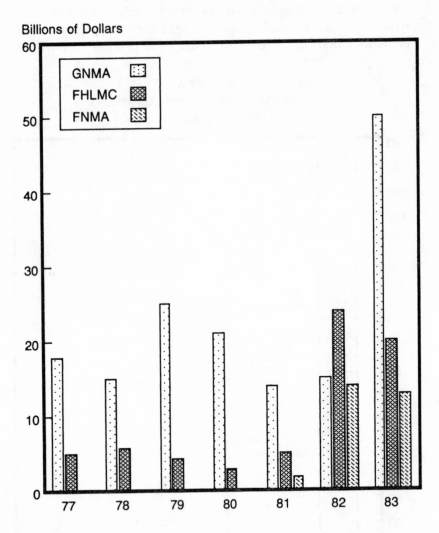

in 1968, returned in 1981 to the secondary market for conventional loans and seasonal FHA and VA loans. The Agencies' issuance of pass-through securities has grown enormously but is still dominated by the GNMA program. Exhibit 6 shows the historical growth of outstanding securities for the issuers.

The Role of the Thrifts

The thrifts' traditional role as the principal portfolio lender of the mortgage industry began its decline as unregulated entities such as money market funds attracted more and more regulated deposits, ending the thrifts' cost advantage relative to other lenders. Eventually, the thrifts were allowed to compete for funds on the basis of price, but that solved only the liquidity problem. A variable rate funding structure cannot finance long-term fixed-rate investments given the capital ratios with which the thrifts entered the free competition era. Core deposits plus access to the secondary market and bond markets assure the thrifts a significant role; however, the traditional long-term bond market lenders must be drawn into the mortgage market over time. The thrifts will also play a major role in the secondary market as they restructure their existing loan portfolios, still the largest component of the mortgage market.

The Role of the Mortgage Bankers

Mortgage bankers have played an increasingly important role in the mortgage markets for three principal reasons:

- The elimination of competitive interest cost advantages of regulated entities such as thrifts and life insurance companies.
- Advances in computer and communications technologies, which have made possible the collection and dissemination of credit information, geographic underwriting data, local competitive rates, national capital market rates, and other pertinent information. Service companies have emerged to provide originators with information required.
- The homogenizing of underwriting standards for the documentation of loans, which allows the repackaging of large numbers of individual contracts into a small number of bond-like investments. Computer technology and applications have helped immensely in this regard.

Those with control of information, dispersed selling networks, and access to low-cost capital market funds will gain shares in the mortgage market. The mortgage bankers, including the thrifts who have developed significant origination-resale capabilities, will assume a larger role in the mortgage industry.

The Role of Life Insurance Companies

The life insurance companies were once more active in supplying funds to the mortgage market. They were the primary source of liquidity to thrifts prior to the evolution of the Agencies. In the mid-1970s, life insurance companies started to come under pressure from disintermediation as policy loans increased and new "high-return" and "variable-return" life insurance products entered the insurance/investment market. These combined to cause an erosion of what had been a stable, low-cost source of funding for portfolio investments. The life companies continue to purchase loans and securities backed by pools of loans. Recently, however, they have focused attention and investment funds on large mortgage loans secured by commercial properties, which in their view carry more attractive terms than conventional mortgages. The life companies could play a key role as bond investors as mortgage-backed bond structures evolve in the capital market.

The Role of Commercial Banks

Many commercial banks, like the thrifts, made direct loans to meet local demand for mortgage credit. While it was never the principal component of their assets, the residential mortgage was nonetheless a significant portfolio investment for most commercial banks. Some large banks have acted as private conduits to the capital markets, issuing mortgage-backed bonds and pass-through certificates and reselling loans in the secondary market. The credit strength of the banks relative to the thrifts and their access to the public and capital private markets assures them of a growing role as mortgage originators and packagers. The recent public acceptance of adjustable-rate mortgages could induce the commercial banks to assume a larger role as a portfolio investor.

The Role of Homebuilders

Homebuilders have evolved over the years from small private operations to large regional and national organizations. The builders were once totally dependent on local lenders to supply mortgage credit to the builders' customers. Homebuilders have formed their own mortgage banking operations or special purpose conduits to directly access the secondary markets and the capital markets. Small builders with common objectives have participated jointly in special purpose entities through which mortgage originations are financed. The willingness to innovate and a marketing orientation have helped gain the homebuilders a growing share of the secondary mortgage market.

The Role of Investment Bankers

In addition to the traditional roles of underwriting bond issues and making secondary markets in pass-throughs and whole loans, several investment bankers have more recently performed a remarketing function driven by the profit potential of arbitrage. Firms purchased GNMA and other pass-throughs via special purpose subsidiaries, reapportioned the projected cash flows to several bond classes to create distinct "maturities," and then sold the bonds to long-term investors who preferred the redesigned maturities. Mortgage-backed bond (as opposed to pass-through) issuance by all types of issuers has reached nearly $15 billion, of which $11 billion was raised by issuing CMOs which were first introduced in June 1983. Investment bankers continue to seek structures that allow public or private placement with long-term investors such as pension funds and trust accounts, which have not historically favored mortgage-related instruments.

Exhibit 7 summarizes the extent of participation in the mortgage market of the various institutions.

EXHIBIT 7
Current Shares of Residential Mortgages

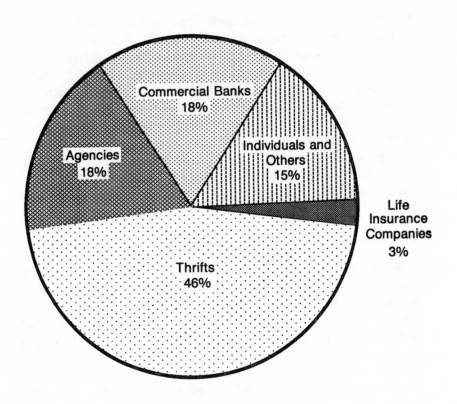

CURRENT DEVELOPMENTS IN THE MORTGAGE MARKET

The secondary mortgage market has evolved into a complex series of pathways for capital flows as demonstrated in Exhibit 8. It has developed some resistance to the effects of high inter-

EXHIBIT 8
The Current Structure of the Mortgage Market

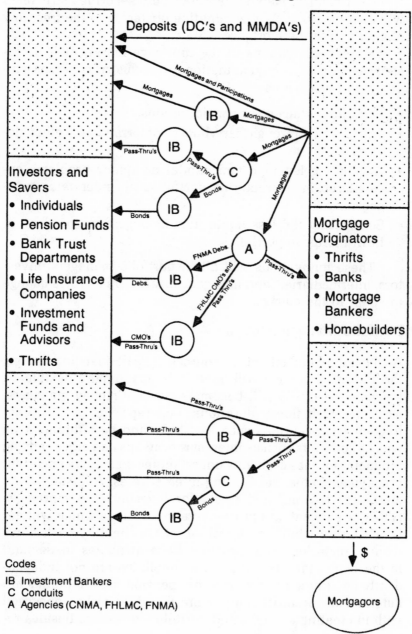

Deposits (DC's and MMDA's)

Mortgages and Participations

Mortgages

IB

Mortgages

Mortgages

IB

Pass-Thru's

Pass-Thru's

C

Mortgages

Bonds

IB

Bonds

Investors and Savers
• Individuals
• Pension Funds
• Bank Trust Departments
• Life Insurance Companies
• Investment Funds and Advisors
• Thrifts

Mortgage Originators
• Thrifts
• Banks
• Mortgage Bankers
• Homebuilders

Mortgages

FNMA Debs.

A

Pass-Thru's

IB

Debs.

FHLMC CMO's and Pass-Thru's

CMO's

IB

Pass-Thru's

Pass-Thru's

Pass-Thru's

IB

Pass-Thru's

Pass-Thru's

Pass-Thru's

C

Pass-Thru's

Bonds

IB

Bonds

$

Mortgagors

Codes
IB Investment Bankers
C   Conduits
A   Agencies (CNMA, FHLMC, FNMA)

est rates, volatility, new competition, legal barriers, and technological change. New issuers and new securities structures will continue to evolve, eliminating obstacles to the free flow of capital into the mortgage market.

Further innovations in the mortgage market will be responses to complex combinations of industry concerns and opportunities such as:

- Portfolio management considerations.
- Tax savings through carrybacks, deferrals, and other devices.
- Accounting leverage and capital adequacy problems encountered in restructuring portfolios of underwater mortgages.
- Securitizing the less liquid, non-homogeneous portions of thrift mortgage portfolios.

These innovations will affect portfolio managers, investors, intermediaries, and mortgage originators as roles change to adapt to the market.

Portfolio Management

As the nature and mix of the sources of thrift financing change, thrift asset structures will have to be made more flexible. In a sense, the thrifts will become more like money managers; matching cash flows, durations, and repricing (rate-setting) frequencies. Securities such as CMOs and pass-throughs, as well as contracts such as interest rate swaps and other hedging products, address cash flow uncertainties created by uncertain prepayment rates and floating interest rates. Adjustable rate mortgages (ARMs) and trusts for investment in mortgages (TIMs) are recent and prospective innovations which will enhance thrifts' ability to match asset and liability cash flows while structuring securities that have attributes in demand in the bond markets. Since thrift liabilities are not independently determined in the way that pension fund liabilities are determined, the thrifts have more variables to be concerned with in creating a "dedicated portfolio" of assets. Besides restructuring assets to match liabilities, thrifts can, to some extent, modify the liability structure.

The increasing internationalization of thrift finance will affect the thrifts' structured transactions. Overcollateralized mortgage-backed bonds and interest rate swaps have given the thrifts access to intermediate-term fixed-rate Eurodollars. The access will broaden as the mystique of mortgages diminishes and understanding of the attributes of mortgage securities grows.

Tax Factors

Many creative transactions have grown out of either corporate tax rules or the tax treatment of particular securities. Federal regulations allow thrifts to carry back losses for ten years and carry forward losses for five years. For institutions that were historically taxpayers, certain transactions that generate tax losses (without accounting losses) can be used to obtain refunds of taxes previously paid. Mergers between thrifts result in the "marking to market" of seasoned mortgage loans for accounting purposes while the loans retain the original tax basis. Such situations lead to sales of loans in the secondary markets so the thrift can potentially recognize tax losses and accounting gains simultaneously. Other thrifts may wish to defer tax losses for as long as possible because they have large tax loss carryforwards. In such instances, a sale of mortgage loans would be less efficient economically than either structuring a bond or preferred stock issue collateralized or supported by the mortgages or selling participations in the loan. In both instances the net economic effect is a sale of the loans allowing the redeployment of funds, while the institution avoids losses or defers the tax losses to a period when they might be used.

Homebuilders have tax incentives to issue bonds backed by mortgages on homes they build. This kind of issue enables them to defer profits for tax purposes by using installment sales treatment on the homes sold, but does not tie up their cash in the mortgages.

Preferred stock investors, largely corporations, who can avail themselves of the 85 percent dividends-received deduction, have been receptive to carefully structured issues by subsidiaries of thrifts. These special purpose companies are organized solely to issue stock and manage assets, e.g., mortgages, pass-throughs, cash, and so on, the income from which will be available to pay dividends on the stock. They have been accorded the highest preferred stock ratings. By issuing stock with dividends that adjust quarterly and giving effect to two tax factors, the thrifts can currently obtain long-term funds at an adjustable rate at a cost lower than could be obtained using the same securities in reverse repurchase agreements. The first effect resulting from the two tax factors is the lower rate on the preferred stock that is accepted in the market due to the dividends-received deductions. The second is that very large tax loss carryforwards have made many thrifts indifferent from a tax point of view to whether their payments on debt or stock are deductible.

These examples represent the early stages of securities development and transaction design.

Accounting Considerations

New accounting regulations established by the Federal Home Loan Bank Board in 1981 allow federally chartered thrifts to amortize accounting losses realized on loan or securities sales over the remaining term of the asset sold. Under the old regulation, losses were recognized immediately with the prospective reduction or elimination of net worth effectively stopping the transaction. The new regulation takes most of the sting out of asset restructuring programs, except for those of publicly held thrifts. These thrifts must report to the public under generally accepted accounting principles (GAAP), which prescribes recognizing the entire loss at the time of the sale.

The accounting treatment for collateralized bond issues, where cash flows from the collateral "exactly" match the debt service of the bonds and where there is no contingent claim on the parent company of the issuer, could affect the volume of CMOs issued in the short term since the mortgage banking and thrift issuers may not be able to support the additional leverage if the issues are deemed consolidated debt.

Purchase accounting in acquisitions has been a major force in eliminating obstacles to free access to the secondary mortgage market. By marking loans to market value in acquisitions, the acquiring company is free to sell the assets without recording losses. Thus, the apparent trend toward consolidation in the industry may well increase the supply of mortgage product for sale in the secondary market.

Packaging Less-Liquid Mortgages

Most securitization emphasis has been placed on single family fixed- and adjustable-rate mortgages. As market participants become more knowledgeable regarding the comparative return, structure, and risk characteristics of the many kinds of mortgages, more creative effort will be applied to the less common, perhaps less-liquid sectors of the mortgage market. Jumbos, manufactured housing, projects, condominiums, second homes, second mortgages, farm mortgages, commercial mortgages, and net lease debt, among others, can be packaged if loss histories or credit support, prepayment statistics or call protection, geographic and other diversification structures, and uniformity of underwriting and documentation standards are provided to prospective investors. Developing secondary markets for these less-liquid portfolio items will be an opportunity in the 1980s.

CONCLUSION

The future growth of mortgage-backed securities is highly dependent on broadening the appeal of mortgage-related instruments to the traditional long-term investors. While pension fund investments in mortgages and mortgage-related securities have increased by more than 50 percent in the last three years to more than $30 billion, this represents less than 6 percent of total pension fund assets of $525 billion. Comparable figures representing mortgage-related penetration in portfolio composition are 3 percent, 8 percent, and 17 percent, respectively, for banks, investment advisors, and insurance companies. These three investor segments represent in the aggregate another $600 billion of assets.

CHAPTER 3

Mortgages

Dexter Senft
Managing Director, Fixed Income Research
The First Boston Corporation

In order to understand and analyze mortgage-related securities, it is necessary to understand how mortgages operate. In this chapter we examine the types of mortgage loans in existence today, their cash flow, and certain other aspects relevant to the analysis of pass-through securities.

WHAT IS A MORTGAGE?

By definition, a mortgage is a "pledge of property to secure payment of a debt." Typically, property refers to real estate, which is often in the form of a house; the debt is the loan given to the buyer of the house by a bank or other lender. Thus a mortgage might be a "pledge of a house to secure payment of a bank loan." If a homeowner (the *mortgagor*) fails to pay the lender (the *mortgagee*), the lender has the right to foreclose the loan and seize the property in order to ensure that it is repaid.

The form that a mortgage loan takes could technically

be anything the borrower and lender agree upon. Traditionally, however, most mortgage loans were structured similarly. There was a fixed rate of interest on the loan for its entire term, and the loan was repaid in monthly installments of principal and interest. Each loan was structured in such a way that the total payment each month (the sum of the principal and interest) was equal, or *level*. We shall refer to this type of loan arrangement as a *traditional* mortgage loan. (There is a growing trend away from this traditional structure, but this is getting ahead of the story.) In a traditional mortgage loan, the terms to be negotiated are the interest rate and the period to maturity. Interest rates vary with the general economic climate, and maturities range from 12 to 40 years, depending on the type of property involved. Most mortgages on single-family homes carry 30-year maturities.

Exhibit 1 illustrates the breakdown of monthly payments between principal and interest on a 30-year, 10 percent traditional mortgage. At first, the mortgage payment is mostly interest. The principal portion increases over time until, at maturity, the payment is almost entirely principal. At all times, however, the sum of the principal and interest payments is the same. Notice that over the course of the loan the borrower pays more dollars as interest than as principal—in fact, total interest is more than twice total principal in this example.

The principal portion of each monthly payment is used to reduce the amount of the loan outstanding. In mortgage terms, the loan is *amortized* over 30 years, and the principal payments each month are known as amortization payments. The amount of the loan that is outstanding at any time is known as the *mortgage balance*. In any month the interest payment equals the interest rate (expressed monthly) times the mortgage balance at the beginning of the month (see Exhibit 2). Often the mortgage balance is expressed as a ratio or percentage of the original loan amount, in which case the mortgage balance runs from 1 (or 100 percent) initially to 0 at maturity. Exhibit 3 shows how the mortgage balance for several possible loans would decline over time. Another way to view the mortgage balance is as the amount of the house

EXHIBIT 1
Monthly Mortgage Payments-Interest/Principal
(30-Year 10 Percent Conventional Loan)

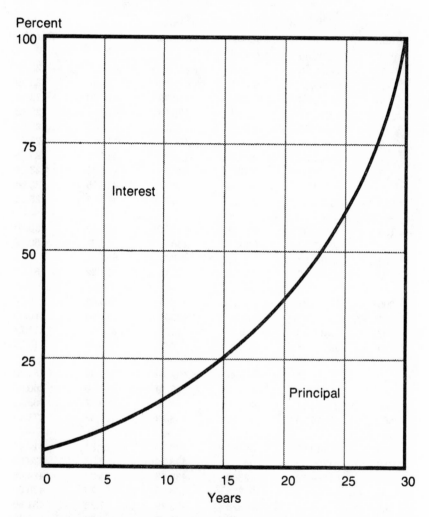

value the home buyer does not yet own. The amount of a home's value that is owned is referred to as the homeowner's *equity*. Equity can be defined as the difference between the current value of the home and the mortgage balance; as the mortgage balance declines, the equity rises. Equity also in-

EXHIBIT 2
Sample Payment Schedule: Traditional Mortgage
(10 Percent Interest Rate, 30-Year [360-Month] Term)

Month	Mortgage Balance		Monthly Payment	Interest	Principal
	Dollars	Decimal			
0	50000.00	1.00000			
1	49977.88	.99956	438.79	416.67	22.12
2	49955.58	.99911	438.79	416.48	22.30
3	49933.09	.99866	438.79	416.30	22.49
4	49910.41	.99821	438.79	416.11	22.68
5	49887.55	.99775	438.79	415.92	22.87
6	49864.49	.99729	438.79	415.73	23.06
7	49841.24	.99682	438.79	415.54	23.25
8	49817.80	.99636	438.79	415.34	23.44
9	49794.16	.99588	438.79	415.15	23.64
10	49770.33	.99541	438.79	414.95	23.83
—	—	—	—	—	—
100	46567.88	.93136	438.79	388.48	50.30
101	46517.16	.93034	438.79	388.07	50.72
102	46466.02	.92932	438.79	387.64	51.14
103	46414.45	.92829	438.79	387.22	51.57
—	—	—	—	—	—
200	38697.88	.77396	438.79	323.44	115.34
201	38581.57	.77163	438.79	322.48	116.30
202	38464.30	.76929	438.79	321.51	117.27
203	38346.05	.76692	438.79	320.54	118.25
—	—	—	—	—	—
300	20651.61	.41303	438.79	174.30	264.48
301	20384.93	.40770	438.79	172.10	266.69
302	20116.01	.40232	438.79	169.87	268.91
303	19844.86	.39690	438.79	167.63	271.15
—	—	—	—	—	—
355	2140.13	.04280	438.79	21.31	417.47
356	1719.18	.03438	438.79	17.83	420.95
357	1294.72	.02589	438.79	14.33	424.46
358	866.72	.01733	438.79	10.79	428.00
359	535.16	.00870	438.79	7.22	431.56
360	0.00	.00000	438.79	3.63	435.16

NOTE: Each month, the interest payment is $\frac{1}{12}$ of 10 percent of the mortgage balance. The principal payment is the total payment less the interest due. The principal balance is reduced by the amount of the principal payment.

EXHIBIT 3
Examples of Mortgage Balances for Various Loans

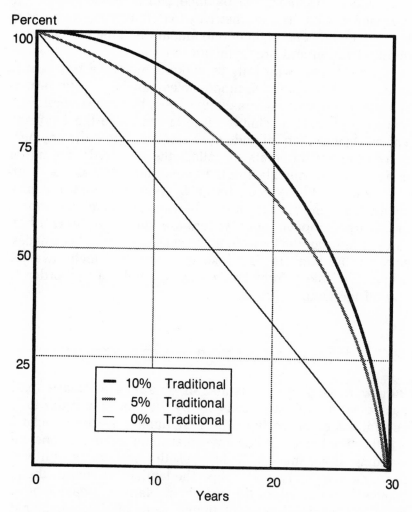

creases if the current value of the home increases, because of home improvements, inflation, and so on.

Sometimes a mortgagor may want to make a monthly payment that is greater than the amount actually due, with the idea of applying the excess payment to further reducing the loan. Such excess principal payments are called *prepayments* and may be made for several reasons. (These reasons will be discussed in detail later.) Prepayments result in a direct reduction of the mortgage balance and a direct increase in the amount of equity. Another way to define mortgage balance is that it equals the original loan amount less the total amount of amortization and prepayments to date.

A mortgagor who fails to make a mortgage payment is said to be *delinquent*. Delinquencies can have a variety of causes—the homeowner may have died, become unemployed, bounced a check, or simply forgotten to make the payment. The mortgagee then reminds the homeowner that the payment is overdue and attempts to collect the money. If the matter is not resolved quickly the mortgagee may assess the mortgagor with a late payment charge. Sometimes there is no quick solution, and the mortgagor may become more than one month in arrears. Although most lenders are willing to allow a borrower a few months leeway, in extreme cases it may be necessary for the bank to foreclose the loan, in which case the property is taken from the mortgagor and sold in order to pay off the loan.

QUALIFYING FOR A MORTGAGE

Borrowers who are interested in obtaining mortgage loans must meet certain standards set by the lender in order to be considered creditworthy. The first thing a lender checks is whether the borrower has any other loans or obligations outstanding; if so, these will diminish the borrower's ability to make mortgage payments. Next the lender determines the income and net worth of the borrower. Many mortgage lenders use these classical rules of thumb to determine whether or not a borrower's income is adequate for the mortgage:

1. The total mortgage payment (principal and interest) should not exceed 25 percent of the borrower's total income less any payments owed for other obligations.
2. Total mortgage payments plus other housing expenses

should not exceed 33 percent of the borrower's income less payments for other obligations. Other housing expenses include such items as taxes, insurance, utilities and normal maintenance costs.

Of course, these percentages may vary depending on the lender and the circumstances. In particular, borrowers with relatively high net worth and/or liquid assets will find lenders to be more flexible. Also, in times of high interest rates and tight money, lenders have been known to bend these rules somewhat in order to maintain a certain level of business.

The buyer is usually required to make a down payment on the property in order to qualify for the mortgage. The down payment might range anywhere from 5 to 25 percent of the purchase price. The reason for requiring a down payment is that in the event the lender is forced to foreclose the loan and sell the property, the mortgage balance will be more easily recovered. In other words, there is room for error if the property is sold—even if it cannot bring the original purchase price on the market, there can still be enough to cover the debt. Lenders use the term *loan to value ratio,* or LTV, to express the amount of protection on the mortgage. LTV is calculated as the ratio of the mortgage balance to the market value of the property and is expressed as a percentage. The lower the LTV, the less the loan amount relative to the property value, and the greater the safety.

The LTV ratio tends to decrease over time. For example, if a buyer makes a 10 percent down payment on a property and mortgages the rest, the LTV is initially 90 percent. Over time, the mortgage balance declines from amortization and prepayments, while the property value tends to increase owing to inflation. Both of these changes serve to lower the LTV.

As with income requirements, down payment and LTV requirements depend on certain circumstances. These include not only the net worth of the borrower but the condition and marketability of the property and the availability of credit. Higher LTV ratios are associated with newer, more marketable properties and with easier credit and lower interest rates.

An important (if not obvious) conclusion about qualifying for a mortgage is that it becomes harder when interest rates rise. Because of the income and LTV requirements, smaller mortgage balances are affordable when rates rise, and yet this is also the time when inflation and therefore home purchase prices are rising. As a consequence, all but those buyers with large amounts of cash or equity are squeezed from the market.

MORTGAGE INSURANCE

There are two types of mortgage insurance that may be used when borrowers obtain mortgage financing. One type is originated by borrowers and the other by lenders. Although both have a beneficial effect on the creditworthiness of the borrowers, the latter is of greater importance from the lender's point of view.

The first type of mortgage insurance is taken out by the borrower, usually with a life insurance company. The policy provides for the continuing payment of the mortgage after the death of the insured person, thus enabling the survivors to continue living in the house. In the sense that the mortgage might just as well have been paid off with part of the proceeds of ordinary life insurance, this form of mortgage insurance is really only a special form of life insurance. It is cheaper than ordinary life insurance, however, because the death benefit, which is equal to the mortgage balance, declines over time.

The other type of mortgage insurance is taken out by the lender, although borrowers pay the insurance premiums. This policy covers some percentage of the loan amount and guarantees that in the event of a default by the borrower the insurance company will pay the amount insured or pay off the loan in full.

An example of how this type of mortgage insurance works is shown in Exhibit 4. Suppose a borrower finances $60,000 of property with a $5,000 down payment and a $55,000 mortgage. The initial LTV ratio is fairly high (91.7 percent), so mort-

EXHIBIT 4
How Mortgage Insurance Works
in the Event of a Default

Situation initially:

$$\text{LTV} = \frac{55{,}000}{60{,}000} = 91.7\%$$

$11,000 Mortgage
insurance obtained

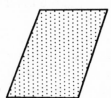 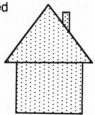

Mortgage:	$55,000	Property value: $60,000
Down Payment	5,000	
Total	$60,000	

Situation after 5 years:
Borrower defaults
Property value falls

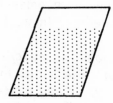 

Mortgage balance: Property value: $50,000
$52,000

Option 1: Insurance company pays claim

Lender has

$ 50,000	Property
11,000	Insurance
(52,000)	Bad debt
$ 9,000	Net profit

Insurance company has   ($11,000) Loss

Option 2: Insurance company takes title to property

Lender has

$ 52,000	From insurer
(52,000)	Bad debt
0	Net profit

Insurance Company has

50,000	Property
(52,000)	Payment to lender
(2,000)	Net loss

gage insurance is obtained in the amount of $11,000 (20 percent of the loan). Suppose the borrower defaults after five years (the mortgage balance having been paid down to $52,000 by then). Suppose further that the property has deteriorated in condition (or perhaps has been partially destroyed), and its market value falls to $50,000. The bank then turns to the insurance company.

Several options are open to the insurance company, perhaps the simplest of which is that it can assist the borrower financially so that the amount in arrears can be paid and no foreclosure is necessary. Assuming this fails, there are two other alternatives. First, the insurance company could pay the claim of $11,000 and let the bank foreclose. The bank, which gets $50,000 for the property and $11,000 insurance, actually makes a profit of $9,000 over the mortgage balance outstanding. A better alternative for the insurance company, however, is to pay off the mortgage balance ($52,000), take title of the property, and sell it (for $50,000). The insurance company thereby loses only $2,000, instead of $11,000. Of course, the insurer could hold the property or even make improvements to it in hope of making a future gain instead of selling it immediately.

The net effect of mortgage insurance from the lender's standpoint is to reduce its risk. The exposure of a lender to loss equals the amount loaned less property value and mortgage insurance. In a sense, the insurance has an effect similar to having a higher down payment because both reduce the lender's exposure to loss. Mortgage insurance is advantageous to borrowers who do not have enough money for a large down payment but who can afford enough down payment and insurance to satisfy the lender.

The cost of the insurance can be passed on to the borrower in several ways. Traditionally, the cost was added to the mortgage rate as an extra one-eighth percent or one-fourth percent, depending on the amount of coverage. As mortgage rates escalated, however, increasing the rate further became less attractive. (In a sense, the insurance company would be increasing the chance of the default it was insuring against.) It has become increasingly common to pay for mortgage insurance in one lump sum at the time of mortgage origination.

It is not necessary to have mortgage insurance in effect for the entire term of a loan. Because the mortgage balance amortizes and the LTV tends to fall over time, the lender may deem mortgage insurance to be unnecessary when the mortgage balance has declined to some predetermined level. At that point, the policy is either cancelled or allowed to expire.

SERVICING

Among the jobs that mortgage lenders must perform in order to ensure that borrowers make timely and accurate payments are sending payment notices, reminding borrowers when payments are overdue, recording prepayments, keeping records of mortgage balances, administering escrow accounts for payment of property taxes or insurance, sending out tax information at year end, and initiating foreclosure proceedings. These functions are collectively known as *servicing* the loans. Many times the original lender, known as the mortgage *originator,* is the one who services the loan, but this is not always the case. Sometimes the mortgage is sold to someone else, and the servicing of the loan may or may not go along with the mortgage.

In the event that one party owns a mortgage and another services it, the servicer receives a fee (the *servicing fee*) for the trouble. Servicing fees usually take the form of a fixed percentage of the mortgage balance outstanding. Although the percentage may vary from one servicer to the next, it is usually in the area of .25 percent to .50 percent. Small servicing fee percentages are usually associated with larger commercial property loans, and larger percentages with smaller residential loans. From the point of view of the owner of the mortgage, the servicing fee comes out of the interest portion of the mortgage payment. For example, if party A owns a 10 percent mortgage being serviced by party B for a three eighths of 1 percent fee, then A is really earning 9⅝ percent (10 percent minus three eights of 1 percent) on the loan.

In addition to servicing fees, there are occasionally other fees that the servicer may keep. For example, some servicers are entitled to keep late-payment penalties paid by the borrower, foreclosure penalties, and certain other penalty fees. The specific types and amounts of fees that servicers are entitled to receive are set forth in a servicing agreement between the mortgage owner and the servicer.

WHERE DOES MORTGAGE MONEY COME FROM?

The largest single originating group is the savings and loan industry. Savings and loans, together with savings banks and credit unions constitute the "thrift industry"—so-called because its funds come from the savings accumulated by thrifty depositors. Commercial banks make up the second largest group of originators, and like thrift institutions, the money they put into mortgages comes primarily from deposits. The third major source of mortgage loans is the mortgage company sector, or mortgage banks. Unlike savings banks or commercial banks, mortgage banks do not have depositors. They are in the business of finding other sources of mortgage money, such as thrifts or insurance companies, and making it available for housing construction and ownership; mortgage bankers' profits come from servicing the loans they originate, plus any profit that can be made from buying and selling the mortgages. The lesser originators of mortgages are the insurance companies, pension funds, and various federal, state, and local entities empowered to make mortgage loans.

Knowing who originates mortgages, however, does not really answer the question of where mortgage money comes from. The real lenders of mortgage money are those who *own* mortgages, who are somewhat different from those who create them. Mortgage bankers, for example, generally do not want to own mortgages at all—once they create them, they sell the mortgages to someone else. Thrifts and commercial banks prove to be the major holders of mortgages, but there are several other notable ones such as life insurance companies and households. The owner category with by far the largest growth is Mortgage Pools and Trusts.

What are these pools and trusts? Essentially, they are collections of mortgages of which shares, or participations, are resold to someone else. (In this sense, Mortgage Pools and Trusts as an ownership category is not very informative.) Mortgage trusts can be created by securities dealers or investment advisors who offer shares in the trust as a form of investment for their clients. Mortgage pools, however, have the lion's share of this category.

WHAT TYPES OF PROPERTIES ARE MORTGAGED?

Virtually all forms of real estate have been mortgaged, but these properties fall into several categories. First, property (and the mortgage on it) can be classified as either residential or nonresidential, depending on whether or not people use the property primarily for living. Residential properties include houses, apartments, condominiums, cooperatives, and mobile homes. These do not necessarily have to be someone's primary residence—for example, summer homes and skiing condominiums are classified as residential properties. Residential properties are subdivided into one- to four-family dwellings and multifamily dwellings for the purposes of Federal Reserve statistics.

Nonresidential properties are subdivided into commercial properties and farm properties. The commercial category encompasses a wide variety of properties, such as office buildings, shopping centers, hospitals, and industrial plants.

NONTRADITIONAL MORTGAGES

The decade of the 1970s saw the advent of many new and different varieties of mortgages. Unlike traditional mortgages, most of these alternative mortgage instruments (AMIs) do not have level monthly payments, but employ some other (often complicated) scheme. One AMI even provides a way for the homeowner to continually take cash out of equity, as opposed to continually putting cash into it.

What was the impetus for the creation of AMIs, and in what ways are they superior to traditional mortgages? The answers to these questions are related to the level and behavior of mortgage interest rates. In the 15 years ending in 1979, mortgage rates doubled from roughly 6 percent levels to 12 percent levels, and by 1981 they had almost tripled to 17 percent. More importantly, the volatility of these rates increased tremendously. Moves of 1 percentage point between the time a loan application was made and the time the loan was closed were not unheard of in 1979. The interest climate resulted in a great deal of risk to both borrower and lender that the rate that seemed plausible one week might be out of line the next week. (Not to mention the next 30 years.) High interest rates combined with the rapid inflation in housing prices to make home financing difficult in general and all but impossible for the first-time buyer. AMIs were created as a way of coping with these problems.

There are literally dozens of different types of AMIs, each with its own peculiar twist. Their names, which are often abbreviated, include GPMs, ARMs, ROMs, RRMs, PAMs, FLIPs, WRAPs, and SAMs. The remainder of this chapter will discuss some of the salient features of the more popular AMIs except ARMs. The next chapter will discuss ARMs.

Graduated-Payment Mortgages (GPMs)

The only essential difference between the GPM and the traditional mortgage is that the payments on a GPM are not all equal. Graduated payment refers to the fact that GPM payments start at a relatively low level and rise for some number of years. The actual number of years that the payments rise and the percentage increase per year depend on the exact type or plan of the GPM. The five major GPM plans work as follows:

Plan	Term to Maturity (years)	Years That Payments Rise	Percentage Increase per Year
I	30	5	2.5%
II	30	5	5.0
III	30	5	7.5
IV	30	10	2.0
V	30	10	3.0

At the end of the graduation period, the monthly payment is held at its existing level for the remainder of the mortgage term. Exhibit 5 shows the payment schedule on a $50,000, 10 percent, Plan III GPM.

The attraction of a GPM is the small payment in its early years. A first-time home buyer who might not be able to afford

EXHIBIT 5

Mortgage Payment Schedule for a $50,000 Plan III GPM (30-Year Term, 10 Percent Mortgage Rate)

Year(s)	Monthly Payment
1	$333.52
2	358.53
3	385.42
4	414.33
5	445.40
6–30	478.81

NOTE: Plan III GPMs call for monthly payments that increase by 7.5 percent at the end of each of the first five years of the mortgage.

payments on a traditional mortgage might be able to afford the smaller payments of the GPM, even if both loans were for the same principal amount. Eventually, when the graduation period has ended, homeowners with GPMs make up the difference by paying larger monthly amounts than the traditional mortgages require. The originators of GPMs reason that most home buyers, particularly young, first-time home buyers, have incomes that will increase at least as rapidly as the mortgage payments increase. Thus they should always be able to afford their monthly payments. Exhibit 6 compares the initial and final payments of a traditional mortgage with the five GPM plans, assuming all mortgages have a $50,000 balance and a 10 percent interest rate. Notice that the lowest initial payment is on the Plan III GPM, and in this example it is about $100 less per month than the traditional mortgage in the first year. The Plan III GPM is the only plan to offer a 7.5 percent graduation rate; this is the maximum graduation rate that federally chartered banks can currently offer.

Because GPMs have smaller initial payments than do traditional mortgages, they do not pay down their mortgage balances as quickly. The interesting feature of GPMs is that in their early years they do not pay down any principal at all—in fact their mortgage balances actually *increase* for a short period of time. Technically, we would say that they experience

EXHIBIT 6
Comparison of Initial and Final Payments:
Traditional Mortgages versus GPMs
($50,000, 10 Percent, 30-Year Mortgages)

Loan Type	Initial Payment	Final Payment
Traditional	$438.79	$438.79
GPM Plan I	400.29	452.88
GPM Plan II	365.29	466.22
GPM Plan III	333.29	478.81
GPM Plan IV	390.02	475.43
GPM Plan V	367.29	493.60

"negative amortization" at the outset. To see how this works, consider the first-month payment on the GPM in Exhibit 5.

Interest due for month one is 10 percent per year for one-twelfth year on $50,000 balance
$$= \$50{,}000 \times \tfrac{1}{12} \times \tfrac{10}{100} = \$416.67$$
Payment on GPM = $333.52
Principal paid = $333.52 − $416.67 = −83.15
New mortgage balance = $50,000 − (−83.15) = $50,083.15

Another way of viewing this situation is as follows: The amount paid on the mortgage ($333.52) was insufficient to cover even the interest due on the loan ($416.67), so the shortfall ($83.15) is lent to the mortgagor. Thus the new mortgage balance is the sum of the original balance plus the new loan:

$500,000 + $83.15 = $50,083.15

Of course, the mortgage balance must eventually be reduced to zero. The annual increases in the mortgage payment eventually catch up to and overtake the amount of interest due, and at that time the mortgage balance begins to decrease. In Exhibit 7 the mortgage balances (expressed as ratios to the original loan amount) are shown at the end of each year, for all five GPM plans as well as for a traditional mortgage. Notice that a Plan III GPM has a balance that rises through the end of the fourth year, at which point it declines to zero over the next 26 years. It is interesting to note that the mortgage balance does not go below 1.0 until some time in the 10th year. Exhibit 8 is a graph of the mortgage balances for a traditional mortgage and a Plan III GPM.

GPMs were first introduced by the Federal Housing Administration (FHA) in November 1976, although various legal and technical matters prevented any large-scale issuance until late 1978. In April 1979 GPMs became eligible for pooling into GNMA pass-through securities, and since that time GPMs have accounted for roughly 25–30 percent of all FHA-insured mortgages. In early 1979 the Mortgage Bankers Association of America had predicted that by the end of 1981 GPMs could

EXHIBIT 7
Graduated Payment Mortgage (GPM) Factor Comparison
for 10 Percent, 30-Year Loans

Year-End Factors	Ordinary Mortgage	Plan I 5-Year 2.5 Percent	Plan II 5-Year 5.0 Percent	Plan III 5-Year 7.5 Percent	Plan IV 10-Year 2.0 Percent	Plan V 10-Year 3.0 Percent
0	1.00000	1.00000	1.00000	1.00000	1.00000	1.00000
1	.99444	1.00412	1.01291	1.02090	1.00670	1.01241
2	.98830	1.00615	1.02258	1.03769	1.01214	1.02335
3	.98152	1.00582	1.02845	1.04949	1.01614	1.03258
4	.97402	1.00281	1.02987	1.05526	1.01853	1.03985
5	.96574	.99678	1.02612	1.05383	1.01909	1.04484
6	.95660	.98734	1.01640	1.04385	1.01759	1.04725
7	.94649	.97691	1.00567	1.03282	1.01376	1.04669
8	.93533	.96539	.99381	1.02064	1.00732	1.04277
9	.92300	.95266	.98071	1.00719	.99796	1.03504
10	.90938	.93860	.96623	.99233	.98532	1.02299
11	.89433	.92307	.95025	.97591	.96902	1.00606
12	.97771	.90591	.93258	.95777	.95101	.98736
13	.85934	.88696	.91307	.93773	.93111	.96670
14	.83906	.86602	.89151	.91559	.90913	.94388
15	.81665	.84289	.86770	.89113	.88484	.91867
16	.79189	.81733	.84140	.86412	.85802	.89082
17	.76454	.78910	.81233	.83427	.82838	.86005
18	.73432	.75792	.78023	.80130	.79564	.82606
19	.70094	.72347	.74477	.76488	.75948	.78851
20	.66407	.68541	.70559	.72464	.71953	.74703
21	.62333	.64336	.66230	.68019	.67539	.70120
22	.57833	.59692	.61449	.63108	.62663	.65058
23	.52862	.54561	.56167	.57684	.57277	.59466
24	.47370	.48892	.50332	.51691	.51326	.53288
25	.41303	.42631	.43885	.45071	.44752	.46463
26	.34601	.35713	.36764	.37757	.37491	.38924
27	.27197	.28071	.28897	.29678	.29468	.30595
28	.19018	.19629	.20207	.20752	.20606	.21394
29	.09982	.10303	.10606	.10892	.10816	.11229
30	.00000	.00000	.00000	.00000	.00000	.00000

EXHIBIT 8
Comparison between Plan III GPM and a Traditional Mortgage

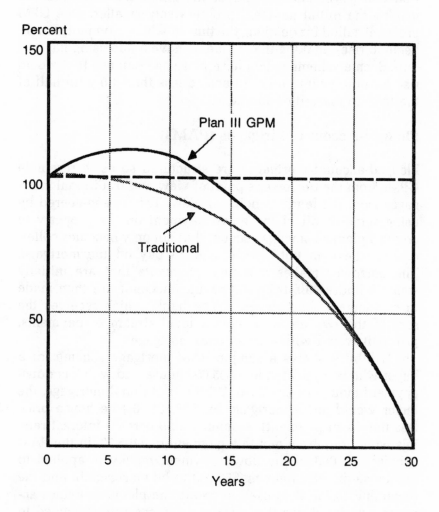

Percent

grow to half of the FHA-insured mortgages; the disarray of the mortgage market since 1979 has postponed such an event, but it still appears feasible.

As interest rates continue to rise, the need for GPMs and similar vehicles becomes increasingly important to the first-time home buyer or those with low cash flows. New varieties and plans of GPMs have been proposed that increase the period that payments rise and/or the graduation rate, thereby making the initial payment progressively smaller. One GPM proposal called for delaying the time at which payments would begin to rise—making the payments have a flat-rising-flat pattern. Such a scheme called for a mortgage balance that would rise for nine years and not become less than 1.0 until half of the term to maturity had elapsed.

Pledged-Account Mortgages (PAMs)

Pledged-account mortgages are structured so as to resemble GPMs from the borrower's point of view and traditional mortgages from the lender's point of view. This is engineered by using some or all of the down payment on the property to create a pledged savings account that not only becomes collateral on the loan but also is used to pay off the mortgage. The borrower makes mortgage payments that are initially small; withdrawals from the savings account are then made to supplement the payments. The bank, which receives the sum of the two amounts, gets a level stream of payments, just as it would with a traditional mortgage.

Exhibit 9 shows a sample PAM mortgage scheme for a buyer who is interested in a $55,000 house and who has down payment money of $8,767.50. With a traditional mortgage, the buyer would get a mortgage for $46,232.50 (the house price less the down payment); assuming a 10 percent interest rate, this would require a monthly payment of $405.73. In the PAM example, $5,000 of the down payment money is applied to the house directly (leaving $50,000 to be mortgaged), and the remaining $3,767.50 is used to create the pledged savings account, which returns the passbook savings rate (assumed to be 5¼ percent in this example). In the first year of the PAM mortgage, the homeowner pays only $327.89 per month, and an additional $110.90 is taken from the savings account each month. The out-of-pocket expense during the first year is $77.84 less than the traditional mortgage, a saving of 19.2 percent. After each of the first five years of this PAM mortgage, the

EXHIBIT 9
Comparison Between a PAM Mortgage and a Conventional Mortgage

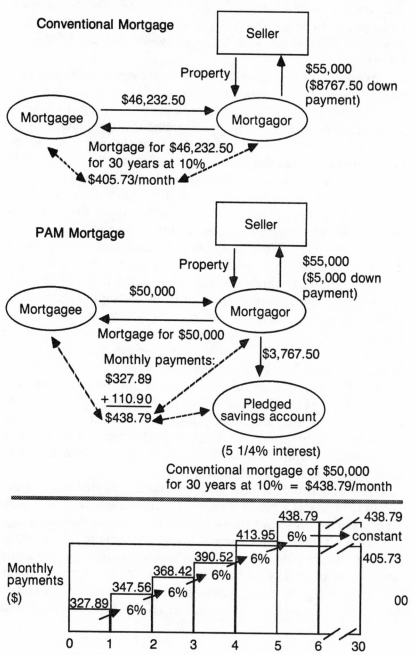

Conventional Mortgage

Seller

Property

$55,000
($8767.50 down
payment)

Mortgagee

$46,232.50

Mortgagor

Mortgage for $46,232.50
for 30 years at 10%
$405.73/month

PAM Mortgage

Seller

Property

$55,000
($5,000 down
payment)

Mortgagee

$50,000

Mortgagor

Mortgage for $50,000

Monthly payments:
$327.89
+ 110.90
$438.79

$3,767.50

Pledged
savings account

(5 1/4% interest)
Conventional mortgage of $50,000
for 30 years at 10% = $438.79/month

Monthly
payments
($)

327.89
6%

347.56
6%

368.42
6%

390.52
6%

413.95
6%

438.79
6%

438.79
constant

405.73

00

0 1 2 3 4 5 6 30

payment from the borrower rises (6 percent in this case), and the saving relative to the traditional mortgage decreases. As with a GPM, when the graduation period is over, the monthly PAM payment is greater than the payment on the traditional mortgage. (The savings in the early years are paid for in the later years.)

While all of this goes on at the borrower's level, the bank receives a constant monthly sum of $438.79—precisely the amount that the monthly payments on a traditional mortgage for $50,000 would be (also the amount the homeowner pays out of pocket in years 6 through 30, after the savings account is exhausted). From the bank's point of view, the total indebtedness of the borrower equals the mortgage balance less whatever money is in the savings account. Because money is withdrawn from the savings account faster than the mortgage balance is paid down, the total indebtedness of the borrower rises for the first five years. This is analogous to the rise in the mortgage balance of a GPM during the period of negative amortization. If, in this example, we assume that the property value remains at $55,000 (no inflation or improvement), the LTV ratio of the mortgage will rise for five years. If the bank had a maximum LTV ratio of 85 percent, then this mortgage would not be feasible because, even though it is low enough in the first year, the LTV rises above .85 in years two through nine. An LTV maximum of 90 percent would be met, however. In making PAM loans, therefore (and GPMs as well), the lender must examine the maximum possible LTV that the loan can reach in order to determine whether the loan meets the lender's standards or whether additional cash for a down payment or mortgage insurance is called for.

The PAM loan is really an ingenious way of trading net worth (or assets) against income. The borrower who has sufficient cash on hand but faces an income or cash flow shortage for the first few years uses the cash to create the savings account, which subsequently subsidizes the monthly payments and lowers the out-of-pocket cost. The price the borrower pays for this privilege is that the savings account interest rate generally does not yield as much as the mortgage rate costs. The additional cost of a PAM loan over 30 years equals the difference between the mortgage rate and the savings passbook rate on the savings balances for the period of graduation. As with GPMs, however, the PAM could be the best buy in the long run despite these added costs because the costs are repaid in the later years of the mortgage; if inflation is sufficiently high, then the homeowner repays current benefits with inflated future dollars.

Like GPMs, PAMs come in a variety of packages with different terms to maturity, graduation periods, and graduation rates. Because PAMs are designed to meet constraints on income to expense ratios and LTV ratios and take into account such factors as mortgage insurance, property insurance, and taxes, the actual payment schedules vary somewhat from the simple pattern shown in Exhibit 9. Although PAMs do not have the same popularity as GPMs right now (primarily because they are not currently eligible for FHA insurance), the PAM is an interesting form of AMI that deserves closer attention in the future.

Buydown Loans

The buydown loan is extremely similar to the PAM loan described previously, except that it is the seller, not the buyer, who places cash in a segregated account that is subsequently used to augment the buyer's mortgage payments. When newly constructed property is financed in this fashion, the loans may be referred to as builder buydowns, since the seller is the home builder. In general, these loans derive their name from the fact that the seller is using cash to buy down the mortgage rate from a high level to a lower level for some period of time.

The buydown loan is very attractive from the buyer's point of view because it provides the benefit of a PAM loan or a GPM at someone else's expense. It might seem that the seller could pass along the cost of the buydown to the buyer by increasing the price of the house; although this may occur to some small extent, it is not true in general because the mortgage lender places constraints on the maximum LTV ratio. The seller of the home cannot arbitrarily hike the price of the property lest there be a difference of opinion with the lender, who bases the LTV ratio on the appraised value of the property.

What motivation does the seller have, then, to give up part of the profit on the sale in order to create a buydown loan? And would it not be simpler just to reduce the price of the property? The answer to both these questions is that the buydown loan is very often the only financing vehicle that can get the property sold because it is the only type of loan that potential buyers may qualify for. Consider a comparison of two possible ways of financing a $60,000 house (see Exhibit 10), using as alternatives a 30-year traditional loan and a buydown loan. In both cases it is assumed that the prevailing mortgage interest rate is 16 percent, that the home buyer has $10,000 down payment money, and that the home builder is willing to give up $3,000 of its profit. The buydown loan shown in the exhibit is of the "3–2–1" variety, meaning that the buyer pays 3 percent less interest the first year (13 percent in this case), 2 percent less the second year, 1 percent less the third year, and all of the mortgage payment thereafter.

If the builder contributes no money to the sale, the monthly payment (on a $50,000 traditional loan) is $672.38. If the builder simply contributes $3,000 to the purchase (by selling the house for $57,000) the monthly payment on the $47,000 loan is reduced to $632.04. If the $3,000 is used to buy down the interest rate from 16 percent according to the 3–2–1 plan, however, the initial monthly payment is only $547.37 and graduates to $672.38 after three years. The buyer of the house can now apply for the loan based on a monthly payment that is roughly 14 percent less than the payment would have been if the price of the property had simply been lowered, and since the seller is the one who is buying down the rate, no increase in down payment is required. Furthermore, if the escrow account in which the seller's funds are placed pays some rate of interest, then not all of the $3,000 will be necessary to buy down the rate (e.g., if the account pays 8 percent, then only about $2,700

EXHIBIT 10
Comparison Between a Buydown Loan and a Conventional Mortgage

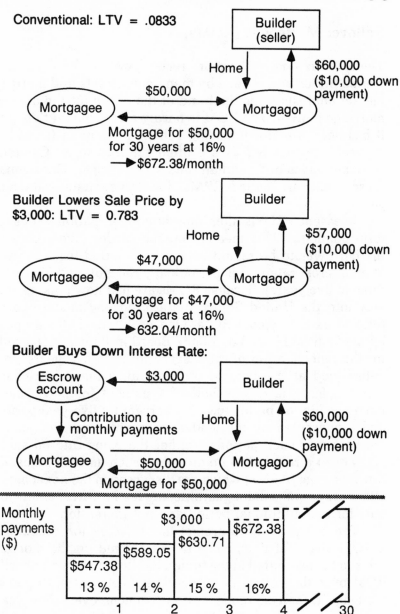

Conventional: LTV = .0833

Builder (seller)

Home

$60,000 ($10,000 down payment)

$50,000

Mortgagee → Mortgagor

Mortgage for $50,000 for 30 years at 16%
→ $672.38/month

Builder Lowers Sale Price by $3,000: LTV = 0.783

Builder

Home

$57,000 ($10,000 down payment)

$47,000

Mortgagee → Mortgagor

Mortgage for $47,000 for 30 years at 16%
→ 632.04/month

Builder Buys Down Interest Rate:

Escrow account ← $3,000 ← Builder

Contribution to monthly payments

Home

$60,000 ($10,000 down payment)

Mortgagee → Mortgagor

$50,000

Mortgage for $50,000

Monthly payments ($)

$3,000

$672.38

$630.71

$589.05

$547.38

13 %   14 %   15 %   16%

1   2   3   4   30

would be needed). Thus the buydown loan can be a cheaper alternative for the seller as well.

Rollover Mortgages (ROMs)

The ROM is one of the more recent AMIs to be used in the United States and is seen by many economists and mortgage-market analysts to be the trend of the future for the domestic mortgage market. The ROM is hardly a U.S. innovation, since it has been a major financing vehicle in Canada for at least 50 years. In fact ROMs are often referred to as Canadian-type mortgages or Canadian rollover mortgages. Occasionally these loans are called RRMs, for "renegotiated-rate mortgages."

In essence ROMs offer long-term amortization with short-term financing. This means that the lender gives money to the borrower to be repaid over a long period (e.g., 30 years) at an interest rate that is periodically renegotiated (e.g., every three to five years). Because ROMs are just now making headway into the United States, there is no one model one can refer to as the typical ROM. One prototype ROM proposed by the Federal Home Loan Bank Board in January 1980 called for the renegotiation of rates every three to five years (to be determined at the time of origination), a maximum change in mortgage rate of one half of 1 percent for each year in the renegotiation period (e.g., 2½ percent for five-year periods) and a guarantee by the lender to provide new financing to the borrower each period at either the going rate on similar loans or at a rate based on an index, such as with adjustable rate mortgage (ARMs) which are discussed in the next chapter. Other proposals call for guaranteeing the borrower a new loan only for one additional period and not thereafter.

There is no way to predict the amortization schedule of a ROM ahead of time, since it will depend on the mortgage rates to be negotiated in the future. Exhibit 11 shows a possible ROM over the course of 30 years. It begins at a 10 percent mortgage rate with renegotiation to occur every five years. In years one through five the payment schedule on the ROM

EXHIBIT 11
Possible $50,000 Rollover Mortgage (ROM)

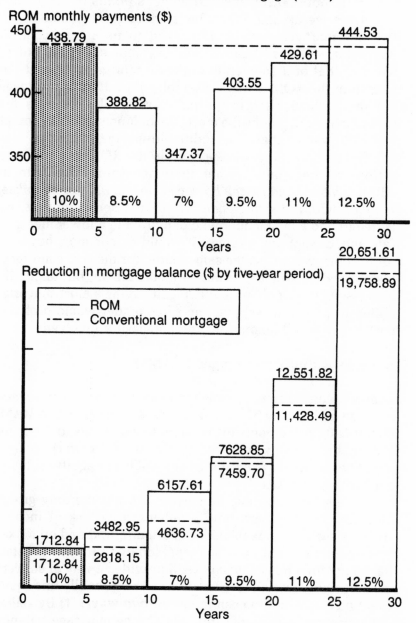

ROM monthly payments ($)

Payment	Rate
438.79	10%
388.82	8.5%
347.37	7%
403.55	9.5%
429.61	11%
444.53	12.5%

Years

Reduction in mortgage balance ($ by five-year period)

— ROM
---- Conventional mortgage

ROM	Conventional	Rate
1712.84	1712.84	10%
2818.15	3482.95	8.5%
6157.61	4636.73	7%
7628.85	7459.70	9.5%
12,551.82	11,428.49	11%
20,651.61	19,758.89	12.5%

Years

exactly corresponds to a traditional 30-year, 10 percent mortgage from both borrower's and lender's points of view. After five years we assume that interest rates have declined, and the new mortgage rate is negotiated to be 8½ percent. At this point and until year 10 the payment schedule exactly matches that of a 25-year, 8½ percent mortgage. Over its 30-year term the ROM always resembles a traditional mortgage, but the particular mortgage that it resembles changes five times. Exhibit 12 graphs the mortgage balance of this hypothetical ROM versus that of a traditional mortgage.

Notice that the mortgage rate on the ROM is always described as negotiated rather than determined (as with an ARM). *This is because the borrower has no obligation to keep the loan with the same lender after each period elapses*, but is free to find a new lender who can provide a lower mortgage rate and/or superior services. It would be common, however, for the borrower to use the same lender for the entire mortgage term. Not only would this be more convenient, but taking the loan elsewhere would probably mean paying a mortgage origination fee, whereas keeping the same lender would probably cost only a small amount for the paperwork involved.

Reverse-Annuity Mortgages (RAMs)

The key word to remember when discussing RAMs is *reverse* because, unlike any of the mortgages discussed so far, RAMs do not call for the homeowner to make payments to the bank. Rather, the homeowner (who is still the borrower) receives monthly payments *from* the bank, while the equity in his or her home *decreases*.

Young and first-time borrowers are not the only groups that tend to have cash flow problems from lack of income. Another such group is the elderly, often retired and on a fixed income. In the event that such a person owns (or has substantial equity in) a house, then a RAM provides a way of converting that equity into an income stream. Traditionally this equity could be converted to cash in one of two ways: (1) By selling the house and paying off any outstanding mortgage balance,

EXHIBIT 12
Comparison between a ROM and a Traditional Mortgage

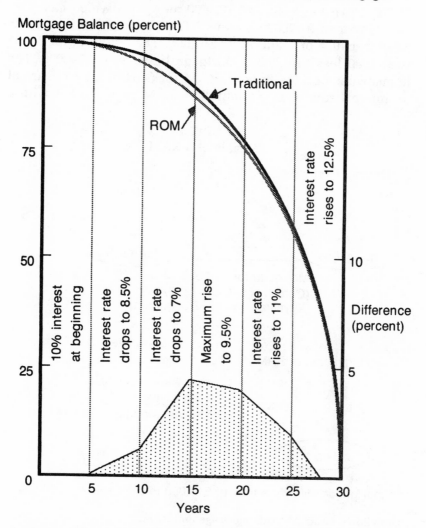

the homeowner realizes the entire equity in the home in cash; or (2) by taking out a new or second mortgage, the homeowner realizes part of the equity in cash. The RAM goes one step further by allowing homeowners to realize part of their equity in a cash stream, paid to them in monthly installments.

Exhibit 13 illustrates a possible RAM. It involves a home-owner who originally bought her home for $25,000—with a $5,000 down payment and $20,000 mortgage, which has been paid down to a $5,000 balance. The price of the house has risen, because of inflation, to $60,000. The equity in the home is $60,000 less the $5,000 mortgage balance, or $55,000. The homeowner decides to get a RAM for $40,000 for 10 years at an interest rate of 10 percent. The RAM provides her with a

EXHIBIT 13
Example of a RAM

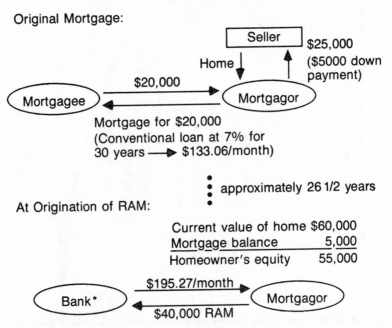

Original Mortgage:

Seller $25,000
($5000 down payment)
Home
$20,000
Mortgagee   Mortgagor

Mortgage for $20,000
(Conventional loan at 7% for
30 years ⟶ $133.06/month)

approximately 26 1/2 years

At Origination of RAM:

Current value of home $60,000
Mortgage balance   5,000
Homeowner's equity   55,000

$195.27/month
Bank*   Mortgagor
$40,000 RAM

The mortgagor will owe a total of $40,000 to the bank after 10 years.

Cash flows associated with mortgage and RAM:

Before RAM:	−133.06	(outflow = monthly mortgage payment)
For 3½ years after RAM:	+62.21	(net inflow)
For remaining 6½ years of RAM:	+195.77	(RAM monthly payment received)

* The "Bank" may or may not be the original mortgagee.

monthly payment of $195.27, which she then uses for food, utilities, home improvements, and/or other expenses. Each year the mortgage balance on the RAM rises to reflect additional payments to the homeowner plus interest on the money lent so far; at the end of 10 years, the mortgage balance is precisely $40,000. Of course, monthly payments on the original mortgage must still be made until it matures. (Often there is no outstanding mortgage when the RAM is originated, so this proviso would not apply.)

From the bank's point of view, the RAM is a continuous series of loans to a homeowner against which the house serves as collateral. Assuming the property keeps the same value, the LTV ratio is continually increasing because the mortgage balance is continually rising. Banks would probably not allow the LTV to get as high as they would for traditional mortgages (i.e., the RAM could not be made for a very high amount relative to the equity) because of the uncertainty of the property value at the end of the RAM's term; as far as the bank is concerned, the property could decline in value and/or deteriorate in condition and marketability.

Shared-Appreciation Mortgages (SAMs)

The SAM loan is another innovation of the early 1980s brought about by high interest rates, and it uses inflation as a way of paying for part of the property. The basic terms are fairly simple. The mortgage lender agrees to provide funds at a greatly reduced rate of interest. In return, the borrower agrees to share part of the increase in the property value with the lender when the loan matures, when the property is sold, or at some other specified time.

At the inception of the SAM program, a one-third participation was popular—the lender would reduce the interest rate by a third (e.g., in a period of 15 percent interest rates the home buyer would obtain a loan at 10 percent) in return for one third of the appreciation in the property value. Over time, the formulas behind SAMs have varied somewhat from the one-third mix. In periods such as 1981 when interest rates were rising in concert with inflation falling, SAM lenders needed to compensate for the imbalance by lowering the percentage reduction in the interest rate, raising the percentage of property appreciation to be shared, or some combination of both.

Exhibit 14 shows the consequences of a SAM loan, assuming the home buyer remains in the home for five years. If the actual percentage increase in the property value (the inflation rate) is close to the prevailing level of interest rates, the cumulative savings over the first five years for the home buyer are roughly the same as the value surrendered at the end of the period. (This example assumes the one-third-type SAM and expresses all costs and benefits in comparable terms.) If inflation turns out to be lower, the homeowner wins in the long run because there is less appreciation in value to surrender; if actual inflation is greater, the homeowner loses. Of

EXHIBIT 14
Traditional Loan versus Shared-Appreciation Mortgage (SAM)

* Traditional loan: $50,000 for 30 years @ 15 percent
* One-third SAM: $50,000 for 30 years @ 10 percent one third of appreciation due on sale

Assume: Inflation rate = 12 percent (1 percent per month).
Homeowner sells after five years.
Original down payment = $10,000.

		Traditional Loan	SAM	SAM Benefit
A.	Monthly payment	($632.22)	($438.79)	$193.43
B.	Total value of payments for five years (assuming 15 percent time value)	(55,998.58)	(38,865.61)	17,132.97
C.	Value of house today	60,000.00	60,000.00	—
D.	Value of house in five years	109,001.80	109,001.80	—
E.	Mortgage balance in five years	(49,360.31)	(48,287.16)	1,073.15
F.	One third of appreciation due to bank on SAM	—	(16,333.93)	(16,333.93)
G.	Net benefit of SAM in five years (B + 3 − F)			1,872.19

course, the homeowner will never have a problem coming up with the funds to pay the lender if the property is sold because they can be taken from the proceeds of the sale. In the event that the SAM matures or whenever the lender must be repaid without the property being sold, it may be necessary for the homeowner to obtain new financing on the property in order to obtain the required funds.

The attractions of the SAM loan are great to both borrower and lender; the borrower is able to purchase the otherwise unaffordable home, and the lender has the potentially lucrative equity kicker, depending on the rate of inflation. Two factors, though, have prevented SAMs from becoming more popular than they already are. First, although the SAM is simple in concept, the fine print can be onerous. The complications created by property additions or home improvements, for example, can cloud the issue of which portion of the overall increase in property value is really owing to inflation and shareable with the lender. Second, SAMs are difficult to package into units and sell as securities because there is such a broad range of formulas and other parameters being used to create them. It is difficult to have mass production of an item for which there is no standardization of parts. Access to the securities markets, which is vital as a liquidity source for mortgage originators, is effectively denied without a fungible product.

CHAPTER 4

Adjustable-Rate Mortgages

Joseph C. Hu, Ph.D.
Vice President
Salomon Brothers Inc

Recently, originations of adjustable-rate mortgages (ARMs) have flourished, exceeding those of long-term fixed-rate mortgages (FRMs). This surge in originations has resulted from aggressive marketing mainly on the part of thrift lenders (savings and loan associations and mutual savings banks), and a confusing array of ARMs is now being offered to prospective home buyers. Because of the low initial rates of ARMs, many prospective home buyers are opting for these mortgages over FRMs, including some who would not have been qualified for FRMs. Thus, ARMs are being created at the expense of FRMs, and this trend will curtail the future supply of FRMs and FRM-backed pass-through securities for longer-term investors. This chapter describes the complex features of ARMs and provides an analysis of their theoretical initial-rate pricing structure. We also discuss the implications of the growing number of ARMs on the housing market, the prospect of a secondary market for ARMs and the potential risk of ARMs as an investment. These discussions are summarized below:

- Newly originated ARMs—currently all conventional loans (not insured by government entities)—have been offered at initial rates of 9¾ percent to 12¾ percent with interest rate adjustment periods ranging from six months to five years.

- ARMs differ in such features as the selection of an index for interest rate adjustments; the charge of origination fees or points; the margin added to the index to establish a new mortgage rate; and the limitations on interest rate or payment adjustments for each period, as well as for the life of the loan.

- Many ARMs allow negative amortization when the monthly payment is insufficient to amortize the loan at the newly established interest rate. This occurs when the interest rate is either adjusted more frequently than the payment or when the necessary increase in the adjusted payment exceeds the amount allowed by the payment cap.

- Several surveys have indicated that one-year ARMs indexed by yields on one-year constant-maturity Treasuries are the most popular variety. The bulk of ARMs, however, are offered with either payment or interest rate adjustment caps.

- For all ARMs, certain relationships among the various features appear to hold true. Given two ARMs with the same loan-to-value ratio and no discounts, the one with the shorter adjustment period will tend to have a lower initial rate under the current environment of a positively sloped yield curve. In addition, the initial rate is often inversely related to the charge of origination fees and the size of the margin. Moreover, ARMs with restrictive caps or possible negative amortization usually carry a higher initial rate than those without such features.

- In an effort to aggressively market ARMs, thrift lenders have apparently made a switch in their lending policy by assuming more credit risk and less interest rate risk. As long as the slope of the yield curve remains significantly positive, ARM financing is likely to continue, which could maintain the strength of single-family housing activity despite rising interest rates. Consequently, new construction and sales of single-family houses are likely to continue at the robust pace of 1983.

- Unlike FRMs, a nationwide secondary market for ARMs has yet to emerge because of their wide variety. ARMs are primarily originated by thrift lenders for their portfolio rather than for sale. Technically, ARMs could be pooled for the issuance of pass-throughs; however, the lack of standardization and volume (with similar features)—the two prerequisites for pass-throughs—has held back such a development.

THE INTRODUCTION OF ARMs

Conceptually, the major difference between an ARM and an FRM is that the former's interest rate is adjusted periodically, whereas the latter's rate remains unchanged for the life of the loan. The idea of financing home purchases with ARMs has been discussed in financial circles since the early 1970s. It was suggested that in an inflationary environment with volatile interest rates, ARMs, because of their reduced exposure to interest rate movements, would be better investments in the long run than FRMs. This suggestion was particularly relevant to thrift lenders, whose liabilities were of much shorter maturity than FRMs.

In reality, however, thrift lenders have made little effort to originate ARMs because of their low profitability relative to FRMs. Borrowers also avoided ARMs because of the uncertainty in the stream of monthly payments associated with interest rate adjustments. Consequently, ARMs comprised only a small portion of newly originated loans during the 1970s. In the early 1980s, as the thrift institutions became unable to continue funding FRMs and long-term interest rates escalated to historically high levels, ARMs began to make inroads as an alternative to FRMs. This development, however, was interrupted in mid-1982, when interest rates declined dramatically and long-term mortgage financing once again prevailed as the main housing finance instrument. It was not until late 1983 that thrifts' aggressive marketing, coupled with the backup of interest rates, enabled ARMs to gain dominance over FRMs.

VARIETY OF FEATURES

The periodic adjustment of interest rates on ARMs creates uncertainty in the stream of their monthly payments. To make ARM financing more attractive, lenders have added various features to reduce this uncertainty. Different combinations of these features have created a wide variety of ARMs in the marketplace. These features are described as follows:

1. **Term of Adjustment.** One of the most important features of an ARM is the frequency of its interest rate adjustment. According to surveys done by the Federal Home Loan Mortgage Corporation and the Federal Home Loan Bank of San Francisco, the most popular term of adjustment is one year. Other terms are usually one month, six months, three years, and five years.

2. **Index of Adjustment.** An index of adjustment is an interest rate series whose maturity usually coincides with the term of adjustment. For one-year ARMs, the index has most frequently been the yield on one-year constant-maturity Treasuries. However, it is not necessary that the term of adjustment match the maturity of the index. The Federal Home Loan Bank Board's (FHLBB) national average mortgage contract rate on the purchase of previously occupied homes, which does not have any definite maturity, has also been used as an index for one-year ARMs. Exhibit 1 shows the interest rate series most often used as indexes: six-month Treasury bill rates (bond-equivalent yield), one-, three- and five-year Treasuries and the FHLBB's national average mortgage contract rate. The FHLBB's average contract rate covers all newly originated mortgages—ARMs as well as FRMs; consequently, as ARM originations ex-

EXHIBIT 1
Historical Yields on Six-Month Treasury Bills, One-, Three- and Five-Year Constant-Maturity Treasuries and Average Mortgage Contract Rate on the Purchase of Previously Occupied Homes, 1974–1983

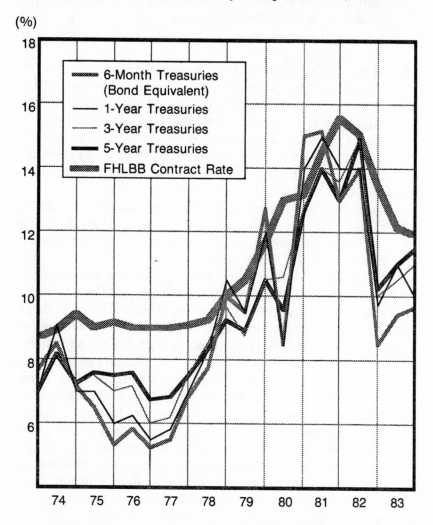

pand, the index is becoming heavily weighted by the initial rates on ARMs.

3. **Initial Rate.** The initial rate is the rate at which the monthly payment for the borrower is established during the initial period before the first adjustment. Among all the features

of ARMs, the initial rate is probably the most important one for the borrower. It enables some borrowers who would not have been qualified for FRMs to purchase homes. In the current pricing of ARMs, discounts or buy-downs have often been provided to qualify borrowers. As a result, the initial rate can be lower than risk-free short-term Treasury yields.

4. **Margin.** The margin is used to determine the new rate on the mortgage at the adjustment dates. For some ARMs, the new rate is established by adding the margin to the interest rate of the index at the time of adjustment. For others, the margin is added to the index only to establish the initial rate; subsequent new rates are then determined by simply adding the change in the index to the initial rate with no further reference to the margin.

5. **Fees.** Lenders charge fees that are a certain percentage of the loan amount (or points) for originating ARMs. Fees for nondiscounted ARMs are slightly lower than those for FRMs currently being offered.

6. **Caps.** Many lenders impose caps on the adjustment of either the interest rates or payments of ARMs to reduce the uncertainty in their payment stream. The caps can be applied to each adjustment period or to the total adjustments for the life of the mortgage or both. For instance, an interest rate cap of one or two percentage points can be applied to each interest rate adjustment, or a 7½ percent annual payment cap can be applied to each payment adjustment. Some ARMs are also subject to a total interest rate adjustment of, for example, five percentage points. Thus, the maximum possible interest rate on the mortgage for some ARMs is the initial rate plus the lifetime cap. For other ARMs (mostly with discounted initial rates), however, the maximum interest rate is the mortgage rate at the first adjustment plus the lifetime cap.

7. **Negative Amortization.** For some ARMs with payment caps or for which the payment is held constant for a longer period of time than the interest rate adjustment period, negative amortization could occur. In other words, if the

monthly payment is held constant so that it becomes insufficient to amortize the loan at the newly established interest rate, the loan balance will not only cease to decline but will begin to increase. In effect, this is equivalent to the lender making additional loans to the borrower. As a result, the loan-to-value ratio is likely to increase as the outstanding loan balance increases during the period of negative amortization. Like FRMs, the ratio of the loan amount to the house price determines the bulk of the underwriting risk of the loan. Historical evidence indicates that, all other things equal, the higher the loan-to-value ratio, the higher the potential risk of the loan and vice versa.

EXAMPLES OF PAYMENT STREAMS

Given the wide variety of ARMs, the stream of monthly payments can be vastly different on two mortgages even if they have the same initial rate. The following example, which is illustrated in Exhibit 2, shows the streams of monthly payments for the first 10 years for 5 one-year ARMs, each with an original loan balance of $50,000. All five start with an initial rate of 7 percent with no discounts, but they differ in the following respects: (1) the selection of an index; (2) the limitations placed on the interest rate or payment adjustment; and (3) the possibility of negative amortization. The new interest rate for each adjustment is assumed to be the level of interest rate on the index plus a margin of 150 basis points. We assume that the five ARMs were originated with the same fees in the beginning of 1974.

ARM1. The interest rate and monthly payment are adjusted annually based on one-year Treasury yields, with no caps of any kind and no possible negative amortization.

ARM2. The interest rate and monthly payment are adjusted annually based on one-year Treasuries with an interest rate cap of two percentage points per adjustment period but no possible negative amortization. There is no cumulative feature for the interest rate cap; that is, any movement in the

EXHIBIT 2
Monthly Payment Streams of Five Hypothetical One-Year ARMs, 1974–1983

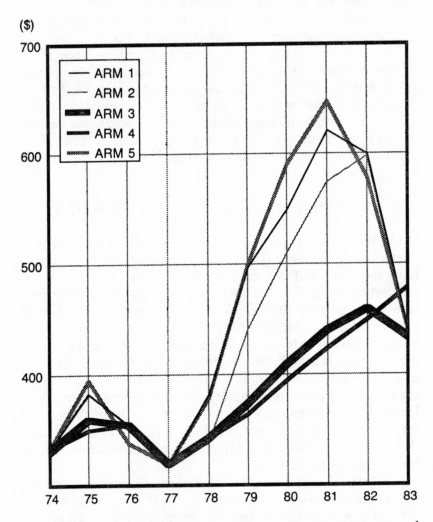

index in excess of the two-percentage-point interest rate adjustment can not be retained and applied to future interest rate adjustments.

ARM3. This loan has the same features as ARM2 except

that the interest rate cap is limited to one percentage point per adjustment.

ARM4. The interest rate and payment are adjusted annually based on one-year Treasuries with a payment cap of 7½ percent per adjustment period. Any necessary payment adjustment in excess of the 7½ percent limit will be added on to the loan balance or, in other words, negatively amortized. The total negative amortization, however, can not exceed 25 percent of the original loan balance. When the 25 percent limit is reached, the 7½ percent cap will no longer be in effect.

ARM5. The interest rate is adjusted every six months based on the six-month Treasury bill bond-equivalent rate. The payment, however, is adjusted annually with no caps. Negative amortization is possible in the second six-month period when the adjusted interest rate exceeds the rate for the first six-month period.

Several observations can be made from Exhibit 2, which charts the monthly payment streams of the five ARMs, and Exhibit 3, which illustrates the unpaid principal balances. First, the payment stream of ARM1, whose rate floats freely according to the index, fluctuates almost as widely as that of ARM5, which is indexed by the more volatile six-month Treasury bill rate. Unlike ARM5, however, ARM1s unpaid principle balance declines steadily without any irregular increases, caused by negative amortization.

Second, when the initial rate is at 7 percent, a one-percentage-point cap (ARM3) is much less restrictive than a 7½ percent payment cap (ARM4), let alone a two-percentage-point cap (ARM2). In fact, unless the initial rate increases to 12 percent, a one-percentage-point cap will always be less restrictive than a 7½ percent payment cap. As a result, in a rising interest rate environment, the payment streams of ARM2 and ARM3 are likely to accelerate much faster than that of ARM4, which resembles a graduated-payment mortgage.

Third, ARM5, which is indexed by the six-month Treasury bill rate, has the widest monthly payment fluctuation despite its one-year constant payment and negative amortization. And

EXHIBIT 3
Unpaid Principal Balance of Five Hypothetical One-Year ARMs,
1974–1983

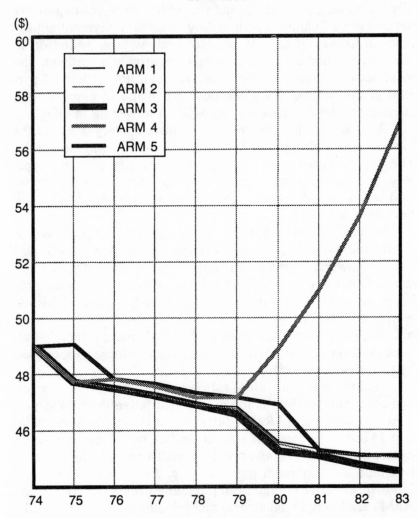

lastly, mortgages with a combination of payment caps and
negative amortization (ARM4 and ARM5) are likely to have
higher year-end unpaid principal balances than those with
interest rate caps. Moreover, ARMs with more restrictive interest rate caps are likely to have lower unpaid principal bal-

ances, because principal paydown is slightly faster at lower mortgage rates.

PRICING ARMs

The pricing of an ARM is basically the setting of its initial rate given all other features. An ARM can be viewed as a short-term mortgage with a 30-year amortization period. In the absence of prepayments and caps on interest rate or payment adjustments, the lender of a three-year ARM will, at the end of a three-year period, reinvest the remaining loan balance at the prevailing interest rate for another three years. Therefore, in an environment of a positively sloped yield curve, an ARM with a shorter adjustment period will have an initial rate lower than that of an ARM with a longer adjustment period. This simple relationship between the initial rate and the term of adjustment is complicated by the provision of discounts, as well as all the other features described in the previous section. In theory, the pricing of an ARM without discounts is shown graphically in Exhibit 4. If other factors such as fees and margins are held constant, based on a yield curve analysis, certain relationships between the level of initial rate and various features are likely to hold true. Results of empirical surveys of ARMs, along with the observations drawn from the previous example of payment streams, appear to bear out these relationships.[1]

ARMs with no limitations on interest rate or payment adjustments should have the lowest initial rate (not considering discounts). As shown in Exhibit 4, the lowest initial rate is measured by the height of the mortgage yield curve at one-year, OA. Furthermore, ARMs with no limitations that are indexed by a more volatile interest rate series will tend to carry a lower initial rate than those with a less volatile index.

---

[1] For a more detailed theoretical discussion on ARM pricing based on the yield curve, see the *Pricing of Alternative Mortgage Instruments* (*AMIs*), Henry Cassidy and Alfred Field, AMIs Research Study, Volume III, Federal Home Loan Bank Board, Washington, D.C., November 1977.

EXHIBIT 4
Yield Curve Analysis of the Pricing of ARMs

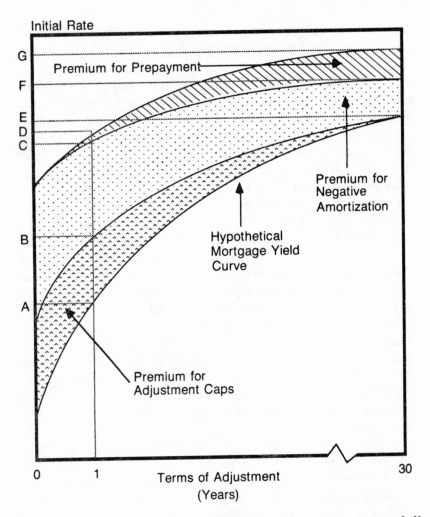

For example, a six-month ARM indexed by the Treasury bill rate should be priced higher than one indexed by one-year constant-maturity Treasuries. As shown in Exhibits 1 and 2, yields on six-month Treasury bills historically have been more volatile than those on one-year Treasury notes, and therefore, monthly payments on ARMs indexed by the former fluctuate more than payments on those indexed by the latter. More important, a more volatile index is likely to be more representative of the prevailing short-term market interest rates. Consequently, ARMs with more volatile indexes require lower initial rates, since rates can be readily adjusted in the future to reflect changes in the lenders' cost of funds.

Given the term of adjustment, a borrower must pay a premium for limiting the interest rate or payment adjustment. The more restrictive the limitation, the higher the level of the initial rate. By way of illustration, consider the extreme case of no interest rate or payment adjustments at all. In this case, an ARM will have the highest initial rate—the same as an FRM—measured by OE in Exhibit 4. As the restriction on the adjustment is eased, the initial rate should be reduced correspondingly as a reward to the borrower for taking on some interest rate risk. The premium charged by the lender for limitations on the adjustment is measured by AB in Exhibit 4. Note that as the term of adjustment lengthens to 30 years, the premium for limitations becomes meaningless and, therefore, is zero.

Negative amortization is generally associated with higher initial rates for all terms of adjustment. As mentioned earlier, negative amortization can be viewed as lenders automatically making loans to borrowers in addition to the original loans. The loan-to-value ratio during the period of negative amortization, therefore, is likely to rise rather than decline. This occurs especially when the house price does not appreciate fast enough to offset the rate of accumulation of the negatively amortized loans. The rising loan-to-value ratio increases the underwriting risk of the mortgage, and as a result, a higher initial rate would be required by the lender. In the hypothetical example of Exhibit 4, a premium for negative amortization, BC (which does not necessarily equal EF in the case of FRMs), is therefore charged by the lender.

Prepayment penalties are usually attached to FRMs as a protection for lenders against early redemption of mortgage loans. For ARMs with very short adjustment periods, the possibility of prepayment should hardly be a concern for lenders and, therefore, has little impact on the level of initial rates. However, it should have some effect on longer-term ARMs, such as the three- and five-year varieties. In Exhibit 4, the largest prepayment penalty is FG—the penalty for an FRM; for a one-year ARM, the possible premium for repayment is measured by CD.

Given the above analysis, we can also conclude that the amount of fees is inversely associated with the initial rate. To a certain extent, lenders that charge a lower initial rate are likely to seek some compensation by requiring a larger fee. Similarly, the size of the margin is generally inversely related to the initial rate. Lenders that set a large markup from the index for interest rate adjustments will have to compensate borrowers by charging lower initial rates for mortgages.

IMPLICATIONS OF ARMs GROWTH

Given the reasons for the recent popularity of ARMs, it is likely that originations will continue to grow in an environment of a positively sloped yield curve. Moreover, as long as thrift institutions' sources of funds remain mostly short dated, thrift lenders will need to originate ARMs. Of course, FRMs will continue to be available to those who prefer certainty in the payment stream provided by fixed-rate financing and who have the qualifying income for such financing. The future volume of newly originated FRMs, however, should be significantly reduced by the surge in ARMs. Already, increasing ARM financing has reduced the volume of FRM-backed pass-throughs and has contributed to the significant tightening of yield spreads between intermediate-coupon pass-throughs and 10-year Governments. In addition, the growth of ARMs originations will have the following important implications.

First, ARMs will sustain housing affordability in an environment of moderately rising interest rates. As shown in Exhibit 5, the number of qualified households at the prevailing FRM rate of 13¼ percent is approximately 24 million. Since

EXHIBIT 5
Sensitivity of Housing Affordability to Changes in Mortgage Interest Rates[a]

Mortage Rate	Monthly Payment	Required Annual Household Income	Qualified Households (Millions)
9%	$521	$25,008	39.0
10	569	27,312	34.9
11	617	29,616	31.3
12	667	32,016	27.8
13	717	34,416	24.6
14	768	36,864	21.7
15	819	39,312	18.9

NOTE: Housing affordability is a measurement of the number of households with the income necessary to qualify under the prevailing mortgage interest rate for a mortgage loan to purchase a median-priced new house. The criterion for determining the required annual income is that 25 percent of the income should be sufficient to cover the annual mortgage payment of principal and interest. The mortgage loan assumes an 80 percent loan-to-value ratio with a 30-year amortization period.

[a] Based on the following assumptions for 1984: The median sales price of a new house is $81,000; household income increases 7 percent across the board over the 1983 distribution, and the number of households increases 2 percent over 1983.

market surveys indicate that initial rates of one-year ARMs are mostly below 11 percent, more than 31 million households would be qualified under such financing for home purchases. While this is an extreme case, it shows that the increasing popularity of ARM financing can significantly alleviate the negative impact of rising long-term mortgage rates on housing affordability. Thus, single-family housing starts for this year are likely to be strong, matching those of the previous year.

Second, the lack of standardization of ARMs hampers the development of a secondary market comparable to that of FRMs. Thus far, ARMs have been originated mostly by thrift institutions for their own portfolios. While some ARMs have been originated for sale by mortgage bankers, they are small in volume with a dizzying variety of features. The Federal National Mortgage Association and the Federal Home Loan Mortgage Corporation have both made a concerted effort to standardize ARMs, and standard ARMs are being purchased by both agencies; however, the transaction volume has been small in relation to their total purchases of FRMs. One of the most important benefits of a fully developed secondary market for FRMs is that it tends to even out regional differences in mortgage rates. Because of nationwide purchases and sales of mortgages, local factors affecting the supply and demand for mortgage credit can have little influence on interest rates on FRMs. Since there is only a limited national market for ARMs, they are likely to be originated under terms dictated by local market conditions. The initial rates of ARMs, along with other features, therefore, are likely to remain significantly different among regions.

Third, by aggressively marketing ARMs, thrift lenders apparently have made a switch in their lending policy by assuming more credit risk and less interest rate risk. In fixed-rate lending, by comparison, thrifts assume all the interest rate risk with minimal credit risk. This is especially true when ARMs share similar underwriting criteria as FRMs. In a rising interest rate environment, the upward adjustment of monthly payments may exceed the borrower's ability to continue servicing the mortgage debt. Two types of borrowers are suspected to be most vulnerable in this environment: those lower-income borrowers who barely qualify for the loan at the low initial rate and those higher-income borrowers who are highly leveraged for the mortgage loan. Thus, ARMs may result in a higher incidence of payment delinquency or even loan default. ARMs that have restrictive limitations on payment or interest rate adjustments, as most of the current ARMs do, may correct the default problem but will adopt the problem of FRMs—that is, the mortgage rate, once it has reached the limitation, can no longer be adjusted upward as interest rates continue to rise.

CHAPTER 5

Housing Finance in a Deregulated Environment

Joseph C. Hu, Ph.D.
Vice President
Salomon Brothers Inc

Since late 1983, the thrift industry (savings and loan associations and savings banks) has operated in a largely deregulated environment. By autumn 1983, interest rate ceilings on virtually all thrift deposits had been eliminated and restrictions on the composition of thrift assets substantially eased. These deregulatory actions have contributed to increasingly shortened deposit maturities, and consequently have pressured the thrifts to invest in interest rate sensitive assets. This pressure, in turn, has led to revolutionary changes in housing finance. (See the appendix for a brief recap of asset and liability deregulation for the thrifts.)

Long-term, fixed-rate mortgages (FRMs), which by and large have been the only instrument for home financing in the past 50 years, have relinquished their dominant role to adjustable-rate mortgages (ARMs). Currently, two thirds of conventional loan originations are ARMs. While the prevailing maturity of ARMs remains unchanged at 25–30 years, interest rates on the underlying mortgage loans have become adjustable, mostly on an annual basis. For the initial year, interest rates on these ARMs have been significantly below those of FRMs. This low-initial-rate inducement has made ARMs widely popular among home buyers, although it has also made some of these extremely attractive ARMs potentially risky for both the lender and the borrower.

In addition, the popularity of ARMs has provided home buyers with a viable alternative instrument of housing finance. Along with recent innovations in the packaging of FRMs for the issuance of collateralized mortgage obligations (CMOs), this new alternative has eliminated certain interest rate premiums traditionally associated with FRMs. Consequently, interest rates on FRMs have been lower than they otherwise would have been. The end result of these developments has been the overall improvement of housing affordability for home buyers, thus adding strength to housing activity.

While ARMs have been popular among home buyers and welcomed by the housing industry, they are not likely to replace FRMs entirely, as the latter instruments still hold certain appeal for borrowers. Depending on the interest rate environment, FRMs could again become the leading mortgage finance instrument. Moreover, with a better understanding of the potential credit risk and drawbacks, the thrifts will become more prudent than they have been in the past in originating ARMs. The future popularity of ARMs, therefore, could diminish considerably. However, it appears that as a result of deregulation, a mechanism is emerging for housing finance under all interest rate scenarios. FRMs and ARMs will alternate as the leading housing finance instrument, depending on the prevailing interest rate environment. Whichever the leading instrument may be, all lenders will rely increasingly on the secondary mortgage market for funding mortgage originations.

In this chapter, we examine the impact of deregulation on housing finance in terms of (1) the popularity and drawbacks of ARMs; (2) the exertion of downward pressure on FRM rates; (3) the reshaping of the residential mortgage market; and (4) the extraordinary strength of current housing activity. Finally, we discuss some of the near-term implications of deregulation on housing finance.

POPULARITY AND DRAWBACKS OF ARMs

Despite their long maturities, ARMs with interest rates that are periodically adjustable are theoretically interest rate sensitive assets. However, ARMs did not become the major investment of the thrifts until late 1983, even though regulators had permitted Federally chartered thrifts to originate ARMs for portfolios since April 1981. Severe disintermediation and historically high interest rates with a flat or negatively sloped yield curve during 1981–82 were the primary reasons behind the lack of enthusiasm for ARMS in the mortgage market.

The deregulation that has prevailed since autumn 1983, however, dramatically changed the fate of ARMs. The December 1982 creation of money market deposit accounts (MMDAs), followed by the October 1983 removal of most interest rate ceilings on deposits, greatly enhanced the thrifts' ability to attract funds. During 1983, the thrifts attracted a whopping $66 billion of net new savings (net of interest credited), 65 percent more than the previous record volume of $40 billion in 1976. For the first seven months of 1984, net new savings exceeded $36 billion.

While these savings flows were huge, they were mostly of short maturities. As shown in Exhibit 1, those accounts that carried market interest rates and that had maturities of less than two and a half years constituted only 49 percent of the thrifts' total deposits in November 1982, the last month prior to the creation of MMDAs. This share rose to 52 percent one month later, increased to 61 percent in October 1983 when most interest rate restrictions were removed, and reached 68 percent in July 1984.

Thus, while the thrifts have always had a need to invest in short-term assets to reduce the maturity gap between assets and liabilities, this need intensified after deregulation. The pressure for the thrifts to put short-term or interest rate sensitive assets on their books forced them to originate ARMs for portfolios. Of course, just as with FRMs, originating ARMs provides the thrifts with fee income and also enables them

EXHIBIT 1

Composition of Deposits at the Thrifts, Selected Months, 1982–1984

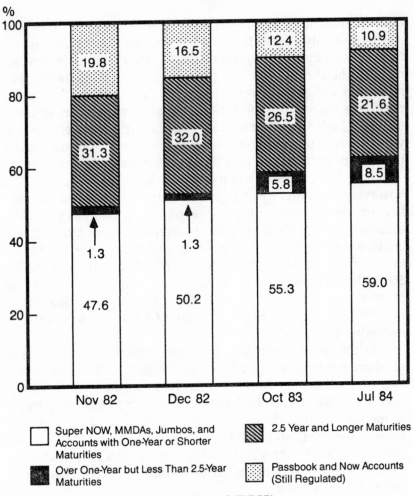

Super NOW, MMDAs, Jumbos, and Accounts with One-Year or Shorter Maturities

Over One-Year but Less Than 2.5-Year Maturities

2.5 Year and Longer Maturities

Passbook and Now Accounts (Still Regulated)

Source: Federal Home Loan Bank Board (FHLBB).

to maintain an active presence in the residential mortgage market.

To market ARMs to prospective borrowers, the thrifts have offered these mortgages in a dizzying variety; the different features include the level of initial rate, index of adjustment, term of adjustment, margin, fees, annual interest rate or payment adjustment caps, and allowance of negative amortization. The most appealing of these enticements has been the level of initial rate. By offering ARMs, the mortgage lenders in theory pass on the interest rate risk to home buyers, who in return receive a certain amount of interest rate concession from lenders for the initial year. This is particularly true in an environment of a positively sloped yield curve, such as that which prevailed during the past two years.

During the initial period of surging ARMs, however, inexperience, earning pressures and intense competition among the thrifts pressed some institutions into offering ARMs with a substantial initial rate concession to home buyers. As a result, although they earned handsome fee income, the thrifts also created many ARMs with "teaser" rates. Because of these rates, ARMs are perceived to be potentially more risky than FRMs, based upon the belief that the potential for "payment shock" after the initial year could lead to an abnormally high incidence of loan defaults.

Recently, there has been a concerted effort on the part of regulators, mortgage insurance companies and agencies (FNMA and FHLMC) to reduce the undue risk of ARMs through "moral suasion," higher insurance premiums and promotion of underwriting guidelines. As a result, it appears that recent ARMs have been created more prudently, and the number of ARMs with teaser rates has been declining. The wide variety of ARMs has been reduced, and most are now offered with annual caps on interest rate or payment adjustments to protect the borrowers. There are also maximum lifetime interest rate adjustments. Maximum negative amortization is provided for those ARMs that have an annual payment cap. These consumer safeguards can also be viewed as investor protection, as they tend to reduce the likelihood of defaults that could result from excessive upward adjustments of monthly payments.

There is, however, an inherent dilemma in the ARM structure. While the various caps are designed to protect borrowers as well as investors, they prevent ARMs from becoming truly

EXHIBIT 2
Quarterly ARM Originations and ARMs as a Percentage of Conventional Loan Originations, First Quarter 1982– Second Quarter 1984

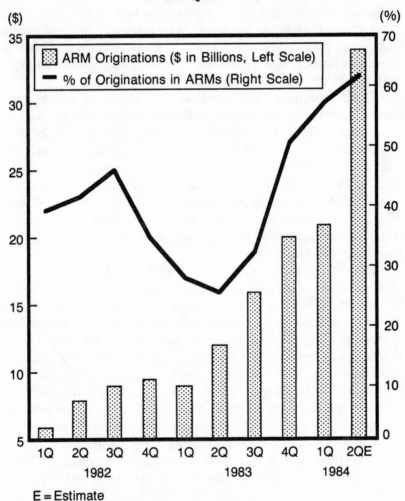

E = Estimate

SOURCES: U.S. Department of Housing and Urban Development (HUD) and FHLBB.

interest rate sensitive assets. Moreover, ARMs may not necessarily be able to match the performance of FRMs in a stable rate environment, much less an environment in which rates are declining. Worse yet, in a rising interest rate environment, ARMs will likely be bested by most floating-rate money market instruments whose interest rates are adjusted more often than once a year, without restrictive limitations. In the long run, these drawbacks will make the thrifts more prudent and less eager to originate ARMs in large amounts for portfolios. The thrifts are likely to insist on fewer interest rate concessions in the initial year.

For example, the initial rate on a desirable and prudently underwritten one-year ARM should probably be 100–150 basis points over the thrifts' marginal cost of funds. (On average, a thrift's overhead costs are about 150 basis points.) Under current market conditions, the initial rate would therefore be at least 12.50 percent, significantly higher than the rate on most current one-year ARMs. The index for the ARM would be the yield on a one-year, constant-maturity Government with a 200-basis-point margin. The annual and lifetime interest rate caps would be two and five percentage points, respectively.

This high initial rate will greatly reduce the popularity of ARMs in the future. For now, however, ARMs have been originated in an increasingly large volume, and the thrifts are directly responsible for about two thirds of this volume. As shown in Exhibit 2, ARMs recently have accounted for more than 60 percent of all conventional loan originations, amounting to $34 billion during the second quarter of this year.

EXERTION OF DOWNWARD PRESSURE ON FRM RATES

Deregulation has had a more indirect than direct impact on the levels of long-term mortgage interest rates, by essentially pressuring the thrifts to invest in interest rate sensitive assets. Thus, ARMs have become viable housing finance alternatives to FRMs in a deregulated environment. Given the desirable interest rate differential between the two types of mortgages, most home buyers have become "risk takers," opting for ARMs, with only a few "risk avoiders" seeking FRMs. Thus, the popularity of ARMs has put downward pressure on long-term mortgage rates.

The introduction of CMOs by FHLMC in June 1983 has greatly reinforced this downward pressure. Since their inception, some $12 billion of CMOs have been offered. In addition to FHLMC, CMO issuers include limited-purpose subsidiaries of investment banking firms, insurance companies, home builders, mortgage bankers, and most recently, a savings and loan association and a commercial bank. CMOs are backed by the cash flows generated from their collateral, which can be either mortgage loans or pass-throughs. Unlike pass-throughs, CMOs have multiple classes of maturity. The fundamental advantage of CMOs is that they can provide investors with a reasonable degree of certainty over the cash flow of their investments through their multiple-maturity classes. Consequently, CMOs allow the mortgage market to reach out to a wider base of investors. More important, for this improved certainty, mortgage investors have been willing to give up a certain portion of yield that they had previously insisted on as compensation for the lack of call protection in mortgage pass-throughs.

By assembling mortgage pass-throughs or whole loans, CMO issuers can realize profits by extracting the yield differential between a series of semi-call-protected CMOs and non-call-protected mortgages. The profit motive on the part of CMO issuers has created an added demand for FRMs or FRM-backed pass-throughs. The combination of the reduced supply of FRMs because of ARMs and increased demand for FRMs because of CMOs has significantly mitigated the upward pressure on long-term mortgage rates in the past year. As shown in Exhibit 3, yield differentials between FRMs and 30-year Governments have narrowed from 298 basis points in January 1983 to less than 100 basis points during May–June 1984, before widening up to the current 225 basis points. The stellar performance of Governments in the most recent market rally, coupled with the lag in the decline in mortgage interest rates,

EXHIBIT 3

Weekly Yields and Yield Spreads Between FRMs and 30-Year Governments, January 5, 1979–September 14, 1984

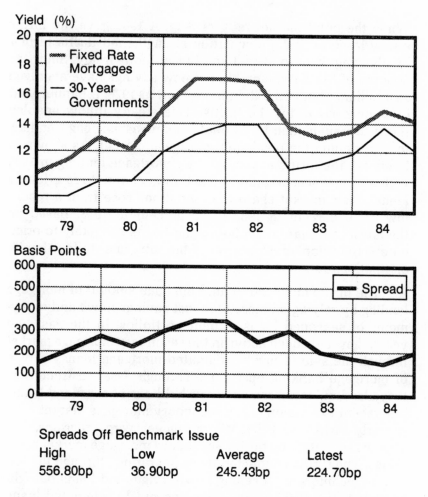

Spreads Off Benchmark Issue			
High	Low	Average	Latest
556.80bp	36.90bp	245.43bp	224.70bp

SOURCES: Federal Home Loan Mortgage Corporation and Salomon Brothers Inc.

had caused the recent widening of yields spreads between the two. However, the current spreads of about 225 basis points are still narrow by historical standards. Previously, when long Governments reached 12.25 percent, the spreads averaged about 300 basis points.

RESHAPING OF THE RESIDENTIAL MORTGAGE MARKET

While the bond market rally of August 1982 gave the thrifts a new lease on life, deregulation strengthened thrifts further by allowing them to attract and invest funds freely. Since the creation of MMDAs, monthly net new savings have averaged $5.3 billion, about $2 billion more than in 1976, a banner year of savings flows for the thrifts. This steady inflow enabled thrifts to resume their traditional function as mortgage lenders, thus reshaping the residential mortgage market. As shown in Exhibit 4, the thrifts expanded their mortgage lending in 1983 with a vengeance, originating $92 billion of one- to four-family loans. Their market share in originations rose from a record low of 40 percent in 1982 to 46 percent in 1983. Based on the latest information available, the thrifts are likely to originate $110 billion, or 52 percent of the total one- to four-family originations for 1984.

The thrifts managed to fund the huge amount of mortgage lending by relying on more than just savings flows and repayments of seasoned loans in their portfolios. In the past two years, they have been active in the secondary mortgage market through the sale of newly originated mortgage loans—a type of mortgage banking operation. Through asset restructuring, they also liquidated some of their holdings of seasoned loans. The recent expansion of the secondary mortgage market, particularly FNMA and FHLMC mortgage swap programs, has greatly facilitated the thrifts' secondary mortgage market operations. The thrifts conducted these operations through the following techniques: (1) selling newly originated loans outright to FNMA and FHLMC; (2) swapping newly originated loans with the two agencies for their guaranteed mortgage pass-throughs for later sale; (3) swapping seasoned loans in portfolio with the two agencies for pass-throughs for possible later sale; and (4) selling seasoned and newly originated loans to other investors. During 1983, the thrifts sold $55 billion of mortgage loans through these operations. Based on their sales activity during the first six months of this year, total loan sales are likely to reach $60 billion in 1984.

EXHIBIT 4

Originations of One- to Four-Family Mortgages and Market Share of Major Lenders, 1970–1984[a]

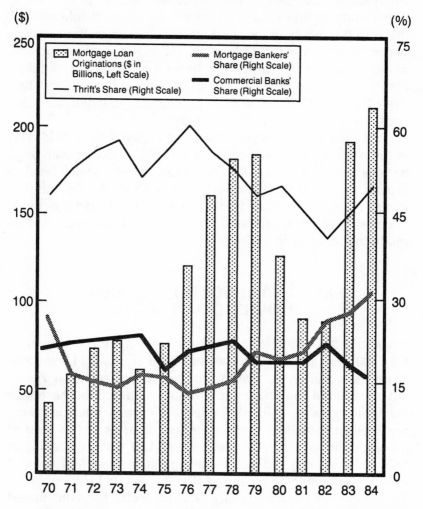

[a] 1984 data are based on the first five months; other lenders account for the remaining 1 percent to 4 percent of the market share.

The thrifts' brisk mortgage banking activity has not affected mortgage bankers adversely. On the contrary, mortgage bankers originated a record $60 billion of loans in 1983, capturing an unprecedented 30 percent of the primary mortgage market. During 1979, a banner year, mortgage bankers created only $45 billion of loans, or 24 percent of the market share. Interestingly, the thrifts' huge appetite for ARMs created an opportunity in late 1983 for mortgage bankers. While competing with the thrifts in the marketplace, mortgage bankers also began to originate ARMs for thrifts. Despite the huge number of loan sales, the thrifts actually became net mortgage purchasers as a result of this hot pursuit of ARMs. For the first time since 1977, the thrifts' mortgage purchases exceeded sales during the second quarter of this year.

As thrifts and mortgage bankers enjoyed their field days in the primary market, commercial banks' share of loan originations contracted in 1983, returning to its normal level of around 21 percent. This could be owing to the fact that in recent years, commercial banks have acquired mortgage bankers as subsidiaries, and as a consequence have been less directly involved in loan originations.

EXTRA STRENGTH IN CURRENT HOUSING ACTIVITY

Since late 1983, long-term mortgage rates have risen by more than 100 basis points to the current level of about 14.5 percent. More importantly, in recent months, initial rates on ARMs have escalated to an average of about 12 percent. These high mortgage rates have finally ended the current housing recovery: Housing starts peaked in the first quarter of this year at a seasonally adjusted annual rate of 1.97 million units. (Up until only recently, however, housing starts had still been at a respectable level of close to 1.8 million units.) Undoubtedly, the strength of the multifamily housing sector has contributed a great deal to the recent strength in housing activity. Nevertheless, single-family housing activity has also been extraordinarily strong. During the past year, single-family housing starts averaged more than 1.1 million units, a level unseen since mid-1979, when long-term mortgage rates were below 11 percent. In comparison, during the past year, mortgage rates have ranged between 12.5 percent and 14.5 percent, hovering mostly around 13.5 percent or higher.

The strength in single-family housing activity in the past year can be attributed to several factors. First, there has been pent-up demand for housing as a result of meager housing production and postponed household formation during 1981–82. During this period, the annual average of single-family housing starts fell to an historically low level of less than 670,000 units. Assuming annual housing demand of 1.6 million

EXHIBIT 5
Monthly Loan-to-Value Ratio for Newly Originated Mortgages on
Previously Occupied **Homes, January 1963–August 1984**

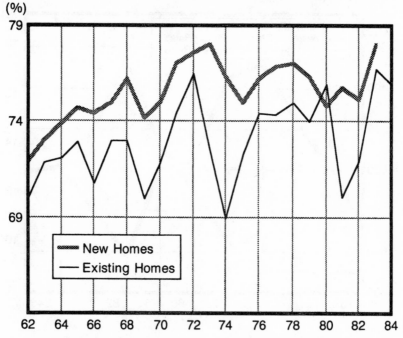

Note: Shaded areas represent periods of housing slowdowns.
SOURCE: FHLBB.

units, and that 60 percent of the demand is for single-family units, the pent-up demand for this type of housing could be about 300,000 units annually. This demand has sustained the number of single-family housing starts in the midst of rising mortgage rates. Second, since the onset of the housing recovery in early 1982, personal income has increased by nearly 20 percent, while housing prices have risen by only 15 percent. The relatively fast growth of income has improved housing affordability for prospective home buyers. Third, mortgage loan underwriting standards in the past year have been more liberal than those of the previous housing recoveries. As shown in Exhibit 5, the average loan-to-value ratio of newly originated

EXHIBIT 6

Quarterly Single-Family Housing Starts and Average Commitment Rates on ARMs and FRMs, First Quarter 1974–Third Quarter 1984[a]

Housing Starts

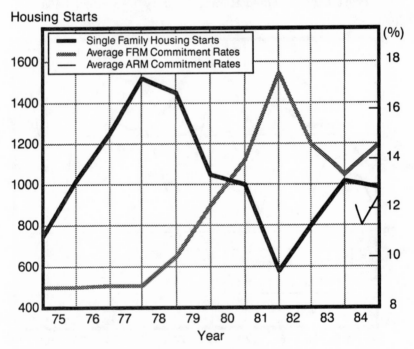

[a] Third quarter is based on estimated data.
SOURCES: U.S. Bureau of the Census and FHLBB.

mortgages on previously occupied homes has exceeded the previous record levels by a significant margin in the past few months.

Finally, and most importantly, housing activity has been increasingly financed by ARMs (see Exhibit 6). Consequently, while long-term rates have been escalating, they have not noticeably dampened the number of single-family housing starts; rather, because of these rising rates, home buyers have opted for ARMs, which have much lower initial rates.

Moreover, as alternatives to FRMs, ARMs have changed the historical relationship between long-term fixed mortgage rates and housing starts. No longer can it be automatically concluded that as long-term mortgage rates rise, single-family housing starts will fall. However, ARMs have not altered the sensitivity of housing activity to overall mortgage rates. It is still true that if an increase in long-term mortgage rates is accompanied by a similar movement in the initial rate for ARMs, as has occurred in recent months, housing activity will undoubtedly decline.

NEAR-TERM IMPLICATIONS

Financial deregulation has greatly enhanced the ability of the thrifts to attract a large amount of savings. However, this has been accompanied by increasing pressure for the thrifts to invest these savings in interest rate sensitive assets. Of all the possible money market assets, the thrifts have chosen to invest mainly in ARMs. In the specific interest rate environment that existed in the past year, ARMs flourished and replaced FRMs as the major housing finance instrument. Their low initial rate provided additional strength to the recovery of single-family housing activity. But, are ARMs going to replace FRMs entirely as the leading instrument of housing finance? We offer "not necessarily" as an answer.

Since the evolution of housing finance from the beginning of the 1970s, we have witnessed the standardization of FRMs, the rapid growth of the mortgage insurance industry, the pooling of FRMs for pass-through securities, the explosive expansion of the secondary market for FRMs, the packaging of FRMs or FRM-backed pass-throughs for CMOs, and now, the wide popularity of ARMs. With further progress on the acceptability between investors and borrowers, the variety of ARMs can be narrowed to a few prototypes. These selected ARMs will then be securitized in large volumes, as has been the case with FRMs. When that occurs, it appears that a complete financing mechanism will be in place for housing activity under all interest rate scenarios. ARMs and FRMs will serve alternately as the leading mortgage instrument. In different interest rate environments, the thrifts and other mortgage lenders will adopt different strategies, providing FRMs or ARMs to finance home buyers.

In a low interest rate environment with a positively sloped yield curve—a situation most advantageous to the thrifts—FRMs would probably comprise the majority of mortgage loan originations. This is primarily because FRMs, with their absolute certainty in constant monthly payments, are still very appealing to most borrowers. With low mortgage rates, a relatively large number of borrowers will have little difficulty qualifying for FRMs. In fact, FRMs would be most popular if borrowers, expecting future rates to rise, decide to lock in low monthly payments. In a high rate environment, however, ARMs would be more appealing than FRMs as long as the yield curve is positively sloped. With a negative yield curve, FRMs might predominate, although overall housing activity would be significantly curtailed.

During the balance of this decade, housing demand—and therefore mortgage credit demand—is expected to be strong. Mortgage lenders will depend increasingly on the secondary mortgage market to fund mortgages, regardless of whether they are ARMs or FRMs. A good case in point is the situation that existed in 1983, when housing demand was financed mostly through FRMs. Lenders, thrifts and mortgage bankers relied heavily on the secondary market for funds through outright selling or securitizing newly originated FRMs. As for 1984, this is clearly the year of ARMs, through which the thrifts

are providing housing finance primarily for their own portfolios. However, despite their enhanced ability to attract savings,
thrifts will not be able to "self-fund" all ARM originations
for an extended period. They will need to sell some ARMs
to the secondary market for replenishment of funds. Although
the securitization of ARMs is now only at an embryonic stage,
these instruments—like FRMs—will most likely be standardized and sold in a securitized form in the future.

APPENDIX
Brief Recap of Asset and Liability Deregulation for the Thrift Industry

Asset

Date	Legislation or Regulation	Effect
March 1980	The Depository Institutions Deregulation and Monetary Control Act of 1980	Expanded authority of Federally chartered savings and loan associations to invest up to 20% of assets in consumer loans, commercial paper, and corporate debt securities; to invest in, sell, purchase, participate, or otherwise deal in real estate loans or interests therein without geographic restriction. Expanded authority of Federally chartered savings banks to invest up to 5% of assets in commercial, corporate and business loans.
April 30, 1981	FHLBB Final Rule—"Adjustable Mortgage Loan Instruments" FR (Federal Register) Docket 81–13094 12 CFR Part 545	The FHLBB authorized Federal associations (Federally chartered savings and loan associations and savings banks) to ". . . make, purchase, participate, or otherwise deal . . ." in adjustable mortgage loan instruments (AMLs). No limitations were placed by the FHLBB on the frequency of interest rate adjustments or on the amount by which the interest rate could be adjusted either at any one time or over the life of the loan.
August 23, 1982	FHLBB Final Rule—"Home Loan Amendments; Adjusted Net Worth" FR Docket 82–22832 12 CFR Parts 545, 555 561, 563 and 570	The individual lender, however, was permitted to place limitations (caps) on the level of interest rates and number of payment adjustments. There were no limits placed on negative amortization, but there was a limit placed on the total term of the loan, which could not exceed 40 years. Interest rate adjustments were to be based on an index that was readily verifiable by the borrower and beyond the control of the lender (i.e., lenders would not be able to use their own cost of funds). Prepayment of the outstanding loan balance could be made without penalty at any time.
October 15, 1982	Garn-St. Germain Depository Institutions Act of 1982	The 20% limitation on investment in commercial paper and corporate debt securities was removed.
May 26, 1983 (Adopted for Implementation)	FHLBB Final Rule— "Implementation of New Powers; Limitation on Loans to One Borrower" FR docket 83–13317 12 CFR Parts 523, 526, 541 545, 555, 561 and 563	The authority of Federal associations was expanded to invest up to 5% of assets, until January 1, 1984, and up to 10%, thereafter, in commercial, corporate, business or agricultural loans. The authority of Federal associations was expanded to invest up to 100% of assets in obligations of state or local governments. The scope of educational loans was broadened to include loans for any educational purpose (not just college loans). The aggregate limit on nonresidential real estate loans was increased from 20% to 40% of total assets; on consumer loans, from 20% to 30% of assets.

Liability

Effective Date	Instrument	Explanation
June 1, 1978	6-Month Money Market Certificates[a]	Interest rate ceiling based on the most recent auction rate of 6-month Treasury bills; $10,000 minimum deposit.
July 1, 1979	2½- to 3½-Year Small-Savers Certificates[a]	Interest rate ceiling based on 2½-year Treasury securities; no minimum deposit.
December 1, 1980	Negotiable Order of Withdrawal Account (NOW)[b]	Interest rate ceiling of 5¼%; available only to individuals and nonprofit organizations.
October 1, 1981	1-Year All-Savers' Certificates[a]	Interest rate ceiling based on 70% of 1-Year Treasury bill rate; no minimum deposit; interest tax-exempt up to $1,000 for individuals and $2,000 for joint returns; expired December 31, 1982.
December 1, 1981	1½-Year or Longer IRA/Keogh Account[a]	No interest rate ceiling; no minimum deposit.
May 1, 1982	3½-Year or Longer Account[a]	No interest rate ceiling; no minimum deposit.
May 1, 1982	91-Day Account[a]	Interest rate ceiling based on 91-day Treasury bill; $7,500 minimum deposit.
September 1, 1982	7- to 31-Day Account[a]	Interest rate ceiling based on 91-day Treasury bill; $20,000 minimum deposit.
December 14, 1982	Money Market Deposit Account[a]	No interest rate ceiling; $2,500 minimum deposit; no minimum term; allows limited third-party transfers; no reserve requirements; a financial institution may guarantee a specific interest rate on the MMDA for a period of up to one month.
January 5, 1983	Super-NOW Account[a]	No interest rate ceiling; $2,500 minimum deposit. No minimum term; allows unlimited checking, but is subject to 12% reserve requirement; available only to individuals and nonprofit organizations.
January 5, 1983	6-Month Money Market Certificate	Minimum deposit lowered to $2,500 from $10,000
	91-Day Account	Minimum deposit lowered to $2,500 from $7,500.
	7- to 31-Day Account	Minimum deposit lowered to $2,500 from $20,000; interest rate ceiling removed.
May 1, 1983	Accounts with Maturities of 2½–3½ Years	The maturity ceiling on regulated rates lowered from 3½ to 2½ years; therefore, accounts with maturities of 2½ years or longer will no longer be subject to rate ceilings.
October 1, 1983	All Fixed-Term Accounts Maturing in More Than 31 Days[c]	Minimum deposit requirements and all interest rate ceilings were removed.

[a] Introduction of new liabilities without deposit rate ceilings or with yields linked to U.S. Treasury obligations of comparable maturity.

[b] Although the NOW account had existed in several northeastern states previously, this marked the first time that an interest-paying transaction account had been authorized on a national basis for individuals and nonprofit organizations. The Garn-St. Germain Depository Institutions Act of 1982 later granted all Federal associations the authority to offer transaction accounts, not only to individuals, but also to corporations, in the form of non-interest bearing demand deposits in connection with loan arrangements. Associations were also permitted to provide NOW accounts to governmental units.

[c] This action leaves passbook, regular NOW and small accounts with maturities of 31 days or less as the only accounts that are still regulated with interest rate ceilings. NOW accounts with less than $2,500 on deposit have an interest rate ceiling of 5¼ percent. Other accounts with less than $2,500 maturing in 31 days or less have an interest rate ceiling of 5½ percent. Effective January 1, 1984, passbook accounts have a ceiling of 5½ percent at thrifts and at commercial banks.

SECTION II

The Securities and Their Historical Performance

CHAPTER 6

Mortgage Pass-Through Securities

Kenneth H. Sullivan
Managing Director and Manager
Mortgage Research and Product Development
Drexel Burnham Lambert

Bruce M. Collins
Analyst
Mortgage Research and Product Development
Drexel Burnham Lambert

David A. Smilow
Analyst
Mortgage Research and Product Development
Drexel Burnham Lambert

MORTGAGE PASS-THROUGH SECURITIES

The largest class of mortgage related securities is the mortgage pass-through certificate. While pass-throughs existed as a legal investment form for decades, they first made sense on a broad scale when several federally supported entities assumed the role of providing credit support and standards of uniformity, which together made the pools of mortgages underlying the pass-throughs more readily marketable. The standardization of mortgage characteristics within pools made the resulting securities easier to analyze, thereby making them more suitable for non-traditional mortgage investors, while the credit support alleviated investor concerns about timely and ultimate collection of amounts due.

Because there are many types of mortgages, e.g., conventional 30-year fixed-rate mortgages, graduated payment mortgages, and 15-year mortgages, among others, a large number of pass-through types have been created. In the following section the principal types traded today are described and compared. The process of creating new kinds of pass-throughs, such as an adjustable mortgage pass-through, continues to the extent that originators require liquidity either through direct sales into the secondary market or by borrowing against pass-through collateral.

This chapter and the one that follows are designed to serve as a general introduction to mortgage-backed securities. In this chapter, we focus on pass-through securities and present an overview of the structure of these securities by analyzing the factors that affect price, yield, and average life. We also present frameworks for analyzing mortgage-backed securities and comparing them with other fixed-income instruments such as Treasury and corporate securities.

TERMS AND FEATURES OF THE DIFFERENT TYPES OF MORTGAGE PASS-THROUGHS

Pass-through securities are formed when mortgages are pooled together and undivided[1] interests in the pool are sold. The sale of a pass-through security represents a sale of assets and is not a debt obligation of the originator.[2] The cash flow from the underlying mortgages is "passed through" to the holders of the securities in the form of monthly payments of interest, principal, and prepayments. Prepayments occur when the holder of an individual mortgage prepays the remaining principal before the final scheduled payment month. Critical to the pricing of pass-throughs are the specific features of that partic-

---

[1] Undivided means that each security holder has a proportionate interest in each cash flow generated in the pool.

[2] The obligation continues to be that of the borrowers collectively, not the originator through whom the loans were made. Payments on the mortgages never become obligations of an originator unless some kind of explicit "first loss" arrangement is formalized.

ular pass-through security. In this section we describe in detail the similarities and differences of various pass-throughs.

Mortgage originators (savings and loans, commercial banks, and mortgage companies) are among the most active in pooling mortgages and issuing mortgage-backed securities.[3] The originator can either issue a private pass-through security or file the necessary documents with a guarantor to issue a pass-through security backed by the guarantor. A GNMA security is an example of the latter case. GNMA guarantees to the investor the timely payment of interest and principal.

A summary of the terms and features of different types of mortgage pass-throughs is found in Exhibit 1. There are four basic types of mortgage pass-through securities—GNMA pass-throughs, FHLMC participation certificates, FNMA mortgage-backed securities and private pass-throughs. While all have similar underlying structures, there are several differences among the four types of pass-throughs.

Government National Mortgage Association Pass-through Securities

The first group of securities is guaranteed by the Government National Mortgage Association (GNMA), commonly known as "Ginnie Mae." The mortgage pools underlying GNMA pass-through securities are made up of FHA-insured or VA-guaranteed mortgage loans. GNMA pass-throughs are backed by the full faith and credit of the United States Government. GNMA is a wholly-owned U.S. Government corporation within the Department of Housing and Urban Development (HUD) and has the authority to fully guarantee the timely payment of principal and interest on its securities. The pass-through secu-

---

[3] Pass-throughs are often an attractive alternative to S&Ls in situations where the loans in a pool would trade below par because of their low coupons. By establishing a pass-through security, an S&L can more readily replenish its funds through reverse repurchase agreements. Also, in situations where an S&L wishes to sell assets, the backing of one of the Federal agencies and liquidity of the trading markets for pass-throughs can often result in the realization of a higher price for the assets sold.

EXHIBT 1
Features of Selected Mortgage Pass-Through Securities

| | GNMA | | | | Mobile Homes | FHA Projects | FHLMC PCs | FNMA MBS |
	GNMA I	GNMA II	GNMA Midgets	GNMA GPM				
Type of Mortgages	Level Payment FHA/VA	Level Payment FHA/VA	Level Payment FHA/VA	Graduated payment loans (mostly 7.5%)	Level Payment FHA/VA	FHA Project FHA/VA	95% single family	Level Payment single family
	New originations	New originations	New originations	New originations	New originations	New originations	New or seasoned conventional loans	New or seasoned conventional loans
Term	90% must be 20 yrs. +	90% must be 20 yrs. +	15 years	30-year Orig. Term	4 types ranging from 12-20 yrs.	Most are 40 years	97½% level payment mostly 30 years (also, a relatively new 15-year term)	30-yr. Orig. Term. 20-yr. Orig. Term (also, a relatively new 15-year term)
Minimum Pool Size	$1 million 12 loans	$7 million	$1 million	$1 million	$.5 million	$.5 million 1 loan	$100 million (except Guarantors Program—$5 million)	$1 million

Geographic Characteristics	Highly regional	May be regional or national	Highly regional	Highly regional	Highly regional	Highly regional	National	National
Mortgage Coupons Allowed (Servicing Fee)	.5% over P-T rate	.5%–1.5% over P-T rate	.5% over P-T rate	.5% over P-T rate	3.25% over P-T rate (Approx.)	.25% over P-T rate	.5%–2.5% over P-T rate	.5%–2.5% over P-T rate
Number of Pools Outstanding	73,000	3,300	1,925	8,600	5,100	600	12,450	8,150
$ Amount Outstanding (Billions)	151.0[a]	8.7[b]	3.4	14.3	3.3[c]	3.0	75.3[d]	33.6[e]
Range of Coupons	5.25%–17.000%	8.00%–14.50%	7.25%–13.50%	9.00%–17.50%	6.00%–16.75%	8.00%–14.25%	4.25%–16.50%	4.00%–17.00%
Stated Delay (days)	45	50	45	50	45	45	75	54
Actual Penalty (days)	15	20	15	20	15	15	45	24

[a] Includes $1.7 billion of buydown pools.

[b] Includes $1.1 billion of GPMs, $661 million of 15-year GNMA IIs, $25 million of Adjustable GNMAs IIs, and $17 million of Mobile Homes.

[c] Includes $17 million of GNMA II Mobile Home pools.

[d] Includes both Regular and Swap/Guarantor PCs, $1.5 billion of 15-year Midgets, $790 million of FHA/VAs, and $385 million of Multifamily PCs.

[e] Includes $3.0 billion of FHA/VAs, $395 million of Intermediate-Term, and $570 million of Long-Term Assumables.

rities guaranteed by GNMA differ according to the nature of the mortgages that comprise the underlying pool.

The GNMA pass-through security is a fully modified pass-through security, which means that regardless of whether the mortgage payment is received, the holder of the security will receive full and timely payment of principal and interest. The original GNMA pass-through is the most common and liquid pass-through security. It constitutes 80 percent of those outstanding in the market. The GNMA II is the most recent GNMA security. While providing the same guarantees as all GNMA certificates, GNMA II has some differences from GNMA I. First, GNMA IIs are based on multiple issuer pools[4] while the original GNMAs are based on single issuer pools. In addition, the mortgage coupon requirements have been relaxed (a wider range of coupons is permitted in a pool), and there is additional delay of five days in passing through principal and interest payments because of centralization of the payment facility.

The four additional GNMA securities summarized in Exhibit 1 include the GNMA Midget, GNMA GPM, GNMA Mobile Homes and GNMA FHA Projects. The GNMA Midget is an intermediate term (15 years) security with an assumed average life of 7 years for purposes of quoting yields. It is similar in structure to the original 30-year GNMA security. The maturity of the underlying mortgages is the primary difference. Because of the maturity difference, which translates into a much shorter average life, the Midget will normally trade at a premium price to a regular GNMA with an equal coupon.

Another security backed by GNMA is the GNMA GPM.[5]

---

[4] Multiple issuer pools can be arranged by GNMA to accommodate many smaller issuers who may not individually generate the minimum volume of $1 million required to participate in GNMA I.

[5] As explained in Chapter 3, Graduated Payment Mortgages (GPM) differ from conventional mortgages because all payments are not level. Payments start out low and rise for a number of years. GPMs are designed to make housing affordable for first time home buyers. Because of the low payments in the initial years, GPMs do not pay down as quickly as traditional mortgages. In fact, the smaller payments in the beginning will cause the mortgage balance to increase. This is known as "negative amortization."

The GNMA GPM pass-through security is based on graduated payment mortgages. This market is smaller and less liquid than fixed-rate single-family GNMAs. In addition, the cash flows are more complex and amortization is initially negative. These features have translated into higher yields for the GNMA GPM. It should be noted that the GPM becomes the equivalent of a fixed-rate, fully amortizing, level payment mortgage after five years. The demographics of the borrowers, however, may be materially different.

The major distinguishing features for GNMA Mobile Home (MH) pass-through securities from the other GNMA pass-through securities lies in the servicing fee. The servicing fee is the difference between the mortgage interest rate and the pass-through coupon rate. The higher servicing fee is the result of several factors. The first is that the "natural" rate for mobile home mortgages is higher than the current production rate for conventional loans. The second factor is that the payments are more difficult to collect from the borrowers, and policing the borrowers can be more costly. It is important to note, finally, that despite the higher underlying coupons on the mortgages, the GNMA MH pass-through does not show a consistent record of higher prepayment rates than conventional pass-throughs. This once again highlights the importance of understanding all of the applicable demographic variables.

The GNMA FHA Projects security is based on longer term (40 years) multi-family project mortgage loans. Pricing is based on an average life assumption of 18 years. An additional feature of these securities is that most of the mortgages in the project pools currently outstanding are "putable"[6] back to HUD 20 years from the date of insurance endorsement. Thus, the mortgage loans have what may be interpreted as a minimum return. GNMA projects have historically traded 10–40 basis points above the original GNMA yields. Today, however, the put option is no longer available. This should have the effect of increasing the yield differential.

---

[6] A putable security is one in which the holder is granted the option to sell the security back to the issuer at a predetermined price.

Federal Home Loan Mortgage Corporation Participation Certificate

Another type of pass-through is the Federal Home Loan Mortgage Corporation (FHLMC) participation certificate or PC. This is commonly known as the "Freddie Mac" PC. The FHLMC is the second largest issuer of pass-through securities. Their PC is based on conventional mortgages (that is, single-family residential mortgages that are *not* guaranteed by VA or insured by FHA). Some of the features that characterize PCs are (i) prepayments are often more consistent than those of GNMAs because the underlying mortgage pools are often larger, (ii) the PC is also a relatively liquid market, although not as liquid as GNMAs, and (iii) FHLMC securities have for most of their history traded at higher yields than GNMAs in the secondary markets. PCs can be purchased in the capital markets and can serve as collateral for other activities (repurchase agreements, for example). Furthermore, FHLMC guarantees the timely payment of interest and ultimate payment of principal on all conventional mortgages that make up the pool. Whereas GNMA and FNMA (discussed next) guarantee the timely payment of interest and principal, FHLMC guarantees only the timely payment of interest and ultimate payment of principal. This means that FHLMC passes through whatever principal it collects and guarantees payment of the remainder within a year.

Federal National Mortgage Association Mortgage-Backed Security

A third type of pass-through security is the Federal National Mortgage Association Mortgage Backed Security (FNMA MBS). FNMA, commonly known as "Fannie Mae," is the newest player in the pass-through security market. They offer a pass-through security similar to the FHLMC PC. FNMA guarantees the timely payment of principal and interest for all securities it issues. Like FHLMC, FNMA offers programs whereby lenders may exchange older mortgages for FNMA MBSs. More recent programs initiated by FNMA include a FHA/VA swap program, an intermediate term (15-year) pass-through program and an adjustable rate mortgage pass-through programs.

Private Pass-Through Securities

The fourth type of pass-through security is a private pass-through. Because of the low volume of private pass-throughs they have not been included in Exhibit 1. Approximately $3.3 billion of private pass-throughs have been issued through year-end 1983 by nine different issuers. Private pass-throughs can be issued without guarantees by independent companies such as commercial banks. This differs from government related institutions such as GNMA and FHLMC. Bank of America and First Federal Savings and Loan of Chicago have both been purchasers or originators of mortgages and issuers of mortgage-backed certificates. In recent years, only Norwest Mortgage, Inc. and Banco Mortgage Co. have used the public pass-through market to any great extent, accounting for $1.33 billion and $300 million of issues, respectively.

MORTGAGE AND MORTGAGE PASS-THROUGH CASH FLOWS

Before one can compare pass-throughs with other fixed income instruments, one must master the details of how the payments work. The analysis of a pass-through security begins with an examination of the cash flow pattern of the mortgages underlying the pass-through assuming that there are no prepayments. This is the simplest case to analyze. In subsequent examples, the effects of servicing fees (an amount retained by a servicer out of the mortgage cash flow, which, therefore, reduces the cash flow to pass-through holders) and simulated prepayments are incorporated into the analysis. The mortgage pool generally used in the following examples to illustrate points is a $1,000,000 pool of 11 percent mortgages with 30-year maturities. The corresponding pass-through certificate has a 10.5 percent pass-through rate and a .5 percent servicing fee typical of a GNMA pass-through. The servicing fee is retained by the originator of the loans both to compensate for the cost of collecting the payments and to ensure that the originator has a continuing interest in monitoring the status of the loans.

As explained in Chapter 3, traditional mortgages are fixed rate loans which are repaid in equal monthly installments of principal and interests. In the early stages of repayment, most of the monthly installment consists of interest. Over time the interest portion of each payment declines as the principal balance declines until, near maturity, almost all of each payment is principal.

Given the assumption that mortgages are homogeneous, the cash flow patterns from a mortgage pool are consistent with individual mortgages. Exhibit 2(a) shows scheduled cash flow patterns for a $1,000,000 pool of 11 percent, 30-year mortgages under the assumption of no prepayments. Because there is a fixed rate of interest on the loan and no prepayments, the mortgage cash flow is level over all periods.

The cash flow patterns of pass-through certificates are related to, but not identical to, the cash flow from the underlying pool of mortgages. The differences are the deduction of servicing fees and a delay in the receipt of payments. While the minimum monthly cash flow from the mortgage pool is level, the corresponding pass-through cash flow is not. The servicing fee is a percentage of the outstanding principal and thus the dollar amount (of servicing fee) is reduced as principal declines. As a consequence, the minimum cash flows for pass-through certificates increase slightly over the term. The cash flow from a pass-through certificate with a 10.5 percent coupon (the difference between the 11 percent and the .5 percent servicing fee) is presented in Exhibit 2(b), which shows that the decline in servicing fees leads to slightly increasing cash flow.

Analysis of the cash flow of both mortgages and pass-through certificates would be straightforward in the absence of prepayments. Since the possibility of prepayments introduces an additional and unpredictable component to cash flow patterns, assumptions must be made concerning the likely prepayment pattern.

Exhibit 3(a) depicts the cash flow patterns for the mortgage pool when prepayments are introduced. Specifically, the cash

EXHIBIT 2
Scheduled Cash Flow Patterns for a $1,000,000 Pool of 11 Percent, 30-Year Mortgage and a 10.5 Percent Pass-Through Certificate

Mortgage Cash Flows (No Prepayment)
Cash Flow (Thousands)

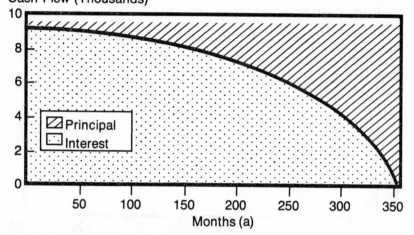

Pass-Through Cash Flows (No Prepayment)
Cash Flow (Thousands)

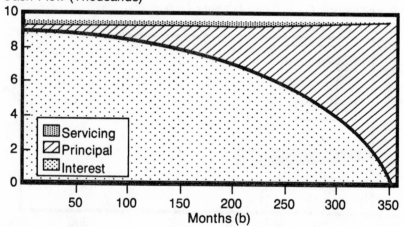

flow pattern shown in the diagram is based on the assumption of a 12-year prepaid life, which is the "industry standard" for quoting mortgage yields. Under this convention, the first 12 years of the mortgage pool are characterized by cash flows that consist of amortized principal and interest on each of

EXHIBIT 3

Scheduled Cash Flow Patterns for a $1,000,000 Pool of 11 Percent, 30-Year Mortgage and a 10.5 Percent Pass-Through Certificate Assuming a 12-Year Prepaid Life

Mortgage Cash Flows (12 Year Life)
Cash Flow (Thousands)

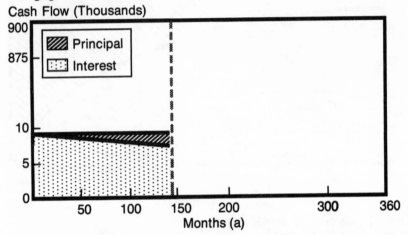

Months (a)

Pass-Through Cash Flows (12 Year Life)
Cash Flow (Thousands)

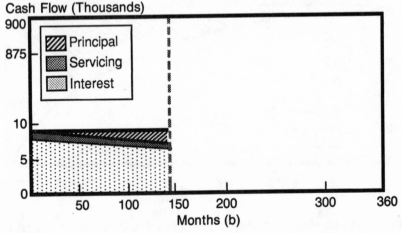

Months (b)

the mortgages in the pool. At the end of the 12th year, the remaining principal balance is assumed to be paid in full. Mortgage yield calculations are made on the assumption of a single prepayment "event," much like the maturity of a bond, which takes place at the end of the 12th year.

The 12-year life assumption was derived from and serves as an approximation for the mortgage termination data compiled by the Federal Housing Administration (FHA) beginning with 1957 originations. The FHA analysis of mortgages indicated that mortgages were prepaid on average in the 12th year. Since the mean (or average) life to prepayment was 12 years, mortgage cash flows have traditionally been evaluated on this basis. The 12-year life assumption was adopted by the pass-through certificate market as well. Mortgage yield is by definition the calculated yield based on a 12-year life assumption. GNMA quotes, for example, refer to mortgage yield and not cash flow yield, which is dealt with in detail below. Exhibit 3(b) shows the cash flow patterns for a pass-through certificate based on a 12-year life assumption.

The mortgage yield convention was not unrealistic prior to the 1970s. The 1970s, however, brought dramatic increases in the level and volatility of interest rates, as well as demographic changes. Higher and more volatile interest rates altered the prepayment process and led to substantial increases in prepayments in the first 12 years. After a period of high interest rates, such as the most recent experience, any reduction in rates will speed up prepayments of mortgages originated near peaks because of the benefits of refinancing at a lower rate. Although the application of the 12-year life assumption may have been appropriate for the past periods of stable interest rates with few refinancing opportunities, this is not the case today as the volatility of interest rates is likely to produce highly volatile prepayment rates. For a mortgage pool, prepayment is not a single event as is the case for an individual mortgage; the prepayments are spread out over time. The shortcoming of the traditional mortgage calculation is that it invariably imposes the same prepayment assumptions regardless of the age and coupon of the mortgage or the interest rate environment. For example, the conventional mortgage calculation would prescribe the use of a 12-year prepaid life to both of the following GNMAs: a GNMA originated in 1974 with a 7 percent coupon and a GNMA originated in 1981 with a 16 percent coupon. In the first case, the effect of seasoning—the ten years that have passed since origination— is that the remaining average life is likely to be substantially less than 12 years. In the latter case, the high prepayment rate one could expect based on current experience indicates that the "correct" life assumption may be as low as five years. The conventional calculation does not allow the analyst to determine a yield based on a probable economic life of the pass-through.

Changes in prepayment rates are fundamentally important for pass-throughs, as they are for mortgage pools, because of their effect on the yield and pricing of these instruments. Accelerating prepayments have an adverse impact on yields for pass-throughs purchased at a premium. The opposite is true for discounts. In the GNMA pass-through market, for example, it is known that high coupon GNMA securities have a faster paydown (prepayment) rate than low coupon GNMAs; therefore, it is highly misleading to compare high and low coupon GNMA yields if both are calculated on a 12-year life.

In summary, the fundamental problem of applying mortgage yields to pass-through certificates is that the cash flow pattern implied by the 12-year life does not conform to the prepayment pattern expected by the marketplace.

There are several alternative methods of addressing the problems associated with the 12-year life assumption. One alternative is to assume the mortgage pool prepays before or after the 12th year. While this method recognizes that there may be a shorter or longer average life than implied by 12-year prepayments, this alternative has some of the same drawbacks. Although the expected number of years to prepayment is critical for yield determination, it is more appropriate to estimate or assume that a portion of the mortgages is terminated each month over the life of the mortgage pool. The industry first attempted to model prepayments by using the FHA experience rate.[7] This measure of prepayment experience is derived from the FHA probability table for mortgage survivals.

---

[7] The FHA provides mortgage protection insurance. Its derivation of FHA experience is intended to be used for actuarial purposes. The FHA is interested in mortgage termination data in order to determine if it is adequately funded and does not promote its survivorship table as an estimate of future prepayment activity.

EXHIBIT 4
Scheduled Cash Flow Patterns for a $1,000,000 Pool of 11 Percent, 30-Year Mortgage and a 10.5 Percent Pass-Through Certificate Assuming .5 Percent of the Outstanding Mortgages Are Prepaid in Full Each Month

Mortgage Cash Flows (.5% CPR)
Cash Flow (Thousands)

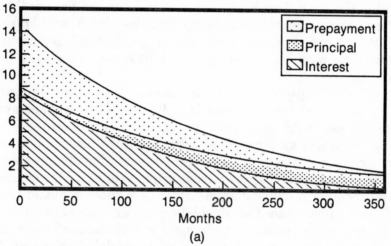

(a)

Pass-Through Cash Flows (.5% CPR)
Cash Flow (Thousands)

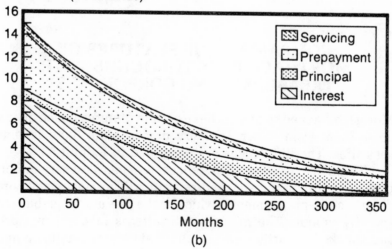

(b)

The problems inherent in the FHA experience rate are discussed in later sections. An alternative measure of prepayment activity is to assume some constant monthly prepayment rate. This measure assumes a constant fraction of the remaining principal is prepaid each month.

The cash flow pattern for a mortgage with a .5 percent constant monthly prepayment assumption is shown in Exhibit 4(a). The cash flow is no longer level over the period. Cash flow commences at a level higher than that which would result if there were no prepayments and gradually declines because the remaining population of level payment mortgages declines.

Exhibit 4(b) shows the cash flow patterns for the corresponding pass-through certificate. Its cash flow declines over the period in the manner of the mortgage cash flows.

Measures such as a constant prepayment assumption are attempts to deal with the inherent problem of predicting future prepayment rates. Meanwhile, attempts to improve the method of modeling prepayments is to define a more realistic cash flow pattern than the single prepayment assumption and thereby generate more meaningful calculations of the rates of return. A yield calculation based on modeled prepayments is called a *cash flow yield*.

COMPARISON OF FEATURES OF MORTGAGE PASS-THROUGHS WITH TREASURIES AND CORPORATES

Mortgage-backed securities have certain features which distinguish them from either Treasury or corporate fixed income securities. The differences are described in Exhibit 5.

There are two basic differences between Treasury or corporates and mortgage-backed securities. The most significant difference is prepayments, which make the mortgage-backed security unique. The prepayment patterns inherent in mortgage-backed securities create uncertainties for maturity and

EXHIBIT 5

A Comparison of the Features of Pass-Throughs with Those of Treasuries and Corporates

Feature	Mortgage Pass-Through Securities	Treasuries	Corporates	Stripped Treasuries
Range of coupons (premium and discount securities)	Full Range	Full range	Full range for a few issuers	Zero coupon; All are discount securities
Maturities available	Limited to Ability to Select Fast Paying Pools or Seasoned (Short Maturity) Pools	Full range	Full range	Full range
Average life	Must be estimated; securities can be prepaid	Very predictable; most are noncallable	Min. average life is predictable and a prepayment penalty helps if called	Predictable
Call protection/ Prepayments	Complex prepayment pattern; coupon selection can help limit the negative effects of prepayments	Noncallable (except for certain 30-year bonds)	Usually callable after an initial period of five to ten years	Noncallable
Frequency of payments	Monthly payments of interest and a portion of principal	Semiannual interest payments	Semiannual (except for Eurobonds which pay annual interest payments)	None until maturity

EXHIBIT 5 (concluded)
A Comparison of the Features of Pass-Throughs with Those of Treasuries and Corporates

Feature	Mortgage Pass-Through Securities	Treasuries	Corporates	Stripped Treasuries
Credit risk spectrum	Generally high grade; range from government guaranteed to A (private pass-throughs)	All are government guaranteed	High grade to speculative	All are backed by government guarantees
Liquidity/ Trading market	Good for many pass-throughs, particularly GNMA, FHLMC, FNMA	Excellent	Limited in most cases	Fair
Basis for quoting yields	Mortgage Yield: monthly payments and a 12-year life (7-year life in certain cases)	Semiannual bond equivalent based on a 365-day year	Semiannual bond equivalent based on a 360-day year of 12 30-day months	Semiannual bond equivalent based on either a 360- or 365-day year depending on the sponsor
Settlement options	Once each month	Any business day	Any business day	Any business day

yield that are not present in Treasuries and are limited in corporates. The range of average lives available for pass-throughs, for instance, is limited by the ability to select pools with expectations of higher or lower prepayments.[8] The average life must be estimated for mortgage-backed securities while it is quite predictable for Treasuries and corporates.

The second principal difference is the frequency of payments. Pass-through securities pay monthly while Treasuries and corporates pay semiannually. This has present value implications for mortgage-backed securities. There are several other factors which must be incorporated into an analysis of pass-throughs as fixed income investments. The most important are discussed in the following sections.

Throughout these sections we use average life, as opposed to duration, half-life, or other measures of term, to compare securities and measure effects of changes in other variables.[9] Duration has gained broad acceptance since it is more easily used to describe the sensitivity of prices to changes in yields; however, it is more difficult to use when comparing mortgage-backed instruments to Treasuries. Treasuries, which are generally bullets (that is, securities that repay the entire principal at maturity), have maturities and average lives that are equal; thus no special calculations are required to derive the average life.

Payment Delay

The first issue to examine is the fact that there is an initial payment delay with mortgage pass-through securities. The first

---

[8] One motivation for the development of collaterized mortgage obligations (CMOs) was the limited range of maturities available with pass-throughs. CMOs enable investors to select from a broader range of maximum maturities.

[9] Average life is the weighted average time to principal repayment. It is useful as an approximation of a single maturity where the mean or average maturity is used to describe the life of the instrument. Duration is calculated by taking a weighted average of the time periods to receipt of the present value of the cash flows from an investment. Half-life is the period until half of the original principal amount of the pool is repaid.

mortgage payment is not due from the homeowner until the beginning of the second month after origination (see Exhibit 6). The holder of the corresponding pass-through does not receive his first payment, however, until some time into the second month.

An investor in a GNMA single family pass-through, for example, does not receive payment until the 15th day of the second month from origination. A GNMA trader will express this 15-day delay as a 45-day delay, indicating the time from origination to first payment. The FNMA security has a stated delay of 54 days. This means the first payment takes place on the 24th day of the second month. A FHLMC security has a 75-day delay.

The effect of delays in payments on a pass-through security's price and yield is indicated in Exhibit 7. For a given mortgage yield, as the delay in payments increases the price of a pass-through declines. At a specific price, a greater delay will decrease the yield.

Monthly Payments

One feature that increases the value of a pass-through of a given coupon compared to traditional corporate or government

EXHIBIT 6
Time Line for a GNMA Pass-Through

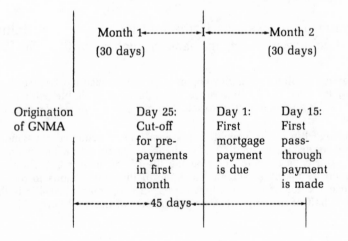

Month 1◄------------►I◄-------------►Month 2			
(30 days)		(30 days)	
Origination	Day 25:	Day 1:	Day 15:
of GNMA	Cut-off	First	First
	for pre-	mortgage	pass-
	payments	payment	through
	in first	is due	payment
	month		is made
◄---------------45 days◄-------------------►			

EXHIBIT 7
The Effect of Delays in Payments on
Pass-Through Price and Yield

Delay (Days)	Price of a 10.5 Percent Pass-Through*		Yield of a 10.5 Percent Pass-Through†	
	($)	Percent Change	($)	Basis Point Change
30	82 23/32		13.60††	
45	82 8/32	− .55	13.50	−10 basis points
50	82 4/32	− .74	13.47	−13
55	81 31/32	− .92	13.44	−16
75	81 12/32	−1.64	13.33	−27

* Assuming a 13.5 percent mortgage yield and .50 percent servicing.

† Assuming a price of 82 8/32.

†† Yield of a 10.5 percent mortgage at a price of 82 8/32 with no delay penalty.

debt is the monthly rather than semiannual payment frequency. This feature provides investors with reinvestment opportunities to compound interest monthly, which are not accorded investors in most corporate or government securities. This monthly compounding gives pass-through securities an advantage over other securities. The quoted mortgage yield, however, does not reflect the advantage.

In order to compare pass-through yields with yields on other securities it is necessary to adjust the mortgage yield upward to its corporate bond equivalent yield (CBE). The CBE allows a standard of comparison for securities with different payment frequencies. In essence, the monthly coupons are treated as if they are collected and reinvested at the mortgage yield rate until the end of each semiannual or other period. The accumulated amount is larger than the face amount of six monthly coupons.

Exhibit 8 shows the upward adjustment of the mortgage yield. The last column indicates the magnitude of the adjustment. The adjustment is absolutely essential for comparing relative performance of pass-through securities for anyone engaged in intermarket transactions.

EXHIBIT 8
Upward Adjustment of Mortgage Yield
Due to Monthly Payments

Mortgage Yield (Percent)	Semiannual Bond Equivalent* (Percent)	Increase In Yield	
		Basis Points	Percent Change
6.0%	6.08%	+ 8	+1.33%
8.0	8.13	+13	+1.63
10.0	10.21	+21	+2.10
12.0	12.30	+30	+2.50
13.5	13.89	+39	+2.89
14.0	14.41	+41	+2.93
16.0	16.54	+54	+3.38
18.0	18.69	+69	+3.83

* The higher semiannual bond equivalent reflects monthly compounding of the mortgage yield at the mortgage yield rate to an equivalent semiannual payment which includes reinvestment income.

A crucial assumption is made when the yield to maturity is used as a measure of how attractive an investment is. The yield to maturity, including both mortgage yield and corporate bond equivalent, assumes that the contractual periodic payments are reinvested at the yield rate. The reinvestment rate subsequently realized could vary considerably from the yield to maturity. Exhibit 9 shows the effect of various reinvestment rates on the yield realized on a security with monthly payment frequency.

When the reinvestment rate is below the quoted yield to maturity, the realized yield to maturity (also known as the adjusted yield to maturity) will be less than the corporate bond equivalent yield. The opposite is true when reinvestment rates exceed the quoted yield to maturity. The last column in Exhibit 9 shows how far the realized yield is likely to vary across a range of reinvestment rate assumptions that do not coincide with the mortgage yield. Careful assessment of mortgage yields requires consideration of the impact reinvestment rate assumptions have on realized return.

EXHIBIT 9
The Effect of Reinvestment Rates
on the Realized Yield
from Monthly Payment Frequency
(10.5 Percent Pass-Through; 13.5 Percent Mortgage Yield)

Realized Reinvestment Rate (Percent)	Semiannual Bond Equivalent* (Percent)	Semiannual Reinvestment Rate of Return† (Percent)	Yield Relative to Semiannual Bond Equivalent (Basis Points)
0%	13.89%	13.50%	−39 basis points
6	13.89	13.67	−22
8	13.89	13.72	−17
10	13.89	13.78	−12
12	13.89	13.84	− 5
14	13.89	13.90	+ 1
16	13.89	13.96	+ 7

* Semiannual bond equivalent is not affected by the reinvestment rate since its assumed reinvestment rate is the mortgage yield.

† Assumes monthly payments of interest and principal are compounded at the realized reinvestment rate to arrive at a semiannual equivalent payment.

Prepayment Effects

The cash flow pattern of a pass-through security is strongly influenced by prepayments. In the following sections we describe the causes and effects of uncertainty as to timing of principal payments and various methods employed to describe or model those prepayments. Exhibit 10 shows the effect of the prepayment rate on yield for three GNMA securities priced above or below par using FHA experience rate as an estimate for prepayments. When the prepayment rate is increased, this shortens average life and skews the cash flow to earlier years. This reduces the investment horizon and affects the realized yield.

If the pass-through security is trading at a premium, an increase in prepayment rates will reduce the yield because the principal is being returned at par earlier than was assumed

EXHIBIT 10
The Effect of Prepayment Rate on Yield When
Pass-Throughs Trade Above or Below Par

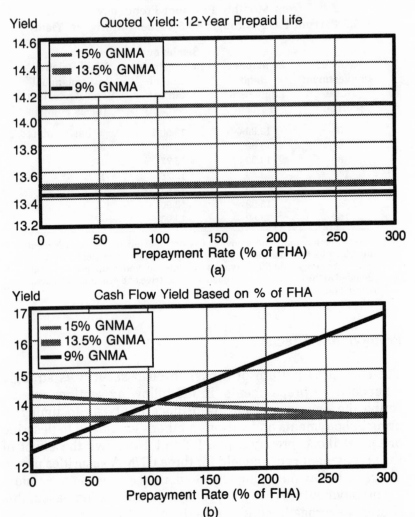

(a)

(b)

in the original yield calculation. It is beneficial for the investor to retain the high coupon interest for as long as possible. In general, for high coupon (premium) pass-throughs, if prepayment rates rise, the average life will fall and the realized yield will be lower than originally anticipated. When pass-through securities are purchased at a discount, increased prepayment rates serve to enhance the yield, due to the early return of principal at par.

Exhibit 10(a) suggests that prepayments (as measured by FHA experience rates) have no impact on yield. The reason is that the table reflects conventional mortgage yields based on a 12-year life assumption. Exhibit 10(b) clearly demonstrates that problems can arise when this assumption is used to estimate yields for all coupons. When the average life is allowed to vary according to the prepayment assumptions, the calculated yields diverge significantly.

Seasoning

Seasoning refers to the time since origination or age of a mortgage or the mortgages in a pool. The average age of the mortgage pool is important because of the implications for average life and yield. Seasoning also affects the assumptions we make with respect to prepayment rates.

Consider, for example, a typical 12 percent GNMA pass-through security priced at 91 and expected to prepay at .01 percent per month. When the underlying mortgage pool consists of new originations, the security has an average life of 22.45 years and a cash flow yield of 13.23 percent. If, however, the underlying mortgages are seasoned 5 years (i.e., 5 years old) and we expect the prepayment rate to increase to .50 percent per month, then the average life falls to 10.72 years while the cash flow yield increases to 13.80 percent. The prepayment assumption is revised upward for the seasoned case because we anticipate an increase in prepayment activity over the low levels associated with the first few years of a mortgage pool. Average life is lower and cash flow yield higher because there are fewer years remaining in the term and principal is recovered more quickly.

Exhibit 11 shows the relationship between seasoning and average life for different pass-through rates and prepayment assumptions. Average life increases with the level of pass-through coupon rates regardless of prepayment assumptions. The reason is that the interest component of the monthly pay-

EXHIBIT 11
The Effect of Seasoning or Age
of the Pool on Average Life

	Average Life (in years)					
	No Prepayment			Prepayment of .50 Percent Per Month		
Pass-Through Rate	New Pool	Aged 5 years	Aged 10 Years	New Pool	Aged 5 years	Aged 10 Years
8%	20.84	16.70	12.78	11.37	10.06	8.52
9	21.38	17.11	13.06	11.57	10.24	8.67
10	21.88	17.49	13.34	11.75	10.41	8.81
11	22.35	17.86	13.60	11.92	10.57	8.95
12	22.78	18.21	13.86	12.07	10.72	9.08
13	23.18	18.54	14.10	12.21	10.86	9.21
14	23.55	18.85	14.33	12.33	10.99	9.32

EXHIBIT 12
The Effect of Seasoning
on Cash Flow Yield

	Age of Pass-Through		
	New	5 Years	10 Years
Remaining Term	30	25	20
Average Life	12.07	10.72	9.08
Cash Flow Yield	13.74%	13.80%	13.91%
Difference Between Remaining Term and Average Life	17.9	14.3	10.9

Assumptions: 1. 12 percent GNMA
2. Purchase price of 91
3. Prepayment Rate of .50 percent per month
4. Mortgages underlying the GNMA were all 12.5 percent, 30-year mortgages.

ment is larger with higher interest rates. Thus, repayment of principal is delayed which increases the average life. As the underlying mortgage pool ages, average life declines. The decline is accentuated when prepayments are introduced. Higher prepayment rates mean that principal is being repaid at a faster rate. This will reduce the time required to repay principal which translates into a shorter average life.

As the remaining term to maturity of a pass-through security decreases, average life declines as it would for a pool that is aging. Remaining term to maturity is simply an alternative way to express age given the initial life of the pool. The effect of seasoning is evident from Exhibit 12. Specifically, for the discount security shown, as the remaining term to maturity is reduced from 30 years to 20 years (i.e., the mortgage pool is aging from new to 10 years), average life of the security falls which will cause the cash flow yield to increase if the price remains the same. Also, over time the difference between average life and remaining term narrows.

PREPAYMENTS AND HOW THEY ARE ESTIMATED

The controversy surrounding pass-through securities has been focused on the methods of calculating yields for these instruments. Typically, a measure of yield involves calculating the rate of discount that equates some sequence of future cash flows with a market price. In the case of Treasury securities the yield measurement is straightforward because the amount and timing of future cash flows are known. With pass-through securities, prepayments create an element of uncertainty which complicates the projection of cash flows and yield measurement. The purpose of this section is to examine the behavior of pass-through yields under different prepayment assumptions.

Twelve-year prepaid life was the first method used to address this issue. In this section two other widely used benchmarks for prepayments are discussed; FHA experience and constant prepayment assumptions.

Causes of Prepayments

Prepayments occur when a homeowner makes a principal payment which exceeds the minimum scheduled amount. Most often, though, loans are repaid in full if prepaid at all, and we focus our analysis exclusively on such terminations.

Prepayments can be separated into two general categories—"economic" and "uneconomic." In the first category we include refinancings. Refinancings occur, with some observable lag, when rates fall below the level of previous originations to the extent that homeowners can more than recoup their expenses of refinancing through lower payments on the new loan. When the home is refinanced, the repayment of the old mortgage causes a flow of cash to be passed on to security holders. Since the future level of interest rates is hard to predict with accuracy, the "economic" component of prepayments will likewise be difficult to predict. Mortgage loans can be prepaid at the homeowner's option at or near the face amount at any time. Therefore, economic prepayments will always be a negative event for pass-through investors since new pass-through coupons will be lower than the coupon previously held.

The second category of prepayments is "uneconomic" prepayments. These occur when a mortgage contract is terminated in an interest rate environment that is not conducive to advantageous refinancings. Uneconomic prepayments include terminations due to default and/or foreclosure, sale of the property (usually a due-on-sale clause is the cause of this kind of prepayment), terminations due to disasters such as floods, fires, and mortgage insurance contracts which pay off balances in the event of a death of a borrower-owner. In general, these are advantageous redemptions for investors since the market value of the mortgage at the time of redemptions will usually be less than the face amount.

Projecting prepayments, i.e., describing prepayments in

the form of a model, is a complex problem which depends on both economic variables such as interest rates, inflation and general affluence, and demographic variables such as frequency of moves and population trends. An additional layer of complexity is contributed by legislative action. For example, recent legislation has upheld the enforceability of due-on-sale clauses. This will have an important effect in "homogenizing" conventional loans across state lines since individual states had heretofore adopted their own positions on this issue. Also, one class of pass-through remains unaffected by due-on-sale clauses. GNMA pools consist of FHA and VA mortgages which by their terms are "assumable." This fact prevents GNMA investors from obtaining the benefit of the largest category of uneconomic redemptions—those forced by due-on-sale clauses. The careful modeling of prepayments, and the analysis and quantification of the factors affecting prepayments, is the topic of Chapter 11. At the very least, the discussion above should alert participants in the mortgage market to the variety of factors that have an impact on investment values and that many of the factors are correlated.

FHA Experience

FHA experience has become the traditional method for estimating prepayments. It is the best known and most widely used prepayment "model." FHA periodically publishes a table of 30 numbers that represent a series of annual survival rates. The table indicates the probability for survival of a mortgage and implicitly tells the percentage of mortgages expected to terminate for any given policy year. The annual rates are interpolated and spread out across each year in monthly intervals. A fundamental problem though is that the FHA experience is based on a single parameter: age of the mortgage. It ignores the coupon and year of origination of the mortgage, among other things. A major consequence of this is that FHA experience more accurately reflects the interest rate environment of the 1960s and 1970s. Furthermore, the usefulness of FHA data is limited in that the statistics are based on assumable

FHA and VA mortgages. Thus, for securities other than GNMAs, such as FHLMCs and FNMAs, the data can be misleading.

To accommodate prepayment experience rates that are either faster or slower than those suggested by the FHA table, prepayment rates are expressed as a multiple of the FHA experience rate. "0 percent of FHA" means no prepayments and "100 percent of FHA" refers to the "normal" rate. Any other rate of prepayment can be expressed as a percentage of the normal rate. "200 percent of FHA" means, for example, that a pool is experiencing prepayment at twice the rate of what appears in the table (i.e., 100 percent of FHA). The use of multiples of FHA experience to adjust for mortgage pools that pay faster or slower is problematic because the pools do not follow a consistent pattern. In other words, fast-paying pools do not increase prepayments proportionately across policy years. Nevertheless, FHA experience is widely used throughout the mortgage-backed securities industry. Therefore, it is important to examine the effect of FHA experience assumptions on variables that affect the pricing of mortgage-backed securities.

Constant Prepayment Factors

An alternative measure for prepayments is to assume that the principal is prepaid at some constant rate, which we call the *Conditional Prepayment Rate* (CPR). Several different expressions have been coined to describe this measure, all of which assume a constant fraction of the remaining principal is prepaid each month (or year). This implies that each individual mortgage that makes up the pool is equally likely to prepay. A major difficulty with this type of measure is that it merely quantifies prepayments. This is a subjective decision and is not based on a predictive model. The advantage of a constant measure is its simplicity. It can easily be incorporated into pricing and yield formulas and it can also be easily adjusted to reflect current prepayment conditions.

PREPAYMENTS, YIELD, AND AVERAGE LIFE

The remainder of this chapter illustrates how prepayments influence variables that ultimately affect the two central considerations for investors—yield and investment horizon.

Since pass-through securities are sustained by the cash flows from an underlying mortgage pool, the effect of prepayments on principal balance will carry from the mortgage pool to the pass-through in the form of earlier payment of principal at par. Whether this is positive or negative to investors is a function of coupon level and security price. The effect of prepayments on principal balance can be illustrated by examining mortgage terminations. Exhibit 13 demonstrates this relationship for 100 percent of FHA experience.

Exhibit 13(a) shows the pattern of terminations as a percentage of the remaining mortgages over the life of a 30-year mortgage pool. The upward sloping line indicates that the likelihood of a mortgage terminating increases over time. According to the FHA experience rate, mortgage terminations are low for the first two policy years, then increase sharply until the 9th or 10th year. Terminations then level off until the 22nd policy year when the rate noticeably increases. The mortality rates are reproduced in the Appendix for both "old" and "new" FHA data. Exhibit 13(b) graphs the pass-through factor over time. The pass-through factor is the ratio of outstanding principal to original principal balance. It declines rapidly over the early periods then levels off before dropping in the later years. This occurs because the paydowns include both scheduled principal payments and prepayments. When there are no prepayments the pass-through factor reflects scheduled principal payments only.

The relationship between prepayment assumptions and average life is illustrated in Exhibits 14 and 15. Exhibit 14 shows the relationship between different magnitudes of FHA experience and average life for a range of coupons. The figure shows that average life is affected by the coupon rate and

EXHIBIT 13
FHA Prepayment Experience and Its Effect on Principal Balances

FHA Prepayment Experience (100 % of FHA Experience)
Terminations as a Percent of Remaining Mortgages

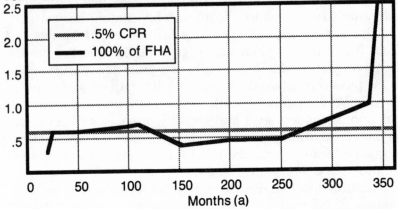

Months (a)

Pass Through Factor (Balance) at 100 % of FHA
Percent of Original Principal Balance

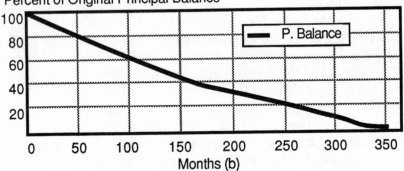

Months (b)

the prepayment rate. In particular, for any given prepayment
assumption, average life increases with coupon rates. This
is because higher rates delay slightly the repayment of principal. Obviously, average life declines as prepayments increase
for a given coupon rate. Exhibit 15 shows the same relationship
between prepayments and average life for a range of coupons

EXHIBIT 14

The Relationship Between the FHA Prepayment Assumption and Average Life for a Range of Coupons
(Assuming 30-Year Remaining Term)

Table of Average Lives (in Years)

Coupon	0 Percent	25 Percent	50 Percent	75 Percent	100 Percent	200 Percent	500 Percent	1000 Percent
				Prepayments Relative to FHA (Percent FHA)				
6	19.66	16.83	14.60	12.81	11.37	7.76	4.20	2.71
8	20.84	17.75	15.32	13.39	11.84	7.97	4.25	2.73
10	21.88	18.55	15.95	13.89	12.23	8.15	4.29	2.74
12	22.78	19.24	16.48	14.30	12.56	8.29	4.32	2.75
14	23.55	19.82	16.93	14.65	12.83	8.41	4.34	2.76
16	24.20	20.31	17.30	14.93	13.05	8.49	4.35	2.77
18	24.76	20.72	17.61	15.16	13.23	8.56	4.36	2.77

133

EXHIBIT 15

The Relationship Between the CPR Prepayment Assumption and Average Life for a Range of Coupons
(*Assuming 30-Year Remaining Term*)

Table of Average Lives (in Years)

Conditional Prepayment Rate (CPR)
(per Month)

Coupon	0 Percent	.1 Percent	.2 Percent	.3 Percent	.5 Percent	1.0 Percent	5.0 Percent	20 percent
6	19.66	17.23	15.21	13.52	10.92	7.07	1.68	.46
8	20.84	18.19	16.00	14.18	11.37	7.27	1.69	.46
10	21.88	19.03	16.68	14.74	11.75	7.44	1.69	.46
12	22.78	19.75	17.26	15.21	12.07	7.57	1.70	.46
14	23.55	20.36	17.76	15.61	12.33	7.68	1.70	.46
16	24.20	20.88	18.17	15.94	12.55	7.76	1.70	.46
18	24.76	21.32	18.51	16.21	12.72	7.82	1.71	.46

using a CPR. These tables are designed to be used to relate average lives to various prepayment rates and can also be used to determine the specific CPR that is equivalent to a FHA speed.[10]

There are a few observations worth noting regarding the tables. The "0 Percent" column is the same for both tables because of the 0 percent prepayment assumption. 100 percent FHA experience, which is the way it is published, is comparable to .5 percent CPR on the basis of average life for newly issued securities. Also, high magnitudes of prepayment dominate the coupon effect since the pool prepays so fast that the interest rate has little impact on the average life of a dollar of principal.

The outstanding balance of a mortgage naturally declines over time. When there are no prepayments, the balance falls slowly at first and rapidly near maturity. Exhibits 16 and 17 illustrate the relationship between different prepayment assumptions and balance outstanding over time. 0 percent of FHA assumes no prepayments and Exhibit 16 shows how the balance outstanding declines based on scheduled payments of principal. This is also true for 0 percent CPR. The two curves are identical because both assume no prepayment activity. The shape of the curve changes as prepayments are introduced. The curve becomes steeper as prepayments get larger, which reflects the speed at which the principal balance declines.

From the previous analyses it is evident that for every combination of average life, remaining term and coupon rate there is a single FHA experience rate and CPR rate. Exhibit 18 shows the relationship between FHA experience and CPR for new 30-year pass-through securities. The table reveals that for a given coupon rate a longer average life is associated with smaller prepayment rates. The table also shows the respective FHA experience rate and CPR (percent per month) required to produce a specific average life. It must also be

---

[10] Factor includes paydowns from both scheduled payments and prepayments.

EXHIBIT 16

**Relationship Between FHA Prepayment Assumption and Balance
Outstanding**

Balance Outstanding by FHA Prepayment Assumption
Balance (Millions)

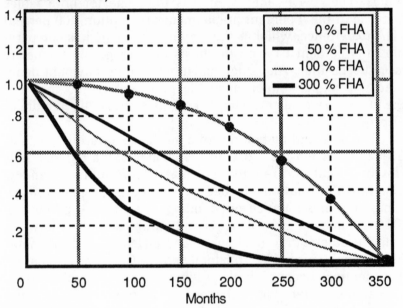

noted that the entire table changes with the age of a pool.
Exhibit 18 is for new originations only.

Exhibit 18 provides ample evidence that the rate of prepayments can demonstrably alter the characteristics of mortgage-backed financial instruments. For the individual investor,
the portfolio manager and the mortgage originator, among others, it is important to try to quantify prepayments. The uncertainty in projecting prepayments translates into greater risk
and a greater need to understand the complexities of the mortgage-backed securities markets in order to control the risk.
The next few illustrations provide some insight into the caution
that must be used when evaluating the return on a mortgage-
related security.

Recent data on prepayment experience are shown in Ex-

EXHIBIT 17
Relationship Between CPR Prepayment Assumption and Balance Outstanding

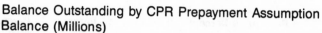

Balance Outstanding by CPR Prepayment Assumption
Balance (Millions)

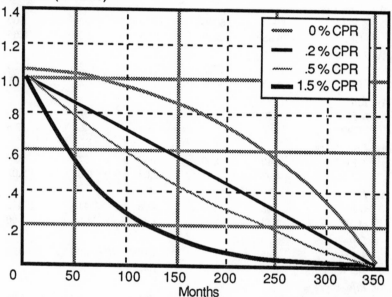

hibit 19 for three mortgaged-backed securities: GNMA-single family, FHLMC–PC, and FNMA–MBS. Generally, higher coupon securities prepay at a higher rate than lower coupon securities. This is particularly true when the security is selling at a considerable premium which reflects market rates lower than the coupon. For similar reasons, discount or low coupon securities are likely to prepay at lower rates. Exhibit 19 suggests, however, that intermediate coupons (10 percent, often 12 percent) prepay at slower rates than lower coupons (8 percent, 9 percent). This can be explained by the age of the underlying mortgage. For example, many 12 percent pass-throughs are based on mortgages with an average age of two years or less. It is known that there are few prepayments in the initial two years because most people will not move within two years

EXHIBIT 18
Relationship Between FHA Experience and CPR for a New 30-Year Pass-Through

	Coupon				
	6 Percent	9 Percent	12 Percent	15 Percent	18 Percent
Av. Life–1 yr.					
% FHA	6000	6000	6000	6000	6000
CPR	8.65	8.65	8.65	8.65	8.65
Av. Life–2 yrs.					
% FHA	1725	1725	1725	1725	1725
CPR	4.25	4.25	4.25	4.25	4.25
Av. Life–3 yrs.					
% FHA	850	850	875	875	875
CPR	2.7	2.7	2.8	2.8	2.8
Av. Life–4 yrs.					
% FHA	540	550	560	570	570
CPR	1.97	2.01	2.03	2.05	2.07
Av. Life–5 yrs.					
% FHA	385	398	405	410	412
CPR	1.54	1.58	1.61	1.64	1.66
Av. Life–6 yrs.					
% FHA	295	306	315	320	323
CPR	1.23	1.27	1.32	1.34	1.36
Av. Life–8 yrs.					
% FHA	190	204	211	216	220
CPR	.84	.89	.93	.95	.97
Av. Life–10 yrs.					
% FHA	130	142	150	156	160
CPR	.59	.64	.67	.82	.73
Av. Life–12 yrs.					
% FHA	89	101	109	115	119
CPR	.41	.46	.49	.53	.55
Av. Life–14 yrs.					
% FHA	58	70	79	85	89
CPR	.27	.33	.31	.34	.42
Av. Life–16 yrs.					
% FHA	34	46	55	61	66
CPR	1.59	.22	.26	.29	.31
Av. Life–18 yrs.					
% FHA	14	26.5	35.5	42	46.5
CPR	0.65	.125	.17	.20	.22

EXHIBIT 18 (concluded)
Relationship Between FHA Experience and CPR for a New 30-Year
Pass-Through

	Coupon				
	6 Percent	9 Percent	12 Percent	15 Percent	18 Percent
Av. Life–20 yrs.					
% FHA	0	10	19	25.5	30.5
CPR	0	.045	.09	.11	.14
Av. Life–25 yrs.					
% FHA	0	0	0	0	0
CPR	0	0	0	0	0

and, in this case, interest rates since 1982 have not presented advantageous refinancing opportunities for mortgages backing 12 percent pass-throughs.

Earlier we discussed the difficulty in measuring yields on pass-through securites. If the yield is calculated based on dif-

EXHIBIT 19
Experience to Date for Selected Mortgage-Backed Securities

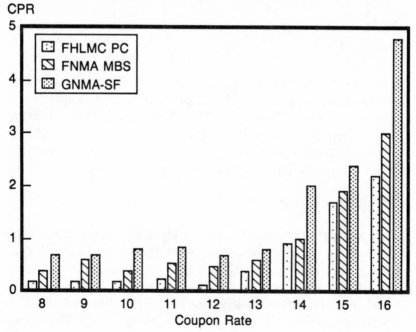

Coupon Rate

EXHIBIT 20

Illustration of the Difficulty of Measuring and Comparing Yield of Discount and Premium Pass-Throughs

Comparison of Yield for Discount & Premium Pass-Throughs

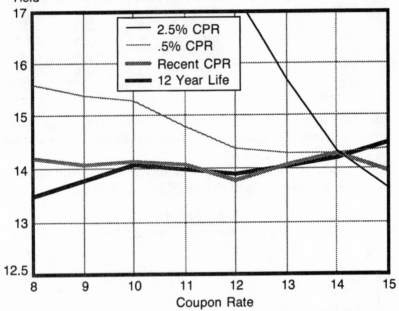

ferent prepayment assumptions, entirely different results may appear. The magnitude of the prepayment assumption will also affect yield. As Exhibit 20 indicates, the effect depends upon whether the security is at a discount or a premium. For discount securities, higher prepayment rates have a positive effect on yield. The opposite is true for premium securities.

Breakeven Prepayment Rates

Prepayment rates will affect both yield and average life. This makes it necessary to evaluate mortgage-backed securities on both a yield and average life basis, i.e., to establish a framework that compares mortgage-backed securities to a Treasury yield for an equivalent average life. The table in Exhibit 21 provides the basis for such a breakeven analysis. The break-

EXHIBIT 21
Derivation of a Breakeven Prepayment Rate for GNMAs

Coupon	Average Age (Months)	CPR (Percent/Mo.)	Latest CPR			Pricing Relative to Treasuries			
			Price	Bond Equivalent Yield	Average Life	Treasury Yield	Required Spread*	Required Yield	Breakeven CPR
8	100	.21	68.3750	14.67	11.55	13.34	100 bp	14.34	.14
9	82	.19	72.6250	14.55	12.85	13.34	100	14.34	.14
10	48	.18	76.6250	14.57	14.87	13.34	100	14.34	.11
11	40	.22	82.3750	14.55	14.84	13.34	100	14.34	.13
12	14	.11	88.6250	14.17	18.68	13.35	100	14.35	.25
13	30	.39	93.6250	14.58	12.99	13.34	100	14.34	.06
14	33	.89	98.8125	14.58	8.14	13.32	100	14.32	—
15	32	1.67	102.4375	14.37	4.86	12.90	100	13.90	2.96

* A single spread is assumed for this example. Actually, the required spread to treasuries varies considerably, depending primarily on whether the pass-through is a discount, current coupon or premium.

141

even prepayment rate is the one which produces a cash flow yield on the pass-through that yields the required spread over Treasuries of that maturity. The user can then assess, based on history and models, whether the actual prepayment rate should be lower or higher than the breakeven.

Exhibit 21 indicates for a given target average life the necessary prepayment rate that must be realized in order to achieve a desired spread.

Both Treasuries and GNMAs are backed by the full faith and credit of the United States Government with respect to the timely payment of interest and principal. Treasuries normally are "bullets" that repay the entire principal at maturity. Treasuries are normally noncallable, i.e., the borrower does not have the option to prepay his debt. Thus, the maturity of a Treasury is also its average life. Pass-through average lives depend on the coupon (to the extent that the coupon is the best indicator of a prepayment rate) and the amortization period. For example, at 100 percent of FHA, the average life of a GNMA–SF 30-year pass-through would be 12 years, while the average lives of Midgets (15-year level pay mortgages) and GPMs (graduated payment mortgages) would be more like 7 and 12 years, respectively.

When the prepayment rate is substantially higher than 100 percent of FHA, as it is for higher coupons, the difference between 30-year and 15-year instruments is diminished because the prepayments tend to dominate the scheduled amortization. The yield curve for GNMAs, however, lies above that of Treasuries primarily because of the risk of adverse changes in prepayments.

The MBS Yield Curve

Another framework for assessing the relative values of the large number of different coupons and structures is the MBS (Mortgage Backed Security) yield curve, which is presented in Exhibit 22. The objective of this framework is to identify points on the maturity spectrum where, based on a projected CPR, the spread between pass-throughs and Treasuries is greatest.

EXHIBIT 22

The GNMA Yield Curve: Recent Pricing Relative to the Treasury Yield Curve

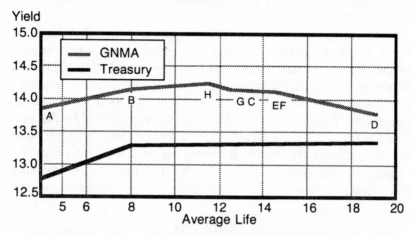

A 15% GNMA @ 102⁷⁄₁₆ with a 1.67% CPR Yields 13.96%; Avg. Life, 4.86 Yrs.
B 14% GNMA @ 98¹³⁄₁₆ with a .89% CPR Yields 14.15%; Avg. Life, 8.14 Yrs.
C 13% GNMA @ 95⅝ with a .39% CPR Yields 14.15%; Avg. Life, 12.99 Yrs.
D 12% GNMA @ 88⅝ with a .11% CPR Yields 13.79%; Avg. Life, 18.68 Yrs.
E 11% GNMA @ 82⅜ with a .22% CPR Yields 14.13%; Avg. Life, 14.84 Yrs.
F 10% GNMA @ 76⅝ with a .18% CPR Yields 14.15%; Avg. Life, 14.87 Yrs.
G 9% GNMA @ 72⅝ with a .19% CPR Yields 14.12%; Avg. Life, 12.58 Yrs.
H 8% GNMA @ 68⅜ with a .21% CPR Yields 14.24%; Avg. Life, 11.35 Yrs.

The GNMA yield curve is humped at a 14 to 15 year average life because the low coupon securities (8 percent, 9 percent) have a shorter average life than intermediate coupon securities because of seasoning and prepayment effects. This curve differs from the Treasury yield curve in that the "maturities" are only best estimates of the average life of the generic coupons. To the extent that the realized average life ultimately differs from this estimate, there is a "reinvestment" or "terminal value" assessment that must be made to compare the pass-through with the analogous Treasury security.

The key to the analysis is to identify the range of prepayment rates that represents the boundary of probable average lives. In other words, by studying the historical stability of the prepayment rates for a coupon group, we can determine the probable minimum and maximum average lives, assess a "penalty" in terms of reinvestment or terminal value for missing the "target" average life, and determine whether the yield spread over Treasuries provides compensation sufficient to match the probable penalty.

Exhibit 23 shows a simplified application of this analysis for a 10 percent GNMA given its historical prepayment rate range. The uppermost line ("A") is the range of yields on a 10 percent GNMA for faster and slower prepayment assumptions which translate into shorter or longer average lives, respectively, then the assumed 10-year hold period. The flat line ("C") is the yield on a 10-year Treasury. The distance between the two lines represents the yield spread. The curve at the bottom of the graph ("D") indicates the penalty for missing the target average life, which increases as the amount by which

EXHIBIT 23
Evaluation of a 10 Percent GNMA Using the Historical Prepayment Rate Range

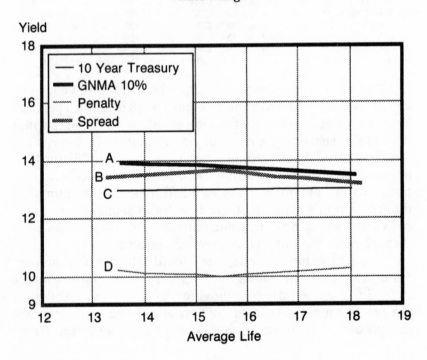

the target average life is missed increases. The penalty represents the negative effects of having reinvested proceeds received early at very low rates or having to sell at a loss an unexpected security balance at the target maturity. The adjusted return on the 10 percent GNMA is depicted by line "B" and represents the probable realized yields to the 10-year horizon (the maturity of the Treasury with which the GNMA is compared).

The MBS yield curve provides a quick measure of yields and whether coupons are rich or cheap. A more comprehensive analysis based on investment horizons and reinvestment rate penalties can then be applied to confirm ideas generated by analyzing spreads off the yield curve. This framework is readily applicable to the mortgage-backed bonds discussed in the next chapter, which provide a greater array of expected average lives across the yield curve.

APPENDIX

A Comparison of the "Old" and "New" FHA Data

	"Old" FHA Data				1983 FHA Data		
Policy Year	Terminations	Factor	Conditional Prepayment Rate (CPR)	Policy Year	Terminations	Factor	Conditional Prepayment Rate (CPR)
1	1126.0	1.000000	.011260	1	2085.4	1.000000	.020854
2	3727.7	.988741	.037701	2	5676.1	.979146	.057970
3	4922.0	.951464	.051731	3	5792.4	.922385	.062798
4	5174.1	.902244	.057347	4	5033.8	.864461	.058231
5	5279.8	.850503	.062079	5	4816.6	.814124	.059163
6	5427.1	.797705	.068034	6	4833.2	.765958	.063100
7	5293.4	.743434	.071202	7	4483.2	.717625	.062473
8	4994.6	.690500	.072333	8	4305.6	.672793	.063996
9	4482.3	.640554	.069975	9	4101.0	.629736	.065123
10	3982.3	.595730	.066847	10	3070.0	.588726	.052146
11	3665.3	.555907	.065934	11	2574.0	.558027	.046127
12	3335.7	.519255	.064240	12	2363.5	.532287	.044403
13	2969.7	.485897	.061118	13	2292.7	.508652	.045074
14	2672.6	.456201	.058584	14	2246.5	.485726	.046250
15	2403.8	.429475	.055971	15	2173.1	.463261	.046909
16	2165.6	.405436	.053414	16	2102.0	.441530	.047607
17	1958.7	.383780	.051037	17	2013.9	.420510	.047892

18	1778.0	.364193	.048820	18	1914.6	.400371	.047821
19	1612.0	.346413	.046534	19	1808.5	.381225	.047439
20	1451.0	.330293	.043931	20	1699.3	.363140	.046795
21	1299.5	.315784	.041152	21	1589.8	.346147	.045928
22	1503.5	.302789	.049655	22	1755.6	.330249	.053160
23	1675.6	.287753	.058230	23	1888.9	.312694	.060407
24	1822.4	.270997	.067248	24	1987.3	.293805	.067640
25	1934.0	.252774	.076511	25	2050.1	.273931	.074840
26	2000.9	.233434	.085716	26	2077.7	.253429	.081984
27	2024.5	.213425	.094858	27	2072.1	.232652	.089064
28	2007.7	.193180	.103929	28	2035.8	.211931	.096060
29	2504.0	.173103	.144654	29	2617.3	.191573	.136622
30	14806.3	.148063	1.000000	30	16540.1	.165401	1.000000

CHAPTER 7

Mortgage-Backed Bonds

Kenneth H. Sullivan
Managing Director and Manager
Mortgage Research and Product Development
Drexel Burnham Lambert

Llewellyn Miller
Vice President
Mortgage Research and Product Development
Drexel Burnham Lambert

Timothy B. Kiggins
Associate
Mortgage Research and Product Development
Drexel Burnham Lambert

Historical Development

Although mortgage pass-through securities have played a vital role in developing and expanding the secondary mortgage market, the monolithic structure of pass-throughs, that is, the payment stream that features a very long life and unpredictable cash flows, has inhibited participation by traditional fixed-income investors such as pension funds, bank trust departments, and fund managers. To attract funds at a lower cost than could be obtained by issuing pass-throughs, holders of mortgages began to design "bond-type" alternatives which reduced the term to maturity and provided some certainty of timing of cash flows. Several varieties of mortgage-backed bonds have evolved since the mid-1970s, with each succeeding structure designed to focus on the key considerations in issuing mortgage-backed bonds:

- Targeting particular investor groups that have preferences for specific maturities or minimum call protection, and thereby lowering the interest cost of the bonds.

- Minimizing the amount of collateral required to support the issue while maintaining the integrity of the credit.
- Taking advantage of favorable tax treatment or avoiding the negative tax consequences of certain structures.
- Minimizing accounting leverage as measured by debt ratios to the extent possible while raising funds in the bond market.

The historical development of the market for mortgage-backed bonds commenced with bond issues by banks and savings and loans, which were backed by mortgages that had an aggregate market value that exceeded, by a substantial margin, the amount of bonds issued. These issues came to be known as Mortgage-Backed Bonds, or "MBBs." The primary reason for the emergence of these bonds was the possibility of raising term funds at a low cost without incurring losses from selling collateral (mortgages) below the value on the books of the issuer. MBBs were popular in the mid-1970s. During this time, the large financial institutions who were the issuers were not under pressure from disintermediation and thus were not collateral-constrained. In the volatile markets of the early 1980s, the MBB disappeared from the new issue market as the thrift industry turned its focus to maximizing the amount of funds that could be raised rather than solely to minimizing costs. Only recently has the MBB structure returned to the new issue market. It has taken two forms: Euro-dollar Mortgage-Backed Bonds and "Controlled" Adjusted Rate Preferred Stocks. Both kinds of financings, which are described later, exhibit the same feature as the old MBBs—a specified percentage of overcollateralization, with the collateral marked to market periodically and with additional collateral provided if necessary. The return of the MBB to the marketplace is symptomatic of renewed emphasis on interest cost minimization in this period of narrow spreads between bond costs and mortgage yields. Other kinds of bonds that are "backed" by mortgages have been developed, but the original term "mortgage-backed bond" has come to mean a bond backed by mortgage collateral of specified market value.

As term funds, the MBBs were cost effective. Two draw-backs, however, were the inefficient use of collateral and the mismatch in cash flow patterns between bonds and mortgages, which exposed the issuer to reinvestment risk. In the early 1980s, market volatility and disintermediation combined to necessitate the design of a more efficient vehicle—the pay-through bond. Economically, the pay-through is similar to a pass-through certificate in that the source of the cash flows to holders of the bonds is collateral, a pool of mortgages. The critical difference between a pay-through and pass-through is that the sale of a pay-through constitutes a secured debt financing while the sale of a pass-through is an asset sale. Thus, a sale of low coupon pass-throughs would require the recognition of a loss by the issuer, while the sale of low coupon pay-throughs would simply increase the amount of debt of the issuer. Because cash flow of the mortgages plus a small safety factor, referred to as overcollateralization, services the bonds on an ongoing basis as opposed to the liquidation con-cept implied by market value overcollateralization, the abso-lute amount of collateral required is reduced substantially. Pay-throughs represented a return to cash flow patterns of the pass-throughs, which were not well designed for the tradi-tional institutional fixed-income market. Another phase of in-novation would be required to reach the pension funds and trusts with a bond.

In mid-1983, FHLMC made a radical contribution to mort-gage-related securities structuring. Its issue of Collateralized Mortgage Obligations ("CMOs") is, strictly speaking, a pay-through bond issue, except that three classes of bonds were issued instead of one. Multiclass pay-through bonds have come to be known as CMOs. The advantage to many issuers is compelling. First, deep discount mortgages can be effectively "sold" to a bankruptcy-proof entity, without recognizing a loss if that entity is part of the consolidated group. In addition, there is no material mismatch between aggregate cash flows on the mortgage collateral and debt service on the CMOs, which helps mitigate interest rate risk for the issuer. Also, the maturities and average lives of the classes can be structured to meet market demands as opposed to issuing a single 30-year pay-through. Finally, the CMO introduced a new concept called "Fast Pay/Slow Pay" bonds, which refers to the prioritization of cash flows to first one class then the next class, and so forth. Each preceding class is retired before any cash flow from the collateral is applied to paying down principal on the next class. In essence, the "Slow-Pay" bonds have a measure of call protection where none had ever before existed with taxable mortgage-related securities. These features combined to produce the results shown in Exhibit 1, which triggered a wave of CMO financings in the wake of the FHLMC issue.

The summary results of the issue were striking. The issue was priced approximately 85 basis points lower than the bond equivalent yield on FHLMCs PCs at the time of pricing. The overall composite issue's spread over Treasuries was only about 75 basis points, a very attractive level to issuers.

In the year and a half following the FHLMC issue, 37 issues aggregating over $12 billion were marketed. The CMOs' appeal was broad, as evidenced by the distribution results in Exhibit 2 reported by FHLMC.

Other innovative structures have been attempted and still others will be developed. Many of these are discussed in the sections that follow. One potential device for creating new mortgage-backed securities is represented in the TIMs legislation (Trusts for Investment in Mortgages). In essence, TIMs would simply be a multiclass pass-through security, which

EXHIBIT 1
Offering Terms of the First CMO

Class	Yield*	Average Life*	Spread Over Treasuries†
A–1	10.70%	3.2 yrs.	+40 b.p.
A–2	11.37	8.6	+54
A–3	11.98	20.4	+85

* Calculated on the basis of 100 percent of FHA experience.
† Selected Treasuries approximating coupons and average lives of the CMO classes.

EXHIBIT 2
Proportion of FHLMC CMO Issue Purchased by Investor Category

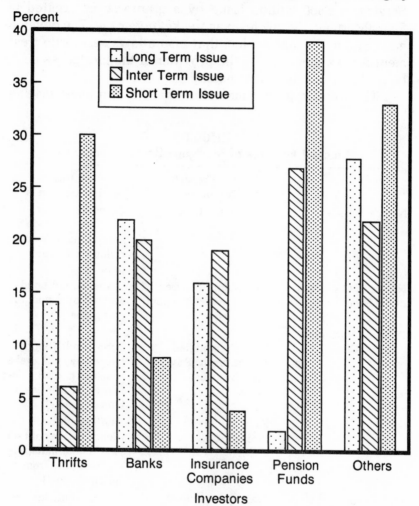

means that issuers could create several maturities out of a
mortgage pool and elect to use either a bond sale (CMO) or
an asset sale (TIMs). The TIMs issue revolves around the tax
treatment of the issuing entity, more specifically the grantor
trust treatment accorded to pass-throughs. To avoid taxation
of trust income, the trust must be passive. The creation of

priority classes, rather than pro rata interests in cash flows, has been determined not to be passive by the Internal Revenue Service. A $500 million issue by a grantor trust created by Sears Mortgage Securities was the keynote case. The development of a multiclass vehicle that also allows asset sale treatment for tax purposes by the provider of the mortgages could be an important new instrument.

The trend toward increasing share of mortgage origina-

EXHIBIT 3
Principal Features of Mortgage-Backed Securities

	Pass-Through Certificates	Mortgage-Backed Bonds
Nature of Issuer	Grantor trust	Corporate issuer, which can include a special purpose corporation ("bankruptcy proof")
Nature of Ownership of the Security	Ownership of a fractional interest in a pool of mortgages	Ownership of bonds secured by a pool of mortgages
Principal Variations Single Class	Partially modified pass-through (Private pass-throughs)	Term bonds (Bonds backed by collateral of specified market value; known as mortgage-backed bonds)
	Fully modified pass-through (GNMA, FNMA)	Pay-through bond (Bonds whose debt service is determined by the cash flow from a collateral pool)
Multiclass	TIMs (prospectively) (To date, the grantor trust structure cannot be employed to create more than one class. TIMs legislation would allow this to be done)	CMOs (Multiclass issue of pay-through bonds where certain classes have maximum maturities and priority as to principal payment)

tions accounted for by adjustable rate mortgages ("ARMs") is going to have a tremendous effect on the mortgage securities market. Of course, ARM pass-throughs will provide an important source of homogeneity and thus liquidity in the form of pass-through trading and use of the ARM pass-throughs in repurchase agreements. It should be noted, however, that many of the factors and issues that caused development of specific types of mortgage-backed bonds related to fixed-rate, level-payment loans will spur the creation of bond-type vehicles in the ARM market also.

Exhibit 3 summarizes the principal structural features of what have or will become generic types of mortgage-backed securities.

In the sections that follow, we discuss the investment characteristics of mortgage-backed bonds and examine how the different structures can be employed to meet specific investment objectives.

MORTGAGE-BACKED BONDS (TERM BONDS)

The common feature of MBBs is that they are all direct obligations of the issuer. Subsidiaries have also been organized to facilitate MBB issues, principally to insulate the bonds from the credit risk of the parent company or to avoid the payment of withholding tax. The MBB is similar to a corporate bond in many ways: Interest payments are generally scheduled semiannually, principal repayment is generally a single payment at a scheduled maturity date, and the bonds may be callable at the option of the issuer prior to the scheduled maturity.

The first issue of MBBs took place in 1975. Since that California Federal Savings and Loan Association issue, more than 75 MBB issues have been sold in public or private transactions. The MBB structure has changed somewhat over time but the essential principle remains the same: A general obligation of a less than first quality issuer can obtain a higher rating by assigning and maintaining a pool of mortgages as security for payments on and redemption of the bonds.

The main considerations continue to be (i) the amount of collateral, (ii) the quality of the collateral, and (iii) the credit quality of the issuer. Quality of the collateral is related most closely with the marketability of the collateral—the ability to raise cash from the sale of collateral. Certain types of collateral are accorded lower discounts in computing a basic maintenance level of value. The amount of collateral of each type must be known so that quality discounts can be applied. The combined effect of these two factors is demonstrated in Exhibit 4 for the recent CoastFed International Finance N.V. note issue due 1988.

The third consideration, the credit quality of the issuer, has assumed greater importance because the increase in volatility and upward trend of rates in the late 1970s and early 1980s have made the valuations of collateral pools more volatile and have undermined the strength of thrifts, the largest group of MBB issuers. The credit strength of the issuer remains important after initial issuance since the issuer may on occasion be required to supply additional collateral. Also, the viability of the issuer could affect the term of the bonds.

The reason for the popularity of MBBs was that lower quality issuers could finance their mortgage holdings with in-

EXHIBIT 4
Quality and Quantity of Collateral—MBBs

Type of Property	Discount Applied to Market Value	Minimum Market Value Required Per $ of Bonds
Cash	None	$1.00
Treasury Securities	10.7–37.5%	$1.12–1.48
GNMA Certificates	27.6%	$1.38
FNMA/FHLMC Certificates	37.5%	$1.48

NOTE: Discounts and Market Values are related to CoastFed's biweekly collateral repricing frequency.

termediate-term bonds in the form of MBBs. Up to that point, few opportunities existed to move either out the yield curve (in maturity) from deposits or down the yield curve (in cost) from pass-through certificates. Many investor groups have a preference for high-quality securities with definite maturities and with final maturities in the 5- to 10-year range. MBBs opened up this market for the thrift industry.

The market value collateral structure has found other applications in reaching particular investor groups. Two examples are MBBs issued through Netherlands Antilles subsidiaries and adjustable rate preferred stocks issued by "controlled" subsidiaries that have limited business activities.

In the first case, the Eurobond issue, the principal attraction to the offering is the low cost of funds. Despite the fact that a Euro-MBB "ties up" as much as $1.40 of collateral for every $1.00 raised, the rates are low when compared to alternative funding sources such as pass-through sales or long-term CDs. The Euromarket is willing to pay higher prices to obtain highly rated securities with call protection and a definitive schedule of interest and principal payments. Most Euro-MBB issues carry final maturities of four to seven years, another preference in the Euromarket.

Adjustable rate preferred stocks of controlled subsidiaries ("CARPs") are the second modern variation of the MBB. While they are not technically bonds—they are stocks—they are a direct issuance by a corporation. The level of assets that must be maintained in the issuing entity is determined in the same fashion as the level of overcollateralization in an MBB issue. Exhibit 5 sets forth the levels that have been established for the recently issued CARPs of CenTrust Capital Corporation, a subsidiary of Dade Federal Savings and Loan Association.

Cost is once again the reason for creating what is essentially a mortgage-backed preferred stock. Corporate investors can take advantage of the 85 percent dividends received deduction, which shelters 85 percent of the dividend income. For 46 percent taxpayers, the after-tax cash yield is increased by a factor of 1.724. This means a 12 percent investment that would normally net 6.48 percent after taxes nets 11.17 percent

EXHIBIT 5
Quality and Quantity of Controlled Assets—CARPs

Type of Property	Discount Applied to Market Value	Minimum Market Value Required Per $ of CARPs
Cash	None	$1.00
Treasury Securities	8.3–38.1%	$1.09–1.62
GNMA Certificates	29.3–30.3%	$1.41–1.43
FNMA/FHLMC Certificates	34.1%	$1.52

NOTE: Discounts and Market Values are related to CenTrust's monthly required asset repricing frequency.

after taxes if it has the benefit of a dividends received deduction, a compelling advantage.

The ability to issue preferred stock is limited in most cases because the dividend is not deductible by the issuer, whereas an interest payment would be. The lack of deductibility increases the cost of money by a factor of 1.852 for a 46 percent taxpayer. Thrifts, however, are issuers that frequently have large tax loss carryforwards that will expire unused. For at least a five-year period the marginal tax rate is zero. Since some of the benefit of the dividends received deduction is reflected in lower required rates on preferred stocks, this lower rate is a net benefit to any issuer who is not a taxpayer.

The preferred stock issues by thrifts to date have been CARPs. There is no requirement that the rate on the preferred be adjustable. It is simply the case that the most attractive terms in the marketplace recently have been those of CARPs rather than fixed rate preferred stocks.

As the quest for lower costs or better portfolio matching continues, new securities will evolve employing the MBB structure.

PAY-THROUGH BONDS (CASH FLOW BONDS)

The pay-through bond is a specialized example of a mortgage-backed bond. Unlike the generic MBB which has a fixed maturity, the pay-through's maturity and principal repayment characteristics are dependent on the payments realized on the mortgage collateral. First issued privately in 1976, the pay-through came into being because it satisfied two concerns. It allowed an issuer to realize in cash the present value of its below-market mortgage assets without selling the assets or significantly overcollateralizing bonds. Stated another way, issuers could obtain nearly 100 percent financing of mortgage assets and avoid the tax and accounting consequences of a sale of assets.

The resolution of numerous legal, tax, rating, and accounting issues delayed introduction of pay-throughs to the public bond market until April 1981 when PHM Credit Corporation brought a $39 million issue to market. Since that time, over $1.5 billion of pay-throughs (excluding CMOs and other serialized bonds) have been brought to market.

The concept behind the pay-through is to determine a bond amount and an interest rate such that absolute minimum payments (zero prepayment assumption) on a mortgage or mortgage pass-through collateral pool will be sufficient to make timely payments on the bonds. In the event that the interest rate on the bonds is lower than the interest rate on the mortgage collateral, the amount of bonds that can be issued is limited to the face amount of the mortgages. This principle must be applied piece-by-piece to the collateral to prevent the situation in which high-coupon mortgages prepay, leaving only low coupon mortgages to service bonds whose interest rate was computed on an average rate on the collateral. The interest and principal payments on the bonds can be designed for monthly, quarterly, semiannual, or other payment periods; however, the reinvestment return assumptions that govern pay-through credit ratings will generally penalize an issuer in terms of the amount of bonds that can be issued as the frequency of payment declines from monthly payments. The required assumption for calculating bond amounts presumes that collections on the collateral are held and reinvested at 5 percent in the first year of the issue, 4 percent in the second year of the issue, and 3 percent thereafter, in which rates are well below the rate at which interest is accruing on the unpaid principal amounts of bonds. At times, certain investor preferences for semiannual payments may result in a cost advantage that may enable the issuer to sell the bonds for a higher percentage of bond value. Exhibit 6 illustrates the relationship between the amount of collateral and the amount of bonds that can be sold for various combinations of bond interest rates and mortgage rates.

This example assumes monthly payments on both the bonds and the mortgages. This simplifying assumption obviated the need for reinvestment of cash balances during interim periods. For the case of semiannual payments on bonds, the bond value as a percentage of the principal amount of mort-

EXHIBIT 6
Relationship Between Bond Value and Principal Amount of
Collateral for an Issue of Pay-Through Bonds with Monthly Payments

Assumes: • Mortgage collateral is uniform (identical coupons and 30 years to scheduled maturity).
   • Payment delay of 30 days between due date on mortgages and availability of cash to make payments on bonds.
   • Servicing fees of .375 percent on the mortgages.
   • Monthly payments on bonds.

Bond Values as a Percent of Mortgage Principal

	Bond Interest Rate				
	10%	**11%**	**12%**	**13%**	**14%**
Net Mortgage Rate*					
6%	67.5%	62.1%	57.5%	53.4%	49.8%
7	75.0	69.1	63.9	59.3	55.3
8	82.8	76.2	70.5	65.5	61.1
9	90.9	83.7	77.4	71.9	67.0
10	99.2	91.3	84.4	78.4	73.1
11	100.0	99.1	91.6	85.1	79.4
12	100.0	100.0	99.0	92.0	85.8
13	100.0	100.0	100.0	98.9	92.3
14	100.0	100.0	100.0	100.0	98.9
15	100.0	100.0	100.0	100.0	100.0

* After deducting servicing.

EXHIBIT 7

Bond Value of an Issue of Pay-Through Bonds with Semiannual Payments

	Bond Interest Rate				
	10%	11%	12%	13%	14%
Net Mortgage Rate					
6%	68.3%	62.9%	58.2%	54.2%	50.6%
7	75.9	69.9	64.7	60.2	56.2
8	83.8	77.2	71.5	66.4	62.0
9	91.9	84.7	78.4	72.9	68.1
10	100.0	92.4	85.6	79.6	74.3
11	100.0	100.0	92.9	86.4	80.7
12	100.0	100.0	100.0	93.3	87.2
13	100.0	100.0	100.0	100.0	93.8
14	100.0	100.0	100.0	100.0	100.0
15	100.0	100.0	100.0	100.0	100.0

gages will decline if the bond interest rate is adjusted upward to the semiannual equivalent of a monthly pay-through. Exhibit 7 sets forth the bond values for a semiannual pay-through. The columns are not directly comparable to the monthly bond values in Exhibit 6. The monthly pay-through will produce a higher return given equivalent rates because of the higher payment frequency.

Investment Characteristics of Pay-Throughs

The important investment characteristics of pay-throughs are the same as pass-throughs: coupon on the bonds, minimum scheduled payments of principal, projected prepayments of principal and the price at which the instrument is purchased. Two additional considerations are the coupon rate (or rates) and other characteristics of the collateral, which will determine the rate at which the bonds will prepay, independent of the coupon on the bonds, and various optional redemption terms that have been used in pay-through bonds. How these factors affect yield, average life, and duration is examined in the following sections.

Effects of Prepayment Rates[1]

For pay-throughs purchased at 100 percent of par, the rate of prepayments on the collateral doesn't affect the cash flow yield on the bonds; however, the average life and duration are affected. For a case in which a pay-through is purchased at 100 percent of par bearing a 13 percent coupon, payable monthly with no delays between mortgage and bond payments, and the collateral consists of mortgages with net interest rates of 9 percent (net of ⅜ percent servicing), the cash flow yield is 13.00 percent. The principal amount of mortgage collateral exceeds the amount of bonds by 34.6 percent. Therefore, if $1.00 of mortgages is prepaid and the entire amount is used to redeem bonds, 34.6 percent more bonds will be redeemed than would be the case if the mortgage amounts and bond amounts were equal. This acceleration effect, which doesn't change the cash flow yield, can drastically alter the average life and duration.

Exhibit 8 shows that the average life is reduced across the board as prepayment rates increase, even if excess cash not required to service bonds is passed back to the issuer. The prepayment rate on the bonds reverts to essentially the same rate as for the mortgage pool. The reduction is especially pronounced for lower coupon collateral pools where all prepayments are used to prepay bonds. Exhibit 9 compares the effect on average life of this "pass-back" or "pass-forward" feature.

To the extent that a pay-through is purchased at a price that differs from the par amount of the bond, the yield is affected by both the speed at which the collateral pays down and the terms of the bond as to whether excess collateral is passed forward or passed back. Exhibit 10 illustrates the combined effect.

Another way to analyze the effect of purchase price on yields is to make an estimate of the probable prepayment

---

[1] For a description of factors relating to the calculation of yields and prepayment probabilities, refer to the relevant sections in Chapter 6.

EXHIBIT 8
Effect of Prepayments on the Average Life of a Pay-Through Bond
(13 Percent Bond Issued at Par)

	Average Life of Bond if Prepayment Rate on Mortgages (Percent/Month) is:				
	0%	.2%	.4%	.6%	.8%
Net Mortgage Rate					
8%	20.27 yrs.	15.95 yrs.	12.62 yrs.	10.26 yrs.	8.54 yrs.
9	21.31	16.31	12.86	10.43	8.66
10	21.82	16.64	13.09	10.58	8.77
11	22.29	16.95	13.29	10.72	8.87
12	22.73	17.23	13.48	10.85	8.96
13	23.13	17.19	13.65	10.96	9.04

rate on the mortgage pool. This price-yield relationship is illustrated in Exhibit 11.

Optional Redemption

A feature of many pay-throughs that is not a factor with pass-throughs is the right of optional redemption frequently retained by the issuer. In some cases, this amounts to no more than a "clean up" provision, e.g., when the amount of the issue declines to 10 percent of the original amount outstanding, the issuer may have the right to call the remaining bonds. This is a relatively harmless condition. In other instances, however, the issuer has the right to call the issue at par plus accrued interest (plus a premium in a few cases) after a specified "non-call" period. This non-call period varies considerably from as low as 4 years in the 1984 issue of American Home Finance Corporation III to 10 or more years in other issues.

The optional call would only be exercised at a time when market rates dropped below the bond rate, precisely the time when the bondholder does not wish to have bonds redeemed. In the absence of this call, the holder would not be prepaid at extraordinary rates if the mortgage collateral interest rates

EXHIBIT 9
Effect of Application of Excess Prepayments on the Average Life
of a Pay-Through Bond
(13 Percent Bond Issued at Par)

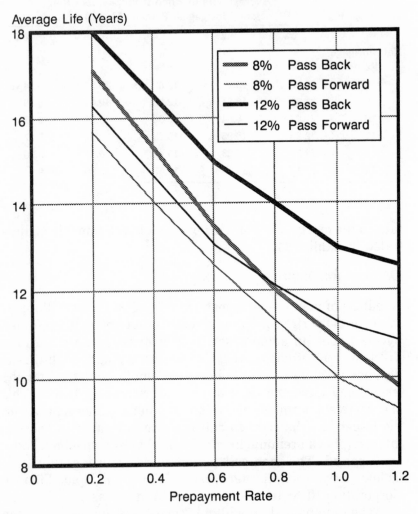

were below the market interest rate level, the low mortgage coupons providing a form of prepayment protection. The effect of the optional call is to limit the potential for appreciation since the issue may trade on the basis of a yield to first call date in declining rate environments.

EXHIBIT 10
Effect of Prepayments on Yields of Pay-Through Bonds
(13 Percent Bond Purchased at 95)

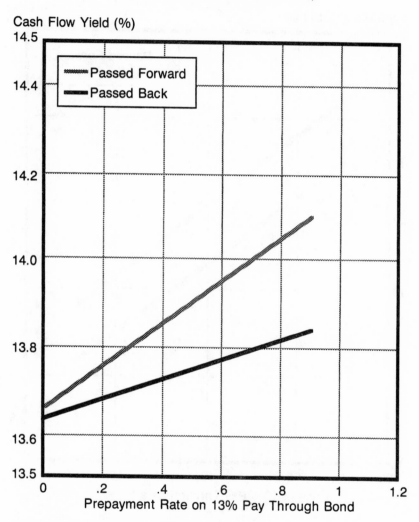

Cash Flow Yield (%)

Prepayment Rate on 13% Pay Through Bond

Prospects for Pay-Through Issues

The pay-through bond has been a useful instrument, particularly for homebuilders. It allows builders to restore liquidity by raising cash approximating the bond value of their collateral, usually GNMAs, without selling the collateral. The sale

EXHIBIT 11
Effect of Purchase Price of Pay-Through Bond on Yield
(8 Percent Mortgage Collateral Prepays at .2 Percent/Month)

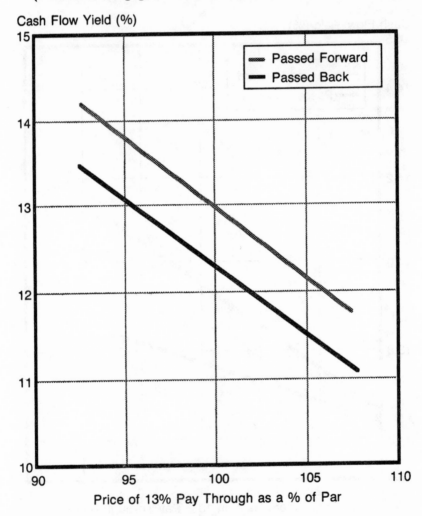

Price of 13% Pay Through as a % of Par

of the collateral would deprive the builder of the ability to use installment sale tax accounting on home sales for which the builder provided the mortgage financing.

Mortgage bankers, thrifts, and others have also availed themselves of this technique. The tax consequences of asset sales versus financings and the ability to utilize tax loss carry-forwards prior to expiration are issues that have a major effect on the merit of a pay-through issue. Accounting and leverage considerations which could affect bond rating bear careful consideration as well.

The greatest contribution of pay-throughs may be that their development paved the way for a much more powerful financing technique and investment vehicle—the collateralized mortgage obligation, which is simply a serial or multiclass pay-through. Its effect on the secondary mortgage market has been felt and will continue to be felt as innovative structures satisfy investment needs of more and more institutional investors.

COLLATERALIZED MORTGAGE OBLIGATIONS

The CMO is a specially designed multiclass pay-through bond. Whereas the term and cash flow patterns of pass-throughs and pay-throughs are similar to those of the collateral, the CMO presents mortgage-backed investments across the entire yield curve. The advantage to investors of a CMO is simply stated: If one wishes to employ funds in a mortgage-related investment over a specific horizon ranging from 2 to 10 years and does not wish to incur substantial price risk from selling off investments that have not matured by the horizon date, CMOs will often be a superior portfolio alternative. Additional considerations, such as the limited degree of call protection that is created by prioritization of cash flows and the effects of various structures on duration uncertainty, are important but are secondary to the fact that CMOs have provided portfolio managers with a new instrument with short- and intermediate-term maximum maturities.

Background

A recent phenomenon, multiclass pay-throughs, were first introduced by Freddie Mac in June of 1983 with an issue of

bonds backed by the cash flow from a specific pool of mortgages. They called the bonds "Collateralized Mortgage Obligations," which has since become the generic name for all multiclass pay-throughs. Since that first issue, approximately $13
billion of CMOs have been issued, dwarfing the volume of

EXHIBIT 12
Cumulative Issuance of CMOs

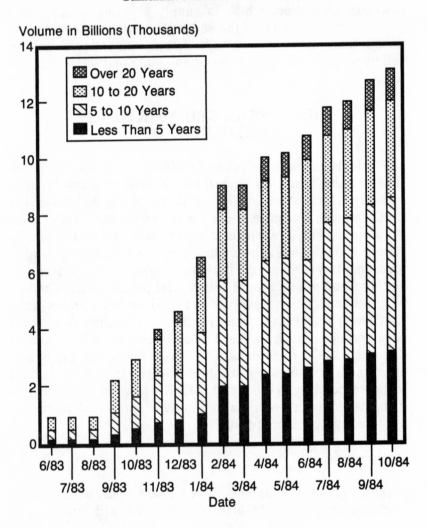

all other mortgage-backed bonds issued in the last ten years. Exhibit 12 shows the volume of issues on a monthly basis.

To investors, the implication of this flow of new issues is that $13 billion of mortgage-type instruments (mortgages and pass-throughs) have been converted to five basic classes of bond-type instruments, with each class determined by maturity. Exhibit 13 illustrates this point.

Without delving into the complexities of analyzing CMOs, the simple stratification by expected average life and maximum maturity shows that a wide variety of bonds have been created, each with its own use in a portfolio. The numerous structures allow portfolio investors a wide array of choices of expected average lives and discounts from par. While opening up opportunities for investors to enhance performance through careful selection, the complexity and variety of CMOs requires that sophisticated techniques be employed to select among CMO alternatives and fixed-income alternatives from other market sectors. Exhibit 14 presents, in matrix form, one view of the current supply of CMOs in a form that is at least a beginning in comparing these bonds to other sectors. It differentiates between bonds priced near par, deeply discounted bonds, and accretion or zero coupon bonds, and is generally

EXHIBIT 13
Conversion of Mortgages to Bonds

Class	Description	Range of Expected Average Lives (Years)	Range of Maximum Maturities (Years)	Cumulative Issuance (Billions)
1	Fast Pay	1.2 to 4.3	Up to 5	$1.6
2	Short Intermediate	1.2 to 8.6	5.1 to 10	2.4
3	Long Intermediate	2 to 14.8	10.1 to 20	5.0
4	Slow Pay	5.33 to 25.6	20.1 to 30	2.7
5*	Zero Coupon	5.7 to 22.6	Up to 30	1.6

* Accretion or compound interest bonds.

EXHIBIT 14
Supply of CMOs by Class and Coupon
($ Millions)

		Expected Average Life (Years)				
Coupon Range	Up to 2.5 years	2.6 to 5.0	5.1 to 7.5	7.6 to 10.0	10.1 to 15.0	More than 15.0
7.1– 8.0	45	0	75	0	80	100
8.1– 9.0	275	50	130	240	45	110
9.1–10.0	25	0	0	0	0	0
10.1–11.0	899	555	105	50	85	230
11.1–12.0	357	740	926	1,647	660	870
12.1–13.0	188	154	690	575	633	729
13.1–14.0	0	0	67	111	83	45
Zero*	0	0	496	0	327	820
Total	1,789	1,499	2,489	2,623	1,913	2,904

* Accretion or compound interest bonds.

a more useful framework for describing the breadth of mortgage-related product made possible by CMOs.

Types of Investors

Mortgage-related instruments have shifted from a thrift portfolio investment to a much more generally utilized portfolio in-

EXHIBIT 15
Investment in Mortgage-Related Securities by Type of Investor

Type of Investor	GNMA	FHLMC-PC	A–1 (Short)	A–2 (Inter- mediate)	A–3 (Long)
Thrifts	37%	53%	30%	6%	13%
Banks			22	20	9
Insurance Cos.			17	19	4
Pension Funds	17	8	2	28	39
Investment Advisors and Others			29	27	33

vestment. Statistics detailing the holders of all CMOs are not available; however, the distribution of the initial Freddie Mac CMO gives us a good indication of the interest of several investor groups in the various CMO classes, and for thrifts and pension funds, a comparison to their historical participation in the pass-through market.

The information is incomplete, but the trend is clear. Investors such as pension funds have preferred the longer maturities, banks and insurance companies have preferred the short and intermediate issues, and thrifts were large purchasers of the short maturity. Experience since the first FHLMC offering suggests that the proportion of longer-term issues purchased by pension funds has increased to more than half the total issued and that insurance companies have accounted for half of the purchases in the intermediate range of average lives

EXHIBIT 16
Investor Appetite for CMO Classes

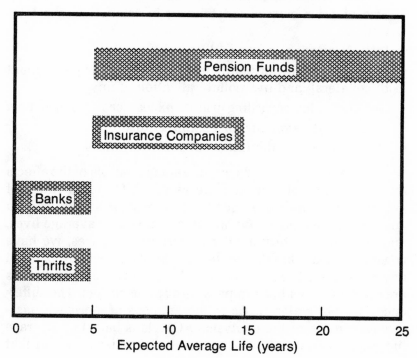

Expected Average Life (years)

(5 to 10 years). Thrifts have participated on a level comparable to the insurance companies and pension funds at average lives of up to three years but have not been a significant factor in issues beyond three years. The segmentation has developed according to portfolio needs and appears to be similar to that shown in Exhibit 16.

Features of CMOs

The basic design of a CMO issue and the prepayment experience realized on the collateral ultimately determine the cash flows of each class of a CMO. While the prepayment experience cannot be predicted with certainty, the structure can be identified and a stream of cash flows can be projected for any given level of prepayments. The principal factors to consider from a structural point of view are:

- Prioritization of cash flows.
- Size of prior classes outstanding in relation to the total issue.
- Price in relation to par and coupon.
- Principal amount of bonds in relation to principal amount of collateral, and overcollateralization, if any.
- Decision rules regarding use of excess cash flow, if any.
- Guaranteed payments, or sinking funds.
- Credit quality of the issuer, in some instances.

The following sections provide some analysis of the effects of the principal structural features of CMOs for a range of prepayment scenarios on quantitative measures such as cash flows, yields, expected average lives, maximum average lives, and maximum maturities. For illustrative purposes, we have generally used simplified collateral pools consisting of level pay mortgages. It should be noted that most collateral pools are not mortgages but are pass-through securities. The differences are not material. As in the analysis of mortgage pass-throughs, much of the analysis of CMOs is based on average life rather than duration. Average life is easier to use in that

Treasury maturities and average lives are readily available for comparative purposes; however, for detailed review, duration is generally preferable.

Prioritization of Cash Flows

The concept behind CMOs is deceptively simple—take a series of cash flows, dedicate portions of them to predetermined holders who indicate a preference for cash flows in specific periods, and price the portions of the cash flows according to the required yields of those investor groups giving consideration to prepayment effects.

The number of classes has ranged from 3 to 10 with maximum maturities of 3 to 30 years. In the early stages of development, CMO classes were often referred to by names like "Fast-Pay," "Slow-Pay," and "Super Fast-Pay." The proliferation of structures has left these distinctions not particularly useful. Groupings by average life prove more useful when trying to compare many CMOs on a quantitative basis.

Exhibit 17 illustrates the concept of prioritization. It compares what would have been the cash flow pattern on a $100 million pool of 30-year 12 percent mortgages to the cash flow patterns of 3 individual classes of CMOs (12 percent 5-year, 12½ percent 15-year and 13 percent 30-year).

The minimum scheduled principal payments on the mortgages serve to retire bonds. First, the Class 1 issue is retired, then Class 2, and Class 3 in order. Since the scenario presented is unrealistic, another model is produced in Exhibit 18. In this scenario, the mortgage and the CMO terms and priorities remain the same, but the prepayment rate is set at 100 percent of the 1981 FHA survivorship tables. The effect is to shorten the life of all of the subject securities, with the hope that the 100 percent of FHA assumption more closely models the future cash flows.

For individual issues, detailed cash flow projections for a large number of scenarios are difficult to derive. Tables are often produced for each issue, which highlight the effects of slower and faster prepayments on the issue. An abbreviated version is presented for the hypothetical issue in Exhibit 19.

EXHIBIT 17
Mortgage and CMO Cash Flows
at a Zero Prepayment Rate

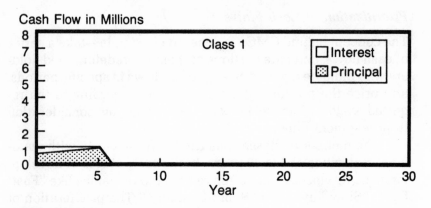

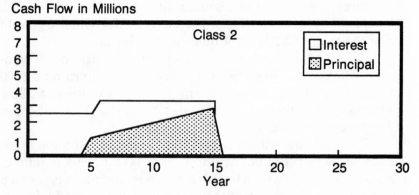

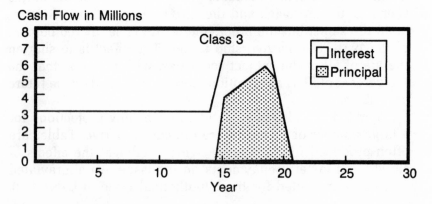

EXHIBIT 18
Mortgage and CMO Cash Flows at a Prepayment Rate of 100 Percent of FHA Experience

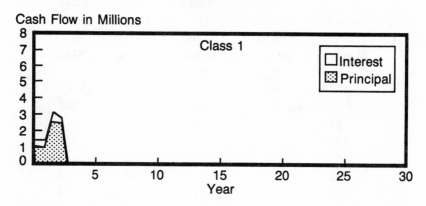

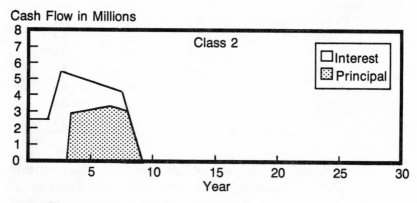

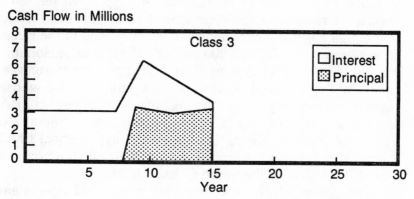

EXHIBIT 19
Summary of Terms of the Hypothetical CMO (Years)

	Class 1	Class 2	Class 3
Coupon	12%	12½%	13%
Principal Amount (000)	$7,500	$40,700	$42,254
Maximum Maturity	5 yrs.	15 yrs.	30 yrs.
Average Life:			
No Prepayments	2.9	11.0	17.5
50% of FHA	2.1	8.5	15.3
75%	1.8	6.9	13.5
100%	1.6	5.9	12.0
125%	1.4	5.2	10.8
150%	1.3	4.3	9.1
200%	1.2	3.7	7.9
Duration:			
No Prepayments	2.4	6.0	7.1
50% of FHA	1.9	5.2	6.8
75%	1.6	4.6	6.5
100%	1.5	4.2	6.2
125%	1.4	3.8	6.0
150%	1.2	3.4	5.5
200%	1.1	3.0	5.1

The concept of limited call protection is demonstrated in Exhibit 20. Technically, each bond class is callable or pre-payable. As a matter of investment strategy, however, each class has a range of probable average lives. If it is determined that a high degree of confidence could be placed in the range of 50 percent of FHA and 200 percent of FHA as reasonable outside limits of prepayment rates for 12 percent mortgages, each CMO class could be viewed as a callable bond whose "equivalent maturity" is the average life at 50 percent of FHA and whose probable non-call period is the average life at 200 percent of FHA. In effect, this makes the hypothetical CMO a bond which begins to amortize after the probable non-call period. This idea is illustrated in Exhibit 20.

The notion of probable non-call period and equivalent

EXHIBIT 20
CMOs Viewed As Callable Bonds

	Class 1	Class 2	Class 3
Coupon (000)	12%	12½%	13%
Principal Amount (000)	$7,500	$40,700	$42,254
Probable Non-Call Period (Average Life at 200% of FHA)	1.2	3.7	7.9
Equivalent Maturity (Average Life at 50% of FHA)	2.1	8.5	15.3

maturity will be central to evaluating CMOs in comparison to other investments. Also, the 50 percent of FHA and 200 percent of FHA limits represent cumulative averages for each of the periods; therefore, temporary aberrations do not necessarily affect the probable non-call period or equivalent maturity.

Relative Size of Classes

The size of each class and the type of class (interest bearing or accreting) will affect the expected average life, the probable non-call period and the equivalent maturity of all of the classes. The presence of an accreting bond class, which earns interest at the coupon rate but does not pay the interest currently, enables an issuer to create a greater amount of shorter maturity bonds by "freeing up" early cash flows. The accreting bonds are often called zero coupon CMOs, Zs, or compound interest bonds. While they are not truly zero coupon bonds, they do have extremely long durations with a high level of reinvestment guarantee. The large class of high priority, short maturity bonds can provide a large buffer, which in effect provides a high certainty that no principal will be prepaid on lower priority issues for a specific period.

The effect of class size and inclusion of an accreting bond (Class Z) is demonstrated in Exhibit 21 for a second hypothetical CMO issue. We have kept the same pool of mortgages (12 percent, 30-year level payment mortgages) and designated

EXHIBIT 21
CMO Cash Flows for the New Four-Class Issue ("B") at a Prepayment
Rate of 100 Percent of FHA Experience

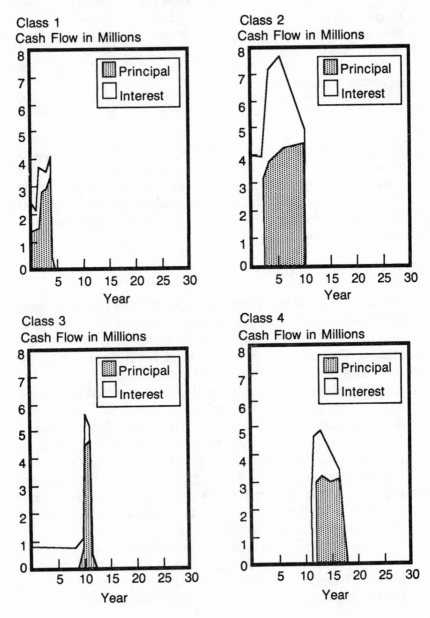

four CMO classes (12 percent 5-year, 12½ percent 15-year, 13 percent 20-year and 12½ percent 30-year "Z").

The amount of bonds in the first two classes increased substantially in the second CMO even though their maximum maturities are identical and the underlying collateral is identical. The effect on these classes is shown in Exhibit 22.

While on the surface Classes A–1 and B–1 appear to be essentially the same, they are not. Classes A–2 and B–2, also apparent equals, are not equivalent from an investment point of view. Classes A–1 and B–1 have probable non-call periods (200 percent of FHA) of 1.2 and 1.4, respectively, a significant difference when comparing them to noncallable Treasuries on a sharply sloped yield curve. Their equivalent maturities (50 percent of FHA) are equal but their expected average lives differ indicating, in substance, that they really are not identical bonds. These differences are more apparent in the comparison of Classes A–2 and B–2, which are partially captured by the .7 year difference in expected average life, but a more complete picture is presented by the addition of the equivalent maturity and probable non-call period, especially if the yield curve is not flat over that range. What we are observing is the effect of having a larger Fast Pay buffer class in Issue B, which delays the return of principal.

EXHIBIT 22
Effect of Bond Class Design on Terms of Early Classes

	Class 1		Class 2	
	Class A–1	Class B–1	Class A–2	Class B–2
Coupon	12%	12%	12.5%	12.5%
Principal Amount (000)	$7,500	$13,351	$40,700	$63,951
Maximum Maturity	5	5	15	15
Average Life at:				
50% of FHA	2.1	2.1	8.5	8.2
100% of FHA	1.6	1.8	5.9	6.6
200% of FHA	1.2	1.4	3.7	5.0

EXHIBIT 23

Class	Coupon	Maximum Maturity	Probable Non-Call Period*	Expected Average Life‡	Equivalent Maturity‡
A–1	12.00	5 yrs.	1.2 yrs	1.6 yrs.	2.1 yrs.
A–2	12.50	15	3.7	5.9	8.5
A–3	13.00	30	7.9	12.0	15.3
B–1	12.00	5	1.4	1.8	2.1
B–2	12.50	15	5.0	6.6	8.2
B–3	13.00	20	8.4	10.8	12.6
B–Z	12.50	30	11.1	14.3	16.6

* Average life at 200 percent of FHA.
† Average life at 100 percent of FHA.
‡ Average life at 50 percent of FHA.

The important features of the two hypothetical CMO issues, except price and yield, are summarized in Exhibit 23.

Nature of the Collateral

In deriving the descriptive information on the holding period of each class, it is essential to perform a detailed analysis of the collateral. There are many factors to be considered, and the most important include:

- Range of coupons and the weighted average coupon.
- Range of maturities and the weighted average maturity.
- Geographic location of mortgagors.
- Assumability of the mortgages and whether "due on sale" clauses are enforceable.
- Proportions of level payment and graduated payment mortgages in the collateral pool.
- Instructions to the Trustee concerning unanticipated excess cash flows as to whether they should be passed forward to retire bonds or passed back to the issuer.

To demonstrate the effects of different coupons on the characteristics of the CMO classes, we have designated another issue of CMOs ("C"), which has the same coupons and final maturities for the first two classes as in Issue A but has underlying collateral of $117 million of 9 percent level payment 25-year mortgages. On a market value basis, the collateral is essentially equivalent to the original collateral in Issue A, which is $100 million of 12 percent level payment 30-year mortgages. One additional assumption must be made regarding the probable minimum and maximum prepayment rates. To the extent that we have assumed that 50 percent and 200 percent of FHA represent the probable range for 12 percent mortgages, the range for 9 percent seasoned mortgages should be considerably lower. In Exhibit 24 the lower and upper bounds on the prepayment rate are assumed to be 40 percent of FHA and 125 percent of FHA. The characteristics of each class are shown, assuming in each case that excess cash flow from the collateral is passed forward to prepay bonds.

Identification of the different characteristics could cause an investor to lean in one direction or another given a preference, for example, for a longer probable non-call period.

The analysis of the coupons on the underlying collateral

EXHIBIT 24
Effect of Current Coupon Versus Discount Collateral
on CMO Characteristics

	Class 1		Class 2		Class 3	
	A–1	C–1	A–2	C–2	A–3	C–3
Principal Amount (000)	$7,500	$6,919	$40,700	$40,042	$42,254	$47,039
Coupon	12%	12%	12½%	12½%	13%	13%
Maximum Maturity	5.0	5.0	15.0	15.0	20.0	20.0
Probable Non-Call Period	1.2	1.1	3.7	3.3	7.9	7.0
Expected Average Life	1.6	1.3	5.9	4.7	12.0	9.9
Equivalent Maturity	2.1	1.7	8.5	6.3	15.3	12.9

is central to determining the appropriate prepayment rate range to use. The other factors cited previously have special effects on the non-call characteristics of the CMO classes. An example of this would be the inclusion of graduated payment mortgages (GPMs) in the collateral. If the entire collateral were GPMs and the GPMs prepaid at extremely low rates in the first five years of their existence, a higher than usual degree of certainty in cash flows would be imparted to the first class in the issue. If prepayment rates then caught up to "normal" levels for fixed payment mortgages after the fifth year when the GPMs level out and become like a fixed payment mortgage, the later classes might be unaffected relative to an issue backed by level payment mortgage collateral.

Geographic differences in mortgage collateral have been documented with certain states recording materially and consistently higher prepayment rates than others. The differences are attributable primarily to demographic and institutional factors. For example, Texas has exhibited prepayment rates that are higher than most states. Demographic and economic factors common to the Sunbelt states could account for much of this, resulting in high housing turnover from both net inflows of people from outside the state and rising affluence and mobility within the state. California mortgages might have performed in a fashion similar to those of Texas; however, until recently state law prevented active enforcement of "due on sale" clauses, which tended to inhibit prepayments.

Price Relative to Par

Like other mortgage-backed securities, CMOs present the analyst with unique problems in comparing yields, particularly when the security is purchased at a price other than par. Unexpected high levels of prepayments can result in increased yields on CMOs purchased at a discount, but only if the prepayment rate is sustained long enough to result in principal repayments of that class. If the prepayment slowed to the point that on a cumulative basis it equated the original expectation and to that point no principal had been repaid, then the realized yield will be the same as originally anticipated.

In this case, the earlier classes will have acted as a buffer, absorbing the volatility in the prepayment rate.

The question still remains, however. What is the relationship between price and quoted yield for any individual class of a CMO? Returning to the earlier examples, the price-yield relationship and sensitivity to the prepayment rate assumption are set forth in Exhibit 25.

Note that since each class has a coupon of 12 percent, each class will yield 12 percent at a price of 100. As the price moves away from par and the assumption concerning prepayments changes, the quoted yield, which is a semi-annual internal rate of return, changes for each class. The relationships among the classes also change since the nature of the collateral was different in each issue. These effects can be even more pronounced for classes with longer average lives. Exhibit 26 presents such a comparison for CMO classes with 12½% coupons and 15-year maximum maturities.

For a given prepayment rate assumption, wide disparities in quoted yield can result. Additionally, one must consider the propriety of comparing CMO A–2 and B–2 (current coupon collateral) to CMO C–2 (seasoned discount collateral) at the same prepayment rate, given that over a sustained period the

EXHIBIT 25
Relationship of Price to
Yield for Selected Short-Term CMO Classes

	Yields								
	50 Percent of FHA			100 Percent of FHA			200 Percent of FHA		
Price	A–1	B–1	C–1	A–1	B–1	C–1	A–1	B–1	C–1
96	14.3	14.30	15.10	14.95	14.51	15.50	16.05	14.70	16.15
97	13.7	13.71	14.40	14.20	14.02	14.55	15.05	14.35	15.10
98	13.10	13.09	13.60	13.45	13.33	13.70	14.05	13.60	14.05
99	12.45	12.63	12.80	12.65	12.67	12.85	12.97	12.80	13.00
100	12.00	12.00	12.00	12.00	12.00	12.00	12.00	12.00	12.00
101	11.45	11.45	11.30	11.30	11.33	11.20	11.05	11.20	11.00
Average Life	2.9	2.1	1.7	1.6	1.8	1.3	1.2	1.4	1.1

EXHIBIT 26
Relationship of Price to Yield
for Selected Intermediate-Term CMO Classes

	Yields								
	50 Percent of FHA			100 Percent of FHA			200 Percent of FHA		
Price	A–2	B–2	C–2	A–2	B–2	C–2	A–2	B–2	C–2
93	13.98	14.00	14.27	14.35	14.21	14.67	15.10	14.55	15.30
94	13.75	13.81	14.00	14.09	13.95	14.35	14.70	14.25	14.90
95	13.52	13.66	13.73	13.80	13.71	14.00	14.30	13.95	14.47
96	13.33	13.33	13.50	13.55	13.45	13.70	13.95	13.65	14.06
97	13.10	13.13	13.23	13.23	13.21	13.40	13.57	13.35	13.65
98	12.90	12.90	13.00	13.00	13.97	13.10	13.20	13.07	13.27
99	12.70	12.70	12.75	12.75	12.73	12.80	12.82	12.80	12.90
100	12.50	12.50	12.50	12.50	12.50	12.50	12.50	12.50	12.50
101	12.30	12.30	12.25	12.25	12.27	12.20	12.15	12.21	12.10
102	12.10	12.10	12.05	12.00	12.04	11.90	11.80	11.68	11.75
103	11.90	11.90	11.75	11.75	11.82	11.63	11.50	11.40	11.40
104	11.70	11.70	11.55	11.50	11.59	11.35	11.15	11.15	11.00
105	11.53	11.51	11.35	11.25	11.38	11.07	10.80	10.85	10.60
Average Life	8.5	8.2	6.3	5.9	6.6	4.7	3.7	5.0	3.3

likelihood is that the cumulative prepayment rate of 12 percent collateral will exceed that of 9 percent collateral.

The sensitivity of CMO prices to quoted yields is apparent from the charts in Exhibit 27. Depending on one's view of interest rates and prepayments, certain of these alternatives will be superior performers.

Average Life and Duration Variability

Other than yield differentials, the principal difference between CMOs (and pass-throughs) and Treasuries is the duration variability. This dimension captures the effects of unpredictable cash flow patterns and also provides a way of comparing the periodic principal payments of mortgage-backed securities to the single payment due at the maturity of most Treasuries.

EXHIBIT 27
Price Sensitivity of CMOs

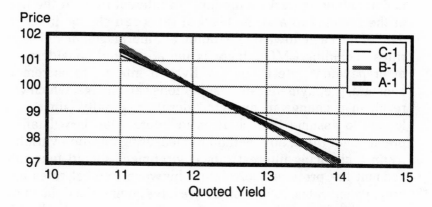

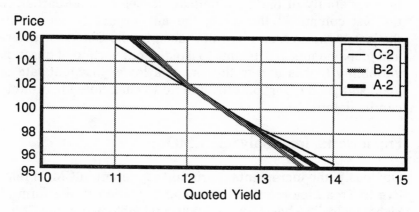

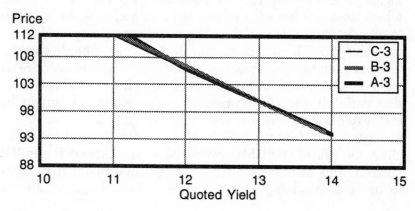

There are several ways to view duration variability. First, in a sense all bonds have some uncertainty since the duration is determined in part by the level of interest rates at the time of the calculation and the level of rates can change independent of the cash flows on the bond. For mortgage-backed securities, including CMOs, there is the additional consideration of prepayment rate scenarios. Even if interest rates remain constant, prepayment rate assumptions can change, which will result in a change in expected duration. Finally, since it is logical to assume that changes in interest levels will affect prepayment rates, any method of measuring duration variability in a changing interest rate environment should take into account the probable correlation between interest rates and prepayment rates. In Exhibit 28, we have summarized the duration variability of the hypothetical classes created earlier. In the last column of the table, the net variability represents the incremental variability introduced by the CMOs' structure and prepayments. It attempts to isolate that portion of duration variability that is due to the use of a lower discount rate or yield so that the portion attributable to cash flow uncertainty can be determined.

Frameworks for Analyzing CMOs

Obviously, the incremental variability inherent in CMOs relative to Treauries requires some compensation in the form of higher yield. The basis for the additional yield is that the CMO, which does not have a definite horizon, exposes the investor to reinvestment rate risk if it pays down too quickly, and terminal value risk if it pays down too slowly. The probable correlation between rapid prepayments and lower reinvestment rates magnifies the problem for mortgage securities with high duration variabilities. The proceeds from prepayments might be reinvested at rates below the initial yield.

Likewise, if interest rates rise and prepayment rates decline, the life of the CMO investment will exceed the initial horizon, and at least a portion of the investment may have to be sold, probably at a loss if rates are higher than the

EXHIBIT 28
Duration Variability for CMO Classes

Class	Coupon	Assumed Price (Percent of Par)	Yield at 100 Percent FHA	Duration at:*			± Variability	Incremental Variability Reliability to Treasury
				200 Percent FHA	100 Percent FHA	50 Percent FHA		
Treasury†	11.875%	101.00%	11.27%	1.84 yrs.	1.83 yrs.	1.83 yrs.	.005 yrs.	—
A–1	12.00	99.86	12.10	1.11	1.48	1.89	.39	.395 yrs.
B–1	12.00	99.85	12.10	1.33	1.61	1.89	.28	.285
C–1	12.00	99.88	12.10	1.05	1.27	1.53	.24	.245
Treasury†	12.75%	101.64%	12.30%	3.99	3.95	3.90	.045	—
A–2	12.50	96.89	13.30	3.03	4.19	5.22	1.095	1.14
B–2	12.50	95.79	13.15	3.75	4.51	5.11	.68	.725
C–2	12.50	97.34	13.30	2.77	3.58	4.39	.81	.855
Treasury†	12.625%	101.91%	12.30%	6.67	6.41	6.15	.26	—
A–3	13.00	96.95	13.70	5.08	6.24	6.82	.87	1.13
B–3	13.00	96.12	13.70	5.30	5.99	6.40	.81	1.07
C–3	13.00	96.30	13.70	6.48	5.75	4.75	.86	1.12
Treasury†	Zero	19.90%	11.87%	14.00	14.00	14.00	0	—
B–Z	12.50%	85.77	13.70	10.73	13.62	15.76	2.89	2.89

* Treasury and CMO durations are calculated assuming a 200 b.p. decline or increase in rates accompanying the 200 percent FHA and 50 percent FHA cases, respectively.

† The Treasury selected approximates a point on the yield curve with a duration equal to the subject CMOs at 100 percent FHA. A 14-year stripped Treasury was selected for comparison with Class B–Z.

initial yield. Again, the greater the variability in duration, the greater the penalty in the event an unfavorable scenario materializes.

Two methods for evaluating CMOs and comparing them with fixed-income alternatives are:

- Horizon Analysis
- Yield Spread—Duration Variability Trade-Offs

Horizon analysis is appealing because it sets a definite time frame to the comparison (the horizon) and selects the better investment by comparing accumulated cash at the horizon date. This accumulated cash is then used to compute a total realized rate of return as if it were the proceeds from a zero-coupon bond. It requires that all coupon income and principal repayments be reinvested as received. It also requires that the analyst specify the rate at which all available cash is reinvested. This can be done simply (just specify), or it can be done in a more sophisticated fashion (develop an implied forward interest rate curve). Finally, a method must be specified for assigning a terminal value to any principal balance at the horizon date. Generally, the remaining scheduled cash flows on any bonds still outstanding at the horizon date will be valued at the assumed then-current interest rate. The values in Exhibit 29 present the results of a simple horizon analysis for our hypothetical CMO classes.

Horizon analysis provides an acid test for the attractiveness of CMOs relative to Tresuries. While the CMO has a quoted yield advantage initially as demonstrated in the last column of Exhibit 29, this yield advantage can disappear in certain negative scenarios. The method is a useful tool for testing relative performance. Its major drawback is that it is difficult to use. To perform the analysis, one must be able to calculate the cash flows of mortgage-backed securities, including CMOs, for a variety of prepayment scenarios. This is a task that cannot be performed either quickly or easily. There is need for a method of comparing CMOs with other investments that does not require calculation of individual cash

EXHIBIT 29
Horizon Analysis for CMOs

Reinvestment Rate Prepayment Rate	10 Percent 200 Percent FHA	12 Percent 100 Percent FHA	14 Percent 50 Percent FHA	Initial Yield to Maturity
Two-Year Horizon				
Treasury	11.18%	11.32%	11.46%	11.27%
A–1	11.18	12.02	11.95	12.10
B–1	11.09	11.98	11.99	12.10
C–1	11.11	12.06	12.49	12.10
Five-Year Horizon				
Treasury	11.80%	12.23%	12.68%	12.30%
A–2	12.19	12.91	12.70	13.30
B–2	12.71	13.10	12.99	13.51
C–2	11.76	12.65	12.82	13.30
Ten-Year Horizon				
Treasury	11.41%	12.18%	12.99%	12.30%
A–3	12.00	12.80	13.61	13.70
B–3	12.06	13.00	13.69	13.70
C–3	10.82	12.96	13.67	13.70
Twenty-Year Horizon				
Treasury	11.31%	11.91%	12.51%	11.87%
B–Z	12.16	13.07	13.70	13.70

flows but produces relative rankings in line with a horizon analysis.

Various forms of analysis have been devised to trade off yield advantage and duration or average life variability. In essence, the goal is to produce a ratio which rewards a security for a yield advantage and penalizes it for incremental variability in duration. A straight linear trade-off is easy to calculate and produces the results shown in Exhibit 30. The higher the ratio of yield advantage to duration variability, the better the CMO.

The ratio is quite useful for comparisons within a given horizon. Use of the ratio to compare Class A–1 to Class A–3 would seem to have little validity, however, because the two classes have such a great difference in duration.

EXHIBIT 30
Yield Spread-Duration Variability Trade-Off

Investment Horizon	Initial Yield	Yield Advantage	Incremental Duration Variability	Yield Spread Variability Ratio
Two-Year Range:				
Treasury	11.27%	—	—	—
A–1	12.10	+83 b.p.	±.395 yrs.	210
B–1	12.10	+83	±.285	291
C–1	12.10	+83	±.245	339
Five-Year Range:				
Treasury	12.30%	—	—	—
A–2	13.30	+99 b.p.	±1.14 yrs.	87
B–2	13.51	+121	±.725	167
C–2	13.30	+99	±.855	116
Ten-Year Range:				
Treasury	12.30%	—	—	—
A–3	13.70	+140 b.p.	±1.13 yrs.	124
B–3	13.70	+140	±1.07	131
C–3	13.70	+140	±1.12	125
Twenty-Year Range:				
Treasury	11.87%	—	—	—
B–Z	13.70	+183 b.p.	±2.89 yrs.	63

All methods of analyzing and comparing CMOs require assumptions. Additionally, the structures of CMO issues vary considerably. For example, certain FHLMC CMOs guarantee minimum payments. This guarantee has value to the investor since it reduces the duration variability, eliminating the risk that the CMO pays down more slowly than expected in a rising interest rate environment. This value inherent in the sinking fund would be captured in both of the methods illustrated.

New security structures and features will appear in future issues, so new methods of comparison will be developed to capture the positive or negative effects of those features. In the past year and a half, the proliferation of structures has been a challenge to the participants in the fixed-income markets. Mortgage securities, with the possibility of high returns relative to the credit risk involved, make the careful analysis required worthwhile.

The Appendixes contain selected terms of CMO issues to date and illustrate the variety of bonds that have been created from mortgage collateral.

APPENDIX I
Selected Terms of Fast Pay CMOs
(Expected Average Life of 1.1 to 3.0 Years)

Issuer and Class		Date Issued	Bond Amount (Millions)	Coupon	Maximum Maturity (Years)	Expected Average Life (Years)	Based on this Percent FHA	Issue Price (Percent of par)	Yield	Spread at Pricing (Basis pts over Treasury)	Use of Excess Cash Flow**	Mortgages as Percent of Bonds	Range of Coupons
Citicorp Home.	A-1	9/20/84	$100.0	11.500%	2.0	1.2	0.50%*	99.844	11.64%	+35 1 yr. T-Bill	PF	111%	9.56-13.875%
Investors GNMA	1-A	9/22/83	25.0	10.000	8.5	1.2	100.00	98.060	11.46	+78 10.875 of 9/85	PB	100	11.50
Travelers M.S.	1-A	2/22/84	270.0	10.625	3.0	1.4	75.00	99.938	10.88	+50 1 yr. T-Bill	PB	104	10.75-12.75
Investors GNMA	A-3	4/6/84	45.0	7.875	6.8	1.7	45.00	93.670	12.01	+35 7.800 of 5/86	PB	100	8.00
Freddie Mac	C-1	1/19/84	129.6	10.750	3.0	1.8	75.00	99.969	10.77	+16 11.875 of 12/85	PB	126	7.50-10.50
Salomon M.S. (83)	1-A	11/17/83	52.3	10.875	5.0	1.8	75.00	99.875	10.96	+30 10.500 of 10/85	PB	102	11.50-12.00
Amer. Southwest	C-1	10/20/83	27.9	10.875	5.0	2.0	75.00	99.750	11.02	+43 10.875 of 9/85	PB	99	9.50-13.00
Investors GNMA	A-5	10/2/84	80.0	10.875	13.6	2.0	60.00	99.670	12.72	+60 11.875 of 9/86	PB	100	11.00
Guaranteed Mtge.	B-1	10/11/83	45.9	11.000	5.0	2.1	75.00	99.781	11.12	+45 10.875 of 9/85	PF	103	9.00-13.50
Guaranteed Mtge.	Q-1	11/23/83	54.0	11.000	5.0	2.1	75.00	99.875	11.07	+49 10.500 of 10/85	PF	102	9.25-13.25
Centex Acc.	D-1	10/21/83	26.0	10.875	5.0	2.1	75.00	99.750	11.02	+43 10.875 of 9/85	PF	103	10.50-13.25
Norwest Conv.	1-A	2/2/84	55.0	11.000	7.0	2.1	100.00	100.000	11.00	+45 10.625 of 1/86	PB	101	12.50-17.38
Ryan Mort. Acc.	2-A	8/21/84	10.0	12.500	14.0	2.1	75.00	99.030	13.53	+65 12.625 of 7/86	PB	100	9.00-13.50
Centex Acc.	E-1	1/17/84	37.5	10.875	5.5	2.2	100.00	99.906	10.93	+43 10.875 of 12/85	PF	101	10.00-12.75
Norwest Mort.	1-A	12/13/83	62.2	11.125	7.0	2.2	75.00	99.750	11.25	+41 10.500 of 10/85	PF	105	11.00-12.50
Norwest Mort.	2-A	2/23/84	23.2	11.250	7.0	2.2	75.00	99.844	11.33	+40 10.875 of 2/86	PB	103	11.00-12.50
Salomon M.S. (84)	1-A	7/3/84	275.0	8.125	9.8	2.2	90.00	90.187	13.77	+61 12.625 of 5/86	PB	101	8.00- 8.25
Ryan Mort. Acc.	1-A	5/22/84	27.6	12.750	6.0	2.3	75.00	99.480	13.04	+50 11.750 of 4/86	PF	100	9.00-13.00
Amer. Southwest	1-A	2/3/84	10.1	10.875	6.5	2.3	75.00	99.813	10.97	+45 10.625 of 1/86	PB	110	10.00-12.88
Centex Acc.	F-1	7/12/84	42.0	13.000	7.0	2.3	75.00	98.187	13.44	+50 13.000 of 6/86	PF	100	10.00-13.50

Guaranteed Mort.	A-1	9/20/84	28.0	12.375	8.0	2.3	100.00	99.937	13.25	+65	11.875 of 9/86	PB	101	9.75–15.25
Investors GNMA	1-B	9/22/83	25.0	10.250	12.7	2.3	100.00	96.840	11.76	+84	11.375 of 8/86	PB	100	11.50
Gen. Homes Fin.	1-A	9/24/84	16.8	12.500	7.7	2.3	75.00	99.810	12.79	+64	11.875 of 9/86	PB	103	10.50–13.50
Freddie Mac	D-1	4/12/84	172.0	11.500	4.0	2.4	100.00	99.797	12.06	+15	11.500 of 3/86	PF	100	12.50–14.00
Amer. Southwest	E-1	6/7/84	38.1	13.000	6.5	2.4	75.00	99.625	13.19	+50	12.500 of 5/86	PB	113	9.00–14.99
L&N Funding	A-1	2/14/84	68.0	11.000	6.5	2.4	100.00	99.750	11.12	+37	10.625 of 1/86	PB	100	12.00–12.25
Int. Mort. Acc.	A-1	2/3/84	17.8	10.875	7.0	2.4	75.00	99.875	10.94	+40	10.625 of 1/86	PB	103	11.00–12.75
Amer. Southwest	F-1	8/23/84	25.4	12.875	7.5	2.5	75.00	99.530	13.10	+65	12.375 of 8/86	PB	109	9.00–15.00
Amer. Southwest	D-1	1/26/84	16.9	11.000	7.5	2.5	75.00	99.906	11.05	+40	10.625 of 1/86	PB	100	9.50–13.25
Sears Mort.	1-A	2/15/84	125.0	11.125	9.2	2.6	100.00	Var.	Var.	+43	10.625 of 1/86	PB	100	12.00
Investors GNMA	A-4	6/13/84	50.0	8.875	11.4	2.7	40.00	89.940	13.66	+55	12.500 of 5/87	PB	100	9.00
Pru Realty II	A-1	1/27/84	126.0	11.000	5.0	2.9	0.00	99.601	11.17	+33	11.000 of 11/86	PB	135	4.50– 8.00

* .50% CRP (monthly prepayment rate).
** PF or PB (pass forward or pass back).

APPENDIX II

Selected Terms of Short Intermediate CMOs
(Expected Average Life of 3.1 to 6.0 Years)

Issuer and Class		Date Issued	Bond Amount (Millions)	Coupon	Maximum Maturity (Years)	Expected Average Life (Years)	Based on this Percent FHA	Issue Price (Percent of par)	Yield	Spread at Pricing (Basis pts over Treasury)	Use of Excess Cash Flow**	Mortgages as Percent of Bonds	Range of Coupons
Citicorp Home.	A-2	9/20/84	$115.0	12.375%	4.1	3.2	0.50%*	99.410	12.61	+50 12.375 of 8/86	PF	111%	9.56–13.88%
Freddie Mac	B-1	9/29/83	147.4	11.000	5.0	3.2	100.00	99.813	11.07	+29 11.375 of 8/86	PF	NA	12.00–14.00
Freddie Mac	A-1	6/7/83	215.0	10.625	5.0	3.2	100.00	99.810	10.70	+40 9.375 of 5/86	PF	NA	11.95–13.50
Guaranteed Mort.	A-1	7/22/83	32.0	11.375	12.0	3.2	100.00	99.938	11.40	+30 9.375 of 5/86	PF	110	11.50–15.00
Investors GNMA	A-2	1/5/84	115.0	11.625	18.8	3.2	100.00	100.000	11.62	+60 11.250 of 12/87	PB	100	12.00
Investors GNMA	1-C	9/22/83	25.0	10.500	15.4	3.3	100.00	96.140	11.97	+81 11.125 of 9/87	PB	100	11.50
Guaranteed Mort.	E-1	6/20/84	38.5	12.500	20.0	3.3	75.00	97.187	13.87	+55 12.500 of 5/87	PF	102	10.00–13.00
Paine Webber	A-1	11/15/83	175.0	11.600	11.5	3.5	100.00	100.000	11.60	+47 11.125 of 9/87	PB	100	12.50
Guaranteed Mort.	C-1	1/12/84	69.0	11.050	6.0	3.8	100.00	99.938	11.08	+35 10.875 of 12/85	PF	102	10.50–13.00
Guaranteed Mort.	B-2	10/11/83	40.8	11.875	7.5	4.1	75.00	99.813	11.93	+58 11.750 of 11/88	PF	103	9.00–13.50
Investors GNMA	1-D	9/22/83	25.0	10.750	17.4	4.1	100.00	95.350	12.27	+92 11.750 of 11/88	PB	100	11.50
Freddie Mac	C-2	1/19/84	86.5	11.350	5.0	4.3	75.00	100.000	11.35	+25 11.250 of 12/87	PB	126	7.50–10.50
Guaranteed Mort.	Q-2	11/23/83	48.0	11.750	7.5	4.3	75.00	99.531	11.87	+57 11.750 of 11/88	PF	102	9.25–13.25
Amer. Southwest	C-2	10/20/83	49.5	11.750	10.0	5.0	75.00	99.375	11.92	+70 11.750 of 11/88	PB	99	9.50–13.00
Centex Acc.	F-2	7/12/84	32.0	13.500	9.5	5.1	75.00	98.344	13.97	+60 13.875 of 8/89	PF	100	10.00–13.50
Investors GNMA	B-5	10/2/84	55.0	10.875	17.5	5.1	60.00	91.670	13.27	+70 12.750 of 11/89	PB	100	11.00
Centex Acc.	E-2	1/17/84	59.0	11.750	10.0	5.3	100.00	99.844	11.79	+50 11.375 of 2/89	PF	101	10.00–12.75
Sears Mort.	1-B	2/15/84	75.0	11.750	12.0	5.3	100.00	Var.	Var.	+48 11.375 of 2/89	PB	100	12.00
Norwest Mort.	1-B	12/13/83	100.0	12.125	12.0	5.3	75.00	99.375	12.29	+63 11.375 of 2/89	PF	105	11.00–12.50
Norwest Conv.	1-B	2/2/84	105.0	12.000	13.0	5.3	100.00	99.750	12.07	+75 11.375 of 2/89	PB	101	12.50–17.38

Ryan Mort. Acc.	2-B	8/21/84	17.0	12.500	20.5	5.3	75.00	96.790	13.53	+75	13.875 of 8/89	PB	100	9.00–13.50
Citicorp Home.	A-3	9/20/84	135.0	12.500	6.5	5.4	0.50*	98.660	12.85	+55	12.750 of 11/89	PF	111	9.56–13.875
Freddie Mac	D-2	4/12/84	188.0	12.375	7.0	5.4	100.00	99.559	12.73	+30	11.750 of 5/89	PF	100	12.50–14.00
Amer. Southwest	E-2	6/7/84	34.9	13.500	9.5	5.4	75.00	97.625	14.15	+50	13.875 of 7/89	PB	113	9.00–14.99
L&N Funding	A-2	2/14/84	72.0	11.875	10.0	5.4	100.00	99.469	12.01	+46	11.375 of 2/89	PB	100	12.00–12.25
Norwest Mort.	2-B	2/23/84	39.3	12.250	12.5	5.4	75.00	100.000	12.25	+59	11.375 of 2/89	PB	103	11.00–12.50
Guaranteed Mort.	A-2	9/20/84	27.0	12.500	11.0	5.4	100.00	98.843	13.76	+75	12.750 of 11/89	PB	101	9.75–15.25
Salomon M.S. (84)	1-B	7/3/84	130.0	8.125	12.3	5.4	90.00	77.500	14.41	+69	13.875 of 8/89	PB	101	8.00– 8.25
Salomon M.S. (83)	1-B	11/17/83	162.9	11.750	12.5	5.4	75.00	99.310	11.93	+53	11.750 of 11/88	PB	102	11.50–12.00
Guaranteed Mort.	C-2	1/12/84	108.0	11.950	10.5	5.5	100.00	100.00	11.95	+45	11.37 of 2/90	PF	102	10.50–13.00
Investors GNMA	1-E	9/22/83	50.0	11.000	20.5	5.5	100.00	94.750	12.45	+93	11.500 of 10/90	PB	100	11.50
Ryan Mort. Acc.	1-B	5/22/84	31.0	13.000	9.8	5.5	75.00	96.530	13.93	+65	11.750 of 5/89	PF	100	9.00–13.00
Centex Acc.	D-2	10/21/83	57.8	11.750	10.0	5.6	75.00	99.375	11.91	+70	11.750 of 11/88	PF	103	10.50–13.25
Amer. Southwest	1-B	2/3/84	22.1	11.875	12.0	5.7	75.00	99.313	12.05	+75	11.375 of 2/89	PB	110	10.00–12.88
Amer. Southwest	F-2	8/23/84	40.8	13.250 Z	12.0	5.7	75.00	99.687	13.33	+70	13.875 of 8/89	PB	109	9.00–15.00
Travelers Mort.	Z-1	2/22/84	455.0	12.000 Z	13.5	5.8	75.00	Var.	Var.		Var.	PB	104	10.75–12.75
Int. Mort. Acc.	A-2	2/3/84	29.1	11.875	12.5	5.9	75.00	100.000	11.88	+60	11.375 of 2/89	PB	103	11.00–12.75
Gen. Homes Fin.	1-B	9/24/84	28.7	12.500	12.9	5.9	75.00	97.810	13.26	+74	12.750 of 11/89	PB	103	10.50–13.50

* .50% CRP (monthly prepayment rate).
** PF or PB (pass forward or pass back).

APPENDIX III
Selected Terms of Long-Term Intermediate CMOs
(Expected Average Life of 6.1 to 10.0 Years)

Issuer and Class		Date Issued	Bond Amount (Millions)	Coupon	Maximum Maturity (Years)	Expected Average Life (Years)	Based on this Percent FHA	Issue Price (Percent of par)	Yield	Spread at Pricing (Basis pts over Treasury)				Use of Excess Cash Flow**	Mortgages as Percent of Bonds	Range of Coupons
Amer. Southwest	D-2	1/26/84	$ 29.5	11.750%	13.0	6.1	75.00%	99.50%	11.87	+56	11.37	of	2/89	PB	100%	9.50-13.25%
Investors GNMA	B-3	4/6/84	75.0	7.875	14.7	6.5	45.00	78.03	13.23	+65	11.75	of	1/91	PB	100	8.00
Investors GNMA	1-F	9/22/83	50.0	11.125	22.8	7.2	100.00	93.83	12.58	+104	11.87	of	8/93	PB	100	11.50
Paine Webber	1-B	11/15/83	125.0	12.250	15.0	7.4	100.00	100.00	12.25	+70	11.50	of	10/90	PB	100	12.50
Guaranteed Mort.	Q-3	11/23/83	144.0	11.875	12.5	7.5	75.00	97.93	12.30	+80	11.50	of	10/90	PF	102	9.25-13.25
Guaranteed Mort.	B-3	10/11/83	119.7	11.875	12.5	7.5	75.00	97.93	12.31	+79	11.50	of	10/90	PF	103	9.00-13.50
Pru Realty II	A-2	1/27/84	120.5	12.000	10.0	7.6	0.00	99.89	12.02	+50	11.75	of	1/91	PB	135	4.50- 8.00
Centex Acc.	E-3	1/17/84	28.6	12.000	11.5	7.7	100.00	99.84	12.03	+55	11.75	of	1/91	PF	101	10.00-12.75
Centex Acc.	F-3	7/12/84	59.0	13.500	13.0	7.7	75.00	96.50	14.26	+80	13.75	of	7/91	PF	100	10.00-13.50
Freddie Mac	C-3	1/19/84	228.7	11.875	10.0	7.8	75.00	100.00	11.87	+37	11.750	of	1/91	PB	126	7.50-10.50
Guaranteed Mort.	C-3	1/12/84	57.0	12.125	12.0	7.8	100.00	99.50	12.23	+55	11.75	of	1/91	PF	102	10.50-13.00
L&N Funding	A-3	2/14/84	58.0	12.000	12.0	7.8	100.00	98.50	12.31	+55	11.75	of	11/93	PB	100	12.00-12.25
Guaranteed Mort.	A-3	9/20/84	25.0	12.500	13.0	7.8	100.00	97.78	14.02	+85	13.75	of	7/91	PB	101	9.75-15.25
Investors GNMA	C-5	10/2/84	50.0	10.875	14.9	7.8	60.00	89.06	13.33	+75	13.75	of	7/91	PB	100	11.00
Investors GNMA	B-4	6/13/84	45.0	8.875	16.3	8.0	40.00	76.00	14.21	+65	11.75	of	11/93	PB	100	9.00
Ryan Mort. Acc.	1-C	5/22/84	22.0	13.000	12.0	8.1	75.00	94.13	14.25	+83	12.38	of	4/91	PB	100	9.00-13.00
Investors GNMA	B-2	1/5/84	150.0	12.000	25.1	8.1	100.00	98.31	12.49	+80	11.75	of	1/91	PB	100	12.00
Salomon M.S. (84)	1-C	7/3/84	195.0	8.125	15.3	8.2	90.00	70.50	14.60	+73	13.13	of	5/94	PB	101	8.00-18.25
Centex Corp.	D-3	10/21/83	27.7	12.000	12.0	8.3	75.00	98.87	12.22	+80	11.50	of	10/90	PF	103	10.50-13.25
Amer. Southwest	E-3	6/7/84	51.7	13.500	12.5	8.3	75.00	95.91	14.36	+90	12.38	of	3/91	PB	113	9.00-14.99

Guaranteed Mort.	E-2	6/20/84	35.0	12.500	21.6	8.4	75.00	91.75	13.87	+75 12.38 of 4/91	PB	102	10.00–13.00
Freddie Mac	D-3	4/12/84	254.5	12.630	10.0	8.6	100.00	99.37	13.10	+42 12.375 of 4/91	PF	100	12.50–14.00
Freddie Mac	A-2	6/7/83	350.00	11.250	12.5	8.6	100.00	99.37	11.37	+54 10.50 of 4/90	PF	NA	11.95–13.50
Freddie Mac	B-2	9/29/83	239.6	11.875	12.5	8.6	100.00	99.37	12.00	+54 11.875 of 8/93	PF	NA	12.00–14.00
Amer. Southwest	C-3	10/20/83	35.8	12.000	12.5	9.0	75.00	98.87	12.23	+80 11.50 of 10/90	PB	99	9.50–13.00
Guaranteed Mort.	A-2	7/22/83	63.4	12.125	19.0	9.0	100.00	99.56	12.21	+60 10.125 of 5/93	PF	110	11.50–15.00
Sears Mort.	1-C	2/15/84	250.0	12.000	17.5	9.3	100.00	Var.	Var.	+65 11.75 of 11/93	PB	100	12.00
Investors GNMA	1-G	9/22/83	50.0	11.250	24.5	9.3	100.00	92.80	12.58	+121 11.875 of 8/93	PB	100	11.50
Ryan Mort. Acc.	2-C	8/21/84	18.0	12.500	24.5	9.5	75.00	94.62	13.38	+85 13.13 of 5/94	PB	100	9.00–13.50
Norwest Conv.	1-C	2/2/84	157.2	12.500	18.0	9.9	100.00	99.72	12.55	+90 11.750 of 11/93	PB	101	12.50–17.38

* PF or PB (pass forward or pass back).

APPENDIX IV
Selected Terms of Slow Pay CMOs
(Expected Average Life of 10.1 to 26.0 Years)

Issuer and Class		Date Issued	Bond Amount (Millions)	Coupon	Maximum Maturity (Years)	Expected Average Life (Years)	Based on this Percent FHA	Issue Price (Percent of par)	Yield	Spread at Pricing (Basis pts over Treasury)	Use of Excess Cash Flow**	Mortgages as Percent of Bonds	Range of Coupons
Amer. Southwest	F-3	8/23/84	$ 83.2	13.250%	17.0	10.3	75.00%	98.750%	13.480	+79 12.630 of 8/94	PB	109	9.00-15.00%
Gen. Homes Fin.	1-C	9/24/84	40.3	12.500	17.2	10.3	75.00	96.125	13.416	+90 12.630 of 8/94	PB	103	10.50-13.50
Amer. Southwest	1-C	2/3/84	36.4	12.375	17.0	10.5	75.00	98.188	12.517	+90 11.750 of 11/93	PB	99	9.50-13.00
Travelers Mort.	1-C	2/22/84	375.0	12.000	16.5	10.7	75.00	96.406	12.623	+73 11.750 of 11/93	PB	104	10.75-12.75
Int. Mort. Acc.	A-3	2/3/84	49.6	12.250	17.5	10.7	75.00	99.500	12.336	+73 11.750 of 11/93	PB	103	11.00-12.75
Norwest Mort.	2-3	2/23/84	86.5	12.250	18.5	10.7	75.00	97.625	12.665	+75 11.750 of 11/93	PB	103	11.00-12.50
Norwest Mort.	1-C	12/13/83	245.0	12.375	18.5	10.7	75.00	97.750	12.770	+84 11.750 of 11/93	PF	105	11.00-12.50
Salomon M.S. (83)	1-C	11/17/83	234.8	12.000	18.0	10.8	75.00	97.375	12.450	+73 11.750 of 11/93	PB	102	11.00-12.50
Amer. Southwest	D-3	1/26/84	48.9	12.250	18.0	11.1	75.00	99.594	12.319	+68 11.750 of 11/93	PB	100	9.50-13.25
Investors GNMA	C-3	4/6/84	40.0	7.875	17.2	11.4	45.00	68.910	13.410	+75 8.750 of 8/94	PB	100	8.00
Investors GNMA	D-5	10/2/84	85.0	10.875	22.9	11.7	60.00	86.260	13.420	+85 13.130 of 5/94	PB	100	11.00
Investors GNMA	1-H	9/22/83	50.0	11.250	25.9	11.8	100.00	91.320	12.880	+129 11.500 of 11/95	PB	100	11.50
Centex Acc.	F-4	7/12/84	25.2	13.000	22.5	13.1	75.00	83.250	14.610	+120 13.750 of 8/04	PF	100	10.00-13.50
Investors GNMA	C-4	6/13/84	45.0	8.875	19.7	13.3	40.00	68.910	14.401	+75 12.630 of 5/95	PB	100	9.00
Guaranteed Mort.	A-3	7/22/83	18.1	12.625	20.5	14.0	100.00	99.875	12.640	+93 11.500 of 11/95	PF	110	11.50-15.00
Guaranteed Mort.	E-3	6/20/84	26.2	12.500	26.0	14.2	75.00	84.687	14.480	+85 13.130 of 5/94	PB	102	10.00-13.00
Investors GNMA	D-3	4/6/84	40.0	7.875	19.3	14.8	45.00	65.400	13.475	+80 7.880 of 2/00	PB	100	8.00
Investors GNMA	C-2	1/5/84	135.0	11.900	28.3	16.0	100.00	95.670	12.750	+100 11.750 of 11/93	PB	100	12.00
Investors GNMA	1-I	9/22/83	100.0	11.375	28.3	16.9	100.00	90.280	13.020	+134 11.125 of 8/03	PB	100	11.50
Investors GNMA	E-5	10/2/84	130.0	10.875	26.1	18.6	60.00	84.800	13.310	+90 13.750 of 8/04	PB	100	11.00

Investors GNMA	D-4	6/13/84	60.0	9.000	22.9	18.7	40.00	67.120	14.285	+80	7.880 of 2/00	PB	100	9.00
Freddie Mac	D-4	4/12/84	109.5	12.900	30.0	18.8	100.00	95.000	13.550	+80	12.380 of 5/04	PF	100	12.50–14.00
Guaranteed Mort	A-4	9/20/84	20.0	12.500	30.0	19.0	100.00	92.250	14.650	+125	13.750 of 8/04	PB	101	9.75–15.25
Investors GNMA	E-3	4/6/84	100.0	7.875	26.0	19.7	45.00	62.770	13.460	+80	10.000 of 5/10	PB	100	8.00
Freddie Mac	B-3	9/29/83	297.7	12.500	30.0	20.4	100.00	99.063	12.630	+97	11.875 of 11/03	PF	NA	12.00–14.00
Freddie Mac	A-3	6/7/83	435.0	11.875	30.0	20.4	100.00	99.250	11.980	+85	10.750 of 5/03	PF	NA	11.95–13.50
Amer. Southwest	E-4	6/7/84	28.0	13.500	30.0	20.7	75.00	84.187	14.740	+125	12.380 of 4/04	PB	113	9.00–14.99
Ryan Mort. Acc.	2-D	8/21/84	55.0	12.500	30.0	21.2	75.00	92.990	13.050	+95	13.750 of 8/04	PB	100	9.00–13.50
Amer. Southwest	F-4	8/23/84	16.6	13.250	30.0	22.0	75.00	90.625	13.840	+120	13.750 of 8/04	PB	109	9.00–15.00
Investors GNMA	E-4	6/13/84	50.0	8.875	24.9	23.2	40.00	64.970	14.280	+80	12.000 of 12/13	PB	100	9.00
Guaranteed Mort.	E-4	6/20/84	75.2	12.500	30.0	23.7	75.00	88.062	14.550	+95	13.250 of 5/04	PB	102	10.00–13.00
Paine Webber	1-D	11/15/83	150.0	12.500	30.0	23.7	100.00	98.250	12.720	+98	12.000 of 8/13	PB	100	12.50
Investors GNMA	F-5	10/2/84	100.0	10.875	29.0	24.6	60.00	83.900	13.310	+90	12.000 of 9/13	PB	100	11.00
Investors GNMA	1-J	9/22/83	100.0	11.375	30.0	25.3	100.00	90.230	12.900	+123	12.000 of 8/13	PB	100	11.50
Investors GNMA	D-2	1/5/84	100.0	11.900	30.0	25.6	100.00	94.340	12.870	+105	12.000 of 8/13	PB	100	12.00

* PF or PB (pass forward or pass back).

APPENDIX V
Selected Terms of Long-Term Zero Coupon CMOs
(Expected Average Life of 10.6 to 22.6 Years)

Issuer and Class		Date Issued	Bond Amount (Millions)	Coupon	Maximum Maturity (Years)	Expected Average Life (Years)	Based on this Percent FHA	Issue Price (Percent of par)	Yield	Spread at Pricing (Basis pts over Treasury)	Use of Excess Cash Flow**	Mortgages as Percent of Bonds	Range of Coupons
Paine Webber	C-1	11/15/83	$ 25.0	12.500% Z	23.5	10.6	100.00%	100.000%	12.50%	+84 11.750 of 11/93	PB	100	12.50
Pru Realty II	A-3	1/27/84	25.0	0.000 Z	12.0	12.0	0.00	25.472	11.75	+39 11.750 of 11/93	PB	135	4.50- 8.00
Guaranteed Mort.	Q-4	11/23/83	54.0	12.000 Z	23.0	13.5	75.00	89.625	12.88	+108 11.875 of 11/03	PF	102	9.25-13.25
Guaranteed Mort.	B-4	10/11/83	48.4	11.875 Z	22.5	14.4	75.00	90.000	12.72	+98 11.875 of 11/03	PF	103	9.00-13.50
Citicorp Home	A-4	9/20/84	150.0	12.500 Z	23.5	14.6	0.50*	93.750	N.A.	— — —	PF	111	9.56-13.87
Paine Webber	C-2	11/15/83	25.0	12.500 Z	27.5	14.8	100.00	100.000	12.50	+84 11.750 of 11/93	PB	100	12.50
Salomon M.S. (84)	1-Z	7/3/84	150.0	8.125 Z	28.3	15.0	90.00	44.250	14.59	+78 12.375 of 5/04	PB	101	8.00- 8.25
Freddie Mac	C-4	1/19/84	80.2	12.100 Z	25.0	16.8	75.00	95.125	12.47	+70 11.875 of 11/03	PB	126	7.50-10.50
Centex Acc.	E-4	1/17/84	35.3	12.000 Z	30.0	17.6	100.00	90.219	12.80	+110 11.875 of 11/03	PF	101	10.00-12.75
L&N Funding	A-4	2/14/84	52.0	12.000 Z	30.0	17.9	100.00	87.438	13.05	+105 11.875 of 11/03	PB	100	12.00-12.25
Gen. Homes Fin.	1-Z	9/24/84	9.7	12.500 Z	29.9	18.5	75.00	85.000	13.76	+135 13.750 of 8/04	PB	103	10.50-13.50
Ryan Mort. Acc.	1-Z	5/22/84	22.2	13.000 Z	30.0	19.1	75.00	81.390	14.74	+125 12.375 of 4/04	PB	100	9.00-13.00
Guaranteed Mort.	C-4	1/12/84	66.0	12.125 Z	25.5	14.6	100.00	90.781	12.94	+105 11.875 of 11/03	PF	102	10.50-13.00
Amer. Southwest	C-4	10/20/83	30.6	12.000 Z	30.0	20.0	75.00	92.375	12.57	+85 11.875 of 11/03	PB	99	9.50-13.00
Centex Acc.	D-4	10/21/84	28.1	12.000 Z	30.0	20.1	75.00	92.375	12.55	+83 11.875 of 11/03	PF	103	10.50-13.25
Sears Mort.	1-D	2/15/84	50.0	12.000 Z	30.0	20.6	100.00	Var.	Var.	+100 11.875 of 11/03	PB	100	12.00
Travelers Mort.	Z-2	2/22/84	150.0	12.000 Z	30.0	21.1	75.00	84.500	13.04	+100 11.875 of 11/03	PB	104	10.75-12.75
Norwest Conv.	1-Z	2/2/84	35.0	12.500 Z	30.0	21.2	100.00	91.625	13.04	+125 11.875 of 11/03	PB	101	12.50-17.38
Amer. Southwest	1-D	2/3/84	7.9	12.375 Z	30.0	21.2	75.00	90.750	12.95	+120 11.875 of 11/03	PB	100	10.00-12.88
Amer. Southwest	D-4	1/26/84	9.8	12.250 Z	30.0	22.1	75.00	90.000	12.85	+110 11.875 of 11/03	PB	100	9.50-13.25
Salmon M.S. (83)	1-Z	11/17/83	50.0	12.000 Z	30.0	22.2	75.00	86.000	12.87	+108 12.000 of 8/13	PB	102	11.50-12.00
Int. Mort. Acc.	A-4	2/3/84	10.8	12.250 Z	30.0	22.2	75.00	90.125	12.85	+110 11.875 of 11/03	PB	103	11.00-12.75
Norwest Mort.	2-D	2/23/84	15.0	12.250 Z	30.0	22.5	75.00	85.500	12.14	+110 11.875 of 11/03	PB	103	11.00-12.50
Norwest Mort.	1-Z	12/13/83	40.0	12.375 Z	30.0	22.6	75.00	82.250	13.28	+117 11.875 of 11/03	PF	105	11.00-12.50

* .50% CRP (monthly prepayment rate).
** PF or PB (pass forward or pass back).

CHAPTER 8

The Historical Performance of Mortgage Securities: 1972–1984[*]

Michael Waldman
Vice President & Manager of Mortgage Research
Salomon Brothers Inc

Steven Guterman
Mortgage Research
Salomon Brothers Inc

The growth of mortgage pass-through securities in the 1970s, and their acceptance as an investment vehicle by a wide variety of institutional investors led Salomon Brothers Inc to introduce a Total Rate-of-Return Index for these securities in March 1979. This Index allows investors to compare the performance of mortgage pass-throughs with alternative fixed income investments, and the performance of their pass-through portfolios with the "market average" return.

The Index covers periods beginning with January 1, 1972 for GNMA pass-throughs, January 1, 1977 for FHLMC PCs, January 1, 1978 for conventional pass-throughs,[1] July 1, 1979 for FHA-insured project mortgage pools, and January 1, 1982 for FNMA Mortgage-Backed Securities.

---

[*] The authors would like to express their appreciation to Matthew Kunka for his invaluable assistance in preparing this chapter.

[1] Conventional mortgage pools originated by "private sector" institutions without a government or agency guarantee.

In previous studies,[2] we analyzed the rate-of-return results through June 1980 and June 1981. The period from mid-1981 through 1984 has been one of extraordinary change for the secondary mortgage market:

- The cumulative amount of mortgage pass-through securities issued expanded from $143 billion to $354 billion. Much of this explosive growth resulted from portfolio restructuring at savings and loan associations, following regulatory accounting changes in the industry and the introduction of mortgage "swap" programs by FHLMC and FNMA.
- New types of pass-through securities such as FHLMC Guarantor PCs, FNMA Mortgage-Backed Securities, and intermediate 15-year mortgage pass-throughs were introduced.
- For the first time, massive refinancing of high-coupon mortgages took place and these issues became utilized as short-term investments.
- Deregulation of liabilities created large deposit inflows at thrifts and they returned as buyers of mortgage investments.
- Adjustable-rate mortgages (ARMs) emerged to dominate the primary mortgage market.
- Collateralized mortgage obligations (CMOs) were developed to more efficiently make use of mortgage cash flows.
- The previous three developments combined to lower mortgage origination costs and promoted the strong housing market in 1983–84.
- Rate ceilings on FHA-insured mortgages were removed.
- The yield spreads between mortgage and bond investments underwent wide swings during this period reaching record wide levels in October 1981 as well as record narrow levels in May 1984.

The purpose of this chapter is to extend the rate-of-return results previously discussed through the end of 1984, and to

[2] Michael Waldman and Steven P. Baum, "The Historical Performance of Mortgage Securities: 1972–1981," Chapter 19 in Frank J. Fabozzi and Irvins M. Pollack (Editors), *The Handbook of Fixed Income Securities* (Dow Jones-Irwin, Homewood, IL).

analyze these results for the various market cycles during the 1972–84 period. Comparisons will be made between the Mortgage Index and the Salomon Brothers High-Grade Corporate Bond Index as well as long and ten-year Treasury securities. Finally, some of the relative performance differences within the mortgage pass-through market will be discussed. Some of the key results from this study are as follows:

- Mortgage pass-through investments outperformed high-grade corporate bonds by 43.4 percent from January 1972 to January 1985.
- Mortgage pass-throughs outperformed long Treasuries by 70.3 percent from September 1974 to January 1985.
- Mortgage pass-throughs outperformed ten-year Treasuries by 24.1 percent from January 1977 to January 1985.

The return advantage of the mortgage investments resulted from their higher yield and their shorter maturity (versus corporates and long Treasuries) during a period of generally rising rates:

- Within the market, high-coupon mortgage securities trailed lower-coupon issues during market rallies, as the threat of homeowner refinancing limited their price gains, but outperformed them during market declines. This performance contrast became magnified when large-scale refinancing actually occurred in 1983.
- Since 1981, the position of discount FHLMC PCs improved relative to discount GNMAs owing to an increase in the FHLMC investor base and a resumption of faster prepayments.
- FNMA securities improved relative to FHLMC securities as the FNMA MBS program gained acceptance.
- FHA project pools outperformed or matched long Treasuries in seven of eight market cycles owing to a higher yield and a mostly narrowing yield spread.
- GNMA–GPMs trailed single-family GNMAs in total return during the early stages of the GPM market, but have outper-

formed them since 1981 owing to an improved relative market position.

THE MORTGAGE
PASS-THROUGH INDEX

The total return of the Mortgage Index is made up of three components: principal return, interest return, and reinvestment return. Principal return is divided into two parts, a return due to price move and a return resulting from the capture of discount (or premium) from principal paydown, which includes normal amortization and prepayments. Since prepayments on mortgages are statistically uncertain, Salomon Brothers maintains a database of monthly paydowns on all mortgage pass-throughs. Thus, the paydown return over any holding period reflects the actual principal payments on all pools covered by the Index. Reinvestment is "back into the market"; that is, each month's payment of principal and interest is reinvested in the pass-through market in amounts weighed by the overall composition of the market that month.

The composition of the Index is shown in Exhibit 1. The Index currently covers about 93,000 pools, representing approximately $312 billion in issued amount. This encompasses about 86 percent of the total of all outstanding mortgage pass-through pools—the difference arises in large part because the Index does not cover "odd coupon" pass-throughs for which there are no regularly available price quotes, nonsingle-family pass-throughs other than FHA-insured project mortgage pools, 15-year intermediate mortgages, adjustable-rate mortgages, or "private sector" pass-throughs for which paydown factors and prices are not readily available.

The Index covers GNMAs from the beginning of calendar year 1972. Since paydown figures for GNMAs were not available until March 1972, it was assumed that the paydowns for January and February of that year were at the same rate as in March. With this exception, the Mortgage Index is based entirely on historical paydowns, prices, and market composi-

EXHIBIT 1
Composition of Salomon Brothers Inc Mortgage Pass-Through Index
(Amount Issued, Dollars in Billions)

January 1	GNMA	FHLMC	Conven-tional	FHA Projects	FNMA	Total
1972	$ 2.4					$ 2.4
1973	3.8					3.8
1974	5.8					5.8
1975	9.1					9.1
1976	16.7					16.7
1977	27.2	$ 0.6				27.8
1978	46.6	5.5	$0.2			52.3
1979	59.6	11.1	0.8			71.5
1980	69.3	15.0	1.2	$0.2		85.7
1981	98.8	17.2	1.4	0.4		117.8
1982	115.3	19.5	1.4	0.9	$ 0.5	137.6
1983	131.5	44.6	1.4	1.5	11.1	190.1
1984	173.6	63.7	1.4	2.1	24.3	265.1
1985	195.0	79.6	1.4	2.1	33.8	311.9

EXHIBIT 2
Annual Total Returns

Year	GNMA	FHLMC	Conven-tional	FHA Projects	FNMA	Mortgage Index
1972	6.1%					6.1%
1973	2.6					2.6
1974	3.9					3.9
1975	10.4					10.4
1976	16.3					16.3
1977	1.5	2.9%				1.6
1978	2.2	4.0	1.9%			2.4
1979	0.2	0.1	0.2			0.1
1980	0.4	0.6	0.0	−1.1%		0.5
1981	1.5	−1.0	0.2	−0.4		1.2
1982	40.1	46.4	41.6	49.0	45.6%	41.4
1983	10.0	12.6	13.9	4.9	13.3	10.9
1984	15.2	17.1	19.9	17.6	16.5	15.8

tions. The yearly total returns for the five major mortgage security categories are summarized in Exhibit 2.

ANALYSIS OF THE RESULTS

A natural starting point for comparisons with the Mortgage Index is the Salomon Brothers High-Grade Corporate Bond Index, an index similar to the Mortgage Index, covering long-term AAA and AA utility and industrial bonds. For the period from January 1972 to January 1985, the Mortgage Index shows a net advantage in total return of 43.4 percent over the High-Grade Corporate Bond Index (See Exhibits 3 and 4). Almost all of this advantage was accrued during market decline periods (1973–74, 1978–81, and 1983). On the other hand, the Bond Index significantly outperformed the Mortgage Index during market rallies (1975–76 and 1982). For 1984, both the Mortgage Index and Bond Index performed similarly, with the Bond Index slightly ahead by 0.6 percent.

EXHIBIT 3
Historical Returns over Calendar Years:
High-Grade Corporate Bonds versus Mortgage Securities

	High-Grade Corporate Bond Index	Mortgage Pass-through Index	Advantage of Mortgage Index
1972	7.3%	6.1%	−1.2%
1973	1.1	2.6	1.5
1974	−3.0	3.9	6.9
1975	14.6	10.4	−4.2
1976	18.6	16.3	−2.3
1977	1.7	1.6	−0.1
1978	−0.1	2.4	2.5
1979	−4.2	0.1	4.3
1980	−2.6	0.5	3.1
1981	−1.0	1.2	2.2
1982	43.7	41.4	−2.3
1983	4.7	10.9	6.2
1984	16.4	15.8	−0.6
13.0-Year Period	135.3%	178.7%	43.4%

EXHIBIT 4
Rate-of-Return by Calendar Year

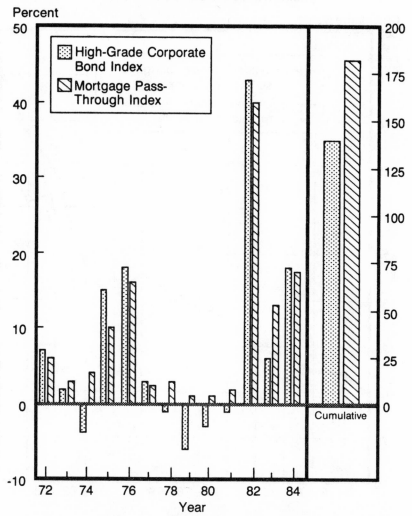

An interesting sidelight to these statistics is that in contrast with the Corporate Bond Index, which produced negative rates-of-return for five of the 13 years shown, the Mortgage Index provided at least a slim positive return in every calendar year from 1972 to 1984.

That the Mortgage Index should enjoy an overall advan-

EXHIBIT 5
Comparative Rate-of-Return Indexes

Cumulative Value

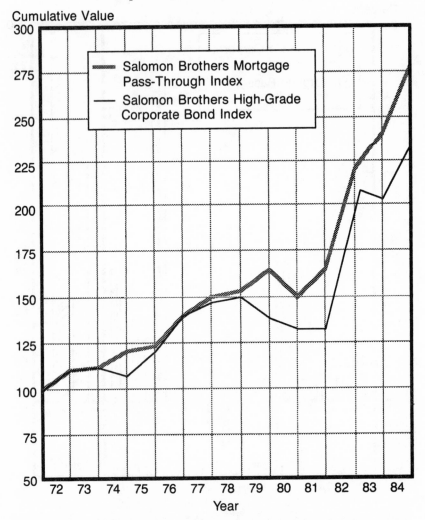

tage during this period is not surprising; the Bond Index represents an average maturity of approximately 23 years, while
as a general rule, mortgages are intermediate investments—
most mortgage pass-throughs are traded to a 12-year prepaid
life. Thus, one would expect the shorter Mortgage Index to
do better during the significant upward trend in interest rates
of the past thirteen years. Exhibit 5 shows the cumulative

EXHIBIT 6
Historical Returns over Market Cycles

Period Ending First of Month	Market Cycle	Months in Cycle	Total Return			
			Corporate Bond Index	Long Treasuries	Ten-Year Treasuries	Mortage Index
Jan 72						
Sep 74	decline	32	−5.4%			−0.1%
Mar 75	rally	6	19.4	14.2%		18.8
Oct 75	decline	7	−2.3	−3.2		−2.6
Jan 77	rally	15	29.6	26.6		25.5
Apr 80	decline	39	−15.8	−18.5	−8.9%	−6.5
Jul 80	rally	3	25.1	24.8	19.0	22.1
Oct 81	decline	15	−21.1	−22.3	−14.8	−19.2
Dec 81	rally	2	19.9	18.3	15.8	21.6
Jul 82	decline	7	−0.0	1.7	2.2	2.7
May 83	rally	10	48.5	41.9	37.2	39.7
Jun 84	decline	13	−10.9	−12.2	−7.8	−2.1
Jan 85	rally	7	24.8	25.6	21.5	21.8
Cumulative Results						
Jan 72–Jan 85			135.3%	108.6%		178.7%
Sep 74–Jan 85			148.7		68.0%	178.9
			64.4	49.0		92.1

value of the two Indexes (January 1, 1972 = 100). One can clearly see the Mortgage Index gaining its advantage during the market declines that occurred during 1973–74, 1975, 1977–80, 1980–81, and finally 1983–84. The market rallies subsequent to each of these declines were able to partially offset, but not reverse, these advantages.

The performance characteristics of mortgage pass-throughs relative to other fixed-income investments become more apparent when one breaks the period under consideration into market cycles. Exhibit 6 gives the rates-of-return for long Treasury and ten-year Treasury securities, as well as for the Mortgage and Corporate Bond Indexes, for 12 market cycles.[3] Each phase represents a period from a peak or trough in interest rates to the subsequent extreme point.

Comparison Versus Treasury Market

Let us focus now on the comparison between mortgage pass-throughs and long Treasury securities (see Exhibits 7, 8, and 9). Over the 10.3-year period from September 1974 to January 1985, the mortgage pass-throughs provided a substantial net 70.3 percent greater total return. Again, the mortgage securities were ahead in all the market decline cycles, as would be expected given their shorter average maturity. However, the pass-throughs also outperformed the long Treasuries in the 1974–75 rally by a considerable 4.6 percent and during the fall 1981 rally by 3.3 percent. How is this explained?

The answer is that there are two key factors that influence the relative performance of these securities other than their maturity differences. First, mortgage pass-throughs enjoyed a yield advantage over long Treasuries throughout this period on the basis of the monthly-compounded quoted yield, which assumes a 30-year maturity and a 12-year prepaid life. By

---

[3] Long Treasuries are analyzed beginning with the rally period starting in September 1974, shortly after the issuance of the Treasury 8½s of May 15, 1999. The analysis of Ten-year Treasuries starts with the cycle beginning in January 1977, about half a year after the 7⅞ percent notes of May 15, 1986, were issued.

EXHIBIT 7
Historical Returns and Spreads over Market Cycles: Long Treasuries versus Mortgage Securities

Period Ending First of Month	Market Cycle	Months in Cycle	Total Return			Yield Spread Relationship			
			Long Treasuries	Mortgage Index	Advantage of Mortgage Index	Long Treasuries Yield	Current Coupon GNMAs	Current Coupon GNMAs Yield[a]	Basis-Point Spread off Long Treasuries
Sep 74						8.70%	9.0%	10.14%	144bp
Mar 75	rally	6	14.2%	18.8%	4.6%	7.83	8.0	8.34	51
Oct 75	decline	7	-3.2	-2.6	0.6	8.55	8.5	9.41	86
Jan 77	rally	15	26.6	25.5	-1.1	7.30	7.5	7.53	23
Apr 80	decline	39	18.5	-6.5	12.0	12.27	12.5	14.26	199
Jul 80	rally	3	24.8	22.1	-2.7	9.94	11.0	11.55	161
Oct 81	decline	15	-22.3	-19.2	3.1	15.20	17.0	18.53	333
Dec 81	rally	2	18.3	21.6	3.3	13.03	15.0	15.19	216
Jul 82	decline	7	1.7	2.7	1.0	13.84	15.0	16.38	254
May 83	rally	10	41.9	39.7	-2.2	10.50	11.5	11.85	135
Jun 84	decline	13	-12.2	-2.1	10.1	13.71	13.5	14.80	109
Jan 85	rally	7	25.6	21.8	-3.8	11.58	12.0	12.58	100
10.3-Year Period			108.6%	178.9%	70.3%				

[a] Bond equivalent yield to 12-year prepaid life.

EXHIBIT 8
Historical Returns over Market Cycles: Long Treasuries versus
Mortgage Securities

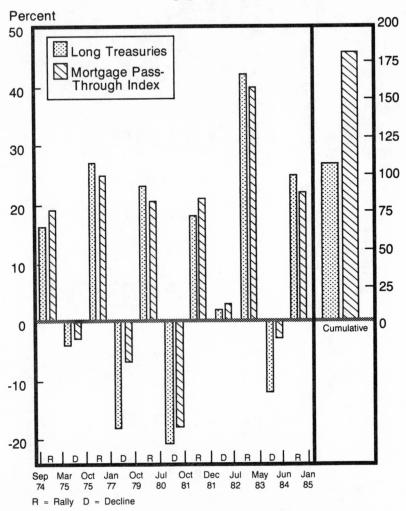

Percent

Long Treasuries

Mortgage Pass-
Through Index

| R | D | R | D | R | D | R | D | R | D | R |

| Sep | Mar | Oct | Jan | Oct | Jul | Oct | Dec | Jul | May | Jun | Jan |
| 74 | 75 | 75 | 77 | 79 | 80 | 81 | 81 | 82 | 83 | 84 | 85 |

R = Rally   D = Decline

stating the quoted yield on a semiannually compounded basis,
this advantage is even greater.[4] Furthermore, the actual prepayments on mortgage securities were often faster than those

───────────

[4] All the yields for mortgage securities shown in the figures, such as
those for current coupon GNMAs in Exhibits 7 and 9, will be bond equivalent
quoted yields.

EXHIBIT 9
**Historical Yield Levels: Long Treasuries versus
Current Coupon GNMAs**

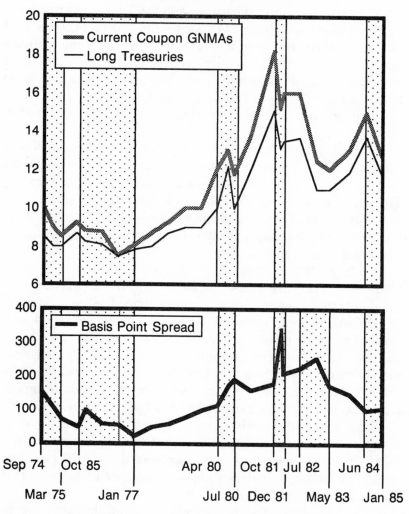

Note: Shaded areas indicate market rally periods.

needed to produce the quoted yield, thereby widening the yield advantage for pass-throughs trading at a discount.

Second, the changing relationship of the yield spread between these two instruments greatly influenced the return of pass-throughs vis-à-vis long Treasuries. This largely accounted for the surprisingly strong showing of the Mortgage Index during the September 1974–March 1975 rally. For this period, the yield spreads between pass-throughs, as represented by GNMA current coupon securities, and the Treasuries narrowed by 93 basis points (from 144 basis points to 51 basis points). This narrowing combined with the pass-throughs' yield advantage more than overcame the greater price volatility of the longer Treasuries in the rally, and allowed the Mortgage Index to outperform the long Treasuries by 4.6 percent.

We briefly discuss below each of the subsequent market cycles.

The long bear market from January 1977 through March 1980, with long Treasury rates rising almost 500 basis points, saw the more defensive mortgage instruments outperform long Treasuries by a cumulative 12.0 percent. For the dramatic market rally in the second quarter of 1980—long Treasury rates fell more than 200 basis points—long Treasuries provided 2.7 percent greater returns.

In July 1980, the market resumed its fall and in October 1981, long Treasury rates reached their highest levels ever at about 15¼ percent. At the same time, the yield spreads of GNMAs to long Treasuries widened to an unprecedented level of more than 300 basis points. Contributing factors were: an inverted yield curve expanded the spreads of all intermediate investments to long Treasuries; high interest rates and the resulting disintermediation removed thrift institutions as purchasers of mortgage securities; mortgage prepayment rates declined to an extremely slow 1 percent pace in a severely depressed housing market, reducing the attractiveness of discount mortgage securities; a fear existed that credit problems might lead to large-scale selling of mortgages from the portfolios of failed institutions.

This widening in yield spreads provided the basis for the Mortgage Index to outperform long Treasuries by 3.3 percent in the fall 1981 rally. The yield spread of GNMAs to long Treasuries narrowed by 117 basis points as the Treasury yield curve flattened and lower rates provided a more favorable environment for prepayments. This process repeated in several ways the developments that took place during the September 1974–March 1975 and spring 1980 market rallies.

For the December 1981–June 1982 period, long Treasury rates rose moderately by 81 basis points and mortgages outperformed long Treasuries by 1.0 percent. Market rates then began to decline in July 1982 and rallied dramatically in August–September. By May 1983, long Treasury rates fell to a cyclical low of near 10¼ percent. For this ten-month period, returns of fixed income investments exploded, reaching levels of 40 percent or more. While the long Treasury return exceeded (by 2.2 percent) that of the Mortgage Index overall, the yield spreads of mortgages to Treasuries narrowed dramatically and many discount mortgage issues outperformed long Treasury bonds.

From May 1983 to June 1984, long Treasury rates rose more than 200 basis points. However, unlike previous market declines, spreads between mortgage securities and long Treasuries tightened considerably. This can be explained by a number of developments that occurred in the housing and mortgage markets. First, the introduction of collateralized mortgage obligations (CMOs) in June 1983 created both a demand for mortgage securities and a direct arbitrage link between mortgage yields and Treasury yields. Second, the deregulation of deposit accounts led to large savings inflows at savings institutions and thrifts reentered the market as purchasers of mortgage securities. Third, adjustable-rate mortgages (ARMs) with low initial rates were aggressively marketed by lenders and became the primary vehicle for housing finance. With ARMs replacing fixed-rate mortgages, the supply of new fixed-rate product was greatly reduced.

Despite the general rise in market interest rates, the average cost of financing a home purchase actually trended downward, because of the tighter spreads between fixed-rate mortgages and Treasuries and the prevalence of low initial rate ARMs. This maintained affordability in the housing market and fostered strong housing activity. As a consequence, mortgage prepayment rates rose, further enhancing the value of discount mortgage securities.

For this period, the Mortgage Index outperformed long Treasuries by a sizable 10.1 percent, because of the shorter maturity of mortgages under rising interest rates and the tightening of spreads.

Some of this advantage was relinquished when the market rallied during the period since June 1984, and—counter to the traditional pattern—yield spreads widened. For the latest seven-month period, long Treasuries returned 25.6 percent versus 21.8 percent for the Mortgage Index.

Comparison versus Ten-Year Treasuries

Turning our attention to the ten-year Treasuries, we see that for the market decline from January 1977 through April 1980, the Mortgage Index had a net return advantage of 2.4 percent (see Exhibits 10, 11, and 12). The sizable yield advantage of the mortgage securities overcame the widening of spreads between the mortgage investments and ten-year Treasuries and provided the pass-throughs with a higher total return. The April–July 1980 rally saw the mortgages maintain their return advantage over the ten-year Treasuries, 22.1 percent to 19.0 percent.

In the July 1980–October 1981 decline, widening yield spreads resulted in a return for Treasuries (−14.8 percent) that was 4.4 percent higher than that of the Mortgage Index (−19.2 percent). The spread between the GNMA current coupon and the ten-year Treasuries expanded from 157 to 277 basis points during this period. This was the only market cycle in which ten-year Treasuries outperformed the Mortgage Index.

Mortgage security yields improved relative to ten-year Treasuries during the October–December 1981 rally—the GNMA current coupon-to-ten-year Treasury yield spread narrowed from 277 basis points to 192 basis points. This improvement and the mortgage pass-throughs' higher yield combined to produce a 5.8 percent greater return for the Mortgage Index.

The pass-throughs maintained a return advantage through the December 1981–July 1982 and July 1982–May 1983 cycles, by 0.5 percent and 2.5 percent, respectively. During the subse-

EXHIBIT 10
Historical Returns and Spreads over Market Cycles:
Ten-Year Treasuries versus Mortgage Securities

Period Ending First of Month	Market Cycle	Months in Cycle	Total Return			Yield Spread Relationship			
			Ten-Year Treasuries	Mortgage Index	Advantage of Mortgage Index	Ten-Year Treasuries Yield	Current Coupon GNMAs	Current Coupon GNMAs Yield[a]	Basis-Point Spread off Ten-Year Treasuries
Jan 77						6.79%	7.5%	7.53%	74bp
Apr 80	decline	39	−8.9%	−6.5%	2.4%	12.60	12.5	14.26	166
Jul 80	rally	3	19.0	22.1	3.1	9.98	11.0	11.55	157
Oct 81	decline	15	−14.8	−19.2	−4.4	15.76	17.0	18.53	277
Dec 81	rally	2	15.8	21.6	5.8	13.27	15.0	15.19	192
Jul 82	decline	7	2.2	2.7	0.5	14.32	15.0	16.38	206
May 83	rally	10	37.2	39.7	2.5	10.18	11.5	11.85	167
Jun 84	decline	13	−7.8	−2.1	5.7	13.78	13.5	14.80	102
Jan 85	rally	7	21.5	21.8	0.3	11.45	12.0	12.58	113
8.0-Year Period			68.0%	92.1%	24.1%				

[a] Bond equivalent yield to 12-year prepaid life.

EXHIBIT 11
Historical Returns over Market Cycles: Ten-Year Treasuries versus Mortgage Securities

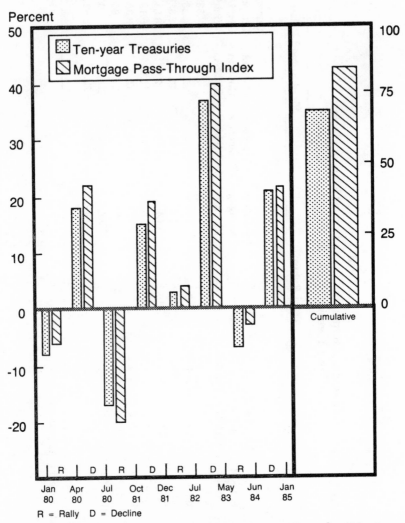

R = Rally   D = Decline

quent market decline of May 1983–June 1984, the Mortgage Index outpaced the ten-year Treasuries by a sizable 5.8 percent. Much of this return advantage was a result of spreads between pass-throughs and ten-year Treasuries sharply tightening by 65 basis points.

For the most recent seven-month period since June 1984,

EXHIBIT 12
Historical Yield Levels: Ten-Year Treasuries versus Current
Coupon GNMAs

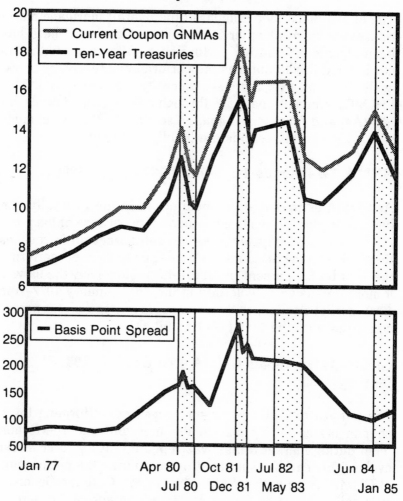

Note: Shaded areas indicate market rally periods.

mortgage investments returned 21.8 percent versus 21.5 percent
for ten-year Treasuries. Overall, the Mortgage Index provided
a 24.1 percent cumulative return advantage for the eight-year
period from January 1977 to January 1985, with a return of
92.1 percent versus 68.0 percent for the ten-year Treasuries.

PERFORMANCE WITHIN THE MORTGAGE SECURITIES MARKET

The above discussion compared the overall mortgage market returns to those of other investments. However, there have been significant relative performance differences within the market. Exhibit 13 outlines the performance record by market cycle for the five mortgage security categories (GNMAs, FHLMCs, conventional pass-throughs, FHA project pools, and FNMAs) and for selected coupon sectors. Particular comparisons over various periods are highlighted below.

GNMA 7½s versus 9s: January 1976–April 1980

As GNMA 9s traded at premium prices in the 1976 rally, they became less attractive to many investors because of the potential losses on prepayments. As a result, prices on 9s rose less than those on the discount GNMAs and the 9s underperformed the 7½s by 3.4 percent in total return. However, the 9s were a more defensive vehicle during the next January 1977–April 1980 market decline, with a return advantage of 1.0 percent compared with the 7½s (see Exhibit 14).

GNMA 11½s versus GNMA 15s: October 1981– January 1985

The pattern of high-coupon mortgages outperforming lower-coupon issues during market declines and underperforming them during market rallies was repeated during later market cycles. This can be illustrated by comparing the performance of GNMA 11½s with GNMA 15s. For the October–December 1981 rally, the 11½s had a return advantage of 2.6 percent, and for the December 1981–July 1982 decline, the 15s had a return advantage of 1.4 percent (see Exhibit 15).

During the next two market cycles, there were enormous swings in the relative total returns of these two issues. From July 1982 to May 1983, market rates fell 400 basis points and GNMA 11½s returned an impressive 39.7 percent. In this envi-

EXHIBIT 13
Historical Returns for Selected Issues

Issue	Jan 72 –Sept 74 Decline	Sep 74 –Mar 75 Rally	Mar 75 –Oct 75 Decline	Oct 75 –Jan 77 Rally	Jan 77 –Apr 80 Decline	Apr 80 –Jul 80 Rally	Jul 80 –Oct 81 Decline	Oct 81 –Dec 81 Rally	Dec 81 –Jul 82 Decline	Jul 82 –May 83 Rally	May 83 –Jun 84 Decline	Jun 84 –Jan 85 Rally
High-Grade												
Corporate Bonds	-5.4%	19.4%	-2.3%	29.6%	-15.8%	25.1%	-21.1%	19.9%	0.0%	48.5%	-10.9%	24.8%
Long Treasuries		14.2	-3.2	26.6	-18.5	24.8	-22.3	18.3	1.7	41.9	-12.2	25.6
Ten-Year Treasuries					-8.9	19.0	-14.8	15.8	2.2	37.2	-7.8	21.5
Mortgage Index	-0.1	18.8	-2.6	25.5	-6.5	22.1	-19.2	21.6	2.7	39.7	-2.1	21.8
GNMA	-0.1	18.8	-2.6	25.5	-6.8	22.3	-19.0	21.5	2.5	38.5	-3.2	22.1
FHLMC					-2.9	20.7	-20.4	22.4	3.9	42.5	0.1	21.7
FNMA										44.2	1.0	20.5
Conventional						23.2	-20.5	21.8	2.6	46.1	0.5	21.4
Discount												
FHA Project	0.7	18.3	-2.5	25.3	-6.6	24.1	-21.8	23.4	3.2	48.0	-9.6	25.6
GNMA 8						23.7	-20.9	20.5	2.5	41.7	-7.4	24.2
FHLMC 8					-3.8	22.3	-23.1	24.0	3.2	45.7	-0.8	23.0
FNMA 8½										46.0	-0.5	21.9
GNMA 9			-0.2	21.5	-7.1	21.9	-19.6	21.6	2.9	42.0	-7.4	24.5
GNMA-GPM 9½						24.0	-21.1	21.4	4.2	45.4	-7.0	23.9
Intermediate-Coupon												
GNMA 11½						19.5	-15.5	22.6	1.7	39.7	-2.7	22.1
FHLMC 12						16.3	-15.9	21.3	4.7	41.5	-0.4	21.6
GNMA 13								22.0	1.6	35.8	1.3	19.4
High-Coupon												
GNMA 15								20.0	3.1	26.3	7.9	15.6
FHLMC 15½								17.4	6.8	22.0	12.9	13.4
FHLMC 16¼								16.7	6.1	17.7	14.9	13.2

EXHIBIT 14
GNMA 7½s versus GNMA 9s: January 1976–April 1980

Period Ending First of Month	Market Cycle	Months in Cycle	Total Return			Yield Spread Relationship		
			GNMA 7½s	GNMA 9s	Advantage of 7½s	GNMA 7½s Yield[a]	GNMA 9s Yield[a]	Basis Point Spread
Jan 76			17.9%	14.5%	3.4%	8.66%	8.73%	7bp
Jan 77	rally	12	−8.1	−7.1	−1.0	7.52	7.99	47
Apr 80	decline	39				13.40	13.78	38
4.3-Year Period			8.3%	6.4%	1.9%			

[a] Bond equivalent yield to 12-year prepaid life.

EXHIBIT 15
GNMA 11½s versus GNMA 15s: October 1981–January 1985

Period Ending First of Month	Market Cycle	Months in Cycle	Total Return			Yield Spread Relationship		
			GNMA 11½s	GNMA 15s	Advantage of 11½s	GNMA 11½s Yield[a]	GNMA 15s Yield[a]	Basis Point Spread
Oct 81	rally	2	22.6%	20.0%	2.6%	18.04%	18.33%	29bp
Dec 81	decline	7	1.7	3.1	−1.4	14.62	15.19	57
Jul 82	rally	10	39.7	26.3	13.4	15.92	16.38	46
May 83	decline	13	−2.7	7.9	−10.6	11.85	14.00	215
Jun 84	rally	7	22.1	15.6	6.5	14.68	15.09	41
Jan 85						12.51	13.84	133
3.3-Year Period			106.9%	94.9%	12.0%			

[a] Bond equivalent yield to 12-year prepaid life.

ronment, many homeowners refinanced their high-rate mortgages—prepayment rates on GNMA 15s rose to a 37 percent
annual rate in early 1983—and the price gains of the 15s stalled
out in the rally. For the period, GNMA 15s returned only 26.3
percent—13.4 percent less than for the 11½s.

On the other hand, for the May 1983–June 1984 market
decline, the 15s—now used as a short-term investment alternative—maintained their price level to a much greater extent
than lower-coupon issues. The 15s provided a positive 7.9 percent return compared with a negative 2.7 percent for the
11½s—an advantage of 10.6 percent.

GNMA 8s versus FHLMC 8s: January 1977–January 1985

A dealer group was established to distribute and trade FHLMC
PCs in January 1977. FHLMC PCs are primarily backed by
conventional loans which often exhibit faster prepayment
rates than the FHA/VA mortgages underlying GNMA pools.
In the initial stages of trading the yield spread between FHLMC
8s and GNMA 8s was a positive 15–30 basis points. As investors recognized the value of the faster FHLMC paydowns,
prices were bid up and the FHLMC discounts started trading
through the GNMAs. Also contributing to the strong performance of FHLMCs during this period was an expansion in
the FHLMC investor base as nontraditional investors became
familiar with the security. For the January 1977–April 1980
market cycle, FHLMC 8s provided a return advantage of 2.8
percent relative to GNMA 8s (see Exhibits 16, 17, and 18).

The yield spread between FHLMCs and GNMAs then
turned positive and widened during the July 1980–October 1981
market decline, peaking at close to 100 basis points when
the market hit bottom in October 1981. This resulted from
FHLMC prepayment rates drastically slowing to the 1 percent
level in the severely depressed housing market and from investors' flight to quality as rates rose to historically high levels.
From April 1980 to October 1981, GNMA 8s outperformed
FHLMC 8s by a cumulative 3.8 percent.

EXHIBIT 16
GNMA 8s versus FHLMC 8s: January 1977–January 1985

Period Ending First of Month	Market Cycle	Months in Cycle	Total Return			Yield Spread Relationship		
			GNMA 8s	FHLMC 8s	Advantage of FHLMCs	GNMA 8s Yield[a]	FHLMC 8s Yield[a]	Basis Point Spread
Jan 77						7.71%	8.05%	34bp
Apr 80	decline	39	−6.6%	−3.8%	2.8%	13.39	13.39	0
Jul 80	rally	3	23.7	22.3	1.4	10.45	10.67	22
Oct 81	decline	15	−20.9	−23.1	2.2	17.11	18.04	93
Dec 81	rally	2	20.5	24.0	3.5	14.21	14.63	42
Jul 82	decline	7	2.5	3.2	0.7	15.16	15.58	42
May 83	rally	10	41.7	45.7	4.0	11.01	11.11	10
Jun 84	decline	13	−7.4	−0.8	6.6	14.40	13.48	−92
Jan 85	rally	7	24.2	23.0	−1.2	12.05	11.44	−61
8.0-Year Period			84.0%	105.8%	21.8%			

[a] Bond equivalent yield to 12-year prepaid life.

225

EXHIBIT 17
Historical Yield Levels: GNMA 8s versus FHLMC 8s

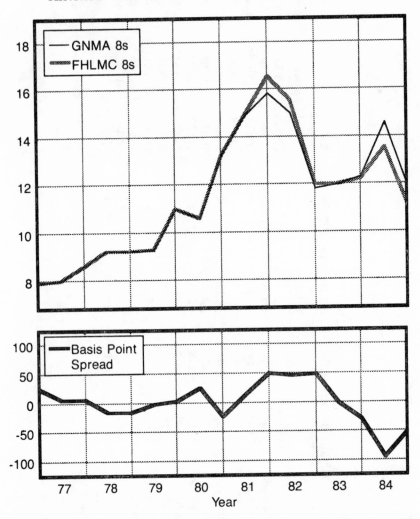

Beginning with the October–December 1981 rally, the yield spread narrowed once again. The strong 1983 housing market brought an increase in mortgage prepayment rates with FHLMC prepayments faster than those of GNMAs. In addition, legislative/judicial and FHLMC policy actions made mortgage due-on-sale clauses generally enforceable for the conventional

EXHIBIT 18
Historical Prepayment Rates: GNMA 8s versus FHLMC 8s

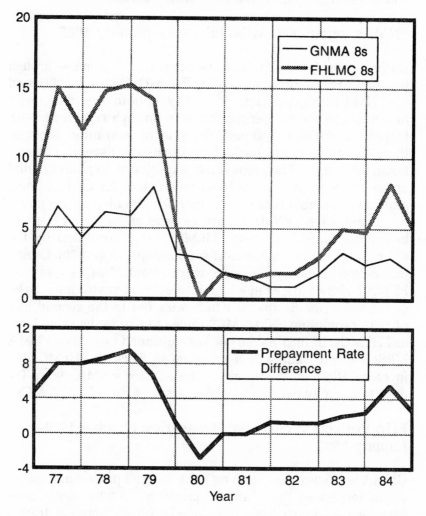

loans backing FHLMC pools while FHA/VA mortgages remained assumable.

The relative position of discount FHLMCs improved further in 1984, with the yield spread between FHLMC 8s and GNMA 8s turning strongly negative at 60–90 basis points. From October 1981 to January 1985, FHLMC 8s outperformed GNMA

8s by a staggering 26.2 percent, owing to faster prepayments and the realignment of relative market levels.

FNMAs versus FHLMCs: July 1982–January 1985

During the second half of 1981, two new mortgage pass-through programs were introduced—the FHLMC Guarantor PC and the FNMA Mortgage-Backed Security. In both programs, pools of mortgages are exchanged for pass-through securities, with FHLMC and FNMA playing the role of guarantor. Most of the pass-throughs are backed by seasoned discount conventional mortgages. The prepayment experience on pools created under these programs has been faster than for GNMA pools and, until the most recent year, than for FHLMC regular pools.

In early 1982, FNMA securities were priced about ⅛-point below comparable coupon FHLMCs (as represented by the 8½ percent coupon securities, see Exhibits 19 and 20). During this period there was some concern about FNMA's credit as FNMA suffered losses in a high interest rate environment. The credit concerns dissipated when rates fell in the second half of 1982, prompting FNMA MBS prices to rise to the same level as FHLMCs. In 1983, as the market continued to mature, FNMA MBSs started trading at a premium in price to FHLMC PCs in recognition of the value of the shorter FNMA delay (54 days to first payment for FNMAs versus 75 days for FHLMCs).

FHA Projects versus Long Treasuries: October 1979–January 1985

GNMA first started auctioning FHA-insured project mortgages originated under the "Tandem program" in 1978. Since then FHA project loans have developed into an actively traded market. The majority of these loans are 7½ percent 40-year mortgages, which trade with an 18-year prepaid life convention. In addition, most of these loans have Section 8 Housing Assistance Payments (HAP) contracts attached. These rent subsidy contracts are either for 5 or 20 years with HUD providing for partial payment of the building tenant's rent.

EXHIBIT 19
FHLMC 8½s versus FNMA 8½s: July 1982–January 1985

Period Ending First of Month	Market Cycle	Months in Cycle	Total Return			Price Spread Relationship[a]		
			FHLMC 8½s	FNMA 8½s	Advantage of FNMAs	FHLMC 8½s Price	FNMA 8½s Price	Price Spread
Jul 82						63–08	63–04	–0–04
May 83	rally	10	44.9%	46.0%	1.1%	82–24	82–24	0–00
Jun 84	decline	13	–0.3	0.5	0.8	71–16	71–28	0–12
Jan 85	rally	7	22.2	21.9	–0.3	80–24	80–28	0–04
2.5-Year Period			76.5%	78.9%	2.4%			

[a] Prices in 32nds.

EXHIBIT 20
Historical Prices: FHLMC 8½s versus FNMA 8½s

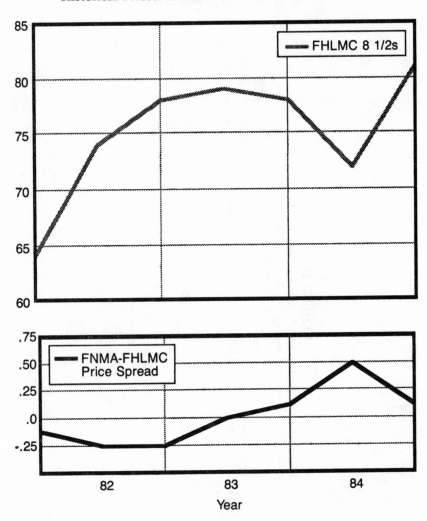

FHA projects have the distinction among standard mortgage products of having the longest maturity, and unlike other
mortgage securities, which trade relative to a ten-year Treasury benchmark, yields are typically compared with long Treasury rates. FHA projects have been used as long-bond sub-

stitutes by total return investors and for dedicated and immunized bond portfolios, which have a need for long-term, call-protected investments. Because of a higher yield and a narrowing yield spread, FHA projects have been able to outperform or match long Treasuries in all market cycles since October 1979, with the exception of the April–July 1980 rally. For the overall 5.3-year October 1979–January 1985 period, the projects provided a cumulative return advantage of 26.2 percent (see Exhibits 21 and 22).

GNMA–GPMs versus Single-Family GNMAs: October 1979–January 1985

HUD first started insuring Graduated Payment Mortgages (GPMs) in 1976. However, it vʼas not until 1979 when they became eligible for GNMA pools, that their volume became significant. To date, $16 billion of GNMA–GPMs have been issued. The majority of these mortgages have 30-year maturities, with annual payment increases of 7½ percent for the first five years and level payments thereafter. The loans have negative amortization for the first few years since the initial GPM payments are not sufficient to cover the interest due. As a result, in the absence of prepayments, a GNMA–GPM will have a slightly longer average life than a single-family GNMA of the same coupon.

GPM prepayments during their early years have been slower than for the corresponding single-family GNMAs. However, the prepayment experience suggests that the prepayment rates of GPMs tend to rise gradually to levels close to those of single-family GNMAs as they approach the end of their five-year graduation period. This trend will bear watching for the next few years as more GPM pools pass over the five-year mark.

In the early stages of the GPM market, GPMs traded 1–2 points below the price of the corresponding GNMA coupon

EXHIBIT 21
Long Treasuries versus FHA Projects: October 1979–January 1985

Period Ending First of Month	Market Cycle	Months in Cycle	Total Return			Yield Spread Relationship		
			Long Treasuries	FHA Projects	Advantage of FHA Projects	Long Treasuries Yield	FHA Projects[a]	Basis-Point Spread off Long Treasuries
Oct 79						9.23%	10.75%	152bp
Apr 80	decline	6	−19.3%	−16.4%	2.9%	12.27	14.01	174
Jul 80	rally	3	24.8	24.1	−0.7	9.94	11.38	144
Oct 81	decline	15	−22.3	−21.8	0.5	15.20	17.71	251
Dec 81	rally	2	18.3	23.4	5.1	13.03	14.71	168
Jul 82	decline	7	1.7	3.2	1.5	13.84	15.67	183
May 83	rally	10	41.9	48.0	6.1	10.50	11.33	83
Jun 84	decline	13	−12.2	−9.6	2.6	13.71	14.52	81
Jan 85	rally	7	25.6	25.6	0.0	11.58	12.20	62
5.3-Year Period			47.4%	73.6%	26.2%			

[a] Bond equivalent yield to 18-year prepaid life.

232

EXHIBIT 22
Historical Yield Levels: Long Treasuries versus FHA Projects

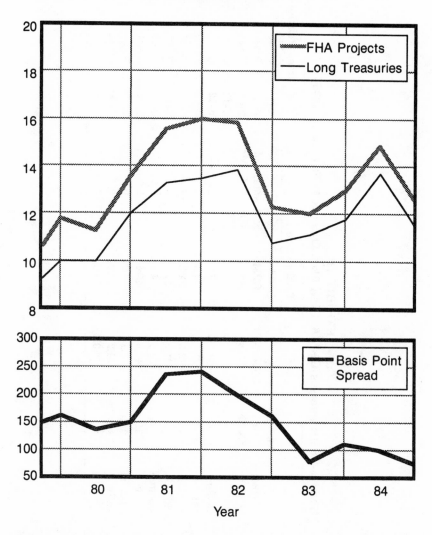

issue. However, the volume and liquidity of GNMA–GPMs were disappointing and during 1980–81, pricing spreads expanded to 3–4 points.

During this period many mortgage market participants focused on the quoted yield based on a 30-year maturity and

EXHIBIT 23
GNMA-SF 9½s versus GNMA-GPM 9½s: October 1979–January 1985

Period Ending First of Month	Market Cycle	Months in Cycle	Total Return			Price Spread Relationship[a]		
			GNMA-SF 9½s	GNMA-GPM 9½s	Advantage of GMNA-GPMs	SF 9½s Price	GPM 9½s Price	Price Spread
Oct 79						92–12	91–20	–0–24
Apr 80	decline	6	–11.9%	–15.5%	–3.6%	76–12	72–28	–3–16
Jul 80	rally	3	21.7	24.0	2.3	90–16	88–00	–2–16
Oct 81	decline	15	–18.8	–21.2	–2.3	62–00	59–00	–3–00
Dec 81	rally	2	21.2	21.4	0.2	73–12	70–00	–3–12
Jul 82	decline	7	2.8	4.2	1.4	69–12	67–08	–2–04
May 83	rally	10	42.5	45.4	2.9	89–20	88–24	–0–28
Jun 84	decline	13	–7.1	–7.0	0.1	72–28	72–12	–0–16
Jan 85	rally	7	24.2	23.9	–0.3	84–00	83–12	–0–20
5.3-Year Period			78.3%	75.2%	–3.1%			

[a] Prices in 32nds.

234

EXHIBIT 24
Historical Prices: GNMA–SF 9½s versus GNMA–GPM 9½s

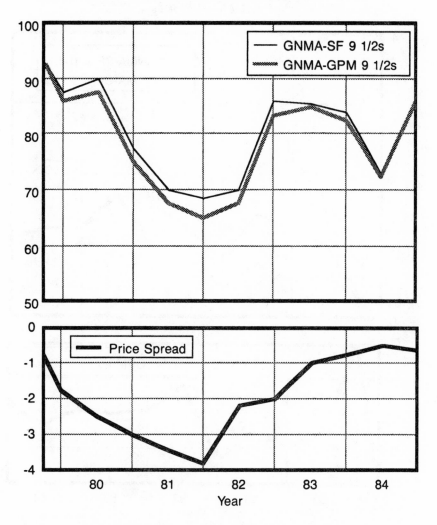

12-year prepaid life. This yield calculation assumes a 30-year maturity regardless of the seasoning of the mortgages.[5] The

---

[5] The quoted yield contains inaccuracies with respect to the assumed prepayment pattern of the loans as well as their assumed maturity. Cash flow yields based on constant prepayment rate estimates utilize a more

EXHIBIT 25
Historical Prepayment Rates: GNMA–SF 9½s versus
GNMA–GPM 9½s

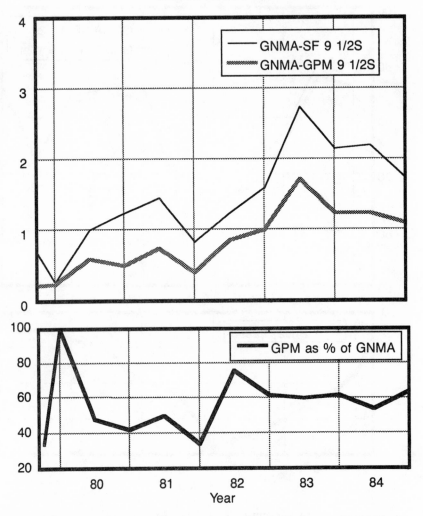

resulting distortion was a minor problem for most GNMA issues in the early 1980s. However, seasoning has a major impact

---

realistic representation of the actual cash flow stream on a mortgage pool
than a one-time balloon prepayment and have come into much wider use
in recent years.

for GNMA–GPMs because of their graduated payment structure. For example, the price of a new 30-year 9½ percent GNMA–GPM would have to be 1¾ points below the price of the comparable single-family GNMA to obtain the same 15 percent bond equivalent quoted yield. However, if both issues have three years of seasoning, the GPM would have to be priced only ½ point below the single-family GNMA.

During 1982, the market began to adjust the price relationships for the seasoning of the older GPM issues. At the same time, the GPM market developed a broader range of participants and a greater degree of liquidity. As a consequence, the price spread narrowed to approximately one point in this period. Whether the trend will continue so that GNMA–GPMs that are past their graduation periods trade at the same dollar price as single-family GNMAs remains to be seen.

GNMA–GPM 9½s thus trailed GNMA 9½s in total return during the early 1979–81 market period, owing to widening price spreads and slower prepayments. Since October 1981, they have outperformed the GNMA 9½s as a result of an improving relative market position (Exhibits 23, 24, and 25).

CONCLUSION

Overall, mortgage securities have outperformed each of the other sectors examined (high-grade corporate bond, long Treasuries, and ten-year Treasuries). The main reasons for this are the high relative yield levels of mortgage securities and their shorter average maturity.

The relative performance of mortgages in market cycles has been greatly influenced by changes in yield spreads. Tightening yield spreads enabled mortgages to outperform other fixed-income sectors during the September 1974–March 1975 and October 1981–December 1981 rallies. Tightening yield spreads also contributed to the sizable performance advantage of mortgages during the May 1983–June 1984 market decline. On the other hand, greater price volatility produced advantages for the longer securities in market rallies when yield spreads failed to narrow. This is evident in the latest June 1984 to January 1985 period.

Much of the improvement in the mortgage market from the low point in the 1981 bear market to date has been the result of structural changes. The deregulation of deposit accounts, the emergence of ARMs as a housing finance force, and the development of CMOs all helped to bring about a housing market recovery and had a direct positive impact on the demand for and supply of mortgage product. The broadened enforceability of mortgage due-on-sale clauses also enhanced the relative value of conventional mortgage-backed securities. These and other developments have created a system of housing finance that should be more resilient in future adverse markets.

There have been wide performance differences within the market. Generally, discount mortgage securities have had the greatest price movements both in market rallies and market declines. Shifts in prepayments have had an important impact on the performance of both high- and low-coupon issues. The posture of thrift institutions has played a major role in the performance of mortgage security investments with the presence or absence of thrift buying being felt most directly in the current coupon sector.

Finally, the pattern of a new security that produces return advantages as it develops market acceptance and liquidity, thereby improving its relative market position, has been repeated several times—first for the GNMA market itself, and then for FHLMC PCs, GNMA–GPMs, FHA project pools, and FNMA MBSs.

SECTION III

Analytical Tools

CHAPTER 9

The Total Return Calculation for Mortgage Pass-Throughs

H. Peter Wallace
Vice President,
Mortgage Portfolio Strategist,
Dean Witter Reynolds

Unlike conventional fixed income securities that offer level semi-annual payments and a lump sum principal payment at maturity (excluding for the sake of example callable, sinking fund, and extendables issues) mortgage-backed securities with variable monthly interest and principal payments are very difficult to analyze in terms of their risk/reward trade-offs. In this chapter, we intend to show how holding period returns can be calculated using forecasts of prepayment rates and terminal yields expected to prevail at the end of the holding period. This methodology will provide the investor with a basis to compare the relative attractiveness of mortgage-backed pass-throughs to one another and also to other fixed income vehicles under the same assumptions of interest rate change over the holding period.

MORTGAGE-BACKED VERSUS CONVENTIONAL BONDS

As with any other mortgage loan, the payment schedule creates a level payment of principal and interest montly. Although

241

the total payment of principal and interest is level, the amounts of principal and interest in the total payment vary from month to month as a function of the amortization schedule. Generally, with level-pay, fixed-rate mortgages, the amount of the monthly interest payments will decrease and the principal component will increase as the loan ages towards maturity. The reason for this is that interest is only paid on the remaining balance of the loan (which is continuously decreasing with the passage of time), leaving the difference between the payment of interest and the total payment to be applied to principal reduction each month.

The potential of principal prepayments occurring from refinancing mortgages at lower interest rates, defaults, changes in family size, relocations, and so on tends to further complicate the cash flow patterns of mortgage-backed securities.

There is obviously a sharp contrast to the relative simplicity of conventional fixed-income securities which offer a level payment of coupon interest paid periodically and the payment of a lump sum of principal on the bond's maturity date. This contrast has led many to believe that mortgage-backed securities are the most difficult fixed-income securities to analyze owing to the complexity and uncertainty of their cash flows.

One can indeed calculate holding period returns on mortgage-backed securities but it is necessary to first understand how the cash flows of mortgages are derived.

MORTGAGE CASH FLOWS

Central to all mortgage cash flows is the need to determine the remaining balance of a mortgage loan at a given point in time reflecting the loan's "normal amortization," which assumes that no prepayments have occurred. For all level-payment fixed-rate loans the remaining balance can be found by using the following formula:

(1) $\quad B_t = 1 - \dfrac{(1+I)^t - 1}{(1+I)^m - 1}$

where B_t = the remaining balance of the mortgage at month t
$\quad\quad$ I = the periodic mortgage interest rate (decimal)
$\quad\quad$ t = the months of mortgage age
$\quad\quad$ m = the months of original maturity

As an example, assume that we wish to find the remaining balance of a 30-year original maturity mortgage that has aged 10 years and bears an interest rate of 10 percent per annum (.00833333 per month):

$$B_{120} = 1 - \frac{(1 + .00833333)^{120} - 1}{(1 + .00833333)^{360} - 1} = .9093802$$

In other words, the remaining balance of $1.00 of original value is now $0.9093802 at the 120th month of mortgage life. To find the actual dollar balance remaining we need only multiply the value of B_t (in this case .9093802) and the original loan amount. This can be expressed as:

(2) $\quad D_t = MB_t$

where D_t = the remaining dollar balance at month t
$\quad\quad$ M = the original loan amount

Using our example and assuming that the original loan amount was $100,000.00:

$D_{120} = 100,000.00 \times .9093802$
$D_{120} = 90,938.02$

CALCULATING THE MONTHLY INTEREST PAYMENT

Once we have calculated the remaining dollar balance of the loan, we can then calculate the monthly interest payment to the investor for the next month (since generally all interest payments on mortgage loans are made in arrears). This is a trivial calculation but first we must determine whether or not the loan is subject to servicing fees. Servicing fees represent the payment made to an intermediary reflecting the cost of

collecting payments from the borrowers, maintaining documentation, record keeping, insurance, and so on. This fee is
applied to the interest portion of the loan payment and represents a reduction of interest to the investor. The result of this
fee is to reduce the interest rate on the mortgage loan or loan
pool. In the case of Government National Mortgage Association pass throughs, the servicing and insurance fee totals .50
percent. This means that the net interest rate on GNMAs is
one-half of one percent lower than the interest rate on the
underlying mortgage collateral of the pool. As an example, a
GNMA pool with a stated coupon rate of 12.00 percent actually
consists of 12.50 percent mortgage loans. Equations (3) and
(3a) show how monthly interest payments may be calculated
excluding and including servicing fees:

For mortgage with no servicing:

(3) $i_{t+1} = D_t I$

where i_{t+1} = Interest payments to be made in month $t + 1$

Using the previous example we can calculate the interest payment due to the investor in the 121st month.

$i_{121} = 90{,}938.02 \times .00833333$
$i_{121} = 757.82$

For mortgages with servicing:

(3a) $i_{t+1} = D_t(I - s)$

where s = periodic servicing expressed as a decimal

To follow the same example again, assume that the annual
service fee is .50 percent:

$i_{121} = 90{,}938.02 \times (.00833333 - .0041667)$
$i_{121} = 719.93$

As can be seen from equations (3) and (3a), interest payments will be different from what is expected if servicing is
included; in the above example the amount of the difference
is $37.89 and, of course, represents the fee paid to the servicer

of the underlying loans. Since most mortgage-backed securities do include some amount of servicing either stated or implied, the investor must be careful to include the amount of servicing in his calculations by increasing the interest rate on the underlying loans to reflect this fee. If this is not done, the normal amortization of the underlying mortgage loans will be overstated. As described above, the gross rate of interest must also be adjusted to derive the correct interest payments. In our example, although the mortgage interest rate is 10 percent if .50 percent servicing is included, the net rate to the investor is 9.5 percent while principal amortization takes place based on a 10 percent mortgage rate.

CALCULATING THE MONTHLY PRINCIPAL PAYMENTS

Monthly principal payments, assuming no prepayments, are also very simple calculations. Principal payments represent the normal amortization of principal to maturity at which time all remaining principal will be exhausted. The calculations reflect only the difference between the remaining dollar balance of the loan or pool between subsequent months. We can state this as:

(4) $p_{t+1} = D_t - D_{t+1}$

where p_{t+1} = the principal payment to be made in month $t + 1$

D_{t+1} = the remaining loan balance at the end of month $t + 1$

Assuming that month $t + 1$ is the 121st month in our example, and finding the remaining loan balance for the 121st month by re-working equations (1) and (2), we calculate the value of D_{t+1} to be \$90,818.26. Solving for p_{t+1} in (4):

$p_{121} = 90{,}938.02 - 90{,}818.26 = 119.76$

CALCULATING THE TOTAL
MONTHLY PAYMENT

Now that both the principal and interest portion of the 121st month's payment have been found, the total monthly payment c_t is nothing more than the sum of the principal and interest payments:

(5) $c_{t+1} = i_{t+1} + p_{t+1}$

For mortgages with no servicing:

$c_{121} = 757.82 + 119.76 = 877.58$

For mortgages with servicing:

$c_{121} = 719.93 + 119.76 = 839.69$

Now that the very basics of mortgage cash flows have been described, we can take one more step and look at the impact of prepayments on the cash flows. In order to do this we will assume that the pass-through security will experience a prepayment rate of .2 percent per month, meaning that .2 percent of principal over and above normal amortization will be prepaid.

Some adjustments must be made to our earlier procedures to reflect the prepayment experience of a given pool on its underlying cash flows. First, we must convert the monthly prepayment rate to a decimal in order to appropriately alter the cash flows. Since the monthly prepayment represents a reduction,

(6) $F = 1 - (mp/100) = .998$

where F = the adjustment to the balance
      mp = the monthly prepayment rate

the decimal equivalent is subtracted from 1. Because the convention for yield price calculations assumes that the particular pool has and will continue to prepay at this rate, we must assume that F has compounded itself over time. For instance, if we take again our 30-year original maturity, 10 percent interest rate loan aged 10 years (120 months), and solve for the remaining balance (assuming that the prepayment rate is .2 percent montly) the general formula is:

(7) $A_t = B_t F^t$

where A_t = the mortgage balance at time t assuming prepayment rate F

In our example:

$A_{120} = .9093802 \times (.998)^{120}$
$A_{120} = .715172$

From this value we can create a hypothetical original balance from which to calculate all further cash flows on the pool by dividing the actual dollar balance outstanding at the 120th month by the mortgage balance at month 120 assuming the given prepayment rate. The formula is:

(8) $M = D_t / A_t$

In our example:

$M = 100,000.00 / .715172$
$M = 139,862.52$

With the original balance calculated, the remaining dollar balances at any month can be found by the following:

(9) $D_t = M(B_t F^t)$

THE TOTAL RETURN CALCULATION

The total return of a mortgage-backed security over a holding period is the sum of the following individual returns:

1. Interest return
2. Principal return (from normal amortization and prepayments)

3.   Reinvestment return
4.   Price return

Because each component of return will vary given a number of conditions such as the age and final maturity of the
pool, the coupon rate and the amount of servicing, the prepayment rate, the reinvestment rate, and of course the prices at
the beginning and end of the holding period, investors in mortgage-backed securities should be familiar with the effects of
each of the above components of return on each security held
in their portfolios. By understanding these components of return and their effect on total return for these securities, investors may make intelligent judgements as to the investment
merits of each mortgage-backed security relative to others and
to conventional fixed income vehicles as well.

In order to perform total return calculations on mortgage-
backed securities and to examine the components of return,
the investor must supply the following information:

1.   Remaining balance of the pool at the time of purchase.
2.   Coupon rate, servicing and delay factor in payments, if
     any.
3.   Assumption of the prepayment rate.
4.   Assumption of the reinvestment rate to be applied to cash
     flows.
5.   Terminal price or yield at the end of the holding period.

Given this information and the procedures outlined above,
the cash flows from the given pool can be calculated and the
components of return derived from those cash flows. By way
of example, assume that we have a GNMA 9.5 percent coupon
pass-through with $90,938.02 balance remaining at the end of
its 120th month of mortgage term. Assume further that we
have paid a price of 85.25 for the pool and expect to sell this
pool six months later at a price of 87.00; in the meantime
we expect the pool to prepay at a monthly rate of .2 percent.
We shall also assume that cash flows will be reinvested at
a nominal annual rate of 12.00 percent, or 1.0 percent per
month. Performing the cash flow calculations as shown above,
we can create the following table of the cash flows:

Month (t)	Principal (p_t)	Interest (i_i)	Cash Flow (c_t)
120	$ 0.00	$ 0.00	0.00
121	301.39	719.93	1,021.32
122	301.54	717.54	1,019.08
123	301.70	715.15	1,016.85
124	301.86	712.76	1,014.62
125	302.03	710.37	1,012.40
126	302.20	707.98	1,010.18
Total	$1,810.72	$4,283.73	$6,094.45

Given the cash flows, the reinvestment income from the cash flows can then be calculated. This becomes a bit more complex as pass-through securities generally have some sort of delay associated with their monthly payments of principal and interest. In the case of GNMA (type I), the stated delay in payment is 45 days. This is somewhat misleading in that payments on mortgage-backed securities are generally made in arrears so that one purchasing a GNMA pool would not normally expect to receive a payment for 30 days anyway, so the effective interest-free delay is only 15 days rather than the stated 45-day delay. The interest-free delay varies from instrument ot instrument, so investors should be aware of the delay period and incorporate the effective delay into their total return calculations as described below. The following table shows how reinvestment income on the above cash flows is calculated:

Month Payment Received	Cash Payment Received	Accumulated Prior Payments	Total Payments + Reinvestment
Month 120	$0(1.005)	+ $0(1.01)	= $0
Month 121	$0(1.005)	+ $0(1.01)	= $0
Month 122	$1,021.32(1.005)	+ $0(1.01)	= $1,026.43
Month 123	$1,019.08(1.005)	+ $1,026.43(1.01)	= $2,061.60
Month 124	$1,016.85(1.005)	+ $2,061.60(1.01)	= $3,104.15
Month 125	$1,014.62(1.005)	+ $3,104.15(1.01)	= $4,154.88
Month 126	$1,012.40(1.005)	+ $4,154.88(1.01)	= $5,213.90
Month 127	$1,005.15	+ $5,213.90	= $6,219.05
Total	$6,089.42		= $6,219.05
		Less total cash flow	− $6,089.42
		Reinvestment income	= $ 129.63

Note that in month 120 no payment is received as the settlement is assumed to take place at month's end with no principal or interest assumed to be owed by the purchaser of the security. No payment is received in month 121. Although earned, it will be received on the 15th of month 122 and will earn 15 days interest in month 122 $(.01 \times 15/30 = .005)$. The payment received in month 127 is the payment attributable to month 126 and is paid after the holding period is over and therefore no reinvestment income is calculated. Note also that the payment in month 127 occurs after the end of our six-month holding period and therefore must be adjusted to reflect only the present value of that amount at the end of month 126. This is accomplished by taking the cash flow amount for month 127 and dividing by the appropriate discount factor. In our example, it is the periodic reinvestment rate multiplied by the ratio of the effective interest-free delay to the number of days in the month. For example:

$$\frac{\$1,010.18}{1 + \left(.01 \times \dfrac{15}{30}\right)} = \$1,005.15$$

As can be seen from the table, the amount of reinvestment income from this particular pool amounts to $129.63 over the six-month holding period, assuming that the cash flows can be reinvested at a nominal annual rate of 12.00 percent.

THE CALCULATION OF TOTAL RETURN

As with any other investment, the total return over a holding period is measured by the sum of all cash flows and the terminal value of the investment at the end of the holding period divided by the initial cost of the investment. Generally this can be described as:

$$(10) \quad \text{Total return} = \frac{(V_e - V_b) + C + R_k}{V_b}$$

where V_b = value of the investment at the beginning of the holding period.

V_e = value of the investment at the end of the holding period.

C = total principal and interest payments received during the holding period.

R_k = total reinvestment income received during the holding period.

In our example:

$V_b = 90,938.02 \times .8525 = 77,524.66$
$V_e = 89,127.30 \times .8700 = 77,540.75$
$C = 6,089.42$
$R_k = 129.63$

$$\text{Total return} = \frac{(77,540.75 - 77,524.66) + 6,089.42 + 129.63}{77,524.66}$$

$\text{Total return} = .0804278 = 8.043\%$

So, through some tedious calculations we have been able to calculate the total return on this security over a six-month holding period given our expectations as to terminal prices, prepayments and reinvestment rates. We may now compare the total return on this security to others in the market place or to alternative investments to determine which offer the most attractive risk/reward trade-offs.

COMPONENTS OF TOTAL RETURN

Now we can consider the components of return that make up total return by studying the individual components of the mortgage-backed security's cash flows and terminal value. This should be done in order to determine from which source the security will derive the majority of its total return.

REINVESTMENT RETURN

The return from reinvestment is quite easily calculated and is simply the amount of reinvestment income received over the holding period divided by the initial value of the investment. We can state the formula for reinvestment return, R_r, as follows:

(11) $R_r = R_k / V_b$

In our example:

$R_r = 129.63 / 77,524.66$
$R_r = .001672 = 0.167\%$

INTEREST RETURN

The return component attributable to interest payments is calculated in the same manner as that of reinvestment income with the exception that we must remember the effect of the interest-free delay and reduce the amount of the last payment in the holding period to its present value as we did when calculating the total cash flow. The interest payments must then be summed, and divided by the initial investment amount. In our example, letting R_i be the return from interest payments, and S_i be the sum of the interest payments (including the last period adjustment):

Interest
Payments

$719.93

717.54

715.15

712.76

710.37

707.98 / 1.005 = 704.46
_____
$4,280.21 total = S_i

Stating the general formula for interest return:

(12) $R_i = S_i / V_b$

Specifically in the current example:

$R_i = 4{,}280.21 / 77{,}524.66 = .05521 = 5.521\%$

PRINCIPAL PAYMENT RETURN

Since unlike conventional bonds, mortgage-backed securities amortize principal over their life, a component of total return is the amount of principal that is returned to the investor at face value (100) during the holding period. This is a result of both normal mortgage amortization and prepayments that increase the "speed" at which principal is returned to the investor. The calculations are exactly like those above for principal return, R_p, letting S_p be the sum of the principal payments:

Principal
Payments

$301.39

301.54

301.70

301.86

302.03

302.20 / 1.005 = 300.70
_____

$1,809.22 total $= S_p$

(13) $R_p = S_p / V_b$

Calculating the actual principal return:

$R_p = 1{,}809.22 / 77{,}524.66$
$R_p = .02334 = 2.334\%$

MARKET VALUE RETURN

The market value component of return is unlike that of conventional bonds owing to the amortizing nature of mortgages. At the end of the holding period there is less principal at risk to changing prices. (This is true only for fixed-rate, level-payment mortgage securities and not for graduated payment loans and some forms of adjustable-rate mortgages where negative amortization may occur.) We can define the market value return, R_{mv}, as:

$$(14) \quad R_{mv} = \frac{D_e \times P_e}{D_b \times P_b}$$

where D_b = Remaining dollar balance at the beginning of the period.

D_e = Remaining dollar balance at the end of the period.

P_b = Price (decimal) at the beginning of the period.

P_e = Price (decimal) at the end of the period.

Calculating the market value return component in our example:

$$R_{mv} = \frac{89,127.30 \times .8700}{90,938.02 \times .8525} = \frac{77,540.75}{77,524.66} = .021\%$$

As can be seen from the market value return calculation, the principal balance of the GNMA declined by an amount that was large enough to almost erase the benefits of a favorable change in price from 85.25 to 87.00 over the six-month period. In fact, the market value component of return is the smallest of the four basic components:

**Components of
Return**

Interest	5.521%
Principal payments	2.334%
Reinvestment income	0.169%
Market value	0.021%
Total*	8.045%

* Answer may not agree with that of formula (10) due to rounding.

CONCLUSION

Although calculating the components of return on pass-through securities is tedious and time consuming, most investors in mortgage-backed securities should take the effort and time to perform the analysis as the components of return are not intuitively obvious and will vary from pool to pool depending on the type of security, age, prepayment assumptions, and expectations of the future level of interest rates.

What should be clear is that each mortgage-backed security is a unique investment and there is little similarity between one mortgage-backed security and another even within the same coupon group and same maturity class. Given this uniqueness, each security must be carefully analyzed to determine its investment merits.

CHAPTER 10

Determining the Yield of a Mortgage Security

Michael Waldman
Vice President & Manager of Mortgage Research
Salomon Brothers Inc

Mark Gordon, CFA
Mortgage Research
Salomon Brothers Inc

The mortgage pass-through market emerged in the 1970s with the establishment of programs by the Government National Mortgage Association (GNMA), the Federal Home Loan Mortgage Corporation (FHLMC), and private sector institutions. The mortgage securitization process has surged in the past three years, in part aided by the introduction of mortgage "swap" programs by FHLMC and the Federal National Mortgage Association (FNMA). Issuance of pass-through securities in 1982–84 totaled over $200 billion—more than the cumulative amount of pass-throughs issued in all previous years. In addition, mortgage securities outperformed fixed-income investments during the period, spurring expanded participation in the market by institutional investors.

This rapid growth has magnified the need for better methods of analyzing the mortgage investment. The problem in assessing mortgage security returns arises because the underlying mortgages of a pass-through pool may prepay at any time, so that the cash flow from the pool is statistically uncertain. Each month, the investor receives the scheduled amortization and interest due on the mortgages still in force, plus any prepayments. Clearly, the amount and timing of these prepayments will affect the yield to the investor.

METHODS FOR EVALUATING MORTGAGE YIELDS

The techniques used for analyzing a mortgage investment have evolved over time. If there are no prepayments, the cash flow from a mortgage is a stream of level payments that amortizes the outstanding balance over the life of the loan (see Exhibit 1).

The earliest model for incorporating prepayments used the "prepaid life" concept. This approach represents all the prepayments on a mortgage pool by one balloon prepayment at a typical or average point in time. A 12-year prepaid life assumption became established as a market convention for quoting yields on 30-year mortgages. Exhibit 2 depicts the mortgage cash flow under a 12-year prepaid life assumption.

While the 12-year life trading convention provides a uniform basis for market quotes, it is unsatisfactory as an investment measure. The assumption that all mortgages prepay after exactly 12 years is not a realistic model of the actual pattern of prepayments on a pool of mortgages. The resulting distortion in yield for mortgage issues trading near par is not serious. However, this convention can significantly misrepresent the yield and other investment characteristics of discount and premium issues.

Cash Flow Yield

Other techniques were developed to estimate the distribution of prepayments over time, thus creating a much more plausible cash flow. A yield based on the cash flow generated by a period-by-period distribution of prepayments is referred to as a "cash flow yield" (see Exhibit 3). Cash flow yields provide a much more flexible and accurate tool for analyzing mortgage

EXHIBIT 1
Mortgage Cash Flow—No Prepayments

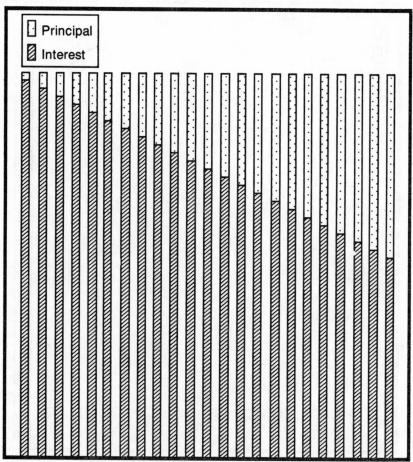

securities than does the quoted yield to 12-year prepaid life, for the following reasons:

1. The prepayment assumption can be varied to appropriate levels for the type of mortgage being considered and for a given set of housing market conditions.

EXHIBIT 2
Mortgage Cash Flow—12-Year Prepaid Life

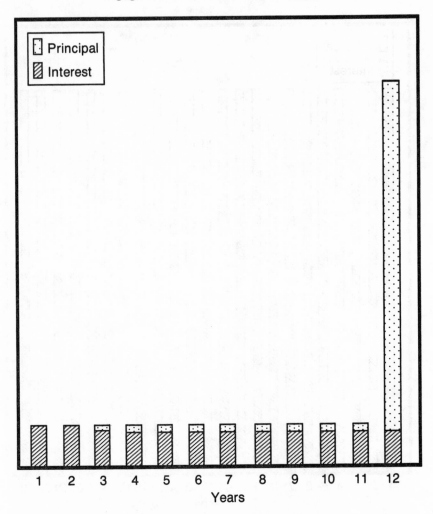

2. Even in the case when the life expectancy of the mortgage population is known to be exactly 12 years, prepayments occurring earlier or later than the 12-year point are treated with more appropriate values—that is, their present values. For mortgages priced at a discount, early retirements boost the value of a stream of prepayments above that indicated by the 12-year life calculation. As a result, the yield to

12-year life understates the yield. (The opposite is true for loans priced at a premium.)

3. A further limitation of the yield to 12-year prepaid life is the way it is applied under the market convention. The quoted yield for older loans assumes a 30-year maturity and a 12-year prepayment regardless of the seasoning of the mortgages. Appropriately used, the cash flow yield is

EXHIBIT 3
Mortgage Cash Flow—Distribution of Prepayments over Time

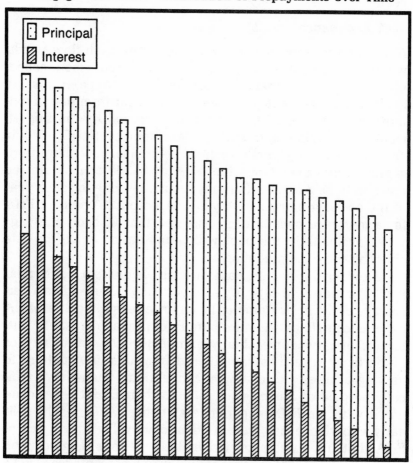

based on the remaining term to maturity in determining yield estimates.

A basic concept underlying the prepayment distribution used for cash flow yield calculations is the prepayment rate. The prepayment rate of a group of loans for a given year is the number of loans that prepay that year expressed as a percentage of the number outstanding at the beginning of the year. For example, a 10 percent prepayment rate for a pool of 100 loans means that 10 loans would terminate during the year.

FHA Experience

A commonly used approach for calculating cash flow yields, which was developed in the 1970s, bases prepayment schedules on "FHA experience." Mortgage pool prepayments are modeled as a percentage of the year-by-year termination patterns of FHA-insured mortgages as observed by the Department of Housing and Urban Development (HUD). While presented as a survivorship schedule—that is, how many mortgages survive over time—the FHA statistics can be viewed essentially as a series of prepayment rates, one for each year of the life of a mortgage. A yield based on 200 percent FHA for a mortgage pass-through assumes that in each mortgage year, the loans in the pool will terminate at twice the rate given by the FHA statistics.

However, projecting pass-through yields from a particular pool's (or mortgage category's) experience expressed as a percentage of the FHA statistics leads to serious difficulties. FHA experience defines an entire pattern of prepayments. The pattern of prepayments actually experienced by various types of mortgage securities has differed from this FHA pattern to varying degrees. For example, conventional loans have typically prepaid at much faster rates in their initial years compared with the FHA experience statistics. As a result, their early experience has translated into very high multiples of FHA that have not persisted in later periods. High-coupon mortgages represent another case in which percentages of FHA experience have been an inappropriate way to analyze the mortgages. Rapid payoffs of these loans take place during periods when lower market rates provide incentives for refinancing, in a pattern bearing no relationship to the FHA experience curve.

To compound the problem, FHA experience changes as HUD updates its statistics every year or two. Exhibit 4 illustrates the prepayment rates embodied in the 1957–81 FHA

EXHIBIT 4
FHA Experience Prepayment Rates
(30-Year Term FHA-Insured Home Mortgages)

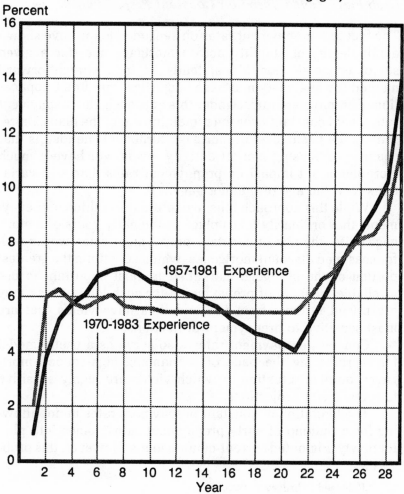

statistics and the latest update[1] covering the shorter 1970–84 period. Each set of statistics has idiosyncracies that reflect the way in which the changes in housing cycles have been incorporated into that particular version. The result is that even for GNMAs—backed by FHA/VA mortgages—prepayments have not tracked the FHA experience statistics. In summary, the percentage of FHA experience has not provided a consistent prepayment measure.

Cash Flow Yields Based on Constant Prepayment Rates

The fact that prepayment rates on seasoned loans have shown a fair degree of stability across mortgage age (for a given set of economic conditions) leads us to a straightforward method for analyzing mortgage securities: the direct application of prepayment rates. Under this approach, the prepayment rate is held constant over the remaining life of the loans, representing the basic level of mortgage turnover. The idea is that changes in housing market activity levels will have a much more important impact on prepayment rates than will variations with the age of the mortgage.

While this approach fails to capture the buildup of prepayments that ordinarily takes place in the early years of a mortgage's life, the use of constant prepayment rates works well for seasoned discount mortgages, which constitute the greatest portion of the mortgage market. It is most important to use a reliable measure of prepayments for such loans, since they are priced farthest from par and thus have yields that are most sensitive to prepayment projections.

Constant prepayment rates also serve as a useful model for representing the pace of refinancing high-coupon mortgages, another situation in which yields are highly sensitive to prepayment projections.

The limitation of constant prepayment rates in not allowing for a buildup of early prepayment rates comes into play for newly originated current-coupon loans. However, this prob-

---

[1] Released February 1, 1985.

lem is less critical, since the loans typically are priced near par so that the inaccuracy in terms of yield is relatively small.

Application to the Market

The prepayment assumption used for a cash flow yield calculation is essentially an estimate of the average prepayment rate expected over a long-term period. We can place the prepayment rate levels of mortgage securities in perspective by viewing the historical data from the pass-through programs.

The prepayment rates of seasoned discount GNMA FHLMC and FNMA pass-through securities are tracked on a monthly basis in Exhibit 5. With mortgage interest rates as the predominant driving force, these prepayment rates follow a clear cyclical pattern: high in an active market in 1973, dropping in recession in 1974–75, peaking in 1977–78, falling to severely low levels in 1980–82, and recovering in 1983. For the period 1975–84 "seasoned discount" prepayment rates averaged 5.2 percent for GNMAs and 7.4 percent for FHLMC PCs.

Cash flow yields based on prepayment rates can be applied as follows. Exhibit 6 shows the market prices of FHLMC 9s and FHLMC 12s on January 4, 1985, with FHLMC 12s the current coupon at that time. According to their quoted yields— assuming a 30-year maturity and a 12-year prepayment— FHLMC 12s outyield FHLMC 9s by 74 basis points.

However, the quoted yields can give a misleading picture of the relative value of these instruments. Exhibit 7 shows that FHLMC 9 percent and FHLMC 12 percent pools experienced average prepayment rates during the immediately preceding 12 months of 6.5 percent and 7.4 percent respectively. We can calculate cash flow yields applying these prepayment rates; the average remaining terms for such pools of 22.3 years and 26.8 years, respectively, are also used in the calculation. The cash flow yields based on the past year's prepayment rate indicate that rather than providing a lower return, FHLMC 9s yield eight basis points more than FHLMC 12s.

Clearly, this advantage would expand or contract if future prepayment rates reached different levels from those of the

EXHIBIT 5
Historical Prepayment Rates of Seasoned Discount
Mortgage Securities[a]
(January 1973–December 1984)

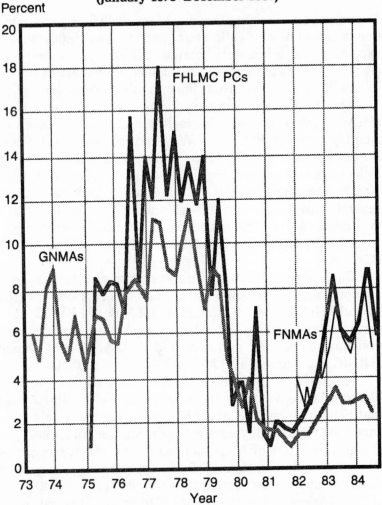

Percent

[a] 3-month moving average for all pools outstanding for two or more years with coupon rates at, or below, the prevailing current coupon.

EXHIBIT 6
FHLMC Yield Profile—Quoted Yield

Issue	Price	Yield to 12-Year Life
FHLMC 9	82⅜	11.66%
FHLMC 12	96⅛	12.40
Yield Spread		− 0.74%

past year. However, the table also indicates that the FHLMC 9s would require a prepayment rate of 6.1 percent to match the 12.51 percent yield on the current-coupon FHLMC 12s. This "break-even" prepayment rate provides a 0.4 percent gap or margin for a prepayment rate decline before the FHLMC 9s would yield less than the FHLMC 12s.

Yield Tables

Salomon Brothers Inc, in conjunction with Financial Publishing Company, recently published a three-volume set of mortgage security yield books. The tables in the book provide the quoted yield, as well as the cash flow yield for various constant prepayment rates. Exhibit 8 is a sample page.

The books also show the *weighted-average life* and *durations* corresponding to each prepayment rate. The weighted-average life is the weighted-average time at which principal is repaid and corresponds to the standard measure of average life for sinking fund bonds. The duration—the average time to receipt of cash flows weighted by the present value of those

EXHIBIT 7
FHLMC Yield Profile—Cash Flow Yield

Issue	Average Remaining Term (yrs)	Prepayment Rate Past 12 Months (Jan–Dec 84)	Cash Flow Yield	Break-Even Prepayment Rate	Gap
FHLMC 9	22.3	6.5%	12.59%	6.1%	0.4%
FHLMC 12	26.8	7.4	12.51		
Yield Spread			+0.08%		

EXHIBIT 8
Sample Page from Yield Book

12½% POOL RATE **YIELD TABLES FOR SINGLE-FAMILY GNMA SECURITIES** **YEARS REMAINING 30**

PRICE	QUOTED YIELD (30/12)	0%	2%	4%	6%	8%	10%
90	14.18	13.92	14.11	14.31	14.52	14.74	14.96
90⅛	14.16	13.90	14.09	14.29	14.49	14.70	14.92
90¼	14.13	13.88	14.07	14.26	14.46	14.67	14.88
90⅜	14.11	13.86	14.04	14.24	14.43	14.64	14.85
90½	14.08	13.84	14.02	14.21	14.41	14.61	14.81
90⅝	14.06	13.82	14.00	14.18	14.38	14.57	14.78
90¾	14.04	13.80	13.98	14.16	14.35	14.54	14.74
90⅞	14.01	13.78	13.95	14.13	14.32	14.51	14.71
DURATION	**5.9**	6.9	6.1	5.4	4.8	4.4	4.0
91	13.99	13.76	13.93	14.11	14.29	14.48	14.67
91⅛	13.97	13.74	13.91	14.08	14.26	14.45	14.64
91¼	13.94	13.72	13.88	14.06	14.23	14.42	14.60
91⅜	13.92	13.70	13.86	14.03	14.20	14.38	14.57
91½	13.90	13.68	13.84	14.00	14.18	14.35	14.53
91⅝	13.87	13.66	13.82	13.98	14.15	14.32	14.50
91¾	13.85	13.64	13.79	13.95	14.12	14.29	14.47
91⅞	13.83	13.62	13.77	13.93	14.09	14.26	14.43
DURATION	**5.9**	7.0	6.1	5.4	4.9	4.4	4.0
92	13.80	13.60	13.75	13.90	14.06	14.23	14.40
92⅛	13.78	13.58	13.73	13.88	14.03	14.20	14.36
92¼	13.76	13.56	13.70	13.85	14.01	14.17	14.33
92⅜	13.74	13.54	13.68	13.83	13.98	14.13	14.29
92½	13.71	13.52	13.66	13.80	13.95	14.10	14.26
92⅝	13.69	13.50	13.64	13.78	13.92	14.07	14.23
92¾	13.67	13.48	13.61	13.75	13.90	14.04	14.19
92⅞	13.64	13.46	13.59	13.73	13.87	14.01	14.16
DURATION	**6.0**	7.0	6.2	5.5	4.9	4.5	4.1
93	13.62	13.44	13.57	13.70	13.84	13.98	14.13
93⅛	13.60	13.42	13.55	13.68	13.81	13.95	14.09
93¼	13.58	13.41	13.53	13.65	13.79	13.92	14.06
93⅜	13.55	13.39	13.51	13.63	13.76	13.89	14.03
93½	13.53	13.37	13.48	13.60	13.73	13.86	13.99
93⅝	13.51	13.35	13.46	13.58	13.70	13.83	13.96
93¾	13.49	13.33	13.44	13.56	13.68	13.80	13.93
93⅞	13.46	13.31	13.42	13.53	13.65	13.77	13.89
DURATION	**6.0**	7.1	6.2	5.5	5.0	4.5	4.1
94	13.44	13.29	13.40	13.51	13.62	13.74	13.86
94⅛	13.42	13.27	13.38	13.48	13.60	13.71	13.83
94¼	13.40	13.25	13.35	13.46	13.57	13.68	13.80
94⅜	13.37	13.23	13.33	13.44	13.54	13.65	13.76
94½	13.35	13.22	13.31	13.41	13.51	13.62	13.73
94⅝	13.33	13.20	13.29	13.39	13.49	13.59	13.70
94¾	13.31	13.18	13.27	13.36	13.46	13.56	13.67
94⅞	13.29	13.16	13.25	13.34	13.43	13.53	13.63
DURATION	**6.0**	7.1	6.3	5.6	5.0	4.5	4.1
95	13.26	13.14	13.23	13.32	13.41	13.50	13.60
95⅛	13.24	13.12	13.21	13.29	13.38	13.47	13.57
95¼	13.22	13.10	13.18	13.27	13.36	13.45	13.54
95⅜	13.20	13.08	13.16	13.24	13.33	13.42	13.51
95½	13.18	13.07	13.14	13.22	13.30	13.39	13.47
95⅝	13.15	13.05	13.12	13.20	13.28	13.36	13.44
95¾	13.13	13.03	13.10	13.17	13.25	13.33	13.41
95⅞	13.11	13.01	13.08	13.15	13.22	13.30	13.38
DURATION	**6.1**	7.2	6.3	5.7	5.1	4.6	4.2
96	13.09	12.99	13.06	13.13	13.20	13.27	13.35
96⅛	13.07	12.97	13.04	13.10	13.17	13.24	13.32
96¼	13.05	12.96	13.02	13.08	13.15	13.22	13.29
96⅜	13.02	12.94	13.00	13.06	13.12	13.19	13.25
96½	13.00	12.92	12.98	13.04	13.10	13.16	13.22
96⅝	12.98	12.90	12.96	13.01	13.07	13.13	13.19
96¾	12.96	12.88	12.94	12.99	13.04	13.10	13.16
96⅞	12.94	12.87	12.92	12.97	13.02	13.07	13.13
DURATION	**6.1**	7.3	6.4	5.7	5.1	4.6	4.2
97	12.92	12.85	12.89	12.94	12.99	13.05	13.10
97¼	12.87	12.81	12.85	12.90	12.94	12.99	13.04
97½	12.83	12.78	12.81	12.85	12.89	12.93	12.98
97¾	12.79	12.74	12.77	12.81	12.84	12.88	12.92
WEIGHTED-AVG. LIFE YEARS		23.0	18.1	14.6	12.0	10.0	8.4

PRICE	QUOTED YIELD (30/12)	0%	2%	4%	6%	8%	10%
98	12.75	12.71	12.73	12.76	12.79	12.82	12.85
98⅛	12.71	12.67	12.69	12.72	12.74	12.77	12.79
98¼	12.66	12.64	12.65	12.67	12.69	12.71	12.73
98⅜	12.62	12.60	12.62	12.63	12.64	12.66	12.67
99	12.58	12.57	12.58	12.59	12.59	12.60	12.61
99¼	12.54	12.53	12.54	12.54	12.55	12.55	12.56
99½	12.50	12.50	12.50	12.50	12.50	12.50	12.50
99¾	12.46	12.46	12.46	12.45	12.45	12.44	12.44
DURATION	**6.2**	7.4	6.6	5.8	5.3	4.8	4.3
100	12.42	12.43	12.42	12.41	12.40	12.39	12.38
100⅛	12.38	12.40	12.38	12.37	12.35	12.34	12.32
100¼	12.33	12.36	12.34	12.33	12.31	12.29	12.26
100⅜	12.29	12.33	12.31	12.28	12.26	12.23	12.21
101	12.25	12.30	12.27	12.24	12.21	12.18	12.15
101¼	12.21	12.26	12.23	12.20	12.16	12.13	12.09
101½	12.17	12.23	12.19	12.16	12.12	12.08	12.04
101¾	12.13	12.20	12.16	12.11	12.07	12.03	11.98
DURATION	**6.2**	7.5	6.7	5.9	5.3	4.8	4.4
102	12.09	12.16	12.12	12.07	12.02	11.97	11.92
102¼	12.05	12.13	12.08	12.03	11.98	11.92	11.87
102½	12.02	12.10	12.05	11.99	11.93	11.87	11.81
102¾	11.98	12.07	12.01	11.95	11.89	11.82	11.76
103	11.94	12.03	11.97	11.91	11.84	11.77	11.70
103¼	11.90	12.00	11.94	11.87	11.80	11.72	11.65
103½	11.86	11.97	11.90	11.83	11.75	11.67	11.59
103¾	11.82	11.94	11.86	11.79	11.71	11.62	11.54
DURATION	**6.3**	7.7	6.8	6.0	5.4	4.9	4.5
104	11.78	11.91	11.83	11.75	11.66	11.57	11.48
104¼	11.74	11.87	11.79	11.71	11.62	11.53	11.43
104½	11.71	11.84	11.76	11.67	11.57	11.48	11.38
104¾	11.67	11.81	11.72	11.63	11.53	11.43	11.32
105	11.63	11.78	11.69	11.59	11.49	11.38	11.27
105¼	11.59	11.75	11.65	11.55	11.44	11.33	11.22
105½	11.55	11.72	11.62	11.51	11.40	11.28	11.17
105¾	11.52	11.69	11.58	11.47	11.35	11.24	11.11
DURATION	**6.3**	7.8	6.9	6.1	5.5	5.0	4.6
106	11.48	11.66	11.55	11.43	11.31	11.19	11.06
106¼	11.44	11.63	11.51	11.39	11.27	11.14	11.01
106½	11.40	11.60	11.48	11.35	11.23	11.09	10.96
106¾	11.37	11.57	11.44	11.32	11.18	11.05	10.91
107	11.33	11.54	11.41	11.28	11.14	11.00	10.85
107¼	11.29	11.51	11.38	11.24	11.10	10.95	10.80
107½	11.26	11.48	11.34	11.20	11.06	10.91	10.75
107¾	11.22	11.45	11.31	11.16	11.02	10.86	10.70
DURATION	**6.4**	7.9	7.0	6.2	5.6	5.1	4.6
108	11.18	11.42	11.27	11.13	10.97	10.82	10.65
108¼	11.15	11.39	11.24	11.09	10.93	10.77	10.60
108½	11.11	11.36	11.21	11.05	10.89	10.72	10.55
108¾	11.07	11.33	11.17	11.02	10.85	10.68	10.50
109	11.04	11.30	11.14	10.98	10.81	10.63	10.45
109¼	11.00	11.27	11.11	10.94	10.77	10.59	10.40
109½	10.97	11.24	11.08	10.91	10.73	10.54	10.36
109¾	10.93	11.21	11.04	10.87	10.69	10.50	10.31
DURATION	**6.5**	8.0	7.1	6.3	5.7	5.2	4.7
110	10.89	11.18	11.01	10.83	10.65	10.46	10.26
110¼	10.86	11.15	10.98	10.80	10.61	10.41	10.21
110½	10.82	11.13	10.95	10.76	10.57	10.37	10.16
110¾	10.79	11.10	10.92	10.73	10.53	10.32	10.11
111	10.75	11.07	10.88	10.69	10.49	10.28	10.07
111¼	10.72	11.04	10.85	10.65	10.45	10.24	10.02
111½	10.68	11.01	10.82	10.62	10.41	10.19	9.97
111¾	10.65	10.98	10.79	10.58	10.37	10.15	9.92
DURATION	**6.5**	8.1	7.2	6.4	5.8	5.3	4.8
112	10.61	10.96	10.76	10.55	10.33	10.11	9.88
112¼	10.58	10.93	10.73	10.51	10.29	10.07	9.83
112½	10.55	10.90	10.69	10.48	10.25	10.02	9.78
113	10.48	10.85	10.63	10.41	10.18	9.94	9.69
WEIGHTED-AVG. LIFE YEARS		23.0	18.1	14.6	12.0	10.0	8.4

cash flows—measures the responsiveness of the price of the investment to interest rate movements.

MATHEMATICAL APPENDIX

Amortization Schedule

The following variables apply to almost every mortgage instrument:

C = gross coupon rate
S = service fee
m = remaining term to maturity in months
n = original term to maturity in months
A = outstanding principal balance

Let variables with lower-case letters represent the monthly decimal equivalents of the annual percentage rates.

$c = C/1200$
$s = S/1200$

Let the monthly balances and cash flows be denoted as follows:

K_i = gross monthly payments by mortgagors in the ith month
CF_i = net cash flow to investors in the ith month
I_i = net interest payment in the ith month
P_i = principal repayment in the ith month
B_i = principal balance at the end of i months

Then we can determine these balances and cash flows month by month in the following manner:

$B_0 = A$

For $i = 1, 2, \ldots, m$:

$CF_i = K_i - s \cdot B_{i-1}$
$I_i = (c - s)B_{i-1}$
$P_i = CF_i - I_i$
$B_i = B_{i-1} - P_i$

To generate this schedule, we need only to define the K_i.

Alternatively, the principal balance at any point can be computed directly as the present value of the future payments:

$$B_i = \sum_{j=1}^{m-i} \frac{K_{i+j}}{(1+c)^j}$$

Mortgage Cash Flow without Prepayments

For a level-payment mortgage, the constant gross monthly payment is:

$$K = \frac{A \cdot c}{1 - (1+c)^{-m}}$$

and $K_i = K$ for all i.

Also,

$$B_i = \frac{K}{c}(1 - (1+c)^{i-m})$$

$$= A\frac{(1+c)^m - (1+c)^i}{(1+c)^m - 1}$$

Graduated-Payment Mortgages (GPMs)

We need some additional variables to describe a GPM:

G = annual percentage increase in monthly payment
D = graduation period in years

For most of the loans in GNMA–GPM pools, G=7½ percent, D=5, and n=360.

Let $g = G/100$
$\quad d = 12 \cdot D$
$\quad h_1 = 1 + g$
$\quad h_2 = 1 + c$
$\quad h_3 = h_1/h_2^{12}$

For a *newly originated* GPM, the initial payment will be:

$$K_o = \frac{A \cdot c}{(1 - h_2^{-12})\left(\dfrac{1 - h_3^D}{1 - h_3}\right) + h_3^D(1 - h_2^{d-n})}$$

The monthly payment K_i in month i is:

$$K_i = \begin{cases} K_0(1+g)^{F(i)} & i \leq d \\ K_0(1+g)^D & i > d \end{cases}$$

where $F(i)$ is the greatest integer less than or equal to i/12.

For a seasoned GPM that is a months old (a=n−m), first compute the payment schedule $\{\tilde{K}_i\}$ of a hypothetical $100 new GPM. The balance of this GPM after a months is:

$$\tilde{A} = \sum_{i=a+1}^{n} \frac{\tilde{K}_i}{(1+c)^{i-a}}$$

Then, the payment schedule of the seasoned GPM is:

$$K_i = \tilde{K}_{i+a} \cdot \frac{A}{\tilde{A}} \qquad \text{for } i = 1, 2, \ldots, m$$

Mortgage Cash Flow with Prepayments

Let variables with asterisks designate the cash flows and balances of the mortgage pool including prepayments. Then the amortization process is as before, and we need only to define the K_i^*, the gross payments made by mortgagors including prepayments.

Constant Prepayment Rate

Suppose a constant annual prepayment rate P is given. To convert P to its monthly equivalent P_M and vice versa:

$$P_M = 100 \left[1 - (1 - P/100)^{1/12}\right]$$
$$P = 100 \left[1 - (1 - P_M/100)^{12}\right]$$

Let p be the monthly decimal prepayment rate. That is:

$$p = 1 - (1 - P/100)^{1/12} = P_M/100$$

Then:

$$K_i^* = (1 - p)^{i-1}(K_i + pB_i)$$

where K_i is the payment and B_i is the principal balance, assuming no prepayments.

Percentages of FHA Experience

While we emphasize the use of constant prepayment rates to analyze mortgage investments, we also describe the calculations with percentages of FHA experience.

Published tables from HUD provide annual survivorship data for FHA-insured mortgages. The tables for the 1957–81 and 1970–84 experience of 30-year term Section 203 home mortgages are shown in Exhibit 9. The exhibit gives the proportion of loans still outstanding after prepayments and defaults, following each year of a loan's term.

Let S_q be the published probability that a loan is still outstanding after q years for $q = 0, 1, \ldots, 30$ ($S_o = 1$).

For a new 30-year loan at 100 percent FHA experience, the probability s_i that the loan will be outstanding after i months is:

$$s_i = S_q\left(\frac{S_{q+1}}{S_q}\right)^{r/12}$$

where $i = 12\,q + r$ and $0 \le r < 12$; $i = 0, 1, \ldots, 360$.

Suppose a multiple x of FHA experience is assumed. Then:

$$s_i = \left[S_q\left(\frac{S_{q+1}}{S_q}\right)^{r/12}\right]^x$$

The age of the loans in a seasoned pool plays an important role in FHA experience calculations. It is customarily assumed that the loans have original terms of 30 years. That is, their age in months is set at:

$$a = \text{Max}(360 - m, n - m)$$

Then:

$$K_i^* = \frac{1}{S_a}[s_{a+i-1}K_i + (s_{a+i-1} - s_{a+i})B_i]$$

where K_i is the payment and B_i is the principal balance assuming no prepayments.

Past Prepayment Experience

We can determine the constant prepayment rate or percentage of FHA represented by a pool's past prepayment experience

EXHIBIT 9
FHA Experience Mortality
Statistics
(30-Year Term)

Year	Surviving at End of Year	
	1957–81	1970–84
0	1.000000	1.000000
1	0.988741	0.981437
2	0.951464	0.923476
3	0.902244	0.864509
4	0.850503	0.816129
5	0.797705	0.771798
6	0.743434	0.726504
7	0.690500	0.682023
8	0.640554	0.643091
9	0.595730	0.606852
10	0.555907	0.573044
11	0.519255	0.541331
12	0.485897	0.511579
13	0.456201	0.483523
14	0.429475	0.457063
15	0.405436	0.432105
16	0.383780	0.408560
17	0.364193	0.386347
18	0.346413	0.365388
19	0.330293	0.345608
20	0.315784	0.326941
21	0.302789	0.309320
22	0.287753	0.290851
23	0.270997	0.271805
24	0.252774	0.252444
25	0.233434	0.233022
26	0.213425	0.213771
27	0.193180	0.194904
28	0.173103	0.176609
29	0.148063	0.156012
30	0.123023	0.135415

Source: U.S. Department of Housing and Urban Development

as follows. Suppose U and V are the principal balances of a pool at the beginning and end of a period, respectively, that the period is k months long, and that the pool has m months remaining at the beginning of the period.

First, compute the principal balance W at the end of the period as if there were no prepayments. For level-payment mortgages:

$$W = U \frac{(1+c)^m - (1+c)^k}{(1+c)^m - 1}$$

Then, the constant prepayment rate in this period is:

$$P = 100 \left[1 - (V/W)^{12/k}\right]$$

Set the age at the beginning of the period to be:

$$a = \text{Max}(360 - m, n - m)$$

Then the multiple of FHA for this period is given by:

$$x = \frac{\log(V/W)}{\log(s_{a+k}/s_a)}$$

To express this result as a percentage, we have:

$$X = 100 \cdot x$$

Quoted Yield

The quoted yield calculation is based on a standard original term to maturity and prepaid life. Exhibit 10 indicates conventions for the assumed maturity, service fee and prepaid life for various types of mortgage securities.

Suppose the following parameters are given:

n = original maturity in months
j = prepaid life in months
D = days to first payment
Y = yield

Let:

$y = Y/1200$
$d = D/30$

EXHIBIT 10
Quoted Yield Conventions for Mortgage Securities

Program	Maturity	Prepaid Life	Service Fee	Days to First Payment[a]
Long-Term				
GNMA (Single-Family)	30 yrs	12 yrs	0.50%	45
GNMA (GPM)	30	12	0.50	45
GNMA (Project Loan)	40	40/18	0.25	45
	35	18	0.25	45
FHLMC PC	30	12	0	75
FNMA MBS	30	12	0	54
FHA Project Pool	40	18	0.07	54
Intermediate-Term				
GNMA (Single-Family)	15 yrs	7 yrs	0.50%	45
GNMA (Mobil Home)	15	7	3.25	45
FHLMC PC	15	7	0	75
FNMA MBS	15	7	0	54

[a] 45 days for GNMA I pools and 50 days for GNMA II pools.

Suppose a cash flow schedule $\{CF_i\}$ and balance schedule $\{B_i\}$ have been developed for a \$100 initial balance pool. Then, the price in general is given by:

$$\text{Price} = \left(\sum_{i=1}^{j} \frac{CF_i}{(1+y)^i} + \frac{B_j}{(1+y)^j} \right) \frac{1+y}{1+d \cdot y}$$

A closed-form solution without any summation exists for level-payment mortgages, as follows:

Let: $u_1 = (1+c)^n$
$u_2 = (1+c)^j$
$u_3 = (1+y)^j$

$$u_4 = \begin{cases} \dfrac{1 - u_2/u_3}{y - c} & y \neq c \\[3mm] \dfrac{j}{1+c} & y = c \end{cases}$$

Price =

$$\left(\frac{100}{u_1-1}\right)\left(\frac{1+y}{1+d\cdot y}\right)\left[\frac{u_1-u_2}{u_3}+\frac{(c-s)u_1(1-1/u_3)}{y}+s\cdot u_4\right]$$

Cash Flow Yield

The cash flow yield is based on the cash flow schedule including prepayments generated by a constant prepayment rate, percentage of FHA experience, or some other assumption. In general, the remaining term of the mortgage pool is used rather than the original maturity. Suppose a cash flow schedule including prepayments $\{CF_i^*\}$ is developed based on a $100 current outstanding balance. Then, using the same notation as before:

$$Price = \left(\sum_{i=1}^{m}\frac{CF_i^*}{(1+y)^i}\right)\frac{1+y}{1+d\cdot y}$$

A closed-form solution without summation exists for level-payment mortgages under a constant prepayment rate assumption.

$$z_1 = \frac{1-\left(\frac{1-p}{1+y}\right)^m}{y+p}$$

$$z_2 = \begin{cases} \dfrac{1-\left(\dfrac{(1-p)(1+c)}{1+y}\right)^m}{y+p+pc-c} & (1-p)(1+c)=(1+y) \\ \dfrac{m}{1+y} & (1-p)(1+c)=(1+y) \end{cases}$$

Price =

$$100\left(\frac{1+y}{1+d\cdot y}\right)\left[\frac{(1+c)^m(p+c-s)z_1+(s-p(1+c))z_2}{(1+c)^m-1}\right]$$

Given a price, the calculation of either quoted yield or cash flow yield requires an iterative process. Starting with a trial yield, the corresponding price is calculated. Using this result, a new yield is selected based on one of several algorithms. In this way, a series of yield estimates is found that produces prices closer and closer to the given price. When the difference between the calculated price and the given price is within allowable limits, the process is done. One simple algorithm is:

Given trial yields y_t, y_{t+1}:

$$y_{t+2} = y_{t+1} + \frac{\text{Target Price} - \text{Price}(y_{t+1})}{\text{Price}(y_{t+1}) - \text{Price}(y_t)}(y_{t+1} - y_t)$$

Bond-Equivalent Yield

The mortgage security yields described above are monthly compounded rates. One can convert a monthly compounded yield to a bond-equivalent yield and vice versa as follows:

Y = monthly compounded mortgage yield
Z = bond-equivalent yield

$$Z = 200[(1 + Y/1200)^6 - 1]$$
$$Y = 1200[(1 + Z/200)^{1/6} - 1]$$

Weighted-Average Life

The weighted-average life is the average time in which principal is repaid. The weighted-average life, expressed in years, is:

$$\text{WAL} = \frac{\sum_{i=1}^{m} P_i^*(i + d - 1)}{12 \cdot A}$$

Duration

The (Macaulay) duration is the weighted average time to receipt of cash flows, weighted by their present values.

$$\text{Duration} = \frac{\sum_{i=1}^{m} \dfrac{CF_i^*(i + d - 1)}{(1 + y)^{i-1}(1 + d \cdot y)}}{12 \cdot \text{Price}}$$

A simple modification of the duration gives the percentage rate of change of price with respect to yield changes.

$$\text{Modified Duration} = \frac{\text{Duration}}{1 + y}$$

CHAPTER 11

Forecasting Prepayment Rates for Mortgage Securities

David J. Askin
Vice President, Mortgage-Backed Securities
Drexel Burnham Lambert

INTRODUCTION

The value of any fixed-income security is determined by the amount and timing of its cash flows, including the proceeds realized at sale, plus the reinvestment income earned on these cash flows over the investment horizon. For highly rated securities, the risk of payment delays or defaults is minimal. With the timely receipt of all contractual payments virtually assured, the only remaining cash flow uncertainty for most fixed-income investments is uncertainty over future reinvestment rates and terminal value if the security is sold before its final maturity.

Mortgage securities are subject to reinvestment risk in the same way as other fixed-income investments. In fact, the problem is magnified because most mortgages produce cash flows monthly, not semiannually. Thus, investors face a reinvestment decision 12 times a year, rather than only twice. However, there is an additional and more important source of cash flow uncertainty for mortgages. This is because of the right mortgagors have to prepay their loans partially or fully at any time, most often without penalty. As a result, the cash flow pattern of any investment in mortgage securities is determined largely by the prepayment experience of the underlying mortgages.

The ability to estimate future prepayment rates accurately is crucial to any investor in mortgage securities. This chapter analyzes current methodologies employed to predict prepayment activity. The organization of the chapter is as follows: First, is a brief discussion of the measurement of prepayment rates. This is followed by a section on the theory that underlies the prepayment decision: how mortgagors evaluate their prepayment options and the factors that determine the outcome. Next is an evaluation of the three basic forecast techniques: econometric models, options pricing models, and models which infer market estimates of prepayment rates from market prices. The final section contains the conclusions.

MEASURING PREPAYMENT RATES

There are three basic ways to measure a mortgage prepayment rate: prepaid life, a multiple of FHA experience, and a conditional prepayment rate. The 12-year prepaid life assumption is the most common prepaid life number in use. This value is based on the early research of the termination experience of FHA mortgages, wherein it was discovered that the mortgages had a weighted average life of approximately 12 years. As a measure of prepayment activity, the 12-year prepaid life assumption posits a situation where all mortgages in a pool return only scheduled principal and interest for the first 143 months. Then, in the 144*th* month all the mortgages prepay fully.

Investors who believe that a given pool will prepay at a different rate can pick a prepaid life number that is higher or lower than 12 years. Regardless of the number chosen, this implausible and arbitrary process is inadequate for evaluating mortgage securities. A prepaid life assumption is a point estimate. It assumes that all prepayments occur at a single moment in time. In reality prepayments occur continuously over the life of the pool. Prepaid life does not describe a realistic series of cash flows that can be discounted over the life of the security. This prevents the determination of an accurate net present value, which is necessary for a valid price and/or yield calculation.

The use of a multiple of FHA experience is better than prepaid life, because it describes a distribution of cash flows over the life of the pool. Therefore, it allows a portion of the mortgages to prepay in each period over the pool's life, rather than forcing all prepayments to occur at some arbitrary end point. However, FHA experience has numerous shortcomings as a measure of prepayment activity. Among the more fundamental problems are that:

- FHA experience is based only on the age of a mortgage and ignores other crucial factors
- It includes only assumable FHA mortgages and not conventional mortgages that typically are not assumable
- It covers only 30-year, single-family, fixed-rate, level payment mortgages and therefore is inappropriate for such instruments as 15-year mortgages, graduated payment mortgages (GPMs), adjustable rate mortgages (ARMs) and multi-family mortgages
- It assumes that each mortgage is acquired when it is newly originated
- There is a proliferation of FHA experience series from which to choose
- Data collection problems exist

These weaknesses have been well documented and need not be expanded upon here.

When it comes to projecting future prepayment rates, there is an additional problem with FHA experience. Many investors still use a multiple of FHA experience to date as a "model" for predicting subsequent prepayment activity. For example, if a pool has prepaid historically at 200 percent of

FHA experience, 200 percent FHA becomes the forecast of future prepayments. This implicitly assumes the fast-paying pools will continue to do so over time. The reasoning behind this assumption is specious and not supported by the evidence. There is no a priori reason why a pool will remain a high (low) prepayment rate pool merely because it has been a fast- (slow-) paying pool so far.[1] In general, individual pools do not follow this kind of consistent pattern. The arbitrary selection of a lower or higher FHA multiple based on the supposition that the prepayment activity will slow down or speed up is an inadequate solution as well.

The use of conditional prepayment rates (CPRs) is the preferred method of measuring prepayment activity. A conditional prepayment rate is the proportion of principal outstanding at the beginning of a particular period that prepays during that period. Since mortgage cash flows occur each month, the purest measure of CPR incorporates these monthly data into a monthly CPR. There are several variations of CPR that are used. Most involve a longer time period, such as a year, but still are based on the monthly CPR.

The CPR is a better prepayment calculation for several reasons. First, it is computed from the actual prepayment activity of the mortgage security so it is not an arbitrary number. Neither is CPR tied to an inaccurate prepayment distribution, as is the case for measures based on FHA experience. Therefore, the resulting cash flow distribution is a better reflection of the real prepayments for that mortgage security. Since CPR is derived from actual pool experience, it is not subject to the periodic revisions that occur with FHA experience. By conditioning the prepayment calculation on the principal balance of mortgages that have survived until the beginning of

---

[1] In fact, the opposite argument sometimes is made; namely that fast-pay pools have a tendency to become slow-pay pools. The "rationale" for this contention is that a point is reached in the life of such a pool when all of the mobile mortgagors have prepaid their loans and only the "slow payers" are left. The important point is the use of only the prepayment history of a pool and ignoring other economic factors does not lead to accurate forecasts of future prepayment activity.

the period, CPRs account for the age of the security. The mortgages are not assumed to be new originations. Finally, CPRs are simple to calculate, understand, and use.

For all its advantages, the use of CPRs still does not in and of itself constitute a forecast model. A constant CPR assumption implies that a fixed proportion of the mortgages outstanding at the beginning of the month prepays each month and that each mortgage is equally likely to prepay. The arbitrary adjustment of CPR to date to express expected cash flows in terms of one or more future CPRs has problems similar to the use of FHA experience as a "model."

A true forecast of future CPRs requires the development of a predictive model. Before a formal model can be created, the factors that determine prepayment behavior must be understood. This is addressed in the following section.

DETERMINANTS OF PREPAYMENT ACTIVITY

The Prepayment Decision

It is useful to recognize that the prepayment decision is part of an evaluation of various financial alternatives. The decision to refinance is made after examining all market opportunities. In many situations, a new mortgage, additional owner's equity, or other financial instruments enable the optimal financing of total household consumption and investment. Often the decision to sell a home is delayed or postponed if acceptable terms cannot be found. If allowed, a mortgage assumption occurs when the combination of cost, remaining term, and principal balance is more attractive to the potential purchaser than that currently available in the market. These components of the prepayment process are discussed in more detail below.

There are several elements to the prepayment decision. The first is whether to refinance. The borrower compares the terms of the existing mortgage to those currently available in the market. If the after-tax cost of the new mortgage is cheaper by enough to allow the recovery of all the transactions costs (both tangible and intangible) required to refinance, then a new mortgage is originated and the old one prepaid.

The second part of the prepayment decision is an evaluation of the home insofar as its ability to meet the housing requirements of the mortgagor is concerned. Once the home fails to meet those needs, it will be sold and the mortgage prepaid. A house can fail to meet a family's housing requirements because it is too large or too small, too expensive, or in an unacceptable location (such as resulting from a job transfer or an undesirable neighborhood).

The third part of the prepayment decision is whether the existing mortgage is assumed if there is a sale. FHA mortgages are assumable by law at the purchaser's option. In this case, the assumability question is an economic one for the new mortgagor, with no input from the lender. Conventional mortgages usually are assumable only at the lender's option, however. Typically, lenders will enforce their due-on-sale rights, so there is no assumption accompanying the sale and a prepayment occurs. With an assumption, there is a home sale but no prepayment.

Events beyond mortgagors' control also can lead to prepayments. Examples are death and natural disasters such as floods and fires. When these occur, there often is insurance in force that is used to pay off the mortgage, resulting in a prepayment.

A final component of the prepayment decision that is often overlooked or treated separately is a default and/or foreclosure situation. If financial reversals occur, the mortgagor must decide whether to default. The decision is primarily financial in nature. If the net cost of defaulting (including the cost of damage to one's credit rating) is less than the cost of saving the home, the default will occur. This often leads to a foreclosure sale and ultimately to a prepayment. Conversely, if the net equity in the home is sufficiently large, the mortgagor will find a way to avoid default. One way to do so is to locate other financial resources that are used to meet the monthly payments. Another is to sell the home. In the first case there is no prepayment, in the latter there is. To investors in guaranteed or insured mortgage securities, the effect of a default often is the same as a prepayment. This is because the mortgage is terminated and the principal repaid sooner than scheduled.

Prepayments are often classified as either economic or uneconomic. The former are prepayments on mortgages with interest rates higher than current market rates by enough to cover the transactions costs associated with refinancing. Conversely, prepayments that occur when the existing mortgage rate is lower than the current market rate are considered uneconomic. Many home sales as well as terminations because of default and/or foreclosure, death, and natural disasters are placed into this category.

This nomenclature is unfortunate because "uneconomic" suggests irrational economic decision making. Yet, the prepayment of a below-market rate mortgage because of a sale due to a job transfer, the ability to afford a more suitable home, or to retain one's home equity and avoid a default hardly are examples of irrational economic behavior. Neither is the decision to allow a default and subsequent mortgage termination because defaulting is deemed the least cost alternative. Further, it is incorrect to assume that refinancings do not occur on mortgages with rates below the current market. For many individuals, the equity in the home is their largest financial asset. Those who have experienced a significant amount of home price appreciation might refinance even at a higher rate to liquefy a portion of this asset. The classification of prepayments as "economic" or "uneconomic" should be avoided because it is misleading and it can cause one to overlook factors that are an important part of the decision process.

There are many complex financial, economic, and sociological factors that interact to determine the prepayment rates for pools of mortgages. The theoretical foundation that underlies this process must be understood if accurate forecasts of CPRs are to be made. Since much of the data that describe the decision process are difficult to obtain, forecast models are often unable to incorporate explicitly each component.

Yet, an acceptable model must account for the impact of each factor, whether included in the model or not.

The Theoretical Foundation

In examining the factors that affect the prepayment rates of mortgage securities, it is useful to think of two general types. First, there are mortgage and/or borrower characteristics that are set at the time the loan is made that determine which mortgagors are more likely to prepay throughout the terms of their mortgages. These variables are often referred to as time 0 variables. The contract rate at which the mortgage is originated is the most obvious example of this kind of factor. Origination year, geographic location, property characteristics, and borrower characteristics are others.

The second general type of factor are those that affect all mortgagors in the same way over time, regardless of mortgage or borrower characteristics at origination. Often these factors are called time t variables. The most important are current mortgage interest rates and mortgage age (seasoning). The prepayment rates of all pools do not move by the same amount as these variables change, but the CPRs all tend to move in the same direction.

The analysis of the factors that determine future CPRs is furthered by classifying them according to the nature of their impact. The five groups of variables used here are: cost of financing, seasoning, macroeconomic, demographic, and geographic. All of the important factors fit into one of these groups. In discussing them and their impact on CPRs, it is useful to consider whether a factor is a time t or a time 0 variable.

Cost of Financing

Cost of financing (or refinancing) variables usually are considered the most important in forecasting CPRs. The theoretical concept is simply stated. When the cost of financing increases, prepayment rates tend to fall. Conversely, prepayment rates rise when the cost of financing falls.

Among the cost of financing variables, the relationship between the current mortgage rate and the contract rate on the mortgage security is crucial to any forecast model. The focus is on the incentive to refinance. From the borrower's perspective, a mortgage is like a callable bond. In a falling rate environment the borrower can call (prepay) the mortgage and refinance at lower cost. When rates rise, the existing mortgage is the lower cost alternative and therefore there is no call (no prepayment). It should be noted that the lender has no such protection against a decline in rates.

The relationship between a change in interest rates relative to the contract rate and CPRs is not symmetric. There is no reason to suppose that prepayment rates increase for a given decline in interest rates to the same extent that they fall when interest rates rise by the same amount. One reason for this is what might be called an inertia or lack of information effect. Many borrowers are not motivated to re-evaluate their mortgages on a regular basis or they may simply have insufficient knowledge or expertise to make the evaluation. Therefore, refinancings do not occur as soon as they become financially advantageous. Second, even for those willing and able to analyze the refinancing option, there is a stochastic element to interest rate changes. It is only with hindsight that peaks or troughs in an interest rate cycle can be identified. Therefore, when rates are falling, mortgagors might delay a refinancing in the hope that rates will decline further. Similarly, when interest rates rise, prepayment activity may continue under the assumption that the increase is temporary.

The final and perhaps most important reason for the asymmetric nature of the interest rate/prepayment rate relationship is the existence of transactions costs. These act as additional cost of financing variables. Discount points, closing costs, application and origination fees, title searches, legal fees, and taxes are among these costs. They are incurred when a refinancing takes place. Any savings to be realized from a reduction in mortgage rates must be sufficient to cover them. If not, there is no incentive to refinance. Thus, prepayment rates vary in an asymmetric way over changes in discount points and related transactions costs, as well as over changes in mortgage rates.

While the inverse relationship between relative interest rates and prepayment rates is universally recognized in forecasting CPRs, the borrowing capacity of the mortgage instrument is a cost of financing effect that often is overlooked. Mortgagors compare not only interest rates (and therefore monthly payments), but the other terms of their existing mortgages to those available in the market. In a similar fashion, lenders evaluate current and expected future market conditions and set the terms of lending accordingly. The more attractive the terms of the existing mortgage relative to available alternatives, the lower the probability of prepayment.

This is an important consideration in the sale and assumption part of the prepayment decision. Low contract rate/high principal balance mortgages are more valuable to homeowners. In a potential assumption situation, the higher the principal balance for a given financing differential (between current rates and the contract rate), the larger the proportion of the value of the house is financed at the lower rate. If an assumption is possible as in the case of an FHA mortgage, high principal balance loans require less cash outlay by the purchaser to effect the assumption. This makes a prepayment less likely. Conversely, the assumption of a mortgage with a low principal balance relative to the value of the house requires a large amount of cash. An assumption is less likely and the probability of a prepayment increases in the event of a sale.

Since it is the size of the principal balance *relative* to the house value that is important, factors which affect the market price of the home must be included. Also, owners of mortgages with favorable terms will attempt to capitalize the value of these attractive mortgages into the selling price of the home. This affects the probability of a sale as well as that of an assumption. In turn, this impacts the probability of a prepayment.

Although the theoretical relationship between the cost of financing and CPRs is fairly intuitive and straightforward, the correct specifications of variables to capture these effects in a forecast model are not. Lack of data often poses a problem. Even when this is not the case, some models try to finesse the issue by ignoring these complex factors. This should not be done casually, since many of these variables have a significant impact on prepayment rates.

Seasoning

Prepayment rates vary systematically with age or seasoning. The general pattern is for CPRs to be low in the early years of the mortgage. The mortgagor has just moved into the home and/or obtained a new mortgage. It is unlikely that in such a short period, there would be a change in financial condition or family circumstance that is sufficiently large to make either the house or the mortgage unacceptable. However, the probability of such a change increases as the mortgage ages. Prepayment rates increase correspondingly. After a number of years prepayment rates tend to level off. This is because once a certain duration in residence is reached, families tend to remain in the existing home. Refinancing incentives still can occur, but family mobility diminishes.

The typical relationship between prepayment rates and seasoning is positive; first at an increasing rate, then at a decreasing rate. At some point, the incremental effect of additional seasoning on CPRs approaches zero. The speed at which CPRs change and then peak in response to the seasoning process varies with the type of mortgage security.

Macroeconomic Effects

General economic and financial conditions impact the prepayment activity for pools of mortgages. They enter the modeling process as time t variables, since they tend to drive prepayment rates in the same direction (although to varying degrees) for all mortgage securities.

As with cost of financing effects, the theoretical relationships between macroeconomic variables and CPRs are straightforward, though the choice of the variable specification may not be. Factors which cause a strong, growing economy, financial strength for borrowers, housing and mortgage markets, and increased borrower mobility lead to higher prepayment rates. Conversely, a weak economy, poor consumer balance sheets, housing and mortgage markets, and reduced borrower mobility cause lower CPRs.

Among the basic macroeconomic variables that often are tried in the modeling process are GNP, housing starts, disposable income, unemployment, home sales, population migration, and net savings. Deposit flows for depository institutions are examined as a possible measure of the availability of mortgage credit. Also, since mortgagors do not respond instantaneously to changes in economic conditions, forecast models often try to incorporate lagged versions of the macroeconomic variables. Classifying the data by the year in which the mortgages were originated also is productive. This is because origination year determines the amount of seasoning at a given point in time and also can serve as a proxy for economic conditions at origination. This, in turn, helps to define the amount of change in the values of important variables over time.

Demographic Variables

Demographic variables are characteristics of individual borrowers that affect their propensities to prepay over time. These characteristics sometimes are referred to as socio-economic factors. They can act either as time 0 or time t variables. Some demographic variables such as age, occupation, number of dependents, and employment history relate to characteristics of the people living in the house or of the family life cycle. Other variables such as income, wealth, and housing expense to income ratio are financial in nature.

The financial characteristics have an intuitively appealing impact on CPRs. Anything that makes mortgagors wealthier or more mobile tends to cause higher prepayment rates and vice versa. The sociological factors are often more difficult to measure, as is their effect on CPRs. For example, younger families tend to be more mobile, with most of the house changes occurring in the early years of family formation. Older families are expected to be more stable in terms of their consumption of housing services. This suggests a negative correlation between borrower age and prepayment activity. Yet, there can be many mitigating factors. Extraordinarily high (low) levels of income or wealth can offset the expected borrower age/ CPR relationship by increasing (decreasing) the affordability of housing and/or borrower mobility. The presence of children or non-traditional living arrangements also can cause significant unanticipated deviations from the norm.

Another complicating factor is that demographic factors can change over time. For example, an income level that was normal when the loan was originated can become much larger or smaller than normal subsequently. Thus, even if demographic data are available at origination, there often is no way to track changes in these variables over time. The result is that demographic factors which are important determinants of future prepayment activity often cannot be included in forecast models.

Geographic Effects

Despite the continuing trend toward nationalization of the mortgage finance markets, housing and mortgage lending largely remain local activities. This results in substantial variations in prepayment rates across geographic regions. There are several reasons for this.

- The strength and diversity of the local economic base
- State and local regulations regarding such things as interest rates, mortgage terms, the applicability of due-on-sale provisions and prepayment penalties, branch banking, interstate banking, loan production offices and foreclosure/forbearance laws
- The viability of the financial institutions that originate mortgages and of their flows of funds
- The strength of local loan demand
- The existence of competing uses of potential mortgage money
- Search costs in obtaining mortgage loans. High search costs often lead to a greater variety of mortgage terms in a local market

All of these factors can have a significant impact on prepayment rates. Yet, they are very difficult to quantify. Therefore, these effects usually are captured in prepayment forecast models by separating prepayment activity for mortgages originated in different states or regions. This often leads to states or regions being classified as "fast-pay" or "slow-pay" areas.

METHODOLOGIES FOR PREDICTING PREPAYMENT RATES

Given the importance of prepayments for determining the value of mortgage securities, there has been surprisingly little empirical work to develop forecast models. Instead, most investors and traders have relied on rules of thumb such as prepaid life assumptions, adjusted multiples of FHA experience, or an examination of the prepayment history of individual pools. Often the prepayment rate "forecast" is nothing more than an extrapolation into the future of past trends, possibly augmented by a subjective adjustment to account for expected interest rate movements over the near-term.

The dramatic growth of the secondary mortgage market fueled by the advent of mortgage-backed securities has increased the incentives to develop formal prepayment models. At present, the GNMA, FNMA, and FHLMC mortgage-backed securities programs are responsible for the issue of more than 100,000 securities representing approximately $400 billion. This would seem to be a sufficiently large body of publicly available data on which to base such a model. Yet, there are several problems that have hampered the research effort.

First, it is very expensive to acquire, maintain, and update a data base of this size. There is a large and growing number of pools outstanding. In addition, the prepayment (factor) information is available monthly. A further complication is that the historical data on GNMA and FHLMC PCs are not readily available back to the beginning of the MBS programs. These mortgage-backed securities were first issued in 1970, but the GNMA and FHLMC factor data bases do not begin until 1979 and 1982, respectively. Thus, for most researchers the data series are incomplete.

A second problem is the absence of mortgage-specific information for the loans that support the mortgage-backed securities. Many of the factors discussed in the previous section that help determine prepayment rates are only obtainable from the individual mortgage documents. This information is lost to the modeler who must rely on the factor data base.

The only information on the mortgage pools known with certainty is the original dollar amount, current factor, issue date (of the MBS only), interest rate (of the MBS only), and security type. Crucial information on the underlying mortgages, such as issue and maturity dates, remaining term to maturity, coupon rate, and property location can only be estimated.[2] This means, for instance, that exact amortization schedules cannot be calculated and therefore historical prepayment rates, seasoning, and relative interest rates also are estimates. Additional cost of financing and demographic information also are unavailable. A desirable alternative would be to use whole loan data. Unfortunately, a sufficiently large, geographically diverse data base of whole loans is hard to find.[3]

The final obstacle is a direct result of the second. Largely because of the data problems inherent in mortgage securities,

---

[2] An exception to this is the certificate rate in the GNMA I program. All of the mortgages in a given pool have the same coupon rate, 50 basis points higher than the certificate rate. However, even though the coupon rate is known, the amortization schedule for each pool still is an estimate because mortgages may be as much as 12 months old when the GNMA is issued. Therefore, the ages are not known with certainty.

[3] FHLMC does have such a data base that could be used. Its loan history file contains borrower demographic information on the mortgage loans that support the PC programs. This data base is available on request from FHLMC. At present, the mortgage corporation only will release data on loans originated through the end of 1980. Therefore, Regular PCs, but not Guarantor/Swap PCs, may be studied. FHLMC may make more current information available at a later date. For a complete discussion of this data base, see Helen F. Peters and David J. Askin, *Average Weighted Life Study of the Federal Home Loan Mortgage Corporation's Conventional Mortgage Portfolio (1973–1980)*, Federal Home Loan Mortgage Corporation, Washington, D.C., January 1984.

most of the models developed to date have not been successful in consistently predicting the CPRs of individual pools.

All is not lost, however. For those fully aware of the data constraints and willing to devote the necessary resources, accurate forecast models can be created. Much of the information embodied in the data that are missing can be provided by using aggregate regional and macroeconomic data. If the pool data are categorized appropriately, CPR forecasts can be produced for groups of pools with characteristics very similar to the individual pool of interest. These CPR forecasts can be used for specific pools with much more confidence than those created by rules of thumb and extrapolation. Further, a formal forecast model allows the user to test the sensitivity of CPR forecasts to a variety of possible economic environments.

Econometric Models

The first and most often used methodology for forecasting CPRs is econometric modeling. Typically, the model is created from an ordinary or generalized least squares regression procedure, although logit models and discriminant analysis have been used as well.

In regression models, the dependent variable usually is a measure of prepayment probability or rate for a group of mortgage securities. As discussed previously, trying to predict the prepayment probability for one mortgage or one pool is unlikely to be successful. Monthly or annualized CPRs are most often used, although multiples of FHA experience also have been employed. CPRs work better.

Whether the data base consists of whole loans or mortgage-backed securities, it is important to aggregate the data into groups. The object of the aggregation is to form cohorts of mortgage securities, where the characteristics that determine the prepayment probabilities of the securities within any cohort are similar. At the same time, the cohorting scheme should allow for significant variation in prepayment probabilities among the various groups.

The best forecast models group the mortgage securities both by the coupon rate and origination date. For example, all of the 8 percents mortgage securities originated in 1973 would be in one cohort, all the 8 percents of 1974 in another, and so forth. This aggregation scheme explicitly recognizes the significance to prepayment activity of relative interest rates and other terms of financing at origination. In addition, it allows the models to capture the impact of changes in important economic and financial variables over time. In situations where the number of observations are sufficient, the data may be broken down further by state or geographic region. If the data do not permit this, geographic effects still may be included by the correct specification of the explanatory variables.

All regression models include an explanatory variable (or variables) to capture the relationship between CPR and the relative level of interest rates. The general form of this factor is the spread between the mortgage rate at the time the prepayment occurred (C_t) and the contract rate on the mortgage security (C_0). However, the exact specification varies. Some models use dummy variables for various subsets over the possible range of spreads. The problem with this approach is that the definition of the ranges for the dummy variables is somewhat arbitrary and the resulting coefficients can be difficult to interpret.

Other models include the absolute level of the spread, $C_t - C_0$, as well as second and higher order polynomial expressions. These specifications are an attempt to account for the nonlinear effect of the interest rate spread on prepayment rates. Unfortunately, the mechanical use of squared or cubed spread expressions provides no theoretical justification for the expected sign of the coefficient on the spread terms. Neither does it account for the asymmetric response function of mortgagors' prepayment activity to a given change in the level of interest rates.

A better specification of the interest rate spread effect is found in a forecast model developed in a study of the conventional loan portfolio that supports the FHLMC regular PC program.[4] The specification is based on the *percentage change* in the interest rate spread, not on the level of the change. This means, for example, that a 100 basis point decrease in mortgage rates from 13 percent to 12 percent will increase prepayment rates by a different amount than will a 100 basis point decline from 15 percent to 14 percent.

The precise form of this effect is:

$$CPR = a \, (PCTSPREAD) + b \, (d \times PCTSPREAD)$$

where

CPR = the conditional prepayment rate for the mortgage cohort;

$$PCTSPREAD = \frac{C_t - C_0}{C_0};$$

d = a dummy variable that equals 1 if PCTSPREAD $\geq$ −5 percent, 0 otherwise;

a,b = the regression coefficients.

This specification accounts both for the nonlinearity and asymmetric response of CPRs to interest rate changes. The cut-off point in the dummy variable definition that is both non-zero and negative recognizes that the incentive to refinance is inhibited until the decline in market rates is below the coupon rate by enough to cover the transactions costs.

The relationship between (annual) CPRs and the percentage change in interest rate spread is shown in Exhibit 1. To the far right of the graph is the situation where the current interest rates are well above the mortgage contract rate. Prepayments are very low but not zero, since some people still move into better houses, get transferred, and so on. As one moves to the left, market rates begin to fall. Refinancing is not yet an important force, but the barriers to moving are lower. More people who are considering this option will do so. At points further to the left, prepayment activity increases at an increasing rate. To the left of zero, the market rate is

---

[4] For a complete description of this model and of the underlying data, see Peters and Askin, *Average Weighted Life Study of the Federal Home Loan Mortgage Corporation's Conventional Mortgage Portfolio (1973–1980)*.

EXHIBIT 1

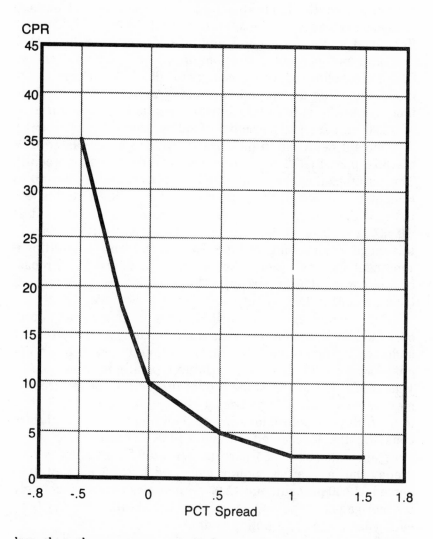

less than the contract rate. Refinancing now is a more important component of the prepayment activity. Beyond the point
where market rates are below the contract rate by more than
5 percent, the curve turns up even more sharply, as the incentives to refinance are very strong.

The estimated values of a and b in this model are -0.537

and 0.392, respectively. This means that if the percentage spread differential is greater than −5 percent, each 1 percent increase (decrease) in the spread variable leads to a decrease (increase) in the forecasted annual CPR by 0.145 (−0.537 + 0.392), or 14.5 percent. For example, if the forecasted annual CPR for a cohort of mortgages given all of the factors in the model including the spread variable is 12 percent, a 1 percent increase in the spread relationship results in a CPR forecast of 10.26 percent [12 percent − (14.5 percent × 12 percent)]. A 1 percent decrease in the spread leads to a forecasted CPR of 13.74 percent [12 percent + (14.5 percent × 12 percent)]. This assumes that the value of all other explanatory variables remain unchanged. If the percentage spread differential is less than (wider) than −5 percent, the regression coefficient is −0.537, a change of 53.7 percent. For spread differentials in this range and a prior CPR forecast of 12 percent, an additional 1 percent increase (decrease) leads to a new CPR forecast of 5.56 percent (18.44 percent). These values are 12 percent ± (53.7 percent × 12 percent).

The second essential variable in most prepayment forecast models is seasoning. This effect usually is captured by including a dummy variable for each time interval. In an annual forecast model, such a variable typically is called *policy year*. Referring to the same model discussed above, prepayment rates start low in the early years, rise rapidly, and peak in the fifth year before leveling off. Holding all other variables constant, the forecasted annual CPRs increase for a given mortgage cohort by 1.55 percent per year for mortgages that prepay during the first policy year and by 5.12 percent, 9.23 percent, 12.30 percent, and 12.97 percent per year, respectively for mortgages prepaying in their 2nd, 3rd, 4th, and 5th (and each year thereafter) policy years.[5]

There is little unanimity among the regression models concerning the inclusion of other variables. In large part, this is because of data availability problems, as discussed previously.

---

[5] Peters and Askin, *Average Weighted Life Study of the Federal Home Loan Mortgage Corporation's Conventional Mortgage Portfolio* (*1973–1980*), p. 14 and pp. 20–21.

Variables such as GNP (in various forms, i.e., real GNP, percentage change in GNP, and so on) disposable income, housing starts, migration, and discount points have been tried as macroeconomic variables. Regionalized variations of these variables also have been employed. The results are mixed. They work in some models, but not in others. Where borrower demographic data are available, earnings, wealth, and borrower age have been the most successful variables. In certain cases, modelers have been able to create successful proxy variables. The usual approach has been to use dummy variables to capture geographic or other qualitative differences and regional/macroeconomic aggregates to capture the effects of variables such as borrowing capacity of the mortgage instrument. Even when these other variables enter significantly into the models, the cost of financing variables and mortgage seasoning are the driving forces behind much of the CPR forecasts.

Options Pricing Models

Options pricing theory, which has been used extensively in finance over the last decade, has been applied to mortgage securities as well. It is predicated on viewing a mortgage as a composite security. One part is a noncallable bond. This is comprised of the scheduled principal and interest payments that must be made every month. The other part is the call option owned by the mortgagor; that is, the right to prepay, usually without penalty. Both pieces of the composite security have value. When accurately calculated and combined, the value of the entire mortgage security is obtained. By valuing the call option inherent in mortgage securities, inferences about prepayment probabilities can be made. This is done by calculating the prepayment rate necessary to produce the market value determined by the options pricing model.

A discussion of the theory supporting options pricing is beyond the scope of this chapter.[6] However, the recognition

---

[6] For a complete discussion of options pricing theory, see Robert Jarrow and Andrew Rudd, *Option Pricing,* Dow-Jones-Irwin, Homewood, Illinois, 1983.

of the option-like feature of the mortgage security has strong intuitive appeal. Most of the work has been done in a continuous time framework, although a discrete time approach has been tried. In the former, the key is to develop a continuous time mortgage pricing model. Instantaneous changes in interest rates and the specification of a risk premium (often assumed to be zero for simplicity) form the information set sufficient to determine the term structure of interest rates and, as a result, the correct pricing mechanism for mortgage securities. The requirements for discrete time options models are similar. However, discrete options models typically are simpler and a bit more flexible, since they do not require the rigorous treatment imposed by stochastic calculus.

The earliest option models were single-state models. That is, they assume that knowledge of the spot (short-term) rate of interest is sufficient to describe the term structure. This rather heroic assumption buys the user a measure of simplicity. More recently, two-state models have been developed, whereby the spot rate and the long-term rate combine to determine the term structure. In exchange for this more realistic construct, an additional layer of complexity is imposed on the model.

With an almost complete reliance on the term structure of interest rates, options models focus on the relationship between CPRs and the spread between market rates and the contract rate to the exclusion of all other factors. The implication is that only the refinancing part of the prepayment decision matters. Home sales caused by job transfers and the desire to upgrade the quality of housing usually are ignored, as are other macroeconomic, demographic, and geographic factors. As a result, most of these models either do not address or do a poor job of providing rationales for the existence of non-zero prepayment rates for deeply discounted mortgages and for the almost $2.4 billion of outstanding principal of GNMA, FNMA, and FHLMC mortgage-backed securities with certificate rates greater than 15 percent.

The empirical testing of CPR forecasts from the options pricing models developed to date has yielded little comfort to investors and traders. Because of the complexity of the models, most empirical work employs simulation techniques or other numerical methods that have minimal linkages to market data. Others have devoted their energies to comparing the magnitudes of the speed of adjustment parameters that govern the interest rate process among the competing options models. To the extent that some models incorporate market price data for empirical testing, they rely heavily on the assumption of perfectly efficient markets for the pricing of mortgage securities. The deviations from this assumption that are observed in the marketplace are sufficient to weaken the empirical results.

The options pricing approach has tremendous potential as an analytical tool. However, the current approach of mechanically applying stochastic calculus to get a default-free rate of interest which is subtracted from a quoted yield to get a market price, which then leads to inferences about the probability of a prepayment by refinancing, must be modified. In particular, adjustments must be made to incorporate other important determinants of prepayments as well as a way to evaluate "uneconomic" calls and non-calls of mortgage securities.

Market Price-Based Models

The third type of approach used to forecast CPRs is one that attempts to infer the market's expectations regarding future CPRs from the market prices of mortgage-backed securities. These models have some similarities to the options pricing approach in that prepayment rate inferences are derived from prices. They differ, however, in that they lack the formal theoretical framework of options models.

Faster prepayments increase the realized yields on discount mortgage-backed securities and lower them for premiums. Prepayments also alter the average lives and durations of these securities and magnify investors' prepayment risk. Rational investors will incorporate these risks into the prices they are willing to pay to own these securities.

Price-based models recognize that prepayment risk is not constant across coupons. The probability of prepayment is much higher for premiums and lower for discounts. However, relatively small changes in CPRs can have a dramatic impact on the price of a discount. Therefore, it is not clear which sector is impacted the most by prepayment uncertainty.

The key to applying the model is to determine the market's required yield on each mortgage security. By combining the current market price and an estimate of required yield, the cash flow stream needed to produce that yield given the price can be derived. The cash flows from a mortgage security consist of scheduled principal and interest plus prepayments. If the mortgage amortization schedule is known, the constant prepayment rate that produces the necessary cash flow over the life of the mortgage security can be calculated. Thus, the prepayment rate imbedded in the current market price is deduced.

The basic limitations of the market price-based models are: a heavy reliance on perfect mortgage market efficiency and on an accurate estimate of required yields, an inability to distinguish between interest rate risk and prepayment risk, and the fact that the CPR forecast produced for a given mortgage security is an average CPR over the remaining life of that security.

Despite a significant and growing number of participants in the secondary mortgage market, there is ample evidence that inefficiencies remain. To the extent that these inefficiencies exist, the CPR forecasts derived from market prices will be biased estimates.

The prices of mortgage securities change in response to interest rate effects in the same way as other fixed-income securities. An additional source of price risk results from prepayment uncertainty. There is a significant correlation between interest rate moves and changes in CPRs, but the correlation is not perfect and changes over time. There is nothing in this modeling technique to distinguish price moves owing to general changes in interest rates from those owing to changes in expected CPRs. This creates a second source of bias in the CPR estimates that are produced.

Market price-based models generate a point estimate; a constant CPR over the remaining term of the mortgage security that is needed to produce the estimate of required yield given today's price. As such, the CPR is an average expected CPR over that term. However, investors have a variety of holding periods and most will sell their investments prior to maturity. It would be useful for the model to be capable of producing a vector of CPR forecasts for different holding periods and under a variety of economic conditions. Market price-based models cannot do this readily, since they assume a fixed required yield over the security's life. The heavy dependence of these models on all relevant information being impounded in market price is somewhat restrictive. It is true that prices change every day, so in principle, the models can be re-estimated daily. But it is unlikely that material changes in prepayment expectations occur that often. Further, most of these models assume the same required yield for all mortgage investments. This is an implication of the assumption of perfect market efficiency, but one that is not supported by the evidence. For example, investors in discount mortgage-backed securities consistently purchase them at lower yields than currents and premiums, in exchange for a greater measure of call protection.

The use of market prices and the prepayment expectations imbedded within them is an appealing framework for forecasting CPRs. These models must be refined before they are capable of consistently providing estimates that are useful for investors and traders under a variety of market conditions.

CONCLUSION

There is great interest in developing models to forecast the prepayment rates of mortgages and mortgage-backed securities. The realized return on an investment in any of these securities is determined by the receipt of cash flows dictated by the prepayment experience. In spite of some rather restrictive informational constraints, models have been created that do credible jobs of providing a framework for predicting the prepayment activity of groups of mortgage securities.

For investors and traders, the important element is not the estimated prepayment rates per se. Rather, it is in obtaining forecasts that can be used for the accurate assessment of investment values. It must be emphasized that most of the existing methodologies should not be used directly to forecast prepayment probabilities for individual mortgages or mortgage pools. The prepayment patterns of many pools show little consistency over time. At the extreme, some observers have concluded that the monthly CPRs of individual pools are essentially random numbers. While there may be an element of truth to this statement, the real problem is largely one of inadequate data. This has discouraged many researchers and prevented some models from being as robust as is desirable. The result is a proliferation of "projected CPRs" that are little more than extrapolations of historical trends and/or pure guesses.

The work done to date makes it clear that prepayment forecast models can be created that are soundly based in theory and produce viable CPR forecasts. The modeling efforts fall into one of three basic categories: econometric models, options pricing models, and market price-based models. Each has significant strengths and some drawbacks as well. However, if properly applied, these models produce prepayment rate forecasts for groups of mortgage securities that are useful for generic pricing. The forecasts also provide guidelines for the evaluation of specific pools.

There is much that needs to be done. This discussion focuses on models that forecast prepayments of fixed-rate mortgages (FRMs) because of their traditional importance in the marketplace. Recently, alternative mortgage instruments, especially adjustable rate mortgages (ARMs), have become a significant part of mortgage finance. The ARM product is too new for an adequate history to exist that could form the basis of empirical testing. Therefore, most of the effort to date has been theoretical, with an emphasis on the options approach.

More empirical work will emerge when there is additional experience with the instrument.

Some analysts argue that ARMs should prepay more slowly than FRMs because the interest/payment adjustment feature removes most of the incentive to refinance. Others feel that with mortgage terms that adjust to current market conditions, there are few impediments to moving inherent in the available mortgage instruments. This should lead to higher CPRs. In addition, a case can be made that many ARMs have been sold at sharply discounted initial rates or to people who prefer FRMs but cannot qualify for them under current conditions. A move to FRMs at the first available opportunity is projected for many of these borrowers. More information and more research in this area are required.

The secondary mortgage market is large and growing. New products which use mortgage securities in a variety of ways, such as CMOs and adjustable rate preferred stocks, continue to develop. The stakes in obtaining valid CPR forecasts for proper security valuation are high as are the rewards. This assures the continuing effort to create better forecasting techniques.

There are two likely paths along which these efforts will proceed: better integration of the modeling frameworks and better data. Many of the strengths of the individual methodologies could be combined so as to complement one another. For example, the theoretical foundation and intuitive appeal of the options pricing approach might be merged with the analytical and applied statistical framework of econometric modeling.

The solution to the data problem is one that is largely exogenous to the decision of selecting a methodology. Most of the data that are publicly available come from the factor data bases provided by GNMA, FNMA, and FHLMC for their mortgage-backed securities. Unfortunately, this data base does not provide all desirable information on the coupons, seasoning, and property characteristics of the underlying mortgages. Modeling and forecasting efforts would be aided significantly by improvements in these data.

Information on whole loan pools of a size sufficient to permit the creation of forecast models is even harder to come by. The localized and fragmented nature of the loan origination process is responsible for this. Although there is a continuing trend toward a greater concentration of the origination and servicing functions, significant progress in this area is unlikely in the near term. The creation of a central information depository would represent a giant step toward a successful resolution.

The cost of improving the information flow for the agency securities, non-agency mortgage-backed securities, and whole loans is large. However, the provision of these data would lead to increased market efficiency. The result would be smaller spreads, increased market liquidity, and ultimately a reduction in the cost of mortgage finance. In the final analysis, the benefits outweigh the cost.

CHAPTER 12

A Framework for Evaluating Treasury-Based Adjustable Rate Mortgages

Michael Waldman
Vice President and Manager of Mortgage Research
Salomon Brothers Inc

Stephen Modzelewski
Vice President, Quantitative Research
Salomon Brothers Inc

Although originations of adjustable-rate mortgages (ARMs) have exceeded those of fixed-rate mortgages, the distribution of ARMs in the capital markets has been severely limited. One reason for this is the confusion caused by the plethora of different ARMs that have been created. ARMs may vary with respect to several features:[1]

- Index;
- Frequency of adjustment;
- Initial rate;
- Reset margin;
- Interest rate caps (yearly and/or lifetime);
- Payment caps; and
- Negative amortization.

A second problem is the difficulty in determining the value of an ARM. There is a great deal of uncertainty about the

---

[1] These features are described in Chapter 4.

way to compare different ARMs, as well as about the way to compare ARMs with alternative fixed-income investments. Along with uniformity of structure, a method for analyzing value is thus critical for the development of the market.

In the first section of this chapter, we analyze one-year ARMs tied to the one-year Treasury rate index for specific interest rate scenarios. The principles apply to other Treasury-based ARMs, as well. In the second section, we will describe our newly developed ARM pricing model, which measures the value of one-year Treasury ARMs using an option-theory approach. It is hoped that these techniques will help market participants to better assess the value of these instruments.

ARMs tied to a cost-of-funds index—the weighted-average cost of the liabilities of thrift institutions—represent another important type of ARM.[2] However, the analysis of these ARMs involves a different set of considerations and, thus, is beyond the scope of this chapter.

SPECIFIC INTEREST RATE SCENARIOS

As with any floating-rate instrument, the cash flows of an ARM are not known in advance but depend on the course of interest rates. The payments on the ARM will rise and fall with changes in the level of the underlying index, subject to the potential limiting effects of any interest rate caps. Thus, a traditional yield-to-maturity calculation is not appropriate.[3]

Since the cash flows of an ARM vary with the value of the index in future years, it makes sense to derive an effective spread or margin over the base index. The idea is to evaluate what the net profit would be if the ARM were financed with a floating-rate liability whose rate matched the index value.

---

[2] According to a survey by the U.S. League of Savings Institutions, nearly half of all ARMs originated by thrift lenders are backed by a cost-of-funds index.

[3] Indeed, even for fixed-rate mortgages the yield cannot be definitively calculated, since the cash flows are not known in advance, as a result of uncertain prepayments.

If the ARM is priced at par, has no caps, no payment delay, and no teaser rate (that is, the initial rate equals the index value plus the margin), the result is very simple: There is an assured profit in each period equal to the stated reset margin. However, if the instrument is priced at a discount (or premium), has caps, or if the initial rate is different from the index value plus the margin, the magnitude of the spread profit is not as clear and may depend upon the actual course of interest rates.

Current Margin

As an initial approach to evaluating the ARM, we can assume that one-year Treasuries remain at their current yield level. Based on this assumption, we can project the cash flows of the ARM and compute the resulting yield (some prepayment assumption must also be made). This yield can then be compared with the current (and constant) one-year Treasury yield. The resulting spread, which we will call the "current margin," shows the yield advantage of the ARM over the base index, taking into account the price, existing coupon, index value, stated reset margin, and time to next reset.[4]

For example, consider an ARM with an initial rate of 10¼ percent and a 200-basis-point stated margin over the one-year Treasury index.[5] Assume no interest rate or payment caps on the ARM and that the current one-year Treasury yield is 11.04 percent.

To calculate the current margin, we project that one-year Treasuries remain constant at 11.04 percent. As shown in Exhibit 1, at the end of the first year, the ARM rate changes to 13.04 percent, and the mortgage payment is recast to fully amortize the loan in the remaining 29 years. For simplicity,

---

[4] A concept very similar to current margin, known as the discounted cash flow margin and its approximation, the adjusted total margin, are often used in the floating-rate note market.

[5] All ARM rates and margins are described on a net-to-the-investor basis.

EXHIBIT 1
ARM Rate Assuming Unchanged Index Value
(10¼ Percent One-Year ARM, No Caps)

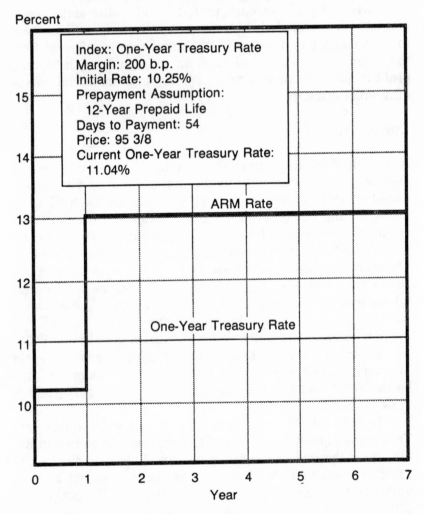

Percent

Index: One-Year Treasury Rate
Margin: 200 b.p.
Initial Rate: 10.25%
Prepayment Assumption:
  12-Year Prepaid Life
Days to Payment: 54
Price: 95 3/8
Current One-Year Treasury Rate:
  11.04%

ARM Rate

One-Year Treasury Rate

Year

we assume a 12-year prepaid life—that is, no prepayments
until a total prepayment at the end of the twelfth year. We
can now calculate the cash flows of this ARM exactly. At a
price of 95⅜, this ARM has a mortgage yield of 13.24 percent,
which, when compared with the constant Treasury yield of

11.04 percent, results in a current margin of 220 basis points.[6] On the other hand, to achieve a current margin of say, 175 basis points, the ARM would have to yield 12.79 percent, which equates to a price of 98.07.

Now, suppose that this same ARM has 2 percent annual and 5¾ percent lifetime caps. These caps mean that the interest rate of the ARM cannot change by more than two percentage points at any annual adjustment, nor can it change in total by more than 5¾ percentage points from its original rate of 10¼ percent. In projecting the cash flows of this ARM assuming a constant index value, the 2 percent annual cap limits the first adjustment, and the ARM rate in the second year is 12.25 percent instead of 13.04 percent. In the third and all subsequent years, the ARM rate fully adjusts to 13.04 percent (see Exhibit 2).

At the same dollar price of 95⅜, this capped ARM has a current margin of 210 basis points—ten basis points lower than that of the uncapped ARM, because of the lower coupon in the second year.

Although this reduction in current margin indicates that the capped ARM is less valuable than the uncapped ARM, it should be clear that the assumption of constant one-year Treasury yields does not evaluate the full "bite" of the caps. To do this, we must relax the assumption of a constant one-year Treasury yield—after all, ARMs were created explicitly to react to *changing* interest rates.

Scenario Margin

Instead of assuming that future one-year Treasury yields are unchanged, we can project an arbitrary scenario of future one-

---

[6] The 220-basis-point current margin compares the monthly compounded yield on the ARM with the (semiannually compounded) bond yield of the one-year Treasury index. A comparison of the bond equivalent yield on the ARM with the bond yield of the one-year Treasury gives a better measurement of the yield advantage provided by the ARM and amounts to 257 basis points in this case. However, it is often helpful for illustrating the concepts to use a mortgage-yield versus bond-yield basis for expressing margins.

EXHIBIT 2
ARM Rate Assuming Unchanged Index Value
(10¼ Percent One-Year ARM, 2 Percent Annual Cap, 5¾ Percent
Lifetime Cap)

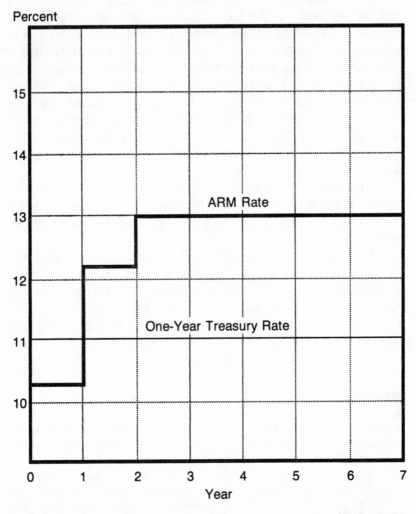

year yields. Given a particular scenario, we can calculate the cash flows of the ARM (as before, some prepayment assumption must also be made, though not necessarily the same for each scenario). For a given price, we can calculate the yield of the ARM under this scenario—the "scenario yield"—but we no longer have a natural choice of index value for comparison.[7]

We can, however, calculate the analogue of current margin as follows: Instead of performing a yield-to-maturity calculation, which uses the same rate for discounting in every year, we must allow our discount rate to vary with the rates in our scenario. For example, to calculate the price of the ARM that provides an advantage to Treasuries of 100 basis points, we calculate the present values of the cash flows of the ARM when the discount rate for each year is 100 basis points greater than the corresponding one-year Treasury yield under the scenario (see Exhibit 3). If the given scenario of one-year yields is 11 percent, 13 percent, 12 percent . . . , then a cash flow of $10 at the end of year three would be discounted back to the present for one year at 13 percent (12 percent + 100 basis points), for a second year at 14 percent (13 percent + 100 basis points) and, finally, for a third year at 12 percent (11 percent + 100 basis points), resulting in a present value of $6.785 (assuming monthly compounding).

For a given price, "scenario margin" is the amount that must be added to the one-year yields so that the price of the ARM is equal to the present value of the cash flows, where present value is calculated as above.

Scenario margin may be interpreted as the break-even financing spread of the ARM under the given scenario. Consider an ARM purchaser who finances this purchase by issuing successive one-year liabilities, each with a net interest cost 100 basis points higher than the then-current one-year Treasury rate. If the ARM has a scenario margin of 100 basis points, then this purchaser will break even if the given scenario comes to pass.

Note that for purposes of the scenario margin calculation, the first scenario rate is the current one-year Treasury yield. Thus, in the above example, the financing for the first year

---

[7] This scenario yield can be used for determining an interesting ARM feature—percent adjustability; see Appendix A to this chapter.

EXHIBIT 3
Scenario Discount Rates

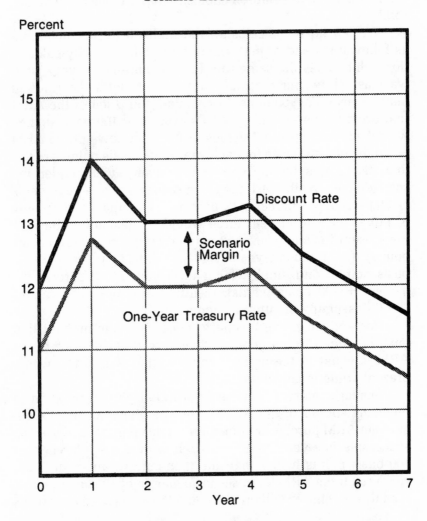

is assumed to be locked in at today's one-year rate. The financing in subsequent years will be determined at the ARM reset points by the future one-year Treasury rates.

The current margin of an ARM is a particular example of scenario margin, where the scenario is chosen to be that of constant index value. We can, however, calculate the scenario margin of an ARM for any given scenario, and thus we can see how the yield advantage of the ARM over Treasuries may vary depending upon the course of interest rates.

For example, consider again the uncapped 10¼ percent ARM described earlier. Since this ARM has no interest rate caps, its advantage relative to Treasuries should be essentially unchanged under different interest rate scenarios.

Suppose we consider simple scenarios where the future one-year Treasury rate remains at some fixed level in future periods, possibly different from the current one-year rate. Exhibit 4 shows the scenario margin on the uncapped 10¼ percent ARM for constant future one-year rates from 8 percent to 16 percent. The scenario margin varies by only three basis points for a wide range of future index values.

We are considering particularly simple scenarios—constant future index values. Of course, we could have examined much more complex index value paths, but the conclusion is the same: For ARMs without interest rate caps, the scenario margin is essentially unchanged and is equal to the easily calculable current margin.

EXHIBIT 4
Scenario Margin for 10¼ Percent ARM
(No Caps)

Future One-Year Treasury Rate	Scenario Margin[a]
8%	221bp
9	221
10	221
11	220
11.04	220[b]
12	220
13	220
14	219
15	219
16	218

[a] Monthly compounded.
[b] Current margin.

Now, if we replace the 2 percent annual and 5¾ percent lifetime caps on this ARM, the current margin declines to 210 basis points, as stated before. We can also consider the results for interest rate levels other than the current index value. For example, Exhibit 5 shows the path of ARM rates, assuming a future one-year Treasury-rate of 13½ percent. Limited by the annual cap, the ARM rate rises from the initial 10¼ percent to 12¼ percent in the second year and to 14¼ percent in the third year. The ARM rate finally reaches the full index plus margin value of 15½ percent in the fourth year and remains at this level in all subsequent years.

The scenario margin, in effect, represents the average of the spreads between the ARM rates and Treasury rates—the differences between the solid and dotted lines of Exhibit 5—appropriately weighted for present value, initial price, and changing principal balance. In this case, the 10¼ percent ARM has a scenario margin of 157 basis points.

Exhibit 6 shows the scenario margin of this capped ARM for future index values from 8 percent to 16 percent. For index values from 8 percent to 10 percent, the scenario margin matches the 221-basis-point margin of the uncapped ARM. However, the scenario margin begins to shrink for future index values above 10 percent and declines rapidly for index values above 14 percent. This occurs because the 2 percent annual caps begin to restrict the ARM cash flows when Treasury rates rise above 10¼ percent, and all of the ARM cash flows become fixed for Treasury rates of 14 percent or higher, as the lifetime cap comes into play.[8]

Exhibit 7 illustrates scenario margins for five representative one-year ARMs in the current market for future one-year rates varying from 8 percent to 16 percent. Each conventional ARM has interest rate caps of 2 percent annually and 5¾ percent over life and a stated reset margin of 200 basis points over the one-year Treasury. The GNMA ARM has caps of 1

---

[8] On the other hand, if initial rates fell sufficiently, the interest rate caps would cause the scenario margin to widen by limiting the downward adjustment of the ARM rate.

EXHIBIT 5
ARM Rate Assuming 13½ Percent Future Index Value
(10¼ Percent One-Year ARM, 2 Percent Annual Cap, 5¾ Percent
Lifetime Cap)

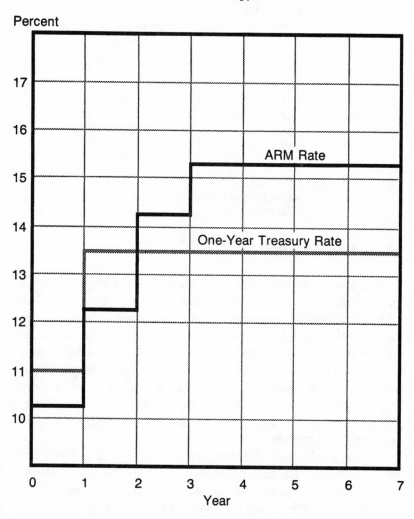

percent and 5 percent and a reset margin of 100 basis points. The scenario margins decline under higher rate levels to a greater extent for the low initial rate ARMs. Exhibit 8 depicts this effect graphically for the conventional mortgage-backed ARMS.

EXHIBIT 6
Scenario Margin for 10¼ Percent ARM
(2 Percent Annual Cap, 5¾ Percent
Lifetime Cap)

Future One-Year Treasury Rate	Scenario Margin[a]
8%	221bp
9	221
10	221
11	210
11.04	210[b]
12	195
13	171
14	143
15	59
16	−25

[a] Monthly compounded.
[b] Current margin.

Yield Curve Margin

While the scenario margin is essentially constant across a broad range of scenarios for ARMs without caps, the addition of caps causes scenario margins to vary considerably. Hence, the question of which scenario to choose as the "base case" becomes relevant. Certainly, the unchanged market scenario, which is used in the calculation of current margin, has the advantages of simplicity and ease of calculation. However, this scenario may not be the best one to use to place the ARM in proper perspective in the market with other fixed-income investments.

It would be useful if the scenario margin of a given instrument reflected its appropriate spread to the Treasury yield curve. For this to be the case, the scenario margins of the various Treasury issues themselves should be zero, since they are, by definition, exactly on the yield curve.

The current margin does not accomplish this result. For example, the 30-year bond at 12.13 percent has a current margin of 109 basis points over the one-year Treasury at 11.04

EXHIBIT 7
Scenario Margin for Five Representative ARM
(12-Year Prepaid Life)

	Conventional				GNMA
	9¼	10¼	11¼	12¼	12
Initial Rate	Percent	Percent	Percent	Percent	Percent
Reset Margin (bp)	200	200	200	200	100
Annual Cap	2%	2%	2%	2%	1%
Lifetime Cap	5¾%	5¾%	5¾%	5¾%	5%
Days to Payment	54	54	54	54	50
Price	92	95⅜	97⅞	100	97⅛
Future One-Year Treasury Rate			Scenario Margin[a]		
8%	260bp	221bp	197bp	182bp	147bp
9	261	221	196	177	135
10	252	221	195	176	135
11	239	210	194	174	136
11.04%	238[b]	210[b]	194[b]	174[b]	136[b]
12	215	195	182	172	136
13	188	171	167	160	136
14	104	143	141	143	122
15	20	59	112	117	107
16	−64	−25	28	87	79

[a] Monthly compounded.
[b] Current margin.

percent. This 109-basis-point advantage is based on the scenario of constant 11.04 percent one-year Treasury yields.

However, there is a scenario that produces zero-basis-point scenario margins over the one-year Treasury for the entire Treasury yield curve. In order to see this, we need to consider the concept of "implied forward rates."

The forward rates implied by the Treasury yield curve are those rates that will bring the returns of any two existing Treasury issues into line when the shorter-maturity issue is

EXHIBIT 8
Scenario Margins for Conventional ARMs[a]
(12-Year Prepaid Life)

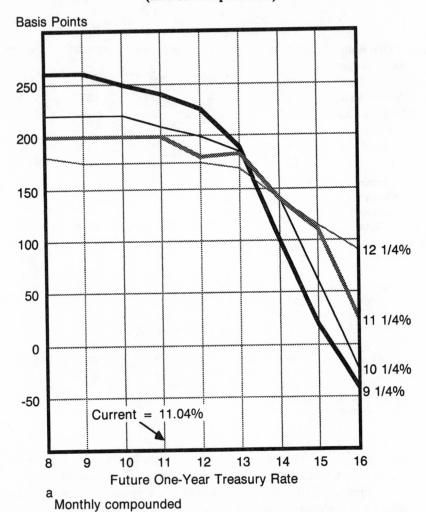

Basis Points

12 1/4%

11 1/4%

10 1/4%

9 1/4%

Current = 11.04%

Future One-Year Treasury Rate

[a] Monthly compounded

rolled at the forward rate to the maturity of the longer issue.
For example, consider one-year and two-year Treasury issues
at 11.04 percent and 11.72 percent, respectively, in the current
market. If the one-year issue is rolled one year from now into
a new one-year Treasury at 12.48 percent, the overall two-

year rate-of-return will just match the 11.72 percent available today in a two-year issue. Thus, the one-year forward rate for one-year Treasury issues implied by today's pricing is 12.48 percent.

Using the Treasury yield curve, we can obtain an entire sequence of implied rates for the one-year Treasury issue for various forward periods: one year from now, two years from now, three years from now, and so on. The implied forward rates have a real financial meaning—at least for situations where actual forward and futures contracts exist—in that differences between the implied forward rates and actual futures prices often indicate arbitrage opportunities.

If we use the sequence of implied forward one-year Treasury rates as our scenario, we find that the 30-year Treasury, in fact all the Treasury issues, will have a scenario margin of zero basis points. Indeed, one way of defining the implied forward rates is the requirement that the scenario margin of the current coupon Treasury market is always zero.

Since the implied forward rates make the values of the various Treasury maturities equivalent, this scenario margin for the ARM represents a spread not just to the one-year Treasury, but to the Treasury yield curve in its entirety. Accordingly, we will single out this particular scenario, and we call the scenario margin determined by the forward rate curve the "yield curve margin" of the ARM.[9]

The implied forward rates also produce scenario margins for other securities that are sensible measures of their spreads to the Treasury curve. For example, a ten-year corporate bond trading at a yield spread of 50 basis points to the ten-year Treasury will have a yield curve margin that is almost exactly 50 basis points. A semiannual floating-rate note spread 45 ba-

---

[9] Although the forward rate scenario is theoretically attractive, minor problems arise in its computation. First, individual forward rates can be very sensitive to minor changes in the yield curve. Fortunately, these effects tend to offset each other, and the scenario margin is not dramatically affected. Second, for a given Treasury curve, the yield curve margin of an ARM can vary slightly, depending upon the particular assumptions and approximations used in the calculation of the forward rates.

sis points over the bond-equivalent yield of the six-month bill
will have a yield curve margin of 45 basis points. In other
words, for many securities, yield curve margin coincides with
the conventional notion of spread to Treasuries.

Using the Treasury yield curve and implied forward rates

EXHIBIT 9
Treasury Yield Curve and Implied Forward One-Year Rates
(12 October 84)

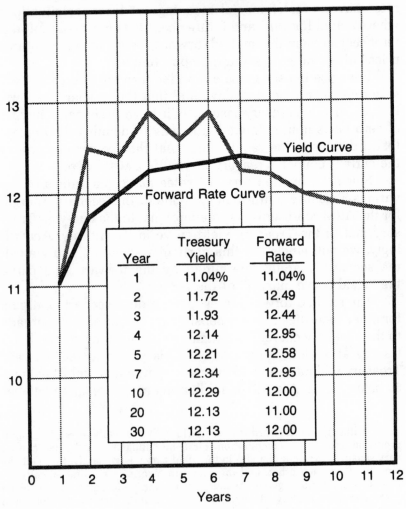

Year	Treasury Yield	Forward Rate
1	11.04%	11.04%
2	11.72	12.49
3	11.93	12.44
4	12.14	12.95
5	12.21	12.58
7	12.34	12.95
10	12.29	12.00
20	12.13	11.00
30	12.13	12.00

Years

EXHIBIT 10
Current Margin and Yield Curve Margin[a]
(12-Year Prepaid Life)

ARM	Initial Rate	Price	Current Margin	Yield Curve Margin
Conventional	9¼%	92	238bp	203bp
Conventional	10¼	95⅜	210	186
Conventional	11¼	97⅞	194	175
Conventional	12¼	100	174	168
GNMA	12	97⅛	136	136

[a] Monthly compounded.

of October 12, 1984, as displayed in Exhibit 9, we calculated the yield curve margins for the five representative ARMs shown earlier. These are compared with the current margins for these investments in Exhibit 10. For example, the 10¼ percent ARM has a yield curve margin of 186 basis points, 24 basis points less than its current margin of 210 basis points. Of course, for the 10¼ percent ARM with no caps, the yield curve margin and the current margin have the same 220-basis-point value.

To summarize, the relative values of different ARMs can be assessed by comparing their scenario margins for a variety of future interest rate scenarios. If a single scenario is chosen as the base case, the yield curve margin, in theory at least, gives a truer picture of the impact of interest rate caps on an ARM than does the current margin.

THE NEWLY DEVELOPED ARM PRICING MODEL

In the first section of this chapter, we described methods for examining the spread of a one-year Treasury-linked adjustable-rate mortgage (ARM) over its base index for specific interest rate scenarios. We showed that the relative values of different ARMs could be assessed by comparing their margins for a range of future interest rate scenarios. We also described how two particular scenarios—the unchanged market and the implied forward rates—lead to simple measures for the value of the ARM: the "current margin" and the "yield curve margin." However, examining the investment results for a single scenario, or even a group of scenarios, is ultimately a limited approach. An overall assessment of the ARM needs to combine these results across the range of potential scenarios.

This problem can be addressed using an options approach. The ARM essentially presents a debt option problem—that is, one involving payments that are contingent upon future interest rate levels relative to certain floors and ceilings established by the caps. For example, the lifetime cap can be represented as a series of puts and calls on one-year Treasury bills.[10]

However, the ARM framework is more complicated than that of the typical option instrument. In the case of an annual cap, it is not only the value of the future interest rate level that matters but also the path along which it reaches its future value. Moreover, there is a series of 29 options points rather than just one. Finally, the ARM involves another interest rate option—the right of the home owner to prepay the mortgage.

To provide a means for assessing the value of these instruments, given the complexities discussed above, we have developed an ARM pricing model. This model analyzes the impact of a full distribution of potential interest rate movements on the cash flows of an ARM. The model is an application of option pricing theory.

The basic technique used is as follows: First, we create a probability distribution of potential future paths for the one-year Treasury rate (index value) based upon an assumed level

---

[10] The lifetime cap creates a ceiling and floor for possible future ARM rates. The loss on the ARM (relative to a pure floating-rate investment) when the index plus margin rises above the ceiling is similar to that on a short position in a one-year Treasury bill put. The profit on the ARM when the index plus margin declines below the floor is similar to that on a long position in a one-year Treasury bill call.

of interest rate volatility.[11] Given this distribution, we perform a Monte Carlo simulation—that is, we randomly select a sufficient number of interest rate paths to closely approximate the impact of the full distribution.[12]

Suppose a desired margin value, say 100 basis points, is given. For each simulated path, we project the cash flows of the ARM (using some prepayment assumption, though not necessarily the same one for each path) and calculate the present value of these cash flows. The discount rates used are the rates along this particular path plus the 100-basis-point desired margin. This present value is calculated for each path, and the average of the present values is the overall value of the ARM. By assessing the results of the ARM along all the paths, this value fully captures the impact of the caps.

For a given price, the process is reversed. Various margins are tried until one is found that makes the average present value match the price. This margin can be termed the "effective margin" or "option-adjusted margin" on the ARM. In a sense, it represents the average of all scenario margins, weighted by their probabilities.

The Interest Rate Distribution

The process described above provides a general technique for evaluating the ARM that takes into account the range of potential interest rate scenarios. We still must decide which interest rate distribution to use.

We would like to define the distribution so that for a given instrument, the effective margin represents a reasonable measurement of its yield advantage versus Treasuries. In the first section, where we looked at specific interest rate scenarios, we found that if we set the future one-year Treasury rates

---

[11] Defined as the standard deviation of the annual percentage change in yield.

[12] For this report, enough simulations were performed so that the standard error of price estimates is less than 0.1 percent.

equal to the forward rates implied by the Treasury yield curve, the resulting scenario margin gave sensible yield spreads to Treasuries for many securities. We therefore referred to this scenario margin as the yield curve margin of the ARM.

We now want to generalize this result for a distribution of future interest rates rather than for just one scenario. We have structured the distribution as follows: The one-year Treasury rate follows a log-normal random walk with standard deviation equal to the assumed level of interest rate volatility. The centers of the distribution are chosen specifically so that the effective margins of the various Teasury issues are zero. This is analogous to centering the distribution around the implied forward rates, but it is not quite the same. Technical details on the structure of the distribution are shown in Appendix B.

By defining the distribution in this way, we obtain logical results for standard fixed-income securities. First, the advantage, as expressed by the effective margin, of Treasury issues themselves to the Treasury curve is zero. Second, the model produces effective margins for other standard securities that correspond to their traditional yield spreads to the Treasury curve. For example, a 20-year corporate bond that yields 12.95 percent when 20-year Treasuries are at 12.10 percent has an effective margin of almost exactly 85 basis points, according to our model. Similarly, a semiannual floating-rate note spread 45 basis points over the bond-equivalent yield of the six-month Treasury bill has an effective margin of 45 basis points. Note that for securities without embedded options, such as noncallable bonds and uncapped floaters, effective margin, yield curve margin, and the traditional yield spread to the Treasury curve are all essentially equivalent.

By using a full distribution of interest rates, however, the model can also evaluate the option features of more complex instruments. In particular, for an ARM, this technique can take into account the impact of all of its potential caps—not just those that come into play under a single scenario. As discussed in Appendix B, this way of calculating the effective margin is also consistent with the theoretical principles for calculating option values that have been developed in the academic literature.

Thus, the effective margin gives the net advantage, in basis points, of the ARM over Treasuries, fully taking into account the impact of the interest rate caps. Furthermore, this spread to the Treasury curve can be sensibly compared with those of other securities.[13]

Exhibit 11 shows the effective margins for five representative one-year ARMs. These values, as well as the other results shown in this report, are based on the Treasury yield curve of October 12, 1984, as displayed in Exhibit 12. Each conventional mortgage ARM has interest rate caps of 2 percent annually and 5¾ percent over the life of the loan and a stated reset margin of 200 basis points over the one-year Treasury. The GNMA ARM has caps of 1 percent and 5 percent and a reset margin of 100 basis points. We have assumed an interest rate volatility of 12 percent and a 12-year prepaid life. For comparison, we have also listed the current margins and yield curve margins for these ARMs. The effective margins are narrower than the yield curve margins in all cases—particularly for the low initial rate ARMs—reflecting the losses that occur under rising rate scenarios.

Exhibit 11 also includes the margins on the uncapped versions of the same ARMs.[14] By comparing the effective margins of the uncapped and capped ARMs, we can now derive the net basis-point cost of the caps to the investor. For example, the 10¼ percent ARM has an effective margin of 220 basis points without caps and 127 basis points with caps. Hence, the caps produce a net negative effect of 93 basis points.

---

[13] Since the effective margin of the ARM gives its advantage over Treasuries, the question may arise as to which Treasury. However, this advantage cannot be related to a single maturity point, but rather it relates to the series of points along the Treasury curve corresponding to various ARM cash flows.

[14] For uncapped ARMs, the scenario margin is essentially independent of the particular scenario chosen hence, all three margin concepts yield the same result (to within a couple of basis points).

EXHIBIT 11
Effective Margin for Five Representative ARMs[a] (12 Percent Volatility, 12-Year Prepaid Life)

ARM	Initial Rate	Price	Reset Margin	Caps		Days to Payment	Uncapped ARM Margin	Capped ARM		
				Annual	Lifetime			Current Margin	Yield Curve Margin	Effective Margin
Conventional	9¼%	92	200bp	2%	5¾%	54	263bp	238bp	203bp	129bp
Conventional	10¼	95⅜	200	2	5¾	54	220	210	186	127
Conventional	11¼	97⅞	200	2	5¾	54	194	194	175	131
Conventional	12¼	100	200	2	5¾	54	174	174	168	133
GNMA	12	97⅛	100	1	5	50	136	136	136	89

[a] Monthly compounded.

EXHIBIT 12
Treasury Yield Curve (12 October 84)

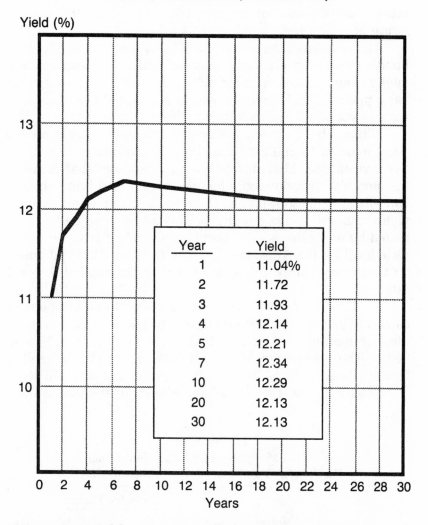

Year	Yield
1	11.04%
2	11.72
3	11.93
4	12.14
5	12.21
7	12.34
10	12.29
20	12.13
30	12.13

Mortgage-Yield versus Bond-Equivalent-Yield Basis

The ARM margins shown in Exhibit 11 are expressed on a mortgage-yield basis. That is, these results reflect comparisons of monthly compounded scenario discount rates with semiannual bond yield index values. This choice has the nice feature

that the margin of an ARM without caps is stable across interest rate scenarios. These instruments thus convey *one* margin
rather than a series of margins that depend on the path of
future interest rates.

The computations could have been done as easily on a
bond-equivalent-yield basis. This would involve using semiannually compounded rates for all the discount rates along scenario paths. In that case, the margin for an ARM without caps
would expand as the underlying index value rises.

Ultimately, we need the bond-equivalent margin on the
ARM in order to make meaningful comparisons with alternative investments. There is a basis-point "add-on" that converts
the monthly compounded effective margin to a bond-equivalent effective margin, just as there is for converting mortgage
yields to bond-equivalent yields. This add-on can be approximated by using the add-on corresponding to a representative
yield level for the ARM: for example, the scenario yield based
on the current index value, or better, on the implied forward
rate path.

For the 10¼ percent ARM with 2 percent and 5¾ percent
caps, a 12 percent interest rate volatility, and a 12-year prepaid
life, the monthly compounded effective margin is 127 basis
points. The scenario yield for this ARM based on the implied
forward rates is 14.12 percent; the add-on at this yield level
is 42 basis points. For the effective margin, the actual add-

EXHIBIT 13
Effective Margin—Bond-Equivalent Basis
(12 Percent Volatility, 12-Year Prepaid Life)

| | | | Effective Margin | |
ARM	Initial Rate	Price	Mortgage	Bond Equivalent
Conventional	9¼	92	129bp	168
Conventional	10¼	95⅜	127	167
Conventional	11¼	97⅞	131	171
Conventional	12¼	100	133	173
GNMA	12	97⅛	89	127

on is 40 basis points, resulting in a bond-equivalent effective margin of 167 basis points. Exhibit 13 shows the effective margins of the five representative ARMs both on a mortgage and bond-equivalent basis. The margins in the subsequent sections of this report will all be expressed on a bond-equivalent basis.

Investment Characteristics of ARMs

The model, by providing the capability to compute ARM prices and effective margins, allows us to examine the nature of these investments in several ways. The parameters that are relevant in describing an ARM investment and that are used in the pricing model include the following:

- Price/effective margin;
- Initial rate;
- Stated reset margin;
- Annual and lifetime caps;
- Current index value;
- Treasury yield curve;
- Interest rate volatility;
- Prepayment assumption;
- Prepayment response to caps; and
- Time to next reset.

We can select any or all of these parameters and examine their impact on the ARM price or effective margin.

Market Interest Rates—Duration: One item of particular interest is the price volatility of the instrument with respect to interest rate movements.

The development of ARMs on a massive scale has been largely a measure to deal with the asset/liability maturity mismatch of thrift institutions. ARMs are seen as interest rate sensitive short-term assets that can be balanced against short-term liabilities. However, for ARMs with caps, this adjustability is limited by the impact of the caps. Given their mixture of floating- and fixed-rate aspects, it is difficult to assess the degree to which these instruments are truly short term in nature.

By using the pricing model, we can examine the (modified)

EXHIBIT 14
Price of 10¼ Percent ARM (167-Basis-Point Effective Margin,
12 Percent Volatility, 12-Year Prepaid Life)

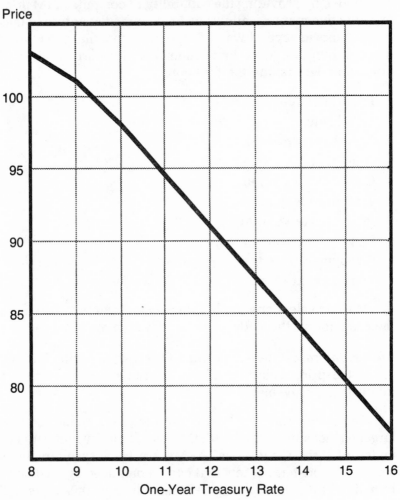

EXHIBIT 15
Duration of Five Representative ARMs at Recent Market Levels
(12 Percent Volatility, 12-Year Prepaid Life)

ARM	Initial Rate	Price	Duration	Equivalent Par Bond Maturity (Years)
Conventional	9¼%	92	3.8	5.5
Conventional	10¼	95⅜	3.3	4.5
Conventional	11¼	97⅞	2.7	3.5
Conventional	12¼	100	2.1	2.5
GNMA	12	97⅛	2.4	3.0

duration[15] —the percentage rate of change of price with respect to interest rate movements—to measure, at least in terms of price responses, the effective length of the investment.

We want to measure the reaction of the price of the ARM to changes in the current index value or short-term interest rate. Since the distribution of future index values depends on the entire yield curve, we will examine the price behavior of the ARM in response to changes in the short-term rate assuming a corresponding parallel shift of the Treasury yield curve.

Exhibit 14 displays the price path of the 10¼ percent ARM for short-term rates between 8 percent and 16 percent for a constant effective margin of 167 basis points. The duration is given by the slope of the tangent to the price curve (divided by the price itself). For a 95⅜ market price, the duration of this ARM is 3.3.

Exhibit 15 shows the durations of each of the five representative ARMs at recent price levels. These durations, with values varying from 2.1 to 3.8, correspond to 2½- to 5½-year maturity bond investments. The durations are longer for the low initial rate ARMs. As market rates rise, these durations will increase, as Exhibit 16 indicates for the 10¼ percent ARM.

---

[15] For the sake of simplicity, we will simply use the term "duration" throughout this chapter.

EXHIBIT 16
Duration of 10¼ Percent ARM
(12 Percent Volatility, 12-Year Prepaid Life)

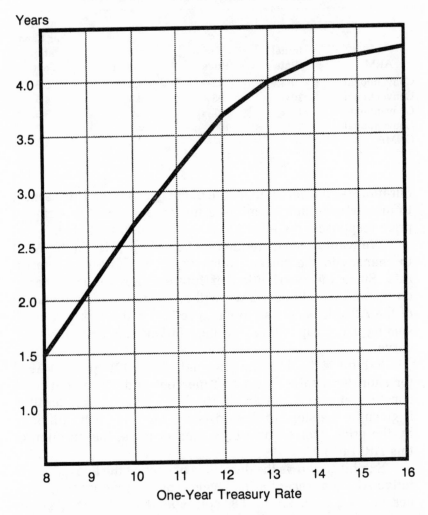

These results have important implications in terms of the balancing of these instruments against short-term liabilities. First, they point out that the appropriate match for these asses-sets is a liability of 2½–5½ years rather than of one year or less. In fact, some one-year ARMs have durations as great as those of 15-year fixed-rate mortgages. Second, the results show that even an appropriately financed position can become vulnerable unless further hedging action is taken, since the duration of the ARM changes as interest rates move.

Effective Margin: The effective margin gives the yield advantage of the ARM over Treasuries and is analogous to the yield spread of a ten-year corporate bond over the ten-year Treasury. Bond spreads are affected by such factors as the supply, liquidity and perceived creditworthiness of the instrument.

A narrowing or widening of the effective margin constitutes a shift in the "basis" of the ARM and has a bigger impact on its price than does a change in market rates. Such a change affects the price of the ARM much like a yield change would affect the price of a fixed-rate mortgage.

Exhibit 17 shows the price of the 10¼ percent ARM for various effective margins and the percentage price change per 1 percent effective margin change. As expected, the percentage price change figures of 5.5 percent–5.8 percent are similar to the durations of fixed-rate mortgages.

Volatility: The assumed market volatility plays an important role in the price of the ARM. As is generally the case for

EXHIBIT 17
Impact of Effective Margin on Price
(10¼ Percent ARM, 12 Percent Volatility,
12-Year Prepaid Life)

Effective Margin[a]	Price	Percentage Price Change Per 1 Percent Effective Margin Increase
100	99.11	5.8%
125	97.68	5.7
150	96.28	5.7
175	94.92	5.6
200	93.58	5.6
225	92.27	5.5

[a] Bond equivalent.

option values, the greater the volatility of interest rates, the greater the potential impact of the annual and lifetime caps. Exhibit 18 displays the volatility of one-year Treasury rates for 40-day periods during the past year. The volatility has varied from 8 percent to 16 percent with an average of about 12 percent for the year. (However, the volatility of one-year

EXHIBIT 18
40-Day Volatility of One-Year Treasury Rates

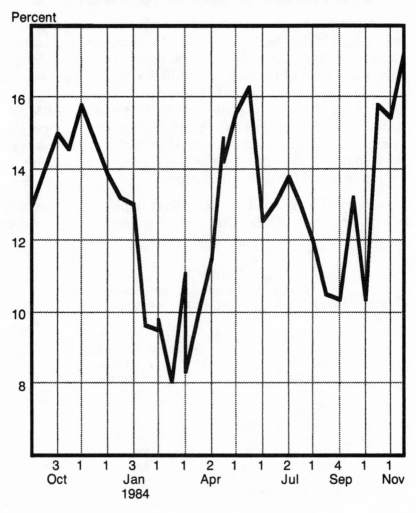

EXHIBIT 19
Impact of Volatility on Price
(10¼ Percent ARM, 167-Basis-
Point Effective Margin, 12-Year
Prepaid Life)

Volatility	Price	Change
9%	96.62	
12	95.38	1.24
15	94.11	1.27
18	92.84	1.27
21	91.58	1.26

Treasury rates has reached significantly higher and lower levels in earlier periods.)

Exhibit 19 shows how the prices of the 10¼ percent ARM vary with market volatility. For each 3 percent increase in volatility, the price declines by about 1¼ points.

Prepayment Assumption: For simplicity, we have assumed a 12-year prepaid life throughout this chapter. Alternatively, we could have used a constant prepayment rate assumption for the ARMs.

Exhibit 20 displays the effective margins of the 10¼ percent ARM for constant annual prepayment rates from 0 percent to 10 percent, as well as for a 12-year prepaid life. At a dollar price of 95⅜, we see the typical pattern for an issue priced at a discount—increasing prepayment rates improve the return on the ARM, although less than for a fixed-rate mortgage at a similar price level. The effective margin expands by four to five basis points for each 2 percent increase in the prepayment rate. In addition, a prepayment rate of about 5 percent produces the same 167-basis-point margin as does a 12-year prepaid life assumption.

Prepayment Response to Caps: The prepayments of fixed-rate mortgages vary in response to interest rate movements. The pace of housing turnover, and hence mortgage prepayment rates, typically slows as interest rates rise, and accelerates

EXHIBIT 20
Impact of Prepayments on Effective Margin
(10¼ Percent ARM, 95⅜ Price,
12 Percent Volatility)

Prepayment Assumption	Effective Margin[a]
12-Year Prepaid Life	167bp
Prepayment Rate	
0%	155
2	159
4	164
6	169
8	173
10	178

[a] Bond equivalent.

when they decline. We may expect the prepayment rates of ARMs to behave similarly.

An even more dramatic response occurs when interest rates decline sufficiently to set off refinancing of fixed-rate mortgages. However, the analogous response for ARMs is likely to be more limited. As long as ARM rates adjust downward to available market rates, significant refinancing will probably not occur. However, if rate caps prevent downward adjustments, some refinancing could take place.

At the opposite end of the scale, if ARM rates are capped out on the upside under rising interest rates, and if the ARMs are assumable (as in the case of the FHA mortgage-backed GNMA ARMs), there may be some decline in prepayments, because of mortgage assumptions.

We have incorporated such "adverse prepayment responses" into the model in order to measure their effect on the return to the investor. There are two prepayment rate adjustments—one for upward rate caps and one for downward rate caps. Using these adjustments, prepayment rates fall when ARM rates cannot fully adjust upward, prepayment rates rise when ARM rates cannot fully adjust downward, and prepayment rates return to normal when the ARM rate fully adjusts.

Exhibit 21 shows the effective margins of the five represen-tative ARMs for a base case of a constant 6 percent prepay-ment rate. It also shows the effective margins still using a basic 6 percent prepayment rate but applying the prepayment rate adjustments. These assume that prepayment rates rise three percentage points when ARM rates hit a floor and that prepayment rates fall 1½ percentage points when ARM rates hit a ceiling. As shown, this prepayment effect reduces the effective margins of these issues by 4–13 basis points. The impact is greater for the ARMs with lower initial rates or tighter annual caps.

Time to Next Reset: The examples used for illustration in this report have been newly originated ARMs with exactly one year to the first reset. ARMs in the actual market may be somewhat seasoned and thus have less than a full year to the first reset.

For a given effective margin, the difference in price be-tween a new ARM and one that is some months old involves several factors. First, there is a "carry" effect—the impact of a difference between the initial ARM rate and the market level (index value plus effective margin) will be in effect for a shorter time period for the seasoned ARM. Second, the distribution of future index values at the reset points is different for the

EXHIBIT 21
Impact of Adverse Prepayment Response on Effective Margin[a]
(12 Percent Volatility)

ARM	Initial Rate	Effective Margin for 6 Percent Prepayment Rate	
		Unadjusted	Adjusted
Conventional	9¼%	180bp	167bp
Conventional	10¼	169	161
Conventional	11¼	168	163
Conventional	12¼	166	162
GNMA	12	130	123

[a] Bond equivalent.

EXHIBIT 22
Impact of Seasoning on Price
(10¼ Percent ARM, 167-Basis-
Point Effective Margin,
12 Percent Volatility,
12-Year Prepaid Life)

Months of Seasoning	Price	Change
0	95.38	
2	96.00	0.62
4	96.62	0.62
6	97.23	0.61
8	97.80	0.57
10	98.36	0.56
12	98.90	0.54

seasoned ARM. The distribution is tighter, because the interest rate volatility has less time to operate; the centers of the distribution take on different values, since they correspond to slightly different points along the Treasury yield curve. Finally, the appropriate short-term rate for the initial period is not the one-year Treasury rate, but that of the shorter Treasury maturing on the first reset date.

Exhibit 22 displays prices for a 10¼ percent ARM, given various months of seasoning, assuming a constant effective margin of 167 basis points. The price increases by approximately ½–⅝ point for each additional two months of seasoning, or about ¼–⁵⁄₁₆ point per month. This increment will be greater for lower initial rate ARMs.

CONCLUSION

The development of a secondary market for ARMs has been hampered by difficulty in determining the value of the investment. There is a great deal of confusion about the way to compare different ARMs, as well as the way to compare ARMs with other fixed-income investments.

In the first section of this chapter, we described a technique—scenario margin—for examining the spread of an ARM over its base index for specific interest rate scenarios. The scenario of forward rates was singled out, since for many securities the resulting measure—yield curve margin—coincides with the usual calculation of spread to Treasuries. However, a more sophisticated approach is needed to make a complete assessment of an ARM that accounts for the impact of the caps across the full range of potential scenarios.

We describe a model that accomplishes this result in the second section of this chapter. The model's measure of value—effective margin—gives the yield advantage of the ARM to Treasuries appropriately adjusted for the options inherent in the caps (and, to the extent incorporated into the model, for those in the uncertain prepayments).

Effective margin is a generalization of the familiar concept of yield spread to Treasuries. The two measures are essentially equivalent for securities without options. For securities with embedded options, such as the ARM, the effective margin fully adjusts for these options and can therefore be sensibly compared with the spreads to Treasuries of other securities.

In addition to providing a valuation tool, the ARM pricing model developed by Salomon Brothers allows us to examine the nature and behavior of ARMs. By using the model to calculate statistics such as duration, we can determine appropriate financing and hedging strategies for these instruments.

We believe that this methodology will fill a gap that currently exists in the ARM market by helping market participants assess and analyze Treasury-based ARMs.

APPENDIX A

Scenario Yield and Percent Adjustability

As we did for scenario margins, we can determine the yield that the ARM will produce under various interest rate scenarios. For each scenario and a given prepayment assumption, we can project the cash flows and compute the resulting "scenario yield."

Consider, for example, the 10¼ percent one-year ARM spread 200 basis points over one-year Treasury rates with 2 percent annual and 5¾ percent lifetime caps. Assume a 12-year prepaid life and that the ARM is priced at 95⅜. Exhibit 23 illustrates the scenario yield of the ARM for assumed future

EXHIBIT 23
Scenario Yield for 10¼ Percent One-Year ARM[a]

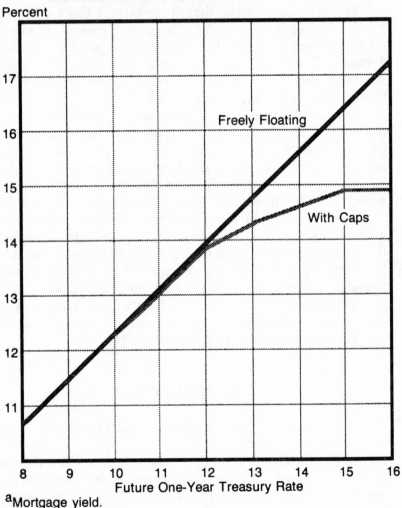

[a]Mortgage yield.

one-year Treasury rates varying from 8 percent to 16 percent. The dotted line shows what the yield would be on a similar ARM without any caps.

For one-year Treasury rates from 8 percent to about 10 percent, the ARM yield moves freely, unhindered by any caps, rising by about 85 basis points for each 100-basis-point rise in the future one-year rate. The ARM yield moves by less than 100 basis points, because a change in the index value affects only the future ARM rates, but not the initial rate. The uncapped ARM continues to rise in yield by approximately 85 basis points for each one percentage point increase in one-year Treasury rates.

However, the yield increases of the capped ARM slow for future index values about 10¼ percent because of the annual cap and stop completely for index values about 14 percent as the lifetime cap takes effect. The relationship of the capped ARM yield increase per 100-basis-point move of the index to that of an otherwise comparable but free floating (uncapped) ARM can be termed its percent adjustability. This measure gives an indication of the extent to which an ARM is responsive to interest rate movements for a given level of the market.

Exhibit 24 shows the percent adjustability for the 10¼ percent ARM for one-year Treasury rates from 8 percent to 16 percent. The percent adjustability holds only for a particular index value region, declining in a series of steps as the index level rises. For a one-year Treasury level of 11.04 percent, the 10¼ percent ARM has a percent adjustability of 83 percent. In other words, for a small rise in interest rates, the yield of this ARM would increase only 83 percent as much as the corresponding cost increase of a freely floating liability.

For a given set of cap and reset terms, the percent adjustability will depend primarily on the difference between the initial ARM rate and the one-year Treasury level—that is, on the depth of the teaser. Exhibit 25 shows the scenario yield and percent adjustability of the five representative ARMs, assuming one-year Treasury rates at 11.04 percent.

The percent adjustability describes an ARM response to a movement in interest rates by measuring the direct impact of such a movement on its cash flows. However, the percent adjustability does not capture the overall impact of an interest rate change on the ARM: It leaves out the extent to which the ARM has moved closer to interest rate caps that do not yet limit its cash flows. This effect is best conveyed in terms of the change in the overall value or price of the ARM, appropriately measured. The price responsiveness of ARMs to inter-

EXHIBIT 24
Percent Adjustability (10¼ Percent ARM, 2 Percent Annual Cap, 5¾ Percent Lifetime Cap)

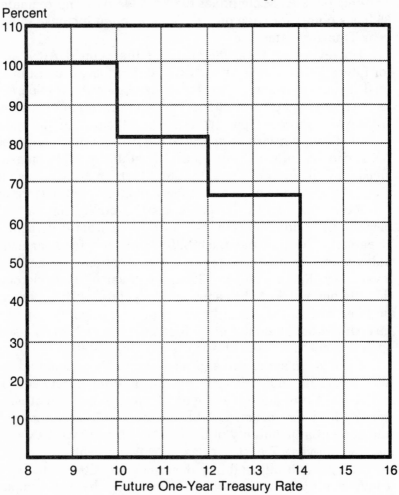

Percent

Future One-Year Treasury Rate

EXHIBIT 25
Scenario Yield and Percent Adjustability
(11.04 Percent One-Year Treasury Rate, 12-Year Prepaid Life)

ARM	Initial Rate	Price	Scenario Yield[a]	Percent Adjustability
Conventional	9¼%	92	13.42%	83%
Conventional	10¼	95⅜	13.14	83
Conventional	11¼	97⅞	12.98	100
Conventional	12¼	100	12.78	100
GNMA	12	97⅛	12.40	100

[a] Monthly compounded.

est rate movements is examined in the second section of the chapter.

APPENDIX B

Theoretical Considerations

While the ARM framework is a complicated type of debt option, the central problem is the same as that encountered in evaluating options on Treasury bonds, notes or bills.

The academic research on the subject of debt options extends the work on stock options pioneered by Black and Scholes, Merton, and others. The basic valuation technique is the riskless hedge approach. To value a stock option, we construct a portfolio of the underlying stock and fixed-income investments so that the performance of this hedge portfolio exactly duplicates the option. If an option is hedged with this duplicating portfolio, the entire position is riskless, and thus the value of the option must equal the cost of maintaining the duplicating portfolio.

One of the results of this theory is that the option value is equal to the expected present value of its exercise proceeds discounted at the short-term interest rate, provided that the distribution of stock price paths is constructed so that the expected short-term rate of return on the stock is equal to the short-term risk-free interest rate. In other words, even though we may believe that the expected rate of return is higher than the short-term risk-free interest rate because of the stock's riskiness, when it comes to valuing derivative securities such as options on the stock, we may nevertheless assume that the stock price distribution reflects "risk neutrality" and value the option as its expected present value.

Following this principle, we decided to set the expected short-term returns of all Treasury securities equal to the short-term rate (both initially and in future periods) and to value the ARM at the expected present value of its cash flows, discounted at the short-term rate as it varies along each scenario path. We have described our distribution in the text as one that gives each Treasury an effective margin of zero, but mathematically, this is equivalent to the condition that the expected short-term return of all Treasuries is equal to the short-term Treasury rate.

Specifically, the model uses one year as its short-term period. That is, the sequence of one-year rates is used for present value discounting, and the expected one-year returns of the Treasury issues are matched to the one-year Treasury rate. Although the procedure we have used here is in the spirit of certain results in the theory of options, the fact that our method is a riskless hedge arbitrage valuation procedure remains to be formally proved.

The exact procedure used for simulating future one-year Treasury rates is as follows: The current one-year rate is given, say R_0. To get the future one-year rates, we use a log-normal random walk:

$$\ln R_i = \ln R_{i-1} + M_i + U_i \quad i = 1,2,\ldots,29$$

The U_i are independent normal shocks, and the M_i are chosen in advance in such a way that all Treasuries have zero effective margin. The standard deviation of each U_i is constant[16] and equal to the volatility of yields. Alternate distributions of future rates could also be explored.

---

[16] The standard deviation of U_1 is reduced appropriately if the time to first reset is less than one year.

SECTION IV

Strategies with Mortgage-Backed Securities

CHAPTER 13

Mortgage-Backed Securities from the Portfolio Manager's Perspective

Richard L. Sega, F.S.A.
Assistant Investment Officer
The Travelers Insurance Companies

The familiar expression, "shooting at a moving target," alludes to the difficulty involved in dealing with a problem where conditions are constantly changing. Consider now a strange situation where the target is fixed, but instead, the gun in your hand is moving and twisting such that you can barely keep your grip on it. If you can imagine this, you begin to appreciate the challange a portfolio manager faces in the use of mortgage-backed securities. However, the yield and flexibility they offer can make the effort well worth it for the astute manager. Realizing these benefits requires careful attention to the particular features of mortgage products.

MORTGAGE-BACKED SECURITIES

Today there is a wide range of issuers of mortgage-backed securities (MBS). By far the most familiar to most portfolio managers are the "agency pass-throughs"—Ginnie Mae, Fannie Mae and Freddie Mac, which have been discussed throughout this book. These securities "pass-through" to the bond-holder the payments made by the individual mortgagors. There are many other issuers of mortgage-backed securities, and many structures other than pass-throughs which occur. One special class, collateralized mortgage obligations (CMOs), will be discussed later in this chapter. All depend on the behavior of the underlying instrument, the residential mortgage, for their value and their special characteristics.

Cash Flows

Cash flows on all mortgage-backed products are driven by the underlying mortgages. Most of the time these loans have level monthly payments for 25 to 30 years. However, seldom (if ever) does the MBS investor see inflows that look very much like level monthly payments based on the stated coupon rate of the pool. It is important to understand the reasons for this.

Prepayments: By far the most important (and also the most complex) reason for variations from the expected level-cash flow pattern is the occurrence of unscheduled payments of principal. Considerable research has been done in an attempt to test for the influences of maturity, mortgage age, type of issuing program, loan-to-value ratio, and a host of other socio-economic variables on the tendency for a borrower to prepay his mortgage. Many of these effects are examined in detail in Chapter 11. Despite the occurrence of mortgage refunding owing to nonfinancial motivations (death, geographical reloca-tion, casualty losses, and so on), the clear front-runner for the portfolio manager's attention is the difference between the rate on the underlying mortgages in the pool and the current market rate for similar financing. This is not to say that other parameters are not important in determining actual prepay-ment rates. Rather, from a portfolio manager's viewpoint, the only factor that can be employed on a cost-effective basis in the face of a volatile interest rate environment is this differ-ential. The other effects are small and are overwhelmed by market rate effects. Some of the other suggested variables (such as housing starts) are themselves very difficult statistics to know with any certainty. For example, insurance company databases are not well suited to the analysis of holdings by geographical location nor are they cross-indexed to economic databases with other necessary data to employ some of the more sophisticated models when making portfolio decisions. For these reasons, most insurance portfolio managers will find the interest rate differential model suitable and sufficient for their purposes.

The customary way to measure prepayment is to calculate the "conditional prepayment rate," i.e., the ratio of face amount prepaying or defaulting in a year to the outstanding balance at the beginning of the year. This ratio can be used directly as a measure of prepayment activity. But, traditionally, it is compared to the history of such ratios compiled by the Actuarial Division of HUD. The HUD table is actually a mortgage survival table called the FHA-experience table, and the percentage of mortgages which do not survive a particular year of age is easily computed. If the ratio described above equals the FHA percentage for the pool's age, it would be said that the prepayment rate is "100 percent FHA." If the pool paid off only half as quickly, 50 percent FHA would be the speed.

A study of the problems caused by the use of FHA-experience is beyond the scope of this discussion, and the reader is referred to Chapter 11. However, for the purposes of portfolio analysis, it is far better to use some measure of prepayment activity that is not tied to an arbitrarily distorted and periodically revised benchmark such as the FHA-experience table. Nevertheless, the FHA-experience table is so entrenched in the MBS market that the portfolio manager should be familiar with its meaning.

Let us assume we have studied GNMA prepayment experience and constructed an extremely simple model for prepayments, i.e., that pools will prepay ½ percent of their principal balances per month for nonfinancial reasons, and an additional ½ percent of their balances for every 100 basis points

EXHIBIT 1
12 Percent GNMA Pool in Several Interest Rate Environments

	Mortgage Yields				
	9 Percent	10 Percent	11 Percent	12 Percent	13 Percent
½ Life*	34 mos	45 mos	67 mos	125 mos	125 mos
Final Maturity	30 yrs	30 yrs	30 yrs	30 yrs	30 yrs
Duration	3 yrs	3.52 yrs	4.26 yrs	5.36 yrs	5.11 yrs
Speed	2%/mos	1½%/mos	1%/mos	½%/mos	½%/mos

* ½ life is the point at which one half of the principal remains; it is a proxy for average life.

the pool rate exceeds the current market rate. Under this model, Exhibit 1 shows a 12 percent GNMA pool in several interest environments.

Exhibit 2 is a similar table for a 12 percent noncallable bond with a similar average life as the pool at par. Note the wide range of durations in the pass-through (Exhibit 1) for a given range of interest rates compared to that of the bond. This instability carries over to the pool's value in the portfolio. The salient point is that MBS present a greater degree of complexity to portfolio management with respect to current and projected interest rate environments. The next section will discuss the effect of this phenomenon on portfolio management decisions.

Before leaving the topic of prepayments, one other area needs to be discussed. That is the relative consistency of various pools' prepayment experience. Much work has been done to isolate "fast pay" pools which, if purchased at a discount, would provide a handsome yield owing to high levels of pre-

EXHIBIT 2
12 Percent Coupon Bond in Several Interest Rate Environments

	Bond Yields				
	9 Percent	10 Percent	11 Percent	12 Percent	13 Percent
Final Maturity	10.5 yrs	10.5 yrs	10.5 yrs	10.5 yrs	10.5 yrs
Duration	6.62 yrs	6.49 yrs	6.36 yrs	6.24 yrs	6.11 yrs

payment at par. The portfolio manager should keep two things in mind. The first is the horizon yield realized after high levels of reinvestment of those prepayments is taken into account, given that the effect occurs and a high yield is obtained on the mortgage pool over a short period. The realized compound yield based on the manager's reinvestment assumptions should be the controlling item.[1]

The second question is whether there are any such "fast payers" that can be found at all. Efforts have been directed at finding these pools by historical observation of their prepayment experience. In fact, some pools will have a somewhat higher content of fast-paying people than others, and this could be observed historically. However, once these fast-paying mortgagors have prepaid and left the pool, you may find that only the relatively slow paying people remain in it. So it may turn out that you have purchased a pool that will be an inordinately slow-payer in the future. Some recent data indicate that in fact there is no measurable consistency of prepayment experience through time, just as this discussion would suggest.

Structure: While prepayments are indeed major, they are not the only reasons that MBS flows do not look like those of level payment mortgages. The structure of the MBS may reorganize the payments, such as in the CMO case. The underlying mortgages themselves may be the source of variation. For instance, while GNMA pools have fairly narrow ranges of final maturities, FNMA rules are not as strict, and a wider range of final maturities (and thus intermediate cash flows) are observed. Another example is the GNMA–GPM program, the graduated payment mortgages. GPM loans feature monthly payments which are increased from 2½ percent to 7½ percent annually for the first five years. Ultimately, the GPM flows look like standard GNMA flows once the graduation period is over.

---

[1] The computation of the realized compound yield is illustrated in Frank J. Fabozzi, "Bond Yield Measures and Price Volatility Properties," Chapter 4 in *The Handbook of Fixed Income Securities*, Frank J. Fabozzi and Irving M. Pollack (Editors), (Dow Jones-Irwin, Homewood, IL, 1983).

Servicing Spread: A relatively small but nonetheless present effect on cash flows is the servicing spread built into the pool rate. For GNMAs this is generally 50 basis points. That means that a 12 percent pool has 12½ percent mortgages in it, and the amortization schedule is so derived. The actual fee is calculated on the outstanding balance and serves to reduce interest paid. Thus as it declines, the total payment to the investor rises slightly over time, absent any prepayments.

FNMA and FHLMC pools have higher servicing spreads than GNMAs, so their underlying mortgages have higher rates and thus may generate higher prepayments than GNMAs. GNMA II pools allow a range of rates and servicing spreads, so they too will ostensibly be subject to higher prepayments than standard GNMAs.

Credit, Expenses, and Other Concerns

Credit analysis, expenses, accounting, and taxation are areas that need special mention with respect to MBS. While in general the same principles apply to investing in MBS as in any other security class, there seems to be an additional layer of complexity whenever mortgages are involved.

Credit: Actually, a large pool of relatively small, diversified debtors is probably one of the more favorable credit situations a lender could find himself in. So, from the standpoint of the underlying mortgages from a well-underwritten bank portfolio, default risk is not a major source of concern. Rather, it is the credit of the issuer of the security which is backed by those mortgages that is important. The investor must be aware of the credit of the issuing entity (e.g., special purpose subsidiary), the trusteeship of the mortgage loans, the paying agent, and the extent of recourse to the parent corporations involved.

In the case of government agency pass-throughs, there is no real default risk. There is, however, a difference in credit. GNMA pools have the full faith and credit of the U.S. Government behind them. FNMA has its own guarantee, with access to U.S. Treasury credit. FHMLC does not guarantee timely principal payments, only that they will be paid in full eventually. While none is likely to default, there may well be delays in forwarding of payments, and opportunity costs as well as processing costs may result.

Expenses: The monthly cash flows of uncertain amounts give rise to considerably high processing and reinvestment expenses compared to ordinary coupon bonds. This should be reflected in the portfolio manager's total return projections and may have an effect on overall strategy.

Accounting: For an insurance portfolio which reports earnings according to generally accepted accounting principles (GAAP), the purchase of discount pass-through securities presents a difficult problem. The amortization of discount against the monthly cash flows and unanticipated prepayments on a constant-yield basis is a complicated calculation beyond the capabilities of many investment accounting systems.

From the GAAP accounting standpoint, amortization of discount on GNMAs generates ordinary income as opposed to capital gains. This is different than the treatment afforded purchases of discount corporate issues. Under some circumstances, such discount accrual is ordinary income for tax purposes as well.

These several examples of special characteristics of MBS are intended not to be comprehensive but only indicative of things which should concern the portfolio manager. Without a full appreciation of these intricacies, the unprepared manager may erode away the yield advantage of his pass-through position through inappropriate accounting, tax, or expense experience. Thorough treatments of these topics can be found in other chapters of this book.

WHY AND HOW TO USE MORTGAGE-BACKED SECURITIES

Meeting Portfolio Management Objectives

The portfolio manager has several objectives which may be brought together in one statement of his general goal: to maximize total return on his portfolio (net of expenses and transaction costs) while remaining within the overall risk tolerance levels of his client (the portfolio's owner). Thus, the portfolio manager seeks high return. He also seeks to minimize his transaction costs and processing expenses. With respect to risk, there are several components to consider and manage. Not only is one interested in the assets' market exposure but also credit, liquidity, and "liability synchronization." The manager does not necessarily wish always to "minimize" risk in the absolute sense. Rather, he needs only to manage and control it. Otherwise, he would find himself wanting to buy exclusively stripped Treasuries with terms matching his liabilities. This approach would minimize risk, but it would fall substantially short of the high return objective.

Let us examine where the MBS asset class (or subclass of the class of fixed-income securities) falls in regard to each of these portfolio management objectives.

Return: MBS have historically yielded more than other fixed income securities of similar quality and maturity.[2] Using GNMAs as an example, typical yield spreads of current coupon GNMAs over the 10-year U.S. Treasury in recent years have ranged from 100 to 250 basis points.

Expenses: MBS have higher expenses associated with them because of several things. The processing of monthly flows can cost as much as 5 to 10 basis points. For accounts subject to state tax, GNMAs and other MBS are taxable, and thus must trade at a higher yield than Treasuries (which are exempt from state taxes) even after accounting for credit and duration risk differences. And MBS positions are management intensive, requiring more time from the portfolio manager, the data processing resource, and the other support areas such as cash management and trading.

Risk: MBS as previously noted do not present any unusual credit or liquidity problems. In fact, if the manager stays within the agency pass-throughs, these two areas are of no real con-

---

[2] For a further discussion of historical returns, see Chapter 8.

cern at all. However, with regard to market exposure, MBS present their biggest problems. The normal interest rate sensitivity associated with fixed income securities of similar duration is exacerbated in the MBS case by the constant fluctuation of that duration, always in the direction disadvantageous to the investor relative to the move in rates. This effect, described mathematically as "negative convexity," will be examined in detail in the next section.

The portfolio manager's task is then to decide if the excess return afforded by MBS is enough to adequately pay for the added expense and risk he will encounter. Many managers have decided that it is, and thus techniques which optimize the features of MBS within various portfolios are constantly emerging. We will examine some of those in the next section.

Managing MBS Positions in Portfolios

Suppose a manager has decided to hold GNMA 12s in his portfolio. What practical steps are involved in the management of that position? A useful way to assess the performance of a security in a portfolio is to view the results of a horizon analysis, i.e., how the security will perform over a certain horizon and a given set of assumptions.[3] We must build a framework of procedures and assumptions that will allow us to answer that question.

Earlier in this chapter, we considered a simple model for GNMA prepayments. We assumed that ½ percent of mortgages would prepay monthly for nonfinancial reasons, and an additional ½ percent would prepay for every 1 percent the pool rate exceeded the market rate for new pools. In practice, the relationship is much more complex. One thing that must be reflected in a prepayment model besides interest rate is the type of MBS you are dealing with. For instance, it has already been discussed that GPMs, FNMAs, and FHLMC pools

---

[3] For a discussion of horizon analysis, see: Martin L. Leibowitz, "Horizon Analysis: An Analytical Framework for Managed Bond Portfolios," Chapter 29 in *The Handbook of Fixed Income Securites.*

will probably behave differently than GNMAs for reasons of structure and servicing spread. Another reason for Fannies and Freddies to pay faster is the existence of "due-on-sale" clauses for some of the loans. States were barred from prohibiting enforcement of these clauses by the 1982 Garn–St. Germaine Act and thus, after a window period, the effect of this law will be felt as higher prepayment rates. For the purposes of illustration in the chapter, we will use our simple model, but the portfolio manager should embellish his with particular information concerning the types of MBS he will be using.

Once the "prepayment algorithm" is developed, it can be used to construct the theoretical cash flow of the MBS through time for a given level of interest rates. Cash flow yields can then be calculated on a more realistic basis. Note that GNMAs and other MBS are quoted in "book yield" terms. This yield assumes no prepayments for a while, then a total lump sum refunding, say at 12 years (for GNMA single family pools; other types might use other terms). For reasonable comparisons with other bonds, these must be converted to realistic yields on a bond-equivalent (semiannual) as opposed to monthly mortgage basis. This is the "honest-to-God" (HTG) yield in the terminology of the First Boston Corporation.[4] Exhibit 3 shows the behavior of our GNMA 12s under changing interest rates using our prepayment algorithm.[5]

Exhibit 3 illustrates several things. The first and most striking is the way the duration (i.e., the price sensitivity to interest rates) changes. The bonds get shorter as rates fall, truncating capital gains. Also, sadly, they get longer to a point as rates rise, expanding capital losses. This is the risk of the unstable duration, the "negative convexity." The patterns also suggest some management opportunities which we will discuss shortly. Another interesting relationship is the difference between the real or "honest-to-god" yield and the book yield

---

[4] See, Dexter Senft, "Pass-Through Securities," Chapter 18 in *The Handbook of Fixed Income Securities.*

[5] For an illustration of how sensitivity analysis can be used, see Chapter 18.

EXHIBIT 3
Behavior of 12 Percent GNMA New Pool under Changing Interest Rates

Realistic (HTG) Mortgage Yield	Paydown Speed Percent Per Month	Price	Duration	Book Yield
8%	2.5%	$110.04	2.61 yrs	10.43%*
9	2.0	108.55	3.00	10.64*
10	1.5	106.56	3.52	10.93*
11	1.0	103.75	4.26	11.34*
12	0.5	99.50	5.36	12.00
13	0.5	94.44	5.11	12.85
14	0.5	89.84	4.89	13.67
15	0.5	85.65	4.68	14.49
16	0.5	81.82	4.49	15.29
17	0.5	78.31	4.31	16.07
18	0.5	75.08	4.15	16.84

* Book yield substantially higher than realistic yield.

under the 12-year prepayment assumption. The manager should not be misled by the cosmetically attractive high yields of the pool relative to the realistic market yields when it is trading at a premium if he believes its average life will actually be much shorter than 12 years.

The next step in the horizon analysis is to establish reinvestment rates and the rate at which the remaining future flows beyond the horizon will be capitalized. Once these assumptions are made, the liability cash flows and expenses can be combined and total wealth at the end of the horizon can be calculated and compared to alternative investments.

To illustrate, let us consider a GNMA 12 percent pool trading at par, and a 12 percent coupon bond also at par so that current yields are comparable. Assume that the market rates for GNMAs and coupon bonds do not change over this horizon. Only the rates in the short-end are allowed to vary. Assume also that there are no liability flows for a 4-year period. The accumulated wealth of the GNMA and coupon bond can be compared via the relationships of their realized compound yields as follows:

Realized Compound Yield Over 4-Years

	Reinvestment Rate (Semiannual)		
	10%	**12%**	**14%**
12 Percent Coupon Bond	11.65%	12.00%	12.36%
	—.35%—		—.36%—
GNMA 12 Percent	11.71%	12.26%	12.82%
	—.55%—		—.56%—

Notice that the GNMA realized yield is higher due to monthly compounding and is more sensitive to the reinvestment rate than that of the coupon bond.

Now assume that there are monthly outflows of 1 percent of the funds:

Cash Flow Yield with Outflows of 1 Percent Per Month

	Reinvestment Rate (Semiannual)		
	10%	**12%**	**14%**
12 Percent Coupon Bond	12.05%	12.00%	11.94%
	—.05%—		—.06%—
GNMA 12 Percent	12.21	12.41	12.63
	—.20%—		—.22%—

While the mortgage pool is still more sensitive than the bond to reinvestment assumption, the range has decreased considerably, and the monthly compounding has increased the effective yield relative to the bond. Add to this a sector spread in yield and the portfolio manager may well choose the GNMA to fund such a liability stream. The exposure to reinvestment risk is reduced while the return is relatively greater than the bond owing to the better matching of asset and liability flows. (The pattern of returns for the coupon bond may be counterintuitive. This phenomenon results from the need to finance the outflows prior to the coupon payment at the reinvestment rate.)

If stochastic interest rate assumptions are made, Monte Carlo simulations can give not only the overall mean return, but also its risk level in terms of standard deviation. Further, the MBS class can be made to fall into line with the portfolio manager's asset allocation procedures.

For many insurance company accounts with high monthly cash flow, such as structured settlements or retired life annuities from pension plans, or for accounts desiring high current taxable yield, MBS present a very viable vehicle with acceptable levels of risk.

The durations and yields shown in Exhibit 3 suggest several other management approaches.

Discounts: The duration pattern of GNMAs in the range of interest rates where they trade at up to several points discount shows great stability. This is because prepayments can approach zero but never become negative. Thus, the yield and cash flow benefits can be obtained without the substantial duration risk by buying discounts. This approach is particularly attractive to "dedicated" cash-matched and horizon-matched portfolios with monthly liability flows. Exhibit 4 shows the low duration risk area for the 12 percent GNMAs.

Premiums: The purchase of premium GNMAs has at times provided a good short-term (1–2 year) return. An attractive side benefit of this approach is seen if the manager's outlook is bearish. Premium GNMAs "cushion" out in price increase after a certain point. Thus, they will hold their value in the face of a run-up in interest rates.

Swapping: An active management program swapping various coupons for added value can be undertaken based on the following analysis. Exhibit 5 illustrates the holding value in a portfolio of the 12 percent GNMA and a 12 percent coupon bond. The bond's term is eight years, so that the durations match at par. The value here is the discounted cash flow of the two instruments at the effective annual interest rate corresponding to the realistic mortgage yield on the horizontal axis. Thus, market spread relationships are not reflected; only the cash flow contribution of each security. Note as GNMA values rise and "cap out," the relative value of the GNMA falls compared to the bond. Under bullish outlooks, the mortgage pools

EXHIBIT 4
Comparative Durations

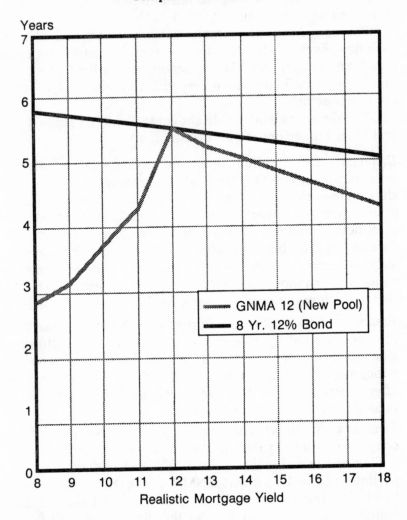

can be sold as they near the peak. Proceeds can be rolled
into other coupons which are relatively less rich, or into another sector. Since the curve shows a low rate of price decline
for the premium pools, rolls into the high coupon area make
sense for bearish investors desiring high current income.

By analysis of horizon returns, realized compound yields,

and relative holding values as shown here, the portfolio manager can compare MBS with alternatives to decide whether to enter the sector at all, and once there how to manage the positions. It is important to understand that the results of these types of analysis are really various expressions of the effects of cash flows, which in turn depend entirely on the prepayment

EXHIBIT 5
Comparative Holding Values

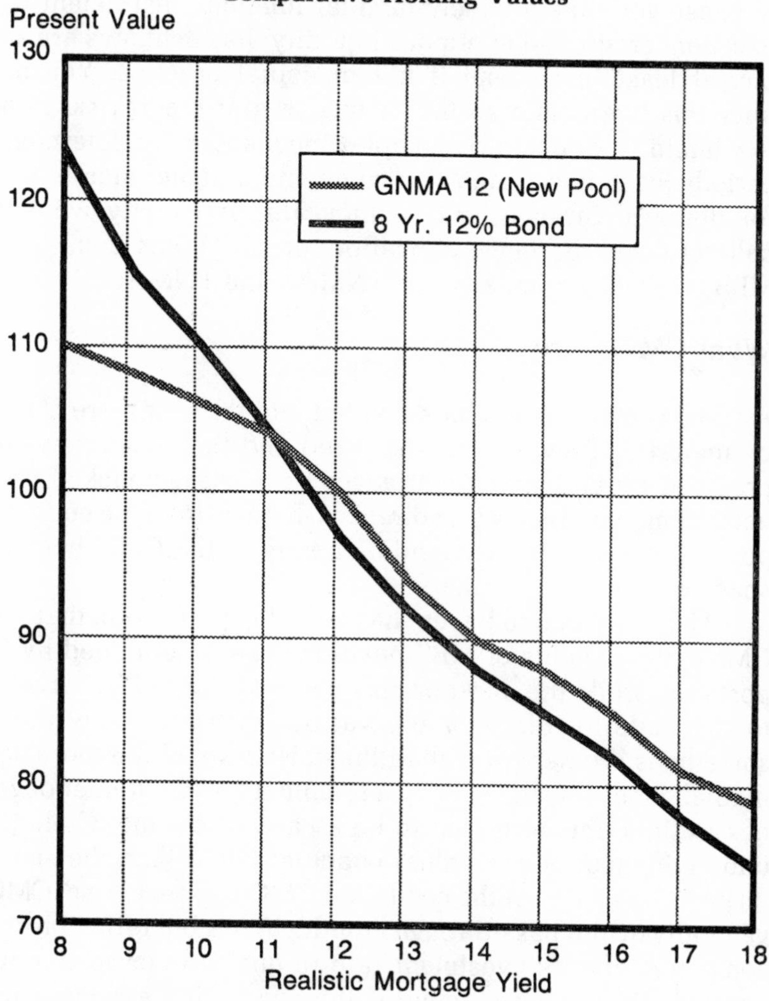
Present Value
130
120
110
100
90
80
70
GNMA 12 (New Pool)
8 Yr. 12% Bond
8
9
10
11
12
13
14
15
16
17
18
Realistic Mortgage Yield

algorithm and interest rate forecast. It should be evident that
the manager who desires a "buy-and-hold" strategy (if there
are any of those left these days) cannot expect to profitably
use the MBS market.

COLLATERALIZED MORTGAGE OBLIGATIONS (CMOs)

Suppose you take a widely familiar financial instrument with
excellent credit and enormous liquidity. Its cashflows are simple, at least in concept if not in actual practice. You now
alter this instrument so that it has greater credit risk, rather
low liquidity, and a fairly complex mechanism for determining
periodic cash flows. *And* you command a higher market price
for doing it. Strange as it sounds, this is exactly what the
collateralized mortgage obligation, or CMO, has done to the
MBS market, particularly for GNMAs and FNMAs.

What CMOs Are

A CMO is a series of bonds divided into three or more classes
by maturity. They are collateralized and their cash flows are
provided by underlying mortgages or mortgage-backed products. Its major effect is to redirect cash flows from the collateral
pool in aggregate to sequential classes of the CMO bonds in
specific order.

The attraction to buyers has been the perception that with
CMOs, the benefits of MBS positions can be obtained by the
portfolio, while the duration risk can be lessened by targeting
to the maturity range of the various classes. These ranges
sometimes are narrower than the variability of the mortgages
in total. Since buyers will pay a premium for this greater degree
of certainty, this turns out to be a case where the whole (the
underlying mortgage's value) is actually less than the sum of
its parts (the value of the combined CMO classes). Also, CMOs
generally do not pass-through monthly flows but rather provide
some minimum reinvestment rate to quarterly or semiannual
periods. This reduces some of the processing expenses normally associated with MBS.

From the issuer's viewpoint, the CMO is an attempt to broaden the appeal of MBS by providing the above features to buyers. There are various accounting and tax considerations in creating a CMO for some issuers, but the most important benefit to early sellers of CMOs was the arbitrage profit involved in acquiring collateral and reselling it, albeit restructured, to the public at a higher price.

It should be clear that in an efficient market, a series of cash flows commands a particular value in the market, regardless of how it is divided. The CMO market has been less than efficient in that the extra price people paid for the more stable maturity classes was not totally offset by the discount on the classes to which that maturity risk was shed. However, there are attractive qualities to both buyers and sellers of CMOs even without the early mispricing effects.

How CMOs Work

CMOs usually have at least three classes of bonds, one or more of which may be "zero-cash flow" bonds. The "zeros" are not zero-coupon bonds, but rather they have a stated coupon which is added to the principal amount outstanding on each coupon date. This simplifies the complications of the zero coupon process which is introduced by the variable maturity date. The bonds are retired in sequence with all payments of principal going to the earliest maturity class until it is gone, then beginning with the next class. (See, for example, Exhibit 6.) Stated maturities are based on either zero or a minimum guaranteed level of prepayments. Prices and yields are based on some specified prepayment assumption. The investor must apply his own analysis to the issue to determine the cash flows he can expect.

CMO bonds will virtually always be retired before their stated maturity. This is because of prepayments, primarily, but there might also be other reasons. Under certain circumstances defined in the indenture, CMO bonds can sometimes be called by the issuer. This is true most often of the longest class, usually a zero. But in some issues with "calamity call" provisions, any class might be partially called if certain levels

EXHIBIT 6
Travelers Mortgage Securities Corporation
Series 1984–1
CMO Analysis
For March 1, 1984

I. *Coupon Groups*

	Face Amount	Coupon	Estimated Speed (as Percent FHA)
1	$505,519,907	11.50%	75
2	28,000,000	12.75	100
3	170,367,264	12.50	100
4	12,000,000	12.25	100
5	121,799,798	12.00	75
6	5,626,382	11.75	75
7	291,317,858	11.50	75
8	145,768,625	11.00	75
9	12,281,559	10.75	75

II. *Issue Description*

	Par Amount	Coupon	Type
A	$270,000,000	10.62%	Coupon
Z–1	455,000,000	12.00	Zero
C	375,000,000	12.00	Coupon
Z–2	150,000,000	12.00	Zero

III. *Cash Flows* (Total)

Period	A	Z–1	C	Z–2
1	$68,478,198	$ 0	$22,500,000	$ 0
2	73,970,867	0	22,500,000	0
3	74,902,527	0	22,500,000	0
4	76,815,401	0	22,500,000	0
5	15,157,648	61,235,266	22,500,000	0
6	0	75,474,484	22,500,000	0
7	0	73,794,805	22,500,000	0
8	0	72,310,885	22,500,000	0
9	0	70,388,108	22,500,000	0
10	0	68,902,682	22,500,000	0
11	0	66,370,853	22,500,000	0
12	0	64,257,612	22,500,000	0
13	0	61,540,861	22,500,000	0
14	0	59,194,531	22,500,000	0
15	0	56,535,789	22,500,000	0
16	0	53,761,705	22,500,000	0
17	0	39,759,968	33,925,289	0

EXHIBIT 6 (continued)

Period	A	Z–1	C	Z–2
18	0	0	71,011,253	0
19	0	0	68,706,392	0
20	0	0	66,591,242	0
21	0	0	64,483,267	0
22	0	0	62,431,225	0
23	0	0	60,411,452	0
24	0	0	58,364,310	0
25	0	0	623,049	55,932,360
26	0	0	0	54,767,164
27	0	0	0	53,129,441
28	0	0	0	51,491,500
29	0	0	0	50,006,141
30	0	0	0	48,512,893
31	0	0	0	47,158,881
32	0	0	0	45,803,049
33	0	0	0	44,556,014
34	0	0	0	43,323,277
35	0	0	0	42,171,786
36	0	0	0	41,158,933
37	0	0	0	40,450,225
38	0	0	0	39,445,826
39	0	0	0	38,705,479
40	0	0	0	37,691,772
41	0	0	0	37,214,992
42	0	0	0	36,814,103
43	0	0	0	36,172,481
44	0	0	0	35,540,117
45	0	0	0	34,680,166
46	0	0	0	33,839,518
47	0	0	0	32,765,370
48	0	0	0	31,713,763
49	0	0	0	30,436,117
50	0	0	0	29,255,517
51	0	0	0	27,934,069
52	0	0	0	26,321,783
53	0	0	0	24,551,635
54	0	0	0	21,554,951
55	0	0	0	16,053,329
56	0	0	0	14,882,709
57	0	0	0	13,431,291
58	0	0	0	12,021,730
59	0	0	0	7,795,281
60	0	0	0	412,670

of prepayments are experienced. This is a safety valve designed to take pressure off the reinvestment process if high prepayments occur early in the coupon period. CMO collateralized by discount mortgages are less susceptible to this, and may not have a calamity call provision at all. Bullish investors concerned about calls resulting from high prepayments should seek out CMOs with substantially discounted collateral.

The "pass-through of spread" also serves to shorten the life of CMOs. The "spread" here is the excess reinvestment earnings on the mortgage flows in the collection account over the assumption in the initial forecasts. In some deals, these funds are used to retire bonds. Deals where the spread is retained by the issuer will be longer for the same level of prepayments than deals where the spread is passed through.

Therefore, if you own an early maturity class of a CMO and you wish to estimate the principal installment on the next coupon date, there are several things you will need to include. The most obvious is the regularly scheduled principal flows of the collateral, and any prepayments you have estimated will have occurred. If any of the later tranches are zero-pay bonds, the amount of interest accrual on them which is added to their principal balances must be included in the retirement of earlier classes. The reason for this is clear if you consider that the total amount of principal outstanding in the CMO relative to that of the collateral cannot be allowed to increase. Thus, if principal is added to one tranche, it must be offset by a reduction in another. Finally, the passing through of spread can be estimated by a forecast of short-term rates. These components plus the effect of any calls (which usually cannot be predicted) make up the next principal installment. The interest component is the full coupon rate applied to the outstanding balance at the beginning of the period.

Considerations in Purchasing a CMO

When considering the purchase of a CMO for a portfolio, the manager must develop the anticipated cash flows which are consistent with his outlook and models. It is also important to measure the sensitivity of those cash flows to variations in assumptions, just as one does for any MBS. This is particularly important for CMOs because the shedding of prepayment risk from one class to another is precisely the reason CMOs have carried their premiums over the underlying mortgages.

Exhibit 7 shows an example of a CMO and the sensitivity of its classes to rate changes as compared to that of a GNMA. While there is a reduction in risk in terms of the possible range of durations of two of the classes, it is not clear what that should be worth in terms of foregone yield spread. That assessment can only be made in light of the corresponding liabilities.

EXHIBIT 7
Effect of CMO Restructuring on Cash Flow
Travelers Mortgage Securities Corporation Series 1984–1*

	GNMA 11.5	A	Z–1	C	Z–2
No Prepayment					
First Payment	0.0 yrs	0.0 yrs	3.0 yrs	13.5 yrs	16.5 yrs
Last Payment	30.0	3.0	13.5	16.5	30.0
Weighted Average Maturity (WAM)	22.6	1.8	9.5	15.2	24.4
Duration	7.5	1.7	7.4	7.2	21.3
Moderate Prepayment (75% FHA)					
First	0.0	0.0	2.5	9.0	12.5
Last	30.0	2.5	9.0	12.5	30.0
WAM	13.1	1.4	5.8	10.7	21.1
Duration	5.9	1.3	5.0	6.2	17.2
Faster Prepayment (200% FHA)					
First	0.0	0.0	2.0	5.5	8.5
Last	30.0	2.0	5.5	8.5	30.0
WAM	8.3	1.0	3.6	7.1	15.1
Duration	4.5	1.0	3.4	4.9	12.4
Maximum Range	30.0 yrs	3.0	11.5 yrs	11.0 yrs	21.5 yrs
Change in WAM	14.3	0.8	9.9	8.1	9.3
Change in Duration	3.0	0.7	4.0	2.3	8.9

* See Exhibit 6 for a summary of the features of this CMO.

The manager's assessment of the CMO should take into account the characteristics of the collateral, such as:

1. ranges and averages of coupons;
2. ranges and averages of maturities, and
3. types of securities or mortgages (i.e., GNMA, FNMA, whole loans, commercial loans, and so on).

Further, the structure of the CMO itself should be studied for the following:

1. degree of overcollateralization;
2. amount of spread-pass-throughs;
3. existence of call provisions;
4. existence of put options, and;
5. existence of guarantees of minimum prepayment rates.

From the credit standpoint, the manager must be aware of:

1. credit rating of issue;
2. minimum reinvestment rates and source of any guarantees (surety bonds, letters of credit, and so on);
3. bondholders' rights to collateral in the event of default;
4. recourse, in the case of a special purpose subsidiary to the parent, and;
5. rating of the trustee and paying agent.

If the issue is satisfactory from the above points of view and is a good fit for the portfolio, the ongoing management of the position is similar to that of other MBS, except that it is unlikely that CMOs will trade with the same degree of liquidity as a more standardized MBS.

The Synthetic Security

While most portfolio management considerations we have looked at view the CMO from the buyer's side, there is a great motivation to consider the issuance of CMOs for the purpose of fitting a specific need. Since the classes can be structured almost at will by varying the percentages of the face amounts in each class, a "synthetic bond" with flows occurring in the years the manager prefers can be built. This class can be retained by the portfolio, and the balance sold to the public.

This was the motivation for the Travelers Mortgage Securities Corporation Series 1984–1 issue considered earlier. There, an existing position in about $450 million of GNMA pools was to be replaced with a security with cash flows concentrated from three to nine years out. A CMO issue of $1.25 billion was required. The collateral was purchased with the cash raised from the sale of the GNMAs, and the proceeds from the sale of the CMO classes A, C and Z–2 to the public. The Z–1, designed to fit cash needs, was retained by the portfolio. Thus, a bond with characteristics not available in the marketplace was synthesized via the MBS market. This type of investment engineering is one of the more promising future applications of CMO issuance for portfolio management purposes.

CONCLUSION

The tremendous growth of the securitized mortgage market during the 1980s is the telling sign of the advantages to be had. For the extra effort required to learn the market, the portfolio manager can reap many times over the benefits that it can often provide.

CHAPTER 14

Financial Futures and Mortgage-Backed Securities

Richard L. Sandor, Ph.D.
Senior Vice President and Manager
Institutional Financial Futures Division
Drexel Burnham Lambert

Norman E. Mains, Ph.D.
First Vice President and Director of Research
Institutional Financial Futures Division
Drexel Burnham Lambert

The relatively brief histories of financial futures and mortgage-backed securities are inextricably intertwined, since the interest rate futures market came into being when the GNMA–CDR futures contract began trading on the Chicago Board of Trade (CBOT) on October 20, 1975. The initial response of capital market participants was less than overwhelming: Daily trading volume averaged less than 400 contracts per day in 1975 while open interest stood at only 1,325 contracts at the end of the year. Nevertheless, the GNMA–CDR contract was the genesis of the interest rate futures market, and financial futures (interest rate, foreign currency, and stock index) currently constitute approximately one-half of all activity in futures markets (Exhibit 1). This chapter will focus on how mortgage-backed security portfolio managers can employ interest rate futures in their day-to-day activities with particular emphasis on hedging the price risk of these securities. It begins with a brief overview of the interest rate futures market. Next, the theory of futures contract pricing is reviewed using the GNMA–CDR contract. This is followed by an introduction to

EXHIBIT 1
Major Financial Futures Contracts

Instrument	Contract Size	Tick Value	Open Interest Contracts (12/31/84)
Short-term interest rate:			
Treasury bills (began 1/6/76)	$1,000,000	$25.00	40,690
CDs (began 7/29/81)	$1,000,000	$25.00	14,593
Eurodollar deposits (began 12/9/81)	$1,000,000	$25.00	85,128
Long-term interest rate:			
GNMAs (began 10/20/75)	$100,000	$31.25	7,636
Treasury Bonds (began 8/22/77)	$100,000	$31.25	202,488
Treasury Notes (began 5/5/82)	$100,000	$31.25	36,000
Stock index:			
Value Line (began 2/24/82)	$88,900 (500 × index)	$25.00	3,888
NYFE (began 5/6/82)	$48,190 (500 × index)	$25.00	7,149
S&P 500 (began 4/12/82)	$82,620 (500 × index)	$25.00	42,191
Major Market (began 7/23/84)	$24,205 (100 × index)	$12.50	13,515
Foreign currency:			
Swiss Franc (began 4/16/72)	125,000 SF	$12.50	17,861
German Mark (began 4/16/72)	125,000 DM	$12.50	33,746
Japanese Yen (began 4/16/72)	12,500,000 JY	$12.50	13,542
British Pound (began 4/16/72)	25,000 BP	$12.50	15,624
Canadian Dollar (began 4/16/72)	100,000 CD	$10.00	7,775

the concept of basis risk. A discussion of the principles of hedging is then presented, and the chapter closes with the review of several applications of strategies that use the hedging techniques introduced in the chapter.

AN OVERVIEW OF FINANCIAL FUTURES

Interest rate futures contracts were spawned in a period in which the U.S. federal government was actively pursuing policies designed to encourage the flow of private capital into the financing of residential properties. One such program was the establishment of the Government National Mortgage Association in 1968 as a wholly owned government corporation within the Department of Housing and Urban Development. A major element authorized by this legislation was the guaranteeing of pass-through securities backed by FHA- or VA-guaranteed mortgages, a program that began in 1970. The payments of principal and interest on GNMA securities represent a commitment of the full faith and credit of the U.S. government, but the response of capital market participants to the GNMA pass-through program was lackluster: less than $12 billion were outstanding at the end of 1974. Nevertheless, as GNMA trading began to grow in the cash (or immediate delivery) market, a nascent forward market in GNMAs also began to flourish. Of course, this was a natural development, since forward markets add a time dimension to cash markets. Futurity and its associated uncertainties have long been recognized as important features of the mortgage industry.

While the emergence of an increasingly active forward market in GNMAs was an important precursor, a futures contract based on mortgages required several aspects in addition to those features that characterize a forward market. Futures markets evolve typically from those forward markets in which participants are especially concerned about the liquidity and default risk of forward contracts. Moreover, the liquidity feature of any instrument is enhanced by creating a vehicle that is homogeneous in grade and quantity with a uniform delivery location and procedure. The delivery mechanism is important since it causes cash and futures markets to converge, although only a small portion of futures contracts are held until delivery, which is almost always contemplated in a forward contract. In addition, futures contracts are traded on a central exchange in which both the standardization of contract terms and exchange rules result in the price of the contract being the only negotiated feature. The standardization of contract specifications also allows for price discovery, since the time-specific profile of prices impounds market participants' best estimates of their expectations.

The central exchange also establishes a clearinghouse that is the responsible opposite party, or third party, in all transactions. Thus, each long contract holder looks to the clearinghouse as the opposite party once a trade has been consummated (that is, the determination of the price of a specific contract) and, likewise, the short contract holder also looks to the clearinghouse. This system requires that exchange members have a high degree of trust in all other members so that the risk of defaulting on the contract specifications is virtually eliminated.

In order to guarantee performance, a clearinghouse requires that both the long and short contract holder deposit margin money called an initial margin deposit, or more appropriately termed a performance bond, in an amount that assumes that either party will receive those funds owing to favorable price movements of the contract. Likewise, the other party must replenish the margin if it drops below prescribed limits. All futures contracts are marked-to-market on a daily basis at closing settlement prices. This allows for the daily transfer of all price gains and losses and thereby minimizes default risk. Many futures contracts specifications also include daily price limits so that exchange members can evaluate their potential exposures on a daily basis and collect additional funds, called maintenance margin, as needed. Failure to meet margin requests can result in the liquidation of the outstanding positions.

The initiation of trading in the GNMA–CDR futures contract was, as many financial innovations, little noticed by many capital market participants in the early days of its trading. Trading volume was light and open interest increased at a relatively slow pace over late 1975 and early 1976. Nevertheless, the new contract added several new important dimensions to the GNMA market such as improved liquidity, relatively low transaction fees, enhanced ability to sell short, and greater transaction discretion. These features did not go unnoticed by an increasing number of major mortgage market participants such as GNMA dealers, large savings and loan associations, and mortgage bankers. Moreover, the breadth of the financial futures market was enhanced with the introduction of the 91-day U.S. Treasury Bill contract on the Chicago Mercantile Exchange in January 1976 and the U.S. Treasury Bond contract on the CBOT in August 1977. Daily trading volume in all financial futures contracts climbed to nearly 4,000 contracts per day in 1977 while open interest (the outstanding number of contracts) aggregated more than 28,000 contracts (Exhibit 2). Nevertheless, these amounts were only a small fraction of the total futures market (nonfinancial plus financial) activity.

A much more extraordinary rise in financial futures activity occurred in the 1978 through 1981 period. A number of new contracts were initiated and several survived during this period, but most of the growth in daily trading volume and open interest occurred in the previously existing financial futures contracts (Exhibit 3).[1] This development was largely in response to the U.S. economy undergoing a further ratcheting up of inflationary pressures throughout most of this period that resulted in an unprecedented escalation in both the level and volatility of U.S. interest rates. This, in turn, caused many financial market participants such as corporate treasurers, portfolio managers, and officers of depositary institutions, to

---

[1] The CBOT started, for example, a second GNMA contract, the Certificate Delivery GNMA, in September of 1978. The CD GNMA contract specifications called for actual GNMA certificates as the delivery instrument. It was discontinued in June 1982.

EXHIBIT 2
Daily Average Trading Volume
in Financial Futures
(Number of Contracts)

Period	Trading Volume*	Memo: Financial as a Proportion of Total Commodity Futures and Trading Volume
1975	940	0.7
1976	3,698	2.5
1977	3,959	2.3
1978	11,670	5.0
1979	26,089	8.7
1980	55,284	15.1
1981	101,148	25.9
1982	156,888	35.2
1983	216,608	39.0
1984	294,658	49.4

* Financial futures include all interest rate, stock index, and foreign currency contracts traded on U.S. futures exchanges. The data exclude all option contracts on financial futures.

EXHIBIT 3
Volume of Selected Longer-Term
Financial Future Contracts
(Number of Contracts)

Year	GNMA CDR	U.S. Treasury Bond	U.S. Treasury Note
1975	20,125	—	—
1976	128,537	—	—
1977	422,421	32,101	—
1978	953,161	555,350	—
1979	1,371,078	2,059,594	—
1980	2,326,292	6,489,555	—
1981	2,292,882	13,907,988	—
1982	2,055,648	16,739,695	881,325
1983	1,692,017	19,550,535	814,505
1984	862,450	29,963,280	1,661,862

Source: Chicago Board of Trade.

seek methods of insulating or enhancing their overall operating results from the consequences of high and volatile interest rates. One of the principal vehicles that these individuals sought out to help them adjust to this new climate of volatility in financial markets was interest rate futures contracts. As a result, both the trading volume and open interest of financial futures expanded rapidly, both absolutely and as a proportion of total futures market activity. Indeed, by 1984 nearly 300,000 financial futures contracts with an underlying market value of more than $75 billion traded daily in the United States. This now represents about one-half of all futures market activity, a phenomenal event to have occurred in only about one decade.

THE GNMA–CDR FUTURES CONTRACT

It is interesting to note from an historical perspective that the origins of the GNMA–CDR futures contract can be traced to a grant in the early 1970s from the University of California at Berkeley, Center for Real Estate in Urban Economics. One result of this study was the conclusion that mortgages were not homogeneous enough to facilitate their incorporation into a futures contract. However, the introduction of the GNMA security itself provided the proper vehicle for the development of this concept. The first draft of the futures contract emerged in May 1972 and called for a 6.5 percent coupon with a par value of $250,000. The size of contract and its coupon reflected the level of interest rates and their volatility at that particular time. After 3 years of additional research and more than 20 separate drafts a final contract emerged.

The GNMA–CDR futures contract is, as all financial futures, a derivative financial instrument based on its underlying instrument: the GNMA security. Since futures contracts must be based on standardized terms for a specific commodity, security, or index, the GNMA–CDR contract is based on GNMA modified pass-through certificates that bear a stated interest rate of 8 percent. As in the cash market, the quotes are based on 30-year FHA/VA mortgages that are presumed to be totally prepaid in the 12th year.[2] The unit of trading for the GNMA contract is $100,000 principal balance, or multiples thereof, and trading is currently conducted in the delivery months of March, June, September, and December. Minimum price fluctuations are multiples of one thirty-second ($\frac{1}{32}$nd) point per 100 points (the par basis) or $31.25 per contract.

Since the GNMA–CDR contract specifications state that the contract grade for delivery is pass-through certificates bearing a stated interest rate of 8 percent, deliverers may, at their option, deliver GNMAs with stated interest rates other than 8 percent provided it bears the same yield as the 8 percent GNMA when calculated at par and under the assumption of a 30-year mortgage with a 12-year life. The price at which GNMAs other than GNMA 8s yields 7.96 percent is found from yield tables, and the CBOT provides GNMA–CDR principal factors for all coupons other than 8 percent that produce the equivalent amounts of these GNMA coupons. For example, $93,167.70 of GNMA 9s yield 7.96 percent, which, expressed as the reciprocal for $100,000 of GNMA 8s, produces an "8s equivalent" factor of .931677. (A table of "8s equivalent" factors for various coupons is shown in Exhibit 4). Packages of GNMAs may be delivered also that include more than one coupon rate.

Contract specifications for the GNMA futures contract call for a collateralized deposit receipt (CDR) to be delivered from the short to the long in the delivery period rather than actual GNMA certificates. The CDRs are certificates that represent GNMAs on deposit at a designated depository—an authorized commercial bank—and approximately $100,000 of GNMA 8 or "8 equivalent" certificates can be obtained by the surrender of the CDR. The receipt is created by a qualified originator: a market participant, typically the short, willing to deposit GNMAs and issue a CDR against the certificates. Once a CDR is surrendered, the delivery of the GNMAs is not made until

---

[2] The actual yield on GNMAs at par is 7.96 precent owing to the 15-day delay in payment of interest and principal to the certificate holder.

EXHIBIT 4
GNMA–CDR Principal Factors

GNMA Coupon Rate	"8s Equivalent" Factor
9	.931677
9-1/2	.900322
10	.841460
10-1/2	.843289
11	.817439
11-1/2	.793021
12	.769724
12-1/2	.747664
13	.726744
13-1/2	.707214
14	.688231
14-1/2	.670578
15	.653595

15 business days later and during this period the originator may swap other GNMAs for those on deposit with the trustee depository.[3]

Upon surrender of the CDR, the originator must deliver GNMA 8s or the equivalent principal balance of another coupon determined by the "8s equivalent" factor within a 2.5 percent tolerance balance ($97,500 to $102,000). This tolerance feature recognizes that the underlying GNMA security is a pool of mortgages that "pay down" their principal balances owing to both scheduled and unscheduled payments. These prepayments can result in the CDR originator being required to replenish the pool with additional GNMAs during the time that the CDR is tendered and the certificates are delivered.[4]

---

[3] The long that has taken delivery of the CDR can elect to hold it and receive $635 per month in interest income until it is surrendered. Holding such a perpetuity can be attractive, although the RP rates applied to the financing of such CDRs typically occur at rates appreciably above RP rates on U.S. Treasury securities.

[4] Since $635 per month translates into an annual yield of 7.62 percent on an investment of $100,000, the originator receives 38 basis points (8.00 minus 7.62 percent) as compensation.

Calculating the Cheapest-to-Deliver Package

The previous section stated that the GNMA–CDR contract specifications allow GNMA packages of various coupons and size to be delivered. Since this is the case, the determination of the package of GNMAs (either one or more coupons) that is *most* attractive for the short contract holder to deliver to the long contract holder determines the market pricing of the GNMA–CDR futures contract. In other words, the pricing of the futures contract will depend primarily on the prices of the GNMA securities that encompass the cheapest-to-deliver package. This point can be illustrated with an example. Since GNMA certificates have a minimum size at par of $25,000 and trade in increments of $5,000, the principal balances and "8s equivalent" balances for several sizes of GNMA 13-1/2s are as follows:

Principal Balance of GNMA 13-1/2s	GNMA–CDR Factor	"8s Equivalent" Principal Balance
$80,000	.707214	$113,120
75,000	.707214	106,050
70,000	.707214	98,980
65,000	.707214	91,910
60,000	.707214	84,840

These data illustrate that an originator would satisfy the specifications of the GNMA–CDR contract by delivering, upon the tendering of the CDR by its holder, only the $70,000 GNMA piece. Neither of the smaller pieces ($65,000 or $60,000) have "8s equivalent" principal balances that are large enough to fall within the tolerance limit of $98,500 to $102,500. In addition, neither of the larger GNMA pieces qualify since each is above the upper-end of the tolerance limit if the principal pool has not been reduced by prepayments. Assuming the price of the GNMA contract settles at par, then the long taking delivery of the CDR can tender it for delivery of the actual GNMA certificates. If the CDR originator elects to deliver a $70,000 piece of 13-1/2s GNMAs, the originator must also settle the difference from par ($1,020) in cash upon delivery.

It was stated previously that the GNMA contract specifications allow for the delivery of more than one coupon. Therefore the originator can assemble various pools for delivery provided that the combinations fall within the tolerance limits after each piece is adjusted by its factor. For example, a $25,000 piece of GNMA 13-1/2s plus a $45,000 piece of GNMA 14-1/2s produces an "8s equivalent" principal balance of $102,456.

GNMA Coupon	Principal Balance	Factor	"8s Equivalent" Principal Balance
13-1/2	$25,000	.707214	$ 25,350
14-1/2	45,000	.670578	67,106
			$102,456

Delivery of this package, assuming the futures contract settled at par and no prepayments, results in the individual tendering the CDR paying the originator $102,456 upon receiving the certificates.

The choice of what coupon or package of coupons that the originator delivers is important if the GNMA futures settles at any price other than par. The contract specifications require the GNMA securities to be priced at the settlement price while the tail is priced at par to yield 7.96 percent. Under these circumstances an originator generally should *overdeliver* when the GNMA contract settles less than par and *underdeliver* when the GNMA contract settles greater than par. GNMA yields have been greater than 7.96 percent over almost the entire period that the GNMA–CDR has been in existence, so coupons or packages producing overdeliveries have generally been the rule. In the above example, the package would be delivered if GNMA 8s were selling at a price below par, since, ceteris paribus, a CDR originator would gain more from an overdelivery rather than underdelivery.

The contract specification giving the seller the right to

substitute coupons other than 8 percent in the delivery process usually assures that the short will select the issue that is "cheapest-to-deliver" in the cash market. As stated previously, it is the "cheapest" coupon or package that will be the most important determinant in the pricing of the GNMA–CDR contract. The "8s equivalent" factors are such that the cheapest-to-deliver issue or package typically has been the one carrying the highest coupon. This was especially true from the inception of the contract until the early 1980s when the secular rise in U.S. interest rates resulted in a rise in the GNMA production rate (50 basis points below the maximum allowable FHA mortgage rate) from 8 percent to as high as 17 percent.[5] This was a period that encompassed declining mortgage security prices for all but relatively brief periods, so market participants had some assurity that the GNMA–CDR contract would be priced off the then-current GNMA production rate.

It can be demonstrated using actual cash and futures market price data that the GNMA–CDR contract typically was priced off high coupon GNMAs in the earlier years of the contract's existence. For example, following prices were recorded on August 25, 1982, at 2:00 P.M. (CST), a day in which the GNMA–CDR contract closed at 70-09/32nds:

Coupon	GNMA Forward Market Price (September Delivery)
16	108-22/32nds
15	104-04
14-1/2	102-21
14	100-31
13-1/2	99-12

It was shown previously that a $70,000 piece of GNMA 13-1/2s produced an "8s equivalent" balance of $98,980 (or an underdelivery of $1,020 per contract). Therefore, example A illustrates that an individual buying the GNMA 13-1/2s in

---

[5] The Housing Act of 1983 eliminated HUD's authority to set an FHA/ VA mortgage rate ceiling.

the forward market at 99-12/32nds and selling the September GNMA–CDR at 67-03/32nds produced a loss of 3-06/32nds assuming that the 13-1/2s were delivered in September.[6] Moreover, the $70,000 price also required that the short settle the underdelivery in cash, so the final result of such a strategy produced a loss of 4-06/32nds (or $4,187.50) per $100,000 par amount.

Coupon	Price	Futures Equivalent Price	Package	GNMA–CDR Futures Price	Cash/ Futures Basis	Basis plus over or under Delivery
Example A:						
13-1/2	99-12	70-09	70-09	67-03	3-06	4-06
Example B:						
13-1/2	99-12 ⎱	70-09	69-11	67-03	2-08	1-16
14-1/2	101-21 ⎰	68-27				
Example C:						
15	104-04 ⎱	67-20	67-28	67-03	0-25	0-01
16	108-22 ⎰	68-02				

The package of 13-1/2s and 14-1/2s discussed previously also produced a sizable difference, 2-08/32nds, in a comparison between the adjusted cash market price and the futures market price (although smaller than the adjusted GNMA 13-1/2s price). Adjusting for the overdelivery, the package produced a difference of 1-16/32nds. Finally, a package of high coupon GNMAs ($35,000 of 16s and $30,000 15s) produced a cash/ futures relationship of 25/32nds without the overdelivery and only 1/32nd when the overdelivery was included. Such high coupon packages showed the highest correlations and smallest price differentials between the GNMA forward and futures markets throughout this period. It seems reasonable, therefore,

---

[6] The results would have been changed only slightly if cash market (or immediate delivery prices) had been substituted for forward prices. When cash market quotes are employed, the value of the GNMAs is calculated on a "cash and carry" basis. In other words, the GNMA's coupon interest and the cost of carrying these securities until the delivery period must be included.

to conclude that market participants focused on these high coupon packages in establishing the futures market price of the GNMA–CDR contract.

THE LINK BETWEEN CASH AND FUTURES MARKETS: THE BASIS

A central concept in all futures markets is the basis relationship between the cash (or forward) market prices and the futures market prices. The cash price minus the futures price equals the basis. The basis relationship must be well understood by hedgers and arbitrageurs. The previous example demonstrated, for example, that a package of high coupon GNMAs, plus the overdelivery allowance, produced a relationship between the cash and futures markets that resulted in only a minor difference. Moreover, if market participants had a high degree of confidence that this difference was likely to remain minimal, then they might be indifferent towards holding either obligation and therefore be willing to substitute freely between the two. It is this principal that allows market participants to continuously price the futures contract: GNMA futures market participants focus on the price of the GNMA or package of GNMAs that is cheapest-to-deliver and then adjust the price of the futures contract to reflect the specifications of the contract. Such an approach is predicated, of course, on the premise that the cash/futures relationship is relatively stable and predictable. This was certainly true in the earlier years of the GNMA–CDR contract. Exhibit 5 depicts, for example, the prices of the GNMA–CDR contract and the package of a $35,000 piece of GNMA 16s and a $30,000 piece of GNMA 15s (plus the overdelivery allowance) over the period from August 1981 through December 1981. The lower portion of Exhibit 5 illustrates that the difference between the price of the package and the futures contract—the *basis*—was relatively minimal (ranging between +14/32nds and −23/32nds) over a period in which the price of the package of GNMA 16s and 15s varied between about 64-3/4 and 56-3/4 (or about 8 full points). The lower portion of the exhibit also demonstrates another important feature of futures markets, namely that the basis relationship erodes to approximately zero at the end of the delivery period.[7] Exhibit 5 illustrates the two principal features of the pricing of a financial futures contract: (1) the high correlation between the futures market price and the cheapest-to-deliver instrument and (2) convergence in the delivery period.

Recent Instability of the GNMA–CDR Basis

The combination of the secular rise in mortgage rates plus the bias toward high coupon GNMA certificates implicit in the GNMA–CDR contract's specifications adequately served the needs of mortgage market participants over most of the early years of the financial futures markets. High coupon GNMAs represented the overwhelming majority of the current production of mortgage bankers and other originators over this period and consequently the GNMA–CDR contract was actively employed by market participants in their hedging and trading activities. However, the relatively small and predictable basis relationship that characterized the late 1970s and early 1980s became volatile and unstable once mortgage prices began to improve from late 1981 onward. The arrest of the upward spiral in inflationary prices in the United States allowed longer-term fixed income prices to increase dramatically in 1982 and into 1983. The impact on mortgage prices was especially dramatic since the overall downward shift in yields

---

[7] Most financial futures contracts do not employ the collateralized depositary receipt mechanism specified in the GNMA–CDR contract. As a result, the delivery procedure typically causes these futures contracts to converge more towards the adjusted cash market prices of the cheapest-to-deliver instruments than in the GNMA–CDR contract. Much of this residual basis risk reflects, of course, the perpetuity feature of the CDR.

EXHIBIT 5

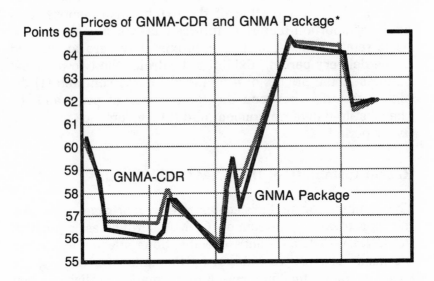

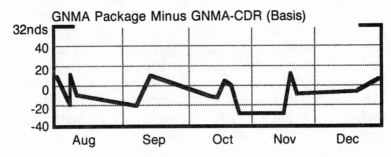

* Package (including overdelivery) consists of a $35,000 piece of GNMA 16s and a $30,000 piece of GNMA 15s.

Note: Position rolled from nearby to first deferred contracts just prior to delivery month.

coupled with the unrestricted prepayment feature of most fixed-rate mortgages caused a large proportion of the outstanding high coupon mortgages to be prepaid as many mortgagers sought to lower their monthly payments. A direct consequence of these actions was a sharp reduction in the expected maturity of high coupon GNMAs from their presumed average life of 12 years. This factor plus steepening in the yield curve resulted in mortgage market participants pricing the higher coupon mortgages as if they were much shorter obligations, and the availability of these coupons was curtailed by prepayments. This impacted the price of the GNMA–CDR futures contract in an important way: It caused the cash/futures basis to become unstable and unpredictable. This greatly complicated the use of the CDR contract in hedging and trading activities since the basis risk became too large for many market participants. This can be seen in Exhibit 6, which displays the price of the high coupon package and the price of the GNMA–CDR futures together with the basis relationship (including the over-delivery allowance) over 1983 and 1984. The lower portion of the exhibit demonstrates that the basis varied widely from a high of 145/32nds to a low of −67/32nds. Such wide swings in the basis relationship were compounded for mortgage originators since the basis relationship for their current production coupons was even more unstable.

The price relationship between high coupon GNMAs and other sectors of the fixed income market shifted as well. An example of this shift can be seen in the spread between the CBOT's Treasury bond futures contract and the GNMA–CDR contract. The spread, called the "intermarket" at the CBOT, widened dramatically in the second half of 1982 as the Federal Reserve shifted to a more accommodative stance and prices of Treasury bond futures rose rapidly while the advance in GNMA–CDR prices was constrained in part by the shift in the cheapest-to-deliver package (Exhibit 7). It then declined from its record high level in early 1983 to a record low level in May of 1984 before retracing a major portion of this change in the latter half of the year.

EXHIBIT 6

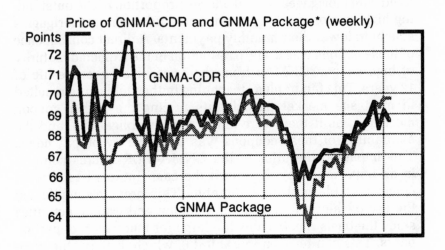

Price of GNMA-CDR and GNMA Package* (weekly)

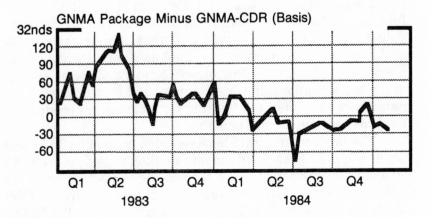

GNMA Package Minus GNMA-CDR (Basis)

* Package (including overdelivery) consists of a $35,000 piece of GNMA 16s and a $30,000 piece of GNMA 15s.

Note: Position rolled from nearby to first deferred contracts just prior to delivery month.

EXHIBIT 7
Spread between Treasury Bond and GNMA–CDR Futures Contracts
(Monthly)

Intermarket Spread (32nds)

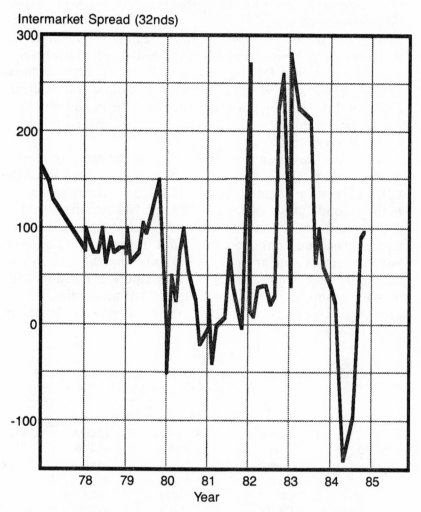

THE GNMA II FUTURES CONTRACT

The inability of the GNMA–CDR contract to track the current production of mortgage originators prompted the CBOT to introduce another mortgage-backed security futures contract, the

GNMA II, on March 22, 1984. The GNMA II contract specifications are such that it is designed to complement the GNMA–CDR contract by incorporating three major changes: (1) it specifies delivery of actual GNMAs, (2) the invoice price for any GNMA delivered is capped at 102-16/32nds to eliminate the delivery of high coupon certificates priced at substantial premiums over par, and (3) the contract allows delivery of those GNMA certificates with coupons at or below the "Current Delivery Rate" during the 4-1/2 months prior to and including the coupon determination day (the 15th of the month prior to the delivery month).

The initial response of mortgage-backed security market participants to the GNMA II contract was favorable as the GNMA II contract traded more than 9,500 contracts per month in the second quarter of 1984 (Exhibit 8). Nevertheless, trading activity in the new contract dropped precipitously in the summer of 1984 and continued moribund in the autumn as well. Several factors appear to have accounted for the lack of success in the new contract, but the most important consideration was the inability of it to track the current production rate of mortgage originators. GNMA mortgage rates were, for exam-

EXHIBIT 8
Trading Volume of Selected Financial Futures Contracts
(Number of Contracts)

| | Monthly Average | | | |
Period	U.S. Treasury Bond	U.S. Treasury Note	GNMA CDR	GNMA II
1983—Q1	1,460,704	70,339	141,658	—
Q2	1,548,983	63,374	159,643	—
Q3	1,832,460	71,771	152,443	—
Q4	1,674,708	66,017	110,261	—
1984—Q1	1,998,790	99,014	118,122	7,114*
Q2	2,678,760	149,816	91,463	9,583
Q3	3,680,144	149,823	56,300	735
Q4	2,630,065	155,301	21,598	50

* Data for eight business days only.
Source: Chicago Board of Trade.

ple, in the range of 13 to 14 percent in the second quarter of 1984, yet the GNMA II contract appeared to track GNMAs with lower coupons.

Also contributing to its apparent demise were several other developments that impacted both the GNMA II and the GNMA–CDR. Originators became reluctant, for example, to create the perpetuity-like CDRs since an increased number of certificate holders retained the obligations rather than tendering them for delivery of the actual certificates. The paydown of high coupon GNMAs also forced many originators to replenish depleted pools and thereby increased their reluctance to increase additional CDR originations.

The overall use of the GNMA futures contracts, both the GNMA–CDR and the GNMA II, also registered an overall decline in trading activity. The inability of either of the GNMA futures contracts to record an acceptable basis risk relationship contributed importantly to a shift towards "cross-hedging" mortgage-backed securities with other than mortgage-based futures contracts. Many mortgage market participants began to employ, for example, U.S. Treasury bond and note futures in the hedging and trading activities as substitutes for GNMA futures. The heightened activity of these contracts is particularly evident in the U.S. Treasury note contract.[8] The monthly average trading activity of the CBOT's Note futures contract surpassed the GNMA contracts in the spring of 1984 and the Note futures have continued to increase in activity while GNMAs have declined since that period (Exhibit 8).

HEDGING WITH INTEREST RATE FUTURES CONTRACTS

It was stated previously that a major impetus for the exceptionally strong growth in financial futures in recent years was

---

[8] The liquidity of the Treasury contracts was facilitated in part by the continued outpouring of new obligations by the U.S. federal government as it recorded unprecedented budget deficits.

the increased level and volatility of U.S. interest rates in the late 1970s and early 1980s. As a result, market participants in both the money and capital markets aggressively sought means of insulating their operating results from the higher volatility of interest rates. Among the solutions that received the largest acceptance was the adoption of hedging programs employing interest rate futures.

The implementation of a hedging program requires a careful and well planned approach; it must be clearly defined and well executed if it is to accomplish its goals. Broadly speaking, the principal objective of a hedging program is to offset changes in either the *values* of assets or liabilities or the interest rate *revenues* or *expenses* of an asset or liability. This objective can be achieved, of course, in various ways, but interest rate futures contracts offer certain distinct advantages (such as cost and flexibility) over alternative strategies. Therefore, the goal of a hedging program using interest rate futures contracts is to fully offset the change in value or flow stemming from a movement in interest rates with a change in the value of the financial futures position.

A well managed hedging program must be constructed in a logical manner. The first step is to *identify* the interest rate risk exposure. How will a movement in interest rates, either short- or long-term, affect the overall results of the entity? A corollary to the identification of the interest rate risk is the *measurement* of the exposure: A relatively precise quantification of the impact of a given change in interest rates is a necessary second step. Once the interest rate risk exposure has been identified and measured, then the individual or group managing the hedging program must *decide* whether to bear the risk (and presumably expect to be compensated for the assumption of the risk) or transfer all or part of it to another financial futures market participant. After the decision is made to hedge all or part of an identified and measured interest rate risk, then the manager or group must focus on *how* to implement the hedging strategy.

It was stated previously that a principal feature of a futures contract is the standardization of contract terms on a good or index that is homogeneous in grade, quantity, delivery location, and procedure. This means that the hedging decision will require, in all likelihood, decisions based on the contract specifications and the maturity, level, and type of interest rate risk that is being hedged. There exists currently in the United States actively traded interest rate futures contracts on 91-day U.S. Treasury bills, 3-month Certificates of Deposits, 3-month Eurodollar deposits, intermediate-term U.S. Treasury notes, long-term U.S. Treasury bonds, and GNMAs. All of these contracts offer relatively liquid markets for the nearby delivery months and varying degrees of liquidity in the back months. Therefore, a manager must decide which contract to use as well as how to structure the hedge.

It should be obvious from the menu of futures contracts that the overwhelming majority of hedging problems involve the assumption of basis risk representing the less-than-perfect correlation between the instrument and the futures contract. As mentioned previously, the goal of the hedge is to substitute the total interest rate risk with a much smaller amount of basis risk, with the second aim of minimizing this risk. Most hedging managers rely heavily on historical interest rate relationships in structuring their hedging solutions. This is, of course, a reasonable approach although one caveat is important to remember: A high correlation between two interest rate series does not necessarily imply a causal relationship between them. Therefore to minimize the possibility of structuring a hedge based on a spurious relationship, the manager should always question the existence of a logical economic relationship between the two series.

In most instances a need to hedge the interest rate risk of a shorter-term asset or liability is best accomplished with a shorter-term interest rate futures contract and likewise for the hedging of a longer-term interest rate risk with longer-term interest rate futures contracts. Nevertheless, it should be clear that large gaps exist in the maturity spectrum of interest rate futures contracts in which the manager must decide which contract or combination of contracts best meets the objective of the hedge. The goal of the hedge is to use the

contract or combination of contracts that will have a change
in value that closely approximates the change in value of the
underlying instrument, so that a hedge likely will have a
weighted maturity or duration that closely approximates that
of the cash market instrument. This will be accomplished in
most cases by the selection of that contract or combination
of contracts that produces the similar duration. For example,
a mortgage-backed security or portfolio with a duration of 5
years could be hedged with either short- or long-term interest
rate futures contracts. While the expected change in the value
of the 5-year obligation could be accounted for by establishing
the proper number of contracts using either the short- or long-
term contracts, the position still would be exposed to a shift
in the profile of the yield curve and this might add to or detract
from the overall efficiency of the hedge. This basis risk might
be partly ameliorated with a hedge that uses both short- and
long-term interest rate futures contracts. Nevertheless, it
should be realized that some residual element of basis risk
is almost always present, and, as stated previously, a major
goal of any hedging program should be to minimize this risk
as much as possible.

Once the decision has been made about which contract
to use, the next issues to be solved are to establish (1) the
number of contracts needed for the hedge, and (2) a determination of which contract months to place the hedge. Both of
these issues require the judgment of the hedge manager. Of
course, the number of contracts to be purchased or sold reflects
the size and interest rate sensitivity of the position to be
hedged. There are a number of methods for estimating the
interest rate sensitivity, and these include: (1) applying the
conversion factor for longer-term contracts, (2) using regression analysis on the historical price series of the contract and
the position to be hedged, and (3) estimating the relative interest rate sensitivities of the cash and futures positions. The
latter of these methods requires that the dollar value for one
basis point change in the cash and futures position be estimated and the hedge then ratioed in an appropriate manner.
The question of which contract months to place the hedge

also requires the judgment of the hedge manager. The nearby contracts are usually the most liquid, and the horizon of the hedge may be such that the nearby contracts are the most appropriate.[9] If a longer-term horizon is called for, the hedge manager must decide between the desirability for extension and the liquidity of the contracts. Sufficient liquidity is needed to both establish the hedge and reverse it such that any price concessions will be minimal.

Examples of Hedges

The following three hedging examples employ some of the principles discussed in this chapter. The simplified examples include a short hedge (that is, the futures market position is short since the contracts have been sold), a long hedge, and an anticipatory short hedge.[10]

Example 1: A mortgage banker held $6.5 million of GNMA 15s on July 1, 1981, but was concerned that long-term interest rates were going to increase further over the next three months.

Solution: The mortgage banker should hedge the $6.5 million of GNMA 15s with the SEP GNMA–CDR contract on July 1st and then roll the short position on August 31st into the DEC GNMA–CDR contract before lifting the hedge on October 1st. GNMA 15s were among the GNMA coupons that were cheapest-to-deliver, and $65,360 of GNMA 15s were equivalent (for delivery purposes) to $100,000 of GNMA 8s.

---

[9] The contract specifications of the longer-term interest rate futures contract typically allow for a delivery period of up to one month. Since this is the case, many market participants will roll their positions from the nearby to the first deferred contract months just prior to the beginning of the delivery month if they have no interest in closing the position or being involved in the delivery process.

[10] The Financial Accounting Standards Board (FASB) recently issued Statement of Financial Accounting standards (SFAS) No. 80, "Accounting for Futures Contracts." SFAS No. 80 resolved many of the conceptual accounting issues regarding financial futures hedges, including qualifications for hedge accounting and characteristics of hedges for anticipated transactions (anticipatory hedges).

Therefore the mortgage banker should sell 100 SEP GNMA–CDR contracts, roll the position on August 31st, and lift the position on October 1st.

Date	Position	Par Amount	Price	Value
July 1, 1981	GNMA 15s	$ 6,500,000	96-00	$6,240,000
	SEP '81 GNMA–CDR	10,000,000	62-01	(6,203,125)
Aug. 31, 1981	SEP '81 GNMA–CDR	10,000,000	56-09	(5,628,125)
	DEC '81 GNMA–CDR	10,000,000	56-22	(5,668,750)
Oct. 1, 1981	GNMA 15s	6,500,000	87-16	5,622,500
	DEC '81 GNMA–CDR	10,000,000	55-11	(5,534,375)

Results: It can be seen from the above data that the price of the GNMA 15s declined 9-1/2 points over the 3-month period from 96-00 to 87-16. This resulted in a decline in the value of the position of —$617,500. Over the same period, however, the gain made on the short GNMA–CDR futures position was $709,375 ($575,000 in the SEP contract plus $134,375 in the DEC contract). The difference between the decline in value in the cash position and the increase in value in the futures position, $91,875, represents a favorable move in the basis relationship.

Example 2: A regional bank has greater interest rate sensitivity in its assets than its liabilities over the next six months. It also regularly lends $10 million in the overnight federal funds market on a daily basis. On October 1, 1984, the bank's asset and liability committee (ALCO) became concerned that short-term interest rates were likely to decline over the next 3 months and this would unfavorably impact the earnings of the bank.

Solution: The ALCO decided to hedge the return that the bank was earning on its sale of federal funds. A hedge ratio of 1.0 was employed since the MAR Treasury bill contract matched the duration of the exposure. The hedge manager purchased 10 MAR T-bill futures contracts on October 1, 1984, and since the exposure declined by definition as the quarter elapsed, one tenth of the hedge was liquidated every 9 days. The final contract was sold on December 31, 1984.

Date	Position	Par Amount	Interest Rate (Percent)
Oct. 1, 1984	Federal Funds	$10,000,000	10.73*
	MAR 81 T-bills	10,000,000	10.57
Dec. 31, 1984	Federal Funds	10,000,000	9.27†
	MAR 85 T-bills	10,000,000	9.08

* Initial interest rate.
† Average interest rate.

Results: The federal funds rate declined from its initial level of 10.73 percent to an average rate of 9.27 percent, a decline of 146 basis points. As a result, the income from this source declined by approximately $36,500 over the period. At the same time the futures position gained by $37,150. This gain more than offset the loss of interest income and reflected a favorable movement in the basis of approximately 3 basis points.

Example 3: On December 1, 1983, a nonbank depository anticipated packaging $100 million par amount of GNMA 10s into a Collateralized Mortgage Obligation (CMO) for issuance on March 1, 1984. In the meantime the institution's ALCO desired to protect the depository from a decline in the value of the GNMAs while it was assembling the collateral for the issue.

Solution: Since the expected duration of GNMA 10s and 10-year Treasury notes are similar, the hedge manager elected to place the hedge in the CBOT's Treasury Notes futures contract because of its enhanced liquidity. Using FHA prepayment experience and the dollar value of a basis point method, a hedge ratio of 0.95 was calculated. Therefore, the institution sold 950 MAR T-Note futures contracts on December 1st and lifted the hedge on March 1st.

Date	Position	Par Amount	Price	Value
Dec. 1, 1983	MAR '84 T-Notes	$ 95,000,000	79-25	($79,781,250)
Mar. 1, 1984	MAR '84 T-Notes	95,000,000	78-23	(78,718,750)
Memo:				
Dec. 1, 1983	GNMA 10s	100,000,000	86-10	86,312,500
Mar. 1, 1984	GNMA 10s	100,000,000	85-01	85,031,250

Results: The memo item in the above data indicates that
the price of the GNMA 10s declined from 86-10 to 85-01 over
the period. The market value of the position would have fallen
by $1,281,250 if the mortgages had been inventoried over the
4-month span. However, the short position of 950 MAR T-Notes
increased by $1,062,500. The difference between the gain on
the futures position and the hypothetical loss on the cash position, −$218,750, represents an unfavorable move in the basis
relationship.

CONCLUSION

This chapter has endeavored to illustrate the widespread use
of interest rate futures contracts by participants in the mortgage-backed securities market. It was stated that the initiation
of the first interest rate futures contract, the GNMA–CDR contract, played an important role in the rapid growth of both
mortgage-backed securities and financial futures. More recently, however, lower mortgage yields, together with specific
features of mortgage-backed futures contracts that favor other-
than-current production coupons, have combined to cause
diminution of hedging and arbitrage activity in the GNMA–
CDR and GNMA II contracts. Many mortgage market participants have elected instead to use the U.S. Treasury Bond and
Note futures contracts more actively, accepting the cross-hedging risk of hedging mortgage and mortgage-backed securities
with U.S. Treasury obligations in return for the enhanced liquidity and depth of these futures contracts. The overwhelming
success of the options on Treasury bond futures contract contributed to this development as well.[11]

It seems highly probable that a well designed mortgage-
backed futures contract which converged on delivery to the
current production rate of mortgage originators would reattract

---

[11] The open interest of the CBOT's option on Treasury bond futures
contract stood at 214,518 as of December 31, 1984. The contract began trading
in the autumn of 1982.

a sizable share of the hedging and arbitrage activities of mortgage market participants. The mortgage-backed security market is growing rapidly and the enormous size of the mortgage-backed securities sector would seem to warrant a futures contract that focuses more narrowly on its needs. A successful mortgage-backed futures contract would also permit the introduction of an exchange-traded options contract based on the mortgage-backed futures contract, a development that would enhance the breadth and liquidity of the market. Whether such a contract is forthcoming is yet to be seen, but one can be assured that market participants in the mortgage-backed securities market will increasingly seek methods to hedge their interest rate risks in today's rapidly changing financial environment.

CHAPTER 15

Return Enhancement: GNMA Time Swap Using Floaters

Ronald J. Ryan, C.F.A.
Managing Director
Ryan Financial Strategy Group

In this chapter, I will illustrate a GNMA time swap. I will further demonstrate that the return on a GNMA time swap can be enhanced under certain conditions by using floaters instead of cash in the swap strategy. Before discussing the GNMA time swap, I will discuss the characteristics of floaters and their performance.

FLOATERS[1]

A floater is a fixed income obligation whose periodic contractual payments can change based on the rate of some financial product. Although floaters have been created with various features and terms since 1979, they do share some of the same

---

[1] For a detailed discussion of floaters, see Frank J. Fabozzi (Editor), *Floating Rate Instruments* (Probus Publishing Co., Chicago, IL, 1985).

general characteristics: (1) the coupon "floats" over some base rate, (2) they tend to perform especially well during "down" markets, and (3) they tend to perform well versus money market equivalents. The base rate of a floater is the rate used in the formula to determine the coupon rate. For example, the base rate can be based on a six-month T-bill rate or LIBOR (London Interbank Offer Rate).

Performance of Floaters

The simple reason for the performance of floaters is their income yield. Their coupon (domestic floaters) is built from a formula that ranges from 50 basis points to 100 basis points over a money market base rate. Moreover, they are priced to usually outyield all other cash equivalents, so their dollar price is normally below par. This income yield advantage accumulates over time and has allowed floaters to outperform all other bond sectors since 1979 as judged by the family of in-

EXHIBIT 1
Total Returns of Floaters and Treasuries

	1980	1981	1982	1983	1984	Cumulative
Treasury 2 year	8.36%	12.97%	21.44%	9.08%	14.64%	85.84%
Treasury 3 year	5.17	12.18	24.78	7.79	14.55	82.02
Treasury 4 year	4.42	9.60	28.28	7.23	14.40	79.97
Treasury 5 year	3.84	8.33	29.94	6.10	15.49	79.83
Treasury 7 year	2.81	6.81	33.89	4.72	15.09	77.08
Treasury 10 year	−0.63	7.36	36.81	4.64	14.27	74.46
Treasury 15 year	−3.42	3.22	40.10	4.07	15.84	68.33
Treasury 20 year	N/A	−2.15	42.89	2.54	15.25	65.19
Treasury 30 year	−2.13	2.73	43.31	−0.40	17.48	68.52
Ryan Index*	2.30	6.65	32.96	5.08	15.27	75.60
Cash Index**	12.06	16.65	14.61	9.06	11.68	82.47
FLOATER Index	9.27	22.47	18.55	16.92	13.39	110.33

* The Ryan Index is an equal weighted average of Treasury yield curve (2 year–30 year).
** Cash Index is the six-month CD.

dexes produced by the Ryan Financial Strategy Group. (See Exhibit 1.)

Floater Pricing

Since the coupon of a floater is not fixed as with most "fixed income" securities, floaters enjoy a rising rate environment— a time when their coupon will rise in step (at coupon change dates) with their base rate (i.e., three-month or six-month T-Bill interest yield equivalent rate). Quite often, if priced at a discount, the floater will actually appreciate in price to maintain the same basis point spread. This quirk is due to the market pricing most securities on a basis point spread instead of a percentage spread, as shown in Exhibit 2.

As shown in Exhibit 2, the floater appreciated in price from $95.65 to $96.30 in a rising rate environment to maintain the same basis point spread over the six-month CD. Notice that the percentage spread collapsed from 9.52 percent higher than the CD rate to only 8.00 percent above it. In a declining rate environment, the floater usually has its most difficult time to perform vis-à-vis the market. Not only is its coupon and income yield being reduced, but to maintain the same basis point spread the price must decline.

EXHIBIT 2
Analysis of a Floater Pricing

	Unchanged	+200 BP	−200 BP
Base Rate	10.00%	12.00%	8.00%
6-Month CD	10.50%	12.50%	8.50%
	(Floater Analysis)		
Floater Coupon	11.00%	13.00%	9.00%
Floater Price	$95.65	$96.30	$94.74
Floater Yield	11.50%	13.50	9.50%
	(Spread versus 6-Month CD)		
Basis Point Spread	100 BP	100 BP	100 BP
Percentage Spread	9.52%	8.00%	11.76%

FLOATER STRATEGY WITH MORTAGE PASS-THROUGHS

With the track record of floaters being a better performer than cash (that is, the Ryan Cash Index which consists of six-month certificates of deposit), they represent an ideal replacement for strategies or investments that involve a cash vehicle. In the mortgage pass-through market, for example, purchases of most coupons can be made with a delayed settlement of one to three months and occasionally six months out. The delay of settlement can be accomplished by using the "forward market." The forward market is a market in which the parties agree to trade "something" at a fixed price for future delivery. When using the forward market, no funds must be put up until settlement.

GNMA Time Swap

The time swap concept has historically been a savings and loan (S&L) investment strategy to enhance the yield on their portfolio without a loss. With this approach, a S&L will sell and buy back the same coupon GNMA at some specified price and settlement date in the future (the forward market). It is assumed that the S&L will invest in some cash equivalent between the sale date and repurchase date. Because S&Ls accounting sees this transaction as "no sale," there is no accounting of a loss or gain on the transaction. This accounting quirk has allowed S&Ls to sell low book yielding assets and to buy higher yielding assets with absolutely no change to the portfolio structure.

Quite often called a "dollar roll," S&Ls will consummate such a transaction basically only when they can pick-up yield. This occurs simply when they can buy back the same GNMA at a lower price in the forward market. The forward market price is determined by two factors: (1) financing costs (the carry) and (2) supply and demand.

Financing costs or the costs of carry calculate the yield differential of holding (warehousing) the GNMA position until settlement date versus the money market rate attainable over that same period time. This yield difference could be positive or negative. Since it is typically a Wall Street investment dealer acting as the principal on the trade, they will set the forward market prices accordingly. If it is favorable (that is, positive carry) for them to warehouse this GNMA trade instead of being in a cash equivalent, they will discount (lower) the forward market price and vice versa.

Supply and demand are always a major consideration. Based on available supply, how traders view the market as well as new pass-throughs being created for forward market settlement will dictate pricing trends.

Pension fund managers as well as aggressive S&Ls have gone well beyond the traditional yield objective of a time swap (dollar roll) to enhance their portfolios. They have found that time swaps offer many values most sought by money managers. These include:

1. Liquidity: transactions can be quite sizeable;
2. Selection: time swaps are available on many coupons and types of mortgage pass-throughs;
3. Leverage: time swaps require no transfer of funds until settlement date, which could be several months away;
4. Quality: time swaps on mortgage pass-throughs deal with only the highest rated securities;
5. Timing: based on interest rate forecasting and/or anticipated flow of funds, investors can time or speculate more efficiently, and;
6. Performance: because a time swap is an over-invested situation where there is ownership of two securities until settlement date, returns can be greatly enhanced. A time swap actually allows one to invest in two different markets at the same time.

Illustration

Let us now take a closer look at the mathematics that support the risk/reward merits of a GNMA time swap. Suppose an investor can sell or give up the opportunity to own GNMA 13.00 percent for immediate settlement in August (cash market) and buy it back or purchase it in November at some specified price (forward market). The basic information for this GNMA time swap and the framework for evaluating this swap is presented in Exhibit 3. In this example, it is assumed that the investor is in a cash equivalent in the meantime (three months) at the yield shown on line G of Exhibit 3. To understand the risk/reward of this swap, the investor simply compares the give-up to the pick-up. The difference is the reward or value added. This is shown on lines N, O, and P of Exhibit 3. As the time swap analysis indicates, a 1.01 percent enhanced return (4.09 percent annualized) can be expected by delaying settlement for three months on this trade. This is an example of an actual trade and strategy that existed on August 3, 1983.

EXHIBIT 3
GNMA Time Swap

A. GNMA coupon	13.00%	
B. Settlement—sale	August	
C. Market price	$96–12.	
D. Forward market (months)	3	
E. Settlement—buy	November	
F. Market price	$94–20.	
G. Cash equivalent yield (CYE)	10.00%	
Sale give-up		
H. Income from GNMA sold	$32,139	
I. Prepayment from GNMA	$0	
J. Total (H + I)		$32,139
Purchase pick-up		
K. Takeout (C − F)	$17,500	
L. Income from CYE	$24,361	
M. Total (K + L)		$41,861
N. Increased return (M − J)	$9,722	
O. Nonannualized percent return	1.01%	
P. Annualized percent return		4.09%

NOTE: Assumes a $1 million position on sale.
SOURCE: Ryan Financial Strategy Group.

Later in this section, I will present the actual performance over the three-month investment horizon.

At the time of this GNMA time swap, the floater market looked attractive as judged by a key issue—Citicorp (FNC) due 5/1/04 whose coupon changed semiannually on May 1 and November 1. Citicorp's coupon was built off a formula that basically took the average interest yield equivalent[2] of the six-month T-bill for a two-week period in April and October and added 105 basis points to this average.[3] On August 13, 1983, the coupon was set at 11.15 percent and due for a change on November 1, which was near the delivery date of the GNMA 13.00 percent (third week in November).

The next step, therefore, was to compare the floater as an alternative to cash for the three-month investment horizon.

Floater versus Cash

Since interest rates at the end of the investment horizon can be either higher, lower, or the same as when any investment strategy is initiated, it is important to appraise a strategy under each interest rate scenario to assess how it will impact total return. The analysis of whether to use a floater or cash under three possible interest rate scenarios at the end of the investment horizon is shown in Exhibit 4.

The analysis in Exhibit 4 indicates that no matter where rates go, the floater returns are higher. Consequently, replacing cash in the GNMA time swap with floaters should enhance expected return even more.

---

[2] The interest yield equivalent is the yield of a security based on the actual proceeds (without a reinvestment assumption). It is computed as follows:

$$\frac{\text{discount per } \$1,000}{\$1,000} \times \frac{360}{\text{No. of days}}$$

[3] Specifically, the coupon formula for the Citicorp (FNC) due 5/1/04 is the interest yield equivalent of the arithmetic average of the weekly market rate for the 181-day U.S. T-Bill as published by the Fed during the 14 calendar days immediately prior to the last 10 calendar days of April and October.

EXHIBIT 4
Analysis of Floater versus Cash

	Unchanged	+50 BP	−50 BP
(Levels)			
6-Month T-Bill	10.10%	10.60%	9.60%
6-Month CD	10.50%	11.10%	10.10%
FNC Coupon	11.15%	11.65%	10.65%
FNC Present Price	$93.38	$93.38	$93.38
FNC Current Yield	11.94%	12.48%	11.40%
FNC Yield versus CD	1.44%	1.38%	1.30%
(At 1.25 percent over CD)			
New FNC Yield	11.75%	12.35%	11.35%
New FNC Price	$94.99	$94.33	$93.83
(3-Month Returns)			
Income Return	2.45%	2.45%	2.45%
Price Return	1.63%	1.02%	0.49%
Total Return	4.08%	3.47%	2.94%
3-Month Cash Return	2.50%	2.50%	2.50%
FNC Return—Cash Return	1.58%	0.97%	0.44%

ASSUMPTIONS: T-Bill to CD spread widens to +50 BP, CD to FNC spread changes to +125 BP, used 3-month CD rate of 10.00 percent for cash return.

Floater Plus GNMA Time Swap

Adding the risk/reward of floaters with an attractive GNMA forward market is quite a "dynamic duo." Once again, this synergistic investment should be evaluated under the three alternative interest rate scenarios.

For the three-month forward market period, the investor will not receive any income from the GNMA position since the investor does not take settlement until November. However, the investor is exposed to price return risk since the November price will change with rates. If interest rates are unchanged at the end of the investment horizon, the November price of 94 20/32 will become the August price of 96 12/32 in November. As a result, it will appreciate 1.85 percent because the forward market becomes or gets marked to the cash market through time. If the August price represents the cash market and the market is unchanged, the cash market, by definition, is unchanged.

As noted earlier, when an investor makes a purchase in the forward market, no funds must be put up until settlement. As a result, the investor owns a floater position in the meantime and will use this floater position as funds to pay for the GNMA 13.00s in November. This creates a temporary over-weighted investment position allowing the investor to add the returns of the GNMA and floater position instead of averaging the two. This extra positioning power allows the dynamic duo strategy to have a considerable head start or extra yield over other investment alternatives. This can be seen in Exhibit 5. The analysis indicates that the dynamic duo strategy has the risk of a 3-month CD but offers the reward of a 30-year Treasury.

EXHIBIT 5
Performance of "Dynamic Duo"
under Three Interest Rate Scenarios
(8/3/83)

	(3-Month Horizon)		
	Unchanged	**+50**	**−50**
GNMA:			
Value of Time Swap	1.85%	1.85%	1.85%
Price Return	0	−2.90	3.05
Total Return	1.85%	−1.05%	4.90%
Floater (FNC 04):			
Income Return	2.45%	2.45%	2.45%
Price Return	1.63	1.02	0.49
Total Return	4.08%	3.47%	2.94%
Total Return (Dynamic Duo)	5.93%	2.42%	7.84%
Investment Alternatives:			
3-Month CD	2.50%	2.50%	2.50%
Treasury 2 Year	2.75	1.97	3.53
Treasury 30 Year	2.97	−0.99	7.28

The Actual Results

Three months later on November 3, 1983—the end of the investment horizon—the dynamic duo strategy was reviewed and the performance evaluated. The results are shown in Exhibit 6.

EXHIBIT 6
"Dynamic Duo" Performance
(8/3/83–11/3/83)

GNMA:	
Value of Time Swap	1.85%
Price Return	2.77
Total Return	4.62%
Floater:	
Income Return	2.45%
Price Return	1.35
Total Return	3.80%
Total Return (Dynamic Duo)	8.42% (Nonannualized)
	38.18% (Annualized)
Investment Alternatives:	
Treasury 2 year = 3.77%	
Treasury 10 year = 4.29%	
Treasury 30 year = 3.24%	

The total return on the GNMA time swap was 8.42 percent (nonannualized) with the GNMA contributing 4.62 percent (nonannualized) and the floater 3.80 percent (nonannualized). The lower panel of Exhibit 6 shows the actual return for alternative investments. As can be seen, the dynamic duo clearly outperformed the return of these alternative investments by a wide margin.

CONCLUSION

Any time a GNMA time swap analysis signals a positive return by extending settlement, the floater market should be reviewed to see if returns can be enhanced further.

CHAPTER 16

OTC Options on Mortgage Securities

Mark Pitts, Ph.D.
Vice President
Shearson Lehman Brothers Inc.

INTRODUCTION

In recent years there has been an explosion in the market for options on debt securities. Options on Treasury bonds, Treasury notes, mortgage securities, and Treasury bond futures now trade on established exchanges or over the counter.[1] With this growth it has been easy to forget that options on mortgage securities have existed for some time. Mortgage lenders made use of "standby" commitments to hedge their interest-rate risk long before other sectors of the debt market even considered adding options to their portfolio. Thus, options on mortgages were the first of many debt options that are now available.

The following discussion provides a non-technical introduction to the over-the-counter (OTC) market in options on mortgage securities. The following sections will also demon-

---

[1] See Frank J. Fabozzi (Editor), *Winning the Interest Rate Game: A Guide to Debt Options* (Probus Publishing, Chicago. IL: 1985).

strate why the market for options on mortgages has grown so substantially in recent years.

OPTIONS IN THE MORTGAGE MARKETPLACE

Options are unique financial instruments. Option contracts entail specific rights and obligations leading to patterns of risk and return that are difficult, if not impossible, to duplicate outside the options market.[2] The unique nature of an options contract arises from the fact that the buyer of an option has most of the rights, while the party that sells the option (i.e. the option *writer*) has most of the obligations and a contingent liability that depends upon whether the buyer chooses to exercise the option. Specifically, the buyer of a *call* option has the right to buy the underlying security at a predetermined *strike* (or *exercise*) price. The buyer of a *put* option has the right to sell the underlying security at the strike price. In either case, the seller of the option must stand ready to sell (in the case of a call) or buy (in the case of a put) the underlying security at the stated strike price.

Most mortgage market participants already have some familiarity with options. Standby commitments are nothing more than put options on mortgage securities. If rates rise and prices of mortgages fall, the standby guarantees that the mortgage can be sold at a predetermined price. The OTC standby market was developed to help lenders hedge the implicit options that they grant to loan applicants: the loan applicant who receives a firm commitment from a lender at a specified rate and is not obligated to take down the loan if rates fall, effectively obtains a put option from the potential lender. If rates increase and prices fall, the potential borrower has the right to sell his mortgage note to the lender at par. Another mortgage option is the homeowner's right to early prepayment

---

[2] Later in this chapter the special characteristics of debt options, and options on mortgage securities in particular, are explained in more detail.

which is, in effect, a call option. The homeowner has the right to repurchase his mortgage at a price equal to the remaining mortgage balance.

While each of these are options on mortgage securities, their terms are quite different. The standby commitment and the right granted to the applicant are usually short-lived options. However, the homeowner's right to prepay is a very long-term option that is in effect until the mortgage is completely paid off. These examples of options on mortgage securities illustrate the different ways in which grantors of options charge for the options they grant. Standby commitments entail a specific option price (or *premium*) that the option buyer agrees to pay the option seller. However, the homeowner and loan applicant do not pay any explicit fee for the options they are granted by the lending institution. Their fee is implicit in the interest rate on the underlying mortgage.

One must conclude that options have been an important part of the mortgage market for some time. Yet, the implicit and explicit options that are granted by mortgage market participants often lead to much unwanted risk. However, since the risk of an options position can be eliminated by taking an offsetting (i.e. opposite) position in an identical option, the OTC market in options on mortgage securities uniquely fills many of the needs of mortgage market participants.

THE OTC MARKET IN OPTIONS ON MORTGAGE SECURITIES

Options on mortgage securities are currently traded only over the counter and share the characteristics of other over-the-counter (as opposed to exchange-traded) securities. Like other OTC markets, there is no central market place at which all transactions take place. A transaction takes place whenever a willing buyer and seller agree to a price over the telephone. Unlike an exchange transaction, the terms, size, and price of the option remain undisclosed to other market participants. Accordingly, the current price for a particular option can be far from obvious. In fact, since two or more identical options could trade simultaneously at different prices, the "current price" of the option is not even well-defined in some cases.

The potential disorder that might arise from such a lack of information in the OTC options market is alleviated to some degree by self-proclaimed market makers. Market makers are typically large security dealers or other financial entities that stand ready to either buy or sell options on mortgage securities. To be effective, the market maker must be willing and able to handle orders in size and must keep the difference between his bid and offer price reasonably small.

Unlike the purchaser of exchange-traded options, the purchaser of options in the OTC market must give considerable weight to the creditworthiness of the option seller. (Since a buyer usually pays for the option at the time of purchase, there is little risk associated with the credit of the buyer.) Entities that sell options frequently have potential liabilities equal to many times their net worth, and, while all but the most risk-loving option sellers establish some type of hedge against their short options position, few hedges are perfect. The seller must therefore have the resources to make good on any shortfall that might result if the option is exercised. Since the seller's liability can equal the total amount by which an option is in the money, the potential liability may far exceed the original premium that the seller receives. Consequently, the selling firm's reputation and resources are of critical importance to the buyer.

Finally, while all markets have illiquid moments and illiquid issues, liquidity is usually more of a problem in the OTC market. Except in rare instances, OTC options are non-negotiable agreements made between a buyer and seller. For example, if one sells an option, the contingent liability cannot be transferred to a third party even if the seller finds a party who is willing to assume that liability (for a price, of course). At best, the seller can buy a similar option from a third party, thus offsetting some of the risk. However, if the credit of the third party is not impeccable or if the offsetting option is not identical, considerable risks may remain. The option buyer faces a similar problem if he decides to close out his option before expiration. Credit risk and the nonnegotiability of the contract may make it difficult for the buyer to cash in on his options position.

The fact that OTC options are nonstandardized contracts aggravates the liquidity problem. Unlike exchange-traded options, OTC options can be specified in any terms that are agreeable to both buyer and seller. Consequently, the underlying security, term, and strike price may vary widely. In some cases, this will make it more difficult for those with options positions to find offsets.

While nonstandardization leads to illiquidity, it provides benefits as well. Many options buyers and sellers take options positions not as a play on options or the market per se, but because the option complements some position or security already in the mortgage portfolio. Since the terms of the option are completely negotiable, the potential buyer or seller has a better chance of creating an options position that exactly meets his needs.

OPTIONS ON BONDS VERSUS OTC OPTIONS ON MORTGAGES

Options on Bonds

Before turning to options on mortgage securities, the value of an option on a straight bond must be clear. In Exhibit 1 the value at expiration of put and call options are shown as a function of the price of the underlying security. As the graph shows, the value can only be positive, reflecting the fact that the owner of the option has the *right* to buy (in the case of a call) or sell (in the case of a put), but is under no obligation to do so if it is not to his advantage. Clearly, the value of the option can be quite large. In the case of a put, the option value could equal the strike price. This might occur, for example, if the option is written on subordinated bonds of a company that falls into bankruptcy. For a call option, the maximum

EXHIBIT 1
Long Positions in Options

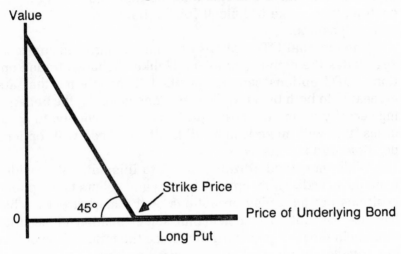

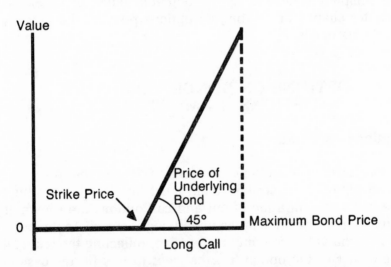

value is constrained only by the maximum possible price of
the underlying security; in the case of a bond, the maximum
price would be obtained if interest rates dropped to 0 percent,
at which point the value of the bond would equal the sum
of all its future cash flows. While this constraint on the maximum price of fixed-income securities has a negligible effect

on the value of an option on long-term bonds, it is quite important for options on short-term instruments.

Exhibit 1 also reflects the fact that if at expiration the price of the bond is less than the strike price, in the case of a call, or greater than the strike price, in the case of a put, then the option will expire worthless. However, if the price of the bond approaches the strike price and moves in the money, the value of the option at expiration moves dollar for dollar with the price of the bond.

The value of a short position in options is the negative, or reverse, of the long position. (See Exhibit 2.) For the option seller or writer, the position can never become an asset since the buyer decides whether the option will be exercised, and will exercise only when the underlying bond is selling for more than the strike price, if the option is a call, or less than the strike price, if the option is a put. The potential losses for the seller are as large as the potential gains for the buyer.

The net effect of an options position when combined with a position in the underlying bond is easily obtained. Exhibit 3 shows the profit or loss associated with a long or short position in the bond itself. By vertical summation, the value of a combined position is derived. For example, if a bond is owned together with a put option having a strike equal to the bond purchase price, then the pattern of return shown in Exhibit 4 is obtained. In this case, the put functions as insurance in that it protects the position from any adverse price change, while preserving the upside potential. Exhibit 5 shows the change in value on a portfolio that is long the underlying bond and short a call on the bond with a strike price just over the purchase price. In this case, the portfolio has significant downside risk, but small upside potential. Other combinations are obviously possible and the payoff schedule for each can be obtained by simply summing the values of the individual securities in the portfolio.

Finally, while the foregoing exhibits show the potential change in value of the bond and option position, they do not indicate the profit on the position. The profit will depend not only on the factors mentioned thus far, but also on the price

EXHIBIT 2
Short Positions in Options

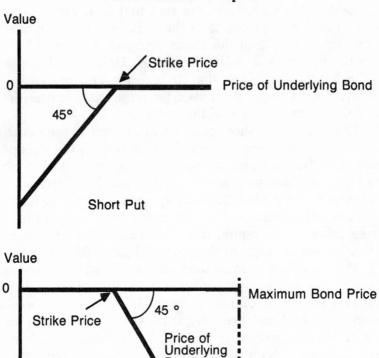

of the options, the coupon income on the bond, and the interest rate (for financing the position and reinvesting coupon income).

OTC Options on Mortgage Securities

The principles underlying OTC options on fixed-rate mortgage securities are, for the most part, no different from options on

EXHIBIT 3
A Position in the Underlying

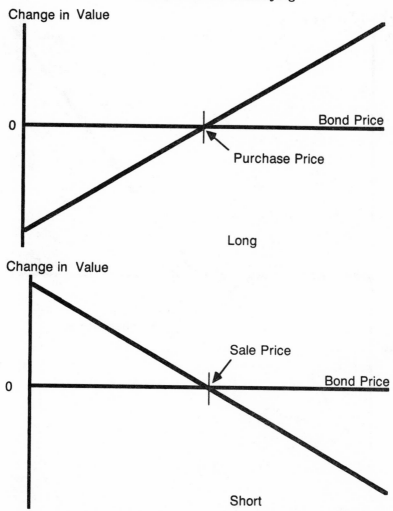

Change in Value

0   Bond Price

Purchase Price

Long

Change in Value

Sale Price

0   Bond Price

Short

bonds. The expiration values of positions containing options on mortgages are the same as those for bonds shown in Exhibits 1–5, except that the horizontal axis would refer to the price of the underlying mortgage security. However, given the unique characteristics of mortgage securities, it would be misleading to not say more about the unique characteristics of OTC options on mortgages. These features arise primarily from the

EXHIBIT 4
Long Bond and Long Put

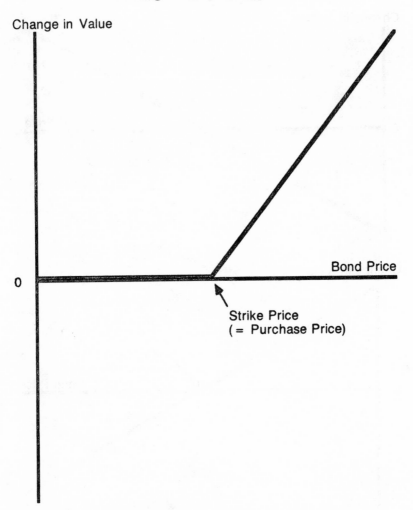

fact that the homeowner has the right at any time to repurchase
the mortgage at par. Thus, if one buys an OTC option on a
mortgage security, one buys an option on a security on which
a call option has already been written. The homeowner's call
option affects the distribution of possible prices for the mortgage security, and thus the potential payoff associated with
the purchase of an option on the mortgage.

EXHIBIT 5
Long Bond and Short Call

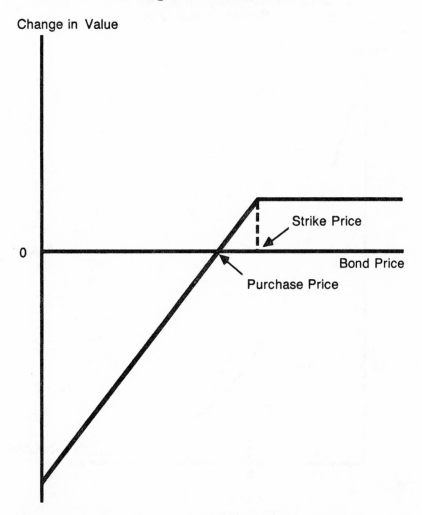

Exhibit 6 shows the relationship between yield and price for a fixed-rate 30-year noncallable self-amortizing loan. If the homeowner is not allowed to prepay (i.e. repurchase) the mortgage, Exhibit 6 would be a completely adequate description of the relationship between a standard mortgage's price and yield. However, because of the prepayment provision, the standard mortgage cannot be treated as a 30-year self-

EXHIBIT 6
Price-Yield Relationship for 30-Year Noncallable
Self-Amortizing Loan

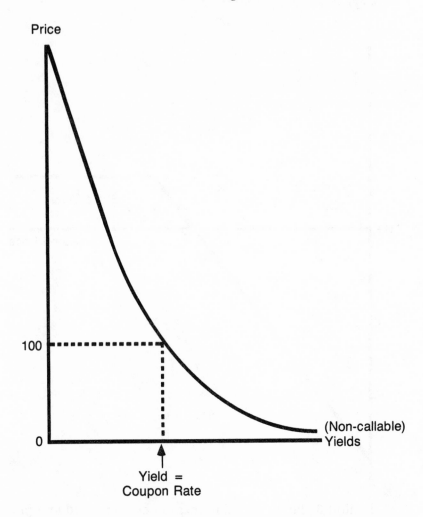

amortizing loan. One way to handle this problem is to break out the mortgage into its component parts—a 30-year noncallable self-amortizing loan and a short call position on that loan struck at par. Exhibit 7 shows the immediate exercise value of the call; it is of course, just the difference between par

EXHIBIT 7
Short Call Position at Expiration
Liability Due to Immediate Exercise

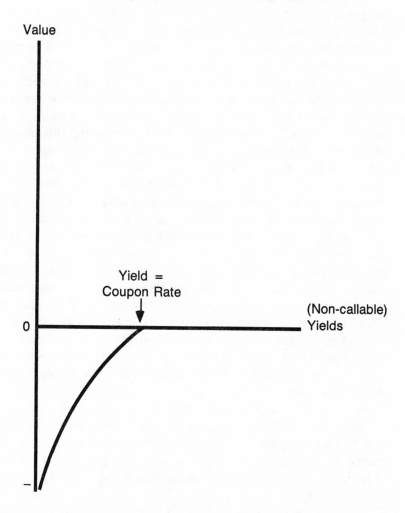

and the price of the (noncallable) security. Combining Exhibits 6 and 7, we derive in Exhibit 8 the price of the callable, or prepayable, mortgage as a function of yields on similar non-callable, or nonprepayable mortgages. Obviously, yields on nonprepayable mortgages cannot be observed directly in the market, but such yields are not difficult to conceptualize.[3] Unfortunately, Exhibit 8 is a gross simplification of the reality of the mortgage security. The value of the homeowner's right to prepay does not equal the value of immediate exercise. First, like other options, the prepayment option has value exceeding the immediate exercise value. Secondly, the homeowner cannot be expected to exercise the call in an "efficient" manner. That is, even if current yields are at or above the coupon rate on the existing mortgage, the homeowner might prepay the mortgage because the family relocates or simply prefers to pay off the loan. Furthermore, assuming the mortgage is insured, "involuntary" prepayments will occur if the property is destroyed or the homeowner defaults on the loan. (In these cases, the appropriate insurance policy pays off the lender.) On the other hand, mortgage loans are often not prepaid even when current yields move below the rate on the existing mortgage. In such cases, the homeowner may be acting irrationally, or may be acting rationally by avoiding refinancing costs (i.e. points, lawyers' fees, policy insurance, time and trouble, etc.). For these reasons, Exhibit 9 more realistically depicts the relationship between the price of a mortgage security and the yield on similar noncallable securities. As indicated in the exhibit, the relationship is an uncertain one, depending upon alternative investment opportunities, expectations of future events, economic conditions, and undoubtedly, numerous other factors. The historical record underscores this uncertainty. In Exhibit 10 recent prices of GNMA 17s are plotted against the yield on ten-year Treasury notes. The ten-year Treasury yields are meant to serve as a proxy for noncallable yields. As the data show, the relationship is at best weak. However, the most important factor

---

[3] This yield should not be confused with the standard mortgage yield that assumes no prepayments until the 12th year, at which time the mortgage is prepaid in full. Since mortgage yields are derived from such unrealistic assumptions, they frequently have little relationship to yields on other fixed-income securities and tell us very little about how a mortgage will move in response to a change in the general level of interest rates.

EXHIBIT 8
Price-Yield Relationship for Noncallable Loan and Short Call Option

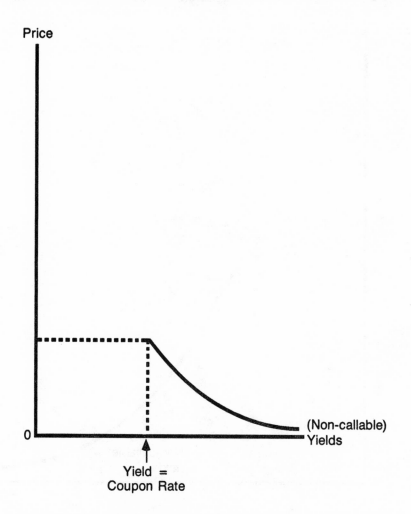

comes through clearly—the price of the mortgage security does not continue to rise as yields fall. At a few points above par, the mortgage securities stall out and do not increase in price even as yields continue to decrease. At very low yields, in fact, prices could *decline* as yields decline. This unusual price-

EXHIBIT 9
Possible Price-Yield Relationship for Mortgages

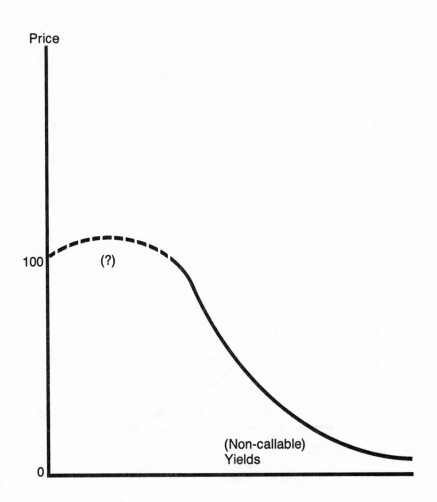

yield pattern is due to the homeowner's right to prepay, that is, the homeowner's call option. Although that option is valued and exercised in a very unpredictable fashion, its net effect—a cap on mortgage prices—is exactly what one would expect.

The impact of mortgage price caps on OTC options on mortgages is significant, especially for calls. While the value

EXHIBIT 10
Price of GNMA 17s versus Yield on 10-Year Treasuries

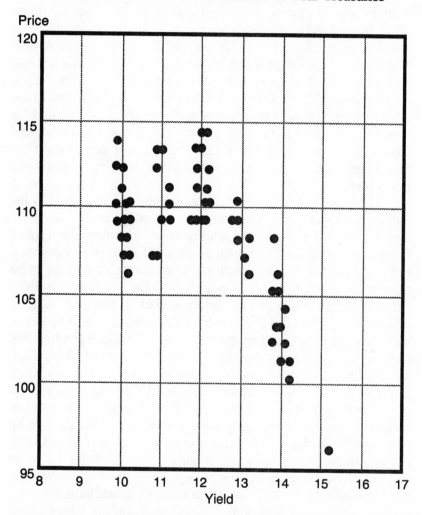

of an OTC call option will increase as long as the price of the underlying mortgage increases, the homeowner's prepayment right severely limits the potential for price appreciation above par. If this factor is ignored, the potential reward from owning OTC call options on mortgage securities will undoubtedly be overestimated.

USING OTC MORTGAGE OPTIONS

Banks (commercial and savings), savings and loan associations, mortgage bankers, pension funds, insurance companies, and home builders are all investors in mortgage securities. Many mortgage originators, such as mortgage bankers and builders, intend to hold their mortgage securities for only a short period of time. Others, such as pension plans and insurance companies, buy mortgages with the intention of making long-term investments. Still others, such as the S&Ls and banks, may hold mortgage securities with the intention of either reselling them in the near future or making a long-term investment.

Since each of these institutions is already involved in the mortgage market, they are in a unique position to use mortgage options. In the subsequent sections we examine the typical fixed-rate single-family mortgage security and show how market participants can use options to reduce risk and/or raise additional income on their positions. The hedging examples that follow illustrate "total" hedges, that is, the positions an institution would take in order to reduce risk as much as possible. As a practical matter, the risks, and therefore the hedging needs, will vary from one institution to the next. A builder, for example, may have a strong incentive to make a rate commitment in order to expedite the sale of the underlying property. Given the gross spread in the transaction, the cost of reducing risk as completely as possible will usually not be prohibitive. On the other hand, a mortgage banker whose primary concern is servicing fee usually does not make the same kind of commitments as the builder, and does not have the profit margin to absorb as much cost in establishing option hedges. Obviously, the cost of OTC options, the firm's profit margins, and the magnitude of the risks are the critical factors in establishing the appropriate hedging program for a given institution.

The following sections illustrate how options can be used to hedge risk or enhance return at each stage in the life of a mortgage. However, since many firms are involved in several stages of the process, this approach maý tend to oversimplify the true situation. While breaking the total picture into parts helps explain the usefulness of options on mortgages, the potential user must not lose sight of the total picture and the net risk of his overall position.

Application and Commitment

The creation, or origination, of mortgage securities consists of several steps, each of which may put the originator at risk. In the initial stage, the potential borrower makes an application for a loan to be collateralized by a piece of property that he wants to purchase. While the application can take many forms, a typical case can be used to illustrate how OTC options can be instrumental in reducing an originator's risk. In particular, consider those applications that are for a fixed amount, but which do not specify the interest rate on the loan. With the interest rate unspecified, the lending institution's primary consideration in accepting or rejecting a particular application will be the creditworthiness of the individual and the market value of the property relative to the loan amount. It is understood that if the application is accepted the rate on the loan will be the "going rate" at the time of acceptance. Until the application is approved, the institution faces no interest-rate risk other than the fact that opportunity losses occur if rates fall while acceptable borrowers are held up in the application stage.

Assuming that property and individual are sound, the lending institution will generally make a *commitment* to the individual. When the commitment is made, the institution obligates itself for a limited period of time to provide the loan at a given rate of interest. Once this rate is set, it cannot be increased over the life of the commitment. Unlike the institution, the potential borrower has no obligation to accept the terms of the loan. Accordingly, if market rates increase substantially the individual has a strong incentive to accept the rate specified in the commitment (which is then below the market rate); but if rates decrease substantially, the individual has a strong incentive not to accept the commitment and to go elsewhere in search of a better rate.

During the commitment stage the institution is, in effect, short a put option on a mortgage security with a coupon rate equal to the rate set forth in the commitment. If rates rise and prices fall, the potential borrower has the right to put, or sell, the mortgage to the institution and receive face value for it in order to purchase the property. The institution has a corresponding windfall if rates fall, and prices rise, only if the applicant closes the loan at the committed rate.

While the commitment risk faced by the institution is structured much like other put options, there are some important differences. Preeminent among these differences is the fact that the homeowner might not exercise the option when it goes in the money, that is, when rates rise. Furthermore, the option might be exercised when it appears irrational to do so, that is, when rates fall. Inefficient exercise arises from the fact that the applicant's situation entails many complications other than the simple economics of the put option. If rates fall the applicant can walk away from the commitment, but then has to begin again the process of applying for a loan. Since rates might go back up by the time a new commitment is granted, this involves time and effort and does not guarantee a lower rate. On the other hand, if rates go up, the homeowner may nonetheless decline the loan. This would occur if the homeowner decides not to purchase the property. The put option cannot be exercised without also purchasing the property, and thus, the applicant must let the put expire unexercised and in the money.

Hedging Optional Commitments with Inefficient Exercise

Despite the dissimilarities between the two types of options, the lending institution's commitments can be hedged using OTC put options on current coupon mortgages. To do so, the lender must first make an estimate of the number of commitments that will be taken down at each rate level. To illustrate,

EXHIBIT 11
The Mortgage Commitment

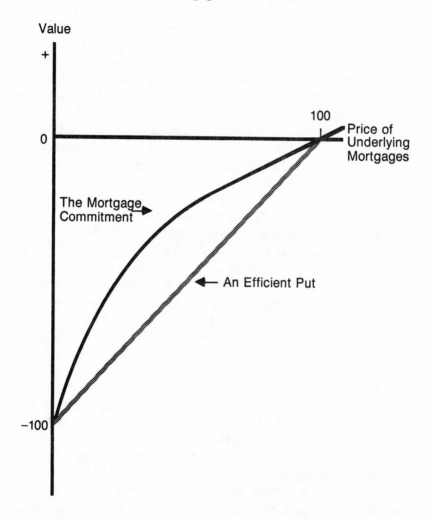

Exhibit 11 shows a hypothetical case. The curved line in the exhibit shows the liability associated with the commitment as a function of the market price of the mortgage the institution has committed to. For a modest fall in prices, the liability is small because of the inefficient exercise discussed earlier. This is evident when the commitment liability is compared to the liability of a totally efficient put, shown as the diagonal straight line in Exhibit 11. As rates rise, it becomes increasingly likely that the applicant will take down the loan. Furthermore, since the commitment liability increases inefficiently for small price declines below par, it is possible that at some point the commitment liability will increase faster than prices decline. This is shown by that portion of the curved line with a slope greater than 1.0. (Accordingly, inefficient exercise can lead to option *deltas* that are greater than 1.0 in absolute value.)

To hedge the (inefficient) commitment option with (efficient) OTC put options, one must approximate the curved liability line shown in Exhibit 11 with linear segments. Obviously, the more linear pieces that are used, the more accurate the approximation. For simplicity we use just three segments as shown in Exhibit 12. The three segments, A–B, B–C, and C–D correspond to three different fall-out rates for three different price intervals, 0–80, 80–92, and 92–100, respectively. Let us also assume that the slope of the line segment C–D is ¾; thus, if prices stay above 92 the rate at which loans are taken down is only 75 percent of the efficient take-down rate. Line segment B–C has a slope of 1.0 so that for prices between 80 and 92, the incremental response of homeowners to an increase in rates is exactly what it would be for an efficient option. (The total take-down rate is still less than efficient because of the inefficient take down at prices above 92.) The line segment A–B has a slope of $^{41}/_{40}$, reflecting the fact that the efficient and inefficient options would entail the same liability as mortgage prices get extremely low.

To hedge the contingent liability of the institution's commitment we hedge only the linear approximation to the curvilinear liability schedule. Since a put on the current coupon mortgage has been granted via the commitment, purchasing puts on the current coupon provides the needed hedge. For example, suppose that the current coupon is 13 percent, then the institution can hedge the commitment by buying puts on 13 percent mortgages in the OTC options market. The only trick is in selecting the right number of options at the right strike prices.

EXHIBIT 12
Linear Approximation to Commitment Liability

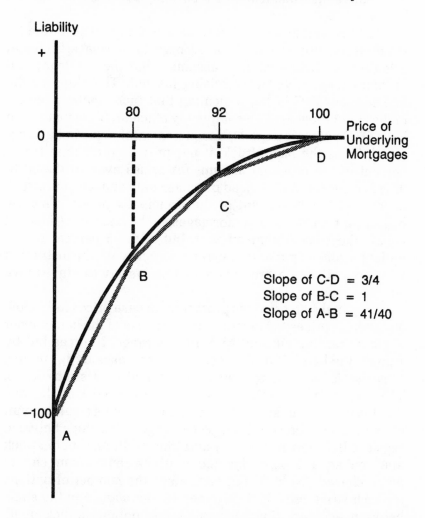

Examination of Exhibit 12 suggests the proper hedging method. By buying a put on 13 percent mortgages struck at par, the purchaser protects against price declines below par. However, since the commitment is exercised at only 75 percent efficiency just below par, the lending institution would purchase only enough puts in the OTC market to cover 75 percent of the face value of the commitment. This purchase would cover the commitment liability as long as prices do not fall below 92.

If, however, additional options are not purchased, the institution remains at risk if the 13 percent mortgage trades at less than 92. Below 92, it is assumed that the applicant will be more responsive in exercising his put. The slope of the line segment B–C is 1.0, indicating that incremental exercise in the 80–92 range will be completely efficient. If the institution buys OTC puts struck at 92, this incremental risk can be eliminated. Since the puts struck at par provide protection for 75 percent of the principal amount for prices even in the 80 to 92 range, the institution need purchase only enough puts struck at 92 to cover 25 percent of the principal amount. Thus, by buying puts on 13 percent mortgages so the underlying amount equals the commitment amount, but with 75 percent of the options struck at par and 25 percent struck at 92, the institution will have adequate protection as long as prices stay above 80.

The final step provides protection in case prices fall below 80. At these prices the incremental response of the homeowner is more than the efficient rate. In this range, if prices fall by 1 point, the liability of the institution increases by $^{41}\!/_{40}$ points. This risk is covered by buying additional puts struck at 80. The options struck at par and at 92 cover most of the risk that the institution faces at prices below 80, but a small amount of extra protection is needed. The change in the slope between segment B–C and A–B is $\frac{1}{40}$, and thus additional puts struck at 80 and equal to $\frac{1}{40}$ of the amount of the commitment should be purchased. (Note that at each stage the number of options for each strike price is determined by the *change* in the slope between adjacent line segments.) The options struck at 80 complete the portfolio of options needed to cover the risks associated with the linear approximation to the commitment liability.

In Exhibit 13, the hedging process is displayed graphically. The options struck at par, 92, and 80 are shown by the solid lines. In each case, the slope of the line is determined by the quantity of each option that the institution purchases (i.e., ¾, ¼, and ¹⁄₄₀). Summing vertically, one derives the dotted line shown in Exhibit 13. The dotted line thus shows the payoff of the portfolio of three OTC options as a function of the price of 13 percent mortgages. However, the dotted line in Exhibit 13 is just the mirror image of the dotted line in Exhibit

EXHIBIT 13
Portfolio of OTC Options on Mortgages

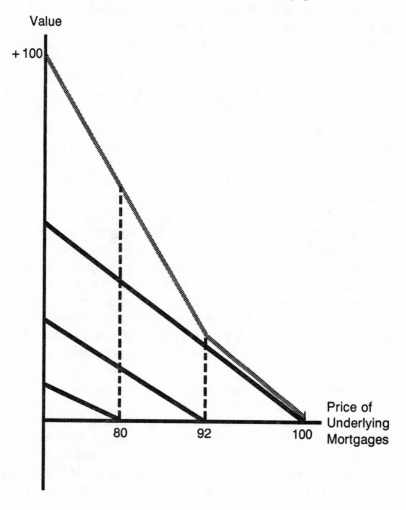

12 showing the approximate commitment liability. Since the values in Exhibit 13 are positive and those in Exhibit 12 are negative, the commitment liability is just offset by the value of the OTC options.

The hedging technique described here does, of course, require some significant simplifications. The liability was approximated by three linear sections. While this leaves much to be desired, the problem can be overcome by using more linear sections. By increasing the number of linear segments, the curvilinear liabilities can be approximated to any degree of accuracy. More serious, however, is the availability of the options needed to carry out the hedging program. As indicated earlier, the OTC market is frequently illiquid in certain issues and certain strikes. For example, it could be difficult to purchase a put struck at 80 when the underlying security is trading at or near par. Consequently, in the foregoing example it might be better to purchase additional options struck at 92 rather than purchasing options struck at 80. Such a strategy covers the downside risk of the commitment liability, but means that the institution buys a little more "insurance" than it needs. (The lender could also simply ignore the incremental risk for prices below 80 since there is very little chance that prices would fall that far during life of the commitment.) Finally, perhaps the most serious threat to a good hedge arises from inaccuracies in the estimated commitment liability. Obviously, the hedge is only as good as the estimate of the liability. While history may be a guide in making this estimate, current economic conditions and the characteristics of the potential mortgages and borrowers are probably the dominant factors determining the commitment liability at each price level.

Warehousing and Price Risk

When a mortgage commitment is made and the applicant accepts its terms, a mortgage loan is created. A new mortgage is then added to the originator's portfolio. Frequently, the originator has no intention of holding the mortgage as a long-term investment, but plans instead to resell it in the near future and use the proceeds to originate new loans. However, in order to resell the mortgages at a reasonable price, the originator usually finds it necessary to collect mortgages in some size and to have them securitized. Until this process is completed and the mortgages resold, the originator faces warehousing risk: the risk that financing rates will increase, and/or mortgage rates will rise and the value of the unsold mortgages will fall.

Let us consider a specific example. Suppose the originator holds a number of mortgages which will be securitized to create 13 percent GNMA pass-through securities. He stands at risk that financing rates will rise before the securities are sold and his incremental cost of carrying the mortgages will wipe out his profit. Unfortunately, OTC options on mortgages are of little help in hedging the financing rate faced by originators. (Futures or options on the financing rate would be the appropriate hedge.) If, however, the originator has not sold the mortgages forward, he also faces the risk that interest rates will rise before the mortgages are sold and that the sale price will be considerably less than the expense of creating the mortgages. Since an active market in OTC options on pass-through securities exists, the originator can hedge his risk by buying put options on 13 percent GNMAs, expiring on or about the anticipated sale date. Unlike the commitment risk discussed in the last section, the price risk of the mortgages can be hedged with an equal face amount of options and just one strike price.

Although the hedging technique is straightforward, the institution must still decide which strike price to use. This is essentially a decision of how much insurance to buy. The lower the strike price the more downside risk the institution faces, but also the lower the cost of obtaining protection.

Usually, there is no such thing as a "correct" strike price for the option used in the hedge. Exhibit 14 illustrates the kind of choices the institution will face. Comparing any two options, the institution will find that one option provides superior results in one rate scenario, and the other option provides superior results in other scenarios. In the exhibit, the line seg-

EXHIBIT 14
Value of Hedged Portfolio for Options with Different Strike Prices

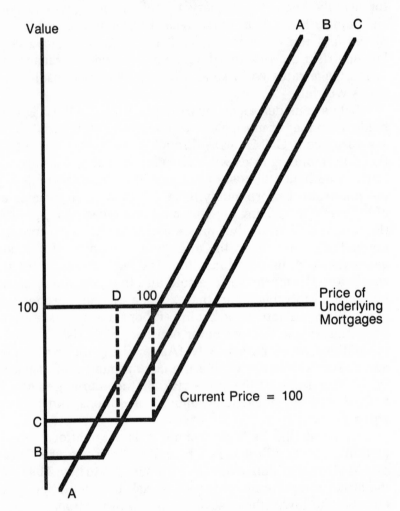

ment C–C shows the value of the mortgage portfolio if hedged
with put options struck at 100, the current price of the mortgages. Segment B–B shows the value if an out-of-the-money
option is used as the hedging vehicle. If the final price of the
mortgage security is above point D in the exhibit, the out-of-
the-money option leads to a greater portfolio value. For prices

below point D, the at-the-money option provides better results. Thus, neither option "dominates" the other; in fact, neither option dominates the unhedged strategy (segment A–A in the exhibit). Similar results would occur no matter which strike prices were considered. In no case would one strategy always lead to superior results. Thus, in the end, the right strike price depends upon management's attitude toward risk and return and their assessment of the consequences of a given gain or loss in the value of the portfolio.

Price Risk and Commitment Risk

As part of their ongoing business, originators typically issue commitments, warehouse mortgages, and securitize and sell mortgage loans. Consequently, commitment risk and price risk of warehoused mortgages are simultaneous risks that the lender faces. Furthermore, the lender is likely to bear the brunt of commitment risk and price risk in the same rate environment, that is, when rates are rising. As discussed earlier, applicants are more likely to take down loans when rates have risen. This adds to the size of the institution's portfolio at a time when prices are falling and the institution would prefer to own fewer, rather than more, mortgage securities. The risks thus seem to compound one another.

Fortunately for the hedger, the risks are strictly additive; that is, the total hedge is just the one needed for the commitments plus the one needed to cover the price risk of the warehoused mortgages. One can simply derive the put positions needed for each type of risk and sum them to obtain the total hedge position. However, when an applicant accepts the terms of a commitment and a new mortgage is created, the institution must recalculate the hedge since commitment risk will have decreased and price risk will have increased. Also, of course, as mortgages are sold the hedge must be recalculated to account for the decrease in the number of warehoused mortgages.

Calculating the hedge needed to cover commitment risk separately from the hedge needed to cover price risk does not ignore the fact that commitments *potentially* lead to price risks. Calculating the hedges separately simply takes into account the fact that potential risks need not be hedged until they become actual risks.

Buying Calls

The institution that faces price risk from its warehoused mortgages has more than one way to hedge its risk. Let us take a specific example. Suppose an institution has $40 million of loans in the mortgage portfolio. When the sum reaches $50 million, the institution plans to securitize the mortgages and resell them in the secondary market. For simplicity, assume that no commitments are outstanding and the only risk is the price risk associated with the $40 million of loans currently in the portfolio.

To hedge the price risk, the institution could buy puts on $40 million worth of mortgages. (See page 438.) However, there is a less expensive alternative. Instead of buying puts, the institution can sell $50 million of mortgage securities in the forward or futures market. This eliminates the price uncertainty associated with the current $40 million portfolio, but exposes the institution to the risk that rates will *decrease* and prices *increase* on the remaining $10 million of mortgage loans. Accordingly, the institution can hedge by buying calls on mortgage securities. If prices increase, the calls will go in the money, offsetting the losses on the uncovered $10 million portion of the forward (or future) sale.

The advantage to this strategy revolves around the fact that by selling forward one can hedge by buying calls on only $10 million in mortgages. If no forward sale is made, puts on $40 million are required to complete the hedge. Thus, the needed protection is acquired at about one-fourth the cost.

Obviously, the relative cost of the two hedging schemes— buying puts versus selling forward and buying calls—depends upon the current size of the portfolio relative to the size of the portfolio at the time of resale. If the previous example is turned around so that only $10 million of loans have been warehoused out of a final size of $50 million, it would be cheaper to buy puts (on $10 million) rather than sell $50 million forward and buy calls (on the uncovered $40 million).

Selling Calls

The lending institution is generally net long mortgages. Accordingly, it can take advantage of covered call writing, that is, selling call options on loans in the portfolio. Covered call writing also appeals to many long-term investors in mortgages since it is a strategy that can be used to raise additional income on a dormant mortgage portfolio. If the institution writes out-of-the-money calls on an existing portfolio, then the option premium is pure income if the options are not exercised; if the options are exercised, the institution keeps the option premium and sells the mortgages at a price above the market price on the day the option is written. While this may appear to be a strategy at which one cannot lose, Exhibit 15 shows that this is not the case. The straight diagonal line (A–A) shows the change in the value of the long position as the price of the security changes. The kinked line (B–B) shows the value of the covered call position. Much like the simple long position, the covered call position has significant downside risk. The downside risk of the covered call is, however, cushioned by the call premium that the writer receives; thus, as prices fall the covered call position will show smaller losses than the simple long position. The "cost" of this cushion on the downside is the give-up on the upside. As prices rise the call option liability increases, and if they rise above the strike price the option may be exercised and the underlying mortgages sold at less than the current market price. Accordingly, the primary cost of covered call writing is the opportunity loss that occurs when prices rise above the strike price. Nonetheless, many institutions are willing to assume a potential opportunity loss in return for immediate income, especially when exercise would mean selling at a price higher than the current market price.

EXHIBIT 15
Long Position versus Covered Call

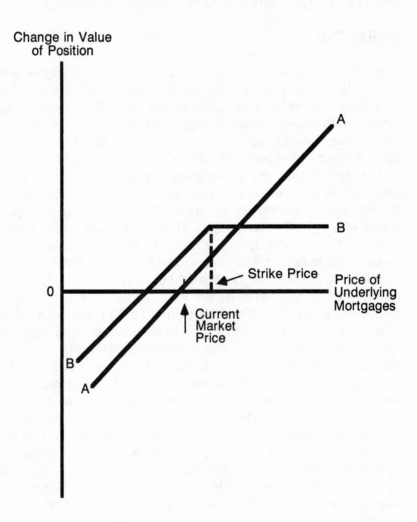

CONCLUSION

Mortgage market participants generally hold mortgage portfolios that are combinations of long and short positions in several
mortgage-related instruments: the (hypothetical) noncallable

mortgage, the homeowner's call on the mortgage, commitments on (callable) mortgages, and futures and forwards on (callable) mortgages. Before taking a position in the OTC options market in mortgages, the investor should examine his position in terms of these component parts. When the simple components have been clearly identified, the individual parts can be summed to obtain a picture of the portfolio or origination process as a whole. This will lead to a better understanding of the change in the value of the position for a given change in yields. The institution will then know whether it is net long or net short, and whether the position is one of balanced risks (such as a simple long or short position) or one of unbalanced risk (such as an option position). Only when the total picture is clear will the institution be able to use the OTC options market to its best advantage.

CHAPTER 17

Hedging the Interest Rate Risk of Fixed Rate Mortgages with Prepayment Rights

Alden L. Toevs, Ph.D.
Morgan Stanley and Co. Inc.

Fixed-rate mortgage production lost substantial market share to several types of adjustable-rate mortgages during the early 1980s. Now we are beginning to observe a reversal in this trend. The resurgence in fixed-rate mortgages (FRMs) has been brought on by at least three factors. First, long-term interest rates have fallen relative to short-term interest rates. Second, the use of teaser rates in adjustable-rate mortgages (ARMs) has moderated. Third, credit losses on some types of ARMs have made lenders and mortgage insurers more cautious of these loans.

There is an additional reason for the renewed interest in FRMs. Some lenders have begun to find effective means by which to hedge the interest rate risk of fixed-rate mortgages. The incentives have been enormous for such a discovery, as innovators can expect to capture a greater percentage of what in the past was once a profitable business. Certainly, most

borrowers have not changed their attitudes during the last
five years; they want stable mortgage payments and many
are more willing than ever to pay premiums for such loan
terms.

This chapter presents a method to estimate the interest
rate risk of FRMs. Because fixed-rate mortgages are such complicated securities, our approach will not be perfect—none
will ever be. Nevertheless, our method can quantify a substantial portion of the interest rate risk of FRMs.

The primary complication to measuring the interest rate
risk of a FRM is the indeterminate maturity date of such a
loan. The typical FRM offers a highly valuable prepayment
right as part of its contractual terms. This right is essentially
a call option that the borrower can exercise at any time by
returning the principal value of the loan, regardless of what
might then be the market value of the remaining contractual
cash flows. Since differences between market values and principal values depend on interest rate levels, prepayment options
affect the effective maturity dates *and* interest rate sensitivities of FRMs.

Call options on debt securities are normally exercised
only when they lead to lower financing costs. FRMs are, however, often prepaid when the principal value exceeds the market value of the remaining cash flows. Due on sale clauses
are one reason for this phenomenon. "Irrational" exercise of
the prepayment (call) option makes the pricing of FRMs more
difficult than other types of callable debt and it alters the
estimated interest rate risk of FRMs. Our methodology ad-
dresses this issue, but space constraints force us to concentrate
primarily on the interest rate risk of FRMs assuming only "rational" refinancing decisions. Such a focus is reasonable at
this stage in the development of interest rate measurement
techniques since if prepayments for loan refinancing cannot
be accurately determined, then there is little hope that complex
combinations of refinancing prepayments and prepayments
for other reasons can be jointly considered.

This chapter is divided into three parts. The first section
discusses the valuation of FRMs with prepayment rights. The

second section measures the interest rate risk of these securities using duration analysis. Our choice of duration as an index of interest rate risk is arbitrary. We have selected it because a growing number of asset/liability managers find duration helpful in measuring the interest rate risk of debt securities. The third section discusses hedging the interest rate risk of FRMs.

VALUATION OF FIXED RATE MORTGAGES WITH PREPAYMENT RIGHTS

Unlike stock options, an option on a debt security normally does not trade separately from the security that is deliverable against the option. Rather, it is an integral part of the security. The purchase, sale, or exercise of an option must be accompanied by the sale, purchase, or delivery of the associated security.[1] The FRM lender, for example, is *long* one unit of the deliverable security and *short* one prepayment (call) option. In this taxonomy, the security deliverable against the option represents the title to the remaining payments of principal and interest of the FRM.

The Basics

Many debt securities contain American call options. These securities permit the issuer to call the bond away from the holder at any date for a specified price. Insurance contracts with cash values have such features. But the traditional FRM represents the most important type of debt security containing an American call option.

---

[1] Bonds issued with detachable warrants are becoming more common, particularly in Europe. Debt issues with detachable options are now being considered in the United States. (See R. Bookstaber, W. C. Haney, and P. D. Noris. *Are Options on Debt Issues Under Valued?* Morgan Stanley, December 1984.) There is growing interest in detachable prepayment options written on mortgage contracts as well.

The market value of a FRM with a prepayment right can be expressed as

$$P_M = P_D + \text{Prem} - P_{PO} \tag{1}$$

P_M is the market value of the FRM. P_D is the present value of the remaining contractual cash flows of the mortgage. It is the present value of the cash flows the lender must exchange for the outstanding principal value should the borrower exercise his or her prepayment right. Prem is the accumulated (realized) payments the lender receives for offering the prepayment option. P_{PO} is the value of the prepayment option as derived from an appropriate option pricing model.

Prepayment Option Premiums

Since the prepayment option is written by the lender to the borrower, its value enters Equation (1) negatively—its value is a cost to the lender. FRM lenders receive a premium for extending a prepayment option to the borrower. At loan origination, much if not all of this premium may be paid by the borrower in up-front points. Afterwards, if the FRM trades in secondary markets, the premium received by the new FRM owner comes in the form of a reduced price relative to the present value of a nonprepayable, but otherwise comparable, debt security.

In the former case, Prem equals the value of the up-front points. As time passes, this fund is invested and grows with the success of these investments. Alternatively, the compensation for the prepayment option may be paid as an adjustment to the yield on a mortgage. This method pays the premium on an installment plan. As these increments are realized (accrue), they can be viewed to be added to a premium pool (Prem) that earns its own return. Title to yield increments not yet realized, however, will have to be surrendered to the borrower if the loan should prepay.[2]

---

[2] It may seem suboptimal to take premiums in the form of uncertain installments rather than in certain up-front payments. Arbitrage trading, however, should equate these forms of payment: Should the prepayment

The pricing of a FRM requires that the three terms in Equation (1) be quantified. The value of the contractual cash flows is obtained by discounting these flows by the rates applicable for noncallable debt with comparable credit risks.[3] This discounting reveals the present value of the remaining premium installments to be paid to the lender in mortgage yield adjustments, if any. At the date of acquisition, the lender must receive an increment in yield plus any initial contribution to Prem that equals P_{PO}. Otherwise, the option would be mispriced. As time passes, P_{PO} may depart from the present value of the premium payments accumulated and to be received. This is just what happens in any option market. As the market changes, the premium remains fixed but the market value of the option may make this sum appear great or small. Once the FRM is resold, however, the new purchaser will receive a new premium commensurate with the then current value of P_{PO}.

Prepayment Option Valuation

P_{PO} is the remaining item in Equation (1) to be valued. The mechanics of option pricing is not the topic of direct concern in this chapter. Rather, we wish to measure the interest rate risk of FRMs with prepayment options using methods comparable to those used on option-free debt securities. Hence, only the necessary items of option pricing will be given here.

---

option go into the money and be exercised, the amount of the up-front premium net of the market loss the lender experiences by "selling" back the title to the remaining cash flows at a below market price will be no different than the loss of remaining yield increments upon delivery of the remaining contractual cash flows.

[3] For GNMAs, the discount rates would be comparable to those derived from a Federal Agency yield curve. These discount rates should be term structure rates (rates on hypothetical zero coupon agency bonds). These can be derived from information on coupon paying bond yields using a number of different empirical techniques. (See, for example, D. R. Chambers, W. T. Carleton and D. W. Waldman, "A New Approach to the Estimation of the Term Structure of Interest Rates," *Journal of Financial and Quantitative Analysis*, September 1984 and G. S. Shea, "Pitfalls in Smoothing Interest Rate Term Structure Data: Equilibrium Models and Spline Approximations," *Journal of Financial and Quantitative Analysis*, September 1984.)

An option can be properly valued only by using a pricing model consistent with the characteristics of the option. These models exist in varying degrees of completeness and accuracy for prepayment options.[4] Values derived from these models combine the intrinsic value of the option with its time value. The intrinsic value of the option is the easier part to value. By definition, it is the larger of zero or P_D − Prin, where Prin is the remaining principal value of the mortgage.[5] (For expositional convenience, prepayment penalties will be viewed to be adjustments to Prin.) In instances where the borrower can prepay and reduce his or her mortgage financing costs, the option is "in the money." Thus,

$$\left.\begin{array}{l} P_{PO} = (P_D - \text{Prin}) + P_{POT} \\[1em] \text{Otherwise, the option has no intrinsic value and} \\[1em] P_{PO} = P_{POT} \end{array}\right\} \qquad (2)$$

where P_{POT} represents the time value of the option.

The time value of any option must be positive. It depends on the expiration date of the option, the current and exercise prices of the security, and the expected volatility of the debt's market value. The longer the period over which an option remains in force, the greater its time value. All other things equal, the more deeply an option is in *or* out of the money, the smaller is its time value. Finally, the more volatile the factors that influence the market value of the cash flows deliverable against an option, the greater the option's time value.

---

[4] See Arden Hall, "Valuing the Mortgage Borrower's Prepayment Option," *AREUEA,* Fall 1985 and R. J. Pozdena and Ben Iben, "Pricing Debt Instruments: The Options Approach," *Economic Review,* Summer 1983, for simple introductions. J. C. Cox, S. A. Ross, and M. Rubinstein, "Option Pricing: A Simplified Approach," *Journal of Financial Economics,* No. 7, 1979, provides a more complex option pricing formulation for American call options.

[5] Intrinsic values are defined to be no smaller than zero because the exercise of an option is voluntary and, normally, out-of-the-money options are not exercised. FRMs differ from more conventional debt securities with options since circumstances exist when the option is exercised even though the option is out of the money. These situations are examined later in the chapter.

In-the-Money Versus Out-of-the-Money FRMs

Using Equation (2) we can rewrite Equation (1) for in-the-money prepayment options as,[6]

$P_M = Prin + Prem - P_{POT}$

For at-the-money or out-of-the-money prepayment options,

$P_M = P_D + Prem - P_{POT}$

(3)

As shown in Equation (3), the market price of a FRM with only rational prepayment becomes either the price of a thirty-year amortizing debt instrument *less* the time value of the call option or its outstanding principal value, adjusted for any prepayment penalties, *less* the time value of the call.

Much as the value of a callable bond depends on adding up the relevant values of its parts, the interest rate sensitivity of the price of a FRM is the sum of the interest rate sensitivities of its parts. Thus, when the FRM is in the money,

$\Delta P_M = \Delta Prin + \Delta Prem - \Delta P_{POT}$

Otherwise,

$\Delta P_M = \Delta P_D + \Delta Prem - \Delta P_{POT}$

(4)

ΔP_M is the dollar change in the market value of the callable bond per basis point change in the "interest rate," and other variables are similarly interpreted.[7]

---

[6] We could have elected not to introduce this dichotomous treatment of FRM prepayment option by keeping the intrinsic and time value of the option aggregated. Such was the methodology employed in A. L. Toevs and J. H. Wernick. "Hedging Interest Rate Risk, Inclusive of Prepayment and Credit Risk," *Identification and Control of Risk in the Thrift Industry*, Proceedings of the Ninth Annual Conference, Federal Home Loan Bank of San Francisco, 1983. Neither approach is perfectly suited for the points we desire to make. The relative advantage of the approach used in Equation (3) is a clearer determination of how the interest rate risk of FRMs change as prepayment options go from deeply in to deeply out of the money.

[7] As mentioned in footnote 3, proper discounting of cash flows should always be done with a term structure of interest rates. We have simplified the discussion in this chapter by assuming that the yield curve is flat and shifts in a parallel fashion. Our results are easily generalized to more sophisticated interest rate environments.

A Graphical Interpretation of FRM Valuation

Exhibit 1 uses a dashed line to depict the relationship between the market value of the contractual cash flows of a FRM including investments of realized premium payments and the level

EXHIBIT 1
Interest Rate Levels and FRM Values

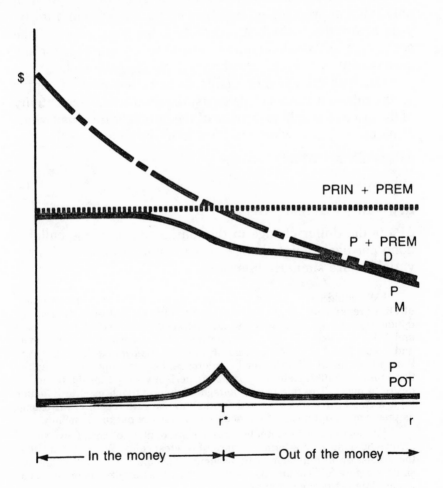

of interest rates (r). This value reaches a maximum when the discount rate (r) equals zero, where it becomes the sum of all the non-discounted contractual cash flows to be received by the lender. As r becomes very high, P_D + Prem tends towards but never reaches zero. These two extreme observations imply that P_D + Prem and r relate to one another in the curvilinear fashion drawn in Exhibit 1. One, but by no means the best, representation of ΔP_D + ΔPrem is the slope of the dashed line in Exhibit 1.

If the mortgage is called, the lender receives Prin + Prem, not P_D + Prem. Since Prin is fixed in value, it is not interest rate sensitive. Exhibit 1 shows this by using the horizontal dotted line. For expositional convenience, we have assumed in the construction of both the dashed and dotted lines that the accumulated realized prepayment premiums are invested in short-term debt, which makes ΔPrem equal to zero.

Normally, an option will be exercised only when interest rates fall below r^*, the rate that equates P_D and Prin. Thus, the present value of the cash flows delivered by the borrower upon prepayment *less* the present value of the intrinsic value of the prepayment option is Prin + Prem for interest rates below r^* and P_D + Prem for rates in excess of r^*. This shift from the dotted line to the dashed line as interest rates rise maps out the value of cash flows of the FRM and premium investments *less* the intrinsic value of the prepayment option.

The solid line at the bottom of Exhibit 1 shows how the *time* value of a prepayment option depends on the level of interest rates. At extreme interest rate levels, the time value of the option is nearly zero. Its value is maximized when the option is at the money. Note how critically the slope of P_{POT} depends on the current level of interest rates. The slope of P_{POT} is found by evaluating P_{POT} at the current interest rate and then again at a rate one basis point higher. The difference defines ΔP_{POT} at the initial interest rate.

While the slope of P_{POT} is small when interest rates are at their extremes, near r^* the slopes of both P_{POT} and the upper solid line in Exhibit 1 are most subject to change (unstable).

Technically, neither is defined at r*.[8] This results in a FRM with an at-the-money prepayment option having an unstable price sensitivity to changes in interest rates.

Exhibit 1 was constructed assuming that the maturity of the FRM, the principal value and the assessment of interest rate volatility remain constant as interest rate levels vary.[9] Changes in any of these values cause the placement of the curves in Exhibit 1 to shift. Consequently, the slopes of the lines in this exhibit, at any given value of r, may also change.

If the time value of the prepayment option is subtracted from the relevant portions of the dashed and dotted lines in Exhibit 1, we obtain a graphical illustration of Equation (3). This subtraction gives the P_M line. Note how the market values of a FRM can differ from the dashed line, a line that represents the values of a noncallable but otherwise comparable mortgage.

Irrational Exercise of FRM Prepayment Options

A borrower often has to prepay a mortgage that would best remain in force to minimize the financing cost of the home with which the mortgage is associated. In large measure, such prepayments occur when the borrower sells the house and the new owner chooses not to assume, or is prevented from assuming, the existing mortgage. Due on sale clauses have notably increased the prepayment of mortgages with below market coupon rates in recent years. A growing number of studies show that many of these home-sale prepayments predictably relate to local mobility patterns, family size changes,

---

[8] While the slopes of the contractual cash flows *less* the *intrinsic* value of the option and the time value of the option are undefined when we are at r*, subtracting the "spike" in P_{POT} from the contractual cash flow less the intrinsic value of the prepayment option leaves a smooth line (P_M).

[9] It may seem odd that if interest rates change dramatically, our assessments of interest rate volatility would not also change. This assumption is made only for convenience and need not be incorporated in any actual analysis. Option pricing becomes, however, more complex when these considerations are added.

the number of years the owner has lived in the house, changes in income, and so on.[10]

Noninterest rate-dependent (static) prepayments can be viewed as simple adjustments to the timing and magnitude of the contractual cash flows to be received from FRM portfolios.[11] Given the new static cash flow pattern, the discounted value of these flows can be computed, as can the value of the prepayment option inclusive of these static prepayments. The valuation of the option will, however, require the use of a more complex option pricing technique.

The new option price should be less than what would be computed without consideration of static prepayments. Lenders realize the prepayment option is less valuable when some borrowers do not optimally refinance their loans. Thus,

$$P^*_M = P^*_D + Prem^* - P^*_{PO} \tag{5}$$

P^*_D is the present value of the contractual cash flows from the mortgage as adjusted for the probable rate of static prepayments. These are the cash flows expected to be delivered should the borrower(s) choose to lower the cost of the existing mortgage by refinancing. P^*_{PO} is obtained from an option pricing model that computes the value of the option relative to the contractual cash flows of the mortgage after they have been adjusted for the probable static loan prepayments. Since P^*_{PO} must be less than the value of P_{PO} in Equation (1), mortgage market competition should force $Prem^*$ to be less than $Prem$.

The adjustments for static prepayments will not be perfect. All that can be done here is to incorporate the best available information on the likely timing of these cash flows into the mortgage valuation procedure before the interest rate sensitivity of the mortgage is determined. Other issues influence FRM pricing. Some truly irrational borrowers will fail to refi-

---

[10] See H. F. Peters, S. M. Pinkus, and D. J. Askin. "Figuring the Odds: A Model of Prepayments," *Secondary Mortgage Markets*, May 1984.

[11] The word "static" in this context does not necessarily mean constant. The rate of prepayment may for demographic reasons first increase and then decrease. Static prepayments are merely those prepayments that cannot be associated with changes in interest rates and the altered incentives such changes bring to refinancing decisions on the existing mortgage.

nance their homes when rates fall to a point that refinancing becomes optimal. Less irrational are those who eventually refinance when rates fall, but do so with a lagged response. Full adjustments for these potentially important sources of error in the techniques suggested will be addressed at another time.

Summary

This section has presented four simple, but fundamentally important concepts: The value of an optioned security is the sum of its parts. The value of these parts can be adjusted for loan prepayments that are determined by factors other than interest rates or changes in interest rates. The quality of these price adjustments will depend on the accuracy with which static loan prepayments can be forecasted. And the interest rate sensitivity of a fixed-rate and prepayable mortgage is the sum of the interest rate sensitivities of the component parts of the mortgage. In the following section the graphical techniques for measuring interest rate sensitivity that were developed above are reexpressed in terms of duration.

THE DURATIONS OF FIXED-RATE MORTGAGES WITH PREPAYMENT OPTIONS

Duration is a statistic that was first developed to measure the life of any series of fixed and known cash flows, such as those arising from an option-free debt security. Term to maturity is an unambiguous measure of the life of a zero coupon bond. But, because term to maturity ignores the amount and timing of all cash flows except the final payment, it incompletely measures the life of other securities. Duration standardizes any debt security's life using a zero coupon bond *equivalent* term to maturity. This approach is compelling because an option-free security can be conceptually viewed as nothing more than a bundle of zero coupon bonds with various maturity (cash flow) dates.

General Characteristics of Duration

Besides providing a means by which average life can be standardized, duration also measures the instantaneous price sensitivity of an option-free security. In its simplest representation,

$$\Delta P_F = -(P_F \times D_F)/(1 + r) \tag{6}$$

where ΔP_F is the dollar price change in an option-free security per unit change in interest rates and D_F is the duration of this security (maturity of an equivalently interest rate sensitive zero coupon bond).

Duration was defined in its simplest context by Macaulay[12] as,

$$D = \sum_{t=1}^{T} w_t \times t, \tag{7}$$

where w_t is the proportion of the market price of the bond maturing at date T contributed by the present value of the cash flow occurring at date t. This formula uses the yield to maturity of the bond when discounting cash flows needed to determine the w's. Macaulay's duration formula is used implicity in this chapter to ease the discussion. This is consistent with the earlier assumption, again made only for expositional convenience, that the yield curve is flat and shifts in a parallel fashion. Other more realistic duration formulas are given elsewhere.[13]

Equation (6) is only an approximation as it measures ΔP_F using what is mathematically equivalent to the slope of a straight line tangent to the price curve of the bond, where an example of such a curve is the dashed line in Exhibit 1. A linear approximation to a curved line has a small error

---

[12] Macaulay, F. R. *Some Theoretical Problems Suggested by the Movement of Interest Rates, Bond Yields and Stock Prices in the U.S. Since 1856.* National Bureau of Economic Research, 1938.

[13] G. O. Bierwag, G. G. Kaufman, and A. L. Toevs. "Duration: Its Development and Use in Bond Portfolio Management," *Financial Analysts Journal,* July/August 1983.

when rates change in small increments, but it grows with the size of the change in interest rates, particularly in instances when the line has a distinct curvature.

One way to describe this approximation error inherent in the duration formulation of Equation (6) is to note that the measured duration value drifts from its original value as rates change. This source of "duration drift" differs from another and more familiar source, the effect of time on duration values: While duration values for zero coupon bonds fall day by day with the passage of time, duration values for coupon paying debt age more slowly. Both sources of duration drift are quite important and their effects must be controlled by rebalancing the portfolio as interest rates change and time passes.

A valuable property of duration is its "additivity" characteristic. A portfolio of two or more option-free securities has a combined duration that equals a value weighted average of the durations of the individual securities. For example, suppose we invest $100 in a four-year duration bond and $200 in a six-year duration bond. One third of the portfolio by value has a four-year duration and two thirds by value has a six-year duration. Thus, the portfolio duration is 5.33 years. The cash flows of this portfolio have an interest rate sensitivity equivalent to that for a 5.33 year zero coupon bond.

Duration analysis can be applied to asset/liability management as well as portfolio management problems. Indeed, a financial institution might best be viewed as a "net bond." Equity claimants own the net cash flow pattern generated by existing assets and liabilities. Understanding the interest rate risk of the market value of equity then becomes one of understanding the zero coupon bond with comparable interest rate risk.[14]

Duration of the Component Parts of FRMs

Recall from Equation (4) that the interest rate sensitivity of a FRM is either $\Delta P_D + \Delta Prem - \Delta P_{POT}$ or $\Delta Prin + \Delta Prem -$

---

[14] This reasoning is developed in A. L. Toevs and W. C. Haney. *Measuring and Managing Interest Rate Risk: A Guide to Asset/Liability Models Used in Banks and Thrifts,* Morgan Stanley, October 1984.

ΔP_{POT}. Now, ΔP_D, ΔPrem, and ΔPrin are the interest rate sensitivities of option-free securities. They are approximated by

$$\Delta P_X = -(P_X \times D_X)/(1 + r) \tag{8}$$

where P_X denotes P_D, Prem, or Prin depending on the cash flow stream of current concern.

The option pricing model that values the prepayment option can also be used to measure the duration of its time value (D_{POT}). In this context, duration can only be interpreted as a measure of the interest rate sensitivity of the option's time value. No reasonable interpretation of duration as the option's "average life" can be made. If D_{POR} equals "ninety years," which we will see to be possible in a moment, then P_{POT} has the interest rate sensitivity of a ninety-year zero coupon bond. As discussed in the prior section, the option pricing model can be used to estimate P_{POT} and, therefore, ΔP_{POT}. After these values have been determined at the current level of interest rates, D_{POT} is obtained by solving for its value using the definitional formula:

$$\Delta P_{POT} = -(P_{POT} \times D_{POT})/(1 + r) \tag{9}$$

Time value durations can be negative in value. Reconsider the line in Exhibit 1 that gives the time values for a prepayment option. When rates are low, a rate increase creates more option time value. Hence, P_{POT} and ΔP_{POT} are greater than zero and, therefore, D_{POT} is negative. A negative value for D_{POT} means that the prepayment option's time value is as sensitive as a *short* position in the zero coupon bond of similar duration. (In a moment, we will provide specific examples of option durations.)

Durations of FRMs

Since there is some zero coupon bond with a similar sensitivity,

$$\Delta P_M = -(P_M \times D_M)/(1 + r) \tag{10}$$

D_M is the duration of the callable security. At the moment, this representation is hypothetical and we cannot use Equation

(10) to determine D_M. But substituting Equations (8), (9), and (10) into Equation (4) and solving for D_M gives, for FRMs with in-the-money prepayment options,

$$D_M = \frac{(P_D \times D_D + \text{Prem} \times D_{\text{Prem}} - P_{\text{POT}} \times D_{\text{POT}})}{(P_D + \text{Prem} - P_{\text{POT}})}$$

Otherwise, for at-the-money or out-of-the-money prepayment options,

$$D_M = (\text{Prem} \times D_{\text{Prem}} - P_{\text{POT}} \times D_{\text{POT}})/(\text{Prin} + \text{Prem} - P_{\text{POT}})$$

$$(11)$$

Equation (11) becomes intuitively appealing when one recalls the additive property of durations. Remember that a FRM represents a portfolio of three securities: either the set of deliverable cash flows or the principal value—perhaps adjusted for prepayment penalties, the cash flows of accumulated premium investments, and the short position in the time value of the prepayment option. The duration formula in Equation (11) is nothing more than the price weighted average of the duration values of these constituent parts.[15]

Reconsider Exhibit 1. At extreme interest rate levels, P_{POT} becomes quite small. Therefore, D_M approaches the duration of the contractual cash flows to the maturity date of the bond for high interest rates and it approaches the duration of the premium investments if the call is exercised at low interest rates. (We have assumed these investments to have a short maturity in constructing Exhibit 1.) For more moderate interest rates, the duration of the callable bond becomes a blend between these two more extreme positions with the duration value itself becoming quite sensitive to the level of interest rates. This reminds us that near-the-money FRMs have relatively unstable interest rate sensitivities. Exhibit 2 illustrates these comments with the dashed line and the reference solid line.

---

[15] The minus signs in the numerator and denominator of Equation (11) denote the short position in the prepayment option. In the second part of Equation (11), the term $\text{Prin} \times D_{\text{Prin}}$ does not appear in the numerator as one might expect. The outstanding principal value has no interest rate risk and, therefore, D_{Prin} equals zero.

EXHIBIT 2
Durations of FRMs and Interest Rate Levels

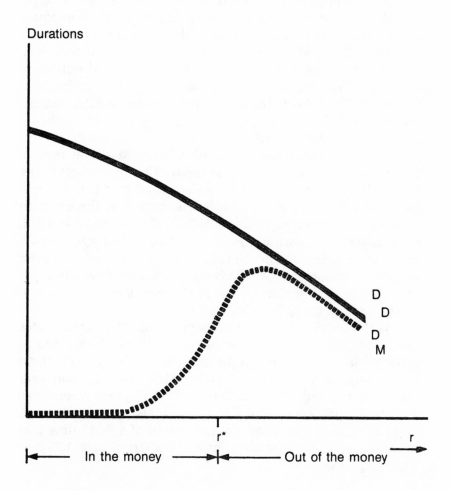

Table 1 gives, for various interest rates, the present values and durations for the components of a 30-year fully amortizing FRM. This mortgage pays a 14 percent coupon and is prepayable without penalty by the return of the outstanding principal balance. This table was constructed assuming that prepayments are fully rational.

When the market interest rate is 14 percent, the FRM is valued at par, provided up-front points of $4.53 per hundred dollars of principal is collected by the lender. At this interest rate the prepayment option has only time value. (This estimate of the time value uses a conservative estimate of mortgage price volatility.) With the collection of the option premium, the lender has effectively lent $95.47 per hundred dollars of face value. The P_{POI} and the P_{PO} columns reports the intrinsic value and the total value of the prepayment option, respectively. The definition of all other variables in Table 1 should be familiar to the reader.

In Table 1 the minimum duration the FRM attains is zero. Rates need to drop only to just below 12 percent before the time value of the option becomes so small that it is optimal to prepay. As rates go to high levels, note how the duration of the FRM converges to the duration of a noncallable FRM. (The noncallable duration is given by D_D.) Mortgage prepayments from forecasted house sales, and so on would, however, keep the duration on most FRMs substantially below this upper bound. And irrational delays of prepayments keep FRM durations from dropping quite so fast to zero.

The interpretation of +50.59 years for D_{POT} when rates are at 14 percent is that for a one basis point increase in rates, the loss in value on an "investment" of the $4.53 premium is comparable to that on $4.53 invested in a fifty-one year zero coupon bond. The duration of −107.43 years when rates are at 13.9 percent is that for a one basis point increase in rates, the *gain* in value on an investment of a $4.10 time premium is comparable to that for $4.10 *shorted* in a 107-year zero-coupon bond.[16]

---

[16] The reason why the duration of the time value of the option gets smaller as the option approaches its at-the-money position, while the slope of the time value line, as depicted in Exhibit 1, gets larger in absolute magnitude, is that the slope of the time value is $-D_{POT} \times P_{POT}/(1 + r)$. That is, the relatively large time value at or near r^* makes the product of the duration and the option value large in magnitude. At high or low rates relative to r^*, the time value of the option falls quicker than D_{POT} rises in absolute magnitude. Thus, the slope of the P_{POT} line goes to zero.

TABLE 1

30 YEAR CALLABLE MORTGAGE*

14%   CONTRACT RATE
$4.53   UP-FRONT PREMIUM
10%   PRICE VOLATILITY

RATE	P D	P PRIN	P POI	P POT	P PO	P M	D D	D PRIN	D POT	D M
10.00	135.02	100.00	35.02	0.00	35.02	104.53	8.49	0.00	0.00	0.00
11.00	124.42	100.00	24.42	0.00	24.42	104.53	8.01	0.00	0.00	0.00
12.00	115.19	100.00	15.19	0.13	15.32	104.40	7.56	0.00	-897.86	1.17
13.00	107.11	100.00	7.11	0.56	7.67	103.97	7.14	0.00	-593.80	3.32
13.10	106.36	100.00	6.36	0.89	7.25	103.64	7.10	0.00	-397.07	3.58
13.20	105.62	100.00	5.62	1.25	6.87	103.28	7.06	0.00	-296.60	3.75
13.30	104.88	100.00	4.88	1.62	6.51	102.91	7.02	0.00	-237.26	3.92
13.40	104.16	100.00	4.16	2.01	6.17	102.52	6.98	0.00	-197.91	4.06
13.50	103.45	100.00	3.45	2.41	5.85	102.12	6.95	0.00	-169.82	4.19
13.60	102.74	100.00	2.74	2.82	5.56	101.71	6.91	0.00	-148.69	4.31
13.70	102.04	100.00	2.04	3.24	5.28	101.29	6.87	0.00	-132.20	4.42
13.80	101.35	100.00	1.35	3.66	5.02	100.87	6.83	0.00	-118.93	4.52
13.90	100.67	100.00	0.67	4.10	4.77	100.43	6.80	0.00	-107.43	4.59
14.00	100.00	100.00	0.00	4.53	4.53	100.00	6.76	0.00	50.59	4.67
14.10	99.34	100.00	0.00	4.31	4.31	99.55	6.72	0.00	50.09	4.75
14.20	98.68	100.00	0.00	4.10	4.10	99.11	6.68	0.00	50.05	4.80
14.30	98.03	100.00	0.00	3.91	3.91	98.66	6.65	0.00	49.57	4.86
14.40	97.39	100.00	0.00	3.72	3.72	98.20	6.61	0.00	49.52	4.91
14.50	96.76	100.00	0.00	3.54	3.54	97.75	6.58	0.00	49.05	4.96
14.60	96.13	100.00	0.00	3.37	3.37	97.29	6.54	0.00	48.99	4.99
14.70	95.52	100.00	0.00	3.21	3.21	96.83	6.51	0.00	48.53	5.04
14.80	94.91	100.00	0.00	3.06	3.06	96.37	6.47	0.00	48.46	5.07
14.90	94.30	100.00	0.00	2.92	2.92	95.91	6.44	0.00	48.20	5.10
15.00	93.71	100.00	0.00	2.79	2.79	95.45	6.40	0.00	47.95	5.13
16.00	88.11	100.00	0.00	1.75	1.75	90.89	6.08	0.00	46.41	5.26
17.00	83.11	100.00	0.00	1.11	1.11	86.53	5.77	0.00	45.09	5.24
18.00	78.62	100.00	0.00	0.72	0.72	82.43	5.50	0.00	43.99	5.14

* THE PRICE VOLATILITY IS THE ANNUALIZED STANDARD DEVIATION OF MORTGAGE RETURNS. THIS VOLATILITY ESTIMATE IS CONSIDERED LOW BY CURRENT MARKET STANDARDS AND IS USED FOR ILLUSTRATIVE PURPOSES ONLY.

THIS MORTGAGE HAS AN INITIAL PREPAYMENT OPTION VALUE GIVEN OUR ASSUMED PRICE VOLATILITY OF $4.53 PER $100 OF FACE VALUE. THE REQUISITE PREMIUM IS OBTAINED IN AN INITIAL UP-FRONT PAYMENT.

DURATION DRIFT AND CURVILINEAR DURATION

The duration concept is an extremely valuable tool because it standardizes the price sensitivity of any option-free fixed-income security using a measure with some intuitive appeal. As we have seen, it also allows the price sensitivity of a FRM to be quickly determined. Against these advantages are three costs. First, the selected duration formula must be consistent with the essential characteristics of the random process generating new interest rates. Second, duration represents only a linear approximation to the true price relationship. Third, irrational prepayments will cause the estimated durations to be unacceptably uncertain unless these prepayments can be determined with a reasonable degree of confidence.

The first problem has been addressed at length elsewhere. This material is, therefore, not repeated here.[17] The second problem, one source of "duration drift," has also been studied in the academic literature.[18] But it is of particular importance when options are present and, consequently, it deserves our attention. The third problem is also important, but the surprising accuracy with which static prepayments can be forecasted gives us some hope for the applicability of our proposed methodology. At a minimum this methodology systematizes the assumptions made in FRM valuation and risk measurement.

Asset-Liability Management

For option-free debt securities, matching the market value and duration of the assets with those of the liabilities minimizes

---

[17] See the development in G. O. Bierwag, G. G. Kaufman, and A. L. Toevs. "Duration: Its Development and Use in Bond Portfolio Management," *Financial Analysts Journal*, July/August 1983.

[18] Miles Livingston, "Measuring Bond Price Volatility," *Journal of Financial and Quantitative Analysis*, June 1979, Jess Yawitz, "The Relative Importance of Duration and Yield Volatility on Bond Price Volatility," *Journal of Money, Credit and Banking*, February 1977, and D. R. Chambers, *The Management of Default-Free Bond Portfolios*. Ph.D. dissertation, University of North Carolina, Chapel Hill, North Carolina, 1981 are representative examples of this literature.

TABLE 2

4.67 YEAR ZERO-COUPON BOND

RATE	FACE	P M	D M
10.00	191.56	120.32	4.67
11.00	191.56	114.87	4.67
12.00	191.56	109.68	4.67
13.00	191.56	104.73	4.67
13.10	191.56	104.24	4.67
13.20	191.56	103.76	4.67
13.30	191.56	103.29	4.67
13.40	191.56	102.81	4.67
13.50	191.56	102.34	4.67
13.60	191.56	101.86	4.67
13.70	191.56	101.39	4.67
13.80	191.56	100.93	4.67
13.90	191.56	100.46	4.67
14.00	191.56	100.00	4.67
14.10	191.56	99.54	4.67
14.20	191.56	99.08	4.67
14.30	191.56	98.62	4.67
14.40	191.56	98.17	4.67
14.50	191.56	97.72	4.67
14.60	191.56	97.27	4.67
14.70	191.56	96.82	4.67
14.80	191.56	96.38	4.67
14.90	191.56	95.93	4.67
15.00	191.56	95.49	4.67
16.00	191.56	91.19	4.67
17.00	191.56	87.08	4.67
18.00	191.56	83.17	4.67

interest rate risk.[19] But this policy prescription can lead to sizable errors when debt securities with options enter the picture. Table 2 reports the prices and durations of a 4.67 year zero coupon bond. At 14 percent interest rates this bond has the same duration as the FRM in Table 1. It also has the same initial value as the FRM and it can be viewed to be a funding

---

[19] For asset managers, the liability of concern in the "bogey" bond with the interest rate risk and return characteristics the asset portfolio is to mirror.

liability. (Technically, the mortgage of $100 requires that the lender find a $95.47 liability, $100 less the $4.53 the lender receives in compensation for writing the prepayment option.)

Notice how the market value of the funding and originally duration-matched zero coupon bond liability begins to depart from the market value of the FRM as interest rates depart from 14 percent. These securities exhibit a growing disparity in market values. This phenomenon can be explained by duration drift because of changes in interest rates. As rates rise from 14 percent, the duration of the zero coupon bond remains constant while the duration of the FRM increases. Conversely, as rates fall, the zero coupon bond continues to have a stable duration while the duration of the FRM falls towards zero. Exhibit 3 retells this story.

Note that the initial duration match at a 14 percent interest rate in Tables 1 and 2 prevents the asset/liability manager from realizing a net gain or loss as rates initially increase. But subsequent rises in rate will cause the net position to lose substantial value if the asset is the FRM and the liability is the zero coupon bond. This is because the sensitivity of the FRM asset exceeds that of the zero coupon bond liability. Alternatively, if rates decline by a small amount from 14 percent, then there will again be an initial wash in the net position. But the duration of the FRM falls while the duration of the zero coupon bond remains stable. Subsequent interest rate declines will again cause losses in the net position because of the growing drift in duration values. Fastidious repositioning of the asset and liability portfolios as interest rates change can minimize the influence of "duration drift" but transaction costs and managerial time commitments will be substantial when the rates-of-duration drift differs substantially on the two sides of the balance sheet.

Straddle Strategies

Some banks, thrifts, and insurance companies have acquired prepayable assets with the proceeds of redeemable (putable) liabilities. In these pairings, an asset/liability structure has been formed with option-free assets and liabilities with what-

EXHIBIT 3
Duration Drift in an Asset/Liability Context

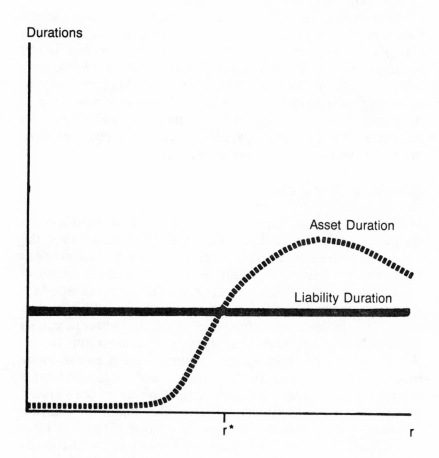

ever interest rate risk they have *plus* a short position in an American "straddle." A straddle is a common option strategy, one where a call and a put are both sold.[20] The straddle gener-

---

[20] Strictly speaking, a short straddle is formed by selling equal numbers of puts and calls of similar terms, including expiration dates. Nevertheless, the essence of the argument still applies.

ates premium income from writing both options. And the strad-dle so written will remain profitable if neither the call on the asset nor the put on the liability goes sufficiently in the money to wipe out the combined premiums.

In essence, the option straddle hidden in the assets and liabilities of many financial portfolios is a bet that financial markets *overestimate* interest rate volatility. Such a bet is ironic as the past five years have been determined to be ones when financial markets got blasted by an unexpected increase in interest rate volatility. Coupling the maturity mismatch in the option-free components of the assets and liabilities with the option straddle strategy helps to explain even more of the recent losses in financial institutions.

Curvilinear Duration

We have seen that adjusting the durations of fixed-income securities with attached options can significantly alter the measured durations of these securities. We have also seen that these new duration estimates can substantially increase the accuracy with which interest rate risk is measured. At a minimum, option adjusted duration values should always be used. Nevertheless, matching asset and liability durations, so adjusted, may not reduce interest rate risk to acceptable levels.

The durations of any coupon paying security moves away from its original value as time passes and as interest rates change. Both sources of duration drift become exaggerated in the presence of options. Of particular importance is the duration drift caused by changes in interest rates. Exhibit 3 dramatically illustrated the differential speed with which dura-tions can drift apart when a prepayable FRM is funded with an option-free liability. Funding prepayable assets with re-deemable liabilities increases the net rate of duration drift. The question is, what can be done about this source of drift?[21]

---

[21] For this asset/liability mix, the rate of duration drift caused by the mere passing of time will be substantial. In 4.67 years time, the liability has matured, but substantial life is left in the FRM. We do not recommend setting durations equal without also considering both their rates of time drift and their rates of interest rate drift.

Duration drift owing to changes in interest rates comes from making the assumption that prices change linearly with interest rates. Such is not the case for either options, particularly at-the-money options, or option-free debt. A step in the right direction is to use a curved representation of duration. This occurs when we set asset and liability durations equal to one another and we also equate the rate of asset duration drift with that for the liabilities. This increases the accuracy of interest rate risk measurement without completely giving up the main advantage of duration matching. This advantage is the added flexibility in the control of interest rate risk relative to a strategy of matching *every* asset cash flow with a liability cash flow and matching *every* asset option with a similar liability option.

Setting the rate of duration drift owing to changes in interest rates of the assets equal to that of the liabilities requires:

$$\sum_{t=1}^{T} a_t \times t^2 + \Delta\Delta P_{TVA} = \sum_{t=1}^{T} l_t \times t^2 + \Delta\Delta P_{TVL} \tag{12}$$

The a_t terms represent the present values of asset cash flows due at time "t" as a proportion of the total market value of the asset. T is the date of the most distant asset or liability cash flow. (These cash flows extend only to the put or call date if the fixed income security has an attached in-the-money put or call.)

Note how close the first expression in Equation (12) is to the duration formula given in Equation (10). The only difference is that these proportional weights multiply t^2 rather than t. The summation on the right hand side of Equation (12) is similarly defined for the liabilities. $\Delta\Delta P_{TVA}$ is the rate by which ΔP_{TVA} changes, where ΔP_{TVA} is the current *slope* of the time value curve for all puts and calls attached to asset securities. $\Delta\Delta P_{TVL}$ is similarly defined for the liability portfolio, if it has option-like features.

Thus, more careful asset/liability matching requires that the option adjusted asset duration equals the option adjusted liability duration *and* that the equality expressed in Equation (12) be met. Exhibit 3 is a circumstance where the option adjusted asset duration equals an option-free liability duration at 14 percent interest rates. Equation (12), however, does not hold at this interest rate. The left hand side of this equation is positive—as interest rates increase, so does asset duration. Conversely, the right hand side of Equation (12) has a value of zero. It is this equation that signals a potentially important source of interest rate risk.

The calculations in Equation (12) systematize what can be done in a simpler manner. As interest rates move from 14 to 14.1 percent in Tables 1 and 2, we observe that the duration of the FRM increases by 0.08 years while the duration of the zero coupon bond remains unchanged. This simple calculation alone is sufficient to caution against using duration matching to hedge interest rate risk. Equation (12) adds value in that computers can be programmed to search for available investment and funding alternatives that match both the durations and the rates of duration drift for the assets and liabilities.

SUMMARY

This chapter has developed a reasonably detailed representation of the components of prepayable fixed-rate mortgages (FRMs). Prepayment rights are American call options that make the effective lives of the associated mortgage uncertain. They also complicate the measurement and control of interest rate risk. In the first section we disaggregated prepayment options into their intrinsic and time values. We then showed how the interest rate risk of a FRM is the interest rate risk of the time value of the option plus the interest rate sensitivity of either the cash flows of the FRM to its maturity date or the interest rate sensitivity of its principal value, which we then argued has no interest rate sensitivity.

In the second section, we converted the interest rate sensitivity analysis of the first section into the duration framework. We noted that the ability of duration analysis to represent the interest rate risk of components of a portfolio with a single number is preserved, although in an altered form, when options are part of the debt security being scrutinized.

In the third section, we discussed the problems that arise in asset/liability management when options are present. We demonstrated that options in this context can cause properly measured durations to drift apart as interest rates change, and they can do so with unacceptable speed. In the third section we also introduced the concept of "curvilinear duration" and showed how it can reduce the problems caused by duration drift, particularly instances when durations of assets and liabilities drift apart owing to changes in interest rates.

CHAPTER 18

Interest Rate Anticipation Strategies

H. Gifford Fong
President
Gifford Fong Associates

Frank J. Fabozzi, Ph.D., C.F.A.
Walter E. Hanson/Peat, Marwick, Mitchell
Professor of Business and Finance
Lafayette College

In a general sense, active management is an approach that will achieve the maximum return for a given level of risk. That is, the emphasis is on return maximization—seeking the highest return possible while not exceeding the desired risk posture. This can be differentiated from passive strategies, namely buy-and-hold and indexing, in which risk aversion dominates and a less than maximum return objective is acceptable. When investment horizons are long or risk tolerances are high, active management is the preferred strategy. Most pension funds and some closed-end mutual funds fit into this category. When this emphasis on expected return emerges, so does the key role of expectations in the process. More precisely, expectations are the prime driving force from which the return sought will be achieved. The uncertainty associated with expectations is also the source of risk in the active management process. How the manager should best make use of expectations in the face of uncertainty can be interpreted as the risk-minimizing dimension of the active strategy.

Active strategies span a wide range of possibilities. The

most widely used are interest rate anticipation strategies. The philosophy in interest rate anticipation strategies is to take advantage of the return implication of expected interest rate change through bond portfolio management. Interest rate change is the dominant source of marginal total return—marginal in relation to the return if no rate change had occurred. As long as there is volatility in rates, this problem will exist. If one is to pursue an active management strategy, there must be an explicit recognition of the effect of interest rate change.

The theme of this chapter is how the manager of a portfolio of mortgage-backed securities can harness interest rate expectations in light of the risk-minimizing dimension of the active strategy. Since a key in interest rate anticipation strategies is the return simulation process, in the next section we provide an overview of the active management process so that the role of return simulation may be better understood.

OVERVIEW OF ACTIVE MANAGEMENT PROCESS

Exhibit 1 describes, in a macro sense, what the active management process is all about. Typically, the manager would begin on the left side of the figure, starting with a portfolio plus a potential purchase list.

The key to this overall process resides in the step identified next: return simulation. Return simulation is the process by which a manager takes a set of expectations and transforms them into expected rates of return. These expected rates of return would capture all the expectations that go into the process, whether they are expectations about interest rate changes, credit risk changes, or spread relationship changes. These all can be finally expressed in a few composite numbers, an expected rate of return for each individual security and the portfolio as a whole.

Portfolio optimization is a direct extention of the results of return simulation. The expected rates of return that have been defined from the return simulation process integrated

EXHIBIT 1
Active Management Framework

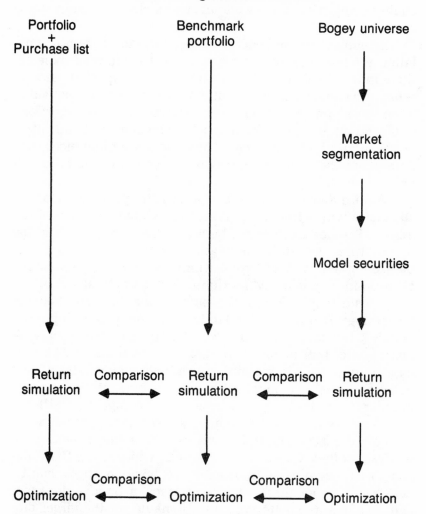

| Portfolio + Purchase list | Benchmark portfolio | Bogey universe |

Market segmentation

Model securities

Return simulation ←Comparison→ Return simulation ←Comparison→ Return simulation

Optimization ←Comparison→ Optimization ←Comparison→ Optimization

with appropriate portfolio policy considerations suggest specific changes to the portfolio. Specific client preference or a particular style that the manager has adopted can be incorporated into the optimization process.

Along with the analysis of the current portfolio, a second step is identified by the center vertical track of Exhibit 1. This is identifying a benchmark portfolio, that is, some "bogey" with which the manager will be comparing the portfolio. This could be any portfolio the manager and client mutually agree upon.

By subjecting the benchmark portfolio to the return simulation process, the manager has again transformed expectations into expected rates of return. These expected rates of return are subsequently subjected to the same policy considerations used for the actual portfolio, resulting in a portfolio optimization analysis. The manager then compares the actual portfolio and identified bogey, evaluates the differences, and determines the potential ability of the actual portfolio to outperform the bogey.

A third active management process for portfolio comparison starts with a bogey universe, the rightmost column of Exhibit 1. The basic difference between this third track and the second track is that, in the bogey universe, the manager may be dealing with a much broader universe of securities instead of those in a benchmark portfolio. For example, the manager may be starting with an index such as the Shearson Lehman Government/Corporate Bond Index. It is comprised of approximately 3,000 to 4,000 securities. That type of bogey may be appropriate, but, in order to subject it to the same kind of expectations transformation and optimization analysis used in the first track, the manager has to do some interim analysis in order to turn that large universe into a manageable portfolio.

What we have identified here is a two-step process. Starting with the 3,000 or 4,000 securities, the manager can do an analysis called market segmentation, which essentially decomposes the universe into sectors. A bogey portfolio can be constructed from these sectors to track a bond index, that can, in effect, replicate the return behavior of the larger universe identified at the beginning. The manager then takes the securities in the bogey portfolio, and subjects them to the return simulation process. That provides the manager with the transformation of expectations into expected rates of return. The manager then can subject that set of expected rates of return to the optimization analysis.

At the optimization level, the manager can do cross comparisons to see how the actual portfolio—before and after the portfolio changes that will be made—compares with a benchmark portfolio or, alternatively, with the bogey universe identified.

This is a rather simplified schematic, and it should be emphasized that much of the essence of the technique is really captured in the return simulation process. Regardless of which active strategy the portfolio manager selects, the important step is subjecting the technique to return simulation.

INTEREST RATE ANTICIPATION
STRATEGIES

As an active management technique, an interest rate anticipation strategy should be concerned with three dimensions: direction of the change in rates; magnitude of the change across maturities; and the timing of the change. If interest rates drop, the price of a fixed income security will rise to reflect the new yield level. Conversely, if rates increase, the price of a fixed income security will decline. The increase or decrease will be directly related to the security's duration. Therefore, the maturity should be lengthened and the coupon decreased—or, equivalently, duration should be increased—when rates are expected to drop, and the opposite action taken when rates are expected to rise.[1] The position of the portfolio along the maturity spectrum should be guided by the shape of the expected yield curve change. Finally, the timing of the expected rate change will be important in evaluating the relative importance of rate change, coupon return, and reinvestment return.

Interest rate anticipation strategies seek to recognize and assess the impact of interest rate changes on the total return

---

[1] The problem of adverse changes in duration for a mortgage-backed security, popularly known as "negative convexity," is discussed in Chapter 13.

of a portfolio over a specified time horizon. For purposes of discussion, the generation of the required interest rate forecast itself will not be covered. It is, at best, extremely difficult to forecast the future direction of rates, much less their magnitude. There are some who would assert that it is impossible. The emphasis here is on how the portfolio manager can harness the forecast once it is determined. To assess the impact and implications of interest rate change, it is useful to evaluate the forecasts of interest rate change relative to a specific portfolio.

Illustration of the Return Simulation Process

Exhibit 2 summarizes inputs suitable for simulating the effect of interest rate change for a portfolio of five GNMAs shown in the lower panel of the exhibit. A framework of one year has been chosen for this illustration, but this would vary according to the portfolio manager's expectations and desires.

Three naive scenarios of interest rate change are shown. These have been derived from historical interest rate change tendencies over the 10 years prior to the analysis. There is a bullish scenario, a market-implicit forecast scenario, and a bearish scenario. The market-implicit forecast is based on a technique known as term structure analysis.[2]

Multiscenario approaches recognize the uncertainty associated with interest rate forecasting and, accordingly, allow a form of sensitivity analysis. In the illustration, these forecasts take the form of the most likely (market-implicit), optimistic (declining rates), and pessimistic (rising rates) cases. The manager's own forecast would be, of course, an alternative. Each scenario is described along with a specified probability. Figures in Exhibit 2 reflect the forecast yield for each scenario as well as the present yield to maturity for each scenario.

Future FHA experience factors were arbitrarily chosen for purposes of this illustration. These are shown for each

---

[2] See Oldrich A. Vasicek and H. Gifford Fong, "Term Structure Modeling Using Exponential Splines," *Journal of Finance* (May 1982), pp. 339–348.

EXHIBIT 2

Interest Rate Projection and Sample GNMA Pass-through Portfolio

Scenario 1 (33.33% probability): falling rates, 10-year historical volatility basis (11/74 to 11/84), reinvestment rate is calculated for each issue.

Scenario 2 (33.33% probability): market-implicit forecast (using term structure analysis), reinvestment rate is calculated for each issue.

Scenario 3 (33.33% probability): rising rates, 10-year historical volatility basis (11/74 to 11/84), reinvestment rate is calculated for each issue.

Interest rate projection: 10-31-84 to 10-31-85

Maturity (years)	Present Yield to Maturity (percent)	Forecast Yield (percent)			Maturity Date	Roll Effect	Forecast Yield Shifts (Basis Points)		
		Scenario 1	Scenario 2	Scenario 3			Scenario 1	Scenario 2	Scenario 3
.250	9.640	7.320	11.830	13.290	1-30-85	.0	-232.0	219.0	365.0
.500	10.140	7.840	11.960	13.730	5- 2-85	.0	-230.0	182.0	359.0
1.000	10.440	8.230	11.820	13.760	10-31-85	-80.0	-312.0	139.0	285.0
2.000	11.090	9.030	11.870	14.090	11- 1-86	-65.0	-286.0	73.0	267.0
3.000	11.340	9.300	11.950	14.000	11- 1-87	-25.0	-231.0	53.0	275.0
4.000	11.510	9.440	11.990	13.960	10-31-88	-17.0	-221.0	44.0	249.0
5.000	11.610	9.630	12.010	13.980	10-31-89	-10.0	-217.0	38.0	235.0
10.000	11.740	9.800	11.960	13.700	11- 1-94	-2.6	-197.4	23.0	201.6
20.000	11.700	10.180	11.870	13.620	10-31- 4	.4	-155.8	17.9	192.8
30.000	11.710	10.240	11.870	13.640	11- 1-14	-.1	-147.6	16.0	192.8

Sample Portfolio

GNMA	10.75%	2/1/98
GNMA	11.75	2/1/98
GNMA	9.75	4/15/98
GNMA	11.50	6/15/13
GNMA	12.50	11/15/13

481

EXHIBIT 3
Future FHA Experience

Issue	Current Pool Factor	Scenario 1 Falling Rates	Scenario 2 Market Implicit Forecast	Scenario 3 Rising Rates	Current FHA Experience
10 ¾'s of '98	.924	165%	165%	165%	165%
11 ¾'s of '98	.949	105	105	105	105
9 ¾'s of '98	.919	195	195	195	195
11 ½'s of '13	.979	100	100	100	100
12 ½'s of '13	.925	125	125	125	125

issue and each scenario in Exhibit 3. In practice, modification of these prepayment expectations by scenario type may be appropriate.

To reflect the effect of quality, issuing, or coupon sectors, additional factors can be imposed which will modify the basic shift represented by the forecast Treasury yield curves in Exhibit 2. For example, a single A rated bond may be expected to shift by 10 percent less than the anticipated shift of a Treasury bond of the same maturity. Assuming the Treasury bond yield was to shift 100 basis points, the modified shift for the single A bond would be 90 basis points. The additional factors of issuing sector and coupon group could further modify the primary shift. All of these factors can be termed *volatility factors*. They modify, on the margin, the anticipated change owing to overall interest rates, and allow the fine tuning of the anticipated reaction to interest rate changes based on the unique characteristics of the bond.

The volatility factor for an issuing sector can be estimated from historical data using the following simple linear regression:

$$\Delta S_t = a + (1 + b)\Delta T_t + e_t$$

where

ΔS_t = change in interest rate for the issuing sector in month t (in basis points)

ΔT_t = change in interest rate for the Treasury issue in month t (in basis points)

e_t = error term in month t

and a and b are the parameters of the model to be estimated. The parameter b is the issuing sector volatility and the parameter a is the issuing sector spread change.

For purposes of this illustration, the volatility factor for GNMAs, b, is assumed to be equal to 0 for all three scenarios. The issuing sector spread change, a, between GNMAs and treasuries is assumed to decrease by 20 basis points in Scenario 1 and increase by 30 basis points in Scenario 3. For Scenario 2, the issuing sector spread is assumed to be 0.

A 45-day payment delay is assumed. Prices are calculated using HTG corporate bond equivalent yield. This is based on the assumed cash flow generated under the specified prepayment rate using monthly compounding. The yields are then adjusted to semiannualized compounding.

Exhibit 4 exemplifies the results of translating interest rate change into expected (composite) rates of return for the five GNMAs in the portfolio. The returns are also presented for each of the three scenarios. The columns are largely self-explanatory, but those of particular importance are described below:

Yield curve   Return due to changes in the nominal yield curve.

Time   Return assuming the initial yield curve remains constant over the projection horizon (i.e., rolling along the yield curve).

Spread change   Return attributable to spread change and volatility effects.

Earned interest   Interest accrued over the projection period.

Maturity/call   Change in principal value for securities projected to be called or to mature. (The price change is separate from that caused by the interest rate effect.)

EXHIBIT 4

Analysis of the Issues of the Portfolio for Each of the Three Interest Rate Forecasts and the Composite
(current date 10/31/84; projection date 10/31/85)

Face Value ($000)	Bond Description			Price (percent)	Yield to Effective Maturity	Components of Return						Total Return (percent)	Effective Maturity Date	Duration (years)
						Yield Curve	Time	Spread Change	Earned Interest	Maturity Call	Reinvestment			
6,072	GNMA		Current:	94.000	12.32MAT								2- 1-98	4.42
5,662	10.7500%	2- 1-98	Scenario 1:	102.406	10.28MAT	7.2	.3	.8	11.0	.4	.8	20.6	2- 1-98	4.41
5,662			Scenario 2:	93.439	12.54MAT	-.8	.3	.0	11.0	.4	.8	11.8	2- 1-98	4.20
5,662			Scenario 3:	86.283	14.61MAT	-7.0	.3	-1.0	11.0	.4	.9	4.7	2- 1-98	4.01
			Composite:	94.043	12.48	-.2	.3	.0	11.0	.4	.8	12.3	2- 1-98	4.21
11,388	GNMA		Current:	98.000	12.39MAT								2- 1-98	4.64
10,785	11.7500%	2- 1-98	Scenario 1:	107.006	10.35MAT	7.7	.1	.9	11.7	.1	.7	21.2	2- 1-98	4.62
10,785			Scenario 2:	97.209	12.60MAT	-.9	.1	.0	11.7	.1	.8	11.8	2- 1-98	4.40
10,785			Scenario 3:	89.428	14.68MAT	-7.4	.1	-1.0	11.7	.1	.8	4.3	2- 1-98	4.20
			Composite:	97.881	12.54	-.2	.1	.0	11.7	.1	.8	12.4	2- 1-98	4.41
3,001	GNMA		Current:	90.000	12.32MAT								4-15-98	4.35
2,773	9.7500%	4-15-98	Scenario 1:	98.106	10.29MAT	7.0	.5	.8	10.4	.8	.8	20.4	4-15-98	4.36
2,773			Scenario 2:	89.651	12.54MAT	-.8	.5	.0	10.4	.8	.8	11.8	4-15-98	4.14
2,773			Scenario 3:	82.872	14.61MAT	-6.8	.5	-1.0	10.4	.8	.9	4.9	4-15-98	3.96
			Composite:	90.210	12.48	-.2	.5	.0	10.4	.8	.8	12.3	4-15-98	4.15
688	GNMA		Current:	94.188	12.88MAT								6-15-13	5.19
655	11.5000%	6-15-13	Scenario 1:	102.525	11.19MAT	7.2	.1	1.1	12.0	.3	.7	21.4	6-15-13	5.43
655			Scenario 2:	93.594	13.04MAT	-.7	.1	.0	12.0	.3	.8	12.4	6-15-13	5.03
655			Scenario 3:	85.272	15.11MAT	-8.0	.1	-1.1	12.0	.3	.8	4.1	6-15-13	4.64
			Composite:	93.797	13.12	-.5	.1	.0	12.0	.3	.8	12.6	6-15-13	5.03
508	GNMA		Current:	98.813	12.99MAT								2-15- 8	4.56
481	12.5000%	11-15-13	Scenario 1:	106.104	11.30MAT	6.1	.0	.9	12.3	.1	.8	20.1	2-15- 8	4.59
481			Scenario 2:	98.194	13.15MAT	-.6	.0	.0	12.3	.1	.8	12.6	2-15- 8	4.33
481			Scenario 3:	90.566	15.22MAT	-6.9	.0	-1.0	12.3	.1	.9	5.4	2-15- 8	4.06
			Composite:	98.288	13.22	-.5	.0	.0	12.3	.1	.8	12.7	2-15- 8	4.33

Reinvestment   Interest on interest earned over the pro-
                      jection period, as well as reinvestment
                      from maturities, calls, puts, sinking fund
                      payments and any other prepayments.
Total return   The sum of all components of return.
Duration   The first figure in the column is current
                      duration; remaining figures are the dura-
                      tion at the end of the assumed holding pe-
                      riod for the particular scenario.

Exhibit 5 summarizes the portfolio return for each scenario
and the composite return for the portfolio for which the return
simulation was performed. In this illustration, the largest component of return in this example is that owing to earned interest
which, for GNMAs, represents payments of both interest and
principal. This component is the same under all scenarios for
each pass-through because the assumed prepayment rates do
not change from one scenario to the next.

The foregoing analysis can be extremely helpful in execut-
ing an effective active management strategy. Analytical insights are achieved by partitioning a set of expected interest
rate changes into implied rates of return. Each graduation provides further insight into the sources and, hence, the causes
of performance. Analysis beyond the total return permits both
the establishment and monitoring of policy. For example, a
manager stressing interest rate anticipation should have the
return due from overall changes in interest rates dominate
the return from spread relationships. Conversely, a manager
with an emphasis on spread relationship exploitation (another
widely used active strategy) should have this component dominate.

In terms of a portfolio perspective, comparing total returns
of securities in the portfolio can be the first step in screening
the most desirable portfolio holdings.

Relative Return Value Analysis

Relative return analysis is a tool that allows a manager to
compare alternative securities systematically. It recognizes

EXHIBIT 5

Summary of Portfolio Return for Each of the Three Interest Rate Scenarios and the Composite (portfolio return on beginning market value—10/31/84 to 10/31/85)

	Yield Change Impact	Time (Roll) Impact	Spread Change Impact	Earned Interest	Coupon Reinvestment	Matured/ Called	Maturity/ Call Reinvestment	Total	Annual Total
Scenario 1 (10-31-85):	7.40%	.22%	.88%	11.36%	.44%	.30%	.29%	20.89%	19.90%
Scenario 2 (10-31-85):	-.86	.22	.00	11.36	.48	.30	.32	11.81	11.48
Scenario 3 (10-31-85):	-7.21	.22	-1.00	11.36	.52	.30	.35	4.53	4.48
Composite (10-31-85):	-.22	.22	-.04	11.36	.48	.30	.32	12.41	12.05

486

EXHIBIT 6
Relative Return Analysis

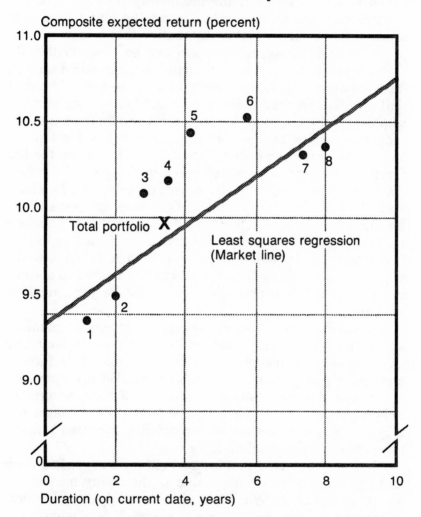

Composite expected return (percent)

Duration (on current date, years)

that choosing the highest expected return security may be inappropriate, since either it may not be the security with the highest realized return, or the level of associated risk may be undesirable. The objective here is to identify the highest expected return security for a given level of risk.

This technique is illustrated in Exhibit 6. Duration is on

the horizontal axis and on the vertical axis is the composite
expected return, which is the probability-weighted return of
each of the three scenario returns from the return simulation
process; however, any other alternative that a manager employs for defining expected return can be used. Within the
diagram is a regression line (dashed line), individual security
representation (dots), and portfolio average return/duration
(letter X). The regression line represents the average relationship between return and duration exhibited by the individual
securities making up the portfolio. Using the regression line
as fair value, we can conclude that securities above the line
are those with greater expected return per unit of duration
than the average relationship; securities below the line have
less return per unit of duration. For example, the best security
for the total expected return and duration optimizer appears
to be security 6. The worst security, as indicated in Exhibit
6, is security 1. An analysis similar to that in Exhibit 4 would
explain why securities G and W would be expected to perform
in this manner. The analysis should also be performed for
each scenario.

Given this kind of two-dimensional framework, a manager
has the ability—at least a first cut—to differentiate the return
characteristics of the securities in a portfolio. This form of
analysis is very similar to the security market line approach,
which is used fairly widely in the analysis of equity securities.[3]
Relative return analysis can be used even if a manager employs some other mechanism for defining expected rates of
return than return simulation.

It should be noted that in the fixed income market, there
is no measure of risk comparable to the equity measure of
market risk or beta.[4] What is used in the analysis is duration,
which is not necessarily a risk measure. It is a measure of
volatility. Although volatility is not the best measure of risk,
duration does quantify risk to the extent that the volatility
is a risk surrogate. Also, duration is a measure of the length

---

[3] William F. Sharpe, *Investments* (Englewood Cliffs, N.J.: Prentice-Hall,
1981), pp. 164–65.

[4] Ibid; pp. 156–59.

of the security—a better measure, in many situations, than maturity. So, duration is a measure for differentiating securities. If, lacking a better summary risk measure, we can use duration (like beta is used on the equity side), we might consider the horizontal axis to be a normalization for volatility, so we can make judgments about any two securities that lie along the same vertical line projecting upward from any given duration level.

Strategic Frontier Analysis

Strategic frontier analysis is a tool for evaluating both the upside and the downside return characteristics of a security. It is a procedure for analyzing the return behavior of securities under alternative interest rate scenarios.

Exhibit 7 provides the display that is employed in strategic frontier analysis. Again we have a two-dimensional framework. The total expected return is shown on the vertical axis. This could be the total expected return of the most likely scenario of interest rate change, or perhaps the return of the most optimistic scenario of interest rate change. On the horizontal axis is the return of the worst case scenario. Again, these scenarios are those used in the return simulation process.

In Exhibit 7 the dots represent the individual security holdings in the portfolio we are analyzing as well as the securities on the potential purchase list. The intersection of the dashed lines in this diagram indicates the portfolio average return, and we can see that this represents a particular position within this framework. Any particular position is defined by the return under either the optimistic scenario or the most likely scenario along one axis, and the returns from the worst case scenario along the other axis.

Once we have this type of framework, we can partition the diagram into quadrants as displayed in Exhibit 7. The portfolio average is at the origin, or center, of the quadrants. Partitioning the diagram into the four quadrants allows a manager to draw conclusions about the return behavior of the securities that fall into each of these quadrants. Let's discuss each of these quadrants.

Securities within quadrant II might be considered *aggres-*

EXHIBIT 7
Hypothetical Upside/Downside Trade-off

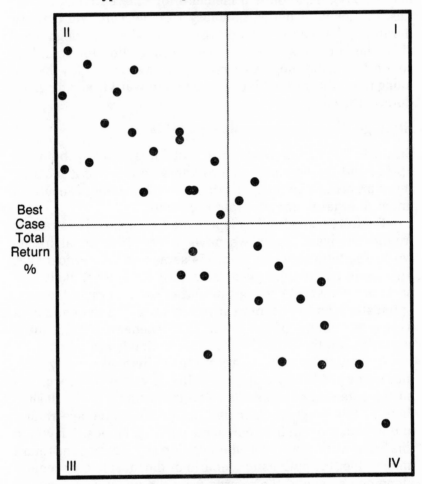

Worst case total return %

sive securities. They are aggressive from the standpoint that, if the best case scenario prevails, a manager would do extremely well. If, however, the worst case scenario were to prevail, a manager would do relatively badly. So, if a manager had very high convictions about the most optimistic scenario, he would tend to choose securities from this quadrant.

In quadrant IV are what might be considered *defensive* securities. They are defensive in that, if the worst case scenario prevailed, a manager would do relatively well. But if the most likely scenario were to occur, a manager would do relatively poorly. So, if a manager wanted to posture his portfolio defensively, he would concentrate it in securities that fall within quadrant IV.

Quadrant III contains securities that might be considered *inferior*. They are inferior because, regardless of scenario outcome—either the best case or worst case—these securities would perform relatively worse than the portfolio average. Securities falling into quadrant III are the potential sales from the existing portfolio since, by definition, they are no-win situations.

That leaves the securities falling in quadrant I. These might be considered *superior* securities because, regardless of scenario outcome, these securities would always outperform the portfolio, providing a no-loss situation. If a manager were to increase his holdings of the securities that fall in this quadrant, he would tend to move the portfolio results to the upper right portion of the quadrant. That would enhance his overall portfolio results, regardless of the scenarios being evaluated.

Exhibit 8 is another characterization of this type of analysis, and what we call a *strategic frontier*. This frontier essentially maps out the upper right region, from which a manager can choose securities that would do the best job, given his convictions. For example, if a manager wanted maximum offense or maximum aggressiveness but was willing to give up the defensive nature of some of the other securities, then he would choose securities along the strategic frontier mapped in or near the upper left quadrant. If a manager wanted a maximum defensive posture and was willing to live with the relatively poor returns should the most likely scenario prevail, then he would choose securities along the frontier in or near the lower right quadrant. Finally, the ultimate objective, especially in the face of the high uncertainty and an unsteady conviction about either scenario, would be to drive the portfolio into the upper right quadrant as far as possible.

EXHIBIT 8
Strategic Frontier Analysis

Total return (composite)

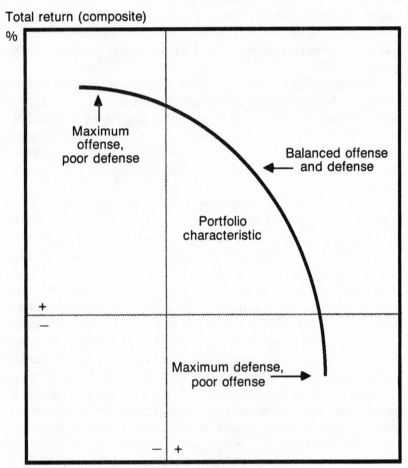

Total return (worst case assumption)   %

SUMMARY

Interest rate anticipation is the key ingredient of active fixed-income portfolio management. Return simulation techniques aid the active manager by transforming interest rate expectations into expected rates of return for individual securities as well as the portfolio as a whole. Systematic comparison of expected security performance forms a basis for portfolio optimization—achieving maximum return for a given level of risk—by isolating securities offering superior and inferior expected returns. Finally, a benchmark portfolio and/or universe can be subjected to the return simulation process, helping the manager assess the impact of anticipated interest rate changes on the market as a whole. The purpose of this chapter is to explain the role of return simulation in the active management process.

SECTION V

Credit Rating and Taxation

CHAPTER 19

The Rating of Mortgage-Backed Securities

David J. Askin
Vice President, Mortgage-Backed Securities
Drexel Burnham Lambert

INTRODUCTION

The issuance, sale and trading of mortgage-backed securities represent one of the most dynamic and fastest growing areas in the investment community. By the end of 1984, the volume of mortgage pass-through securities issued since inception should exceed $350 billion. The comparable figure four years earlier was less than $100 billion. These numbers do not include securities such as pay-throughs, collateralized mortgage obligations (CMOs) and mortgage-backed bonds, which often use mortgage pass-throughs or whole loans as collateral to support the sale of other mortgage-backed securities.

To date, less than 25 percent of the residential mortgage debt outstanding has been securitized. The Public Securities Association projects that over the next decade $4 trillion will be needed to finance housing in the U.S. and that more than three quarters of this amount will be financed in the secondary mortgage market. Further, thrift institutions have begun to restructure their balance sheets, leading to an increase in loan sales or the use of old loans as collateral for borrowings and the issuance of new mortgage-backed securities to finance their lending and investment activities. This points to continued growth of the secondary mortgage market.

Typically, mortgage-backed securities are supported by high-quality assets. However, these instruments are fraught with structural and legal complexities that make their evaluation difficult, even for sophisticated investors. These problems are in addition to the usual economic uncertainties faced by all investors in fixed-income securities.

Just as unsecured corporate debt and preferred stock are rated by nationally recognized rating agencies, so too, are mortgage-backed securities. These ratings are not intended to identify good and bad investments. Rather, the ratings attempt to quantify the relative credit quality and identify potential risks or weaknesses in the securities. This allows informed investors to make distinctions among potential investments. The resulting evaluations by large numbers of investors help the financial markets to allocate capital more efficiently by adjusting the cost of capital to issuers on the basis of perceived differences in credit quality.

A rating is not the only determinant of the quality and therefore, the price of a fixed-income security. Many unrated securities are sold in a variety of markets. However, a rating is an important factor that influences price, and most of the fixed-income securities sold (in terms of dollar volume) are as rated securities. The purpose of this chapter is to describe how the rating process is applied to mortgage-backed securities.

The Rating Process—An Overview

The Rating Agencies

The nationally recognized rating agencies have made the logical extension of their rating systems for unsecured corporate debt to mortgage-backed securities. These securities often are referred to as structured transactions. Moody's Investors Service and Standard & Poor's Corporation are the two rating agencies that dominate the fixed-income market generally. They also dominate the rating of mortgage-backed securities. These transactions also have been rated by Fitch Investors Service.

A rating issued by any of these agencies applies to the securities that are issued, not the issuing company. The agencies reserve the right to rate debt offerings and preferred stock issues they feel are important to financial markets, even without a request by the issuer. As a practical matter, virtually all public offerings of any size are rated by one or more of the agencies. Many private placements also are rated but usually only upon the issuer's request. In most cases, the ratings of public issues are published while those of private placements are not.

The rating process involves a continuous dialogue between the issuer, its representatives (e.g., investment bankers, lawyers, and accountants), and the analytical staff(s) of the rating agency(ies). The purpose is to explain the key functional elements of the proposed transaction. These include the financial, legal, and accounting details as well as the operating characteristics (past, present, and future) of the issuer. Many documents are reviewed, such as the prospectus or offering circular, financial statements, bond indentures, articles of incorporation, by-laws, other SEC registration documents, legal opinions, and printouts of computer analyses. Any of the information that is of a sensitive or proprietary nature is used only to determine the rating and is kept strictly confidential by the agencies.

Rated mortgage-backed issues are structured transactions in the sense that the issuer has a large degree of control in designing the transaction so as to achieve the desired rating. For example, support elements can be added to the collateral that prevent investors from incurring losses under a variety of possible circumstances. The process of determining the quantity and quality of the support elements and thus, the rating level of the security itself embodies many elements of a negotiation. This is different than the procedure for an unsecured debt rating. There is little a company can do in the short run to alter significantly the credit quality and therefore, the rating of its securities.

The methodologies employed by each agency need not be identical. Yet, for the ratings to be meaningful and useful, they must be credible. Credibility implies that the varying methodologies produce similar ratings for similar transactions. This means that the ratings of a single agency should be consistent across transactions. Also, when a transaction is rated by more than one agency, there should be no appreciable difference between the ratings.

There have been no significant differences to date in the final ratings on specific mortgage-backed security transactions. This is because there is general agreement among the agencies on the key characteristics that determine quality, even if these characteristics are incorporated into the various rating frameworks in different ways. The following discussion of the criteria used to rate mortgage-backed securities does not focus on the views of a particular rating agency. Rather, it is on an analysis of the characteristics used by all agencies to determine the ratings and on how the characteristics are used. Since the structural framework in developing these criteria was based on taxable mortgage-backed security financings which employed residential, single-family mortgage loans, the same framework is used here.

The Role of the Federal Agencies in the Secondary Mortgage Market

Originally, the secondary mortgage market consisted largely of mortgage originators, primarily thrifts, selling whole loans to portfolio lenders such as life insurance companies or other thrifts. The explosive growth of mortgage-backed securities which followed can be traced to the development of secondary market programs by the three government-supported housing agencies: the Government National Mortgage Association (GNMA or "Ginnie Mae"), the Federal Home Loan Mortgage Association (FHLMC or "Freddie Mac"), and the Federal National Mortgage Association (FNMA or "Fannie Mae").

GNMA is a federal agency and is part of the Department

of Housing and Urban Development (HUD). Although the largest contributor to the secondary market for mortgage-backed securities, GNMA issues no securities. Rather, it guarantees the full and timely payment of all principal and interest on GNMA certificates, which are issued by thrifts, mortgage bankers, home builders, and other approved mortgage originators. The certificates are supported by pools of FHA-insured and VA-guaranteed mortgages. GNMA's guarantee is backed by the full faith and credit of the United States Treasury. By the end of June 1984, GNMA had guaranteed the issue of approximately $208 billion of mortgage-backed securities.

FHLMC is a federally chartered institution which is owned by the 12 Federal Home Loan Banks. FHLMC began its secondary mortgage market program in 1970. The bulk of the securities issued by FHLMC are called participation certificates (PCs). By the end of the first half of 1984, FHLMC had issued roughly $71 billion of PCs. FHLMC guarantees the timely payment of interest and the ultimate (but not timely) payment of principal on its PCs. The guarantee is that of FHLMC, not that of the United States Treasury.

FNMA is a shareholder-owned public corporation that was federally chartered. Originally, FNMA's basic business was to purchase mortgages from thrift institutions and hold them in its portfolio. Late in 1981, FNMA began a mortgage-backed securities program. FNMA guarantees its mortgage-backed securities for the timely payment of all principal and interest. As with the FHLMC guarantee, this is not a guarantee of the United States Treasury. By the end of June 1984, FNMA had issued over $36 billion of mortgage-backed securities.

The agency mortgage-backed securities are generally considered to be of the highest quality, yet technically they are unrated. This is because it is considered inappropriate to apply a credit rating, which implies a non-zero probability of default, to securities issued or guaranteed by the United States Treasury or one of its agencies. However, the agency pass-through securities have provided the support for the vast majority of debt and preferred stock issues that have been rated and the use of the agency securities provides a firm base for obtaining the highest rating. GNMA, FHLMC, and FNMA are expected to continue their significant roles in the secondary market. However, private issuers are becoming more important, and this trend is expected to become more pronounced in the future.

An Assessment of Mortgage-Backed Securities

Properly structured mortgage-backed securities qualify for the highest rating categories. To date, virtually every rated structured transaction involving mortgage-backed securities has received a rating of double A or triple A. This is because of the high quality of the underlying support for these transactions—the single-family residential first mortgage.

There is a large body of data available on single-family residential mortgages originated in the United States. The cash flow behavior of these mortgages has been studied under a variety of economic conditions. The timing of the receipt of principal and interest from a pool of mortgages varies depending on the incidence of prepayments. However, the ultimate receipt of all money owed is extremely likely and the distribution of cash flows is predictable with a high degree of precision. This predictability can be enhanced by the way in which individual mortgages are aggregated into pools. The inclusion of a large number of mortgages in the pool, diversification by geographic location and mortgagor characteristics, and standardizing the terms of the mortgages are some of the ways of increasing forecast accuracy. To the extent that risks remain, additional support elements can be provided to enhance the rating potential of the transaction.

Four basic risks are inherent in mortgage-backed securities: market risk, maturity risk, default risk, and delinquency risk. Market risk is the uncertainty over time concerning the market price of the security. Always important, this risk becomes even more so if an investor has to sell the security, rather than hold it to maturity. Maturity risk arises because of the uncertainty over the rate of repayment on a pool of mortgages. Investment decisions involving fixed-income securities are based in part on investors' investment horizons. Securities are sometimes chosen with maturities that match the desired horizon. In the case of mortgage securities, nominal (latest possible) maturities are known but the actual maturities are not. This makes the reinvestment problem inherent with all interest-bearing debt securities considerably more complex. With corporate bonds, the timing and amount of the cash flows to be reinvested (absent insolvency) are known even though future reinvestment rates are not. For mortgage securities, these factors must be estimated or forecasted. Default risk is the risk that some or all of the principal and/or interest owed will not be paid. Delinquency risk is the possibility that monies owed will not be paid on time.

It is the quantification of these latter two risks that is the basis of the rating process for mortgage-backed securities. The estimation of the probabilities of late payments and the failure to pay determine credit quality. Though important for investment decisions, neither market risk nor maturity risk are in any way factored into the rating.

In developing a rating system for mortgage-backed securities, each rating agency wanted to create one that was consistent with that used for rating long-term debt obligations. The systems that have emerged recognize that individual mortgage loans have a slightly higher delinquency risk than corporate bonds. However, this increased risk is offset by a lower default risk during the term of the mortgage-backed security. Further, while the probability of default on a corporate bond can increase over time due to adverse changes in the financial condition of the issuer, default risk should decrease over time for mortgage-backed securities as the equity in the underlying mortgages increases.

Mortgage-backed security transactions, when properly structured, qualify for the highest ratings. The explosive growth in the secondary mortgage market has led to the development of liquid trading markets. Realized rates of return to investors in these securities have been attractive relative to other securities of comparable risk. However, mortgage-backed securities are structurally and legally complex. The balance of this chapter discusses the ways in which the rating agencies analyze these complexities and incorporate them into the rating process.

RATING CLASSIFICATIONS

Types of Mortgage-Backed Securities

The type of analysis employed in the determination of a rating depends, in part, on the type of mortgage-backed security to be rated. There are three basic classes of mortgage-backed securities: mortgage-backed bonds, mortgage pass-throughs and mortgage pay-throughs (cash flow bonds). A collateralized mortgage obligation is a type of pay-through bond which is discussed as a special case. Other financing vehicles brought to market recently, such as collateralized certificates of deposit and commercial paper, collateralized Eurodollar deposits, and adjustable rate preferred stock supported by mortgage assets, are treated for rating purposes as modifications of one of the three basic classes.

Mortgage-Backed Bonds

A mortgage-backed bond is a general debt obligation of the issuer which is collateralized by a pool of mortgages. Mortgage-backed bonds are designed to resemble tradition corporate bonds—they pay semi-annual interest and have a specified maturity. The underlying mortgage assets are not sold, but rather are used as collateral for the borrowing. Therefore, losses are not realized by the issuer if low-coupon mortgages are used in the collateral pool. The quantity of mortgages needed for the collateral pool is based on the current market value of the mortgages, which is determined at specified intervals. If the current value of the mortgages falls below some predetermined level, additional collateral must be provided by the issuer. Pledged collateral may be released if market values rise sufficiently. To allow for declining prices between evaluation dates, substantial overcollateralization on a market value basis is required.

Pass-Throughs

A mortgage pass-through security represents an ownership interest in the underlying mortgage loans and thus, in the cash flow that these mortgage loans produce. A mortgage pass-through is treated as a sale of assets to investors. Therefore, the seller records a profit (or loss) when the transaction is closed. Sale treatment allows the transaction to be recorded off the balance sheet of the issuer. Inflows of principal and interest from the mortgages are "passed through" to investors on a monthly basis. This continues either until the mortgages are completely repaid or until the debt issue is retired by the issuer. Retirement occurs either at the bonds' stated final maturity or upon the exercise of the call provision (if created at the time of issue) by the issuer.

Pay-Throughs

A pay-through is a hybrid security. Like a pass-through, cash flows from the pledged mortgage collateral are "paid through" to investors to meet the debt service requirements. Like a mortgage-backed bond, however, a pay-through usually is a debt offering, not a sale of assets. The debt financing is designed to customize the payout characteristics of the bond to meet investor requirements. This makes pay-throughs easier to market at attractive yields.

Collateralized Mortgage Obligations (CMOs)

A CMO is a pay-through security with multiple bond classes. Unlike other mortgage-backed securities, principal repayments are not made to all bondholders on a pro rata basis. Instead, bond repayments are prioritized according to bond class. That is, bondholders of one class are paid off entirely before the next class of bondholders receives any principal repayments.

The first CMO was issued by FHLMC in June 1982. Since that time, many others have been issued. The most popular type seems to be a CMO with four bond classes, each bearing its own rate of interest. The last class often has been a zero coupon or deferred interest class. The zero coupon class accrues interest, but none is paid until the other bond classes have been repaid in full. Collateral cash flow available to meet the deferred interest on the zero coupon class is used to make larger principal payments on other bond classes. The result is that the zero coupon class shortens the maturity of the other bonds classes.

CMOs have several advantages over traditional pay-through bonds. First, investors' repayment schedules are more predictable. The knowledge that no principal will be received until all holders of prior classes have been repaid in full provides a measure of call protection to holders of later classes. Second, CMOs appeal to a wider spectrum of investors owing to the presence of a variety of maturity classes. Investors can choose the class that meets their maturity objectives. Third, CMOs are cost effective when the yield curve is positively sloped. The price paid for an expected yield on a given class can be tied to the portion of the yield curve that matches its expected maturity. This reduces the overall cost of the financing to the issuer. Finally, CMOs can be an effective asset/liability management tool for many classes of issuers.

When CMOs were first issued, they were treated either as a sale of assets or a debt financing, depending on the issuers' preferences. Home builders, who have been active issuers of CMOs, prefer sale of asset treatment in order to take advantage of certain provisions in the tax code. Mortgage bankers and investment banking firms also prefer sale of asset treatment in order to remove the transactions from their balance sheets. Thrifts, on the other hand, prefer to treat CMOs as a debt financing. This is to avoid the recognition of losses that would occur if the use of low-coupon, deeply discounted mortgage securities were treated as a sale. More recently, the Financial Accounting Standards Board (FASB) has attempted to standardize the accounting treatment of CMOs. Rulings to date indicate that in most instances CMOs are to be treated as a debt financing. However, under certain circumstances, CMOs might qualify as a sale of assets. This issue will evolve further as rulings are finalized.

Philosophical Approach

To determine the final rating, the various elements that comprise the mortgage-backed security transaction must be combined in some fashion. This requires a unifying theme to serve as an analytical framework. Two basic frameworks have evolved, the building block approach and the weak-link approach. Moody's employs the former and Standard & Poor's the latter.

The building block approach recognizes that the various elements contained in a transaction are mutually supportive. This means that weaknesses in one element can be offset by strengths in another to achieve the targeted rating. As a result, total risk in the transaction can be less than the risk inherent in any one element of support viewed in isolation.

The key determinant of the risk reduction that is possible is the correlation of various credit characteristics. As long as these characteristics are not perfectly correlated, risk reduction is possible. In statistical terms, the joint probability of failure of independent credit variables can be less than joint probability of credit variables which are highly correlated.

In applying this technique, each support element in the transaction is identified and the level of risk of each is determined. Weights are assigned to each credit characteristic depending upon its importance to the transaction. The extent to which the credit variables are then related to one another is assessed. The performance of these interrelated variables within the context of the proposed structure are assessed under a variety of adverse economic conditions. The evaluation of this performance leads to the determination of credit quality and hence, of the rating.

In its pure form, the weak-link approach suggests that the final rating of a transaction can be no higher than rating quality of the weakest element that supports the transaction. An implicit assumption of this philosophy is that all of the credit characteristics are nearly perfectly correlated. In other words, if one of the support elements fails, others will fail as well. A modification of the weak-link approach recognizes that not all of the credit elements are equally important to the transaction. Under the appropriate conditions, one or more factors with low weights can be of slightly lower quality without requiring a lower rating. Still, all the key support elements must be of credit quality no worse than that target level.

The foundation of any mortgage-backed securities transaction is the underlying pool of mortgages. The probability of significant delinquencies or defaults for a transaction supported by a high quality, well-diversified pool of mortgages is relatively low even in the absence of additional protective elements. However, to achieve the highest ratings, additional support elements are needed to reduce further the delays and losses that would be imposed by delinquencies and defaults. Examples of these elements are insurance policies, overcollateralization, servicer and issuer obligations, and other forms of guarantees.

The building block approach infers that the probability of loss for a transaction is reduced sufficiently to justify a high grade rating, even when the entities providing the additional support carry a slightly lower rating. This is because the likelihood that the mortgage pool will prove to be significantly weaker than anticipated at the same time that the support elements fail is relatively low. This would not be true under the weak-link approach because of the assumption that joint probability of simultaneous failure is high.

There has been a high degree of consistency to date in the ratings of similar transactions, despite different implications of the two approaches. In large part, this is due to variations in the assessment of credit quality of the mortgage insurance industry by the rating agencies. Moody's and Standard & Poor's agree that the support provided by mortgage insurance companies carries high weight in determining the final rating for mortgage-backed securities. The indications are that Moody's believes that the firms in the mortgage insurance industry are of lower credit quality than does Standard & Poor's and there is more variation in credit quality among the mortgage insurance companies. Under the building block approach the credit quality of the mortgage insurer can be one level below the rating target without necessarily jeopardizing the rating. The weak-link approach requires the mortgage insurer to have a rating no lower than that desired. Thus, Standard & Poor's seems to rate the members of the industry higher than does Moody's. There are also differences, albeit relatively small ones, in the agencies' view of overcollateralization standards and the credit quality of servicers and issuers. However, when incorporated into the differing philosophical approaches, the methodologies still lead to similar rating conclusions.

Debt Rating Definitions

The rating agencies have applied their corporate debt rating definitions to mortgage-backed securities. Moody's has nine general classifications, while Standard & Poor's has ten. The precise definitions of the rating classifications are given below. However, since mortgage-backed securities have attained the highest ratings, only the definitions for the three highest classifications are included.

Moody's[1]	*Standard & Poor's*[2]
Aaa	AAA
Bonds which are rated "Aaa" are judged to be of the best quality. They carry the smallest degree of investment risk and are generally referred to as "gilt edged." Interest payments are protected by a large or an exceptionally stable margin and principal is secure. While the various protective elements are likely to	Debt rated "AAA" has the highest rating assigned by Standard & Poor's. Capacity to pay interest and repay principal is extremely strong.

---

[1] *Moody's Bond Record,* August 1984, Volume 51, Number 8, p. 1.

[2] *Standard & Poor's Credit Overview: Corporate and International Ratings,* August 1983 (New York), p. 87.

change, such changes as can be visualized are the most unlikely to impair the fundamentally strong position of such issues.

Aa

Bonds which are rated "AA" are judged to be of high quality by all standards. Together with the Aaa group they comprise what are generally known as high-grade bonds. They are rated lower than the best bonds because margins of protection may not be as large as in Aaa securities, fluctuation of protective elements may be of greater amplitude, or there may be other elements present which make the long-term risks appear somewhat larger than the Aaa securities.

AA

Debt rated "double A" has a very strong capacity to pay interest and repay principal, and differs from the highest rated issues only in a small degree.

A

Bonds which are rated A possess many favorable investment attributes and are to be considered upper-medium-grade obligations. Factors giving security to principal and interest are considered adequate, but elements may be present which suggest a susceptibility to impairment some time in the future.

A

Debt rated "A" has a strong capacity to pay interest and repay principal although it is somewhat more susceptible to the adverse effects of changes in circumstances in economic conditions than debt in higher rated categories.

Both agencies use modifiers to indicate relative standings in the major rating categories. Moody's applies numerical modifiers 1, 2, and 3 for each rating classification from Aa to B. The modifier 1 indicates that the security is in the higher end of its rating category, modifier 2 indicates a mid-range ranking, while modifier 3 indicates that the security ranks in the lower end of its rating category. Standard & Poor's uses a plus or minus for the upper and lower ranking, respectively. The mid-range ranking has no modifier.

Types of Underlying Security (Collateral)

There are two general types of mortgage loans that are used to support rated transactions—residential mortgages and commercial mortgages. By far the most important category has been residential mortgage. This group includes fixed-rate, level payment mortgages (FRMs), graduated payment mortgages (GPMs), growing equity mortgages (GEMs), and adjustable rate mortgages (ARMs). All but ARMs have been used as collateral for rated mortgage-backed securities.

The basis for the criteria used to rate all mortgage-backed securities is the FRM on single-family dwellings. This is because far more is known about the prepayment, delinquency, and default characteristics of this instrument than any other. A few rated transactions have been done using manufactured housing. The rating criteria are based on the fixed-rate mortgage, because the available data on manufactured housing are not extensive. It is likely that there will be a slight increase in the number of ratings on this type of transaction in the future. Ratings supported by mortgages on multi-family properties are being considered.

Recently, there also has been much discussion of the possibility of developing pass-through or pay-through securities supported by commercial real estate loans. Unfortunately, these loans are too heterogeneous and the data too sparse to permit the necessary standardization that leads to a framework for rating analysis. However, given the volume of these loans and the large size of the players in this market, the development of criteria for rating these types of securities is to be expected.

EVALUATION OF THE CREDIT RISK OF THE UNDERLYING ASSETS

The rating agencies have determined the essential factors that impact the quality of the underlying mortgage assets and therefore, the ratings of mortgage-backed securities. In some instances, these factors are applied uniformly to all types of ratable securities, while in others they are applied differently to allow for the special characteristics of the various securities. For example, whole loans and mortgage-backed securities are treated differently when used as the underlying collateral. There is much less standardization of individual mortgage loans than for GNMA and FNMA pass-throughs or FHLMC PCs. Mortgage-backed securities are more marketable and easier to price than whole loans because of the existence of deep secondary markets. Additional legal analysis also is needed for whole loans. The rating process is affected accordingly.

Besides the evaluation of underlying mortgage assets, there are additional support elements that must be evaluated as well. Over-collateralization is one of these support elements. The rating potential is enhanced if an issuer is willing to overcollateralize. In many transactions, overcollateralization is required for any kind of rating to be obtainable. The presence of an equity position is a second structural element that can improve a rating. Cash or a letter of credit are two ways of providing such equity. A governmental guarantee is another support element. Finally, insurance protection often is present as a way of further enhancing the transaction.

The quality of the underlying mortgage assets and of the incremental support elements are crucial to the rating process. The evaluation of both components is discussed in this section.

Quality of the Mortgage Pool

Prime Quality Mortgages

There are certain characteristics that are essential for a high quality rating on any mortgage-backed security transaction. The presence of these characteristics does not guarantee the highest ratings, nor does their absence preclude them. Transactions without them might still qualify. However, substantial additional analysis and incremental support will be required. The presence of these characteristics establishes a solid starting point for the achievement of a high-grade rating.

These basic characteristics of the mortgages in the pool are:

1. Properly recorded first mortgage loans on single-family residential detached units on properties located in the United States;
2. Fully amortizing mortgage loans;
3. Owner-occupied dwellings that serve as the primary residence of the occupant; and
4. Loans with original maturities of no more than 30 years.

Mortgages of this kind are most frequently originated in the market. Adequate data exist to permit a detailed analysis of their expected behavior over time. Mortgages with these characteristics are more liquid if they must be sold. They have the lowest rates of default and delinquency. The relative safety and predictability of their cash flows make them most suitable for use in transactions designed to achieve high ratings.

The absence of proper recording and of first lien on the underlying real estate make high-grade rating a virtual impossibility. Attached units, such as townhouses and condominiums, have become more acceptable as mortgage collateral for structured transactions in recent years. Some adverse early experience and the relative scarcity of data make these types of loans less useful for high ratings. Much the same can be said for vacation and second homes, multi-family units, balloon loans, non-owner-occupied housing, manufactured housing, mobile homes, and mortgages with maturities greater than 30 years. It must be stressed that the use of these kinds of assets does not preclude the highest ratings. Rather, it means that additional support elements must be provided. Although in principle this support always can be provided, the cost of doing so might make the transaction economically infeasible.

The basic characteristics listed above can be thought of as somewhat qualitative in nature. There is an additional set of preferred characteristics desirable for high ratings. Safe, stable cash flows and high predictability are associated with these characteristics, just as with the basic ones. However, with the preferred characteristics things are not so absolute. Every mortgage in the pool need not embody all of these characteristics. Instead, specified proportions of the pool should qualify and there is more flexibility to substitute incremental support in other areas.

The preferred characteristics are:

1. Fixed-rate, level payment mortgages;
2. Original loan-to-value ratios of not more than 80 percent;
3. Seasoning (more than 6 years is preferred);
4. Adequate geographic dispersion;
5. Loan size reasonable, relative to comparable mortgages from the same location;
6. High quality underwriting and servicing combined with an experienced originator; and
7. Mortgage coupons that are reasonable, relative to the market.

Although trade-offs against these criteria are possible, the rating agencies limit the extent to which failures to adhere to these preferred standards can be offset and highest ratings still achieved.

Fixed-Rate Level Payment Mortgages. FRMs are preferred as the underlying mortgage asset. This is because far more is known about this mortgage and its cash flow characteristics than any other type of mortgage instrument. The result is higher credit quality. Therefore, it is easier to obtain the highest ratings with FRMs, although as more is learned about the newer alternative mortgage instruments, the gap between them and FRMs might narrow.

Loan-to-Value Ratio. The decision to default on one's mortgage is essentially financial. Individuals who get into financial difficulty will sell the house and prepay on the mortgage rather than default, if they have a positive net equity position. If, on the other hand, the amount that could be realized upon the sale of the home is insufficient to pay off the outstanding mortgage plus the associated transactions costs, then mortgagors will default. Studies of mortgage defaults have consistently used loan-to-value ratio as a crucial component of the net equity variable.[3]

In general, default probabilities increase as loan-to-value ratios increase. This effect is pronounced for ratios above 80 percent. Mortgage loans often are classified by loan-to-value ratio in 5 percent increments starting at 80 percent (e.g., 80–85 percent, 85–90 percent, and so on). Standard mortgage contracts require primary mortgage insurance on loans with loan-to-value ratios greater than 80 percent. This insurance usually covers each loan down to the 75 percent level.

The rating agencies favor pools with large numbers of mortgages having ratios below 80 percent. Even with the presence of primary mortgage insurance on high loan-to-value ratio loans, there are limits on the number of such loans that can be in the pool if a high grade rating is sought. The preferred limit on high ratio loans is 25 percent. It should be noted that primary coverage is not required unless the loan-to-value ratio

---

[3] For a description of an explanatory model of mortgage default for conventional mortgages, see Helen F. Peters, Scott M. Pinkus, and David J. Askin, "Default: The Last Resort," *Secondary Mortgage Markets*, Vol. 1, No. 3 (August 1984), pp. 16–20. An alternative approach is found in Tim S. Campbell and J. Kimball Dietrich, "The Determinants of Default on Insured Conventional Residential Mortgage Loans," *Journal of Finance*, Vol. 38 (December 1983), pp. 1569–1581. Examples of default models for FHA mortgages are found in George M. Von Furstenberg, "Default Risk on FHA-Insured Home Mortgages as a Function of the Terms of Financing: A Quantitative Analysis," *Journal of Finance*, Vol. 24 (June 1969), pp. 459–477, and Helen F. Peters, "Termination Distributions of FHA-Insured Residential Mortgages," Unpublished Ph.D. dissertation, University of Pennsylvania, 1979.

exceeds 80 percent, but if it does, coverage is required below 80 percent, down to 75 percent. This suggests that the agencies believe a greater amount of insurance is needed to offset the higher probability of default on mortgages with loan-to-value ratios greater than 80 percent.

Seasoning. Mortgage defaults are most likely to occur within the first 5 years after origination.[4] Default is particularly likely between the second and fourth policy years. This is because in the early years, there is little time for mortgages to accumulate a significant amount of equity, either through the paydown of principal or price inflation. Therefore, if a problem arises during this time, there could be little financial incentive to avoid default. In later years as equity accumulates, mortgagors are more likely to sell the property to save their equity or to make alternative financial arrangements in order to continue making the monthly payments. Seasoning also is valuable to the rating agencies because it provides payment histories for mortgagors and thus, evidence on creditworthiness.

Seasoning is valued for the mortgages in the pool as a way of reducing the exposure to the risk of default, especially if it takes the mortgages beyond the fifth policy year. For GPMs and other alternative instruments that allow negative amortization, seasoning well beyond the fifth year is necessary to achieve a significant amount of risk reduction. Little additional credit is given for seasoning on FRMs beyond the eighth or ninth year, since little risk reduction is achieved beyond this point. The value of seasoning in the reduction of default risk

---

[4] A detailed analysis of the default experience of conventional mortgages is given in Helen F. Peters and David J. Askin, *Average Weighted Life Study of the Federal Home Loan Mortgage Corporation's Conventional Mortgage Portfolio: 1973–80* (Washington, D.C.: Federal Home Loan Mortgage Corporation, January 1984). This is found in the section titled "Phase II: Estimation of FHLMC Termination Distributions." A shorter version also is in Helen F. Peters, Scott M. Pinkus and David J. Askin, "Prepayment Patterns of Conventional Mortgages: Experience from the Freddie Mac Portfolio," *Secondary Mortgage Markets,* Vol. 1, No. 1 (February 1984), pp. 6–11. Similar distributions for FHA mortgages is examined in Peters, "Termination Distributions of FHA-Insured Residential Mortgages."

is such that it often can offset the negative effects of undesirable characteristics, such as high loan-to-value ratios.

Seasoning also affects the ratings of mortgage-backed securities through its impact on prepayment rates. Prepayments tend to rise in the early policy years, reach a plateau and stay relatively constant thereafter.[5] This also is referred to as the "duration in residence" effect. Since the distribution of cash flows over the life of the mortgage as well as the ultimate return of principal are crucial for the ratings, the impact of seasoning on prepayments is incorporated into the analysis.

Geographic Dispersion. Diversification is one of the best ways to reduce risk. Mortgage defaults are thought to be highly correlated with one another because changes in the economy tend to have somewhat similar effects on everyone's financial condition. Still, diversification within a pool is possible and yields material benefits in the rating process.

The first step toward geographic dispersion is the size of the pool. The rating agencies prefer each pool to contain at least 300 mortgages. Five or six hundred mortgages are desirable to assure adequate nation-wide dispersion.

Numbers alone do not guarantee proper dispersion, however. The agencies impose additional restrictions in order to minimize the pool's exposure to individual financial adversities that could lead to significant losses. These restrictions are expressed in the following terms:

- The number of geographic regions in which mortgages are originated.

- Absence of state concentrations; i.e., no more than 10 percent of the mortgages come from any one state.

---

[5] See Peters and Askin, *Average Weighted Life Study of the Federal Home Loan Mortgage Corporation's Conventional Mortgage Portfolio: 1973–80,* pp. 2–46 of "Phase II: Estimation of FHLMC Termination Distributions," for tables and a complete description of the prepayment experience of a large, geographically dispersed portfolio of conventional mortgages. Peters, Pinkus, and Askin, "Prepayment Patterns of Conventional Mortgages," contains a shorter description.

- Strong, diversified regional economic base; to the extent that the mortgage pool is concentrated geographically, the region should not be dominated by one industry, the failure of which could jeopardize the financial strength of large numbers of mortgagors.
- Absence of local concentration; no more than 5 percent of the properties should be located in the same zip code.
- Areas with known problems should be avoided altogether, i.e., depressed housing markets, locations with adverse environmental conditions, or states and/or municipalities with onerous legal restrictions (such as anti-deficiency statutes or restrictive foreclosure/forebearance laws).

As with other criteria, these are guidelines, not absolute requirements. Trade-offs with other areas of strength are possible up to a point. Still, adherence to these guidelines makes it more likely that a high-grade rating will be achieved.

Size of Loan. The rating agencies require additional coverage on large loans owing to the associated increase in default risk. This increased risk is attributed to lower liquidity for large loans in the event that they must be sold to raise cash. A loan which does not exceed the FNMA/FHLMC limits (currently $114,000) can be sold to one of the government agencies. If the loan qualifies otherwise, this creates a ready market for quick sale that often results in the best price as well.

Loans that do not qualify for sale to FHLMC or FNMA still can be sold in the secondary mortgage market. However, as the loan size increases, sale becomes increasingly more difficult. Fewer participants are able to buy very large loans and those who can might be willing to do so only if the loan is discounted. This means that fewer dollars than expected will be realized by the seller, given the face amount of the loan.

The size of the mortgage relative to comparable properties also is a rating concern. A loan that is too large could indicate that the buyer overpaid for the property. Even if the loan is reasonable for the intrinsic value of the property, the full intrinsic value might not be realized if the property is sold. In either case, the jumbo loan embodies a higher degree of risk and the rating agencies require additional support.

In quantifying the additional coverage required, the rating agencies have created classes of loans by size. The break points are similar but not identical across agencies. In general the classes are: less than $150,000, $150,000–$250,000, $250,000–$500,000, and greater than $500,000. Loans of less than $150,000 generally require no additional coverage. Jumbo loans larger than $500,000 are rare and typically are not used in collateral pools. Among the other categories, the amount of additional coverage depends on the size mix within the pool, and strengths and weaknesses in the other criteria.

Underwriting/Servicing Standards and Originator Experience.   Quality underwriting is crucial to credit quality. Superior underwriting requires a combination of valid underwriting standards, implementation of those standards, careful monitoring, and improvements based on experience. These criteria apply as well to the servicing operation.

This is an area that is not easily quantified. The rating agencies rely on adherence to FNMA/FHLMC or FHA-approved underwriting and servicing standards where appropriate. Deviations from these standards make high-grade ratings harder to obtain. The rating agencies also will evaluate the experience and track record of originators and servicers. Delinquency and default statistics as well as payment processing information may be analyzed.

One characteristic of the underwriting process that lends itself to quantification is income coverage ratios. For FNMA/FHLMC conforming loans, the current standards are 28/36, meaning that the ratio of the mortgagor's gross monthly income to monthly housing expense cannot exceed 28 percent and that the ratio of income to total monthly debt obligations cannot exceed 36 percent. The rating agencies typically are more liberal for mortgage pools. They rely on standards such as 33/38 or 34/39. Some variations within the mix of mortgages in the pool are allowed, as are trade-offs.

Of special concern to the rating agencies are seller-provided financing incentives. Buydown mortgages are one example. Buydown is where the seller, typically a homebuilder or its agent, subsidizes the mortgagor by permitting mortgage payments that are less than those scheduled for the stated interest rate and maturity of the loan. The seller pays the shortfall. This is done so that homebuyers can qualify for mortgages (and then buy homes) for which they would otherwise be ineligible. The buydown period usually is much shorter than the maturity of the loan. When the buydown period expires, the mortgagor assumes the full scheduled payment.

The rating agencies prefer that the buydown period last no longer than 3 years. If the buydown mortgage is part of a GNMA pool, then GNMA's guarantee applies and nothing more is required. Otherwise, the full amount of the seller's subsidy payment would have to be guaranteed in some way such as with cash or a letter of credit of suitable quality. The agencies also must have some assurances that the underwriting process takes account of the mortgagor's ability to meet the higher monthly payments when the buydown period ends.

Mortgage Coupon. The coupon rates at which the mortgages are written are important because prepayment rates and the market value of the pool depend on the relationship between current interest rates and mortgage rates.[6] Prepayment experience determines the distribution of cash flows over the life of the pool. The degree of interest rate protection afforded the pool and its cash flows is determined in large part by the coupon. For instance, a large increase in rates relative to those of the mortgage collateral would result in a large decline in market value of the mortgages. For transactions supported by this market value, such a loss in value could strain the ability of the issuer to provide additional collateral needed to avoid an event of default. The rating agencies evalu-

---

[6] For a detailed description of this relationship, see "Phase III: The Development of the Forecast Model," in Peters and Askin, *Average Weighted Life Study of the Federal Home Loan Mortgage Corporation's Conventional Mortgage Portfolio: 1973–80.* The following paper by Peters, Pinkus, and Askin presents much of the discussion in a more abbreviated form: "Figuring the Odds: A Model of Prepayments," *Secondary Mortgage Markets,* Vol. 1, No. 2 (May 1984), pp. 18–23.

ate the interest rate protection inherent in the mortgage coupons in determining the amount of incremental support required for the rating level desired.

Mortgage coupons also are important because high coupon mortgages result in larger monthly payments. This can lead to higher default rates. Studies have found evidence that the rate at which a mortgage is written relative to others in the same region at the same time can act as a proxy for the lender's evaluation of a mortgagor's creditworthiness.[7] Since the mortgage coupon has a significant impact on the rate of principal reduction of mortgages in the pool as well as credit quality and market value of the pool, the rating agencies examine mortgage coupons quite closely.

Alternative Mortgage Instruments

The basis of the rating criteria established to date is an analysis of the 30 year, fixed-rate, level payment mortgage. As financial institutions moved toward deregulation and interest rate volatility increased, a variety of alternative mortgage instruments emerged. Not all of these alternative instruments have been equally successful in the market. Yet, the rating agencies have attempted to incorporate them into their rating frameworks.

Although there are numerous alternative mortgage instruments for single-family residential property, they can be condensed into four general types for rating purposes: level payment mortgages that amortize fully in less than 30 years (midgets), graduated payment mortgages (GPMs), growing equity mortgages (GEMs), and adjustable rate mortgages (ARMs).

Midgets

With proper underwriting, midgets pose no special rating concerns. Higher monthly payments are called for owing to shorter

---

[7] See, for example, "Phase III: The Development of the Forecast Model," in Peters and Askin, *Average Weighted Life Study of the Federal Home Loan Mortgage Corporation's Conventional Mortgage Portfolio: 1973–80.*

maturity, but if mortgagors are qualified for these mortgages at higher payment levels, there is no rating penalty for their use. Mortgages with maturities of 15 years are the most popular of the midgets in use today.

GPMs

A GPM is a mortgage with early payments that are insufficient to cover the interest on the outstanding loan balance. Negative amortization results, since the shortfall between the interest owed and the interest actually paid is added to the principal balance outstanding. The monthly payments are increased periodically until such time as each period's interest obligation can be met. The now higher principal balance is amortized at a rate sufficient to retire the loan by the original maturity date.

A GPM is a fixed-rate loan, since nominal interest rate does not change over the life of the instrument. However, it obviously is not a level payment mortgage since payment amounts increase over its life. The typical GPM is a 30-year mortgage, with lower initial payments that are increased annually at a rate of 7½ percent at the end of each of the first five years. The payment that results at the end of year five is unchanged over the remaining 25 years of the mortgage. Other GPMs may have different maturities, frequencies or rates of payment adjustment, or durations of payment adjustment periods. However, the fundamental concept is the same.

There are three basic rating agency concerns with GPMs. First is the fact that mortgagors are qualified for mortgages at the lower first-year payment level. Many of these borrowers would be unable to qualify for mortgages at the higher payment amount. The hope is that the mortgagor's income will increase sufficiently over time to handle the new monthly payments. However, most underwriting standards do not explicitly evaluate the likelihood that this will occur.

The second concern, which is related to the first, is the possibility of payment shock that can arise because the monthly payments will increase five times over the life of the loan. By the time the payment becomes fixed at the end of the fifth year, monthly payments are greater than they would have been under a FRM. If borrower income does not rise sufficiently to cover increases, the probability of default rises dramatically.

Finally, there is concern over the negative amortization feature. Negative amortization requires each mortgagor to pay a larger sum of money over the life of the loan than under a FRM. Also, negative amortization greatly reduces and can even eliminate totally borrowers' equities in their properties in the early years of the mortgage. As discussed previously, the risk of default is greatest in these early years. Negative amortization exacerbates the problem.

The use of GPMs does not preclude the highest ratings. Rather, the rating agencies prefer to limit the maximum proportion of GPMs in the pool to 25 percent or less. Additional support such as extra pool insurance or a higher level of cash flow overcollateralization may be required. Further, the cumulative amount of negative amortization that can occur over the lives of mortgages must be fully covered. This is done by establishing a debt service fund into which cash, a letter of credit, or some form of guarantee of suitable quality is placed.

GEMs

GEMs, like GPMs, are fixed-rate, non-level payment mortgages. Unlike GPMs, however, GEMs involve no negative amortization. Monthly payments are increased each year. The original scheduled principal payment as well as the entire amount of the payment increases are dedicated to reducing the outstanding principal balance. This serves to shorten the actual maturity of the loan. The most common form of GEM calls for a monthly payment during the first year that is the same as a FRM. At the end of the first year, and each year thereafter until the loan is retired, the monthly payment is increased by 4 percent. Since all of these payment increases are applied against the principal balance on the loan, it is fully repaid in slightly less than 13 years.

The only rating agency concern with GEMs is the possibility of payment shock. Mortgagors are qualified at the same level as borrowers with FRMs. If the usual underwriting standards are applied, there is no anticipated problem initially. However, mortgagors are committed to a 4 percent increase in monthly payments each year over the life of the loan. Although the reduction in loan maturity is of some benefit, there still is no guarantee that mortgagors' incomes will rise sufficiently to accomodate the higher payments each year. As with GPMs, the rating agencies limit the proportion of GEMs allowed in the mortgage pool and often require additional support elements to cover the increased risk of default.

ARMs

An adjustable rate mortgage is one with an interest rate that is changed with some frequency over its life. The monthly payment can be fixed for this kind of mortgage if the maturity is continually adjusted to reflect changes in the interest rate. In practice, most ARMs have a fixed maturity and instead, the payments are adjusted to reflect the interest rate changes.

The interest rate adjustments are tied to an index, such as a Treasury security index, a Federal Home Loan Bank Board (FHLBB) index, or the lender's cost of funds. ARMs often are written with caps on the increase in interest rates or on payments. Interest rate caps limit the change in interest rates for any adjustment as well as over the life of the loan. Payment caps limit the amount of increase in monthly payments over any adjustment period and over the life of the loan. Some ARMs are written with caps on both the interest rate and the monthly payment or without any caps at all. While ARMs have been an important instrument in the primary mortgage market, there has been little securitization to date involving them. A major obstacle to securitization has been lack of standardized instruments. This, in turn, makes it difficult to establish consistent rating criteria.

Recently, the rating agencies have begun to address this problem by identifying the risks inherent in ARMs and analyzing the incorporation of these risks into the rating process. Five types of risk are recognized in evaluating ARMs: payment shock, negative amortization, equity shock, spread and servicing risk, and legal risks.

Payment shock is the most widely recognized of the risk categories. Like GPMs and GEMs, ARMs involve periodic adjustments to monthly payments. Unlike other alternative mortgage instruments, the monthly payments on ARMs can decline. This is not a concern to the rating agencies. What is a concern is that when a payment increase occurs, its size is not known in advance. Periodic and lifetime caps help to some extent, but much uncertainty still remains. The problem is exacerbated by questionable underwriting tactics employed by some institutions. In the attempt to build large ARM portfolios quickly in a period of excess liquidity, many lenders offered the loans at deep discounts. Unfortunately, borrowers often were qualified for the mortgages at these "teaser rates" rather than at current market rates. Many borrowers are unable to meet their monthly payments once the adjustments take place, even when no increase in the index occurs. Higher rates of defaults have been observed for ARMs than for otherwise comparable FRMs. This trend is expected to continue in the future unless stricter underwriting criteria are applied.

Negative amortization is possible with some ARMs, when the new monthly payment called for in an adjustment period cannot be raised by the full amount due to payment caps. Negative amortization increases the outstanding principal balance of the mortgage. Also, it reduces the mortgagor's equity in the property, sometimes causing it to turn negative. This leads to a greatly increased risk of default. Most ARMs limit the maximum amount of negative amortization that can occur to 125 percent of the original principal balance. Once this limit is reached, no further negative amortization is permitted. This is advantageous to borrowers; however, the incentive to default remains high if financial adversity occurs.

There is negative amortization with GPMs, but the pattern of negative amortization is known at the beginning of the loan. With ARMs, the occurrence and amount of negative amortization are uncertain. Negative amortization is more likely during periods of sharply rising interest rates. Such periods often are

followed by an increase in unemployment and depressed housing markets. Personal financial difficulties and the inability
to sell homes quickly at reasonable prices are precisely the
circumstances that lead to increases in defaults.

Equity shock is a situation where the nominal equity in
a property is greater than the real equity. This creates problems
if the home must be sold to avoid default. Equity shock often
happens when financing packages are offered to the borrower
to subsidize a home purchase. If the costs of the subsidy are
passed on to the buyer in the form of a higher purchase price,
the price paid for the home overstates the true market value
of the property. If the financing subsidies cannot be transferred
to new buyers when the house is resold, the original buyers
may find that the "equity" assumed to be present is reduced
or even nonexistent. This situation occurs most often with
builder buydowns on new homes or condominium sales.

Spread and servicing risks affect investors and servicers
of ARMs, but not borrowers. Discounted ARMs must be on
the books at higher market rates for relatively long periods
of time in order to earn back the original discount. This imposes a greater risk to servicers relative to FRMs. Even in
stable interest rate environments, ARM adjustments to market
rate levels can take several years. This takes even longer in
a rising rate scenario. The result is reduced profitability of
ARMs to investors. The possibility of prepayment further increases this risk. Servicing risk arises because of the frequent
adjustments required on ARMs. These adjustments and the
associated monitoring of indexes serve to increase servicing
costs. If higher servicing spreads are not charged, the profit
potential of ARMs is reduced commensurately.

There has been much debate and confusion over the advantages and disadvantages of ARMs. Many borrowers do
not understand how ARMs work and are often uncertain over
the future implications of the different features. There are indications that some originators, servicers, and investors do not
fully understand ARMs either. The results are dissatisfaction,
controversy, and ultimately the proposal of restrictive regulations and laws. Lawsuits have arisen from borrowers claiming
to have been misled by lenders. Political pressure has been

exerted for state and federal intervention. This situation is fraught with uncertainty. Uncertainty leads to increased risk.

The Federal housing agencies are formulating guidelines for underwriting ARMs and creating ARM-backed securities. The rating agencies have begun to develop standards for the incorporation of ARMs into the rating process. As with other mortgage assets that are not considered prime quality, the guidelines impose limitations on the proportions of non-prime mortgage securities in mortgage pools, requirements of additional incremental support, or outright prohibition in some cases.

The rating guidelines developed to date include the following characteristics:

1. Greater geographic diversification is required than for FRMs;
2. Restrictive caps are required on interest rate changes, such as 1 to 2 percent per year and 5 percent over the life of the loan;
3. Loans permitting negative amortization will be greatly restricted or eliminated altogether until more is known about likely default experience;
4. Borrowers must qualify for the loans in accordance with strict underwriting standards at current market rates, not at teaser rates;
5. First year rate discounts would be severely limited to a maximum of 2 to 3 percent;
6. Greater amounts of cash flow overcollateralization and/ or pool insurance coverage will be required;
7. Loan documents must clearly describe and demonstrate the potential impact of maximum future payments adjustments;
8. Quality of the servicer must be higher than for FRMs;
9. Liquid secondary markets for the ARMs included in the pool must exist for transactions in which the liquidation of the mortgage assets might be required.

These standards will be continually monitored and updated as more is learned about ARMs and ARM-backed securities.

TYPES OF PROTECTION AGAINST LOSS

The previous section discussed the rating agencies' analysis of the cash flow and market value protections inherent in the individual mortgage securities. This section considers loss protection generated from structural features in the transaction. These protections arise either internally through the mortgage pool or from external sources. The types of protection included are government guarantees, mortgage insurance, reinvestment income, overcollateralization, other types of insurance and cash advance provisions.

Government Guarantees

At the whole loan level a basic distinction is made between mortgages that carry some form of government insurance or guarantee and those that do not. The former are represented by FHA-insured and VA-guaranteed mortgages. The latter usually are referred to as conventional mortgages. In the rating process, credit is given for government guaranteed or insured mortgages. Conventional loans that conform to FNMA/ FHLMC underwriting standards are favored as well. Conventional loans that do not conform to these standards are likely to be at a rating disadvantage.

The guarantees of the Federal housing agencies for mortgage-backed securities were described previously. The GNMA guaranty, which is backed by the full faith and credit of the United States Treasury, is considered to be free of default risk. The guarantees of FNMA and FHLMC, although not wholly default free, are still considered to be of quality comparable to that of triple A-rated securities. FNMA's guarantee has slightly greater value in supporting a transaction than FHLMC's, since it includes the timely payment of principal as well as interest.

Mortgage Insurance

Mortgage insurance often is the most important incremental support element in a structured transaction. Generally it is used to supplement mortgagors' equities in their properties or to enhance the cash flow overcollateralization of a pool of mortgages. With high interest rates and a general trend of increasing home price inflation, the proportion of high loan-to-value ratio loans has increased leading to a corresponding increase in the proportion of conventional loans insured by mortgage insurance companies.

Primary Mortgage Insurance

Primary Mortgage Insurance is applied on an individual loan basis. There are two general types: basic and supplemental. Basic primary mortgage insurance is used to insure loans with loan-to-value ratios in excess of 80 percent. The coverage extends down to 75 percent of the appraised property value. Standard mortgage loan contracts require this insurance as a condition of the loan. It provides loss protection to the lender and ultimately to the investor in the securities. In certain transactions, specific types of mortgages included in the collateral pool have been covered 100 percent by primary mortgage insurance in order to secure the targeted rating. Mortgages most often subject to this requirement are loans on second and vacation homes, rural properties, and properties located in high default risk areas.

Supplemental mortgage insurance often is obtained by lenders for seasoned mortgage loans with loan-to-value ratios in excess of 75 percent that have not been insured previously. This insurance is required if the loans are to be sold to FNMA or FHLMC.

Pool Insurance

Pool insurance is an aggregate default coverage on a pool that supplements the primary insurance on individual loans. The amount of pool insurance varies, depending on the amount of support needed to obtain the desired rating level. The rating agencies analyze pool characteristics such as types of mortgage loans, geographic distribution, loan-to-value ratios, and so on. Deviations from the basic or preferred characteristics cause an increase in the risk exposure through an increase in the probability of default, resulting in higher required levels of pool insurance coverage. Cash flow overcollateralization generated by the mortgage pool can substitute for pool insurance.

Insurance Endorsements and Indemnity Bonds

Insurance endorsements and indemnity bonds often are used to provide additional protection for structured transactions involving conventional mortgages. These policies may cover losses in situations where: a mortgage loan becomes immediately due and payable as a result of, say, faulty documentation; mortgage loans become delinquent and funds must be advanced to the servicer; losses occur owing to any adjustment in monthly payments of the loan resulting from bankruptcy proceedings; and there is a failure of a servicer to perform under the servicing agreement.

Quality of Mortgage Insurers

The rating agencies consider not only the types and quantities of mortgage insurance provided, but also the quality of the mortgage insurer. As discussed previously, the weak-link and building block theories permit insurers of different credit quality to support a given rating. In practice, consistent ratings on the transactions have been produced. However, there have been structured transactions involving large proportions of non-prime mortgage loans. These can usually obtain higher ratings only if the mortgages are covered 100 percent by mortgage insurance. In this case, the transaction's rating would be that of the mortgage insurer. This could lead to a split rating if there was a difference of opinion concerning the credit quality of the mortgage insurer.

In rating the insurers, industry risk, company characteristics, underwriting performance, investment activities, non-insurance activities, earnings protection, leverage, financial flexibility, and evaluation of management are the factors that are evaluated. Many companies also have secondary support in the form of reinsurance agreements and relationships with other affiliate companies. These forms of support are recognized explicitly in the rating process.

Reinvestment Income

In most mortgage-backed securities transactions there is a period of time between the receipt of income from the mortgage assets and the payment of funds to investors. The existence of this "float" creates an opportunity for funds to be reinvested at interest and thus, provide additional cash to support the transaction. In general, the rating agencies allow these investments to be in assets of the same credit quality as that of the transaction. If the maturity of the reinvestment is short, less than 6 months or a year, the credit quality of the investment may be one full rating level below that of the transaction.

The rating agencies also allow credit in performing certain calculations for reinvestment income that can be derived from any guaranteed minimum cash flow to be produced by the mortgage assets. For example, the scheduled principal and interest that will be generated by a GNMA security can be used to support a bond transaction, as well as reinvestment income on those funds during the period of time between their receipt and when they must be paid to investors. The reinvestment rate assumption used by the rating agencies for these calculations is conservative. It is 5 percent or 5½ percent per annum (depending on the agency) during the first year of the transaction, 4 percent per annum during the second year, and 3 percent per annum during the third year and every year thereafter. Any funds held for the benefit of the investor that are reinvested still must be readily available as cash on the day when the payment is due. In most instances, this means that any eligible investments must mature no later than the day before the relevant payment due date.

In some transactions the issuer may issue more bonds if reinvestment rates greater than those assumed by the rating agencies are assured. One way to do this is the guaranteed investment contract. Under such a contract, an independent entity such as a bank or an insurance company guarantees to pay some rate of interest on reinvestable funds. The guarantor must have a credit rating at least as high as that of the structured transaction.

Overcollateralization

Most mortgage-backed securities transactions involve overcollateralization to some degree. Overcollateralization means that the value of the assets or of the cash flow generated by the assets that support a transaction is greater than the value of the outstanding liability or of the cash flows that must be generated to honor the obligation. In using the word "collateralization," it is recognized that not all transactions use pledged collateral in the legal sense of the word. An investor in a pass-through, for example, has an ownership interest in the assets and hence collateral per se is not present. Similarly, there are preferred stock transactions where mortgage assets and their resulting cash are used to support preferred stock dividends and to redeem the stock, if necessary. The mortgage assets are not collateral in this case, either. In the rating context, overcollateralization refers to asset support in excess of that required by the terms of the liability itself.

Overcollateralization is expressed in terms of the percentage of par of the liability. Thus, asset coverage that is 1½ times as great as the liability is expressed as 150 percent overcollateralization, while coverage that is twice as great as required is 200 percent overcollateralization. The overcollateralization required for any transaction depends on the structure of the transaction as well as the credit quality of the issuer. Most taxable structured transactions done to date involve either an unrated or a low-rated issuer. These entities require a higher level of overcollateralization.

There are two ways to determine the overcollateralization: based on the current market value or on the cash flows generated by the assets and liabilities. Mortgage-backed bonds and "collateralized" preferred stock typically use a market value basis. Here, the presence of overcollateralization assures the ability to liquidate the assets in an amount sufficient to pay accrued interest (dividends) and to redeem the debt (pre-ferred stock) if the issuer becomes insolvent. Mortgage pay-throughs usually use a cash flow overcollateralization. Here the overcollateralization creates a reserve of cash sufficient to cover delinquencies, delays, and defaults.

Market Value Overcollateralization

There are five factors that determine the quantity of required overcollateralization when done on a market value basis: type of collateral, target rating, frequency of evaluation of the collat-eral, maximum cure period, and quality of the issuer. The best collateral to use for high ratings on a structured transaction are those that are themselves of high quality. These assets have liquid secondary markets should liquidation of the collat-eral become necessary. Not suprisingly, mortgage-backed se-curities and whole loans are used most often in structured transactions. In determining overcollateralization require-ments, distinctions are made among and between those two collateral classes. Mortgage-backed securities issued and/or guaranteed by government agencies usually are valued more highly than those issued by private companies because of the lower probability of delays and defaults. Also, the use of mort-gage-backed securities typically results in a lower overcol-lateralization requirement than whole loans. The reason is not credit quality so much as it is liquidity of secondary mar-kets. In most instances a mortgage-backed security can be sold at a favorable price more quickly than can a pool of whole loans.

The desired rating for a transaction also affects the amount of overcollateralization required. The higher the de-sired rating, the greater the amount of overcollateralization that is necessary. The overcollateralization requirement can be reduced by evaluating the collateral more frequently. Whenever collateral is valued, if the market value exceeds the required level, nothing more is done. If there is a deficiency, sufficient collateral must be added to bring the total market value back to the required level. In determining overcollaterali-zation standards, the rating agencies assume that interest rates

increase by some large amount (and therefore, the value of
the assets decreases by a large amount) between evaluation
dates. They then test to see if enough market value of assets
would remain in the pool at the end of the evaluation period
to redeem the outstanding liabilities.

The issuer is free to choose the length of time between
evaluation dates. The shorter this period, the less overcollateralization required. In computing the amount of collateral
needed, the maximum cure period is included. For example,
if collateral is marked to market monthly and an additional
30 days are allowed to cure any deficiencies that occur, then
a two month period is used in determining the overcollateralization level.

Issuers that are themselves of lower credit quality must
post higher levels of overcollateralization than high-quality
issuers. This is because for the former, there is a higher probability of becoming insolvent. If this happens, there is no one
available to provide additional collateral that might be needed.
It should be noted that the governing documents in these types
of transactions typically require the immediate liquidation of
collateral and concurrent redemption of all liabilities if the
issuer becomes insolvent.

Moody's and Standard & Poor's both publish extensive
tables of their overcollateralization standards under most variations of the important criteria. A few examples are provided
below. For a triple A rating Moody's requires 160, 180, and
200 percent for monthly, bi-monthly, and quarterly evaluations
respectively, when whole loans are used as the collateral. For
a double A rating the standards would be 155, 175 and 190
percent, respectively. The maximum cure period is assumed
to be 30 days. If GNMA certificates were used for a structured
transaction of a non-investment grade issuer, Standard &
Poor's would require 135 percent overcollateralization with
daily evaluation (1-day cure), 140 percent for weekly evaluation (2-day cure), 145 percent for monthly evaluation (2-day
cure), 150 percent for monthly evaluation (1-month cure), 155
percent for bi-monthly evaluation (1-month cure), and 160 percent for quarterly evaluation (1-month cure) for a triple A rat-

ing. The analogous six overcollateralization levels for a double A rating would be 130, 135, 138, 140, 145, and 150 percent. These examples are meant to be illustrative, not exhaustive. Differences in overcollateralization requirements exist for the 2 rating agencies. However, these differences are small and usually do not materially affect the final rating.

Cash Flow Overcollateralization. The basic concept behind a pay-through bond is to take monthly cash inflows from mortgage assets and to restructure them into cash outflows that more closely match investors' needs. Investors are willing to pay a premium for this customization of cash flows. The premium flows to the issuer in the form of reduced financing cost. The rating agencies are concerned that the requisite amounts of cash are available at each point in time over the life of the transaction. Merely having enough cash to retire the bonds at the final maturity is not sufficient. The cash flow overcollateralization concept is used in rating these securities. The rating agencies are not concerned with the market value of the collateral. Rather, it is with the cash flows generated by the mortgage pool that support the transaction and its rating.

Pool insurance often may be used interchangeably with cash flow overcollateralization. Regardless of which method is chosen to overcollateralize, the amount required is tied to the expected levels of delinquencies and defaults under a "worst case" scenario. The cash flow available in each time period must be sufficient to sustain this adverse situation and still meet all required payments to investors in a timely fashion.

Any mortgage pool will have mortgages with delays and defaults. Therefore, even the highest quality pools are required to overcollateralize to some degree. In most cases, 5 percent overcollateralization is the starting point for a triple A rating, while 4 percent is used for a double A. Additional overcollateralization may be required to the extent that the mortgages in the pool deviate from the basic and preferred characteristics. The characteristics are evaluated independently as well as within the context of the structure of the transaction. This allows interactive effects among the various characteristics to be included.

As an example, consider a pass-through certificate of an issuer desiring a double A rating. The certificates are collateralized by 30-year fixed-rate conventional mortgage loans that are well diversified geographically. The mortgages are new originations. Builder buydowns account for 5 percent of the loans. Half of the loans are from $200,000 to $300,000 in size. Half of these have loan-to-value ratios of less than 80 percent. Of the remaining loans which are under $200,000 in size, half have loan-to-value ratios in the 80 to 90 percent range. Since a double A rating is sought for the transaction, the overcollateralization analysis starts with the basic 4 percent requirement. Given the combination of unseasoned loans, builder buydowns, jumbo loans and loans with high loan-to-value ratios, additional overcollateralization of approximately 3 percent is likely to be required. Therefore, the final overcollateralization amount needed for a double A rating for this transaction is 7 percent.

A Special Case: Collateralized Deposits.   A spin-off from collateralized mortgage transactions are collateralized deposits. There are two general types of these: collateralized certificates of deposit and collateralized Eurodollar deposits (or bonds). Both of these result in special overcollateralization issues.

Collateralized certificates of deposit usually are issued domestically by institutions insured by the Federal Deposit Insurance Corporation (FDIC) or the Federal Savings and Loan Insurance Corporation (FSLIC). Each certificate holder's interest in the institution's deposits is insured up to the insurance limit (currently $100,000), less any deposits of that institution held by the certificate holder acting in the same legal capacity. The rating on these transactions pertains to the full amount of principal invested, the largest interest payment possible on the deposit and the allowance of an additional 30 days of interest resulting from possible delays in the payment of insurance coverage by the FDIC or FSLIC. This last factor often is called post-default interest. The rating agencies require disclosure to investors that the rating is based primarily on the deposit insurance coverage and that amounts held in excess of the applicable limits are not covered by the rating.

The overcollateralization calculation is performed by multiplying the per annum interest rate on the certificate of deposit times the outstanding principal amount and then dividing by the proportion of a year covered by the interest payment. Thirty days of interest then is added to this amount. This total figure divided by the outstanding principal amount yields the overcollateralization requirement expressed as a percentage of par. The coverage allows for the possibility that the institution issuing the certificates of deposit will become insolvent on the last day of the period when the interest payment is due and that in addition, the FDIC or FSLIC takes the full 30 days to honor investors' insurance claims.

Eurodollar bond transactions are overcollateralized in a similar manner. Eurodollars, of course, are issued overseas rather than domestically. Deposit insurance is not a factor here. Therefore, the original principal amount of the transaction must be collateralized by the mortgage assets or similar securities. Overcollateralization is required on the principal to the extent that adverse price movements of the collateral could affect the coverage. Also, the maximum interest payment amount is covered by overcollateralization as is interest over the maximum cure period after a mark-to-market evaluation is done. This latter factor is somewhat analogous to post-default interest for domestic collateralized certificates of deposit.

At the present time there are several regulatory and legal issues outstanding concerning collateralized Eurodollar transactions, especially U.S. withholding tax regulations for foreign investors. The successful resolution of these issues is expected. Most collateralized deposit transactions done to date have been rated triple A.

Cash Flow Coverage of Reinvestment Risk

An important part of the cash flow coverage of a structured transaction is for reinvestment risk. Reinvestment risk occurs

Chapter 19

when mortgage assets prepay and the proceeds must be reinvested for some period of time before being used to redeem bonds. In this instance, there is always the chance that the available reinvestment rates on eligible investments will be less than the bond rate. This can lead to an interest shortfall. It should be recognized that funds received upon mortgage foreclosures also may be subject to reinvestment risk.

The key considerations in evaluating reinvestment risk are the level of mortgage prepayments, the length of time exposure to reinvestment risk, the minimum assumed reinvestment rate, and the interest rate on the bond liability. If no mortgages prepay, there is no investment risk. At the other extreme, the potential for reinvestment risk is maximized when all of the mortgages prepay at the beginning of a given time period. Historically, the rating agencies have assumed this worst case. In other words, 100 percent of the mortgages outstanding in the pool at the beginning of a period are assumed to prepay at the beginning of that period. More recently, Moody's relaxed this standard somewhat after an extensive review of the prepayment experience of mortgage-backed securities. For transactions rated double A and lower, Moody's allows the assumption that 80 percent of the outstanding principal balance in a pool prepays at the beginning of the period.

An assumption of anything less than 100 percent prepayment creates the theoretical possibility that the realized prepayment experience exceeds the assumed. It must be realized, however, that the prepayment rate assumption is only one part of the protection. The timing of the prepayments, as well as the reinvestment rate available at that time, also determines whether sufficient protection is provided. A prepayment experience in excess of 80 percent could occur without creating an interest shortfall, as long as the time exposure to reinvestment risk and/or the reinvestment rate available are favorable. As discussed below, the assumptions regarding the time exposure and reinvestment rate are very conservative as well.

The rating agencies assume that all prepayments occur at the beginning of the time period. Thus, the time exposure to reinvestment risk is the maximum period in which a prepayment could be reinvested pending the redemption of a corresponding amount of bond liability. This period is determined by the interval between bond redemption dates. This interval is specified in the bond indenture or other documents governing the transaction. The actual time exposure to reinvestment risk is reduced the closer prepayments occur to the redemption cutoff date (the last day on which a prepayment could be received yet still used to redeem bonds on the next redemption date). For example, the actual time exposure is one half of the maximum period, if prepayments are evenly distributed over the time period.

The reinvestment rates allowed in quantifying reinvestment risk are the same as discussed previously for calculating reinvestment income on float. These rates are 5 percent per annum (Standard & Poor's allows 5½ percent per annum) during the first year of the transaction, 4 percent per annum the second year, and 3 percent for the third and all the subsequent years. These rates are quite low compared to recent experience. However, the rating agencies are understandably reluctant to forecast interest rates for transactions with final maturities of 30 years. Guaranteed insurance contracts of suitable credit quality are allowed to substitute for the reinvestment rate assumption. The credit quality of the guarantor would have to be monitored continuously.

The bond rate also is an important determinant of reinvestment risk. Higher bond rates increase the interest liability, leading to higher reinvestment risk. For CMOs and other multiple-class securities, the highest bond rate is used in computing reinvestment risk exposure.

Many structured transactions allow excess cash to be released to the issuer. The rating agencies also permit this. However, high reinvestment rates realized in the past cannot be used to subsidize future reinvestment rates. This means the issue must realize a reinvestment rate in *each* period that is at least equal to the assumed rate.

The reinvestment risk can be quantified as

$$RISK = (HBR-RR) \times TE \times BO \times PA$$

where

RISK = potential reinvestment risk loss,
HBR = highest bond rate (on a monthly basis),
 RR = assumed reinvestment rate (on a monthly basis),
 TE = time exposure to reinvestment risk (in months),
 BO = outstanding bond amount, and
 PA = assumed prepayment rate expressed as a decimal (e.g.,
        100% = 1.0, 80% = .8).

As an example, assume $100,000,000 of bonds outstanding at
13.5 percent per annum (1.125 percent per month). With an
assumed reinvestment rate in the third year of 3 percent (0.25
percent per month), a six month time exposure and a prepayment assumption of 80 percent, the potential reinvestment risk
of loss is [(1.125% − 0.25%) × 6 × $100,000,000 × .8] =
$4,200,000.00.
    There are several special considerations in calculating
the time exposure to reinvestment risk. Interest on whole loans
ceases to accrue on the date the mortgage prepays. With an
assumption that prepayments occur at the beginning of the
period, there is no interest accrual on prepayments. Therefore,
there is no need to adjust the maximum time exposure for
whole loans. For mortgage-backed securities, security holders
receive 30 days of interest on the previous month's security
balance regardless of the amount or timing of any prepayment.
This guarantee of a full 30-days' interest enables the assumed
time exposure to be reduced by one month from the total time
between interest payment periods. The terms of the bond indenture also may affect the calculation of interest on the bonds.
For example, many bonds have payments on the 25th of each
month, but interest payments are required only through the
end of the previous month on the bonds to be redeemed. In
this case, the assumed time exposure is reduced by the length
of a lag, 25 days in the example. Finally, internal reserve funds
may be created when there will be available one or more
extra monthly payments from the mortgage collateral to pay
any bond interest owed. Internal reserves are created by allowing the mortgage assets to generate cash inflows for one

or more months before the start of the first payment period on the mortgage-backed security.

In many of the early structured transactions, a reserve fund was created into which were put the funds required to cover the potential loss owing to reinvestment risk. These funds usually took the form of cash or a letter of credit issued by a guarantor of suitable credit quality. More recently, issuers have chosen to institute a special mandatory redemption feature that reduces the time exposure to reinvestment risk, while limiting the amount of cash coverage required. A typical special redemption feature calls for the bond trustee to determine each month whether the cash on hand from mortgage prepayments and reinvestment income are required to redeem bonds, so that collateral cash flow will be adequate to meet the debt service on the bonds. To make this determination, the trustee examines the bond value of the remaining mortgage collateral plus any investments on hand and calculates whether these are sufficient to support the outstanding bond balance if no redemptions are made. If they are, then nothing is done on this evaluation date. If the test fails, then available cash is used to redeem bonds in an amount sufficient to assure that the outstanding bond balance after the redemption can be supported by the remaining assets.

The special redemption test is performed every month, regardless of the length of time between interest payment periods called for in the bond indenture. This creates the possibility that special mandatory redemptions will occur between the scheduled bond payment dates. This reduces the call protection afforded to investors, but the cost of this feature to the issuer in most instances is less than that of providing cash up front or paying for a letter of credit. There are many variations of these calculations that have been used in transactions done to date. The most efficient of these recognize that minimum scheduled cash flows to be generated during the next month plus reinvestment income on these funds at the minimum assumed reinvestment rate can be given credit in determining the amount of cash that will be on hand to support the bond liability. This serves to increase the reinvestment risk coverage and reduce the probability that a special redemption will be required.

Other Insurance

There are several other types of insurance typically required in the rating of mortgage-backed securities transactions. One of these is regular hazard insurance. This is the standard fire and theft protection that is part of homeowners' insurance policies. It is required by lenders at the time the original mortgage loan is closed, so it is not a rating agency concern. Another is federal flood insurance. Certain locales have been designated as high risk flood damage areas. Homeowners living in these areas are eligible for federal flood insurance. Any mortgage on a property in one of these areas is required to carry federal flood insurance prior to being placed into a mortgage collateral pool. Therefore, except for the requirement that this insurance be in force, flood insurance is not a rating agency concern.

Special hazard insurance is required on a pool to protect against losses due to certain acts of nature such as earthquakes and mudslides. Historically, claims against this kind of coverage have been virtually non-existent. Yet, it is required as a worst case protection in the event that a loss is incurred for one of these reasons and other forms of coverage have been exhausted previously. The coverage requirement is straightforward, being equal to the greater of 1 percent of the dollar amount of principal in the pool or two times the largest loan in the pool.

Bankruptcy bond coverage or Chapter 13 coverage as it is often called, has gained increased attention in recent years. This coverage is designed to cover the situation when an individual files for personal bankruptcy and goes before a bankruptcy court which then has the power to renegotiate the outstanding mortgage debt. To protect against losses to investors from this occurrence, the rating agencies require Chapter 13 coverage in an amount equal to the greater of 1 percent of the outstanding principal balance of the pool or the largest loan. Upward adjustments sometimes are made for pools of mortgages that include relatively large proportions of mortgages secured by investor, vacation, or multi-family properties. The percentages of required coverage may be revised downward, if the insurance policy is replenished each year.

Other types of insurance policies such as errors and omissions policies, fidelity bonds, and surety bonds sometimes are needed to provide the incremental support to achieve the desired rating. In effect, these policies guarantee the performance of the issuer, servicer, or third party obligor that might be involved in a structured transaction. Usually they are required only when the particular party is small or relatively inexperienced. These policies should be unconditional, noncancellable and written with appropriate mechanisms in place to assure timely payment.

One additional incremental coverage feature is cash advance coverage. Although not an insurance policy, it functions similarly. To achieve a desired rating level, some issuers must post cash for the next required interest payment sometime in advance of the interest payment date. The calculation of the cash advance requirement involves an assessment of the additional foreclosure and delinquency loss exposure.

INFRASTRUCTURE

The quality of the mortgage assets and the additional support elements that protect against losses are critical parts of the rating determination. Even if the quality of these factors is known, the rating cannot be assigned without an analysis of the infrastructure of the transaction. The infrastructure elements support the transaction, but unlike those discussed previously are somewhat more qualitative in nature. The five components covered are the issuer, the servicer, the trustee, the mortgage documents, and the audit process.

The Issuer

Most mortgage-backed securities transactions are structured so the creditworthiness of the issuer does not adversely affect the rating. In fact, a high-quality issuer could well enhance the rating of a structured transaction. Most issuers, even those that are unrated or don't qualify for high ratings, can obtain the highest ratings for mortgage-backed securities issues. Still, the rating agencies are not totally indifferent with respect to the creditworthiness of the issuer. Often the agencies desire a reasonable level of confidence that the financial condition of the issuer indicates the issuer is likely to remain viable for the life of the proposed transaction. This is true even though the governing documents of most structured transactions make provisions for the continuation of the transaction in the event of issuer insolvency.

In evaluating the viability of the issuer, the factors analyzed include: the implementation of underwriting standards that assure the ability to originate high-quality mortgages; the issuer's track record in originating and servicing similar mortgages; the issuer's financial condition; the ability to advance cash or substitute additional mortgage collateral if necessary; and the relationship of the issuer to other affiliates or a parent corporation, if relevant.

Issuers subject to the bankruptcy code should be limited to single-purpose subsidiaries unless the unsecured debt rating of the issuer is at least as high as that desired for the subject transaction. This is because in a bankruptcy proceeding the court could disrupt the cash flows generated by the collateral pool and thus prevent payments to investors in the contractually agreed upon manner.

The use of a wholly owned, single-purpose subsidiary to administer the collateral pool and issue securities represents an attempt to make the actual issuer insolvency-resistant. Although no entity is completely insolvency-proof, the rating agencies examine these subsidiaries to determine whether everything has been done to minimize the likelihood of insolvency. Some criteria have emerged from case law that the rating agencies have adopted as guidelines for insolvency-resistant subsidiaries. The legal documents creating the issuer, such as articles of incorporation or by-laws, should clearly state that the issuer is a single-purpose corporation. The issuer should be capitalized or have the ability to generate sufficient funds from operations to pay any fees, taxes or transactions costs. The issuer should be prohibited from incurring additional debt that is not subordinated to the rated transaction and the filing of a voluntary petition of insolvency should not be permitted. Existing creditors, including the issuer's parent, should agree in writing not to petition the issuer into bankruptcy.

In addition to minimizing the possibility of the issuer's insolvency, steps should be taken to minimize the possibility of a substantive consolidation of the issuer with the parent in the event of the latter's insolvency. Substantive consolidation would result in a court's consolidating the assets and liabilities of the issuer with those of the parent. Establishing a legitimate business purpose for the issuer and maintaining the separation of boards of directors, assets, business records, and operating premises reduce the likelihood that a substantive consolidation could occur.

Single-purpose subsidiaries may not be needed in instances where the issuer's insolvency would not come under the bankruptcy code. For example, federally insured institutions such as banks and thrifts could issue the bonds directly. Not being subject to the bankruptcy code, their insolvency should not prevent performance as contracted under the bond indenture. In the event of an insolvency, the FDIC or FSLIC would be appointed receiver. The insurance funds should allow the bond trustee to continue to perform as before. There could be an acceleration of the issuer's obligation, but investors should not be penalized.

Although many insured financial institutions can issue securities directly, many still choose to employ a special purpose subsidiary. This reduces the likelihood of a delay if there should be an insolvency. The federal insurance agencies have indicated that documents governing the transaction should preserve agencies' flexibility to operate in the event of insolvency of the parent. This means that an acceleration of the liability should not be required. Rather, the agency should have the option to accelerate or to allow the liability to continue to perform. The insurance agencies have indicated that the collateral would not be liquidated in a situation where its market value was less than the amount of the debt outstanding. In this case, the liability would resemble a legally defeased bond. Legally, there would be no debtor and bondholders would have an interest only in the collateral.

The possibility of acceleration in the event of the insolvency of an insured institution should be clearly disclosed to investors. This is because the creditworthiness of the issuer or its parent impacts the call protection inherent in the investment, even though the investment itself is not materially at risk. Also, it should be noted that some residual uncertainty remains when the issuer of structured securities is an insured financial institution. In the first place, FDIC and FSLIC differ in certain technical areas in terms of their likely responses in the event of an insolvency. More importantly, there have been no test cases to assess their actual behavior against what they have indicated to be likely. Certainly no one is anxious to witness an insolvency that would serve as a test case, but there is always the possibility that practice would differ from theory.

The Servicer

The quality of the servicer is an important support element for structured transactions. The basic function of this servicing is to assure that there are no delays in the ultimate movement of funds to investors.

The issuer or one of its affiliates often acts as the servicer. The servicer need not obtain a long-term debt rating from one of the rating agencies. However, the creditworthiness of the issuer is important because of the three main functional concerns that involve the servicer in the rating process. The first, and most often cited, is the servicer's cash advance capability. Payment delays owing to mortgagor delinquencies, defaults, or unavoidable obstructions in transmitting funds usually result in a requirement that these funds be advanced to the trustee by the servicer. This is true at least to the extent that the funds ultimately are recoverable from mortgage insurance policies. In some transactions, servicers are required to advance funds regardless of whether or not they are ultimately recoverable. Even if there is mortgage insurance coverage, mortgage insurance companies pay claims only when the title to the property is transferred. Often this process can take several months or longer. Under any or all of these circumstances, it is the servicer's cash advance capability that assures the timely payment to investors. Cash reserves or a surety policy can supplement or substitute for the servicer's cash advance capability. Regardless of the mechanism employed, sufficient funds ultimately must be available to cover loans that will eventually foreclose as well as those that are merely temporarily delinquent.

The second functional concern is over segregation of cash. The trustee, who administers funds for the benefit of the investors, has control of the cash generated by the mortgage assets only when in physical possession of the funds. Even though money handled by the servicer does not belong to it, if the servicer becomes insolvent after accumulating funds but before they have been transferred to the trustee, costly delays or losses may be realized by investors. The implication of this is that servicers should be required to remit to the trustee all cash received (less the servicing fee) immediately upon receipt. In situations where funds are not transferred as received, the servicer should be required to keep mortgagor payments physically separate from the general operating funds. This money should be protected against losses in the event of insolvency of the institution into which they are deposited. Deposit accounts with highly rated depositaries or trust or investment arrangements limiting the funds to eligible investments are acceptable ways of meeting this requirement.

The third concern is with the servicer's compensation and overall profitability of its operations. The servicer should be paid a fee that is sufficient to provide the necessary incentives to assure the timely performance of its duties. Adequate compensation also makes it easier to hire a replacement servicer if this becomes necessary. The overall profitability of the servicer's operation provides assurances that the servicer will remain solvent during the life of the transaction.

The Trustee

The basic function of the trustee is to carry out provisions of the governing documents of the transaction and to act as a fiduciary that protects the interests of the investors. In this role the trustee holds mortgage documents, monitors and controls the flow of cash, inspects mortgage documents, and acts as back-up servicer.

The rating agencies carefully review all documents that control the rights and responsibilities of the trustee. The experience and expertise of the trustee and of its staff are prime considerations in evaluating acceptability. Since the trustee controls the cash, restrictions on accounts and eligible investments that control the trustee's behavior are imposed.

The trustee's compensation should be adequate to stimulate compliance with all duties and responsibilities and to assure the ability to find a replacement if this becomes necessary. Trustees often require that their compensation be granted a lien on the mortgage assets or on the cash flows generated. If this is done, the lien should be subordinate to that of the investors.

Mortgage Documents

Often there are twenty or more documents involved when whole loans are used to collateralize a structured transaction. Documentation is extensive even if mortgage-backed securities are used. As mentioned above, all mortgage documents should be physically held by the trustee. The assignment of these mortgage documents to the trustee should be recorded. The original mortgage loans themselves also should be recorded. If this is impractical, then the loans should be held in recordable form and an unqualified legal opinion so stating should be obtained.

The loan documentation procedure is more complex when

a participation sale is involved. Under a participation, the originator sells most of its interest in the loan, while retaining a portion for itself. In most cases, the participation interest sold is 90 percent or greater. It is possible either for the participation interest sold or the retained portion to be used as collateral in a mortgage-backed transaction. A thorough legal review is required to ascertain that investors' interests are fully protected. This means that the investors must have a valid, perfected first security interest in the collateral property.

Of particular importance in the mortgage documents are the representations and warranties. These explicitly state all information pertaining to the mortgage loans and promise that this information is true and correct. Compliance with all laws and regulations and the ability and authority of all parties to perform any duties promised also are guaranteed. Provisions for corrective action in the event that any defect in any loan is found subsequent to closing are made. Extensive legal review obviously is required for rating agency acceptance of the representations and warranties.

The Audit Process

Mortgage-backed securities always have been complex transactions. If anything, the complexity seems to be increasing. This creates the need for a significant amount of accounting and cash flow verification. Auditing is required both at closing and over the life of the transaction.

Typically, the governing documents stipulate that the issuer must submit reports to the trustee on a regular basis. These reports include information on the status of the collateral, cash inflows and outflows, and the performance of complex tests such as those which determine whether excess cash exists that may be released to the issuer and whether bonds must be redeemed. In some cases, the trustee is required to prepare reports as well. Independent accountant verification of the adequacy of the collateral and its cash flow is a precondition for closing the transaction. Issuer and trustee reports performed subsequent to closing must be audited as well. Some of the verification may rely on raw data provided by the issuer such as maturity, interest rate, and principal balance on the mortgages. The balance of the audit requires detailed analysis and calculations made directly by independent accountants. The accuracy of any computer programs used to process the data should be tested. The frequency and scope of the audit process is determined by the actual structure of each issue.

VALUATION OF THE COLLATERAL

Once the credit risk of underlying securities and incremental support elements have been evaluated and the infrastructure of the proposed transaction has been analyzed, the actual evaluation of collateral must be performed. In general, there are two ways to do this: the aggregate cash flow method and the bond value method. These two approaches are discussed in this section as are some special considerations that impact the final evaluation.

Aggregate Cash Flow Method

Under the aggregate cash flow approach, the aggregate scheduled cash flow of the collateral pool must be sufficient to meet the bond debt service in each period over the life of the instrument. Only scheduled cash flow from the mortgage collateral may be used. There can be no reliance on any mortgage prepayments for required payments on the debt. In calculating the cash flows available for debt service, only net cash flows are allowed. In other words, servicing fees and other nonsubordinated or uncovered expenses are deducted.

A special concern is to eliminate the subsidy effect of premium interest income. Premium interest income is interest received on mortgage collateral having an interest rate higher than the lowest bond rate in the transaction. Although premium interest income can be used to support bond debt service if there are no prepayments, this is not the case if any mortgage having a higher interest rate prepays at any time during the life of the transaction. The interest cash flow from high coupon mortgages subsidizes the issuance of more bonds than actually can be supported if prepayments occur. Since the rating agencies cannot assume that prepayments will not occur, this subsidy must be eliminated.

A simple example demonstrates the subsidy effect. Assume a collateral pool of $100,000,000 of 30-year, level-pay fixed-rate mortgages with no servicing fee. Half of these mortgages bear coupons of 15 percent and the other half 10 percent. Assume further that these mortgages are used to issue $100,000,000 of 30-year fully-amortizing, monthly-pay bonds bearing an interest rate of 12 percent per annum. With no prepayments, the monthly collateral cash flow generated by the mortgages is $1.071 million, which is equal to the amount needed for the monthly bond debt service. However, if the 15 percent mortgages all prepay just after closing, the $50,000,000 original principal amount of 10 percent mortgages generate only $438,600 in the first month. This amount is insufficient even to service the interest obligation on the corresponding $50,000,000 of 12 percent debt, which comes to over $520,000.

There are three possible solutions to the subsidiary problem: all collateral must have interest rates higher than the highest bond rate, all collateral must bear interest rates lower than the lowest bond rate, or the positive spread on high rate collateral must be excluded when computing available cash flows to support bond debt service. The third solution must be chosen if the collateral has mixed interest rates.

There are two special situations that can occur when the aggregate cash flow approach is used. The first is that excess cash flow can be generated when mortgage prepayments occur. Excess cash flow is defined as cash flow received in a given bond debt service period that is not needed to support the bond. Since excess cash flows are not required to support the bonds, they can be released to the issuer. An aggregate cash flow report must be provided to the trustee that verifies excess cash flow calculations before the funds may be released to the issuer. The second special situation is ability to substitute collateral after the transaction has closed. Often issuers desire to preserve the right to substitute for collateral placed in the pool originally. This is allowed if an aggregate cash flow report is produced that verifies that substituted collateral generates at least as much cash flow for each period over the life of the transaction as the collateral being replaced.

Bond Value Method

Under the bond value approach an individual bond value is calculated for each mortgage in the collateral pool. The individual bond value equals the amount of bonds supported by the scheduled cash flow of that mortgage. By summing the individual bond values for all of the mortgage assets, the total amount of bonds that can be issued is determined. Any individual bond value cannot exceed the unpaid mortgage balance. This is often referred to as the "par cap." If the par cap were violated, the bond value that exceeds the mortgage balance would be lost when the mortgage prepaid. The total bonds outstanding then might not be supportable by the remaining mortgage collateral. This is an event of default that is not permitted for high-grade ratings. There are three general ways to compute bond value: the coupon-to-coupon method, the modified coupon-to-coupon method, and the present value method.

Coupon-to-Coupon Method

The coupon-to-coupon method sometimes is referred to as the inverse coupon method. Under this procedure, the bond value of each mortgage asset is defined as the mortgage coupon net of the servicing fee divided by the highest bond rate times the unpaid mortgage balance, or

$$BV_{it} = \frac{I_i - SF_i}{HBR} \times OB_{it}$$

where

BV_{it} = the bond value of the ith mortgage at the beginning of period t;

I_i = the interest rate on the ith mortgage;

SF_i = the servicing fee on the ith mortgage;

HBR = the highest bond coupon rate; and

OB_{it} = the outstanding mortgage balance for the ith mortgage at the beginning of period t.

In applying this formula, the individual bond value cannot be greater than the unpaid mortgage balance.

Using this procedure, interest payments on the mortgages are sufficient by themselves to cover bond interest payments on a period-to-period basis. In addition, the payments of mortgage principal in each period are always adequate to repay the bonds in full as long as all mortgages mature on or before the bond maturity and there are no required sinking fund payments. If either of these two conditions are violated, mortgage principal scheduled to be paid after the bond maturity or the amount of the scheduled sinking fund payment are ignored in performing the bond value calculation. In other words, the additional mortgage principal must be provided so that the bond value relationship is fulfilled without reliance on the additional principal required to fulfill these special conditions.

As an example of the bond value calculation, assume a $100,000 fixed-rate, level-payment, 30-year mortgage at 12.5 percent with a 50 basis point servicing fee. This mortgage is to support a 14 percent, 30-year bond. Then

$$\text{Bond Value} = \frac{(12.5\% - 0.5\%)}{14\%} \times \$100,000 = \$85,714.28.$$

The bond value calculations must be updated on each interest payment date in order to determine whether the remaining mortgage collateral will support the current bond amount outstanding. If not, bonds must be redeemed out of cash on hand at least until the point when the bond value of the mortgages is no smaller than the outstanding bond balance. More bonds, but not less, than required may be redeemed.

Modified Coupon-to-Coupon Method

The modified coupon-to-coupon method recognizes explicitly that, at a minimum, scheduled mortgage principal will be paid during each payment period and this principal will be available to support bonds. The result is some additional computational complexity in exchange for a more efficient transaction in that more bonds can be issued originally than under the "unmodified" coupon-to-coupon method. In the formula defined previously, the first term on the right hand side of the equation that defines the relationship between the net mortgage coupon and the highest bond coupon is adjusted by a factor that recognizes this minimum monthly scheduled principal. The new formula is:

$$BV_{it} = \frac{[\frac{1}{12} \times (I_i - SF_i)] + F_{im}}{(\frac{1}{12} \times HBR) + F_{im}} \times OB_{it}$$

where

F_{im} = the factor for the ith mortgage in first month of the current payment period = the smallest monthly scheduled principal payment on the mortgage during the payment period as a percentage of the mortgage balance at the beginning of the month.

All other terms are as defined previously. As before, bond value is constrained to be less than or equal to the unpaid mortgage balance.

This procedure uses some mortgage principal to pay bond interest. The minimum amount of principal payment owed the bondholders is the bond value percentage (defined as the bond value divided by the unpaid mortgage balance) times the mortgage principal payments received. Therefore, the largest amount of mortgage principal ever used to pay bond interest is the product of the mortgage principal payments received and the difference between 100 percent and the bond value percentage. As in the coupon-to-coupon method, full repayment of the bonds out of mortgage principal always is assured as long as all mortgages mature on or before the bond maturity and there are no scheduled sinking fund payments. If these latter conditions do not hold, the same corrective measures as described in the coupon-to-coupon method are applied.

An example of this procedure is shown below. All values are identical to the previous ones, but now the factor representing the smallest monthly scheduled principal payment is included.

$$\text{Bond Value} = \frac{[\frac{1}{12} \times (12.5\% - 0.5\%)] + .0256\%}{(\frac{1}{12} \times 14\%) + .0256\%} \times \$100,000$$
$$= \$86,021.02$$

Using the modified coupon-to-coupon method, $306.74 more bonds can be issued.

Present Value Method

Under the present value method, the bond value of an individual mortgage is defined as the present value of that mortgage's scheduled cash flow, net of its servicing fee, and discounted at the highest bond rate over the greater of (A) the life of the bonds or (B) the life of the mortgage. As always, the bond value of an individual mortgage cannot exceed the unpaid mortgage balance. The cash flows used to determine the present value only are those that come directly from the mortgages. In other words, no reinvestment income is assumed. This definition can be expressed as the following formula.

$$BV_{it} = \sum_{t=1}^{m} \frac{SCF_{it}}{(1 + HBR)^t}$$

where

SCF_{it} = the scheduled cash flows from mortgage i in month t,

m = the greater of the life of the bonds or of the mortgage.

All other terms are as before.

Using the same numerical values as in the previous example, the bond value calculation under the present value method leads to the issuance of $86,764.92 of bonds. It should be noted that the present value method can be used for CMOs only if all of the mortgage cash flows are discounted at the highest bond rate.

Special Considerations

There are several special situations that must be recognized in performing bond value calculations. One of these is the need to project scheduled cash flows over the entire life of the transaction. This must be done under the modified coupon-to-coupon and present value methods. Not only the total monthly payments, but also the distribution between scheduled principal and interest for each monthly payment is required. When mortgage-backed securities such as GNMAs, FHLMC PCs, and FNMA MBSs are used as collateral, sufficient information about each underlying mortgage loan is not always available. This is because the final maturity of the mortgage-backed security is the longest maturity of any mortgage in the pool. This is not the same as final maturity for *each* mortgage in the pool, since not all mortgages represent new originations. In addition, for all but the GNMA I program, the exact mortgage coupon on each individual mortgage is not known. Under the GNMA II program, the highest mortgage coupon, after the 50 basis point servicing fee is netted out, may be up to 100 basis points above the security rate. For regular FHLMC PCs and FNMA MBSs, the net coupon on the mortgage with highest interest rate may be up to 200 basis points above the security rate.

With the final maturities and possibly interest rates of the underlying mortgages uncertain, scheduled cash flows can only be estimated. In making these estimates, the rating agencies have chosen the most conservative method, whereby the estimated cash flow can be no greater than the securities' actual cash flow. This is done by calculating the amount of cash flow needed to amortize fully the outstanding principal balance of the security on a level-pay basis through its final maturity date. The smallest amount of principal that could be received also is assumed. Using the maximum possible interest rate on any mortgage-backed security to determine the amortization schedule assures the minimum scheduled principal payment.

A second special consideration is the frequency of compounding used in calculating the discounted cash flow from the mortgages. This is relevant only in the present value method. The rating agencies usually assume that frequency of the bond payments should be equal to compounding frequency for present value calculations. This means that if bond payments are made semi-annually, the scheduled collateral cash flows should be discounted over their remaining lives on a semi-annual basis. The presumption is that the compounding frequency should reflect the frequency with which the collateral cash flows are being used to redeem bonds or the maximum maturity of reinvestment of the float from mortgage collateral. This is a conservative assumption because the collateral cash flows are usually never invested beyond the next bond payment date.

Assume a $100,000,000 30-year FRM at 12 percent with no servicing. The monthly payment on this mortgage is $1,067.26. With a 15 percent discount rate, the bond value of the mortgage if discounted monthly is $84,405.30. However, the bond value if discounted semi-annually (6 payments of $1,067.26 each over sixty periods at half of 15 percent) is $84,266.71, a difference of $131.59.

Another important point is that in computing the initial bond value under the present value method, explicit credit can be given to reinvestment income derived from the scheduled cash flow received between bond payment dates. The period over which this reinvestment income is earned varies depending on the structure of the transaction and the type of mortgage collateral used. This interest income allows an increase in the amount of bonds that can be issued over that which would be possible if the income was ignored.

Partial mortgage prepayments can cause problems when the present value method is used to calculate bond value and the bonds are level-pay and fully amortizing with the issuer withdrawing excess scheduled collateral cash flow. In certain situations the partial prepayment can cause the underlying mortgage to mature before its associated bond value. This can happen because the standard industry practice in the event of a partial prepayment is to keep the monthly mortgage payment fixed and instead, shorten maturity of the mortgage. With no modification of the typical bond structure, the dollars obtained from partial prepayment would be used to redeem bonds, the monthly bond payments would remain the same, but the remaining life of the prepaid mortgage used to compute the bond value would be shortened. When the mortgage coupon (on a bond equivalent basis) exceeds the bond rate, partial prepayment causes the mortgage to amortize faster than its bond value over the remaining life. Therefore, some of the bond value will remain outstanding after the mortgage loan associated with it has been fully repaid.

The rating agencies have suggested a modification of the bond structure to prevent a partial prepayment from creating an event of default in this situation. First, a minimum prepayment value is computed. This value is the amount of bond value that must be redeemed in order for the remaining cash flow of the mortgage that is partially prepaid to be sufficient to support its remaining bond value. If a partial prepayment occurs, then the minimum prepayment value is compared to the amount of partial prepayment to determine which is greater. This is the amount to be redeemed from the bond value associated with the partially prepaid mortgage balance. It prevents the mortgage from maturing before its bond value.

The minimum prepayment value exceeds the amount of the partial prepayment when the mortgage coupon is greater than the bond rate. There may be insufficient money available to fund this difference when the partial prepayment occurs. Therefore, the bond indenture should be modified to enable this difference to be amortized over time from cash flows to be received in later periods. The portion of the unamortized minimum prepayment value continues to accrue interest at the bond rate until it is fully repaid. With this modification, over time there always will be sufficient money available to fund the minimum prepayment value.

LEGAL AND REGULATORY ISSUES

The credit and structural elements for mortgage-backed securities are very complex. In addition, there are several legal concerns addressed by the rating agencies before the final rating is determined. The ones discussed below are those that arise most often in rating mortgage-backed securities. Many others can occur for specific transactions. Some of the issues discussed are well resolved, while others are in a state of flux. Any legal or regulatory matter can change owing to new court decisions, legislation, or administrative actions.

Perfected Security Interest

In most structured transactions, mortgage securities and/or other fixed-income securities are pledged as collateral to support the issue. One of the first things the ratings agencies address is whether the trustee has a valid, perfected, first security interest in that collateral as well as any additional collateral that may be added to the pool. For this to occur, assurances must be given that the issuer has good and marketable title to the collateral that is pledged. The rating agencies prefer the trustee to have physical possession of the collateral to support further the trustee's valid, perfected, and first security interest.

The Bankruptcy Code

There are two aspects of the bankruptcy code that are of particular interest to the rating agencies. One is the possibility that the bankruptcy of an issuer can cause delays in payments to creditors. In some instances the code imposes an automatic stay upon the filing of the bankruptcy petition. This can prevent creditors from obtaining possession of the collateral that was pledged to support obligations to them. The rating agencies believe that an indenture trustee should be able to petition the bankruptcy court and get the stay lifted in a very short period of time. The basis for this belief is a principal of law that grants relief from the automatic stay because of lack of "adequate protection." This has been interpreted in the courts to mean that secured creditors are not adequately protected unless they can either liquidate the collateral or continue to receive the cash flows generated by the collateral. Once the stay is lifted, the indenture trustee would have the ability to use the collateral for the interests of the security holders.

Preferential transfers are another concern that can arise in bankruptcy. The bankruptcy code provides for situations when a bankruptcy trustee can recover transfers of property which occurred shortly before the filing of the petition of bankruptcy. Such recoveries are possible if they were made within 90 days of the filing of the bankruptcy petition, if they allow the creditor to receive more than would have occurred in liquidation and if they were made as a result of a preexisting debt.

In situations where the rating agencies believe that a preference problem can arise owing to the bankruptcy of the issuer, additional collateral sufficient to cover the preference period often is required. When federal law governs, the preference period is 90 days. Therefore, collateral sufficient to cover any contractual obligations must be available for 90 days longer than the period contemplated in the bond indenture. When state law governs, the preference period applicable under the laws of that state are applied.

The Role of Legal Opinions

The rating agencies have employed legal experts to assist in the formulation of many of their policies concerning legal and regulatory matters. For most transactions, legal opinions from issuer's counsel are strongly recommended or required in order to obtain a high grade rating. Unqualified legal opinions asserting the existence of a valid, perfected first security interest in the collateral are given for most transactions. Similar opinions concerning the existence of good and marketable title, that all governing documents and agreements are legal, valid, binding and enforceable, and that all relevant parties are legally empowered to perform their duties as contracted often are incorporated into the structure as well. Some transactions require legal opinions on the legal jurisdictions that would be involved in the event of bankruptcy and on whether a preference problem can arise. The rating agencies prefer that these unqualified legal opinions be provided by nationally recognized experts in their fields and that they either be addressed to the rating agency or state that the rating agency may rely on the opinions.

Taxes and Financial Reporting

Taxes often are a concern to investors in and issuers of mortgage-backed securities. Among the tax issues that arise are the tax treatment of original issue discount bonds (OIDs) and deferred compound interest bonds (DCIBs), whether cash flow payments to investors are considered taxable or tax-exempt, and withholding taxes applied against securities purchased by foreign investors. In most cases, these tax issues are not rating agency concerns, except to the extent that the agencies require adequate disclosure to investors in the governing documents.

However, one tax issue that directly concerns the rating agencies is the treatment of discounted mortgage collateral in the event of an insolvency of the issuer. In many instances, the insolvency may require the immediate liquidation of mortgage collateral. If this occurs, the governing documents should call for payments to investors from such originally discounted collateral only at their accrued market value to the date of insolvency, not at the par or maturity value of the collateral. This becomes particularly relevant for multiclass securities such as CMOs that have accrual or "zero coupon" bonds. Since these bonds do not pay interest during their lives but rather, accrue interest over time, they are placed into multiclass securities at discounts. If the issuer becomes insolvent and payments to investors at par were required, insufficient funds would be available to pay all of the bondholders, due to the discrepancy between the par value and current market value of the accrual bonds. Full payment to the holders of accrual bonds would result in a wealth transfer to them at the expense of the holders of the zero coupon bonds. Therefore, payments are made only to the extent of the accrued value of the bonds to the date of the insolvency.

A second important tax issue is whether CMOs and certain other structured transactions ought to be considered a financing or a sale of assets for tax purposes and for financial statements. Originally, many virtually identical transactions were treated as debt by some issuers and as asset sales by others. In fact, some issuers accounted for their securities as sales for financial statements and financings for tax purposes. This led to much controversy within the industry. At present, the Financial Accountings Standards Board (FASB) has recommended that CMO-like issues be presumed to be debt financings unless the issuer (and its accountants) can prove otherwise. FASB and the rest of the industry continue to analyze this situation, however.

Another controversial issue is the use of the multi-class structure in the form of a grantor trust. This was done by the Sears Mortgage Securities Corporation in a $500,000,000 CMO issue early in 1984. This CMO was sold as a grantor trust on the basis of an unqualified legal opinion by issuer's counsel. Previously, it was assumed that the Treasury Department would treat this structure as a taxable association. This would have made the transaction economically infeasible. The first deal was closed and sold, however, when Sears Mortgage attempted to close a second transaction, the Treasury Department intervened. This effectively ended, for the time being, the ability to issue a multiclass pass-through security with taxes owed only by investors and not by the trust as well. A revision of the tax code and/or a change of heart by the Treasury Department would be required for this structure to become viable again.

Mortgagor Insolvency

The insolvency or bankruptcy of individual mortgagors recently has become an issue. Preference and adjustment of the debt are the basic concerns. If high-quality underwriting standards are used by the originator, then a successful preference claim should not be possible since the fair market value of the mortgaged property should never be less than the amount of the mortgage debt. This removes the necessary criterion (for a successful preference claim) that investors in the mortgage-backed security received more than they would have received in liquidation.

The adjustment of the debt is not so easy to dismiss, however. Chapter 13 of the bankruptcy code allows debtors, subject to court approval, to renegotiate their debts. This can adversely affect the position of secured creditors. Modified repayment schedules may be called for on mortgages securing second homes as well as on principle residences. Bankruptcy bonds usually are employed to cover this situation. The bond covers an amount equal to the difference between the court's valuation of the property and the outstanding amount of the debt. Protection against a reduction in the contractual rate of interest also is provided. This coverage is required only when conventional whole loans are used as collateral, since government or agency guaranteed mortgage-backed securities provide payment guarantees to holders under all circumstances.

State Real Property Law

The real property laws of all relevant states must be analyzed in the rating process. Some states have restrictive foreclosure laws that may impair the ability of various parties within a structured transaction to perform in accordance with their contracts. State anti-deficiency laws also limit creditors' recourse to mortgaged property. Mortgage pools containing loans from problem states typically require additional collateral or other forms of support if high-grade ratings are to be obtained. A detailed legal analysis is part of this evaluation process.

CONCLUSION

Mortgage-backed securities are very complex as is the rating of them. Many analytical, structural and legal issues are examined at length before the rating agencies determine rating for each transaction. In addition to these issues, the interrelationships among the variables affecting the credit quality of the support elements are evaluated. In spite of these complexities, a rating process has emerged that is consistent with existing ones for long-term unsecured debt and preferred stock. In most instances, mortgage-backed securities transactions qualify for high ratings. (See Appendix A for ratings and descriptions of several recent transactions.) Structures containing significant weaknesses have not received lower ratings; rather, they have not been rated at all.

The frameworks used by the rating agencies originally were based on taxable structures involving single-family, residential mortgage loans. These frameworks now are being extended to include multifamily loans, commercial real estate, tax-exempt securities and other structures that may not involve mortgage collateral at all. Short-term securities such as collateralized commercial paper have extended the rating process in other directions. Each new structure involves its own peculiarities. Still, the analytical framework discussed in this chapter based on an evaluation of the underlying assets, the quality of incremental support, structural concerns and legal protections is at the heart of the analysis and ultimately, of the ratings.

The turbulent economic conditions experienced over the last decade have affected the issue and rating of all fixed-income securities. However, mortgage-backed securities and other structured transactions have been affected less by the high volatility of interest rates, deregulation and increased global interdependence than other rated securities. This is because securitized, structured transactions possess a greater degree of flexibility. Adverse economic occurrences in one area lead to new product developments in others. The provision of additional support often can cover a potential weakness and cause a security to qualify for a higher rating. A by-product of this is that the declining credit quality that has afflicted fixed-income securities generally has not been a problem for structured transactions. However, financial markets dislike uncertainty. The perception of inadequate call protection, the proliferation of alternative mortgage instruments and

questionable underwriting practices on the part of a few originators have caused some investors and potential issuers to
shy away from this market. Yet, if the future of mortgage-
backed securities in any way resembles its past, new products
and structures are likely to be developed that will bring many
of these players into the market while maintaining the highest
ratings.

APPENDIX A
A Sample of Rated Mortgage-Backed Security Transactions

Issuer	Issue Date	Rating	Type	Collateralized Mortgage Obligations Collateral						Class	Bonds			
				Mortgages as a Percentage of Bonds Issued	Percentage of GPMs	Range of Coupons	Weighted Average Coupon	Remaining Terms	Excess Cash Flow		Amount (000s)	Coupon	Stated Maturity (Years)	Expected Average Life (Years)
Prudential Realty Securities II, Series A	Jan. 1984	Aaa Moody's AAA S & P	Conventional & FHA/VA whole loans	135%	0%	4.50–8.00%	5.77%	24–276 months	Returned to Issuer	A-1 A-2 A-3	$126,000 120,500 25,000 $271,500	11.000% 12.000 11.750	5.0 10.0 12.0	2.9 7.6 12.0
Norwest Conventional I	Feb. 1984	Aa2 Moody's AA S & P	Conventional whole loans	101	0	12.50–17.38%	13.71	Weighted average term in excess of 28 years.	Returned to Issuer	A B C Z	$ 55,000 105,000 157,200 35,000 $352,200	11.000 12.000 12.500 12.500	7.0 13.0 18.0 30.0	2.1 5.3 9.9 21.2
Travelers Mortgage Securities Series 1984-1	Feb. 1984	Aaa Moody's AAA S & P	GNMAs FNMAs	104	0	10.75–12.75%	11.66	Weighted average remaining term in excess of 28.5 years.	Returned to Issuer	A Z-1 C Z-2	$270,000 455,000 375,000 150,000 $1,250,000	10.625 12.000 12.000 12.000	3.0 13.5 16.5 30.0	1.4 5.8 10.7 21.1
American Southwest Financial Corporation Series E	June 1984	AAA Fitch AAA S & P	Conventional whole loans, GNMAs, FNMAs, FHLMC, PCs	113	19	8.00–14.99%	12.11	Weighted average remaining term in excess of 29.6 years.	Returned to Issuer	E-1 E-2 E-3 E-4	$ 38,086 34,860 51,751 28,016 $152,713	13.000 13.500 13.500 13.500	6.5 9.5 12.5 10.0	2.4 5.4 8.3 20.7
Centex Acceptance Corporation, GNMA, Collateralized Bonds, Series F	July 1984	Aaa Moody's AAA S & P	GNMA Is, GNMA IIs, including GNMA midgets	100	31	10.00–13.50%	12.30	Weighted average remaining term in excess of 28 years.	Used to redeem bonds	F-1 F-2 F-3 F-4	$ 42,000 32,000 59,000 25,200 $158,200	13.000 13.500 13.500 13.000	7.0 9.5 13.0 22.5	2.3 5.1 7.8 13.1

Mortgage-Backed Bonds

Issuer	Issue Date	Rating	Collateral Type	Frequency of Collateral Evaluation	Overcollateralization Requirement	Amount of Bonds Issued (000s)	Bond Coupon	Bond Maturity
First Nationwide Savings	July 1979	Aa1 Moody's	Whole loans	Quarterly	150%	$ 75,000	9.50%	1989
Great Western Savings and Loan	June 1979	Aaa Moody's AAA S & P	Whole loans	Quarterly	200	$200,000	9.50	1989
Washington Mutual Savings Bank	August 1979	Aaa Moody's	Whole loans	Quarterly	200	$ 50,000	9.70	1989

Adjustable Rate Preferred Stock

Issuer	Issue Date	Rating	Annual Dividend Rate	Number of Shares (000s)	Amount Issued (000s)	Security Type	Frequency of Security Evaluation	"Overcollateralization" Requirement
Coast Capital Corporation	March 1984	"aaa" Moody's	Initial—10.375% (Caps—6.50-12.50% (200 basis pts. below Treasury Index)	3,500	$175,000	GNMAs, FHLMC PCs, FNMAs, Treasury Securities, Short-term money market instruments	Monthly (with a 22-day cure period)	1.04%-158%
PSFS Finance, Inc.	April 1984	"aaa" Moody's	Initial—11% (Caps—6.50-13.00% (200 basis pts. below Treasury Index)	4,000	$200,000	GNMAs, FNMAs, FHLMC PCs, Treasury Securities, Short-term money market instruments	Monthly (with an 18-day cure period)	106-162%

567

APPENDIX A (concluded)

Mortgage Pass-Throughs

Issuer	Issue Date	Rating Moody's	Type
Sears Mortgage Securities Corporation Series 1984-1	Feb. 1984	Aaa	GNMA Is GNMA IIs

Collateral

Mortgages as a Percentage of Bonds Issued	Percentage of GPMs	Range of Coupons	Weighted Average Coupon	Remaining Terms	Excess Cash Flow
100%	0%	12.00%	12.00%	Weighted average remaining term in excess of 29 years.	Returned to Issuer

Bonds

Class	Amount (000s)	Coupon	Stated Maturity (Years)	Expected Average Life (Year)
1-A	$125,000	11.125%	9.2	2.6
1-B	75,000	11.750	12.0	5.3
1-C	250,000	12.000	16.5	9.3
1-D	50,000	12.000	30.0	20.6
	$500,000			

Issuer	Issue Date	Rating	Interest Rate
American Savings International, N.V.	April 1984	Aaa	12.00%

Collateralized Eurodollar Bonds

Dollar Amount (000s)	Collateral Type	Frequency of Evaluation	Overcollateralization Requirement	Maturity
$125,000	GNMAs, Treasury and U.S. Agency Securities	Weekly (with a one-week cure period)	150%	1989

CHAPTER 20

Federal Income Tax Treatment of Mortgage-Backed Securities

James M. Peaslee
Partner
Cleary, Gottlieb, Steen & Hamilton

INTRODUCTION

This chapter surveys the principal U.S. federal income tax rules governing investments in mortgage-backed securities. As will be seen, the law in this area is not altogether clear. The uncertainty is attributable both to a spate of recent—and therefore little understood—tax legislation affecting debt securities generally, and to the fact that progress in the application of the tax law to mortgages and their offspring has lagged behind market developments.[1]

The mortgage-backed securities considered here are those which are supported exclusively (or almost so) by (i) payments made on a fixed pool of mortgages, or (ii) payments on a fixed pool of mortgages together with earnings from the reinvestment of those payments over a limited period (generally, not

---

[1] The discussion below is current through March, 1985, and is, of course, subject to change through subsequent judicial decisions, legislation or administrative actions.

more than six months).[2] These securities have two payment features that distinguish them from conventional publicly-held debt obligations: their principal amount is payable in installments, and they are subject to mandatory calls to the extent the mortgages which fund them are prepaid. Distinguishing characteristics of a legal nature will also be present if the mortgage-backed security is of a type that is treated as an ownership interest in the underlying mortgages. In that event, to the extent the underlying mortgages finance personal residences, the mortgaged-backed security will represent an ownership interest in debt obligations of individuals. Discount income that is realized when principal payments on an obligation are received or come due is taxed differently depending on whether the debtor is an individual, or a corporation or other legal entity. In the hands of institutional investors, a mortgage-backed security that is treated as an ownership interest in mortgages may also qualify for certain tax benefits associated with investments in real property mortgages.

The federal income tax questions peculiar to mortgage-backed securities relate either to the features described above or to the legal structures that are used in transforming whole mortgages into such securities.

TYPES OF MORTGAGE-BACKED
SECURITIES

The holder of a mortgage-backed security is likely to display greater interest in the timing and amounts of the payments to be received thereon than in its legal form. Nonetheless, in order to understand how such a security is taxed, it is necessary to be aware of the available legal structures and the tax reasons for their use.

The objective in creating derivative mortgage securities is to repackage whole mortgages in a manner that increases

---

[2] Thus, debt obligations that are secured by mortgages, but have payment terms unrelated to those of the mortgage collateral, are not addressed.

their attractiveness as investments without at the same time incurring material additional costs by comparison with a direct investment in whole mortgages. This goal could hardly be achieved if the legal wrapping used to convert mortgages into securities resulted in the imposition of incremental taxes in more than trivial amounts. For example, if mortgage-backed securities were required to take the form of stock in a corporation that was taxable at current corporate tax rates of up to 46 percent on the gross income from the mortgages that it held, without offsetting deductions for dividends paid on the securities, such securities would never have been introduced into the market.

The principal types of mortgage-backed securities that are currently available are pass-through certificates and pay-through bonds. The legal arrangements used in creating these two classes of securities successfully address the problem of incremental taxes, although in different ways. Pass-through certificates are generally issued by a trust that is not considered to be a taxable entity; indeed, for almost all federal income tax purposes, the trust is simply ignored. Pay-through bonds, on the other hand, are generally issued by a corporation that is subject to the corporate income tax. The burden of that tax is largely eliminated, however, through deductions allowed to the corporation for interest payments made to holders of the bonds.

The section which follows describes more fully the tax implications of the arrangements used to create pass-through certificates and pay-through bonds.

Pass-Through Certificates

In their most common form, pass-through certificates are issued by a trust[3] that holds a fixed pool of mortgages. The arrangement is brought into being by a sponsor, who transfers the mortgages to the trust against receipt of the certificates,

---

[3] In some cases, the trust is replaced with a custodial arrangement, but in terms of tax analysis, the difference is mostly in the name.

and then sells all or a portion of the certificates to investors. The certificates evidence ownership by the holders of specified interests in the assets of the trust. Most often, each certificate represents a *pro rata* interest in the mortgage pool. Thus, if 1,000 such certificates are issued, each would represent a right to 1/1,000th of each payment of principal and interest on each mortgage in the pool.[4] The mortgage payments passed through to certificate holders are reduced by fees for mortgage servicing, pool administration and any applicable guarantees or pool insurance. These fees are fixed in advance over the life of the pool so that certificate holders can be guaranteed a fixed "pass-through rate" of interest on the principal balance of the certificates, representing the earnings on the mortgages net of such fees. The power of the trustee to reinvest mortgage payments received by the trust, or proceeds of the sale of mortgages held by the trust, is severely limited in order to avoid possible classification of the trust as an association taxable as a corporation[5] under the Treasury's entity classification regulations.[6] As a result, payments to certificate holders are

---

[4] Pass-through certificates representing different proportionate interests in mortgage principal and interest are considered in the discussion of the bond stripping rules below. *See also* footnote 16 for a description of tax constraints imposed on the issuance by a single trust of multiple classes of pass-through certificates having different payment priorities.

[5] If the trust were classified as an association taxable as a corporation, it is likely that the income realized by the trust with respect to the mortgages, net of fees paid by the trust, would be subject to the corporate income tax. The balance of such income remaining after payment of the corporate tax would be treated as taxable dividends when distributed to certificate holders.

[6] The classification for tax purposes of an unincorporated entity such as a trust is not controlled by what it is called, but depends instead on its functional characteristics and activities. Under Treasury Regulation §301.7701-4, entities that qualify as trusts under state law are generally classified as trusts for tax purposes if they are passive and merely hold property to protect and conserve it; by contrast, they are classified as associations taxable as corporations if they engage in a profit-making business. In particular, an investment trust holding mortgages would be classified as an association if there was any significant power to vary the investment of the trust beneficiaries (*e.g.*, by reinvesting mortgage payments in other mortgages). However, the Internal Revenue Service has ruled that the trustee of a trust holding mortgages that makes quarterly distributions to certificate

usually made monthly in parallel with ᵗhe receipt of mortgage payments by the trust.

A trust used in any commercially available pass-through arrangement will not have investment powers that risk classification of the trust as an association. Instead, it will qualify as a trust for tax purposes, and, in particular, will be a "grantor trust" taxable under section 671.[7] Consequently, for federal income tax purposes, the trust will effectively be ignored and

---

holders can reinvest monthly mortgage payments in high quality obligations if the obligations mature prior to the next distribution date and are held to maturity. Revenue Ruling 75–192, 1975–1 C.B. 384. It is also permissible for the proceeds of a sale of pass-through certificates held by the trustee to be used to acquire mortgages not specifically identified at the time of funding of the trust (Revenue Ruling 75–192, 1975–1 C.B. 384; General Counsel's Memorandum 38456, July 25, 1980), for a trustee to accept an offer by a debtor to exchange old debt for new debt if the debtor is in default or default will probably occur in the reasonably foreseeable future (Revenue Ruling 73–460, 1973–2 C.B. 424), and foᵣ a trustee to accept new mortgages in exchange for defective mortgages in the mortgage pool that did not conform to representations and warranties made upon transfer of the mortgages in trust for some initial period following the date of the transfer (Revenue Ruling 71–399, 1971–2 C.B. 433; substitution permitted for a period of two years).

[7] Except as otherwise noted, all section references herein are to the Internal Revenue Code of 1954, as amended (the "Code"). For federal income tax purposes, a trust is usually recognized to be a taxpayer and is subject to tax, at the rates applicable to individuals, on that portion of its income which it does not distribute currently to beneficiaries. Income distributed to beneficiaries is taxable to them. In order to prevent the separate tax identity of a trust from being used to shift income to lower bracket taxpayers (*e.g.*, from wealthy parents to a family trust or to its beneficiaries) in cases where the grantor (the person creating the trust) retains an economic interest in, or significant rights of control over, the trust, the so-called "grantor trust" rules were created. These rules, which are found in sections 671 through 679, provide that if the grantor of a trust retains specified interests in the trust, including a right to income, then he is treated for tax purposes as the owner of the assets of the trust in which he has such interests and is required to include income from those assets in his own tax return. To that extent, the trust is ignored for tax purposes. While the holder of a pass-through certificate issued by a trust holding mortgages is not, strictly speaking, the grantor of the trust, the grantor trust rules have been seized upon by the Internal Revenue Service as a basis for disregarding the issuing trust and treating certificate holders as tax owners of the mortgages, according to their interests.

certificate holders will be recognized to be the owners of the mortgages held by the trust.

One consequence of disregarding the separate existence of a pass-through trust is that certificate holders who report income for tax purposes under a cash method of accounting (which would be true of virtually all holders who are individuals) must report income based on the timing of receipts of mortgage payments by the trust and not on the timing of distributions made to them by the trust.[8] The trustee is viewed as an agent collecting mortgage payments on the certificate holders' behalf. While certificate holders are obliged to include in income the gross amount of interest on the mortgages, they are allowed deductions for mortgage servicing and other fees paid out of such interest, again on the theory that those amounts are paid on their behalf.

Public rulings have been issued by the Internal Revenue Service which confirm the consequences described above in the case of pass-through certificates guaranteed by the Government National Mortgage Association,[9] the Federal Home Loan Mortgage Corporation[10] and the Federal National Mortgage Association[11] and certificates representing interests in pools of conventional mortgages that are supported by private mortgage insurance.[12]

Because the holders of pass-through certificates are treated as the owners of the assets of the issuing trust, to the extent those assets include mortgages on personal residences that are loans to individuals, the holders are subject

---

[8] Similarly, accrual method holders would report income as it accrues on the mortgages, as distinguished from the certificates, although the difference between the two should not be substantial.

[9] Revenue Ruling 70–544, 1970–2 C.B. 6, and Revenue Ruling 70–545, 1970–2 C.B. 7, both modified by Revenue Ruling 74–169, 1974–1 C.B. 147.

[10] Revenue Ruling 71–399, 1971–2 C.B. 433, amplified by Revenue Ruling 81–203, 1981–2 C.B. 137, Revenue Ruling 80–96, 1980–1 C.B. 317, Revenue Ruling 74–300, 1974–1 C.B. 169, Revenue Ruling 74–221, 1974–1 C.B. 365, and Revenue Ruling 72–376, 1972–2 C.B. 647.

[11] Revenue Ruling 84–10, 1984–1 C.B. 155.

[12] Revenue Ruling 77–349, 1977–2 C.B. 20.

to a special rule, described below,[13] regarding the character of discount income that is realized as principal is paid. For the same reason, institutional investors that derive tax advantages from the direct ownership of real property loans[14] benefit equally from the ownership of pass-through certificates evidencing interests in those loans. The existence of Federal Housing Administration insurance on, or a Veterans' Administration guarantee of, the mortgages underlying pass-through certificates, or of a guarantee of the certificates by the United States or a U.S. sponsored agency, is not considered to transform the certificates into government securities for these and most other tax purposes.[15]

Pay-Through Bonds

Unlike pass-through certificates which represent an ownership interest in mortgages, a pay-through bond is a debt obligation of a legal entity (typically a corporation) which is collateralized by mortgages. A holder is considered to own the bond, but not an interest in the underlying mortgages, in the same way that the holder of, for example, a public utility bond would be considered the owner of the bond but not of the power generating station that secures it. Although the payment terms of a pay-through bond and of the underlying mortgage collateral are not identical, the relationship between them may be quite close. In most cases, the mortgages, and earnings from the reinvestment of mortgage payments over a short period,

---

[13] *See* footnote 21 below.

[14] *See* the discussion of special rules for certain institutional investor below.

[15] However, the Internal Revenue Service has ruled that pass-through certificates guaranteed by the Government National Mortgage Association are not to be treated as "mortgage notes (not including bonds) secured by real property" under the tax treaty in effect between the United States and the Netherlands Antilles, on the ground that, because the certificates are marketable, highly liquid investments and are issued in registered serial form, they more closely resemble "bonds". Revenue Ruling 79–251, 1979–2 C.B. 271. The treaty provides more favorable treatment for bonds than mortgage notes.

are expected to be the sole funding source for payments on the bonds, and mortgage prepayments are "paid-through," in whole or in part, to bondholders in the form of mandatory calls on the bonds.

A collateralized mortgage obligation, or "CMO," is a type of pay-through bond which is divided into classes having different payment priorities. CMOs are typically issued by a corporation organized by a sponsor. The sponsor initially contributes a nominal amount of cash to the corporation in exchange for its stock. The proceeds of sale of the CMOs, together with additional capital contributed by the sponsor or other purchasers of the corporation's stock, are used by the corporation to acquire the mortgage collateral that will be held by the corporation and used to repay the CMOs. Such collateral often takes the form of pass-through certificates guaranteed by the United States or a U.S. sponsored agency, although the CMOs themselves are not government guaranteed.

CMOs are a more recent innovation than pass-through certificates. They are similar to pass-through certificates in that they bear interest at a fixed rate and are funded primarily out of payments received on a fixed pool of mortgages or interests in mortgages. They differ from pass-through certificates in that they generally provide for quarterly or semiannual payments, with the issuing corporation being responsible for reinvesting monthly receipts on the mortgages until the next CMO payment date. More importantly, CMOs are divided into "fast-pay" and "slow-pay" classes which have different priorities as to the receipt of principal and in some cases interest. All principal payments (including prepayments) are made first to the class having the earliest maturity date until it is retired, and then to the class with the next earliest maturity date until it is retired, and so on. It is also common to have one or more "interest accrual" classes which receive no payments of interest or principal until all prior classes have been fully retired. Until that time, the interest that accrues on an interest accrual class is added to its outstanding principal balance and a corresponding amount is paid as additional principal on prior classes.

The reason why pay-through bonds were chosen over pass-through certificates as the vehicle for creating mortgage-backed securities with different payment priorities is tax related. If a trust issued multiple classes of pass-through certificates having different maturities, the trust could be classified as an association taxable as a corporation, with the holders of the certificates being treated as its shareholders rather than as creditors.[16] In that event, the trust would be subject to corporate income tax on the income from the mortgages it holds without an offsetting deduction for "dividends" paid to certificate holders. While a corporation that issues CMOs is acknowledged to be subject to tax on its taxable income, a deduction is allowed in computing taxable income for interest paid to CMO holders since the CMOs are debt obligations of the corporation rather than stock. Thus, only the spread between the yields on the mortgages and the CMOs—representing earnings on the capital invested in the corporation by the sponsor and other shareholders—becomes subject to an entity level tax.

Because pay-through bonds are debt obligations of the corporation which issues them and not ownership interests in the mortgage collateral, the holders are taxed based on the payments they are entitled to receive on the bonds rather than on the payments received by the corporation on the un-

---

[16] On April 27, 1984, the Internal Revenue Service proposed an amendment to the trust classification regulations described above in footnote 6 that would require classification of a trust or other similar "arrangement" as an association if it has more than one class of ownership interest. These regulations were directed in part at an issue of pass-through certificates sponsored by Sears Mortgage Securities Corporation which had a "fast-pay," "slow-pay" class structure similar to CMOs. However, they have broader implications and may, for example, prohibit the creation of two classes of interests in a trust holding mortgages that are identical except for the subordination of one to the other. The regulations contain an exception for "mere custodial arrangements formed to allow investors to own specifically identifiable stripped coupons or stripped bonds" subject to the bond-stripping rules of section 1286 of the Code. It is likely that this exception will be construed to permit different fixed percentage interests in principal and interest on mortgages to be created, as discussed later in this chapter, without jeopardizing the non-association status of the arrangement.

derlying mortgages. For the same reason, pay-through bonds are not treated as obligations of individuals or real property mortgages for tax purposes.

Trust for Investment in Mortgages

The Report of the President's Commission on Housing, dated April 1982, proposed that the Code be amended to create a new pass-through vehicle designed specially for mortgages. The new vehicle was labelled a Trust for Investment in Mortgages or "TIM". A TIM would be able to issue multiple classes of ownership interests and would be allowed to reinvest mortgage payments. A TIM would not itself be taxable; rather, all of its income would be reported by the holders of ownership interests in the TIM.

Legislation providing for creation of TIMs (S. 1822) was introduced by Senators Garn and Tower in August of 1983. In hearings in November of that year, the Treasury supported the TIMs concept but not the Garn-Tower bill. In particular, the Treasury wished to prohibit the use of TIMs to repackage interests in mortgages with guarantees by the United States or U.S. sponsored agencies. A Treasury alternative bill was widely distributed at the beginning of 1984, but a decision was ultimately made by the Administration to drop the TIMs initiative until, at the earliest, 1985. It would not be surprising if the TIMs concept is revisited in future years.

Other Available Structures

It may be possible to create mortgage-backed securities in the form of partnership interests, or stock or other ownership interests in a real estate investment trust ("REIT") taxable under sections 851–859. In either case, the mortgage-backed security would represent an ownership interest in a legal entity that is not generally ignored for tax purposes. Thus, in contrast to pass-through certificates, the holder of a partnership interest or stock or other equity interest in a REIT would not necessarily be treated as the owner of an interest in the mortgages held by the partnership or REIT. On the other hand, no significant entity level tax would be imposed. A partnership is not itself subject to income tax. Instead, its income flows through to the partners who are required to report such income on their own tax returns. A REIT is taxable as a corporation, but a special deduction is allowed in computing its taxable income for dividends paid to the holders of REIT stock, provided certain technical requirements are met (including a requirement that it distribute substantially all of its income currently).

No extended discussion of the tax treatment of equity interests in partnerships and REITs is included here, for the reason that, to date, no public offerings of mortgage-backed securities in that form have been made.[17] If, however, such securities become available at a future date, readers should not assume that the rules described below governing pass-through certificates and pay-through bonds would apply.

TAXATION OF HOLDERS

Overview

As the discussion above indicates, the mortgage-backed securities that are currently available are treated as debt obligations for tax purposes. Pass-through certificates are ownership interests in mortgages which are, of course, debt obligations of the mortgagors. CMOs and other pay-through bonds are

---

[17] Pay-through bonds and common stock have been offered to the public by Investors GNMA Mortgage-Backed Securities Trust, Inc., which is a corporation that elected to be taxed as a REIT. However, in that case, the stock is more akin to true common stock than to a mortgage-backed security. The stock does not guarantee a return of principal, or income at a fixed rate, but instead represents an interest in cash flow from the mortgages held by the corporation, and from any reinvestment thereof, remaining after the payment of debt service on the bonds.

debts of the corporation or other legal entity that issues them.[18] Accordingly, except for the need to take account of the distinguishing characteristics of mortgage-backed securities referred to in the introduction to this chapter, the Code rules governing conventional publicly-held debt obligations apply. Thus, for example, interest earned on a mortgage-backed security is taxable as ordinary income. Upon sale of the security, gain or loss is recognized in an amount equal to the difference between the net proceeds of such sale and the seller's "tax basis" in the security (generally, his cost for the security, adjusted for the amortization of discount or premium). Any such gain that is not characterized as interest income, and any loss, is treated as capital gain or loss, respectively, if the security is held as a "capital asset," which would be the case unless the holder is a dealer in securities.[19] Capital gain is long term, and thus is taxable at reduced rates,[20] if the security has been held at the time of sale for a minimum period, which is six months in the case of a security acquired after June 22, 1984 and before January 1, 1988 and otherwise one year. An amount

---

[18] The issuer of pay-through bonds could theoretically be organized as a partnership rather than as a corporation. In that event, the discussion below of the tax treatment of such bonds would still apply, except that the election to amortize premium under section 171, described later in this chapter, would not appear to be available since it is limited by its terms to obligations of corporations and governments.

[19] Holders that are banks or thrift institutions, however, always recognize ordinary income or loss from sales of debt obligations under section 582(c).

[20] Non-corporate taxpayers are allowed a deduction equal to 60 percent of any net capital gain income, producing an effective maximum rate of tax on such income of 20 percent given the current maximum tax bracket for such taxpayers of 50 percent. Net capital gain is the excess of net long-term capital gain (long-term capital gain reduced by long-term capital loss) over net short-term capital loss (short-term capital loss reduced by short-term capital gain). The tax imposed on corporate taxpayers having net capital gain income is the lesser of (i) the regular corporate tax (currently at a maximum rate of 46 percent on taxable income including net capital gain, and (ii) the sum of the regular corporate tax applied to taxable income exclusive of net capital gain and 28 percent of net capital gain. Net capital gain is a tax preference item for purposes of computing the alternative minimum tax imposed on non-corporate taxpayers and the minimum tax applicable to corporations.

paid as accrued interest upon the sale of a mortgage-backed security between interest payment dates is treated as interest income by the seller and may be offset by the purchaser against the interest received on the next interest payment date.

In order to apply the rules described above and below to a pass-through certificate, it must be kept in mind that such a certificate is not generally considered a single security for tax purposes, but instead represents an ownership interest in each of the mortgages held by the issuing trust. Technically, the holder of a pass-through certificate should calculate income or loss with respect to each mortgage separately by allocating among the mortgages, in proportion to their respective fair market values, the price paid for the certificate and the price received on resale. Such an allocation is rarely necessary in practice, however, because in most instances the tax results obtained by viewing the mortgages, alternatively, in isolation or as a group would be the same. For convenience, the discussion below of the tax treatment of mortgage-backed securities will proceed as if the security in question were in all cases a debt obligation of one debtor (either an interest in a single mortgage or a single pay-through bond).

If a mortgage-backed security is purchased at its principal amount, its tax treatment is relatively straightforward. The only income to be realized by the holder is stated interest; as principal payments are received, they represent a return of the investor's cost and do not give rise to gain or loss. This is true regardless of whether principal is paid when due or before. Gain or loss is recognized if the security is sold for more or less than its principal balance at the time of the sale and is generally capital gain or loss if the security is held for investment.

The tax treatment of a mortgage-backed security is more complex when it is purchased at a price different from its principal amount, *i.e.*, at a discount (a price below such amount) or a premium (a price above such amount). If a mortgage-backed security is purchased at a discount, and the holder subsequently receives its full principal amount, the excess of the principal received over the cost of the security will represent additional income. A question then arises as to the proper timing of recognition of that income and as to its character as ordinary income or capital gain. Similar issues exist regarding the use of premium to offset income or increase loss. Discount is more prevalent than premium, in part because of upward trends in market interest rates, and because investors are understandably reluctant to purchase at a substantial premium a mortgage-backed security that offers, as most do, limited or no call protection.

Treatment of Discount

Coming to grips with the tax treatment of discount is, regrettably, a formidable undertaking. First, it is necessary to distinguish between original issue discount (which, as the name implies, is discount at which a debt obligation is originally sold to investors by the issuer or, in a public offering, by the underwriters) and market discount (generally, discount arising from decreases in the market value of a debt obligation following its issuance). A major difference between original issue discount and market discount is that, in general, original issue discount is includible in income by the holder of a discount obligation as the discount accrues, whereas market discount is taxable only when principal payments are received or come due or the obligation is sold. The rule requiring the current inclusion in income of original issue discount has applied to corporate obligations since 1969, but was first extended to obligations of individuals by the Tax Reform Act of 1984 ("TRA 1984"), effective for obligations issued—which in the case of mortgages means closed—after March 1, 1984.

If a debt obligation has market discount, it must be determined whether the obligation was issued after July 18, 1984, the date of enactment of TRA 1984, or on or before that date. Gain from a sale to a new holder of a mortgage-backed security issued after July 18, 1984 is ordinary interest income to the extent of the market discount that accrued during the period the seller held the security rather than capital gain as was generally true under prior law. The manner in which market discount is allocated among principal payments will also differ depending on whether TRA 1984 applies.

A further distinction to keep in mind in determining the tax treatment of market or original issue discount is whether the debtor is an individual or a corporation or other legal entity. Gain realized upon the receipt of a payment of principal on an obligation of an individual (representing market discount, or original issue discount not previously included in income) is *always* ordinary income, whereas gain from the payment of principal on an obligation of a corporation or other legal entity may be capital gain if the obligation is held as a capital asset.[21]

The distinction between original issue discount and market discount is blurred by the "bond stripping" rules of section 1286. These rules apply when rights to principal and interest on a debt obligation are sold separately or in different proportions and are likely to play a significant role in the taxation of a number of common mortgage pass-through certificate arrangements. If rights to payments on a debt obligation qualify as "stripped bonds," all discount at which the obligation is purchased (including discount attributable to declines in market value) is treated as original issue discount.

The discussion below will address, in order, original issue discount, market discount and the bond-stripping rules. In each case, it will be assumed that the mortgage-backed securities under discussion have an original term to maturity of more

---

[21] This distinction is based on a technical quirk in the Code. In order for gain to be capital gain, it must result from a "sale or exchange" of a capital asset (*see* the definitions in section 1222). Under case law dating back to the early days of the tax law, gain from the extinguishment of a contractual claim, including gain realized upon retirement of a debt obligation, is not considered to result from a sale or exchange unless there is a Code provision which so states. Section 1271(a)(1) treats amounts received by the holder on retirement of a debt instrument as amounts received in exchange therefor, but this section does not apply to obligations of individuals (*see* section 1271(b)(1)). Since amounts received in retirement of an obligation of an individual are not received in a sale or exchange of the obligation, any resulting gain is ordinary income. On the other hand, if such an obligation is actually sold to a new holder, the sale or exchange requirement is satisfied and income from the sale can be capital gain.

than one year. A different tax regime, which is of little rele-
vance to mortgage-backed securities, applies to discount on
short-term obligations.[22]

1. Original Issue Discount

Original issue discount is defined as the excess of the "stated
redemption price at maturity" of an obligation over its "issue
price".[23] In the case of an obligation which bears interest at
a fixed rate which is payable at fixed intervals of not more
than one year over the entire term of the obligation, the stated
redemption price at maturity of the obligation is its principal
amount. The issue price of an issue of publicly offered obligations is the initial offering price to the public (excluding bond
houses and brokers) at which a substantial amount of the
obligations is sold. Thus, neither the price at which the obligations are sold to the underwriters by the issuer, nor the price
at which any particular obligation is sold to an investor, determines the issue price.

(a) Pay-Through Bonds: It is not uncommon for pay-
through bonds to be issued at a substantial discount, particularly where the mortgages pledged as collateral for the pay-

---

[22] In brief, the holder of a debt obligation that has an initial term of
one year or less ("short-term obligation") is not required to include the
original issue discount, if any, relating to the obligation in income as it
accrues unless such holder is an accrual basis taxpayer, a bank, a dealer
holding the obligation in inventory or another class of holder specified in
section 1281. Holders not described in section 1281 will include accrued
original issue discount on a short-term obligation in income only when the
obligation is sold or matures, but may be required under section 1282 to
defer deductions for interest paid on any related borrowings under rules
similar to those that apply to leveraged investments in long-term market
discount obligations described below. While a mortgage-backed security
will typically have an initial term well in excess of one year, it is possible
that the Internal Revenue Service will take the position that any principal
installments due within one year after the issue date should be considered
separate short-term obligations for purposes of determining the tax treatment
of any related discount income.

[23] Section 1273(a). Under a *de minimis* rule, if the discount as so defined
is less than ¼ of one percent of the stated redemption price at maturity
times the number of complete years to maturity, original issue discount is
considered to be zero.

through bonds are themselves purchased at a discount. In that event, the pay-through bonds will have original issue discount, even though the discount mirrors market discount on the mortgages, because the pay-through bonds are new securities distinct from the collateral. Furthermore, an interest accrual class of CMOs (a class that bears interest at a fixed rate but does not provide principal or interest payments until all prior classes have been retired) is *always* considered to have original issue discount, even if the obligations are initially offered to investors at their principal amount; the original issue discount equals the excess of the aggregate amount of all principal and interest payments to be made on the obligations over their issue price.[24] For tax purposes, interest payments are converted into additional principal and all of the interest income to be reported by the holders assumes the guise of original issue discount.

An investor who purchases a pay-through bond having original issue discount at a yield not less than the yield at which it was initially offered must include in income in each taxable year that he holds the bond the portion of the original issue discount that is considered to accrue in such year (regardless of whether he otherwise reports income under a cash or accrual method of tax accounting). As explained in more detail below, the portion of the original issue discount on a bond that is considered to accrue in any period generally equals the amount by which the value of the bond would increase during such period if it continued at all times to have a yield to maturity equal to its yield to maturity at the time

---

[24] The reason for this result is as follows: Original issue discount is defined as the excess of the stated redemption price at maturity of an obligation over its issue price. Section 1273(a)(2) defines the stated redemption price at maturity of an obligation to include all payments made on the obligation other than interest based on a fixed rate which is payable unconditionally at fixed periodic intervals of one year or less during the entire term of the obligation. Since interest is not paid on an interest accrual class of CMOs until prior classes have been retired (and thus is not paid at least annually over the entire term of the obligations), the stated redemption price at maturity of such obligations includes interest and all other payments to be made thereon.

of issuance calculated based on its issue price. This method of accruing original issue discount is known as the "constant yield" or "scientific" method.[25] It gives effect to the compounding of interest by adding original issue discount to principal as it accrues. The method results in a greater allocation of discount to each period over time as the outstanding principal balance, adjusted for accrued original issue discount, grows.

The yield to an investor of a debt obligation purchased at a discount is greater the shorter the assumed life of the obligation. In the case of most pay-through bonds, it is highly probable that principal will be prepaid to some degree. While it would be possible to accrue original issue discount on a bond based on an average life which reflects the most likely rate of prepayment of the bond, there are many tax advisors who believe that under present tax law accruals of discount should be calculated on the assumption that no prepayments will be made.[26] This view finds support in the statutory require-

---

[25] The constant yield method was introduced into the tax law by the Tax Equity and Fiscal Responsibility Act of 1982 and first applied to corporate and government obligations issued after July 1, 1982. In the case of obligations issued on or prior to that date, original issue discount was accrued under a straight-line method, which allocated the same portion of the discount to each year.

[26] Although the propriety of a zero prepayment assumption is accepted by many tax advisors, there appears to be no direct authority under current law either approving or disapproving the assumption as applied to obligations such as mortgage-backed securities that are likely to be prepaid. Moreover, the Internal Revenue Service could adopt regulations under the authority of section 1275(d) requiring account to be taken of anticipated prepayments in determining the rate of accrual of original issue discount. It is unlikely, however, that any such regulations would apply to obligations issued before the date on which the regulations are first published. One objection to a zero prepayment assumption that has been voiced is that it permits too large a portion of the original issue discount on a mortgage-backed security to be converted into capital gain taxable when principal payments are received or the security is sold. The Internal Revenue Service might attempt to thwart such conversion by arguing that the expectation of some level of prepayments evidences an intention on the part of the issuer to call the security before maturity, with the result that such gain would be ordinary income. *See* discussion of the intention to call rule in footnote 34 below. Such an argument seems unlikely to prevail, particularly in view of the fact that prepayments of mortgage-backed securities are based largely on actions taken by the individual mortgagors on the underlying mortgages that are outside of the control of the issuer of the securities.

ment that accruals be based on the yield "to maturity" of an obligation.[27] In common understanding, the maturity of an obligation is not affected by the existence of optional call rights. If original issue discount on an obligation is accrued based on the obligation's yield to maturity, and the obligation is in fact prepaid, then a holder of the obligation who purchased it at a discount would recognize gain at the time of the prepayment at least equal to the amount of original issue discount that would have been included in his income in future periods with respect to the prepaid principal if he had held the obligation to maturity and it had not been prepaid. Thus, there is a direct relationship between the rate of accrual of original issue discount and the tax consequences of prepayments.

The detailed workings of the original issue discount rules can most readily be understood by first examining an obligation that provides for a single payment of principal. The principal of most pay-through bonds is payable in installments, and the arithmetic refinements necessary to take account of multiple payments of principal are considered next. The discussion of original issue discount concludes by analyzing the effect on the rate of accrual of such discount of an acceleration in the due date of a future installment of principal that is caused by the prepayment of the underlying mortgage collateral.

(i) *Single Payment Obligations*

Accrual of original issue discount. Consider a bond having a principal amount of $1,000 that was issued at a price of $770.60 on April 1, 1985, bears interest at an annual rate of 8 percent of principal payable on April 1 and October 1, and matures on April 1, 1995. No principal is due prior to maturity. The bond has original issue discount of $229.40. The yield to maturity of the bond, based on semiannual compounding, is 12 percent.[28]

A holder of the bond is required to include in gross income in each taxable year the sum of the "daily portions" of original

---

[27] *See* section 1272(a)(3)(A)(ii).

[28] In other words, the present value of all interest and principal payments due on the bond, calculated using a discount rate for each semiannual period of 6 percent, equals the $770.60 purchase price.

issue discount for each day during the taxable year on which he holds the bond.[29] In the case of an investor who purchased the bond in the initial offering at the issue price, two steps are needed to determine the daily portions of original issue discount. First, a calculation is made of the portion of the original issue discount that is attributable to each "accrual period" during the term of the bond. An accrual period is a six-month period (or shorter period from the issue date of the bond) which ends on a day in the calendar year corresponding to the maturity date of the bond or the date six months before such maturity date.[30] Second, the portion of the original issue discount attributed to each accrual period is allocated ratably to each day during the period to determine the daily portion of original issue discount for that day.

The amount of original issue discount on a bond that is attributed to each accrual period is the excess of (i) the yield to maturity of the bond, determined on the basis of compounding at the end of each accrual period, multiplied by the "adjusted issue price" of the bond at the beginning of such accrual period, over (ii) the sum of the amounts payable as interest during such accrual period. The adjusted issue price of a bond at the beginning of an accrual period equals its issue price, increased by the aggregate amount of original issue discount on the bond attributed to all prior accrual periods, if any. Thus, it represents the first purchaser's capital investment in the bond, adjusted for the amount of original issue discount that has been earned and included in income for tax purposes but not yet paid.

Since the bond in the example above matures on April 1, 1995, the accrual periods for the bond are the six-month

---

[29] Section 1272(a).

[30] Section 1272(b)(5). This definition was introduced by TRA 1984. For an obligation issued before January 1, 1985, the term accrual period is defined as a one-year period (or shorter period to maturity) beginning on the day in the calendar year which corresponds to the issue date of the obligation. Both the new and old definitions are subject to change through Treasury regulations. It seems likely that regulations will eventually authorize use of a quarterly or monthly accrual period in the case of obligations that provide for quarterly or monthly payments of debt service, respectively.

periods ending October 1 and April 1. The semiannual yield to maturity of the bond, based on compounding at the end of each accrual period, is 6 percent.[31] Thus, the original issue discount allocable to the first accrual period ending October 1, 1985 is $6.24 (the adjusted issue price, which for the first accrual period equals the issue price of $770.60, times 6 percent, or $46.24, less $40.00, the interest payable in such period). The corresponding amount for the second accrual period ending April 1, 1986 is $6.61 [($776.84 × .06) − $40.00]. If the initial holder of the bond reports income based on the calendar year, he would include in income for 1985 the sum of all daily portions for the first accrual period ending October 1, 1985 ($6.24) and the sum of the daily portions for the days in the second accrual period which are on or prior to December 31, 1985. The second accrual period includes 182 days of which 91 are on or prior to December 31, 1985. Thus, the sum of the daily portions of original issue discount for the days in such accrual period which are on or prior to December 31, 1985 is $\frac{91}{182}$ times $6.61, or $3.31. The total amount of original issue discount includible in income by such holder in 1985 is therefore $9.55 ($6.24 plus $3.31). The adjusted issue prices for the bond at the end of each accrual period are plotted as the upward sloping line in Exhibit 1.

The example above involves an investor who purchased the bond in the initial offering at the issue price. The daily portions of original issue discount would be calculated in the same manner for a subsequent holder if such holder purchased the bond at a price not exceeding its adjusted issue price on

---

[31] If the first accrual period is a short period of less than six months, it is not entirely clear how the yield to maturity should be calculated. It seems likely, however, that the Internal Revenue Service will allow yield to be computed in such a manner that the percentage yield for the short accrual period is $100 \times \left[\left(1 + \frac{Y}{100}\right)^F - 1\right]$, where Y is the yield for a full accrual period expressed as a percentage and F is the fraction of a full accrual period represented by the short accrual period. Thus, if the yield for a six-month accrual period was 6 percent, the yield for a short-period of three months would be 2.96 percent, which is computed using the formula and values of 6 and .5 for Y and F, respectively.

EXHIBIT 1
Adjusted Issue Price at the End of Each Accrual Period

Adjusted Issue Price

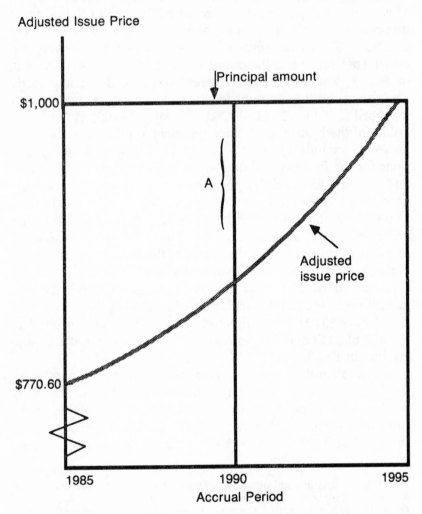

the date of purchase. On the other hand, an investor who bought the bond at a price exceeding its adjusted issue price at the time of purchase (and thus at a yield lower than the bond's initial yield to maturity) would be allowed to offset that excess amount (which will be referred to as a "purchase premium") against the daily portions of original issue discount calculated as described above.[32] In particular, each of those daily portions would be reduced by an amount equal to the product of such daily portion and a fixed fraction. The numerator of the fraction is the purchase premium and the denominator is the sum of the daily portions of original issue discount (determined without regard to any purchase premium adjustment) for all days after the purchase date through the maturity date of the bond. Thus, if the purchase premium for any bondholder represents 25 percent of the aggregate amount of original issue discount that remains to be accrued after the purchase date, the amount of original issue discount that would otherwise be required to be included in the holder's income for any day would be reduced by 25 percent.

Gain on prepayment. The tax basis of a holder of a bond having original issue discount is increased by the amount of such discount that is included in the holder's income.[33] Thus, an investor who purchased such a bond at a price not less than its adjusted issue price at the time of the purchase and received its principal amount at maturity would have no gain as a result of the principal payment; he would already have included the remaining discount in income and therefore his tax basis in the bond at maturity would equal its principal amount. On the other hand, if the principal amount of the bond were paid prior to maturity, the investor would recognize gain equal to the amount of original issue discount that would have been included in such investor's income after the date of the prepayment if the bond had not been prepaid and he had held it to maturity.

To illustrate the calculation of gain on prepayment of an original issue discount obligation, return to the bond in the example above which has a $1,000 principal amount, is issued on April 1, 1985 and matures on April 1, 1995. In the case of an investor who purchases the bond at a price equal to its adjusted issue price, the gain on prepayment is represented in Exhibit 1, for a prepayment occurring at any time shown

---

[32] *See* section 1272(a)(6).

[33] Section 1272(d)(2).

on the horizontal axis, as the vertical distance between the horizontal line at $1,000 and the upward sloping line representing the adjusted issue price of the bond. For example, if the bond were called on April 1, 1990, such an investor would recognize gain of $147.20, the excess of $1,000 over $852.80, the adjusted issue price of the bond on that date. This gain is shown as line A in the exhibit.

The gain equal to the unaccrued original issue discount that is taken into income when an original issue discount bond prepays is generally taxable as capital gain, provided the bond is held for investment and is not the obligation of an individual.[34] The difference in the character of such income is a major point of distinction between a pay-through bond issued by a corporation, and a pass-through certificate evidencing an ownership interest in home mortgages which are loans to individuals.

(ii) *Installment Payments of Principal*

Pay-through bonds differ from the bond in the example above in that they generally provide for more than one payment of principal. In applying the original issue discount rules to such a security, each installment payment of principal would be treated as if it were a separate obligation.[35] Consequently, each such payment would have its own stated redemption price at maturity and issue price, and the difference between the two would represent the discount at which the payment is considered to be issued. The adjusted issue price of the

---

[34] As indicated above in footnote 21, gain recognized upon the retirement of an obligation of an individual is always ordinary income. One further requirement for capital gain treatment is that there not have been, at the time of original issuance of the bond, an intention to call the bond prior to maturity. If such an intention existed, gain upon the retirement or sale of the bond would be taxable as ordinary income up to the amount of original issue discount remaining unaccrued at the time of the retirement or sale. *See* section 1271(a)(2). In order for such an intention to exist, there must have been an understanding between the bond issuer and any original purchaser that the call right would be exercised. Such an understanding will rarely be found to exist in the case of publicly offered bonds, unless the issuer represents in the offering documents that it intends to call the bonds prior to maturity. *See* Treasury Regulation §1.1232–3(b)(4)(ii).

[35] *See* Treasury Regulation §1.1232–3(b)(2)(iv).

payment would equal the sum of its issue price and the amount of accrued original issue discount relating to the payment.

To illustrate, imagine a bond that has a principal amount of $1,000 and bears interest of 8 percent per annum payable semiannually. One $500 principal payment is due five years after issuance of the bond and a second $500 principal payment is due five years thereafter. The bond would be analyzed as if it consisted of two separate $500 obligations. Each obligation would have a stated redemption price at maturity of $500 and would bear interest at an 8 percent rate on its unpaid principal amount. The issue prices for the two $500 obligations would be determined by allocating the issue price for the bond between them. It is not entirely clear how this should be done under current law, but the approach that has gained the widest acceptance assumes that each $500 obligation has an initial yield to maturity equal to the initial yield to maturity of the bond. Under this assumption, the issue price of each $500 obligation would equal the present value on the issue date of the payments of principal and interest to be made on such obligation, calculated using a discount rate equal to the initial yield to maturity of the bond. Thus, if the bond were issued at a price of $811.70 to yield 12 percent, the issue price of the $500 obligation with the earlier maturity would be $426.40, and that of the second $385.30. The $188.30 of original issue discount would be allocated $73.60 to the first payment and $114.70 to the payment due after ten years.

In theory, the original issue discount accruing on the bond should be determined by summing the amounts of original issue discount accruing separately on the two $500 obligations. However, if the issue price of each obligation is calculated as described above, its initial yield to maturity would be the same as the initial yield to maturity of the bond. Since the other factors used in the calculation of accrued original issue discount for the two obligations (adjusted issue prices and interest payments) will, when added together, equal the same factors determined for the bond, it is apparent that the original issue discount accruing on the bond in any period can be calculated directly based on the yield to maturity and adjusted issue price of, and the interest payments on, the bond. For example, the original issue discount that accrues on the bond in each of the first two years after its issuance would be $17.93 and $20.14, for a total of $38.07. These figures were calculated in the manner described above as if the bond provided for a single payment of principal at maturity. If the first payment of principal is paid on its due date, the amount of that payment would reduce, dollar for dollar, the adjusted issue price of the bond on that date.

A separate calculation of the adjusted issue prices of the two principal installments would be required only if the bond is partially prepaid. In that event, a holder who purchased the bond at its adjusted issue price would recognize gain equal to the excess of the principal received over the adjusted issue price of the principal installments that are considered to have been prepaid. The adjusted issue price of the bond would be reduced by the adjusted issue price assigned to the prepaid installments.

The adjusted issue price assigned to the prepaid installments can be calculated by identifying which installments have been prepaid and then aggregating the issue prices and accrued original issue discount determined separately for those installments. If the method described above is used in calculating the issue prices of the principal installments, however, an alternative and possibly simpler method of computing the adjusted issue price of any prepayment would be to discount the amounts that are prepaid. In particular, such adjusted issue price would equal the present value, on the prepayment date, of the future payments of principal and interest on the bond that are not required to be made because of the prepayment, calculated using as the discount rate the original yield to maturity of the bond. The gain from the prepayment, represented by the excess of the amount of the prepayment over the adjusted issue price as so determined, would be adjusted downward in the case of an investor who purchased the bond at a price greater than its adjusted issue price.[36]

---

[36] The gain would be reduced by the same fraction that is applied to reduce the daily portions of original issue discount. *See* the text at footnote 32 above.

To illustrate the effect of a partial payment of the bond described above, suppose that on the second anniversary of the issue date, the holder of the bond receives a prepayment of principal in the amount of $750. Assume that under the terms of the bond, prepayments are credited against future principal installments in inverse order of maturity.[37] Accordingly, the prepayment will first be applied against the $500 payment due at the end of year ten and the remainder will reduce the payment due at the end of year five, leaving a $250 balance due on the bond at the end of year five. The adjusted issue price of the bond at the end of the second year, before taking account of the prepayment, is $849.77. Using the alternative method referred to above, the adjusted issue price of the prepayment will equal the present value at the time of the prepayment (the end of year two) of the future payments otherwise due on the bond that are satisfied through the prepayment (*i.e.,* principal payments of $250 at the end of year five and $500 at the end of year ten, together with interest thereon of 8 percent). This present value, calculated using a discount rate of 12 percent which is the initial yield to maturity of the bond, is $624.35. Thus, a holder who purchased the bond in the initial offering at its issue price would recognize gain from the prepayment of $125.65 ($750, the amount of the prepayment, less $624.35). The adjusted issue price of the bond, for purposes of calculating the accrual of original issue discount in years three through five, is reduced by $624.35, the adjusted issue price assigned to the prepayment, from $849.77 at the beginning of year three to $225.42. The amounts of original issue discount accruing in those years, calculated as described above, will be $24.58, assuming no further prepayments. The sum of this amount, the original issue discount of $38.07 that accrued on the bond in the first two years and $125.65, the gain recognized as a result of the prepay-

---

[37] The order in which prepayments are credited against future amounts due on a bond will, of course, vary from one debt obligation to another. The ordering rule will determine which future installments of principal are considered to be prepaid and thereby affect the tax consequences of the prepayment.

ment, fully accounts for, as it should, the $188.30 of original issue discount on the bond.

In the event the bond described above is sold, or is prepaid in whole, gain or loss can be calculated by comparing the adjusted tax basis of the bond as a whole with the principal received or the amount realized in the sale.

The method described above for calculating accruals of original issue discount and gains from partial prepayments can be applied regardless of the number of principal installments. For example, it would apply to a loan that is amortized through level payments of principal and interest and therefore provides for a payment of some amount of principal on each payment date.

(iii) *Changes in Scheduled Payment Dates*

As explained above, it is generally believed that for purposes of determining the rate of accrual of original issue discount, the yield of a discount obligation should be calculated assuming no prepayments, even if there is a high probability that some prepayments will occur. If a zero-prepayment assumption is appropriate under current law, a question still remains as to whether the rate of accrual of original issue discount should be adjusted where the dates on which principal installments are scheduled to be paid shift forward as a result of prepayments that have already occurred. The problem addressed here involves a change in the timing of payments of a given amount of principal that remains outstanding before and after the change occurs, not the effect of a partial retirement of an obligation through a principal prepayment.

The question has arisen primarily in analyzing CMOs. To illustrate, assume that two classes of CMOs, A and B, are issued against a pool of mortgages. The mortgages have a principal balance of $100 million, bear interest at a 12 percent rate, and will be retired through equal monthly payments of principal and interest over a thirty-year period unless prepaid. Each of the two classes of CMOs bears interest of 12 percent and has a principal balance of $50 million. Interest is paid currently on both classes of CMOs, but principal received on the mortgages is used solely to pay principal on Class A until that class is fully retired.

If a mortgage prepays and the amount of the prepayment is passed through as a principal prepayment on Class A, the life of Class A will obviously be shortened. However, the prepayment will also shorten the life of Class B, even if no additional prepayments are made. In order to see why, consider a representative mortgage in the collateral pool. If there are no prepayments, Class A will be entitled to the first 50 percent of the principal payments on that mortgage and Class B will be entitled to the balance. Assume, however, that immediately after the CMOs are issued, $25 million of the mortgages prepay, reducing the principal balance of Class A to $25 million. After giving effect to that prepayment, Class A will be entitled to only the first one-third of the principal payments on each of the remaining mortgages and Class B to the remaining two-thirds. Accordingly, the scheduled debt service on Class B has been accelerated from one based on the timing of the last half of the principal payments on a thirty-year mortgage to one based on the last two-thirds. In the extreme case where prepayments eliminate Class A soon after the CMOs are issued, Class B would take on the payment characteristics of a thirty-year mortgage.

If Class B is issued at a discount, the rate of accrual of such discount should be determined initially assuming that no prepayments on the mortgages will be made, for the reasons given above. To the extent, however, that prepayments have in fact been made and passed through to Class A, the schedule of future payments on Class B, calculated assuming no additional mortgage prepayments, will also be advanced. While the question remains to be resolved authoritatively, many believe that the rate of future accruals of original issue discount on Class B should be accelerated to take account of the reduction in its remaining life.[38] Since the deductions claimed by the issuer of the CMOs for original issue discount would also

---

[38] This would be accomplished by calculating original issue discount for future periods as if Class B had been reissued with a revised payment schedule. The issue price for the "new" Class B would be considered to equal the adjusted issue price of the "old" Class B at the time the adjustment is made.

be accelerated if the adjustment were made,[39] most recent CMOs prospectuses state that the issuer will make the adjustment, for purposes of filing its own tax return and reporting income of holders to the Internal Revenue Service, unless and until it is authoritatively determined that the adjustment is improper.

(b) Pass-Through Certificates: Original issue discount is not likely to be encountered in connection with an investment in pass-through certificates unless the stripped bond rules apply, or, as discussed below, interest payments on the underlying mortgages increase over time. The exchange of pass-through certificates for mortgages is not treated as the creation of a new debt security for tax purposes, so that the existence or not of original issue discount is not affected by the price at which the certificates are originally sold. Rather in testing for the presence of original issue discount, it is necessary to look to the terms of the original loan between the mortgagor and the mortgage originator, and mortgages are not typically originated at a discount.[40] In any event, the original issue dis-

---

[39] Section 163(e) requires the issuer of discount bonds to use the same method of calculation of accruals of original issue discount as the holders.

[40] While it is common for a mortgage lender to charge the borrower "points" in connection with the origination of a mortgage, such points are often paid out of the mortgagor's own funds and represent a prepayment of interest rather than original issue discount. *See* section 461(g) (special rule allows a cash basis mortgagor a deduction for prepaid interest paid in the form of points on a loan to finance a principal residence if the number of points does not exceed the number generally charged in the area in which the mortgage is originated). Moreover, even if the points were viewed as discount, the points may be less than a *de minimis* amount, at least with respect to the portion thereof allocable to principal payments due more than one year after issuance (see footnote 23 above), so that they would be disregarded in determining whether the mortgages are subject to the original issue discount rules of the Code. If mortgages are originated with a view to their being immediately transformed into pass-through certificates and sold in a public offering, an argument could be made that the originator is acting in the same manner as an underwriter in a conventional offering of newly issued securities. Under that view, the issue price of the mortgages for purposes of determining original issue discount might be considered to be the initial offering price of the certificates to the public. In most cases, this argument would not be compelling in view of the warehousing and pricing risks assumed by the originator and the other services it performs.

count rules of the Code would not apply to whole or pro rata interests in mortgages which are obligations of individuals if those mortgages were originated before March 2, 1984.[41] TRA 1984 extended those rules to obligations of individuals for the first time, effective for obligations issued on or after that date. As noted above, a pass-through certificate would not fail to qualify as an interest in obligations of individuals because the mortgages or the certificates are guaranteed by the United States or a U.S. sponsored agency.

In the case of a residential mortgage originated after March 1, 1984, original issue discount will exist if the amount unconditionally payable as interest in each year, expressed as a percentage of the outstanding principal balance of the loan, increases over the term of the loan. Thus, a mortgage will be considered to have original issue discount if it provides for negative amortization of principal or bears interest payable at rates that are *scheduled* to increase (in contrast to rates that are merely variable according to an external index) over the life of the loan.[42] The effect of applying the original issue

---

[41] *See* section 1272(a)(2)(D). It appears that those rules would apply, however, to a non-pro rata interest in a residential mortgage that is acquired after March 1, 1984, regardless of the actual date of origination of the related whole mortgage. As described later in this chapter such acquired interest would be treated as an obligation newly issued on the acquisition date under the bond-stripping rules of the Code.

[42] The reasoning supporting this conclusion is as follows: Original issue discount exists if the stated redemption price at maturity of an obligation exceeds its issue price. Thus, a mortgage that is purchased by the first buyer at its principal amount will have original issue discount if its stated redemption price at maturity is greater than its principal amount. This will be true only if the stated interest payments on the mortgage are included to some extent in the stated redemption price at maturity. The stated redemption price at maturity includes all payments made on an obligation with the sole exception of interest based on a fixed rate which is payable unconditionally at least annually during the entire term of the obligation. A negative amortization mortgage may bear interest at a fixed rate over its entire term, but interest is actually payable at a rate below the stated rate during the negative amortization period. During that period, the accrued and unpaid interest is added to principal. If a rate of interest payable was calculated for each year of the mortgage by dividing the interest payable during that year by the outstanding principal amount of the mortgage at the beginning of the year, and the lowest rate of interest payable in any year was then

discount rules to such loans will be to require holders (i) in the case of a negative amortization loan, to include stated interest in income as it accrues, and (ii) in the case of a loan which bears interest at increasing rates, to take into income interest that accrues based on the yield to maturity of the loan (*i.e.*, a yield representing a blend of the stated interest rates). Original issue discount is present in such loans because some part of the stated interest payable thereon is treated as additional principal for tax purposes. Determining which stated interest payments will be recharacterized as principal is somewhat complex. The choice of which mortgage interest payments are to be recharacterized should not, however, affect the current interest income (stated interest plus accrued original issue discount) reported by holders in any taxable year. On the other hand, if a mortgage that is considered to have original issue discount is acquired with additional market discount, it may be necessary to know the extent to which each interest payment is treated as principal in order to determine the timing of recognition of the market discount income.[43]

---

determined, the amounts payable as interest in each year would be included in the stated redemption price at maturity to the extent they were payable at a rate greater than that lowest rate. Similarly, if a mortgage provided for payments of interest currently as the interest accrued but the stated rate of interest increased over the life of the loan, interest paid at a rate greater than the lowest rate would be included in the stated redemption price at maturity and hence would represent original issue discount. The inclusion of interest payments on a home mortgage in the stated redemption price at maturity may result in the postponement of interest deductions by the mortgagor since deductions for original issue discount would be allowed only when the principal to which such discount is allocated is paid. *See* section 1275(b).

[43] The method of determining the interest payments on a mortgage that are includible in its stated redemption price at maturity is outlined in footnote 42 above. The breakdown of mortgage payments between amounts treated as interest and amounts included in the stated redemption price at maturity should not affect the reporting of current interest income by holders (including both stated interest and accrued original issue discount). For any accrual period, such interest income would always equal the product of (i) the yield to maturity of the mortgage and (ii) its adjusted issue price. The calculation of the yield to maturity does not depend on the characterization of loan payments as principal or interest. The same is true for the adjusted issue price. If an amount paid as interest in any accrual period

If a mortgage provides for interest determined in whole or in part by reference to an index of market interest rates, it is not clear how the original issue discount rules would be applied. One possible approach would be to treat the mortgage as if it provided for fixed interest payments equal to the interest that would be paid if the value of the index were frozen at its value on the date of origination of the mortgage. Under that approach, the mortgage would be considered to have original issue discount only if the terms of the mortgage provide for a scheduled increase in interest rates not dependent on an increase in the index.

In the event that the holder of a pass-through certificate is required to include in income an amount representing unaccrued original issue discount upon prepayment of an underlying mortgage that is an obligation of an individual, such income would be ordinary income. This result contrasts with the treatment of a pay-through bond issued by a corporation, in that gain from prepayment of such a bond would generally be capital gain if the bond is held as a capital asset.

2. Market Discount

Overview. Any discount at which an obligation is purchased below its principal amount (if the obligation has no

---

is recharacterized as principal, the stated interest payable in that period would be reduced, and the accrued original issue discount (which equals the total interest for the period less payments of stated interest) would be increased, in the amount of the recharacterized payment. While the adjusted issue price would be increased by the additional amount included in income as accrued original issue discount, it would then be reduced in the same amount by the additional principal repayment, for a net adjustment from the recharacterization of the payment of zero. While the recharacterization as principal of interest payments on a mortgage would not affect the current interest income reported by a holder, if the mortgage is acquired with market discount, then the holder may be required to allocate market discount among all amounts treated as principal for tax purposes, including interest recharacterized as principal, and to include the discount allocated to each payment in income as the payment is received. In that event, the recharacterization of interest payments would, alter the timing of reporting of market discount income. However, the holder could argue that only stated principal should be treated as principal for this purpose. This problem exists, of course, only for mortgages originated after March 1, 1984 to which the original issue discount rules potentially apply.

original issue discount), or below its adjusted issue price (if the obligation does have original issue discount), is considered to be market discount. The treatment of market discount has been significantly altered by TRA 1984.

Prior to enactment of TRA 1984, market discount on a mortgage-backed security was generally allocated among all principal payments in proportion to their amounts regardless of when they were due. The discount was included in income as principal payments were received or came due or when the security was sold. Thus, if an obligation having an outstanding principal balance of $1,000 was purchased by an investor for $750, the investor would report 25 percent of each principal payment as income when the payment came due or was received while he held the obligation. Such income was ordinary income (although not interest income) if the obligation was the debt of an individual; otherwise, it was generally capital gain, assuming the obligation was held as a capital asset. Given the same assumption, gain realized upon sale of the obligation was always capital gain. Such gain would reflect any market discount allocated to the principal of the obligation that remained unpaid at the time of the sale, since the seller's tax basis for purposes of computing gain would equal the portion of the initial purchase price, as reduced by the market discount, that was allocated to such unpaid principal.

TRA 1984 does not change the rule of prior law that permitted the reporting of market discount on an obligation to be deferred until the obligation is disposed of or principal thereon is paid or comes due. The new law does, however, characterize market discount income reported by the holder of an obligation as ordinary interest income for tax purposes to the extent of the portion of the discount that accrued while the holder held the obligation. It also provides rules to ensure that accrued market discount will not be exempted from tax under certain nonrecognition provisions in the Code. Finally, TRA 1984 defers deductions for all or a portion of the tax losses that might otherwise be generated by borrowing at market rates to finance low-coupon market discount obligations, claiming current deductions for interest expense on the borrowing and deferring the inclusion in income of the market discount until the obligation is disposed of or repaid. The new market discount rules do not apply to obligations that have an original term of one year or less.

While TRA 1984 does not generally treat market discount in the same manner as original issue discount, it does offer investors a new election, in section 1278(b), to treat market discount as original issue discount. Market discount obligations affected by the election are not subject to the income conversion and loss deferral rules described below. The election applies to all obligations acquired after the first day of the first taxable year to which the election applies, regardless of whether those obligations were issued before or after the date of enactment of TRA 1984, and continues in effect unless permission to terminate the election is obtained from the Internal Revenue Service. Barring unusual circumstances,[44] this election is unlikely to be made since it would result in the acceleration of income and in some cases greater conversion of capital gain into ordinary interest income.

Detailed Discussion. TRA 1984 adds to the Code a new section 1276, which applies to obligations *issued* after July 18, 1984, the date of enactment of the legislation. The new section provides that gain from a sale or other disposition of an obligation acquired with market discount,[45] presumably including a partial disposition of such an obligation in the

---

[44] These circumstances might include the availability of expiring net operating loss carryovers.

[45] Market discount is defined in section 1278(a)(2) as the excess of the stated redemption price at maturity of an obligation over its basis immediately after its acquisition by the taxpayer. However, in the case of an obligation issued at a discount, the stated redemption price at maturity is replaced by the sum of the obligation's issue price and the portion of the original issue discount thereon that has accrued to the acquisition date. This rule has the effect of excluding unaccrued original issue discount from the definition of market discount. Also, under a *de minimis* rule, market discount is considered to be zero if it is less than ¼ of 1 percent of the stated redemption price at maturity multiplied by the number of complete years to maturity (after the taxpayer acquired the obligation).

form of payment of an installment of principal, will be treated as ordinary income (generally interest income) to the extent the gain does not exceed the portion of the market discount that is considered to have accrued from the acquisition date to the time of the sale or other disposition. Subject to certain exceptions,[46] such income is recognized notwithstanding other nonrecognition rules in the Code. Thus, for example, a holder who makes a donative transfer of a market discount obligation would recognize income up to the amount of accrued market discount even though gifts do not ordinarily trigger the recognition of gain.

Market discount will be considered to accrue under a straight-line method[47] unless the holder elects, on an obligation-by-obligation basis, to use a constant yield method.[48] If the election is made, accrued market discount for any period will equal the portion of such discount that would have been included in the holder's income during that period as accrued original issue discount under the rules described above if the market discount had been original issue discount. Most sophisticated investors will make a constant yield election for all of their market discount bonds since the election will have the effect of slowing the rate at which market discount accrues.

In the case of a market discount obligation on which principal is payable in installments, such as most mortgage-backed securities, an election to accrue discount under a constant yield method should determine not only the rate at which the market discount allocated to a given principal payment accrues, but also the manner in which market discount is allo-

---

[46] *See* section 1276(d). These exceptions allow, among other things, certain transfers of obligations to and from corporations or partnerships, or in connection with a corporate reorganization, without triggering recognition of accrued market discount income.

[47] Under this method, accrued market discount is calculated by multiplying the market discount by a fraction, the numerator of which is the number of days the holder has held the obligation and the denominator of which is the total number of days after the holder acquired the obligation to and including the maturity date. *See* section 1276(b)(1).

[48] *See* section 1276(b)(2).

cated among principal payments.[49] It is not clear how market discount should be allocated among principal payments if no election is made, so that market discount is required to be accrued on a straight-line basis. One allocation method that is a straight-line method but gives some effect to the timing of payments is a "bond-years" approach under which each principal payment is weighted by the length of the period from the date of acquisition of the obligation to the date on which such payment is due.

In the case of a residential mortgage which is the obligation of an individual, the new rules will not significantly alter the character of discount income realized upon receipt of principal payments from the mortgagor. Such income would be ordinary in any event, although the characterization of such income as interest under section 1276 does represent a change. On the other hand, section 1276 may convert capital gain into ordinary interest income in the event of a sale at a profit of the mortgage to a third party. The method of allocation of discount among principal payments will also be affected by section 1276, at least if an election is made to calculate accrued market discount under a constant yield method. If such an election is made, discount will be allocated to a greater extent to later payments than under a *pro rata* approach with the result that the reporting of discount income will be deferred by comparison with old law.

As already noted, section 1276 applies only to obligations issued after July 18, 1984. Thus, the section will apply to all pay-through bonds issued after that date. By contrast, it should apply to pass-through certificates issued after July 18, 1984 only to the extent they evidence interests in mortgages originated after that date. In other words, the pass-through certificates should not be viewed as new obligations-distinct from the underlying mortgages for this purpose.

In addition to changing the character of market discount income, TRA 1984 requires the deferral of tax losses that would otherwise result from financing an investment in market dis-

---

[49] *See* the text immediately following footnote 35 above.

count obligations with debt that bears interest at a current
market rate. This is accomplished by new section 1277, which
applies to obligations that are *acquired* after July 18, 1984
(regardless of when those obligations were issued).

Section 1277 allows a deduction in any taxable year for
"net direct interest expense" with respect to a market discount
obligation only to the extent such expense exceeds the market
discount that accrues during the days in such year on which
the taxpayer held the obligation. The rate of accrual of market
discount is determined under the rules of section 1276 described above (including the election to use a constant yield
method). Net direct interest expense is the excess of the interest paid or accrued during the taxable year on debt incurred
or continued to purchase or carry the market discount obligation over the aggregate amount of interest on the obligation
(including original issue discount) includible in gross income
for the taxable year by the holder. The "incurred or continued
to purchase or carry" standard used to link a borrowing with
an investment in market discount obligations is amorphous
and yet familiar, having been used for many years in determining whether investments in tax-exempt bonds are debt
financed.[50] A special interest expense allocation rule applies
to banks and thrifts.[51]

The deductions for net direct interest expense on a market
discount obligation that are disallowed under section 1277 are
allowed (i) when the market discount obligation is disposed

------

[50] It is likely that the guidelines for determining whether a tax-exempt
bond is debt financed set forth in Revenue Procedure 72–18, 1972–1 C.B.
740, will also be followed in applying section 1277.

[51] In calculating net direct interest expense, a bank or thrift is required
to allocate to each market discount obligation that it holds a portion of
its interest expense on all outstanding borrowings, including deposits, determined by multiplying such expense by a fraction the numerator of which
is the tax basis of the market discount obligation and the denominator of
which is the tax basis of all of its assets. While this rule will ensure an
allocation by such an institution of some interest expense against any holdings of market discount obligations, the institution's average cost of funds
may be significantly lower than the rate of interest payable on any specific
borrowing that might otherwise be matched against the market discount
obligations under a facts and circumstances test.

of in a taxable transaction,[52] or (ii) if the taxpayer so elects,[53] to the extent necessary to offset any net interest income on the obligation (the excess of the interest income over interest expense on related borrowings) recognized in subsequent years. While the character of the gain recognized upon the disposition of a market discount obligation issued prior to July 19, 1984 is not affected by section 1276, such gain is treated as ordinary income under section 1277(d) to the extent of the ordinary deduction for disallowed interest expense that is allowed with respect to the obligation in the year of its disposition. The purpose and effect of this rule is to ensure that the market discount income and deferred interest deduction offset each other in the holder's tax return in much the same manner as if the deferred interest expense had been capitalized and added to the tax basis of the market discount obligation.

The policy underlying section 1277 is that deductions for apparent losses resulting from a leveraged investment in a market discount obligation should be deferred, if and to the extent the losses are offset economically by the accrual of market discount, until the accrued market discount is included in income. Thus, if an investor borrows at 12 percent to finance the purchase of an 8 percent mortgage that has a yield, taking account of market discount, of 11 percent, the investor's economic loss is only 1 percent, the amount by which the rate of interest paid on the borrowing exceeds the yield on the mortgage. Income and expense would obviously be mismatched if a deduction were allowed for the apparent additional 3 percentage point loss before the corresponding amount of accrued market discount income is recognized.

---

[52] If a market discount obligation is disposed of in a transaction in which gain or loss is not fully recognized, a deduction for the previously disallowed interest expense is allowed up to the amount of gain recognized in the transaction. The balance is preserved as a future deduction by the new holder of the obligation if his basis in the obligation is calculated by reference to its basis in the hands of the former holder, and otherwise will be available to the prior holder upon disposition of the property received in exchange for the market discount obligation.

[53] *See* section 1277(b)(1).

3. Bond Stripping Rules

Section 1286, which was first enacted in 1982 as section 1232B, contains special rules governing the taxation of stripped bonds and stripped coupons. A stripped bond is defined as a bond issued with coupons (which, for this purpose, includes any rights to receive stated interest), where there is a separation in ownership between the bond and any coupons that have not yet come due. A stripped coupon is a coupon relating to a stripped bond. The tax treatment of stripped bonds and stripped coupons is the same, and the term stripped bond will be used in this discussion to refer to both.

The classic example of a bond stripping transaction is a sale by the owner of a bond of one or more unmatured interest coupons, with the seller retaining any remaining coupons and all rights to principal. The bond stripping rules also extend, apparently, to less dramatic situations where different percentage interests in rights to principal and interest on an obligation are sold. Thus, if the holder of an obligation sells to an investor a 10 percent participation interest in each and every payment of principal and interest due on the obligation, the bond stripping rules would not come into play because corresponding rights to principal and interest are being sold. By contrast, if a right to 10 percent of each principal payment and 12 percent (or any other percentage which is not 10 percent) of each interest payment is sold, it appears that each payment due on the obligation would be transformed into a stripped bond.

The principal effect of section 1286 is to transform the entire discount at which a stripped bond is purchased into original issue discount which is taken into income as it accrues in the manner described above. More specifically, section 1286(a) provides that if a person purchases a stripped bond, then the stripped bond will be treated, while held by that person, as a bond originally issued on the purchase date having original issue discount equal to the excess of the face amount of the stripped bond over its purchase price. If a number of stripped bonds are purchased together at one price, which is often the case, the purchase price is allocated among the stripped bonds in proportion to their fair market values.[54]

In the mortgage-backed securities area, the bond stripping rules are most likely to be encountered where pass-through certificates are created evidencing non-pro rata interests in a pool of mortgages. Suppose, for example, that a bank holds a pool of mortgages bearing interest at a rate of 10 percent (net of servicing) and that a current rate of interest for pass-through certificates is 12 percent. The bank could sell pass-through certificates with a 10 percent rate of interest at a discount. If, however, the market would assume a lower pre-payment rate, and thus require a greater discount in the purchase price to produce a 12 percent yield, than the bank thinks is reasonable, the bank may prefer to retain the discount for its own account. It could do this by retaining a right to ⅙ of each principal payment on the mortgages and selling pass-through certificates with no discount at a 12 percent rate. Since the purchasers of those certificates would acquire a right to 100 percent of the interest payments on the mortgages but only ⅚ of the principal, their rights to receive payments on the mortgages would be stripped bonds. Similarly, if the bank held premium mortgages and wished to sell pass-through certificates based on those mortgages with a current market pass-through rate of interest, it could accomplish its objective by selling all of the principal payments but only a fraction of

---

[54] The stripped bond rules also affect the computation of gain and loss by the seller by requiring that he allocate his basis in the obligation that is stripped between the stripped bonds that are sold and those that are retained in proportion to their respective fair market values. *See* section 1286(b). Thus, it is no longer possible, as it may have been before 1982, to allocate basis solely to rights to principal with no allocation being made to rights to interest payments regardless of their value. The basis allocated to the stripped bonds that are sold is compared with the proceeds of the sale to determine the seller's gain or loss from the sale. The seller is treated as having purchased the stripped bonds which he retains at a price equal to the basis allocated to those stripped bonds. The difference between that purchase price and the face amount of the stripped bonds is treated as original issue discount under the rule of section 1286(a) described above in the text.

the interest. Again, this transaction would call the bond stripping rules into play.[55]

Another example of a pass-through arrangement that may
be subject to the stripped bond rules is one in which the underlying mortgages have a range of stated interest rates. In order
to be able to quote to investors a single pass-through rate of
interest that will apply over the life of the pool regardless
of prepayment experience, it is common in these circumstances
for the pool sponsor or the servicer to receive an "excess
servicing fee." This fee is payable out of interest received
on the higher coupon mortgages and equals the excess of the
interest received on those mortgages over the interest that
would have been received if those mortgages paid interest
at the lowest rate of interest borne by any mortgage in the
pool. Although this fee is labelled a servicing fee, it could
also be characterized as an ownership interest in a fixed percentage of each interest payment on the higher coupon mortgages. Under that view, the certificate holders' interests in
the higher coupon mortgages would be stripped bonds.

To the extent that the stripped bond rules apply to a mortgage, the interest income earned by the holder of the mortgage
will consist entirely of original issue discount. This will be
true regardless of whether the price paid by the holder equals,
or is less or greater than, the principal payments on the mortgage to which the holder is entitled, and the rules governing
market discount and premium discussed herein will not apply.
Under the original issue discount rules, the holder will report
interest income in each taxable year based on the yield to
maturity of the mortgage to such holder. Such interest income
will approximately equal the interest income the holder would
have reported if he had purchased a hypothetical mortgage
(i) having a principal amount equal to the price which he actually paid for the mortgage subject to the stripped bond rules
(the "stripped mortgage") and (ii) bearing interest at a rate

---

[55] Revenue Ruling 71–399, 1971–2 C.B. 433, analyzes the tax treatment
of non-pro rata interests in interest and principal payments on mortgages
in a pool under the law in effect before enactment of the bond stripping
rules.

equal to the yield to maturity of the stripped mortgage.[56] In the event that the stripped mortgage prepays, the holder would have additional ordinary income or ordinary loss (assuming the mortgage is the obligation of an individual) equal to the difference between the then outstanding principal amounts of the stripped mortgage and the hypothetical mortgage.

An example may help to illustrate the principles discussed above. Consider a 30-year mortgage having a principal balance of $1,000 which pays interest at a 14 percent rate and provides for equal monthly payments of principal and interest. Assume that the entire mortgage is sold to an investor, except that the seller retains a right to $\frac{2}{14}$ of each interest payment. The investor would be entitled to receive payments in increasing amounts from one month to the next reflecting the greater amounts of principal included in the monthly payments on the 14 percent mortgage. If the mortgage is purchased by the investor for $1,000, it would have a yield to maturity of 12 percent. Since the investor is entitled to a lesser percentage of interest than principal payments, the bond stripping rules would apply. Consequently, the mortgage would be treated as a collection of zero coupon bonds, each yielding 12 percent, and all of the interest income to be reported by the investor would take the form of original issue discount. The amount includible in the investor's income in each taxable year as accrued original issue discount would closely approximate the stated interest he is entitled to receive. No additional gain or loss would be recognized if the mortgage prepaid. The only practical effect of applying the stripped bond rules in this situation would be to require interest on the mortgage to be reported as it accrues, even if the investor is otherwise a cash basis taxpayer.

---

[56] The stripped mortgage would not ordinarily provide for equal monthly payments, and this would have to be reflected in the terms of the hypothetical mortgage. For example, if the whole mortgage that is stripped provides for equal monthly payments of principal and interest, the holder of the stripped mortgage would receive increasing monthly payments if he is entitled to a greater percentage of principal payments than interest payments and decreasing monthly payments if he is entitled to a lesser percentage of principal than interest.

If the investor purchased the mortgage for $950, he would have a yield to maturity of 12.689 percent. The amounts that he would include in income as accrued original issue discount would closely approximate the interest he would be entitled to receive if the mortgage had a principal amount of $950 and bore interest of 12.689 percent (but continued to provide the same schedule of payments as the investor will actually receive). If the mortgage prepaid, he would have additional income equal to the excess of the amount of the prepayment actually received over the remaining principal amount at the time of the prepayment of the hypothetical 12.689 percent mortgage. For example, if the mortgage prepaid at the end of three years, the investor would have gain of $48.10 (the excess of $991.91, the actual amount of the prepayment, over $943.81, the remaining principal balance of the hypothetical mortgage). Similarly, if the mortgage were purchased at a price greater than $1,000, the hypothetical mortgage would have a principal amount equal to the purchase price and an interest rate less than 12 percent, and the holder would have an ordinary loss if the mortgage prepaid equal to the excess of the outstanding principal amount of the hypothetical mortgage over the amount received.

Treatment of Premium

If a corporate obligation, such as a pay-through bond, is purchased at a premium, the holder can elect under section 171 to amortize the premium as an offset to interest income. Any method of amortizing bond premium regularly employed by the holder can be used, provided such method is reasonable; in all other cases, premium is amortized under a straight-line method.[57] A straight-line method would result in more rapid amortization of premium than, for example, a constant yield method.

Section 171 does not apply to obligations of individuals. Thus, a premium paid upon purchase of a residential mortgage

---

[57] *See* Treasury Regulation §1.171–2(f).

(or a pass-through certificate evidencing an interest in such a mortgage) cannot be amortized. Instead, such premium is allocated among principal payments, generally in proportion to their amounts without regard to the time of payment, and is deductible as an ordinary loss as the payments to which the premium is allocated are made or come due.

Special Rules for Certain Institutional Investors

Thrifts are required to hold a minimum percentage of their assets in certain investments, including real property loans, in order to qualify for special bad debt reserve deductions under section 593. Similarly, a real estate investment trust will be eligible to deduct dividends paid to shareholders only if it holds a large percentage of its assets in the form of real property assets, including real property loans (*see* sections 856(c)(3) and (5)). In general, pay-through bonds do not qualify as real property loans for these purposes, since they are merely collateralized by such loans, whereas pass-through certificates do so qualify since the holder of such certificates is treated for tax purposes as the owner of the underlying mortgages.

The general rules of the Code relating to the accrual of discount and the amortization of premium on debt securities do not apply to life insurance companies. Under section 811(b), they are generally required to take discount and premium into account under the method which they regularly employ in maintaining their books if such method is reasonable.

Rulings and Treasury regulations[58] authorize mutual savings banks, building and loan associations and cooperative banks to amortize mortgage premiums and discounts on a composite basis (*i.e.*, ratably over an assumed average life of the loans). It appears that the TRA 1984 amendments extending the Code rules governing original issue discount to residential mortgages, and the new rules relating to market discount, would supersede these earlier authorities to the extent they produce conflicting results.

---

[58] Revenue Ruling 54–367, 1954–2 C.B. 109; Revenue Ruling 216, 1953–2 C.B. 38, and Treasury Regulation §1.1016–9(c).

Foreign Investors

Prior to TRA 1984, foreign investors not engaged in trade or business within the United States were generally subject to a 30 percent tax on United States source interest income. This tax was generally collected through withholding. Interest paid on an obligation of a U.S. person (including an individual who is a citizen or resident of the U.S. and a corporation organized in the U.S. that derives at least 20 percent of its income from U.S. sources) would ordinarily be treated as being derived from U.S. sources.[59] Thus, foreign investors were typically subject to the 30 percent tax with respect to interest on U.S. mortgage-backed securities unless such tax was reduced or eliminated under a tax treaty.

TRA 1984 eliminates the 30 percent tax with respect to certain "porfolio interest" paid on obligations issued after July 18, 1984. The repeal will generally apply to pay-through bonds issued by corporations after that date. In Temporary Regulations issued in August, 1984,[60] the Internal Revenue Service took the position that the repeal does not extend to obligations of individuals. Under this view, interest paid on residential mortgages directly to the holders of such mortgages would continue to be subject to the 30 percent tax. On the other hand, it appears that if such mortgages are exchanged for pass-through certificates which are of a type that are publicly traded, then the interest received by the holder of the certificates would be eligible for the repeal, but only to the extent the underlying mortgages were originated after July 18, 1984.[61]

The Foreign Investment in Real Property Tax Act of 1980 enacted section 897 which for the first time subjects to U.S. tax gain on sales of certain real property interests held by foreign investors that are not engaged in trade or business

---

[59] An exception to this rule applied to certain bank deposits under sections 861(a)(1)(A) and 861(c).

[60] 49 F.R. 33228 (August 22, 1984).

[61] *See* Joint Committee on Taxation, General Explanation of the Revenue Provisions of the Deficit Reduction Act of 1984, at 396 (December 31, 1984).

or otherwise present within the United States. This legislation does not apply to interests in real property that are solely creditor interests with no participation in the income, revenues or appreciation of the property. Thus, foreign investors holding mortgage-backed securities lacking any such participation feature would not be affected by this legislation.

GLOSSARY OF TERMS*

Accretion: The process or effect of accumulating accrued coupon payments as additional principal.

Average Life: The weighted average time to principal repayment. It is useful as an approximation of a single maturity where the mean or average maturity is used to describe the life of the instrument. (See "Duration" and "Half-Life.")

Bankruptcy Proof Entity: A legal entity whose asset/liability structure is such that under all realistic scenarios, proceeds from sale or utilization of assets are sufficient to meet all liabilities.

Bond Value: The amount of bonds of a given structure that will be supported by a mortgage's scheduled cash flow, but the amount is limited to the unpaid mortgage balance.

Breakeven Prepayment Rate: The prepayment rate which produces a required cash flow yield on a pass-through security. It can also refer to a cash flow yield that satisfies the required spread over treasuries of specified average life or duration.

Cash Flow Bond: See Paythrough Bond.

Cash Flow Yield: A monthly internal rate of return of an investment in a projected stream of monthly principal and interest payments. The yield will vary with the prepayment assumption that determines the cash flow pattern.

Collateralized Mortgage Obligation: A type of mortgage-backed corporate bond (also known as CMOs, Fast-Pay/Slow-Pay Bonds, and Serialized Mortgage-Backed Securities), characterized by a multiclass (or multitranche) prioritization structure. Such issues are partitioned into several classes of a ranked priority by which bonds are redeemed. A given class is not redeemed until all bonds of an earlier priority have been redeemed. This creates a series of bonds of distinct expected maturities.

---

* Prepared by Kenneth Sullivan, Managing Director and Manager, Mortgage Research and Product Development, Drexel Burnham Lambert.

Conditional Prepayment Rate (CPR): A measure of prepayment which assumes that each month a constant proportion of then outstanding mortgages will prepay.

Corporate Bond Equivalent Yield: An upward adjustment to reflect monthly payment of interest rather than semiannual payment of interest which is the convention in the Corporate and Government bond markets.

Coupon Rate: The annual interest paid on a fixed-income instrument.

Delay: This refers to the "stated" delay time elapsed to the first payment of principal and interest (GNMAs—45 days, FHLMC PCs—75 days, FNMA MBSs—54 days, conventional pass-throughs—54 days). The "actual" delay, or penalty, is 30 days less than the "stated" delay.

Due-on-Sale Clause: A clause in a loan agreement that requires the payment of the remaining loan balance upon a sale or other transfer of title of the underlying collateral, such as real estate.

Duration: A measure of the sensitivity of an instrument's price to changes in yields. It is calculated by taking a weighted average of the time periods to receipt of the present value of the cash flows from an investment. (See "Average Life" and "Half Life.")

Duration Variability: A measure of the extent to which the duration of a cash flow may vary from its expected value owing to fluctuation in yields and/or prepayment rates.

Factor: The outstanding principal balance in decimal form. The proportion of the original principal balance still outstanding.

Fast-Pay Bonds: Bonds of a high priority class with respect to redemption priority over other bonds in an issue. As a result, they will be redeemed at a faster rate than others in the same issue.

Federal Home Loan Mortgage Corporation: Also known as "FHLMC" and "Freddie Mac." FHLMC is a private corporation authorized by Congress, which sells participation certificates and collateralized mortgage obligations backed by pools of conventional mortgage loans.

Federal Housing Administration: The FHA is a division of the Department of Housing and Urban Development, whose business includes insuring residential mortgage loans under a nationwide system.

Federal National Mortgage Association: Also known as "Fannie Mae" and "FNMA." FNMA was created by Congress to support the secondary mortgage market. A private corporation, it buys and sells residential mortgages insured by FHA or guaranteed by VA. FNMA also issues mortgage-backed securities backed by conventional mortgages.

FHA Experience: A statistical series, revised periodically, which represents the proportion of mortgages that "survive" a given number of years from their origination.

FHLMC Participation Certificates: Securities backed by a pool of mortgages owned by FHLMC. Certifies ownership interests in the specific pool of mortgages.

Fully-Modified Pass-Through: A pass-through for which the timely payment of principal and interest is guaranteed by the issuer. A GNMA is an example of a fully-modified pass-through.

Government National Mortgage Corporation: Also known as "Ginnie Mae" or "GNMA." A wholly-owned U.S. government corporation. As part of the Department of Housing and Urban Development, GNMA issues and guarantees mortgage-backed securities which are backed by the full faith and credit of the United States government.

Graduated Payment Mortgages (GPM): Mortgages which differ from conventional mortgages because not all payments are equal. There is a graduation period where payments start at a relatively low level and rise for some number of years.

Grantor Trusts: Trusts whereby the grantor (certificate holder) retains control over the income or assets, or both, to such an extent that such grantor will be treated as the owner of the property (mortgage assets) and its income for tax purposes. The result is to make the income from a grantor trust taxable to the grantor but not to the trust which receives it.

Half-Life: The period until half of the original principal amount of the pool is repaid. (See "Duration" and "Average Life.")

Midgets: GNMA pass-through security with an intermediate term (15 years). It is similar in structure to the original 30-year GNMA security.

Mortgage-Backed Bond: A bond whose payments are secured by a set of mortgages.

Mortgage Yield: An industry convention. An internal rate of return calculation based on a 12-year life assumption (for most securities).

Optional Redemption: An optional call provision reserved by the issuer which becomes exercisable after a certain number of years from issue date. This provision allows the "clean-up" of small amounts of remaining principal with thin marketability.

Overcollateralization: The extent to which the bond value of the assets or the cash flow produced by the assets (collateral) exceed the liability or the cash flow required to meet liability obligations. It is usually expressed as a percentage of par amount of the liability. (See Bond Value.)

Pass-Back: A feature of a collateralized bond that provides that some fraction (possibly all) of the "excess" cash flow from collateral is passed to the issuer. (See Pass Forward, Bond Value, Overcollateralization.)

Pass-Forward: A feature of a collateralized bond that provides that some portion (possibly all) of the "excess" cash flow from collateral is used to redeem outstanding bond principal. Excess cash flow is the proceeds from collateral beyond that required to maintain the overcollateralization ratio.

Pass-Through Security: A security which derives its cash flow from underlying mortgages where the issuer passes through to the investor the principal and interest payments made on the mortgages on a monthly basis.

Pay-Through Bond (Cash Flow Bond): A debt obligation secured by a mortgage pool. They are fully amortizing instruments whose principal and interest payments closely track the cash flow of the collateral in that scheduled amortization of the bonds is met by scheduled collateral cash flows, and mortgage prepayments accelerate redemption of bonds.

Principal Balance: The actual balance of an obligation exclusive of accrued or unpaid interest.

Prioritization: The ranking or ordering of security classes for sequence in which they are to be redeemed, such as in a multiclass bond issue.

Seasoning: The aging of a mortgage. The amount of time that has elapsed since origination.

Servicing Fee: The fee withheld by the servicer from the monthly interest payments made by the mortgagors. The balance of the interest and all of the principal is passed through to the holders of the security.

Sinking Fund: The obligation to retire liabilities according to a schedule, which results in a substantial, partial redemption of the issue before final maturity.

Slow-Pay Bonds: Bonds in a low priority class compared with bonds in other classes with respect to the order of redemption, which results in slow redemption when compared to the other classes.

T.I.M.S.: (Prospective) Trusts for investment in mortgages are entities structured as non-taxpaying entities limited to active investing in residential mortgages and mortgage-backed securities and issuing multiple classes of ownership interests and are prohibited from active business such as mortgage origination or servicing.

Twelve-Year Life: The assumption that the cash flow associated with a mortgage will consist of level payments until the 12th year, when the remaining principal balance is paid in full.

Yield to Average Life: The yield to maturity of a bond with a maturity that is the same as the average life of a corresponding pass-through.

Yield to Half Life: Yield to the point at which half of the original principal has been paid.

Yield to Maturity: An internal rate of return calculation on a security held to maturity.

Zero Coupon CMOs: CMO bonds that are either true zero coupon instruments or accrual bonds. An accrual bond (or compound interest bond) is a coupon bond that during some part of its life, accumulates accrued interest as increased principal rather than as cash paid. This accumulation is called accretion.

INDEX

A

Accounting, 355
Accounting, regulations, 26–27
Accrual of original issue discount, 587–592
Active management process, overview of, 476–479
Adjustable rate mortgage (ARMs), 24, 79–86, 90–92, 93–95, 155, 202, 215, 304–305, 447, 511, 521, 524–527
  consumer safeguards of, 83, 85–86
  drawbacks of, 81–85
  evaluation framework for, 307–346
  features of, 63–78, 307–308, 331–340
  framework, 345–346
  growth, 76–78
  interest rates of, 66–69
  investment characteristics of, 331
  payment streams of, 69–73
  popularity of, 81–85
  pricing of, 73–76
  pricing model, 323–324
  rating guidelines for, 527
  risk in, 524–527
Adjustable rate preferred stocks of controlled subsidiaries (CARPs), 150, 157–158
Adjustment
  frequency of, 307
  index of, 66
  terms of, 66
Age of mortgage; see Seasoning
Agencies, role of the, 15–19
"Agency pass-through," 349–350
Aggregate cash flow method, 550–552
Aggressive securities, 489–490
Alternative mortgage instruments (AMIs), types of, 42–61, 521–527
American call option, 449–450, 472
American Home Finance Corporation III, 163
American straddle, 469

AMIs, see Alternative mortgage instruments (AMIs)
Amortization, 242–243
  payments, 30
  schedule, 269–270
Anticipatory short hedge, 397–400
Arbitrage trading, 450–451
ARMs, see Adjustable rate mortgage (ARMs)
Askin, David J., 293, 298, 457, 515–517, 520–521
Asset and liability committee (ALCO), 399
Asset-liability management, 466–468
Audit process, 549–550
Average life, 119, 125–127, 131–134, 140, 184, 186–187

B

Banco Mortgage Company, 109
Bank of America, 109
Bankruptcy, 562–563
  bond coverage, 542–543
  code, 559–560
Basic primary mortgage insurance, 529
Basis, 386–387
Baum, Steven P., 202
Bearish scenario, 480
Benchmark portfolio, 478
Beta, 488–489
Bierwag, G. O., 459, 466
Black and Scholes, 345
Bogey, 478
  bond, 466–467
  portfolio, 478
  universe, 478
"Bond stripping" rules of Section 1286, 583–584, 608–612
Bond(s), 1–3, 449; see also Conventional bonds
  equivalent yield, 277
  mortgage-backed, 149–191, 504
  options on, 417–420

Bonds *(Cont.)*
  portfolio management, 476
  rate, 539
  term, 155–158
  value calculations, 556–558
  value method, 552–555
"Book yield" terms, 358–359
Bookstaber, R., 449
Bullish scenario, 480
"Buy and hold strategy," 364
Buydown loan, 51–54
Buydown mortgage, 519–520
Buying calls, 442–443

C

"Calamity call," 365
California Savings and Loan Association, 155
Call option, 414
  American, 449–450
  buying of, 442–443
  selling of, 443
Canadian-type mortgages, 54
Capital gain, 580–583
Caps, 68
Carleton, W. T., 451
CARPs; *see* Adjustable rate preferred stocks of controlled subsidiaries (CARPs)
Cash flow(s), 109–116, 350–354
  aggregate, 550–552
  bonds, 158–167
  coverage, reinvestment risk, 537–542
  overcollateralization, 535–536
  prepayments with, 271
  prepayments without, 270
  priorization of, 173–177
  yield, 116, 258–267
Cash market, 386–387
Cash, floater versus, 409–410
Cassidy, Henry, 73
CBOT; *see* Chicago Board of Trade (CBOT)
CenTrust Capital Corporation, 157–158
Chambers, D. R., 451, 466
Chapter 13 coverage, 542–543, 563
Cheapest-to-deliver package, calculation of, 382–386
Chicago Board of Trade (CBOT), 373, 377, 389, 391–393, 397
Chicago Mercantile Exchange, 377
Classes, relative size of, 177–180
CMOs; *see* Collateralized mortgage obligations (CMOs)
CoastFed International Finance 156

Code rules, 580, 583, 599, 602–604, 613
Collateral, nature of, 180–182
Collateral, types of, 511–512
Collateral, valuation of, 550–558
Collateralized deposits, 536–537
Collateralized mortgage obligations (CMOs), 24, 27, 80, 86, 119, 151–154, 159, 167–200, 350, 364–371, 497, 505–506, 561–562, 576–577, 579, 585, 596–597
Commercial bankers, 90
Commercial banks, role of, 20–21
Commercial properties, definition of, 42
Committment risk, 441–442
Conditional prepayment rate (CPR), 130–131, 133–135, 138–139, 282–283, 285–296, 351
Constant prepayment factors, 130–131
Constant prepayment rate, 264–265, 271
"Controlled" adjustable rate preferred stocks, 150, 157–158
Conventional bonds, mortgage-backed bonds versus, 241–255
Conventional mortgages, 49–53
Corporate bond equivalent (CBE), 121
Corporate Bond Index, 206–238
Corporates, pass-throughs versus, 116–119
Coupons, 520–521
Coupon-to-coupon method, 552–553
Covered call writing, 443
Cox, J. C., 452
CPR; *see* Conditional prepayment rate (CPR)
Credit, 354–355
Credit risk, 416–417, 451
Current margin, 309–311
Curvilinear duration, 466, 470–472

D

De minimis rule, 584, 598
Debt rating definitions, 509–511
Defaults, 36–39, 83, 284–285, 515–517
Defensive securities, 491
Deferred compound interest bonds (DCIBs), 561
Delinquency risk, 503
Delinquent, definition of, 34
Demographic variables, 290–291
Department of Housing and Urban Development (HUD) 262–263, 272
Deregulation, 79–97
  thrift industry, 93–95
Discounts, 361
  treatment of, 582–612

Disintermediation, 14–20
Diversification, 517
Documents, 548–549
Down payment, 35
"Due on sale" clauses, 358
Duration, 119, 267, 277, 331, 363, 485, 487–489
  characteristic of, 459–460
  drift, 466
  FRMs components of, 460–465
  variability, 184, 186–187
"Dynamic duo," 410–412

E

Earned interest, 483
Econometric models, 294–301
Effective margin, 335
Equity
  definition of, 31–33
  securities, analysis of, 489–491
  shock, 525–526
Eurodollar
  bond transactions, 537
  mortgage-backed bonds, 150–157
Exercise price, 414
Expenses, 355–356

F

Fabozzi, Frank J., 413
"Fannie Mae," 16, 108, 500
"Fast pay/slow pay" bonds, 152
Federal Agencies, role of, 500–502
Federal Deposit Insurance Corporation (FDIC), 536–539
Federal flood insurance, 542
Federal Home Loan Bank Board (FHLBB), 16, 26, 54, 66, 82, 84, 91, 96, 524
Federal Home Loan Bank System, 16
Federal Home Loan Mortgage Corporation (FHLMC), 15–16, 66, 574
Federal Housing Administration (FHA), 16, 45, 47, 575; see also FHA
Federal income tax treatment of mortgage-backed securities, 569–615
Federal National Mortgage Association (FNMA), 15–17; see also FNMA
Federal Reserve, 389
Federal Savings and Loan Insurance Corporation, 536–537
Fees, 68
FHA, 103–108, 113–116, 129–130, 133, 136, 142, 146–147, 176, 178, 202, 204, 220, 227–228, 230–231, 238, 262, 264, 272–273, 275, 338, 375, 380, 384; see also

FHA (Cont.)
  Federal Housing Administration (FHA)
FHA experience, 123, 125, 128–132, 135, 138–139, 262–262, 272–273, 281–283, 288, 294, 351, 482
FHLBB; see Federal Home Loan Bank Board (FHLBB)
FHLMC, 77, 83, 88, 104–105, 108, 130, 137, 151–153, 156, 158, 171, 190, 201–203, 220–230, 238, 257, 265, 267, 275, 292, 300, 305, 354, 357, 500–502, 505, 512, 518–519, 528–529, 556; see also Federal Home Loan Mortgage Corporation (FHLMC)
Field, Alfred, 73
Financial Accounting Standards Board (FASB), 397, 506, 561
Financial deregulation; see Deregulation
Financial futures; see Futures
Financial Publishing Co., 267
Financial reporting, 561–562
First Boston Corporation, 358
First Federal Savings and Loan of Chicago, 109
Fitch Investors Service, 499
Fixed rate mortgages (FRMs), 63, 65, 75–81; see also FRMs
Floaters, 403–413
FNMA, 77, 83, 88, 103–105, 108, 120, 130, 137, 154, 156, 158, 201–202, 220, 228–230, 238, 257, 265, 275, 292, 300, 305, 353–354, 357–364, 500–502, 512, 518–519, 528–529, 556; see also Federal National Mortgage Association (FNMA)
Fong, H. Gifford, 480
Foreclosure, 284–285
Foreign Investment in Real Property Tax Act of 1980, 614–615
Foreign investors, 614–615
"Freddie Mac," 108, 167, 171, 349–350, 500
FRMs, 85–87, 92–95, 304–305, 511, 514–515, 523, 526–527, 556; see also Fixed rate mortgages (FRMs)
  duration of, 461–466
  in-the-money, out-of-the-money versus, 453
  interest rate risk of, 447–473
  prepayment rights with, 447–473
  rates, 85–87
  resurgence factors of, 447–449
  valuation of, 454–456
Futures, 373–401

G

GAAP; see Generally Accepted Accounting Principles (GAAP)
Gain on prepayment, 591–592
Garn-St. Germain Depository Institutions Act of 1982, 96, 358
Garn-Tower bill, 578
Generally accepted accounting principles (GAAP), 26, 355–364
Geographic dispersion, 517–518
Geographic effects, 291–292
"Ginnie Mae," 103–107, 349–350, 500
GNMA, 103–109, 113, 120, 130, 137, 141–145, 154, 156, 158, 165, 201, 203–205, 212–216, 219–228, 231–238, 244, 257, 264–265, 268–275, 292–293, 300, 305, 327, 338, 351–361, 364, 371, 375, 377, 379–393, 395, 379, 480–481, 483–485, 500–502, 512, 520, 528, 531, 534, 556, 574–575; see also Government National Mortgage Association (GNMA)
  FHA projects, 106–107
  GPM, 106–107
  Midget, 106
  Mobile Homes, 106–107
  Mortgage-Backed Securities Trust, Inc., 579
  pass-throughs, 103–107
  time swap, 403–412
  II, 106, 391–393
GNMA-CDR futures contract, 373–400
Government guarantees, 528
Government National Mortgage Association (GNMA), 15–18, 21; see also GNMA
GPMs; see Graduated-payment mortgages (GPMs)
Graduated-payment Mortgages (GPMs), 42–51, 106–107, 182, 203, 231–235, 270, 281, 353, 357, 521–523
"Grantor trust," 573
Growing equity mortgages (GEMs), 523–524

H

Hall, Arden, 451
Haney, W. C., 449, 460
HAP; see Section 8 Housing Assistance Payments (HAP)
Hazard insurance, 542–543
Hedges, example of, 397–398
Hedging interest rate risk of FRMs, 447–473

Hedging with interest rate futures, 393–397
Hedging with OTC options, 432–445
High Grade Corporate Bond Index, 206–238
Holders, taxation of, 579–582
Homebuilders, role of, 21
"Honest to God" (HTG) yield, 358
Horizon analysis, 188–189, 357–360
Housing Act of 1983, 384
Housing finance in deregulated environment, 79–97
HUD, 103, 228, 351, 375, 384, 501; see also U.S. Department of Housing and Urban Development (HUD); see also Department of Housing and Urban Development (HUD)

I

Ibsen, Ben, 452
In-the-money versus out-of-the-money FRMs, 453
Incremental insurance coverage, types of, 543
Indemity bonds, 530
Index, 307
Inferior securities, 491
Infrastructure, elements of, 543–550
Initial rate, 67–68, 82–83, 307
Insolvency; see Bankruptcy
Institutional investors, special rules for, 613
Instrinic values, 452
Insurance
  endorsements, 530
  mortgage, 36–39, 529
  quality of, 530–531
  types of, 542–543
Interest payment, calculation of, 243–245
Interest rate, 286–289
  anticipation strategies, 457–493
  caps, 307, 524
  ceilings, 79
  changes, 358–361
  distribution, 325–329
  exposure, 394
  futures contracts, 393–397
  market, 331
  prepayment rate relationship, 286–289
  risk, 447–473
  return, 204, 252
  scenarios, 308–309
Internal Revenue Code of 1954, 573
Internal Revenue Code rules; see Code rules

Internal Revenue Service, 154, 573–574, 576–577, 603, 614
Investment bankers, role of, 21–22
Investment horizon, 131–145
Investors, types of, 170–172
Issuer, 543–546

J

Jarrow, Robert, 299

K

Kaufman, G. G., 457, 559, 466
Kunka, Matthew, 201

L

Legal issues, 558–563
Legal opinions, role of, 560–561
Legal risk, 525
Leibowitz, Martin L., 357
Less-liquid mortgages, 27
Life insurance companies, role of, 20
Liquidity, 416–417
Livingston, Miles, 466
Loan, size of, 518–519
Loan to value (LTV) ratio, 35–36, 39, 50–52, 92–93, 515–517
Local primary mortgage market, 11
London Interbank Offer Rate (LIBOR), 404
Long bond and long put, 422
Long bond and short call, 423
Long hedge, 397–400
Long positions in options, 418–420
Loss, types of protection against, 528–543
LTV ratio, see Loan to value (LTV) ratio

M

Macaulay, F. R., 459
Macroeconomic effects, 289–290
Margin(s), 68, 307, 309–318, 335
"Market average" returns, 201
Market
  discount, 601–603
  implicit forecast scenario, 480
  interest rates, 331
  mortgage 7–28; see mortgage market
  mortgage securities performance, 220–238
  price-based models, 301–303
  risk, 488–489, 502
  value return, 253–254
Maturity/call, 483
Maturity risk, 502
MBBs; see Mortgage-backed bonds (MBBs)

Midgets, 521–522
MMDAs; see Money market deposit accounts (MMDAs)
Modified coupon-to-coupon method, 553–555
Money market deposit accounts (MMDAs), 81, 88, 97
Monte Carlo simulation, 325, 360–361
Monthly payments, 120–123
  breakdown of, 30–32
  calculations of, 246–247
Moody's Investors Service, 498, 507–511, 534, 538
Mortgage
  ages of; see Seasoning
  balance, definition of, 30
  bankers, 19–20, 90
  cash flows, 242–243
  coupons, 520–521
  definition of, 29
  documents, 548–549
  Index, 203–238
  insurance, 36–39, 528–529
  insurers, quality of, 530–531
  less-liquid, 27
  market, 7–28
  money origination, 40–41
  nontraditional, 42–61
  originators of, 431
  pool; see Pool(s)
  properties, 41–42
  qualifying for, 34–36
  types of, 29–61, 101–102
Mortgage pass-through(s); see pass-through(s)
  cash flows, 109–116
  features of, 102–109
  Index, 203–238
  long Treasury securities versus, 210–216
  securities, 101–145
  ten-year Treasury securities versus, 216–219
  terms of, 102–109
  total return calculations for, 241–255
  types of, 102–109
Mortgage-backed bonds, 149–191, 504; see also bonds
Mortgage-backed securities (MBS); see also Mortgage securities assessment of, 502–504
  features of, 154
  Federal income tax treatment of, 569–615
  financial futures and, 373–401

Mortgage-backed securities (*Cont.*)
  legal issue of, 558–563
  market for, 1–3
  portfolio management of, 349–371
  rating of, 497–568
  regulatory issue of, 558–563
  risks in, 502–503
  types of, 504–506, 570–579
  yield curve, 142–145
Mortgage Bankers Association of America, 47
Mortgage securities; see also Mortgage-backed securities
  forcasting prepayment rates for, 279–306
  historical performance of, 201–238
  market, performance within, 220–238
  OTC options on, 413–445
  yield determination of, 257–277
Mortgage yield
  equivalent-yield basis versus, 329–331
  methods of evaluating, 258–269

N

National primary mortgage market, 12–13
"Negative amortization," 45, 68–69, 75, 307, 525–526
"Negative convexity," 357–358, 479
Negotiable Order of Withdrawl account (NOW), 97
91 day account, 97
Nonresidential properties, 42
Nontraditional mortgages, 42–61
"Normal amortization," 242–243
Norris, P. D., 449
Norwest Mortgage, Inc., 109
NOW accounts, 97

O

1 year all savers' certificate, 97
½ year or longer IRA/Keogh account, 97
Optional redemption, 163–165
Options, 414–415
  bonds, OTC options versus, 417–420
  pricing models, 299–301
OTC; see Over-the-counter
Original issue discount, 584–601
Original issue discount, accrual of, 587–592
Original issue discount bonds (OIDs), 561
Originator, 39–41, 102, 109, 125, 431
Overcollateralization, 532–533, 537
Over-the-counter (OTC)
  characteristics of, 421–430

Over-the-counter (OTC) (*Cont.*)
  hedging, uses of, 432–445
  market, 415–417
  mortgages on, 417–420
  options, 413–445

P

PAMs; see Pledged-Account Mortgages (PAMs)
Par, price relative to, 182–184
Participation certificate (PC), 108
Pass-through certificates, 571–575, 598–601
"Pass-through of spread," 368
Pass-throughs, 1–3, 505; see also Mortgage pass-throughs
  corporates versus, 116–119
  GNMA, 103–107
  private, 109
  total return for, 241–255
  Treasuries versus, 116–119
Past prepayment experience, 272–273
Pay-through bonds, 158–167, 575–578, 584–598
Pay-throughs, investment characteristic of, 161–167, 505
Payment caps, 307
Payment delay, 119–120
Payment schedule, 32
"Payment shock," 83, 524–525
Payment streams, example of, 69–73
Payments, monthly, 243–247
PC; see Participation certificate (PC)
Peters, Helen F., 293, 298, 457, 515–517, 520–521
PHM Credit Corporation, 159
Pinkus, Scott M., 457, 515–517
Pledged-Account Mortgages (PAMs), 42, 48–51
Policy year, 298
Pollack, Irving M., 353
Pool(s), 41, 111–112, 282, 293, 513–521
  insurance, 529–530, 535
Portfolio management, 24–25, 349–371, 475–493
Pozdena, R. J., 452
Premiums, 361, 415, 612–613
Prepaid life assumption, 280–281
"Prepaid life" concept, 258
Prepayment(s), 33–34, 102, 109, 114, 116, 123–125, 127–128, 130–145, 350–353, 357–358, 423, 538–539
  activity, 283–292
  algorithm, 358
  assumptions, 337

Prepayment(s) (*Cont.*)
  causes of, 128–129
  decision, 283–286
  effects, 123–125
  estimation of, 127–128
  gain on, 591–592
  options, 450–458
    FRMs, 458
    premium, 450–451
    valuation, 451–452
  penalities, 75–76
Prepayment rate(s), 264–267
  breakeven, 140–142
  effects of, 162–163
  factors affecting, 285–292
  forecasting of, 279–306
  measuring of, 280–283
  methodologies for predicting, 292–306
  pool, 282
  prediction of, 292–306
  response to caps, 337–338
  rights, FRMs with, 447–473
Present value method, 555
Price-based models; *see* Market price-based models
Price caps, 428
Price relative to par, 182–184
Price risk, 438–442
Pricing model, 452
Pricing model, ARMs, 323–324
Primary mortgage
  insurance types of, 529
  market evolution of, 10–13
Prime quality mortgages, characteristic of, 513–514
Principal
  calculations of, 245
  installment payment of, 592–596
  payment return, 253
  return, 204
Private pass-throughs, 109
Properties, types of, 41–42
Public Securities Association, 497
Put option, 414
Putable security, 107

Q
Quoted yield, 274–276

R
RAMs; *see* Reverse-annuity mortgages (RAMs)
Rating
  agencies, 498–502, 538–539
  classifications, 504–527

Rating (*Cont.*)
  frameworks for, 507–511
  mortgage-backed securities, 497–568
  process, an overview of, 498–500
Real estate investment trust, 578–579
Real property laws, 563
Refinancing costs, 286–289
Regression models, 294–301
Regulation Q ceiling, 9
Regulatory issues, 558–563
Reinvestment
  income, 531–532
  rate, 122–123, 360–364
  return, 204, 252
  risk, evaluation of, 537–542
"Renegotiated-rate mortgages" (RRMs), 54
Report of the President's Commission on Housing, 578
Reset margin, 307
Residential mortgage(s), 7–9, 88–93, 350, 497
Residential properties, definition of, 41
Return(s), 356
  enhancement, 403–412
  simulation, 476–478, 489
  types of, 204–206, 247–254
Reverse-annuity mortgages (RAMs), 56–59
Risk, 356–357, 487–489
  committment, 441–442
  credit, 416–417, 451
  interest rate, 466–467
  market, 488–489
  price, 441–442
  types of, 502–503, 524–527
Riskless hedge, 345–346
Rollover mortgages (ROMs), 54–56
ROMs; *see* Rollover mortgages (ROMs)
Ross, S. A., 452
RRMs; *see* Renegotiated-rate mortgages (RRMs)
Rubinstein, M., 452
Rudd, Andrew, 299
Ryan Financial Strategy Group, 405–406

S
Salomon Brothers High Grade Corporate Bond Index, 203, 206–238
Salomon Brothers Inc., 201, 205, 267, 341
SAMs; *see* Shared-appreciation mortgages
Savings and loans, 103
Scenario margin, 311–318

Scenario yield and percent adjustability, 341–342

Scheduled payment rates, changes in, 596–598

Sears Mortgage Securities Corporation, 154, 562

Seasoning, 125–127, 289, 298, 516–517

Secondary mortgage market
evolution of, 13–21
role of Federal agencies in, 500–502

Section 8 Housing Assistance Payments (HAP), 228

Section
171, 612
593, 613
811, 613
856, 613
897, 614–615
1273, 584–585
1277, 606–607
1276, 603–607
1286, 583, 608

Securities; see Mortgage securities and see Treasury securities
mortgage-backed, 1–3
pass-through, 101–145
types of, 489–491

Security market line approach, 488–489

Senft, Dexter, 358

Servicer, 546–548

Servicing, 39–40
fee, 107, 109, 243–244
spread, 354
standards, 519–520

7 to 31 day account, 97

Shared-appreciation mortgages (SAMs), 59–61

Sharpe, William F., 488

Shea, G. S., 451

Shearson Lehman Government/Corporation Bond Index, 478

Short hedge, 397–400

Short positions in options, 419–420

Simulation return process, 480–485

Single family housing, 90–93

Single payment obligations, 587–591

Single-state models, 300

Six-month money market certificates, 97

Sociological factors, 290–291

Special redemption test, 538–542

Spread and servicing risk, 525

Spread change, 483

Spread relationship exploitation, 485

Standard and Poor's Corporation, 498, 507–511, 534, 539

Stanley, Morgan, 449, 460

State real property laws, 563

Statement of Financial Accounting Standards (SFAS), 397

Static prepayments, 457–458

Straddle strategy, 468–470

Strategic frontier analysis, 489–491

Strike price, 414

"Stripped bonds," 583–584, 608–612

Structure, 353

Super NOW account, 97

Superior securities, 491

Supplemental mortgage insurance, 529

Swapping, 361–362

Synthetic security, 370–371

T

"Tandem program," 228

Tax Equity and Fiscal Responsibility Act of 1982, 586

Tax factors, 25–26

Tax Reform Act of 1984 ("TRA 1984"), 582–583, 599, 602–603, 605, 613–614

Taxation of holders, overview of, 579–582

Taxes, 561–562

"Teaser rates," 83

Term bonds, 155–158; see Mortgage-backed bonds

Term structure analysis, 480

The Depository Institutions Deregulation and Monetary Control Act of 1980, 96

Thrift(s), 90
deregulation of, 79–97, 93–95
industry, 40, 90–95
institutions, 10–12
role of, 19

Time, 483
next reset, 339–340
O variables, 286, 290
swap, 406–412
T variables, 286, 290

TIMs; see Trusts for investment in mortgages (TIMs)

Toevs, A. L., 453, 459–460, 466

Total monthly payment, calculations of, 246–247

Total Rate-of-Return Index, 201

Total return, 485
calculations of, 247–251
components of, 251–254

Traditional mortgage loan, 29–32

Transaction costs, 287–288

Travelers Mortgage Securities Corporation Series 1984–1 issue, 371

Treasuries, pass-throughs versus, 116–119

Treasury securities, 319–329, 335–337, 343–346, 377, 391–393, 395, 398–400

Treasury securities, mortgage pass-throughs versus, 210–219

Trust for investment in mortgages (TIMs), 24, 152–154, 578

Trustee, 548

Trusts, 41

12 year prepaid life, 111–114, 127–128

2½–3½ year small-savers certificate, 97

U

U.S. Department of Housing and Urban Development (HUD), 84 see also HUD

U.S. Federal income tax, rules of, 569–615

U.S. League of Savings Institutions, 308

U.S. Treasury; see Treasury

Underlying assets, credit risk of, 512

Underwriting, 519–520

"Uneconomic," 128, 285

University of California at Berkley, Center for Real Estate in Urban Economics, 379

V

VA, 129–130, 375, 380, 384; see also Veteran's Administration (VA)

Valuation of collateral, 550–558

Vasicek, Oldrich A., 480

Veterans' Administration (VA) loans, 16–17

Veterans' Administration (VA), 575; see also VA

Volatility 335

Volatility factors, 482–483

Von Furstenberg, George M., 515

W

Waldman, D. W., 451

Waldman, Michael, 202

Warehousing, 438–441

Weighted average life, 267, 277

Wernick, J. H., 453

Y

Yawitz, Jesse, 466

Yield(s), 111, 113, 116, 121–123, 126–127, 131–145, 423–428

bond equivalent, 277

cash flow, 258–267, 276–277

curve 483

curve margins, 318–323

curve, MBS, 142–145

mortgage, 258–269

spread-duration variability trade-offs, 188–191

tables, 267–269